ENCYCLOPEDIA OF
AMERICAN WAR HEROES

Major Bruce H. Norton, USMC (Ret.)

EDITOR AND COMPILER

Facts On File, Inc.

Encyclopedia of American War Heroes

Copyright © 2002 by Bruce H. Norton

Facts On File, Inc.
132 West 31st Street
New York NY 10001

Library of Congress Cataloging-in-Publication Data

Norton, B. H. (Bruce H.)
    Encyclopedia of American War heroes/Bruce H. Norton,
       p. cm.
    Includes bibliographical references and index.
    ISBN 0-8016-4637-9
       1. United States—History, Military—Encyclopedias. 2. Heroes—United States—
Biography—Encyclopedias. 3. Women heroes—United States—Biography—
Encyclopedias. 4. United States—Biography—Encyclopedias. I. Title.

E181. N88 2002
920.073—dc21   2001057517

Facts On File books are available at special discounts when purchased in bulk quantities for businesses, associations, institutions, or sales promotions. Please call our Special Sales Department in New York at (212) 967-8800 or (800) 322-8755.

You can find Facts On File on the World Wide Web at http://www.factsonfile.com

Text design by Joan M. Toro
Cover design by Cathy Rincon

Printed in the United States of America

VB Hermitage 10 9 8 7 6 5 4 3 2 1

This book is printed on acid-free paper.

To my own heroines and hero;
Darice, Elizabeth, and Bruce II.

CONTENTS

✯ ✯ ✯ ✯

Photo Credits
vii

Acknowledgments
ix

Introduction
xi

Awards, Decorations, and Honors
xvii

Entries A–Z
1

Appendix: American War Statistics
275

Bibliography
277

Index by Era
281

Index
287

PHOTO CREDITS

★ ★ ★ ★

The illustrations on the following pages are courtesy of the author: 23, 105, 130, 139, 167
Courtesy of the Library of Congress are illustrations on page 208
Courtesy of the National Archives are illustrations on pages 41, 100, 128, 147
Courtesy of the US Navy Historical Center are illustrations on page 190
All other illustrations are courtesy of the Congressional Medal of Honor Society and the
Marine Corps Historical Center Archives

ACKNOWLEDGMENTS

★ ★ ★ ★

Ms. Crystal M. Lottig; Mr. Andrew H. Zack; Mr. Fredrick J. Graboske, Head Archivist, Marine Historical Center; Col. Thomas Palmer, USMC (Ret.); Captain John Dunn, USMC (Ret.); Maj. Gen. John S. Grinalds, USMC (Ret.); Mr. Ron Huegel; Mr. Paul Keaveney; Mr. John B. Hagerty; Mr. Kevin Jandreau; Lt. Col. Frank E. Thompson, USAF (Ret.); Col. John "Tony" Lackey, USA (Ret.); Major Rick Spooner, USMC (Ret.); Mr. Eugene D. Foxworth III; Mr. Terry Joyce, *Charleston Post & Courier*; Mr. Russell K. Pace; The Legion of Valor Association; The Medal of Honor Society; The Force Recon Association; First Recon Battalion Association; Third Recon Battalion Association; The Marine Corps League; Daniel Library, The Citadel, Charleston, South Carolina; *Leatherneck* magazine; and the *Gazette*.

INTRODUCTION

☆ ☆ ☆ ☆

For decades there has been a compelling need for an encyclopedic listing of many of those American service personnel who have distinguished themselves on the battlefield in the many military campaigns in which our nation's people have fought since the founding of our great country. *Encyclopedia of American War Heroes* helps to fulfill that need and serves as a ready historical reference, not only for those brave individuals and their families, but for many others who are interested in our nation's military history and in the individual heroic achievements recognized by the armed forces.

Because of the immensity of such a project, this encyclopedia contains only a sampling of the valiant deeds of Americans who have been recognized as heroes since 1675. Described are the deeds of American patriots; Native Americans; Union and Confederate officers and enlisted personnel; military leaders who made great contributions to our nation's war efforts; and hundreds of American service personnel cited individually for their heroic actions.

The information contained in this publication has been gleaned from many primary and secondary sources, including official U.S. Department of Defense, army, navy, Marine Corps, air force, and Coast Guard releases, reports, and memorandums, either wholly or partially emanating from their respective decorations and medals branches. Additionally, I have included source references—authors, titles, and dates of additional publications—hoping to guide the reader in new directions of reading, research, and discovery. Because of a devastating fire at the National Personnel Records Center in St. Louis during the 1970s, many personnel records were lost. Therefore the dates of birth and death for many service personnel in this volume were not available. When I first considered the criteria for "Who is a war hero?" I asked Lt. Col. Alex Lee, USMC (Ret.), formerly my company commander during the Vietnam War and later, as a lieutenant of marines, my battalion commander, for his opinion on the question and for the names of some of his heroes who would immediately come to mind. His reply, reproduced here, helped set the stage for the selection and inclusion of many of the heroic individuals listed in this work. Lt. Col. Lee's impressive military credentials squarely place him in a position to assist in the selection process.

A fifth-generation Californian, Alex Lee was commissioned on graduation from Stanford University, in Palo Alto, California, in 1956. As a marine infantry and reconnaissance officer, he served with distinction in operational and command billets throughout the world, including 39 months of command special field assignments during combat operations in the Republic of Vietnam.

He served a total of more than nine years in special operations assignments, which required operational service—openly and/or covertly—in 44 countries for various agencies of the United States government. He served two tours in research and development of special mission equipment, including operational analysis, combat equipment evaluation, test parachute work, test deep diving work, and test explosives work. Additionally, Lee served two tours at Headquarters, United States Marine Corps—one in a managerial position in the procurement process and the second as the developer of combat readiness evaluation systems for deploying Marine expeditionary units.

Lt. Col. Lee attended numerous military schools, including the Test Parachute School, the Airborne Course, Diving School, Special Forces School, High-Altitude Free-Fall School, Jungle Survival School, British Warfare School and the Australian Jungle Warfare School. His personal awards and decorations include the Silver Star, the Bronze with Combat "V" (Valor) Device, the Legion of Merit with Combat "V" Device, Purple Hearts (2), Navy Commendation Medal with Combat "V" Device (2) the Combat Action Ribbon, Vietnamese Cross of Gallantry (3). His unit awards include the Presidential Unit Citation (3), Navy Unit Citation (2), Meritorious Unit Citation, and, for Third Force Reconnaissance Company, the Valorous Unit Citation, for service in Vietnam in 1969/70. Only two units in the entire history of the United States Marine Corps have received this coveted unit award.

Lt. Col. Lee replied:

I know far more than 10 men who fit the definition of the word "hero." Marine Colonel John Ripley, for example, made all the right decisions and would never have been criticized by anyone had he not gone out on the bridge at Dong Ha ... but, no Medal of Honor! There is an aviator, an air force officer, who saw his wingman crash-land at Ta Bat (yes, our own Ta Bat in the A Shau Valley), and despite a heavy volume of enemy ground fire, he chose to land and fly his buddy out on the wing of his AD-5 as he hung precariously to the canopy rail. He made all the right decisions and could have elected to stay safe. Jim Tull, a marine tanker at the Chosin Reservoir in 1950, was on the last tank out of the Tok Tong Pass with no ammunition left, so he jumped off his tank and borrowed a 3.5-inch rocket launcher and dropped back behind the column. He knocked out at least a platoon of Chinese Communists, dashed back to his tank, and got a Bronze Star Medal for his heroic efforts. I have enough ego to put my day on Operation UTAH up as a demonstration of someone who goes forward, against all odds, with almost a certain death in the offing ... yet goes on to do the job. I know many young marines, 18 and 19 years old, who choked down their vomit, stood up, and went forward. In their hearts they were almost sure of dying, but having no choice, they went forward anyway. Just go back and look at Iwo Jima, or Tarawa, or Pelilieu ... just walking forward made heroic figures of those marines who did so.

Personally, I do not agree with the awarding of the Medal of Honor to those who jumped on hand grenades at the cost of their own life, nor awards of valor given to regimental commanders far from riflemen in their fighting holes, and a flock of aviation "b——" medals. I hark back to the Navy Cross awarded to the pilot in the OV-10 Bronco, given for his support of the Marine rifle company from 3/3 (Third Battalion/Third Marine Regiment) that was surrounded and cut up badly. While I got a very nice ride in the back seat of the same aircraft, while firing seven batteries of Marine artillery to help the company, we got 37 bullet holes in the aircraft and both of us could have died; however, the Navy Cross? No way. It was not a heroic act, period. It was the young Marine Pfc. on the ground, acting as the air liaison officer, who was a real hero, coming through, no matter the difficulty.

In my view, accidental heroics top out at the Navy Cross level. If I want someone to be a hero, he must have seen the need for action (above and beyond the call of duty), known that it was almost certain death to go do whatever was required, while knowing full well that a failure to perform the act would never receive critical comment by those who were not there, yet he gets up and goes out in the wind of shot and shell, and does what it takes to pull off the action. It is deep in my heart that knowing you need not go out there and die, but going anyway, after you know the fact—is what sets the act apart from what is normally demanded in close combat. Fixing bayonets when the enemy comes through the wire is nice, Distinguished Service Cross–level work, but leaving a safe fire-base and crossing through enemy lines to join a beleaguered unit about to be destroyed, and knowing that you don't have to do this thing, there is a heroism.

I could go on and, on, but I think that after 33 years you know me well enough to see the logic I use in seeking the "knowing" part of action in combat, as opposed to just fighting back hard when your unit is being chopped to bits. In fact, it is knowing that you really need not go out there and die that I use for rough criteria for the title heroic act.

I would suggest that anyone should read Stephen E. Ambrose's book *Band of Brothers: E Company, 506th Regiment, 101st Airborne from Normandy to Hitler's Eagle's Nest* about the company in the 101st Airborne from D-Day to the end of World War II. He has a lot of good information about "heroism," yet the men who did those brave deeds got little or no recognition. As you may remember, the U.S. Army's Second Rangle Battalion at Point du Hoc, on D-Day, dared greatly, yet few received any medals for their heroism. Hell, look at the paucity of medals for Third Force Reconnaissance Company Marines [during the Vietnam War] who did it all, no matter the cost.

No, astronauts are not heroes—brave men and women, hell yes, but not heroes. They are just brave individuals taking chances in a highly technological world. In many ways the 22-year-old line cop in South Chicago, East Los Angeles, or walking a beat in East Harlem is far closer to being a hero. He could quit the force on any day and become an office manager for a finance company, yet he goes out night after night and does his best, knowing that he could die and that no one would be critical if he gave up law enforcement and went to work in that finance office for about the same amount of money. The same applies to firemen who make their choices and do the work, knowing the inherent danger—neither cops nor firemen are often accidental heroes.

I really love the idea of this book, but it will be a tough one to do and it will be criticized for years. Douglas MacArthur was a brave and *perhaps* a heroic officer in World War I, but generals at their maps, who maneuver their armies over vast expanses of ground, should be evaluated for their failures … heroic actions are not a part of their act. While MacArthur was a bold, innovative, clever, and ego-mania–driven man—and a far better commander than many Marine Corps historians give him credit for— "hero" is not the right descriptive word for him.

Good luck on writing a reference book that should be mandatory reading by every American high school student—finally, a place where examples of our nation's true role models can be found.

—A. Lee, Marine

My own perspective on individual heroism is not based solely on historical research, but also on my 24 years of military service, first as a navy corpsman assigned to a Marine force reconnaissance team during the Vietnam War and later as an infantry officer in the United States Marine Corps, from 1974 to 1992.

Having been in combat as a corpsman during the Vietnam War; having been in combat against a numerically superior enemy force on numerous occasions; having been wounded in combat; having been decorated for heroism under fire; and having seen brave men perform heroic deeds under fire, I keep my own definition of who deserves the title of war hero.

At a minimum, the majority of the individuals listed in this work meet my criteria:

1. That the individual cited has taken the enemy under fire using small-unit, organic weapons, such as the rifle, pistol, and bayonet, fighting knife, ax, or club
2. That multiple witnesses observed that individual's actions, if possible
3. That the individual cited is usually wounded or killed in the action
4. That the individual cited is (usually) an officer in the grade of lieutenant colonel (O-5) or below or an enlisted man in the grade of staff sergeant (E-6) or below

There are, of course, exceptions to these criteria.

In our nation's early history military leaders left the job of killing to the enlisted men. They usually "observed the fray" from a removed and elevated position, usually one that guaranteed their survival. Unfortunately, success in battle was credited to the officer(s) in charge, and those individuals who made up the majority of the enlisted ranks were seldom mentioned for their individual heroic deeds.

Contained within these pages are also complete, albeit short, biographical sketches of great American military leaders who also, by their boldness, exceptional judgment, tactical expertise, strategy, efficiency, ego, and arrogance, must be viewed as fitting the term *heroic*. And, although it is a very small percentage of those rare individuals who have actually participated in close combat, those who survived and were awarded medals of distinction for their heroic actions would quietly tell us that they were simply "doing their job."

Recently, I enjoyed reading *The Spirit of America*, by William J. Bennett, the former secretary of education and chairman of the National Endowment for the Humanities under President Ronald Reagan, and a man whom I consider to be a 'national hero' in his own right. In his introduction, Mr. Bennett states,

> It is necessary for each generation of Americans to look at ourselves, since, as President Abraham Lincoln warned, the great deeds and virtues of the founding generation "grow more and more dim by the lapse of time." How can Americans fully know this country and themselves without knowing at least a little about the men and women who pledged and risked their "lives," "fortunes," and "sacred honor" for the blessings of liberty we enjoy today?
>
> Lately, Americans have become worried about the state of the culture and, in my opinion, rightly so. I have argued for years that it is not the economy that is the source of our present discontent. And most Americans now agree, citing moral decline as our chief malady. We have fallen way short of our duties and aspirations, and I do not exempt myself in this regard. We need to engage in a relearning—to borrow novelist's Tom Wolfe's phrase, "a great relearning." We also need to restore this nation's

sense of greatness, to learn once again about the great deeds and the great men and women of our past so that we might move forward.

The intent of this encyclopedia is to provide the reader with a reference of American war heroes. It does not include every recipient of the Medal of Honor, Navy Cross, Distinguished Service Cross, Silver Star, or Bronze Star but does provide a worthy sampling of those men and women who have distinguished themselves in combat, and by their exceptional leadership, throughout our nation's history. I believe this collection of American heroes will serve as a positive reflection of who we are as a nation. Although some survived their ordeals, many did not. These men and women are the role models whose examples of heroism will withstand the tests of time.

— Maj. Bruce H. Norton, USMC (Ret.)

AWARDS, DECORATIONS, AND HONORS

★ ★ ★ ★

One of the oldest traditions in the profession of arms is the recognition of heroic feats against an armed enemy. The ancient Greeks awarded crowns, the Romans, torques and decorative disks. A wreath made from branches of laurel was the greatest award a Roman citizen could win because it meant that he was the best, the most outstanding in his field. It was not given only to brave soldiers. It could be won for making a great speech, writing a great play, or winning a race. At the Olympic Games, the winner is still crowned with a laurel wreath.

The coins of the day were decorated with the emperor's head, and usually he was wearing a laurel wreath. As time passed, the wreath was moved off the head and placed on the obverse of the coins. Looking closely at the back of an American penny, you will see two small branches rising from the bottom. They are all that remain of the laurel wreath after 2,000 years.

This ancient tradition is carried on in the United States's awards and decorations system, which includes six medals that recognize heroism on the field of battle. To these are added two other types of awards, one recognizing meritorious service that is a response to the importance of administrative and logistical efficiency in modern warfare, the other recognizing participation in campaigns and completion of overseas tours of duty.

It is quite natural that the first award of honor for the common soldier was given in the United States, where the conception that all men are created equal is fundamental to our way of life.

The American system of military decorations began in 1782, when George Washington established the Badge of Military Merit to recognize "instances of unusual gallantry" as well as "extraordinary fidelity" and "essential service." The actual decoration was a heart-shaped piece of purple cloth that was sewn to the recipient's uniform coat. General Washington issued an order in 1782 that any soldier who showed outstanding bravery "shall be permitted to wear on his left breast the figure of a heart in purple cloth or silk edged with narrow lace.... The road to glory is thus opened to all."

In addition to the Purple Heart, six special medals were awarded during the American Revolution, three to generals and three to privates. General Washington received one for his "beating the British at Boston." Gen. Horatio Gates received one for winning the Battle of Saratoga and Gen. "Light Horse" Harry Lee, father of Gen. Robert A. Lee, received one for his participation in battle at Paulus Hook, New Jersey. The other three medals went to militiamen who captured the British spy Major John André while he was carrying the plans of West Point, which he had received from Benedict Arnold.

Except for these six medals, no recognition was given to hundreds of brave men during the American Revolution, the War of 1812, the Mexican War, and the early years of the Indian wars in the west. These men were unsung heroes because most citizens believed that wearing medals was not proper for Americans. They said, "If European soldiers wear medals, it's a good reason why Americans soldiers should not. We want no kings, no nobles, and no medals. Medals are not democratic."

Largely forgotten after the Revolutionary War, the decoration for honor was revived by the War Department as the Purple Heart in 1932, the 200th anniversary of George Washington's birthday. In its new form, this decoration recognizes military personnel wounded or killed in combat and does not itself constitute an award for heroic action.

America's highest award for gallantry, the Medal of Honor (often mistakenly called the Congressional Medal of Honor), was established during the Civil War, in 1862. Originally, it was used to recognize both gallantry in combat and meritorious performance, but by the end of the 19th century the standard for awarding this medal had become "conspicuous gallantry and intrepidity at the risk of life above and beyond the call of duty."

During World War I, two more decorations (Crosses) for heroism were added. The Distinguished Service Cross (Army), the Navy Cross, and the Air Force Cross (added in 1960) all recognize bravery that falls short of that action required for the Medal of Honor. The second medal, the Silver Star, is awarded by all services for gallantry that is less noteworthy than that required for a service cross.

Finally, there are three other decorations that recognize varying degrees of gallantry in combat: the Distinguished Flying Cross (authorized by Congress in 1926), the Bronze Star (authorized by executive order in 1944), and the Air Medal (established by executive order in 1942). All three of these medals may also be used to recognize outstanding service or special achievements that do not necessarily entail bravery in the face of an armed enemy. When the Bronze Star is awarded for heroic action, it is worn with a small bronze V device that stands for "valor." Without the V, the Bronze Star recognizes meritorious service in support of combat operations. Multiple awards of all decorations are indicated through a system of small metallic oak clusters and stars that are affixed to medals. In addition to medals recognizing heroism in combat, each service has a decoration for heroism and risk of life outside combat: the Soldier's Medal, the Navy and Marine Corps Medal, and the Airman's Medal.

Modern combat units became increasingly dependent upon support forces, whose personnel came to outnumber those in combat commands by nearly 10 to 1. Moreover, throughout the cold war, crews manning strategic weapons systems endured long hours on alert or patrol with virtually no opportunity to perform a heroic feat of arms. The need to recognize the contributions of personnel in noncombatant roles gave rise to a second set of military decorations.

The highest-ranking award in this second set is the Defense Distinguished Service Medal, bestowed by the secretary of defense. Just below this decoration are the army Distinguished Service Medal (DSM) and the navy DSM, established by Congress in 1918 and 1919, respectively; an air force DSM was added in 1960. These medals call for "specially meritorious service to the Government in a duty of great responsibility." Rounding out this set of awards are several other Department of Defense decorations and military service medals that recognize lower levels of achievement and meritorious service. Finally, the Air Force Combat Readiness Medal was established to recognize the sacrifice of service members who spent much, if not all, of their professional careers in roles related to deterring nuclear war.

The expansion of the U.S. overseas service requirement was accompanied by a steady rise in the number of decorations recognizing such factors as participation in a campaign and completion on overseas deployment, even in peacetime. This began in 1898, when the Dewey Medal was authorized for those who participated in the Battle of Manila Bay. Another form of participatory award is the unit citation, which recognizes those who serve in a unit that accomplished its mission in a superior manner. An example of this type of award is the Presidential Unit Citation.

Medals are usually worn only on ceremonial occasions. For routine, daily wear, each medal has a small oblong swatch that matches the pattern of the suspension ribbon.

Napoleon Bonaparte's comment to the effect that soldiers will risk their lives for a little piece of colored ribbon indicates the extreme importance the military attaches to its decorations for combat heroism. However, the criteria for awarding medals are highly subjective. Controversies relating to U.S. military decorations can be traced back as far as the Civil War, when the Medal of Honor was awarded under questionable circumstances on several occasions. During World War II, the number of decorations awarded raised serious questions about the significance of medals. In the course of this war, the army (which still included the Army Air Forces [AAF] gave out a total of 1,800,729 medals. Of these, 1,314,000, or 73 percent, went to personnel of the AAF, although they accounted for only 28 percent of the total personnel strength of the army. Similar problems have occurred right down to the Persian Gulf War of 1991.

As the ratio of support forces to combat forces increased dramatically in the 20th century, new awards to recognize and motivate support personnel proliferated, skewing the awards and decorations system toward meritorious service and mere participation in military activities. By the mid-1900s, the situation had reached the point where medals recognizing heroic combat service were often lost among the multiple rows of ribbons worn by virtually every career member of the armed services, the vast majority of whom had never been subjected to enemy fire. The U.S. awards and decorations system had yielded much of its traditional function of recognizing those who demonstrated extraordinary courage in combat.

The Medal of Honor

The first formal system for rewarding acts of individual gallantry by the nation's fighting men was established by General George Washington on August 7, 1782. Designed to recognize "any singularly meritorious action," the award consisted of a purple cloth heart. Records show that only three persons received the award: Sergeant Elijah Churchill, Sergeant William Brown, and Sergeant Daniel Bissel Jr.

The Badge of Military Merit, as it was called, fell into oblivion until 1932, when General Douglas MacArthur, then army chief of staff, pressed for its revival. Officially reinstituted on February 22, 1932, the now familiar Purple Heart was at first an army award, given to those who had been

The Air Force Medal of Honor, the Army Medal of Honor, and the Navy Medal of Honor

wounded in World War I or who possessed a Meritorious Service Citation Certificate. In 1943, the order was amended to include personnel of the navy, Marine Corps, and Coast Guard. Coverage was eventually extended to include all services and "any civilian national" wounded while serving with the armed forces.

Although the Badge of Military Merit fell into disuse after the Revolutionary War, the idea of a decoration for individual gallantry remained through the early 1800s. In 1847, after the outbreak of the Mexican War, a "certificate of merit" was established for any soldier who distinguished himself in action. No medal was awarded. After the U.S.-Mexican War, the award was discontinued; that meant there was no military award with which to recognize the nation's fighting men.

Early in the Civil War, a medal for individual valor was proposed to General in Chief of the Army Winfield Scott. But Scott felt medals smacked of European affectation and killed the idea. The medal found support in the navy, however, where it was felt recognition of courage in strife was needed. Public Resolution 82, containing a provision for a navy medal of valor, was signed into law by President Abraham Lincoln on December 21, 1861. The medal was "to be bestowed upon such petty officers, seamen, landsmen, and Marines as shall most distinguish themselves by their gallantry and other seamanlike qualities during the present war."

Shortly after this, a resolution similar in wording was introduced on behalf of the army. Signed into law July 12, 1862, the measure provided for awarding a Medal of Honor "to such noncommissioned officers and privates as shall most distinguish themselves by their gallantry in action, and other soldierlike qualities, during the present insurrection."

Although it was created for the Civil War, Congress made the Medal of Honor a permanent decoration in 1863.

Almost 3,429 men and 1 woman have received the award for heroic actions in the nation's battles since that time.

(Quoted passages are from American Forces Information Service. *Armed Forces Decorations and Awards,* Washington, D.C., Department of Defense, 1989.)

THE DISTINGUISHED SERVICE CROSS

Description: A cross of bronze, 2 inches in height and 1 $^{13}/_{16}$ inches in width, with an eagle on the center and a scroll below the eagle bearing the inscription "FOR VALOR." On the reverse side, the center of the cross is circled by a wreath with a space for engraving the name of the recipient.

Criteria

The Distinguished Service Cross is awarded to a person who, while serving in any capacity with the army, distinguishes himself or herself by extraordinary heroism not justifying the award of a Medal of Honor; while engaged in an action against an enemy of the United States; while engaged in military operations involving conflict with an opposing/foreign force; or while serving with friendly foreign forces engaged in an armed conflict against an opposing armed force in which the United States is not a belligerent party. The act or acts of heroism must have been so notable and have involved risk of life so extraordinary as to set the individual apart from his or her comrades.

The Distinguished Service Cross

Background

a. The Distinguished Service Cross was established by President Woodrow Wilson on January 2, 1918. General Pershing, commander in chief of the Expeditionary Forces in France, had recommended that recognition other than the Medal of Honor be authorized for the armed forces of the United States for service rendered, in like manner to that awarded by the European armies. The request for establishment of the medal was forwarded from the secretary of war to the president in a letter dated December 28, 1917. The act of Congress establishing this award (Public Law 193, 65th Cong.) dated July 9, 1918, is contained in Title 10 *United States Code (USC)* 3742. The establishment of the Distinguished Service Cross was promulgated in War Department General Order No. 6, dated January 12, 1918.

b. The first design of the Distinguished Service Cross was cast and manufactured by the United States Mint at Philadelphia. The die was cast from the approved design prepared by Lt. Aymar E. Embry, Engineers Officer Reserve Corps. Upon examination of the first medals struck at the mint, it was considered advisable to make certain minor changes to add to the beauty and the attractiveness of the medal. Because of the importance of the time element involved in furnishing the decorations to General Pershing, 100 of the medals were struck from the original design and numbered 1 to 100. These medals were furnished with the provision that these crosses be replaced when the supply of the second design, which would also be numbered 1 to 100, was accomplished.

c. Title 10, *USC* 3991, provides for a 10 percent increase in retired pay for enlisted personnel who have retired with more than 20 years of service if they have been awarded the Distinguished Service Cross.

d. Order of precedence and wear of decorations are contained in Army Regulation (AR) 670-1. The policy for awards, approving authority, supply, and issue of decorations, is contained in AR 600-8-22.

The Distinguished Service Cross (DSC) was established by order of the president January 2, 1918, and confirmed by Congress July 9, 1918. It is awarded to members of the United State Army serving after April 6, 1917, who distinguish themselves by "Extraordinary Heroism in Connection with Military Operations Against an Opposing Armed Force." Second and subsequent awards are denoted by bronze Oak Leaf Clusters; a silver Oak Leaf Cluster is worn in lieu of five bronze. Designed by Captain Aymar Embury, sculpted by Corporal P. L. Gaetano Cecere, it was awarded to United States Air Force personnel until 1960.

THE NAVY CROSS

The Navy Cross was established on February 4, 1919, with the passage of Public Law 193, by the 65th Congress of the United States. Until then there was

The Navy Cross

but one medal, the Medal of Honor, also known as the Congressional Medal of Honor because it was awarded in the name of the Congress.

Established in 1861, the Medal of Honor was awarded "for gallantry in action and other seaman-like (soldier-like) qualities." With this broad criterion, 2,625 Medals of Honor were awarded between 1862 and 1916, when a permanent Medal of Honor Board was established as part of a sweeping review of the entire award and decorations procedures of the military. Nine hundred ten awards of the Medal of Honor were recalled (864 of those recalled had been awarded to members of one regiment, the 27th Maine, by President Lincoln as inducement to continue guarding the capitol past the approaching end of their enlistment). No awards to navy personnel were, or have since been, recalled.

It had become clear during the First World War that one medal alone could not effectively recognize the full range of exceptional service, including heroism. So the criterion of the Medal of Honor was elevated; it was to be awarded to "one who shall in action with an enemy, distinguish himself conspicuously by gallantry and intrepidity at the risk of his life above and beyond the call of duty." Stringent requirements for documentation were imposed, and new awards were created in a descending order of precedence.

The Navy Cross came into existence at this time along with the Navy Distinguished Service Medal, the Army Distinguished Service Cross and Service Medal, and the Silver Star Certificates (later to become the Silver Star Medals). These were the frameworks of a graduated system of recognition, which had not existed previously.

From the awards' inception, the distinction between the Navy Cross (originally intended for combat bravery only) and the Navy Distinguished Service Medal became blurred. For many years the Navy Cross was ranked third in order of precedence below the Medal of Honor and the Navy Distinguished Service Medal. With the passage of Public Law 702, on August 7, 1942, the issue was resolved. This act clarified the criterion, which now states that the award for the Navy Cross shall be to

> any person while serving in any capacity with the Navy or Marine Corps who distinguishes himself with extraordinary heroism not justifying the award of the Medal of Honor while engaged in an action against an enemy of the United States; (2) while engaged in military operations involving conflict with an opposing foreign force; or (3) while serving with friendly foreign forces engaged in an armed conflict against an opposing armed force in which the United States is not a belligerent party. To warrant this distinctive decoration the act should involve risk of life so extraordinary as to set the person apart from his contemporaries. An accumulation of minor acts of heroism does not justify the award.

Congress also specified that the Navy Cross was to rank (along with the Army Distinguished Service Cross and now the Air Force Cross) as the second highest honor the nation can bestow for combat heroism.

The Navy Cross, made of bronze, was designed by James Earle Fraser. It is a broad-faced cross patee with the ends of the arms rounded. The cross is one and one-half inches wide with a circle in the middle of the cross encompassing the design of a sailing vessel. Laurel leaves are represented at each joining of the arms about the center. In the center of the circle on the reverse side of the medal are crossed anchors and the letters *USN*. The Navy Cross has not been numbered; nor has it usually been engraved with the name of the recipient.

The medal is suspended by a thin half-inch ring from a one-and-three-quarter-inch-wide ribbon on navy blue moire silk and a quarter-inch-wide white center stripe. Through World War II the metal used was a dark bronze. Since then the cross has been made of a lighter, brighter colored metal.

Sources
Chamber, John Whiteclay II. *The Oxford Companion to American Military History.* New York: Oxford University Press, 1999.

Kerrigan, Evans E. *War Medals and Decorations.* New York: Viking, 1990.

Stevens, Paul Drew, ed. *The Navy Cross—Vietnam: 1964–1973.* Forest Ranch, Calif.: Sharp & Dunnigan, 1987.

Werlich, Robert. *Orders and Decorations of All Nations: Ambient and Modern, Civilian and Military.* Washington, D.C.: Quaker Press, 1964.

Wyllie, Robert E. *Orders, Decorations, and Insignia, Military and Civil.* New York: G. P. Putnam's Sons, 1921.

AIR FORCE CROSS

The Air Force Cross is awarded to U.S. and foreign military personnel and civilians who have displayed extraordinary heroism in one of the following situations: while engaged in action against a U.S. enemy, while engaged in military operations involving conflict with a foreign force, or while serving with a friendly nation engaged in armed conflict against a force in which the United States is not a belligerent party.

The Air Force Cross is awarded when the heroic actions fall short of warranting the Medal of Honor.

Prior to 1960, when Congress established the Air Force Cross, enlisted men were decorated with the Distinguished Service Cross for heroic actions.

The Air Force Cross

THE SILVER STAR

Description
A gold star, $1\frac{1}{2}$ inches in circumscribing diameter with a laurel wreath encircling rays from the center and a $3/16$-inch-diameter silver star superimposed in the center. The pendant is suspended from a rectangle-shaped metal loop with rounded corners. The reverse has the inscription "FOR GALLANTRY IN ACTION."

Criteria

The Silver Star is awarded to a person who, while serving in any capacity with the United States Army, is cited for gallantry in action against an enemy of the United States while engaged in military operations involving conflict with an opposing foreign force or while serving with friendly foreign forces engaged in armed conflict against an opposing armed force in which the United States is not a belligerent party. The required gallantry, although of a lesser degree than that required for award of the Distinguished Service Cross, must nevertheless have been performed with marked distinction. Soldiers who received a citation for gallantry in action during World War I may apply to have the citation converted to the Silver Star Medal.

The Silver Star

Background

a. The Citation Star was established as a result of an act of Congress on July 9, 1918 (65th Cong. 2nd Sess., Ch. 143, p. 873) and was promulgated in War Department Bulletin No. 43, dated 1918. It was retroactive to include those cited for gallantry in action in previous campaigns back to the Spanish-American War. A letter from General Jervey, Office of the Chief of Staff, dated February 26, 1926, is quoted in part:

> The Secretary of War directs as follows—The following is the amended version of paragraph 187 of Army Regulation. "No more than one Medal of Honor or one Distinguished Service Cross or one Distinguished Service Medal shall be issued to any one person, but for each succeeding or act sufficient to justify the award of a Medal of Honor or Distinguished Service Cross or Distinguished Service Medal, respectively, a bronze oak leaf cluster, shall be issued in lieu thereof; and for each citation of an officer or enlisted man for gallantry in action, published in orders from headquarters of a force commanded by a general officer, not warranting the issue of a Medal of Honor, Distinguished Service Cross or Distinguished Service Medal, he shall wear a silver star, $^3/_{16}$ inch in diameter, as prescribed in Uniform Regulations.

Army Regulation 600-40, par. 48, September 27, 1921, specified that the Citation Star would be worn above the clasp, on the ribbon of the service medal for the campaign for service in which the citations were given.

b. On July 19, 1932, the secretary of war approved the Silver Star medal to replace the Citation Star. This design placed the Citation Star on a bronze pendant suspended from the ribbon design. The star was no longer attached to a service or campaign ribbon.

c. Authorization for the Silver Star was placed into law by an act of Congress for the navy on August 7, 1942, and an act of Congress for the army on December 15, 1942. The primary reason for congressional authorization was the desire to award the medal to civilians as well as army personnel. The current statutory authorization for the Silver Star Medal is Title 10, *U.S. Code*, Sec. 3746.

d. Order of precedence and wear of decorations are contained in Army Regulation 670-1. Policy for awards, approving authority, supply, and issue of decorations is contained in Army Regulation 600-8-22.

e. The design is by Bailey, Banks, and Biddle.

THE DISTINGUISHED FLYING CROSS

The Distinguished Flying Cross

Description

A bronze cross patee on which is superimposed a four-bladed propeller, 1 $^{11}/_{16}$ inches in width. Five rays extend from the reentrant angles, forming a one-inch square. The medal is suspended from a rectangle-shaped bar.

Criteria

The Distinguished Flying Cross is awarded to any person who, while serving in any capacity with the armed forces of the United States, distinguishes himself or herself by heroism or extraordinary achievement while participating in aerial flight. The performance of the act of heroism must be evidenced by voluntary action in recognition of sustained operational activities against an armed enemy.

Background

a. The Distinguished Flying Cross was established in the Air Corps Act, on July 2, 1926, Public Law 446, 69th Congress. The extraordinary achievement must have resulted in an accomplishment so exceptional and outstanding as to set the individual clearly apart from comrades or other persons in similar circumstances. Awards will be made only to recognize single acts of heroism or extraordinary achievement and will not be provided as an award "to any person, while serving in any capacity with the Air Corps of the Army of the United States, including the National Guard and the Organized Reserves, or with the United States Navy, since the 6th day of April 1917, who has distinguished, or who, after the approval of this Act, distinguishes himself by heroism or extraordinary achievement while participating in an aerial flight."

b. Various designs from the U.S. Mint, commercial artists, and the Office of the Quartermaster General were submitted to the Commission of Fine Arts on May 31, 1927. The commission approved a design submitted by Arthur E. Dubois and Elizabeth Will.

c. Initial awards of the Distinguished Flying Cross were made to persons who made record breaking long-distance and endurance flights and who set altitude records. The secretary of war authorized the first Distinguished Flying Cross to Capt. Charles A. Lindbergh in a letter dated May 31, 1927. With the support of the secretary of war, the Wright brothers retroactively received the Distinguished Flying Cross. This award required a special act of Congress, since the law precluded awarding it to civilians.

d. The current statutory requirements for award of the Distinguished Flying Cross to army personnel are contained in Title 10, *U.S. Code* Sec. 3749; Sec. 6245 for navy personnel; and Sec. 8749 for air force personnel. Enlisted personnel may be entitled to a 10 percent increase in retirement pay under Title 10, *U.S. Code,* Sec. 3991, when credited with heroism equivalent to that required for the award of the Distinguished Service Cross.

e. Order of precedence and wear of decorations are contained in Army Regulation 670-1. Policy for awards, approving authority, supply, and issue of decorations is contained in Army Regulation 600-8-22.

THE BRONZE STAR

Description

A bronze star $1^1/_2$ inches in circumscribing diameter. In the center thereof is a $^3/_{16}$-inch-diameter superimposed bronze star; the center line of all rays of both stars coincides. The reverse has the inscription "HEROIC OR MERITORIOUS ACHIEVEMENT" and a space for the name of the recipient to be engraved. The star is suspended from the ribbon by a rectangle-shaped metal loop with the corners rounded.

Criteria

a. The Bronze Star Medal is awarded to any person who, while serving in any capacity in or with the military of the United States after December 6, 1941, distinguished himself or herself by heroic or meritorious achievement or service, not involving participation in aerial flight, while engaged in an action against an enemy of the United States; while engaged in military operations involving conflict with an opposing foreign force; or while serving with friendly foreign forces engaged in an armed conflict against an opposing armed force in which the United States was not a belligerent party.

The Bronze Star

b. Awards may be made for acts of heroism, performed under circumstances described, that are of lesser degree than required for the award of the Silver Star.

c. Awards may be made to recognize single acts of merit or meritorious service. The required achievement or service, although of lesser degree than that required for the award of the Legion of Merit, must nevertheless have been meritorious and accomplished with distinction.

Background

a. General George C. Marshall, in a memorandum to President Roosevelt dated February 3, 1944, wrote: "The fact that the ground troops, Infantry in particular, lead miserable lives of extreme discomfort and are the ones who must close in personal combat with the enemy, makes the maintenance of their morale of great importance. The award of the Air Medal may have had an adverse reaction on the ground troops, particularly the Infantry Riflemen who are now suffering the heaviest losses, air or ground, in the Army, and enduring the greatest hardships." The Air Medal had been adopted two years earlier to raise airmen's morale.

b. President Roosevelt authorized the Bronze Star Medal by Executive Order 9419 dated February 4, 1944, retroactive to December 7, 1941. This authorization was announced in War Department Bulletin No. 3, dated February 10, 1944. The executive order was amended by President Kennedy, per Executive Order 11046, dated August 24, 1962, to expand the authorization to include those serving with friendly forces.

c. As a result of a study conducted in 1947, a policy was implemented to authorize the retroactive award of the Bronze Star Medal to soldiers who had received the Combat Infantryman Badge or the Combat Medical Badge during World War II. The basis for doing this was that the badges were awarded only to soldiers who had borne the hardships that motivated General Marshall's support of the Bronze Star Medal. Both badges required a recommendation by the commander and a citation in orders.

d. Order of precedence and wear of decorations is contained in Army Regulation (AR) 670-1. Policy for awards, approving authority, supply, and issue of decorations is contained in AR 600-8-22. The design was created by Bailey, Banks, and Biddle.

THE PURPLE HEART

Originally established by General George Washington on August 7, 1782, at Newburgh on the Hudson, New York, as an award for outstanding military merit, or the Badge of Merit, the decoration was in the form of an embroidered

heart-shaped badge of purple cloth, only three noncommissioned officers received the order at that time. Though never officially abolished, it was not again awarded for almost one hundred and fifty years. Upon its revival in 1932, as the Purple Heart, the decoration was to be awarded to members of the United States Army in two categories: "For being wounded in action in any war or campaign under conditions which entitle the wearing of a wound chevron" and "For those persons who perform any singularly meritorious act of extraordinary fidelity or essential service."

In 1942, President Franklin D. Roosevelt issued an executive order that provided that the Purple Heart would

The Purple Heart   be made available to members of all the United States armed services who were wounded in action. Since then the Purple Heart has become one of the most highly respected decorations of the U.S. armed forces. The decoration holds a unique position in that it can be earned in only one way, by being wounded. An attendant requirement is that the wound must have been received as a direct result of enemy actions. Second and subsequent awards are denoted by bronze Oak Leaf Clusters; a silver Oak Leaf Cluster is worn in lieu of five bronze Oak Leaf Clusters. The medal was designed by Elizabeth Will and sculpted by John Sinnock.

A

Abrams, Creighton Williams, Jr. (1914–1974) *One of the leading United States Army generals of the 20th century.*

Born in Springfield, Massachusetts, on September 15, 1914, Abrams earned an appointment to West Point and graduated 185th of 276, in the famous class of 1936 that produced 60 wartime general officers, and was commissioned a second lieutenant of cavalry. He was promoted to captain and transferred to armor in 1940, commanding tank units during World War II and winning distinction as commander of the 37th Tank Battalion.

Aboard his tank named Thunderbolt, Abrams led the column of Fourth Armored Division into Bastogne on December 26, 1944, relieving the beleaguered 101st Airborne Division. He was commended publicly by Gen. George S. Patton, who said, "I'm supposed to be the best tank commander in the Army, but I have one peer—Abe Abrams." Promoted to temporary colonel in 1945, he served as director of tactics at the Armor School, Fort Knox, Kentucky, from 1946 to 1948. Abrams graduated from the Command and General Staff School in 1949, then served as a chief of staff for the I, X, and IX Corps successively during the Korean War (June 1950–July 1953). He attended the U.S. Army War College in 1953 and was promoted to brigadier general (1956) for reserve components on the Army General Staff. He was promoted to the grade of major general in May 1960, having served in a variety of command and staff positions; he was commander Third Armored Division (1960–1962) and later led troops in quelling disturbances over civil rights in Mississippi from September 1962 to May 1963.

Abrams was promoted to lieutenant general and made commander of V Corps in Germany in August 1963. He was promoted to the grade of general and made army vice chief of staff in September 1964. As deputy commander U.S. Military Assistance Command Vietnam (MACV) in May 1967, he directed operations in northern South Vietnam during the Tet Offensive (January 30–February 29, 1968) and its aftermath (March 1–April 15, 1968). He succeeded Gen. William C. Westmoreland as commander of U.S. MACV and remained in that post, directing the "vietnamization" of the war and the disengagement of American forces, until his appointment as chief of staff of the army in July 1972. General Abrams died while serving in that post on September 4, 1974.

An aggressive but thoughtful commander, Abrams had experience and skill in conventional mechanized warfare that did not leave him well equipped for the military peculiarities of the Vietnam War; despite this handicap he worked diligently to ready the South Vietnamese forces to fight on their own and shifted away from General Westmoreland's massive "search and destroy" operations to a war of patrols and ambushes, endeavoring to destroy the Viet Cong–North Vietnamese army military support system. He was particularly sensitive to the war's effects on the Vietnamese people.

In the last two years of his life, as army chief of staff, he was determined to rebuild the army in a way that would ensure its decisive use in future engagements. His vision is widely credited with creating the foundation for the 1991 Desert Storm victory over Iraq during the Persian Gulf War. His insistence on joining superbly trained soldiers to multiple and synergistically devastating equipment led to the development of the air land battle, the strategy that produced the most lopsided military victory in history in 1991.

Additional Reading
Dupuy, Trevor N. *The Harper Encyclopedia of Military Biography.* Edison, N.J. Book Sales Inc., 1995.
Millet, Allan R. *A Short History of the Vietnam War.* Bloomington: Indiana University Press, 1978.
Palmer, David R. *Summons of the Trumpet.* Novato, Calif.: Presidia Press, 1978.

Abshire, Bobby W. *Corporal, United States Marine Corps, was awarded the Navy Cross for his heroic action, in the Republic of Vietnam, on May 21, 1966.*

Citation: "For extraordinary heroism as Crew Chief of a UH-1E helicopter while serving with Marine Observation Squadron TWO during operations against the enemy in the vicinity of Da Nang, Vietnam on 21 May 1966. When a platoon from Company A, First Battalion, Ninth Marines was pinned down in an open rice paddy by heavily armed North Vietnamese and Viet Cong forces, Corporal Abshire's medical evacuation helicopter was assigned the mission of recovering the casualties, which included over half the men of the platoon. Despite vicious incoming fire, which damaged the helicopter, a successful landing was made on the second attempt. Since remnants of the platoon were too heavily committed to assist in the evacuation, Corporal Abshire jumped from the helicopter and gallantly carried two wounded Marines into the aircraft while enemy rounds struck all around him. When it became necessary to return to the home field to replace the battle-damaged helicopter, he quickly transferred equipment to a new aircraft and volunteered to return. On each of the eight trips by his aircraft into the besieged zone, Corporal Abshire ignored enemy fire to assist in loading wounded and dead Marines. On one occasion, he swiftly silenced an enemy machine gun with accurate fire from a grenade launcher. His fearless and determined efforts contributed in large measure to the success of the mission, in which twenty-three casualties were evacuated. His courage in the face of hostile fire and his compassion for his wounded comrades were an inspiration to all who observed him. By his daring actions and devotion to duty in spite of great personal risk, Corporal Abshire reflected great credit upon himself and upheld the highest traditions of the Marine Corps and the United States Naval Service."

Source and Additional Reading
Navy Cross Citation.
Stevens, Paul Drew, ed. *The Navy Cross: Vietnam: Citations of Awards to Men of the United States Marine Corps, 1964–1973.* Forest Ranch, Calif.: Sharp & Dunnigan, 1987.

Adams, John T. *Corporal, USMC, was awarded (posthumously) the Navy Cross for his heroism in combat, in the Republic of Vietnam on June 16, 1966.*

Citation: "For extraordinary heroism while serving with the First Platoon, Company C, First Reconnaissance Battalion in Vietnam on 16 June 1966. Corporal Adams was a member of a reconnaissance team occupying an observation post on Hill 488, Quang Tin Province, deep in enemy controlled territory. During the early morning hours the platoon of 18 Marines was subjected to an intense assault by an estimated North Vietnamese unit of battalion size. As the members of his team were withdrawing to a predesignated defensive perimeter, Corporal Adams braved the withering small-arms fire and returned accurate rifle fire which momentarily slowed the enemy assault force and enabled his companions to reach the relative safety of the defensive position. Firing out all of his ammunition, Corporal Adams fearlessly charged directly into the assaulting horde and, using his rifle as a club, killed two of the enemy soldiers before he was struck down by automatic weapons fire. Severely wounded, the once again engaged an enemy soldier in hand-to-hand combat, and in a final effort, killed his foe. As a result of his courageous action and fighting spirit, his comrades were able to rally and withstand the onslaught of the numerically superior enemy. Corporal Adams upheld the highest traditions of the Marine Corps and the United States Naval Service. He gallantly gave his life in the cause of freedom."

Source and Additional Reading
Navy Cross Citation.
Stevens, Paul Drew, ed. *The Navy Cross: Vietnam: Citations of Awards to Men of the United States Marine Corps, 1964–1973.* Forest Ranch, Calif.: Sharp & Dunnigan, 1987.

Adams, Laurence R., III *Captain, United States Marine Corps, was awarded the Navy Cross for his heroic actions in combat, in the Republic of Vietnam, on January 12, 1969.*

Citation: "For extraordinary heroism on 12 January 1969, as a pilot in Medium Helicopter Squadron 165, Marine Aircraft Group 16, First Marine Aircraft Wing, in connection with combat operations against the enemy in the Republic of Vietnam. Assigned the emergency mission of extracting an eight-man reconnaissance team which had been engaged in combat with a numerically superior hostile force for twenty-four hours in a densely-jungled, mountainous area southwest of An Hoa, Captain Adams piloted his transport helicopter to the designated area and maintained his craft in a hover above tall trees while a cable ladder was lowered to the ground. Undaunted by the extremely heavy volume of enemy fire which caused extensive damage to his helicopter, he remained in this dangerously exposed position and then inadvertently lifted out of the hazardous area with only five of the eight members of the reconnaissance team on the ladder. Informed that three Marines still remained on the ground, Captain Adams resolutely elected to return to the perilous area after disembarking the five patrol members. Despite deteriorating weather conditions, approaching darkness, and a lack of adequate support from the helicopter gunships which had expended nearly all of their ordnance, he established a hover on his third approach, after twice being driven back by the intense enemy fire, and succeeded in rescuing the three remaining Marines. A subsequent investigation revealed that his aircraft had sustained a total of twenty-three hits and over eighty grenade fragment holes from its extended exposure to the enemy fire. By his courage, superior airmanship, and dedication, Captain Adams was directly instrumental in saving the lives of eight fellow Marines and upheld the highest traditions of the Marine Corps and of the United States Naval Service."

Source and Additional Reading

Navy Cross Citation.

Stevens, Paul Drew, ed. *The Navy Cross: Vietnam: Citations of Awards to Men of the United States Marine Corps, 1964–1973*. Forest Ranch, Calif.: Sharp & Dunnigan, 1987.

Adams, Stanley T. (b. 1922) *Master sergeant (then Sfc.), United States Army, Company A, 19th Infantry Regiment, so distinguished himself in combat, during the Korean War, that he was awarded the Medal of Honor for his heroic actions.*

Born: May 9, 1922, DeSoto, Kans.; **Entered service at:** Olathe, Kans.; **Place and date:** Near Sesim-ni, Korea, February 4, 1951. G.O. No.: 66, August 2, 1951.

Citation: "M/Sgt. Adams, Company A, distinguished himself by conspicuous gallantry and intrepidity above and beyond the call of duty in action against an enemy. At approximately 0100 hours, M/Sgt. Adams' platoon, holding an outpost some 200 yards ahead of his company, came under a determined attack by an estimated 250 enemy troops. Intense small arms, machine gun, and mortar fire from 3 sides pressed the platoon back against the main line of resistance. Observing approximately 150 hostile troops silhouetted against the skyline advancing against his platoon, M/Sgt. Adams leaped to his feet, urged his men to fix bayonets, and he, with 13 members of his platoon, charged this hostile force with indomitable courage. Within 50 yards of the enemy M/Sgt. Adams was knocked to the ground when pierced in the leg by an enemy bullet. He jumped to his feet and, ignoring his wound, continued on to close with the enemy when he was knocked down 4 times from the concussion of grenades which had bounced off his body. Shouting orders he charged the enemy positions and engaged them in hand-to-hand combat where man after man fell before his

Stanley T. Adams

terrific onslaught with bayonet and rifle butt. After nearly an hour of vicious action M/Sgt. Adams and his comrades routed the fanatical foe, killing over 50 and forcing the remainder to withdraw. Upon receiving orders that his battalion was moving back he provided cover fire while his men withdrew. M/Sgt. Adams' superb leadership, incredible courage, and consummate devotion to duty so inspired his comrades that the enemy attack was completely thwarted, saving his battalion from possible disaster. His sustained personal bravery and indomitable fighting spirit against overwhelming odds reflect the utmost glory upon himself and uphold the finest traditions of the infantry and the military service."

Source

Medal of Honor Citation.

Allen, Ethan (1738–1789) *Revolutionary War hero, leader of the Green Mountain Boys, and captor of Fort Ticonderoga, 1775.*

Born in Litchfield, Connecticut, on January 21, 1738, Allen was prevented from completing formal education by his father's death in 1755, but he read widely. He served at Fort

William Henry during the French and Indian War in 1757. He acquired land, in 1769, with four brothers in the New Hampshire Grants (now Vermont, but then a disputed area between New York and New Hampshire). Allen organized resistance to New York settlement in the Grants and led the Green Mountain Boys, a specially raised defensive militia group, in guerrilla attacks on the area. His activities were so notorious that Governor Tryon of New York offered £100 for his capture. Accompanied by Benedict Arnold, Allen led his Green Mountain Boys to seize Fort Ticonderoga in a surprise assault early on the morning of May 10, 1775. Voted out of command of the Green Mountain Boys when he joined the Continental Army, he served on the expedition against Canada and was captured in an ill-advised assault on Montreal on September 25, 1775. Sent in chains to England, but returned on parole in October 1776, Allen was formally exchanged for a British officer on May 6, 1778, and reported to General George Washington's headquarters at Valley Forge. Given the rank of brevet colonel in the Continental Army, he returned to Vermont in the summer of 1778. After failing to arouse congressional interest in his cause of statehood for Vermont, he entered into negotiations with the British commander at Quebec to make Vermont a British colony. These plans never materialized, and Allen died in Burlington, February 11, 1789.

A talented guerrilla leader and a cantankerous, controversial individual, Ethan Allen was devoted to Vermont but was relatively indifferent to the United States.

Source

Allen, Ethan. *The Narrative of Colonel Ethan Allen.* 1779. Reprint Bedford, Mass.: Applewood Books, 1987.

Holbrook, Stewart Hall. *Ethan Allen.* New York: Macmillan, 1940.

Allex, Jake (b. 1887) *Corporal, United States Army, Company H, 131st Infantry, 33d Division, awarded the Medal of Honor during World War I.*

Born: July 13, 1887, Prizren, Serbia; **Entered service at:** Chicago, Illinois; **Place and date:** At Chipilly Ridge, France, August 9, 1918. **G.O. No.:** 44, W.D., 1919.

Citation: "At a critical point in the action, when all officers with his platoon had become casualties, Corporal Allex took command of the platoon and led it forward until the advance was stopped by fire from a machine-gun nest. He then advanced alone for about 30 yards in the face of intense fire and attacked the nest. With his bayonet he killed 5 of the enemy, and when it was broken, used the butt of his rifle, capturing 15 prisoners."

Source
Medal of Honor Citation.

Alspaugh, Timothy D. *Seaman (SN) United States Navy, so distinguished himself in combat, in the Republic of Vietnam, that he was awarded the Navy Cross for his heroic actions.*

Citation: "For extraordinary heroism during operations against an armed enemy in the Republic of Vietnam on 25 September 1969. SN Alspaugh was the after .50 caliber machine gunner aboard PBR 677, which had inserted in a night waterborne guard post on the north bank of the Cai Lon River in support of interdiction operations in Kien Giang province. His boat was acting as a cover boat and had taken a position about fifty yards astern of the patrol's lead boat, with its starboard side to a heavy growth of nipa palm along the river bank. Shortly past midnight, after several hours of waiting quietly in the darkness to detect enemy movement on the water, SN Alspaugh observed what he believed to be a sampan on the river upstream from his boat. Alerting his Boat Captain and bringing his machine gun to bear over the port quarter, he was concentrating on the barely visible craft when he was struck on his left side by an object that he instinctively recognized as a grenade thrown from the underbrush. He immediately shouted a warning to his fellow crewmembers, at the same time bending down to search for the grenade, which had come to rest on the pump covers on the far side of his gun mount. Despite the extreme darkness and the imminent danger of an explosion, SN Alspaugh succeeded in locating the grenade and quickly threw it back into the small clearing from which it had been thrown. Even before the grenade exploded near the enemy's position, he was firing his .50 caliber machine gun into the brush, continuing until the boats were clear of the area. Because of SN Alspaugh's quick reaction and disregard for his own personal safety, the patrol escaped without casualty. His extraordinary courage and selfless devotion to duty reflected great credit upon himself and were in keeping with the finest traditions of the United States Naval Service."

Source
Navy Cross Citation.

Ambrose, Gerald D. *Lance corporal, USMC, was awarded the Navy Cross for his heroic action in combat on the night of January 8, 1970, in the Republic of Vietnam.*

Citation: "For extraordinary heroism while serving as a Squad Leader with Company M, Third Battalion, First Marines, First Marine Division in connection with combat operations against the enemy in the Republic of Vietnam. On the night of 8 January 1970, Lance Corporal Ambrose was leading a ten-man joint combat patrol consisting of four United States Marines and six Republic of Vietnam Regional Forces soldiers, when the unit came under a heavy volume of fire from approximately twenty-five enemy soldiers near the village of Chau Son (1) in Quang Nam province. Ignoring the hostile rounds and grenades impacting around him, Lance Corporal Ambrose quickly deployed his men and initiated an aggressive assault against the enemy positions. When a hand grenade exploded near him, he sustained several wounds, but steadfastly refused medical attention. Shouting encouragement to his men, he relentlessly pressed the advance, personally accounting for five enemy killed. During the ensuing fierce fire fight, he repeatedly exposed himself to the hostile fusillade as he called directions to his companions and maintained the momentum of the attack until the enemy was forced to retreat, abandoning numerous weapons, documents containing information of intelligence value, and four troops who were captured. Although suffering intense pain and bleeding profusely, Lance Corporal Ambrose again refused medical assistance and, with his last remaining strength, led his unit, and the four captured wounded enemy, safely back over 1,200 meters of heavily booby-trapped enemy territory to a secure base. His heroic and resolute actions inspired all who observed him and were instrumental in defeating a determined numerically superior hostile force. By his courage, aggressive fighting spirit, and unwavering devotion to duty, Lance Corporal Ambrose contributed significantly to the accomplishment of his unit's mission and upheld the highest traditions of the Marine Corps and of the United States Naval Service."

Source
Stevens, Paul Drew, ed. *The Navy Cross: Vietnam: Citations of Awards to Men of the United States Marine Corps, 1964–1973*. Forest Ranch, Calif.: Sharp & Dunnigan, 1987.

Anderson, Beaufort T. (b. 1945) *Technical sergeant, U.S. Army, 381st Infantry, 96th Infantry Division, awarded the Medal of Honor for his heroic actions during World War II.*
     Born: Eagle, Wis.; **Entered service at:** Soldiers Grove, Wis.; **Place and date:** Okinawa, April 13, 1945. **G.O. No.:** 63, June 27, 1946.

Citation: "He displayed conspicuous gallantry and intrepidity above and beyond the call of duty. When a powerfully conducted predawn Japanese counterattack struck his unit's flank, he ordered his men to take cover in an old tomb, and then, armed only with a carbine, faced the onslaught alone. After emptying 1 magazine at pointblank range into the screaming attackers, he seized an enemy

mortar dud and threw it back among the charging Japs, killing several as it burst. Securing a box of mortar shells, he extracted the safety pins, banged the bases upon a rock to arm them and proceeded alternately to hurl shells and fire his piece among the fanatical foe, finally forcing them to withdraw. Despite the protests of his comrades, and bleeding profusely from a severe shrapnel wound, he made his way to his company commander to report the action. T/Sgt. Anderson's intrepid conduct in the face of overwhelming odds accounted for 25 enemy killed and several machine-guns and knee mortars destroyed, thus single-handedly removing a serious threat to the company's flank."

Source
Medal of Honor Citation.

Anderson, Johannes S. (unknown) *First sergeant United States Army, Company B, 132d Infantry, 33d Division, awarded the Medal of Honor for his actions in World War I.*
     Born: Finland; **Entered service at:** Chicago, **Place and date:** At Consenvoye, France, October 8, 1918. **G. O. No.:** 16, W. D. 1919.

Citation: "While his company was being held up by intense artillery and machine-gun fire, 1st Sgt. Anderson, without aid, voluntarily left the company and worked his way to the rear of the nest that was offering the most stubborn resistance. His advance was made through an open area and under constant hostile fire, but the mission was successfully accomplished, and he not only silenced the gun and captured it, but also brought back with him 23 prisoners."

Source
Medal of Honor Citation.

Anderson, Richard Heron (1821–1879) *General officer, Confederate States Army.*

Born in Sumter County, South Carolina, on October 7, 1821, Anderson was the son of a physician. He graduated from West Point in 1842 and was commissioned in the dragoons. He "served with distinction" under Gen. Winfield Scott during the Mexican War and was breveted first lieutenant for bravery at San Agustin Atlapulco on August 17, 1847. He served in Pennsylvania, Kansas, and Nebraska, rising to the grade of captain in 1861. He resigned from the United States Army and accepted the colonelcy of the First South Carolina Infantry in March of that year. His unit supported the siege of Fort Sumter

(April 12–14), and he was promoted to brigadier general in July 1861. He became the brigade commander of James Longstreet's division in the Army of Northern Virginia in the spring of 1862 and again "fought with distinction" at the Seven Pines (Fair Oaks) May 31–June 1 and Seven Day's Battles, June 25–July 1. As a major general, Anderson led a division at Second Bull Run (August 29–30) and at Antietam on September 17, when we was wounded. He fought again at Chancellorsville (May 1–6, 1863) and served in General A. P. Hill's corps at Gettysburg, where he captured Seminary Ridge. As a temporary lieutenant general, he replaced the wounded Longstreet as commander of I Corps in May 1864. He occupied Spotsylvania Court House after a night march on May 7 and held that important position throughout the ensuing battle (May 8–12). He then led I Corps during the Battle of Cold Harbor (June 3–12) and conducted offensive operations south of Petersburg from June to October. He relinquished I Corps command when General Longstreet recovered and reverted to his divisional command and rank. He suffered his only defeat at Sayler's Creek, where he halted his men to cover Lee's retreat on April 6, 1865. He extracted the remnants of his command with difficulty and rejoined the Army of Northern Virginia, but reorganization left him without a command. After the war, Anderson returned to South Carolina to work as a railroad official and a phosphate inspector. He died in Beaufort, South Carolina, on June 26, 1879.

Additional Reading

Catton, Bruce. *The Army of the Potomac Trilogy.* New York: Anchor Books, 1962.

Dupuy, Trevor, N. *The Harper Encyclopedia of Military Biography.* Edison. N.J.: Book Sales Inc.; 1995.

Freeman, Douglas Southall. *Lee's Lieutenants.* 3 vols. New York: Charles Scribner's Sons, 1944.

Warner, Ezra. *Generals in Gray.* Baton Rouge: Louisiana State University Press, 1978.

Anderson, Robert (1805–1871) *General officer, Union army*

Born near Louisville, Kentucky, on June 14, 1805, to a prominent Virginia family, Anderson graduated from West Point in 1825 and was commissioned as an artillery officer. He served for a time as secretary to his brother, the minister to Colombia, before assuming his military duties.

As a colonel of Illinois Volunteers during the Black Hawk War (April–August 1832) he was breveted a captain for his heroic conduct during service in Florida against the Seminoles (1836–38). He served under General Winfield Scott during the Mexican War, winning a brevet to major for his actions on September 8, 1847, at Molino del Rey, where he was wounded. Selected to command forts around the harbor of Charleston, South Carolina, partly because of his southern and proslavery sentiments, he moved his headquarters from the indefensible Fort Moultrie to Fort Sumter in Charleston Harbor after South Carolina's secession from the Union, December 20, 1860.

He pursued a conciliatory attitude toward Charleston authorities, and although he refused to surrender, he also did not assist the federal supply ship *Star of the West* when it was shelled by shore batteries manned by Citadel cadets on January 9, 1861. His second refusal to surrender, on April 11, provoked the bombardment of April 12–13, which rendered Fort Sumter indefensible. Anderson surrendered the fort on April 14, 1861. Promoted to the grade of brigadier in May, he commanded the Department of Kentucky until he fell gravely ill in October. Anderson retired from active duty in October and was breveted major general in February 1865. He raised the Union flag at Fort Sumter on April 14, 1865. While on a trip to Europe, Anderson died in Nice, France, on October 26, 1871.

Revered as a heroic, competent, and resourceful officer, he performed well in a difficult position requiring diplomatic and political skills as well as acute military sense.

Source

Dupuy, Trevor N. *The Harper Encyclopedia of Military Biography.* Edison, N.J.: Book Sales Inc., 1992.

Andrews's Raiders *The first men to be awarded the Medal of Honor, during the American Civil War, for actions against the Western and Atlantic Railroad in Georgia in April 1862*

Ross, Marion A.   Sergeant major, Second Ohio Infantry

Pittinger, William   Sergeant, Company G, Second Ohio Infantry

Bensinger, William   Private, Company G, 21st Ohio Infantry

Buffum, Robert   Private, Company H, 21st Ohio Infantry

Knight, William   Private, Company E, 21st Ohio Infantry

Parrott, Jacob   Private, Company K, 33d Ohio Infantry

During the Civil War, 19 of 22 men (including 2 civilians) who, by the direction of Maj. Gen. Don Carlos Buell, penetrated nearly 200 miles south into the enemy's territory and captured a railroad train at Big Shanty, Georgia, distinguished themselves heroically, in an attempt to destroy the bridges and railroad track between Chattanooga and Atlanta.

The daring mission was conceived and led by James J. Andrews, a civilian spy for the federal government, who recruited 19 volunteers from an Ohio brigade in the Army of the Tennessee to accompany him. They and two other civilians were to infiltrate the Confederate lines in small groups in civilian clothes, posing as Kentuckians traveling to Atlanta, Georgia, to join the Confederate army. Once in Atlanta, they were to hijack a Confederate train and take it northward toward Chattanooga, Tennessee, tearing up the railroad tracks and burning the railway bridges behind them, cutting off the main supply line for the besieged city of Chattanooga. They initially succeeded in hijacking the train, powered by a locomotive named *The General,* but the plan was foiled by the conductor of the train, William Fuller, who after being left behind immediately went in pursuit, first on foot, then by handcart, then by a small switch engine, and finally by catching up to another locomotive, named *Texas.* Fuller and the crew of the *Texas* managed to stay close enough behind Andrews and his raiders on *The General* that the raiders were never able to stop long enough to inflict significant damage on the railroad. With Fuller sounding the alarm while in close pursuit, Confederate cavalry troops were able to head off *The General.* Andrews and all of his raiders abandoned the train and fled. All were captured within a week. Andrews, the other two civilians, and five of the soldiers were eventually hanged as spies. The others endured whippings and other torture but managed to escape en masse after a few months. The six men listed here were recaptured and subjected to more beatings and other torture before finally being freed in a prisoner exchange. These men were the first recipients of the Medal of Honor. There were no provisions for a posthumous award; it is assumed that the soldiers who were executed might have also received it.

Source

Above and Beyond. A History of the Medal of Honor from the Civil War to Vietnam. Boston: Boston Publishing, 1985.

Antonio, Joseph J. (b. 1950) *Sergeant, United States Army.*

Born February 17, 1950, in Westboro, Massachusetts, Joseph Antonio joined the army as a private, in 1969. He saw combat duty in Vietnam in 1970–71 and during this time was awarded four Bronze Stars, the Purple Heart, and one Air Medal.

First Bronze Star Citation: "Sergeant Joseph J. Antonio distinguished himself by valorous actions on 25 May 1970, while serving as an assistant Patrol Leader with Company B, 1st Battalion (Airborne) 503d Infantry in Northern Phu My District, Republic of Vietnam. On this date Sergeant Antonio's patrol engaged an enemy base camp. After silencing two enemy soldiers, Sergeant Antonio's patrol was subjected to intense enemy small-arms fire and hand grenades, and was forced to withdraw. Although wounded by fragments from an enemy grenade, Sergeant Antonio refused medical attention and led a reinforcing element in an assault on the heavily fortified enemy position, exposing himself repeatedly to intense hostile fire. Sergeant Antonio's personal bravery and devotion to duty were in keeping with the highest traditions of the military and reflect great credit upon himself, his unit, and the United States Army."

Second Bronze Star Citation: "The Bronze Star Medal (First Oak Leaf Cluster) is presented to Sergeant Joseph J. Antonio, United States Army, who distinguished himself by outstanding meritorious achievement in connection with military operations against a hostile force in the Republic of Vietnam. During the period of 28 February 1970, to 3 September 1970, he consistently manifested exemplary professionalism and initiative in obtaining outstanding results. His rapid assessment and solution to numerous problems inherent in a combat environment

Antonio, Joseph J.

greatly enhanced the allied effectiveness against a determined and aggressive enemy. Despite many adversities, he invariably performed his duties in a resolute and efficient manner. Energetically applying his sound judgment and extensive knowledge, he has contributed materially to the successful accomplishment of the United States mission in the Republic of Vietnam. His loyalty, diligence and devotion to duty were in keeping with the highest traditions of the military service and reflect great credit upon himself and the United States Army."

Third Bronze Star Citation: "For heroism in connection with ground operations against a hostile force in the Republic of Vietnam. Sergeant Antonio distinguished himself by exceptionally valorous actions on 19 September 1970. On this day, while on a mission to search a cave complex being used by the enemy as a POW Compound and a Viet Cong Infrastructure Headquarters, Sergeant Antonio exposed himself to enemy fire on many occasions. At every opportunity he volunteered to go into the cave to search for enemy soldiers, documents and weapons. On one of his many trips down into the cave Sgt. Antonio exposed himself to deadly accurate enemy fire to retrieve a wounded comrade. Without regard for his own safety, Sergeant Antonio moved about the cave to complete the mission successfully. As a result of Sergeant Antonio's efforts, thirty pounds of documents, fifteen rucksacks, and several enemy weapons were captured. Sergeant Antonio imparted a sense of urgency, purpose and determination to the men of Company B, that subsequently played a key role in the success of the company's mission. His valorous efforts and high morale in the face of the enemy helped to disrupt the enemy's mission and indirectly saved the lives of many other comrades. Sergeant Antonio's extraordinary heroism and concern for the accomplishment of the mission were in keeping with the highest traditions of the military service and reflect great credit upon himself and his unit, and the United States Army."

Fourth Bronze Star Citation: "The Bronze Star Medal is presented to Sergeant Joseph J. Antonio, United States Army, who distinguished himself by outstanding meritorious service in connection with military operations against a hostile force in the Republic of Vietnam. During the period February 1970 to February 1971, he consistently manifested exemplary professionalism and initiative in obtaining outstanding results. His rapid assessment and solution to numerous problems inherent in a combat environment greatly enhanced the allied effectiveness against a determined and aggressive enemy. Despite many adversities, he invariably performed his duties in a resolute and efficient manner. Energetically applying his sound judgment and extensive knowledge, he has contributed materially to the successful accomplishment of the United States' mission in the Republic of Vietnam. His loyalty, diligence and devotion to duty were in keeping with the highest traditions of the military service and reflect great credit upon himself and the United States Army."

Air Medal Citation: "By Direction of the President, the Air Medal is presented to Sergeant Joseph J. Antonio, United States Army, who distinguished himself by meritorious achievement, while participating in sustained aerial flight, in support of combat ground forces in the Republic of Vietnam. During the period of 20 February 1970 to 3 September 1970, he actively participated in more than twenty-five aerial missions over hostile territory in support of operations against communist aggression. During all of these flights, he displayed the highest order of air discipline and acted in accordance with the best traditions of the service. By his determination to accomplish his mission, in spite of the hazards inherent in repeated aerial flights over hostile territory, and by his outstanding degree of professionalism and devotion to duty, he has brought credit upon himself, his organization, and the United States Army."

Source
Staff.
United States Army Citations.

Antrim, Richard Not (b. 1907) *Commander, United States Navy,; awarded Medal of Honor for heroic actions during World War II.*

Born: December 17, 1907, Peru, Ind.; **Entered service at:** Indiana; **Place and date:** Makassar, Celebes, Netherlands East Indies, April 1942.

Citation: "For conspicuous gallantry and intrepidity at the risk of his life above and beyond the call of duty while interned as a prisoner of war of the enemy Japanese in the city of Makassar, Celebes, Netherlands East Indies, in April 1942. Acting instantly on behalf of a naval officer who was subjected to a vicious clubbing by a frenzied Japanese guard venting his insane wrath upon the helpless prisoner, Comdr. (then Lt.) Antrim boldly intervened, attempting to quiet the guard and finally persuading him to discuss the charges against the officer. With the entire Japanese force assembled and making extraordinary preparations for the threatened beating, and with the tension heightened by 2,700 Allied prisoners rapidly closing in, Comdr. Antrim courageously appealed to the fanatic enemy, risking his own life in a desperate effort to mitigate the punishment. When the other had been beaten unconscious by 15 blows of a hawser and was repeatedly kicked by 3 soldiers to a point beyond which he could not survive, Comdr. Antrim gallantly stepped forward and indicated to the perplexed guards that he would take the remainder of the punishment, throwing the Japanese completely off balance in their amazement and eliciting a roar of acclaim from the suddenly inspired Allied prisoners. By his fearless leadership and valiant concern for the welfare of another, he not only saved the life of a fellow officer and stunned the Japanese into sparing his own life but also brought about a new respect for American officers and men and a great improvement in camp living conditions. His heroic conduct throughout reflects the highest credit upon Comdr. Antrim and the U.S. Naval Service."

Source
Medal of Honor Citation.

Archer, James Jay (1817–1864) *General officer, Confederate States Army.*

A lawyer and Mexican War veteran, James Archer resigned his captain's commission in the regular army on March 14, 1861, to receive the same rank in the Confederate service two days later. Although a Marylander, Archer was appointed colonel, fifth Texas, a regiment organized in Richmond from independent companies, on October 2, 1861. He commanded his regiment, and sometimes the brigade, at the batteries at Evansport along the Potomac and on the Peninsula in the actions at Eltham's Landing and Seven Pines. He was promoted to brigadier general, Confederate States Army (CSA), June 3, 1862, and given command of Hatton's old brigade of Alabama, Georgia, and Tennessee troops (Hatton had been killed at Seven Pines). The Georgians were eventually transferred out and replaced by more Alabamians, but the brigade became known as the Tennessee Brigade. Archer's commands in the Army of Northern Virginia included Tennessee Brigade, A. P. Hill's division (June 3–July 1862); Tennessee Brigade, A. P. Hill's division, Jackson's corps (July 27, 1862–May 30, 1863); Tennessee Brigade, Heth's division, A. P. Hill's corps (May 30–July 1, 1863); and Archer's and Walker's brigades, Heth's division, A. P. Hill's corps (August 19–October 24, 1864).

Commanding his brigade, Archer took part in actions at Beaver Dam Creek, Gaines' Mill, Frayer's Farm, Cedar Mountain, second Bull Run, the capture of Harpers Ferry, Antietam, Fredericksburg, and Chancellorsville.

On the first day at Gettysburg an Irishman in the Union's Iron Brigade, captured Archer, the first general taken from the Army of Northern Virginia since Lee had taken command. While imprisoned at Johnson's Island, Ohio, Archer let the Confederate War Department know through a paroled prisoner that the guards could be overwhelmed but the southerners would have no way of getting off the island. On June 21, 1864, Archer was ordered sent to Charleston Harbor to be placed under Confederate fire in retaliation for southern treatment of prisoners. Later exchanged, Archer was ordered to the Army of Ten-nessee for duty on August 9, 1864, but he was redirected to the Army of Northern Virginia 10 days later.

He was assigned command of his own as well as Walker's brigades, which had been temporarily consolidated. Suffering from the effects of his imprisonment and the rigors of the Petersburg trenches, including the Battle of Peebles' Farm, Archer died on October 24, 1864.

Source and Additional Reading
Boatner, Mark M. *The Civil War Dictionary* Rev. ed. New York: David Mckay Co., 1988.
Freeman, Douglas S. *Lee's Lieutenants.* 3 vols. New York: Charles Scribner's Sons, 1944.

Armistead, Lewis Addison (1817–1863) *Brigadier general, Confederate States Army*

Lewis A. Armistead nearly scuttled his military career when he broke a plate over the head of a fellow cadet, Jubal A. Early, and was expelled from West Point. He was, however, commissioned directly into the infantry in 1839 and served in the Mexican War, being wounded at Chapultepec and earning two brevets. He resigned his captaincy on May 26, 1861, and headed back east to offer his services to the Confederacy. His assignments included major, Infantry (from March 16, 1861); colonel, 57th Virginia (September 23, 1861); brigadier general, Confederate States Army (CSA) (April 1, 1862); commanding brigade, Department of Norfolk (ca. April 1–12, 1862); commanding brigade, Huger's division, Department of Northern Virginia (April 12–July 1862); commanding brigade, Anderson's division, First Corps, Army of Northern Virginia (July–September 17, 1862); and commanding brigade, Pickett's division in First Corps, Army of Northern Virginia (October 1862–February 25, 1863, and May–July 3, 1863), in the Department of Virginia and North Carolina (February 25–April 1, 1863), and in the Department of Southern Virginia (April 1–May 1863).

After serving in western Virginia, he was given command of a brigade in the Norfolk area and later served with it on the Peninsula, seeing action at Seven Pines and in the Seven Days. He fought at second Bull Run and Antietam, where he was wounded. After being lightly engaged at Fredericksburg, he went to southeastern Virginia, in his home state, with Longstreet. Returning for the invasion of Pennsylvania, he fell mortally wounded among the guns of Cushing's battery during Pickett's Charge at Gettysburg. He died two days later in Union hands.

Source and Additional Reading
Coddington, Edwin B. *The Gettysburg Campaign.* New York: Scribner, 1968.

Freeman, Douglas S. *Lee's Lieutenants*. 3 vols. Scribners, New York, 1942–1944.

Armstrong, Russell P. *Staff sergeant, United States Marine Corps, was awarded the Navy Cross for his heroic actions in combat on September 7 and 8, 1967, in the Republic of Vietnam.*

Citation: "For extraordinary heroism while serving as a Platoon Commander with Company I, Third Battalion, Twenty-sixth Marines, Third Marine Division in the Republic of Vietnam on 7 and 8 September 1967. While moving toward the battalion perimeter near Con Thien, Company I came under a heavy volume of rocket, mortar and artillery fire supporting an attack by a reinforced North Vietnamese Army company which caused numerous casualties and separated the friendly unit into two groups. Rapidly assessing the situation, Staff Sergeant Armstrong fearlessly raced across the fire-swept terrain as he consolidated his position and organized a defensive perimeter. Shouting words of encouragement to his men and directing their suppressive fire against the enemy, he was supervising the movement of the more seriously wounded Marines to the center of the position when he was severely injured in both legs by a hostile mortar round impacting nearby. Unable to walk, he dragged himself across the hazardous area by the use of his arms alone and resolutely directed his platoon in successfully joining with the main body of the company. Although in great pain, Staff Sergeant Armstrong steadfastly refused medical evacuation and skillfully began coordinating artillery and mortar fire against the enemy soldiers, frequently adjusting the rounds to within 50 meters of friendly lines. Although periodically lapsing into unconsciousness, he continued his determined efforts throughout the night, crawling among his men to encourage them and to ensure that every possible avenue of enemy approach was effectively covered by firepower. Upon the arrival of a relief force in the early hours of the following morning, he permitted himself to be evacuated only after ascertaining that all of his Marines were accounted for and the more seriously injured had been removed. His heroic and decisive actions were instrumental in his unit's accounting for over 60 of the enemy killed. By his courage, aggressive leadership and selfless devotion to duty, Staff Sergeant Armstrong upheld the highest traditions of the Marine Corps and the United States Naval Service."

Source and Additional Reading
Navy Cross Citation.
Stevens, Paul Drew, ed. *The Navy Cross: Vietnam: Citations of Awards to Men of the United States Marine Corps, 1964–1973*. Forest Ranch, Calif.: Sharp & Dunnigan, 1987.

Ashby, James W. (d. 1967) *United States Navy hospital corpsman awarded the Navy Cross, posthumously, for his heroic actions on June 1, 1967, in the Republic of Vietnam.*

Citation: "For extraordinary heroism on 1 June 1967, while serving as a corpsman with Company 'L', Third Battalion, Ninth Marines, Third Marine Division (Rein), FMF, in the Republic of Vietnam. During a search and destroy operation, Petty Officer Ashby's company came under intense fire from a large North Vietnamese Army force deeply entrenched in a cleverly-concealed and heavily defended bunker complex, and suffered heavy casualties during the first few minutes of the fierce battle. Responding immediately, Petty Officer Ashby dashed from his position of relative safety and, seemingly impervious to the murderous hostile automatic-weapons fire sweeping the area, moved through the open terrain, treating and encouraging the wounded. Completely aware of the grave danger involved in remaining in a position exposed to the withering enemy fire, he staunchly refused to seek cover while there were wounded Marines in need of assistance, placing the welfare of his wounded comrades above his own personal safety. As he knelt over a seriously wounded Marine, shielding the Marine with his own body while administering lifesaving first aid, Petty Officer Ashby was mortally wounded by enemy sniper fire. By his inspiring courage in the face of great personal danger, his deep compassion for his comrades-in-arms, his outstanding professional ability, and his unfaltering devotion to duty, he succeeded in saving the lives of many Marines and upheld the highest traditions of the United States Naval Service."

Source and Additional Reading
Navy Cross Citation.
Stevens, Paul Drew, ed. *The Navy Cross: Vietnam: Citations of Awards to Men of the United States Marine Corps, 1964–1973*. Forest Ranch, Calif.: Sharp & Dunnigan, 1987.

* * * *

Badnek, Samuel J. *Private, United States Marine Corps, was awarded the Navy Cross for his heroic actions, in August 1965, in the Republic of Vietnam.*

Citation: "For extraordinary heroism while serving with Company 'H', Second Battalion, Fourth Marines, during Operation STARLITE near Chu Lai, Vietnam, on 18 August 1965. Private Badnek's platoon was temporarily pinned down by intense automatic weapons, mortar and grenade fire delivered by an insurgent communist (Viet Cong) assault force. In the early moments of the engagement, two enemy grenadiers were silenced, causing the Viet Cong to fall back and regroup, all the while keeping the Marines under intense fire. Realizing the seriousness of the situation, and with total disregard for his own safety, Private Badnek stripped all combat equipment from his body and boldly dashed forty-five yards through heavy fire to reach the enemy. Hurling several grenades into the enemy position, he personally killed eight of the guerrillas. Stunned by his one-man assault, the remaining enemy forces rapidly became disorganized and were unable to conduct a counterattack on the Marines now advancing upon them. Although he sustained a head wound during his heroic act, Private Badnek remained undeterred as he continued to ferociously engage the enemy, directing accurate and effective rifle fire into the enemy position. Later, after withdrawing to a helicopter evacuation site, he assisted in loading his wounded comrades aboard the aircraft, refusing evacuation himself until all other casualties had embarked. Private Badnek's courageous actions, inspiring combative spirit and loyal devotion to duty reflect great credit upon the traditions of the United States Marine Corps and the United States Naval Service."

Source
Navy Cross Citation.

Stevens, Paul Drew, ed. *The Navy Cross: Vietnam: Citations of Awards to Men of the United States Marine Corps, 1964–1973.* Forest Ranch, Calif.: Sharp & Dunnigan, 1987.

Baker, Thomas A. *Sergeant, United States Army, Company A, 105th Infantry, 27th Infantry Division, distinguished himself in combat and was awarded (posthumously) the Medal of Honor for his heroic actions during World War II.*
    Born: Troy, N.Y.; **Entered Service at:** Troy, N.Y., **Place and date:** Saipan, Mariana Islands, June 19 to July 7, 1944. **G.O. No.:** 35, May 9, 1945.

Citation: "For conspicuous gallantry and intrepidity at the risk of his life above and beyond the call of duty at Saipan, Mariana Islands, 19 June to 7 July 1944. When his entire company was held up by fire from automatic weapons and small-arms fire from strongly fortified enemy positions that commanded the view of the company, Sgt. (then Pvt.) Baker voluntarily took a bazooka and dashed alone to within 100 yards of the enemy. Through heavy rifle and machine-gun fire that was directed at him by the enemy, he knocked out the strong point, enabling his company to assault the ridge. Some days later while his company advanced across the open field flanked with obstructions and places of concealment for the enemy, Sgt. Baker again voluntarily took up a position in the rear to protect the company against surprise attack and came upon 2 heavily fortified enemy pockets manned by 2 officers and 10 enlisted men which had been bypassed. Without regard for such superior numbers, he unhesitatingly attacked and killed all of them. Five hundred yards farther, he discovered 6 men of the enemy who had concealed themselves behind out lines and destroyed all of them. On 7 July

1944, the perimeter of which Sgt. Baker was a part was attacked from 3 sides by from 3,000 to 5,000 Japanese. During the early stages of this attack, Sgt. Baker was seriously wounded but he insisted on remaining in the line and fired at the enemy at ranges sometimes as close as 5 yards until his ammunition ran out. Without ammunition and with his own weapon battered to uselessness from hand-to-hand combat, a comrade, who was then himself wounded, carried him about 50 yards to the rear. At this point Sgt. Baker refused to be moved any farther stating that he preferred to be left to die rather than risk the lives of any more of his friends. A short time later, at his request, he was placed in a sitting position against a small tree. Another comrade, withdrawing, offered assistance. Sgt. Baker refused, insisting that he be left alone and be given a soldier's pistol with its remaining 8 rounds of ammunition. When last seen alive, Sgt. Baker was propped against a tree, pistol in hand, calmly facing the foe. Later Sgt. Baker's body was found in the same position, gun empty, with 8 Japanese lying dead before him. His deeds were in keeping with the highest traditions of the U.S. Army."

Source
Medal of Honor Citation.

isolated troops. Aware that leaving the position would sever contact with the 8,000 Marines trapped at Yudam-ni, and jeopardize their chances of joining the 3,000 more awaiting their arrival in Hagaru-ri for the continued drive to the sea, he chose to risk loss of his command rather than sacrifice more men if the enemy seized control and forced a renewed battle to regain the position, or abandon his many wounded who were unable to walk. Although severely wounded in the leg in the early morning of the 29th, Captain Barber continued to maintain personal control, often moving up and down the lines on a stretcher to direct the defense and consistently encouraging and inspiring his men to supreme efforts despite the staggering opposition. Waging desperate battle throughout 5 days and 6 nights of repeated onslaughts launched by the fanatical aggressors, he and his heroic command accounted for approximately 1,000 enemy dead in this epic stand in sub-zero weather, and when the company was relieved, only 82 of his original 220 men were able to walk away from the position so valiantly defended against insuperable odds. His profound faith and courage, great personal valor, and unwavering fortitude were decisive factors in the successful withdrawal of the Division from the death-trap in the Chosin Reservoir sector and reflected the high-

Barber, William E. (b. 1919) *Captain, United States Marine Corps.*

Born in Dehart, Kentucky, Bill Barber was the commanding officer of Company F, Second Battalion, Seventh Marines, First Marine Division, at the Chosin Reservoir area, in Korea, in late 1950, when he distinguished himself heroically in combat and was awarded the Medal of Honor.

Citation: "For conspicuous gallantry and intrepidity at the risk of his life above and beyond the call of duty, as commanding officer of Company F in action against enemy aggressor forces. Assigned to defend a 3-mile mountain pass along the division's main supply line and commanding the only route of approach in the march from Yudam-ni to Hagaru-ri, Captain Barber took position with his battle-weary troops and, before nightfall, had dug in and set up a defense along the frozen, snow-covered hillside. When a force of estimated regimental strength savagely attacked during the night, inflicting heavy casualties and finally surrounding his position following a bitterly fought 7-hour conflict, Captain Barber, after repulsing the enemy, gave assurance that he could hold if supplied by airdrops and requested permission to stand fast when orders were received by radio to fight his way back to a relieving force after 2 reinforcing units had been driven back under fierce resistance in their attempts to reach the

William E. Barber

est credit upon Captain Barber, his brave officers and men, and the United States Naval Service."

Source and Additional Reading
Blakeney, Jane. *Heroes: U.S. Marine Corps 1861–1955*. Washington D.C.: Guthrie, 1957.
Medal of Honor Citation.
Saluzzi, Joseph. *Red Blood . . . Purple Hearts: The Marines in the Korean War*. Brooklyn, N.Y.: Eagle Production, 1990.

Barnum, Harvey C., Jr. (b. 1940) *Captain (then 1st lt.), United States Marine Corps, Company H, Second Battalion, Ninth Marines, Third Marine Division (Rein), so distinguished himself in combat, during the Vietnam War, that he was awarded the Medal of Honor for his heroic actions.*

Born: July 21, 1940, Cheshire, Conn.; **Entered service at**: Cheshire, Conn.; **Place and date**: Ky Phu in Quang Tin Province, Republic of Vietnam, December 18, 1965.

Citation: "For conspicuous gallantry and intrepidity at the risk of his life above and beyond the call of duty. When the company was suddenly pinned down by a hail of extremely accurate enemy fire and was quickly separated from the remainder of the battalion by over 500 meters of open and fire-swept ground, and casualties mounted rapidly, Lt. Barnum quickly made a hazardous reconnaissance of the area, seeking targets for his artillery. Finding the rifle company commander mortally wounded and the radio operator killed, he, with complete disregard for his safety, gave aid to the dying commander, then removed the radio from the dead operator and strapped it to himself. He immediately assumed command of the rifle company, and moving at once into the midst of the heavy fire, rallying and giving encouragement to all units, reorganized them to replace the loss of key personnel and led their attack on enemy positions from which deadly fire continued to come. His sound and swift decisions and his obvious calm served to stabilize the badly decimated units and his gallant example as he stood exposed repeatedly to point out targets served as an inspiration to all. Provided with 2 armed helicopters, he moved fearlessly through enemy fire to control the air attack against the firmly entrenched enemy while skillfully directing 1 platoon in a successful counterattack on the key enemy positions. Having thus cleared a small area, he requested and directed the landing of two transport helicopters for the evacuation of the dead and wounded. He then assisted in the mopping up and final seizure of the battalion's objective. His gallant initiative and heroic conduct reflected great credit upon himself and were in keeping with the highest traditions of the Marine Corps and the U.S. Naval Service."

Harvey C. Barnum Jr.

Source
Marine Corps Historical Center.
Medal of Honor Citation.

Barton, Clarissa "Clara" Harlow (1821–1912)
"The Angel of the Battlefield" during the American Civil War and founder of the American Red Cross.

Clara Barton was born on December 25, 1821, in North Oxford, Massachusetts. She was the youngest of five children of Stephen and Sarah (Stone) Barton. Her father was a veteran, a prosperous farmer, and a sawmill operator. Her mother was a homemaker.

Her older brothers and sisters provided much of Barton's education, and while still a teenager she started to teach in Massachusetts. In 1850, she took a break to attend the Liberal Institute of Clinton, New York, an advanced school for women educators. She resumed her teaching career in New Jersey, where, in 1852, she founded one of that state's first public schools in Bordentown. She started this school with six students, and by the close of the year there were six hundred attending.

In February 1854, she resigned from her teaching post and moved to Washington, D.C., where she took a job as a copyist in the U.S. Patent Office. She was the first woman to hold an independent clerkship in the federal government. She served from 1854 until 1857 and then again in 1860.

During the early years of the Civil War, she began to accumulate first-aid supplies because she was concerned about the plight of the soldiers on the battlefield. She gained her first experience with the wounded when the casualties from the secessionist attack on the sixth Massachusetts were taken to the capital from Baltimore. At the bloody Battle of Antietam her wagon followed the Union Second Corps onto the battlefield. A surgeon was killed while taking a drink of water from her, and she even operated on one of the wounded soldiers, extracting a bullet from his cheek.

Despite the initial opposition of both the War Department and many field surgeons, she and a few friends began to distribute first-aid supplies to field hospitals, camps, and battlefields. In addition to distributing supplies, she nursed wounded soldiers. She continued with her efforts in the field until the summer of 1864, when she became superintendent of Union nurses.

At the close of the war, at the request of President Lincoln, Barton became involved in finding information on missing Civil War soldiers. She helped to identify and mark the graves of almost thirteen thousand Union prisoners buried at Andersonville, Georgia. She also drew up lists and gathered information on other missing soldiers and had the information published in northern newspapers, where friends and relatives of the soldiers might see it.

From 1866 to 1868, Barton spent much of her time giving speeches about her wartime experiences. As a lecturer, she visited Dansville, New York, where she was later to settle for a time. By 1869 she suffered a physical breakdown and was advised by her doctors to go to Europe to rest.

Barton's time of rest was short-lived. While visiting Switzerland, she found out about the International Committee of the Red Cross, and in 1870–71 she aided in their efforts during the Franco-Prussian War.

"The Angel of the Battlefield" went on to found the American Red Cross in 1881 and served as its president from 1882 to 1904. Under her leadership, the focus of the committee grew from warfare to include natural disasters.

Source and Additional Reading

Barton, William Eleazar. *The Life of Clara Barton, Founder of the American Red Cross.* New York: Free Press, 1994.

Dubowski, Cathy East. *Clara Barton: Healing the Wounds.* New York: Silver Burdett Press, 1991.

Oates, Stephen. *A Woman of Valor: Clara Barton.* New York: HarperCollins, 1994.

Ross, Isabel. *Angel of the Battlefield: The Life of Clara Barton, Notable American Women.* Vol. 1, New York: Harper & Row, 1956, pp. 103–108.

Basilone, John (1916–1945) *Gunnery sergeant, United States Marine Corps, awarded the Medal of Honor for his heroic actions on Guadalcanal in 1942 and the Navy Cross for his actions in the Iwo Jima campaign, in which he was killed in action.*

Born: November 4, 1916, Buffalo, N.Y.; **Entered service at:** Raritan, N.J.; **Place and date:** Guadalcanal, Soloman Islands, October 24–25, 1942.

At Guadalcanal, where he was serving with the First Battalion, Seventh Marines, First Marine Division, Basilone used a machine gun and a pistol to pile up 38 Japanese bodies in front of his emplacement and to be awarded his nation's highest military decoration.

On Iwo Jima, Sergeant Basilone again distinguished himself, single-handedly destroying a Japanese blockhouse while braving a smashing bombardment of enemy heavy-caliber fire. For this exploit he was posthumously awarded the Navy Cross. While on Iwo Jima, he was

John Basilone

attached to the First Battalion, Twenty-seventh Marines, Fifth Marine Division. The son of an Italian-born father, Basilone had spent nearly six years in the U.S. armed forces and is credited with playing a major role in the virtual annihilation of an entire Japanese regiment. He was a sergeant at the time.

President Franklin D. Roosevelt signed the citation, which accompanied the Medal of Honor.

Citation: "For extraordinary heroism and conspicuous gallantry in action against enemy Japanese forces, above and beyond the call of duty, while serving with the 1st Battalion, 7th Marines, 1st Marine Division in the Lunga Area, Guadalcanal, Solomon Islands, on 24 and 25 October 1942. While the enemy was hammering at the Marines' defensive positions, Sgt. Basilone, in charge of 2 sections of heavy machine-guns, fought valiantly to check the savage and determined assault. In a fierce frontal attack with the Japanese blasting his guns with grenades and mortar fire, one of Sgt. Basilone's sections, with its guncrews, was put out of action, leaving only 2 men able to carry on. Moving an extra gun into position, he placed it in action, then, under continual fire, repaired another and personally manned it, gallantly holding his line until replacements arrived. A little later, with ammunition critically low and the supply lines cut off, Sgt. Basilone, at great risk of his life and in the face of continued enemy attack, battled his way through hostile lines with urgently needed shells for his gunners, thereby contributing in large measure to the virtual annihilation of a Japanese regiment. His great personal valor and courageous initiative were in keeping with the highest traditions of the U.S. Naval Service."

The story about the 38 Japanese bodies is from Pfc. Nash W. Phillips, of Fayetteville, North Carolina, who was in the same organization with John Basilone on Guadalcanal.

"Basilone had a machine gun on the go for three days and nights without sleep, rest or food," Phillips recounted. "He was in a good emplacement, and causing the Japs lots of trouble, not only firing his machine gun but also using his pistol."

Basilone's buddies on Guadalcanal called him "Manila John" because he had served with the army in the Philippines before enlisting in the Marine Corps.

John was one of a family of 10 children. Hi father, Salvatore Basilone, was born just outside Naples, Italy, and immigrated to the United States at an early age. He operated a one-man tailor shop in Somerville, New Jersey. The Marine hero's mother, Mrs. Dora Basilone, was born in Raritan, New Jersey, where the family had settled.

John Basilone had five brothers and four sisters. Two brothers followed John into the Marine Corps, George William and Donald Francis; and, Alphonse, served with the army in Iceland.

John Basilone was born in Buffalo, New York, on November 4, 1916. He attended St. Bernard Parochial School in Raritan, New Jersey, before enlisting in the army at the age of 18. After completing his three-year enlistment he returned home to work as a truck driver in Reistertown, Maryland.

In July 1940, Basilone enlisted in the Marine Corps at Baltimore. Before going to the Solomon Islands he saw service at Guantanamo Bay, Cuba, in addition to training at the Marine Barracks, Quantico, Virginia; Marine Barracks, Paris Island, South Carolina; and at New River, North Carolina.

On July 10, 1944, John Basilone and Sergeant Lena Riggi of Portland, Oregon, formerly a member of the Marine Corps Women's Reserve, were married. Mrs. Basilone was presented the posthumously awarded Navy Cross.

After World War II, Gunnery Sgt. John Basilone's remains were reinterred in the Arlington National Cemetery; in July 1949, the USS *Basilone*, a destroyer, was commissioned in his honor at the Boston Naval Shipyard.

Source and Additional Reading
Documentation; Headquarters Marine Corps.
Boswell, Rolfe. *Medals for Marines.* New York: Vail-Ballou Press, 1945.

Bearss, Hiram Iddings (1875–1938) *Brigadier general, United States Marine Corps, awarded the medal of honor for heroism in the Samar campaign in the Spanish-American War.*

Born: April 13, 1875, Indiana; **Entered service at:** May 27, 1898; **Place and date:** Samar, Philippine Islands, November 17, 1901.

Bearss was appointed a second lieutenant in the Marine Corps in the Spanish-American War, May 27, 1898, and was honorably discharged February 21, 1899. He was appointed a first lieutenant in the Marine Corps, June 2, 1899; was promoted to captain July 23, 1900; to major, May 16, 1915; to lieutenant colonel, August 29, 1916; and to colonel (temporary), July 1, 1918. He was placed on the retired list, incapacitated for active service by a Marine Retirement Board by reason of physical disability incident to his service, and was advanced to the rank of brigadier general on the retired list, January 16, 1936, by reason of having been specially commended for heroism in combat in World War I (Act of January 16, 1936). He died August 27, 1938.

Early in his career, he served in the Philippine Islands from December 1899 to May 1902. During this period he served with Major Waller's battalion in Samar from October 1901 to March 1902. Much later, his extraordinary heroism during the Samar campaign was rewarded with the Medal of Honor presented to him on March 13, 1934.

Citation: "For extraordinary heroism and eminent and conspicuous conduct in battle at the junction of the Cadacan and Sohoton Rivers, Samar, Philippine Islands, 17 November 1901. Col. Bearss (then Capt.), second in command of the columns upon their uniting ashore in the Sohoton River region, made a surprise attack on the fortified cliffs and completely routed the enemy, killing 30 and capturing and destroying the powder magazine, 40 lantacas (guns), rice, food and cuartels. Due to his courage, intelligence, discrimination and zeal, he successfully led his men up the cliffs by means of bamboo ladders to a height of 200 feet. The cliffs were of soft stone of volcanic origin, in the nature of pumice, and were honeycombed with caves. Tons of rocks were suspended in platforms held in position by vine cables (known as bejuco) in readiness to be precipitated upon people below. After driving the insurgents from their position, which was almost impregnable, being covered with numerous trails lined with poison spears, pits, etc., he led his men across the river, scaled the cliffs on the opposite side, and destroyed the camps there. Col. Bearss and the men under his command overcame incredible difficulties and dangers in destroying positions which, according to reports from old prisoners, had taken 3 years to perfect, were held as a final rallying point, and were never before penetrated by white troops. Col. Bearss also rendered distinguished public service in the presence of the enemy at Quinapundan River, Samar, Philippine Islands, on 19 January 1902."

Later, he served in Panama, from December 1903 to March 1904; in Cuba in February, March, and April 1913; in Mexico during the occupation of the city of Vera Cruz and during the engagement incident thereto; and in Santo Domingo from June 1916 to May 1917.

During World War I, General Bearss served with distinction in various capacities. He arrived in France in August 1917 and was in command of the Base Detachment, Fifth Marine Regiment, until October 1917. He commanded the Third Battalion, Ninth Infantry, in the Toulon-Troyon Sector southeast of Verdun, France.

In the St. Mihiel Operation, he commanded the leading elements of the 51st Brigade, 26th Infantry Division, in a bold and successful march southeast of the Rupt Sector through Dommartin-la-Montagne, the Grande Tranchee de Calonne, Vigneulles-les-Hattonchatel, advancing from the south, and thus completed the reduction of the Mt. Mihiel salient. He was cited in General Orders No. 112, Headquarters, 26th Division, and was highly commended by General Pershing, the commanding officer of the division and the Commanding General of the 51st Brigade. He served in France from August 20, 1917, to December 14, 1918, and was awarded the following decorations: The Distinguished Service Medal (Army G.O. 89); Distinguished Service Medal (Navy); Distinguished Service Cross—"For extraordinary heroism in action at Marcheville and Riaville, France, September 26th, 1918, while commanding the 102d Infantry, U.S. Army. Colonel Bearss' indomitable courage and leadership led to the complete success of the attack by two battalions of his regiment on Marcheville and Riaville. During the attack, these two towns changed hands four times finally remaining in our possession until the troops were ordered to withdraw. Under terrific machine gun and artillery fire, Colonel Bearss was the first to enter Marcheville where he directed operations. Later, upon finding his party completely surrounded, he personally assisted in fighting the enemy off with pistol and hand grenades."

He was also awarded the croix de guerre with palm, a second croix de guerre with palm, and the croix de guerre with silver star.

Source
Marine Corps Historical Center.
Medal of Honor Citation.

Beaudoin, Raymond O. (d. 1946) *First lieutenant, United States Army, Company F, 119th Infantry, 30th Infantry Division, distinguished himself heroically in combat and was awarded (posthumously) the Medal of Honor for his actions during World War II.*

Born: Holyoke, Mass; **Entered service at:** Holyoke, Mass; **Place and date:** Hamelin, Germany, April 6, 1945. G.O. No.: 9, 25 January 1946.

Citation: "He was leading the 2d Platoon of Company F over flat, open terrain to Hamelin, Germany, when the enemy went into action with machine-guns and automatic weapons, laying down a devastating curtain of fire which pinned his unit to the ground. By rotating men in firing positions he made it possible for his entire platoon to dig in, defying all the while the murderous enemy fire to encourage his men and to distribute ammunition. He then dug in himself at the most advanced position, where he kept up a steady fire, killing 6 hostile soldiers, and directing his men in inflicting heavy casualties on the numerically superior opposing force. Despite these defensive measures, however, the position of the platoon became more precarious, for the enemy had brought up strong reinforcements and was preparing a counterattack. Three men, sent back at intervals to obtain ammunition and reinforcements, were killed by sniper fire. To relieve his command from the desperate situation, 1st Lt. Beaudoin decided to make a 1-man attack on the most damaging enemy sniper nest 90 yards to the right flank, and thereby divert attention from the runner who would attempt to pierce the enemy's barrier of bullets and secure help. Crawling over completely exposed ground, he relentlessly advanced, undeterred by 8 rounds of bazooka fire, which threw mud and stones over him, or by rifle fire which ripped his uniform. Ten yards from the enemy position he stood up and charged. At point-blank range he shot and killed 2 occupants of the nest; a third, who tried to bayonet him, he overpowered and killed with the butt of his carbine; and the fourth adversary was cut down by the platoon's rifle fire as he attempted to flee. He continued his attack by running toward a dugout, but there he was struck and killed by a burst from a machine-gun. By his intrepidity, great fighting skill, and supreme devotion to his responsibility for the well-being of his platoon, 1st Lt. Beaudoin single-handedly accomplished a mission that enabled a messenger to secure help which saved the stricken unit and made possible the decisive defeat of the German forces."

Source
Medal of Honor Citation.

Beauregard, Pierre Gustave Toutant
(1818–1893) *General, Confederate States Army.*

The services of "the Hero of Fort Sumter," Pierre G.T. Beauregard, were not utilized to their fullest as a result of bad blood between the Confederate general and Jefferson Davis. The native Louisianan had graduated second of forty-five in the 1838 class at West Point. There he had become a great admirer of Napoleon and been nicknamed "the Little Napoleon." Posted to the artillery, he was transferred to the engineers a week later. As a staff officer with Winfield Scott in Mexico he won two brevets and was wounded in battle at both Churubusco and Chapultepec. In the interwar years he was engaged in clearing the Mississippi River of obstructions. In 1861, he served the shortest term ever, January 23–28, as superintendent at West Point. Southern leanings probably resulted in his prompt removal from this position. On February 20, 1961, he resigned his captaincy in the engineers and offered his services to the South.

Beauregard's Confederate assignments included brigadier general, Confederate States Army (CSA)(March 1, 1861); commander, of Charleston Harbor (March 3–May 27, 1861); commander, Alexandria Line (June 2–20, 1861); commander, Army of the Potomac (July 20–October 22, 1861); general, CSA (August 31, 1861, to rank from July 21); commander, Potomac District, Department of Northern Virginia (October 22, 1861–January 1862); commander, Army of the Mississippi (March 17–29 and April 6–May 7, 1862); commander, Department of South Carolina, Georgia, and Florida (August 29, 1862–April 20, 1864); commander, Department of North Carolina and Southern Virginia (April 22–September 23, 1864); commander, Military Division of the West (Octo-

ber 17–March 16, 1865); and second in command, Army of Tennessee (March 16–April 26, 1865).

Placed in charge of the South Carolina troops in Charleston Harbor, he won the nearly bloodless victory at Fort Sumter, ("and Great Creole" was hailed throughout the South. Ordered to Virginia, he commanded the forces opposite Washington, D.C., and created the Confederate Army of the Potomac. Reinforced by Joseph E. Johnston and his Army of the Shanandoah, Beauregard was reduced to corps command under Johnston the day before First Bull Run. However, during this battle Beauregard, being familiar with the field, exercised tactical command while Johnston forwarded troops to the threatened left flank. Both officers later claimed that they could have taken the Union capital if they had been properly supplied with rations for their men. This was one of Beauregard's first conflicts with Jefferson Davis. Nonetheless, he was named a full general from the date of the battle and early in 1862 was sent to the west as Albert Sidney Johnston's second in command.

Utilizing Napoleonic style, he drafted the attack orders for Shiloh and took command when Johnston was mortally wounded on the first day of the battle. On the evening of the first day, he let victory slip through his fingers by calling off the attack. Controversy over his decision has raged on this day. The next day he was driven from the battlefield by General Grant's and Buell's combined armies.

He defended Charleston brilliantly from late 1862 to 1864. In May 1864, he defeated the Union general Benjamin F. Butler in front of Petersburg, Virginia, he then became commander of the Division of the West and fought under General Joseph E. Johnston at war's end.

After the war, Beauregard became a railroad company president and recouped his fortunes as manager of the Louisiana lottery and head of New Orleans public works. He wrote frequently about the war and ghostwrote a biography of himself.

Sources and Additional Reading
Roman, Alfred. *The Military Operations of General Beauregard.* 2 vols. 1883. Reprint, New York: Da Capo, 1994.
Williams, T. Harry. *P. G. T. Beauregard: Napoleon in Gray.* Baton Rouge: Louisiana State University Press, 1954.

Benavidez, Roy P. (b. 1935) *Master sergeant, Detachment B-56, Fifth Special Forces Group, Republic of Vietnam, so distinguished himself in combat in the Republic of Vietnam that he was awarded the Medal of Honor for his heroic actions.*

Born: August 5, 1935, DeWitt County, Cuero, Tex.; **Entered service at:** Houston, Tex., June 1955; **Place and date:** West of Loc Ninh, May 2, 1968.

Roy P. Benavidez

Citation: "Master Sergeant (then Staff Sergeant) Roy P. Benavidez United States Army, distinguished himself by a series of daring and extremely valorous actions on 2 May 1968 while assigned to Detachment B56, 5th Special Forces Group (Airborne), 1st Special Forces, Republic of Vietnam. On the morning of 2 May 1968, a 12-man Special Forces Reconnaissance Team was inserted by helicopters in a dense jungle area west of Loc Ninh, Vietnam to gather intelligence information about confirmed large-scale enemy activity. This area was controlled and routinely patrolled by the North Vietnamese Army. After a short period of time on the ground, the team met heavy enemy resistance, and requested emergency extraction. Three helicopters attempted extraction but were unable to land due to intense enemy small arms and anti-aircraft fire. Sergeant Benavidez was at the Forward Operating Base in Loc Ninh monitoring the operation by radio when these helicopters returned to off-load wounded crewmembers and to assess aircraft damage. Sergeant Benavidez voluntarily boarded a returning aircraft to assist in another extraction attempt. Realizing that all the team members were either dead or wounded and unable to move to the pickup zone, he directed the aircraft to a nearby clearing where he jumped from the hovering helicopter, and ran approximately 75 meters under withering small arms fire to the crippled team. Prior to reaching the team's position he was wounded in his right leg, face, and head. Despite these painful injuries, he took charge, repositioning the team members and directing their fire to facilitate the landing of an extraction aircraft, and the loading of wounded and dead team members. He then threw smoke canisters to direct the aircraft to the team's position. Despite his severe wounds and under intense enemy fire, he carried and dragged half of the wounded team members to the awaiting aircraft. He then provided protective fire by running alongside the aircraft as it moved to pick up the remaining team members. As the enemy's fire intensified, he hurried to recover the body and classified documents on the dead team leader. When he reached the leader's body, Sergeant Benavidez was severely wounded by small arms fire in the abdomen and grenade fragments in his back. At nearly the same moment, the aircraft pilot was mortally wounded, and his helicopter crashed. Although in extremely critical condition due to his multiple wounds, Sergeant Benavidez secured the classified documents and made his way back to the wreckage, where he aided the wounded out of the overturned aircraft, and gathered the stunned survivors into a defensive perimeter. Under increasing enemy automatic weapons and grenade fire, he moved around the perimeter distributing water and ammunition to his weary men, reinstilling in them a will to live and fight. Facing a buildup of enemy opposition with a beleaguered team, Sergeant Benavidez mustered his strength, began calling in tactical air strikes and directed the fire from supporting gunships to suppress the enemy's fire and so permit another extraction attempt. He was wounded again in his thigh by small arms fire while administering first aid to a wounded team member just before another extraction helicopter was able to land. His indomitable spirit kept him going as he began to ferry his comrades to the craft. On his second trip with the wounded, he was clubbed from additional wounds to his head and arms before killing his adversary. He then continued under devastating fire to carry the wounded to the helicopter. Upon reaching the aircraft, he spotted and killed two enemy soldiers who were rushing the craft from an angle that prevented the aircraft door gunner from firing upon them. With little strength remaining, he made one last trip to the perimeter to ensure that all classified material had been collected or destroyed, and to bring in the remaining wounded. Only then, in extremely serious condition from numerous wounds and loss of blood, did he allow himself to be pulled into the extraction aircraft. Sergeant Benavidez' gallant choice to join voluntarily his comrades who were in critical straits, to expose himself constantly to withering enemy fire, and his refusal to be stopped despite numerous severe wounds, saved the lives of at least eight men. His fearless personal leadership, tenacious devotion to duty, and extremely valorous actions in the face of overwhelming odds were in keeping with the highest traditions of the military service, and reflect the utmost credit on him and the United States Army."

Source and Additional Reading
Medal of Honor Citation.
Above and Beyond. Boston: Boston Publishing, 1985.

Benfold, Edward C. (1931–1952) *Hospital corpsman third class United States Navy, attached to a company in the First Marine Division, so distinguished himself in combat, during the Korean War, that he was awarded (posthumously) the Medal of Honor for his heroic actions.*

Born: 1931, Staten Island, N.Y.; **Entered service at:** Philadelphia, Pa.; **Place and date:** Korea, September 5, 1952.

Citation: "For gallantry and intrepidity at the risk of his life above and beyond the call of duty while serving in operations against enemy aggressor forces. When his company was subjected to heavy artillery and mortar barrages, followed by a determined assault during the hours of darkness by an enemy force estimated at battalion strength, Petty Officer Benfold resolutely moved from position to position in the face of intense hostile fire, treating the wounded and lending words of encouragement. Leaving the protection of his sheltered position to treat the wounded when the platoon area in which he was working was attacked from both the front and rear, he moved forward to an exposed ridgeline where he observed two Marines in a large crater. As he approached the two men to determine their condition, an enemy soldier threw two grenades into the crater while two other enemy charged the position. Picking up a grenade in each hand, Petty Officer Benfold leaped out of the crater and hurled himself against the on-rushing hostile soldiers, pushing the grenades against their chests and killing both the attackers. Mortally wounded while carrying out this heroic act, Petty Officer Benfold, by his great personal valor and resolute spirit of self-sacrifice in the face of almost certain death, was directly responsible for saving the lives of his two comrades. His exceptional courage reflects the highest credit upon himself and enhances the finest traditions of the U.S. Naval Service. He gallantly gave his life for others."

Source
Medal of Honor Citation.

Bennett, Steven L. (1946–1972) *Captain, United States Air Force, 20th Tactical Air Support Squadron, Pacific Air Forces, so distinguished himself in aerial combat that he was awarded (posthumously) the Medal of Honor for his heroic actions in the Republic of Vietnam.*

Born: April 22, 1946, Palestine, Tex.; **Entered service at:** Lafayette, La.; **Place and date:** Quang Tri, Republic of Vietnam, June 29, 1972.

Citation: "Capt. Bennett was the pilot of a light aircraft flying an artillery adjustment mission along a heavily defended segment of route structure. A large concentration of enemy troops was massing for an attack on a friendly unit. Capt. Bennett requested tactical air support but was advised that none was available. He also requested artillery support but this too was denied due to the close proximity of friendly troops to the target. Capt. Bennett was determined to aid the endangered unit and elected to strafe the hostile positions. After four such passes, the enemy force began to retreat. Capt. Bennett continued the attack, but, as he completed his fifth strafing pass, his aircraft was struck by a surface-to-air missile, which severely damaged the left engine and the left main landing gear. As fire spread in the left engine, Capt. Bennett realized that recovery at a friendly airfield was impossible. He instructed his observer to prepare for an ejection, but was informed by the observer that the force of the impacting missile had shred his parachute. Although Capt. Bennett had a good parachute, he knew that if he ejected, the observer would have no chance of survival. With complete disregard for his own life, Capt. Bennett elected to ditch the aircraft into the Gulf of Tonkin, even though he realized that a pilot of this type aircraft had never survived a ditching. The ensuing impact upon the water caused the aircraft to cartwheel and severely damaged the front cockpit, making escape for Capt. Bennett impossible. The observer successfully made his way out of the aircraft and was rescued. Capt. Bennett's unparalleled concern for his companion, extraordinary heroism and intrepidity above and beyond the call of duty, at the cost of his life, were in keeping with the highest traditions of the military service and reflect great credit upon himself and the U.S. Air Force."

Source
Medal of Honor Citation.

Bertoldo, Vito R. (b. 1916) *Master sergeant, United States Army, Company A, 242d Infantry, 42d Infantry Division, distinguished himself in combat and was awarded the Medal of Honor for his heroic actions during World War II.*

Born: December 1, 1916, Decatur, Ill.; **Entered service at:** Decatur, Ill.; **Place and date:** Hatten, France, January 9–10, 1945. **G.O. No.:** 5, January 10, 1946.

Citation: "He fought with extreme gallantry while guarding 2 command posts against the assault of powerful infantry and armored forces which had overrun the battalion's main line of resistance. On the close approach of enemy soldiers, he left the protection of the building he defended and set up his gun in the street, there to remain for almost 12 hours driving back attacks while in full view of his adversaries and completely exposed to 88-mm, machine-gun and small-arms fire. He moved back inside the command post, strapped his machine-gun to a table and covered the main approach to the building by firing through a window, remaining steadfast even in the face of 88-mm fire from tanks only 75 yards away. One shell blasted him across the room, but he returned to his weapon. When 2 enemy personnel carriers led by a tank moved toward his position, he calmly waited for the troops to dismount and then, with the tank firing directly at him, leaned out of the window and mowed down the entire group of more than 20 Germans. Some time later, removal of the command post to another building was ordered. M/Sgt. Bertoldo voluntarily remained behind, covering the withdrawal of his comrades and maintaining his stand all night. In the morning he carried his machine-gun to an adjacent building used as the command post of another battalion and began a daylong defense of that position. He broke up a heavy attack, launched by a self-propelled 88-mm. gun covered by a tank and about 15 infantrymen. Soon afterward another 88-mm. weapon moved up to within a few feet of his position, and, placing the muzzle of its gun almost inside the building, fired into the room, knocking him down and seriously wounding others. An American bazooka team set the German weapon afire, and M/Sgt. Bertoldo went back to his machine-gun dazed as he was and killed several of the hostile troops as they attempted to withdraw. It was decided to evacuate the command post under the cover of darkness, but before the plan could be put into operation the enemy began an intensive assault supported by fire from their tanks and heavy guns. Disregarding the devastating barrage, he remained at his post and hurled white phosphorous grenades into the advancing enemy troops until they broke and retreated. A tank less than 50 yards away fired at his stronghold, destroyed the machine-gun and blew him across the room again but he once more returned to the bitter fight and, with a rifle, single-handedly covered the withdrawal of his fellow soldiers when the post was finally abandoned. With inspiring bravery and intrepidity M/Sgt. Bertoldo withstood the attack of vastly superior forces for more than 48 hours without rest or relief, time after time escaping death only by the slightest margin while killing at least 40 hostile soldiers and wounding many more during his grim battle against the enemy hordes."

Source
Medal of Honor Citation.

Bigelow, Elmer Charles (1920–1945) *Watertender first class, United States Naval Reserve, so distinguished himself in combat during World War II that he was awarded (posthumously) the Medal of Honor for his heroic actions.*

Born: July 12, 1920, Hebron Ill.; **Entered Service at:** Illinois.

Citation: "For conspicuous gallantry and intrepidity at the risk of his life above and beyond the call of duty while serving on board the U.S.S. *Fletcher* during action against enemy Japanese forces off Corregidor Island in the Philippines, 14 February 1945. Standing topside when an enemy shell struck the *Fletcher,* Bigelow, acting instantly as the deadly projectile exploded into fragments which penetrated the No. 1 gun magazine and set fire to several powder cases, picked up a pair of fire extinguishers and rushed below in a resolute attempt to quell the raging flames. Refusing to waste the precious time required to don rescue-breathing apparatus, he plunged through the blinding smoke billowing out of the magazine hatch and dropped into the blazing compartment. Despite the acrid, burning powder smoke, which seared his lungs with every agonizing breath, he worked rapidly and with instinctive sureness and succeeded in quickly extinguishing the fires and in cooling the cases and bulkheads, thereby preventing further damage to the stricken ship. Although he succumbed to his injuries on the following day, Bigelow, by his dauntless valor, unfaltering skill and prompt action in the critical emergency, had averted a magazine explosion which undoubtedly would have left his ship wallowing at the mercy of the furiously pounding Japanese guns on Corregidor, and his heroic spirit of self-sacrifice in the face of almost certain death enhanced and sustained the highest traditions of the U.S. Naval Service. He gallantly gave his life in the service of his country."

Source
Medal of Honor Citation.

Bird, William C. *Private first class, United States Marine Corps, was awarded the Navy Cross for his heroic actions on May 15, 1969, in the Republic of Vietnam.*

Citation: "For extraordinary heroism while serving as a Rifleman with Company E, Second Battalion, 5th Marines, First Marine Division, in the Republic of Vietnam on 15 May 1969. The First Platoon of Company E was assigned the mission of relieving a friendly unit heavily engaged in combat with a North Vietnamese Army battalion near An Hoa, in Quang Nam Province. As the point squad of Company E crossed an open field, it came under a heavy volume of rocket and automatic weapons fire from a large hostile unit occupying well-camouflaged bunkers. Alertly observing two wounded Marines lying dangerously exposed to enemy fire, Private First Class Bird, despite the intense volume of hostile rounds impacting near him, pulled his comrades to a position of relative safety. Reacting instantly, he fearlessly stood up and, effectively firing his M-16 rifle, provided enough covering fire to enable a Navy corpsman to reach the wounded Marines. Continuing to expose himself to the intense hostile fire, he delivered accurate covering fire for the corpsman as he moved throughout the hazardous area and administered emergency medical treatment to all the wounded. At dusk, another reaction force and two supporting tanks were deployed from the company command post. Alertly observing that the tank commanders were having difficulty discerning the enemy targets because of the approaching darkness, Private First Class Bird unhesitatingly climbed aboard the lead tank, despite the intense volume of enemy fire directed at him, and skillfully pointed out the hostile positions to the tank commander, and was instrumental in bringing devastating fire to bear upon the enemy. As the platoon withdrew to a night defensive position, Private First Class Bird personally carried two wounded Marines to the friendly perimeter and subsequently assisted in loading the remainder of the casualties aboard the tanks for rapid evacuation. When an enemy rocket impacted on one of the tanks, seriously wounding the driver, Private First Class Bird positioned himself between the tank and the nearby hostile emplacement and, accurately firing his rifle, suppressed the enemy fire while the tank crew reorganized and continued firing. Private First Class Bird was directly responsible for saving the lives of six Marines. His courage, aggressive fighting spirit and unwavering devotion to duty upheld the highest traditions of the Marine Corps and the United States Naval Service."

Source and Additional Reading
Navy Cross Citation.
Stevens, Paul Drew, ed. *The Navy Cross: Vietnam: Citations of Awards to Men of the United States Marine Corps, 1964–1973.* Forest Ranch, Calif.: Sharp & Dunnigan, 1987.

Black Hawk (Ma-ka-tai-me-she-kia-kiak)
(1767–1838) *American Sauk and Fox war chief.*

Born in 1767 into the Sauk and Fox tribe at Sauk village, Illinois, Black Hawk succeeded his father as chief, in 1788. Having developed a long and friendly trading relationship with the Spanish, he conceived a deep hatred for the American settlers when they displaced the Spanish in the old Northwest. He refused to sign the Treaty of 1804, which ceded tribal lands east of the Mississippi to whites.

Black Hawk fought with the great Shawnee chief Tecumseh on the side of Britain during the War of 1812. His hatred for Americans increased when they enlisted the aid of Keokuk, a rival Sauk chief, from 1815 to 1825. Black Hawk peacefully led his tribe back to their lands in Illinois, but the move was interpreted as hostile, and troops under the command of General Henry Atkinson opposed it. When Native American peace envoys were killed by U.S. troops, Black Hawk declared war, early in 1832. Although he won a few skirmishes, his tribe was virtually destroyed at Bad Axe River, on August 2, 1832. He survived the battle but was later captured and imprisoned. Black Hawk met with President Andrew Jackson and later dictated his autobiography. Placed under Chief Keokuk's charge as a hostage in 1834, he sustained a blow to his pride that destroyed him, and he died in Keokuk's village on the Des Moines River, Iowa, on October 3, 1838. Black Hawk is to be remembered as a noble and fierce Native American warrior. Resentful of American encroachment on Sauk land and the destruction of their way of life, he resisted violently. His autobiography stands as a classic statement of the Native American point of view, in the struggle against white oppression.

Source and Additional Reading
Black Hawk. *Autobiography of Ma-Ka-Tai-Me-She-Kia-Kiak, or Black Hawk, . . .* Edited by Antoine Le Clair and interpreted by J. B. Patterson. St. Louis, Mo.: St. Louis Continental Printing, 1833. Reprint.
Dupuy, Trevor N., Curt Johnson, and David L. Bongard. *The Harper Encyclopedia of Military Biography.* New York: HarperCollins, 1992.
Goodrich, Samuel G. *Lives of Celebrated American Indians.* 1843. Reprint, Temecula, Calif.: Reprint Services Corp: 1999.
Wood, Norman. *Lives of Famous Indian Chiefs*, Aurora, Ill: American Indian Historical Publishing Co., 1906.

Bolton, Cecil H.
First lieutenant, United States Army, Company E, 413th Infantry, 104th Infantry Division, so distinguished himself in combat, during World War II, that he was awarded the Medal of Honor for his heroic actions.

Born: Crawfordsville, Fla.; **Entered service at:** Huntsville, Ala.; **Place and date:** Mark River, Netherlands; November 2, 1944. **G.O. No.:** 74, September 1, 1945.

Citation: "As leader of the weapons platoon of Company E, 413th Infantry, on the night of 2 November 1944, he fought gallantly in a pitched battle which followed the crossing of the Mark River in Holland. When 2 machine-guns pinned down his company, he tried to eliminate, with mortar fire, their grazing fire which was inflicting serious casualties and preventing the company's advance from an area rocked by artillery shelling. In the moonlight it was impossible for him to locate accurately the enemy's camouflaged positions; but he continued to direct fire until wounded severely in the legs and rendered unconscious by a German shell. When he recovered consciousness he instructed his unit and then crawled to the forward rifle platoon positions. Taking a two-man bazooka team on his voluntary mission, he advanced chest deep in chilling water along a canal toward 1 enemy machinegun. While the bazooka team covered him, he approached alone to within 15 yards of the hostile emplacement in a house. He charged the remaining distance and killed the 2 gunners with hand grenades. Returning to his men he led them through intense fire over open ground to assault the second German machinegun. An enemy sniper who tried to block the way was dispatched, and the trio pressed on. When discovered by the machinegun crew and subjected to direct fire, 1st Lt. Bolton killed 1 of the 3 gunners with carbine fire, and his 2 comrades shot the others. Continuing to disregard his wounds, he led the bazooka team toward an 88-mm. artillery piece which was having telling effect on the American ranks, and approached once more through icy canal water until he could dimly make out the gun's silhouette. Under his fire direction, the two soldiers knocked out the enemy weapon with rockets. On the way back to his own lines he was again wounded. To prevent his men being longer subjected to deadly fire, he refused aid and ordered them back to safety, painfully crawling after them until he reached his lines, where he collapsed. 1st Lt. Bolton's heroic assaults in the face of vicious fire, his inspiring leadership, and continued aggressiveness even though suffering from serious wounds, contributed in large measure to overcoming strong enemy resistance and made it possible for his battalion to reach its objective."

Source
Medal of Honor Citation.

Bolton, Gilbert CWO-4, *Marine gunner, United States Marine Corps, awarded the silver star for conspicuous gallantry and intrepidity while serving in the Republic of Vietnam in 1967.*

Born in Ohio, he attended Portsmouth High School and enlisted in the Marine Corps in 1959. Initially, he served with both the First Battalion, Seventh Marine Regiment, at Camp Pendleton and the First Battalion, Third Marines, Third Marine Division, on Okinawa until 1963.

He was reassigned to Marine Barracks Yokosuka, Japan, in 1963, at returned to MCRD, San Diego, in 1964, where he served as a drill instructor until ordered to duty in Vietnam in 1966.

Arriving in Vietnam, he was assigned to the Third Battalion, Seventh Marine Regiment (3/7), First Marine Division, where he served as a rifle platoon sergeant, and a rifle platoon leader. While with the Second Platoon, "M" 3/7, he was recommended for a battlefield commission and was awarded the Silver Star and the Purple Heart for his heroic actions in November 1967.

In 1968, he returned to the Marine Corp Recruiting Depot (MCRD), San Diego, as a drill instructor until commissioned as a Second lieutenant. He completed his tour as a recruit series commander and assistant director of the Recruit Special Training Branch.

In 1970, as a first lieutenant, he served as the combat cargo officer aboard the USS *Paul Revere,* LPA-248 until ordered to Weapons Training Battalion, at Edson Range, Camp Pendleton, California, in 1972. Prior to leaving the ship, he requested to be reverted from temporary officer to permanent warrant officer. As a designated chief Marine gunner, CWO2, 0302 infantry warrant officer, he served as a recruit range officer at Edson Range until reassigned to the Infantry Training School, Camp Pendleton, in 1975.

While at the school, he served as Officer in Charge (OIC), Recruit Entry Level Training Section; 52 area guard officer; and OIC of the Weapons Training Section until ordered to the Third Marine Division, in 1979.

On Okinawa, he served at the Northern Training Area as both Assistant OIC and OIC until reassigned to the Infantry Training School in 1980. At the school, he reassumed his duties as OIC, Weapons Training Section, until his transfer on May 20, 1987 to the Advanced Infantry Training Company, as the commanding officer.

On March 1, 1990, Gunner Bolton retired from active duty with more than 30 years of distinguished service to his corps and country.

Silver Star Citation: "For conspicuous gallantry and intrepidity in action while serving as a Platoon Sergeant with Company M, Third Battalion, Seventh Marines, First Marine Division in connection with operations against insurgent communist (Viet Cong) forces in the Republic of Vietnam. Very early in the morning on 2 November 1967, Staff Sergeant Bolton's platoon, occupying its combat base on Hill 25, came under intense small arms, automatic weapons and mortar fire from a force composed of an estimated 100 Viet Cong soldiers. In the initial moments of the vicious attack, the platoon command post was destroyed by an enemy satchel charge. Escaping from the burning and collapsing command bunker and realizing that the unit's primary radio was inoperable, Staff Sergeant Bolton fearlessly maneuvered through intense enemy fire to the bunker where the second radio was located. Encouraging his men, he then quickly manned the radio and called in and adjusted an artillery illumination mission over the area, which revealed the enemy penetrating the defensive wire. Without hesitation, Staff Sergeant Bolton organized a blocking force and succeeded

Gilbert Bolton

in stopping the penetration at one point, but failed to drive the enemy back. As the determined Viet Cong continued to surge over the hill, he realized that drastic measures were required to save his platoon. Displaying bold initiative and extraordinary courage, Staff Sergeant Bolton, unable to contact the platoon commander, directed his men into their bunkers and, with exceptional composure, called for six 105 mm variable timed fuze fire missions on his own position. After the fire missions were completed and the remaining Viet Cong had been driven from the hill, he rallied his men, directed the recovery of casualties and assisted in reorganizing the platoon's defensive perimeter. His decisive actions and sound judgment were instrumental in repulsing the enemy assault and in preventing additional casualties in his platoon. By his extraordinary courage, superb leadership and selfless devotion to duty at great personal risk, Staff Sergeant Bolton upheld the highest traditions of the Marine Corps and of the United States Naval Service."

Source and Additional Reading
Silver Star Citation.
The Marine Corps Mustang Association. *U.S. Marines, Mustangs of the Corps.* Dallas, Tex.: Taylor Publishing, 1991.

Bondsteel, James Leroy (b. 1947) *Staff sergeant, United States Army, Company A, second Battalion, second Infantry, First Infantry Division, so distinguished himself in combat in the Republic of Vietnam that he was awarded the Medal of Honor for his heroic actions.*

Born: July 18, 1947, Jackson, Mich.; **Entered service at:** Detroit, Mich.; **Place and date:** An Loc Province, Republic of Vietnam, May 24, 1969.

Citation: "For conspicuous gallantry and intrepidity in action at the risk of his life above and beyond the call of duty. S/Sgt. Bondsteel distinguished himself while serving as a platoon sergeant with Company A, near the village of Lang Sau. Company A was directed to assist a friendly unit which was endangered by intense fire from a North Vietnamese Battalion located in a heavily fortified base camp. S/Sgt. Bondsteel quickly organized the men of his platoon into effective combat teams and spearheaded the attack by destroying 4 enemy occupied bunkers. He then raced some 200 meters under heavy enemy fire to reach an adjoining platoon, which had begun to falter. After rallying this unit and assisting their wounded, S/Sgt. Bondsteel returned to his own sector with critically needed munitions. Without pausing he moved to the forefront and destroyed 4 enemy occupied bunkers and a machine gun, which had threatened his advancing platoon. Although painfully wounded by an enemy grenade, S/Sgt. Bondsteel refused medical attention and continued his assault by neutralizing 2 more enemy bunkers nearby. While searching one of these emplacements S/Sgt. Bondsteel narrowly escaped death when an enemy soldier detonated a grenade at close range. Shortly thereafter, he ran to the aid of a severely wounded officer and struck down an enemy soldier who was threatening the officer's life. S/Sgt. Bondsteel then continued to rally his men and led them through the entrenched enemy until his company was relieved. His exemplary leadership and great personal courage throughout the 4-hour battle ensured the success of his own and nearby units, and resulted in the saving of numerous lives of his fellow soldiers. By individual acts of bravery he destroyed 10 enemy bunkers and accounted for a large toll of the enemy, including 2 key enemy commanders. His extraordinary heroism at the risk of his life was in the highest traditions of the military service and reflect great credit on him, his unit, and the U.S. Army."

Source
Medal of Honor Citation.

Bonnyman, Alexander, Jr. (1910–1943) *First lieutenant, United States Marine Corps Reserves, awarded the Medal of Honor (posthumously) for his heroic actions in World War II.*

Born: 2 May 1910, Atalanta, Ga. **Accredited to:** New Mexico.

Citation: "For conspicuous gallantry and intrepidity at the risk of his life above and beyond the call of duty as Executive Officer of the 2d Battalion Shore Party, 8th Marines, 2nd Marine Division, during the assault against enemy Japanese-held Tarawa in the Gilbert Islands, 20–22 November 1943. Acting on his own initiative when assault troops were pinned down at the far end of Betio Pier by the overwhelming fire of Japanese shore batteries, 1st Lt. Bonnyman repeatedly defined the blasting fury of the enemy bombardment to organize and lead the besieged men over the long, open pier to the beach and then, voluntarily obtaining flame throwers and demolitions, organized his pioneer shore party into assault demolitionists and directed the blowing of several hostile installations before the close of D-Day. Determined to effect an opening in the enemy's strongly organized defense line the following day, he voluntarily crawled approximately 40 yards forward of our lines and placed demolitions in the entrance of a large Japanese emplacement as the initial move in his planned attack against the heavily garrisoned, bombproof installation which was stubbornly resisting despite the destruction early in the action of a large number of Japanese who had been inflicting heavy casualties on our forces and holding up our advance. Withdrawing only to replenish his ammunition, he led his men in a renewed assault, fearlessly exposing himself to the merciless slash of hostile fire as he stormed the formidable bastion, directed the placement of demolition charges in both entrances and seized the top of the bombproof position, flushing more than 100 of the enemy who were instantly cut down, and effecting the annihilation of approximately 150 troops inside the emplacement. Assailed by additional Japanese after he had gained his objective, he made a heroic stand on the edge of the structure, defending his strategic position with indomitable determination in the face of the desperate charge and killing 3 of the enemy before he fell, mortally wounded. By his dauntless fighting spirit, unrelenting aggressiveness and forceful leadership throughout 3 days of unremitting, violent battle, 1st Lt. Bonnyman had inspired his men to heroic effort, enabling them to beat off the counterattack and break the back of hostile resistance in that sector for an immediate gain of 400 yards with no further casualties to our forces in this zone. He gallantly gave his life for his country."

Source
Medal of Honor Citation.

Boyd, Belle (1843–1900) *Confederate spy.*

One of the most famous of Confederate spies, Belle Boyd served the Confederate forces in the Shenandoah Valley. Born in Martinsburg—now part of West Virginia—she operated her spying operations from her father's hotel in Front Royal, providing valuable information to Generals Turner Ashby and "Stonewall" Jackson during the spring 1862 campaign in the valley. The later general then made her a captain and honorary aide-de-camp on his staff. As such she was able to witness troop reviews. Betrayed by her lover, she was arrested on July 29, 1862, and held for a month in the Old Capitol Prison in Washington. Exchanged a month later, she was in exile with relatives for a time but was again arrested in June 1863 while on a visit to Martinsburg. On December 1, 1863, she was released, suffering from typhoid, and was then sent to Europe to regain her health. The blockade runner she attempted to return on was captured, and she fell in love with the prize master, Samuel Hardinge, who later married her in England after being dropped from the navy's rolls for neglect of duty in allowing her to proceed to Canada and then England. Hardinge attempted to reach Richmond, was detained in Union hands, but died soon after his release. While in England Belle Boyd Hardinge had a stage career and published *Belle Boyd in Camp and Prison.* She died while touring the western United States.

Sources
Scarborough, Ruth, *Belle Boyd: Siren of the South.* Macon, Ga. Mercer University Press, 1983.
Sigaud, Louis A. *Belle Boyd, Confederate Spy.* Richmond, Va.: Dietz Press, 1945.

Boyington, Gregory (b. 1912) *Major, United States Marine Corps Reserve, Marine Squadron 214, so distinguished himself in aerial combat against the enemy, during World War II, that he was awarded the Medal of Honor.*

Born: December 4, 1912, Coeur d'Alene, Idaho; **Entered service at:** Washington; **Place and date:** Central Solomons area, from September 12, 1943, to January 3, 1944. **Other United States Navy award:** Navy Cross.

Citation: "For extraordinary heroism and valiant devotion to duty as commanding officer of Marine Fighting Squadron 214 in action against enemy Japanese forces in the Central Solomons area from 12 September 1943 to 3 January 1944. Consistently outnumbered throughout successive hazardous flights over heavily defended hostile territory, Maj. Boyington struck at the enemy with daring and courageous persistence, leading his squadron into combat with devastating results to Japanese shipping, shore installations, and aerial forces. Resolute in his efforts to inflict crippling damage on the enemy, Maj. Boyington led a formation of 24 fighters over Kahili on 17 October and, persistently circling the airdrome where 60 hostile aircraft were grounded, boldly challenged the

Japanese to send up planes. Under his brilliant command, our fighters shot down 20 enemy craft in the ensuing action without the loss of a single ship. A superb airman and determined fighter against overwhelming odds, Maj. Boyington personally destroyed 26 of the many Japanese planes shot down by his squadron and, by his forceful leadership, developed the combat readiness in his command which was a distinctive factor in the Allied aerial achievements in this vitally strategic area."

Sources and Additional Reading
Marine Historical Center.
Medal of Honor Citation.
Boyington, Col. Gregory. *Baa Baa Black Sheep*. Fresno, Calif.: Wilson Press, 1958.
Gamble, Bruce. *The Black Sheep*. Novato, Calif.: Presidio Press, 1998.

Bradley, Omar Nelson (1893–1981) *World War II commander and first chairman of the Joint Chiefs of Staff. One of only nine five-star generals, he was known as "the GI General."*

During World War II, Bradley commanded the U.S. 12th Army Group in Europe. By the spring of 1945 this group consisted of four field armies, 12 corps, 48 divisions, and more than 1,300,000 men, the largest exclusively American field command in U.S. history. A mild-mannered man with a high-pitched voice, General Bradley created the impression less of a soldier than of a teacher, as he actually was during much of his early career in the army at the U.S. Military Academy at West Point and at the Infantry School, Fort Benning, Georgia. Yet he earned a reputation as an eminent tactician and as a "soldier's soldier," a general with whom the lower ranks could readily identify.

Bradley was born in Clark, Missouri, on February 12, 1893. He moved with his family 15 years later to Moberly, Missouri, where he met the woman he eventually married, Mary Quayle. He graduated from the U.S. Military Academy in 1915. During World War I, Bradley rose to the temporary rank of major while serving with the 14th Infantry Regiment. Early in World War II he served as commandant of the Infantry School, commanded an infantry division in training, and in the spring of 1943 commanded the Second Corps in North Africa and later in Sicily.

The supreme Allied commander, Gen. Dwight D. Eisenhower, selected him to command the First United States Army, the American contingent during the invasion of Normandy in June 1944. As the size of U.S. forces increased, Bradley was appointed to command the 12th Army Group. His troops broke out of the Normandy beachhead, liberated Paris, defeated a German counteroffensive during the winter of 1944–45, seized the first

bridgehead over the Rhine River, and drove through central Germany to establish the first Allied contact with troops from the Soviet Union.

Bradley missed the full encirclement of a German army in Normandy, but this was generally attributed to the delayed advance of troops under British command. He failed to detect German preparations for the winter counteroffensive, but this was a general failure throughout the Allied command. General Bradley was proudest of Operation Lumberjack, the campaign he launched to reach the Rhine after the German counteroffensive.

For two years after World War II, Bradley served as administrator of veterans' affairs before becoming chief of staff of the United States Army early in 1948. The following year he became the first chairman of the Joint Chiefs of Staff in the newly created Department of Defense, the highest military position open to a U.S. officer. In September 1950, while chairman of the Joint Chiefs, he became the fourth officer to reach the five-star rank of General of the Army. He also served as the first chairman of the Military Committee of the North Atlantic Treaty Organization (NATO), consisting of the military chiefs of staff of the nations united in that organization for common defense. After relinquishing the NATO Military Committee chairmanship in 1950, he continued until mid-1953 as a U.S. representative on the committee and on its Standing Group. Late in 1953 he became chairman of the board of the Bulova Watch Company.

General Bradley died in New York City on April 8, 1981.

In his memoir, *A Soldier's Story* (1951), Bradley sharply criticizes the British field marshal Montgomery for his "misrepresentation" of U.S. and British roles in the German winter counteroffensive.

A modest and unassuming man, Bradley was one of the most successful generals of World War II. Although not considered to be brilliant or highly imaginative, he was a superb military tactician, planner, and administrator. He was known both for his calm confidence under extreme stress and for his concern for the welfare of his men.

Source
Bradley, Omar N. *A Soldier's Story*. New York: Holt, 1951.

Brady, Patrick Henry (b. 1936) *Major, United States Army, Medical Service Corps, 54th Medical Detachment, 67th Medical Group, 44th Medical Brigade, so distinguished himself in combat that he was awarded the Medal of Honor for his heroic actions during the Vietnam War.*

Born: October 1, 1936, Philip, S.D.; **Entered service at:** Seattle, Wash.; **Place and date:** Near Chu Lai, Republic of Vietnam, January 6, 1968.

Citation: "For conspicuous gallantry and intrepidity in action at the risk of his life above and beyond the call of duty, Maj. Brady distinguished himself while serving in the Republic of Vietnam commanding a UH-1H ambulance helicopter, volunteered to rescue wounded men from a site in enemy held territory which was reported to be heavily defended and to be blanketed by fog. To reach the site he descended through heavy fog and smoke and hovered slowly along a valley trail, turning his ship sideways to blow away the fog with the backwash from his rotor blades. Despite the unchallenged, close-range enemy fire, he found the dangerously small site, where he successfully landed and evacuated 2 badly wounded South Vietnamese soldiers. He was then called to another area completely covered by dense fog where American casualties lay only 50 meters from the enemy. Two aircraft had previously been shot down and others had made unsuccessful attempts to reach this site earlier in the day. With unmatched skill and extraordinary courage, Maj. Brady made four flights to this embattled landing zone and successfully rescued all the wounded. On his third mission of the day Maj. Brady once again landed at a site surrounded by the enemy. The friendly ground force, pinned down by enemy fire, had been unable to reach and secure the landing zone. Although his aircraft had been badly damaged and his controls partially shot away during his initial entry into this area, he returned minutes later and rescued the remaining injured. Shortly thereafter, obtaining a replacement aircraft, Maj. Brady was requested to land in an enemy minefield where a platoon of American soldiers was trapped. A mine detonated near his helicopter, wounding two crewmembers and damaging his ship. In spite of this, he managed to fly 6 severely injured patients to medical aid. Throughout that day Maj. Brady utilized 3 helicopters to evacuate a total of 51 seriously wounded men, many of whom would have perished without prompt medical treatment. Maj. Brady's bravery was in the highest traditions of the military service and reflects great credit upon himself and the U.S. Army."

Source
Medal of Honor Citation.

Bragg, Braxton (1817–1876) *General, Confederate States Army.*

Of the eight men who reached the rank of full general in the Confederate army Braxton Bragg was the most controversial. The North Carolinian West Pointer (1837) had earned a prewar reputation for strict discipline as well as a literal adherence to regulations. At one time, the story goes, he actually had a written dispute with himself while serving in the dual capacity of company commander and post quartermaster. His pre–Civil War career was highly distinguished. After seeing action against the Seminoles, he went on to win three brevets in the Mexican War, in which his battery of "flying artillery" revolutionized, in many respects, the battlefield use of that arm. In 1856 he resigned his captaincy—he was a lieutenant colonel by brevet—in the Third Artillery and became a Louisiana planter.

His Confederate assignments included those of colonel, Louisiana Militia (early 1861); major general, Louisiana Militia (early 1861); commander, Department of Louisiana (February 22–March 1861); brigadier general, Confederate States Army (CSA) (March 7, 1861); commander Pensacola, Florida (March 11–October 29, 1861); major general, CSA (September 12, 1861); commander, Department of Alabama and West Florida (October 14, 1861–February 28, 1862); commander, Army of Pensacola (October 29–December 22, 1861); commander, Army of the Mississippi (March 6–17, May 7–July 5, August 15–September 28, and November 7–20, 1862); commander, Second Corps, Army of the Mississippi (March 29–June 30, 1862); general, CSA (April 12, 1862, to rank from April 6); commander, Department of the East Tennessee (June 17–October 24, 1862, and November 3, 1862–July 25, 1863); commander, Army of Tennessee (November 20, 1862–December 2, 1863); commander, Department of Tennessee (August 6–December 2, 1863, except briefly in August); commander, Department of North Carolina (November 27, 1864–April 9, 1865, but under Joseph E. Johnston from March 6, 1865); and supervisor, Hoke's division, Hardee's corps, Army of Tennessee (April 9–26, 1865).

Initially commanding in Louisiana, he was later in charge of the operations against Fort Pickens in Pensacola Harbor. Ordered to northern Mississippi in early 1862, he briefly commanded the forces gathering there for the attack on Grant at Shiloh. During the battle itself he directed a corps and was later rewarded with promotion to full general. As such he relieved Beauregard when he went on sick leave and was then given permanent command in the west.

Having served during the Corinth siege, he led the army into Kentucky and commanded at Perryville, where he employed only a portion of his force. On the last day of 1862 he launched a vicious attack on the Union left at Murfreesboro but failed to carry through his success on the following days. Withdrawing from the area, he was driven into Georgia during Rosecrans's Tullahoma Campaign and subsequent operations.

In September he won the one major Confederate victory in the west, at Chickamauga, but failed to follow up his success. Instead he laid siege to the Union army in Chattanooga and merely waited for Grant to break through his lines. In the meantime he had been engaged in a series of disputes with his subordinates, especially

Leonides Polk, James Longstreet, and William J. Hardee, that severely injured the effectiveness of the Army of Tennessee. Several top officers left the army for other fields, and Longstreet and Simon B. Buckner were dispatched into east Tennessee. With the army thus weakened, Bragg was routed at Chattanooga and was shortly removed from command. Almost immediately he was appointed as an adviser to Jefferson Davis, his staunch supporter, and maintained an office in Richmond. Ineffective in the position of quasicommander in chief, he was dispatched to North Carolina in the waning days of the war. The forces under his command remained inactive during the second attack on Fort Fisher, allowing it to fall. When Joseph E. Johnston assumed command of all forces in North Carolina on March 6, 1865, Bragg was soon relegated to supervision of Hoke's division from his old department. In that capacity he surrendered near Durham Station. For a time after the war he served as Alabama's chief engineer and then settled in Galveston, Texas, where he died September 27, 1876, while walking down the street with a friend. He is buried in Mobile, Alabama. He was the brother of the Confederate attorney general, Thomas Bragg.

Source and Additional Reading

McWhiney, Grady C. *Braxton Bragg and Confederate Defeat.: Field Command.* New York, Columbia University Press; 1969.

Brandtner, Martin L. *Lieutenant general, United States Marine Corps, twice awarded the Navy Cross.*

A native of Minneapolis, Minnesota, he was commissioned a second lieutenant via the Naval Reserve Officer Training Course (NROTC) Regular Scholarship Program after graduation from the University of Minnesota in June 1960. He also earned a master's degree from George Washington University (1973).

After graduation from the Basic School, Quantico, Virginia, in March 1961, General Brandtner remained at Quantico, where he was assigned to the Officer Candidates School, serving as a platoon leader until January 1962.

Reassigned to the First Marine Brigade, Fleet Marine Force (FMF), in February 1962, he served with the First Battalion, Fourth Marines, as a rifle platoon leader, battalion staff officer, rifle company executive officer, and rifle company commander, respectively.

In February 1965, Brandtner was assigned to the First Marine Aircraft Wing, Iwakuni, Japan, serving as the S-1 (personnel officer)/ Adjutant of Marine Wing Headquarters Group 1. Deploying to the Republic of Vietnam in April 1965, he assumed additional duties as area defense coordinator for the Wing Headquarters compound at Da Nang Airbase.

Returning from overseas in April 1966, he reported to the Landing Force Training Command, Pacific, where he served as branch head of the Basic Amphibious Training Branch.

In July 1968, General Brandtner returned to the Republic of Vietnam, where he joined the First Battalion, Fifth Marines, serving as a rifle company commander and, on promotion to major in November 1968, as battalion operations officer and executive officer. While serving as commanding officer, Company D, he was wounded in action and awarded the Navy Cross, twice, within an eight-day period, for his heroic actions during the month of September 1968. He is one of only two Marines to be awarded two Navy Crosses during the Vietnam War.

Citation: "For extraordinary heroism while serving as Commanding Officer of Company D, First Battalion, Fifth Marines, First Marine Division, in connection with operations against the enemy in the Republic of Vietnam. On 3 September 1968, while conducting a reconnaissance in force near the village of Lan Phouc in Quang Nam Province, the lead platoon of Company D became pinned down by intense automatic weapons fire from a large North Vietnamese Army force. As he moved forward to assess the situation, Captain Brandtner was wounded by grenade launcher fire from an enemy soldier standing in a nearby trench. With complete disregard for his own safety, Captain Brandtner boldly exposed himself to the hostile fire and hurling a hand grenade, killed the North Vietnamese soldier. Suddenly, the Marines came under an intense North Vietnamese hand grenade attack, and when one of the lethal objects landed at Captain Brandtner's feet, he unhesitatingly seized the grenade and threw it back at the enemy. On two more occasions he completely disregarded his own safety to seize hand grenades that were thrown near his position and hurl them toward the hostile force. When another grenade landed in the midst of four nearby Marines, Captain Brandtner fearlessly rushed to their position, picked up the lethal object and hurled it away from his companions. Then, concerned only for the welfare of his fellow Marines, he knocked two of the men to the ground and quickly placed himself on top of them, thereby absorbing the fragments from the exploding grenade in his protective armor and preventing possible death or serious injury to his companions. Realizing the numerical superiority of the enemy, he consolidated his company's position and skillfully adjusted effective supporting arms fire, which caused the hostile force to flee and enable his Marines to overrun the objective. By his courage, intrepid fighting spirit, and selfless devotion to duty at the risk of his life, Captain Brandtner sustained and enhanced the traditions of the Marine Corps and of the United States Naval Service."

Second Award. Citation: "For extraordinary heroism in action while serving as the Commanding Officer, Company D, First Battalion, Fifth Marines, First Marine Division (Reinforced) in the Republic of Vietnam on 11 September 1968. Assigned a mission to conduct a search and destroy operation near the village of My Binh, Quang Dia Loc District, Quang Nam Province, Captain Brandtner selected his defensive position and began deploying his platoons for their assigned night activities. As the First Platoon departed, en route to their night ambush site, they began receiving intense small arms, automatic weapons and rocket fire from a numerically superior North Vietnamese Army force. Simultaneously, the enemy, approximately the size of the two North Vietnamese Army companies, began an attack on the Command Group with 82 mm mortars, intense automatic weapons fire and P-40 rockets. Quickly analyzing the situation and immediately realizing the seriousness and danger involved, Captain Brandtner disregarded his own personal safety and moved forward to an extremely exposed position in order that he could personally control the battle at hand. When the enemy began the first of a series of "human wave" sapper attacks against the company's position, he calmly and with outstanding presence of mind moved from position to position reorganizing, encouraging and rallying his outnumbered and dazed company into an inspired fighting unit which completely stopped the momentum of the enemy attack and forced them to withdraw. Realizing the enemy was regrouping for subsequent attacks, he calmly adjusted his supporting artillery fire to within 200 meters of his lines, again raising havoc and confusion within the enemy's ranks. When the North Vietnamese Army units began their second attack, the devastating fires of a well-organized Marine Corps rifle company caught them off balance and inflicted heavy enemy casualties. Twice more, the determined enemy launched massive "human wave" assaults on the perimeter of Company D, but the steadfast efforts of the men of the company proved to be too much for the now overwhelmed and demoralized enemy. After more than two hours of persistent attempts to overrun the company, the enemy broke contact. Daylight revealed 67 North Vietnamese dead as mute testimony to the ferocious encounter that had taken place. The number of enemy dead and wounded evacuated could not be estimated. Company D suffered only one Marine killed and fourteen wounds serious enough to require evacuation. By his outstanding courage, superb leadership and unswerving devotion to duty, Captain Brandtner served to inspire all who observed him and upheld the highest traditions of the Marine Corps and the United States Naval Service."

In August 1969, General Brandtner returned to the United States and assumed duties as the inspector-instructor, 26th Rifle Company, USMCR, Minneapolis, Minnesota, where he served until selected to attend the Naval War College of Command and General Staff, at Newport, Rhode Island, in 1972.

Again being assigned overseas, he reported to the Third Marine Division, on Okinawa, Japan, where he served as the G-3 operations officer until he returned to the United States in July 1977. While overseas he was promoted to lieutenant colonel in April 1977.

From July 1977 to June 1980, General Brandtner was assigned to the Marine Corps Recruit Depot, San Diego, California, where he served initially as the executive officer, Headquarters and Service Battalion. He subsequently was assigned as the commanding officer, First Recruit Training Battalion, where he served until selected to attend the Air War College in July 1980.

Graduating with distinction from the Air War College in July 1981, General Brandtner was selected to be the senior military assistant to the under secretary of defense for policy, a position in which he served until July 1984. During his tour of duty he was promoted to colonel in July 1982.

Returning to the Fleet Marine Force (FMF), General Brandtner was assigned as the assistant chief of staff, G-4, Marine Amphibious Force, Camp Pendleton, where he served until May 1985. The following month, he assumed command of the Fifth Marine Regiment. In July 1986, he was assigned as chief of staff, First Marine Division, FMF. While serving in this capacity, he was selected for promotion to brigadier general. He was assigned duty as the assistant division commander, Second Marine Division, FMF, Atlantic, Camp Lejeune, North Carolina, on June 1, 1988, and advanced to brigadier general on July 25, 1988; he was assigned duty as the commanding general, Second Force Service Support Group, at Camp Lejeune.

From December 1988 through February 1989, General Brandtner served as the commanding general, 10th Marine Expeditionary Brigade, at Camp Lejeune. Advanced to major general on May 11, 1990, he was assigned duty as the vice-director for operations, J-3, Joint Staff, on July 3, 1990. General Brandtner was promoted to lieutenant general on March 11, 1991, and assumed duty as director for operations, J-3, Joint Staff, Washington. He served in that capacity until his retirement from the Marine Corps on June 1, 1993.

Source and Additional Reading

Marine Corps Historical Center.

Navy Cross Citations.

Stevens, Paul Drew, ed. *The Navy Cross: Vietnam: Citations of Awards to Men of the United States Marine Corps, 1964–1973.* Forest Ranch, Calif.: Sharp & Dunnigan, 1987.

Brittin, Nelson V. (d. 1951) *Sergeant first class, United States Army, Company One, 19th Infantry Regiment, distinguished himself in combat during the Korean War and was awarded (posthumously) the Medal of Honor for his heroic actions.*

Born: Audubon, N.J.; **Entered service at:** Audubon, N.J.; **Place and date:** Vicinity of Yonggong-ni, Korea, March 7, 1951 G.O. No.: 12, February 1, 1952.

Citation: "Sfc. Brittin, a member of company I, distinguished himself by conspicuous gallantry and intrepidity above and beyond the call of duty in action. Volunteering to lead his squad up a hill, with meager cover against murderous fire from the enemy, he ordered his squad to give him support and, in the face of withering fire and bursting shells, he tossed a grenade at the nearest enemy position. On returning to his squad, he was knocked down and wounded by an enemy grenade. Refusing medical attention, he replenished his supply of grenades and returned, hurling grenades into hostile positions and shooting the enemy as they fled. When his weapon jammed, he leaped without hesitation into a foxhole and killed the occupants with his bayonet and the butt of his rifle. He continued to wipe out foxholes and, noting that his squad had been pinned down, he rushed to the rear of a machine gun position, threw a grenade into the nest, and ran around to its front, where he killed all 3 occupants with his rifle. Less than 100 yards up the hill, his squad again came under vicious fire from another camouflaged, sandbagged, machine gun nest well flanked by supporting riflemen. Sfc. Brittin again charged this new position in an aggressive endeavor to silence this remaining obstacle and ran direct into a burst of automatic fire, which killed him instantly. In his sustained and driving action, he had killed 20 enemy soldiers and destroyed 4 automatic weapons. The conspicuous courage, consummate valor, and noble self-sacrifice displayed by Sfc. Brittin enabled his inspired company to attain its objective and reflect the highest glory on himself and the heroic traditions of the military service."

Source
Medal of Honor Citation.

Bronson, Deming (b. 1984) *First lieutenant, United States Army, Company H, 364th Infantry, 91st Division, distinguished himself heroically in combat and was awarded the Medal of Honor for his action in September 1918.*

Born July 8, 1894, Rhinelander, Wis.; **Entered service at:** Seattle, Wash.; **Place and date:** Near Eclisfontaine, France, September 26–27, 1918. **G.O. No.:** 12 W. D., 1929.

Citation: "For conspicuous gallantry and intrepidity above and beyond the call of duty in action with the enemy. On the morning of 26 September, during the advance of the 364th Infantry, 1st Lt. Bronson was struck by an exploding enemy hand grenade, receiving deep cuts on his face and the back of his head. He nevertheless participated in the action, which resulted in the capture of an enemy dugout from which a great number of prisoners were taken. This was effected with difficulty and under extremely hazardous conditions because it was necessary to advance without the advantage of cover and, from an exposed position, throw hand grenades and phosphorous bombs to compel the enemy to surrender. On the afternoon of the same day he was painfully wounded in the left arm by an enemy rifle bullet, and after receiving first aid treatment he was directed to the rear. Disregarding these instructions, 1st Lt. Bronson remained on duty with his company through the night, although suffering from severe pain and shock. On the morning of 27 September, his regiment resumed its attack, the object being the village of Eclisfontaine. Company H, to which 1st Lt. Bronson was assigned, was left in support of the attacking line, Company E being in the line. He gallantly joined that company in spite of his wounds and engaged with it in the capture of the village. After the capture he remained with Company E and participated with it in the capture of an enemy machine gun, he himself killing the enemy gunner. Shortly after this encounter the company was compelled to retire due to the heavy enemy artillery barrage. During this retirement, 1st Lt. Bronson, who was the last man to leave the advanced position, was again wounded in both arms by an enemy high-explosive shell. He was then assisted to cover by another officer who applied first aid. Although bleeding profusely and faint from the loss of blood, 1st Lt. Bronson remained with the survivors of the company throughout the night of the second day, refusing to go to the rear for treatment. His conspicuous gallantry and spirit of self-sacrifice were a source of great inspiration to the members of the entire command."

Source
Medal of Honor Citation.

Brown, Jacob Jennings (1775–1828) *Hero of the War of 1812 and commanding general, United States Army, 1821–1828.*

A successful farmer and land speculator in the frontier region of upper New York State, Pennsylvania-born (1775) Jacob Brown—despite a complete lack of military training—was elected colonel of militia in 1808 for the district of Brownville, New York, a town he had founded.

It was a fortuitous choice because Brown, though a Quaker, proved to be an instinctive soldier, rivaled only by Andrew Jackson as a battle leader. Appointed militia brigadier general in 1811, Brown was in command of a large area along the New York–Canadian frontier when the War of 1812 between Britain and the United States broke out the following year. Rallying his command of 500 militiamen and 400 regulars to the successful defense of Sacketts Harbor (New York) on Lake Ontario in May 1813, Brown repulsed a British invading force. The following year he was appointed a major general in the United States Army and led an abortive invasion of Canada; he was severely wounded at the Battle of Niagara on July 25, 1814. Despite his wounds Brown took charge of the successful defense of the recently captured Fort Erie in August and September 1814, an engagement that ended the fighting in the north. Remaining a soldier after the war Brown was appointed commanding general of the United States Army in 1821, a post he held until his death in 1828.

Source
Army Historical Center

Browner, Ralph L. *Private first class, United States Marine Corps, so distinguished himself in combat during World War II that he was awarded the Navy Cross for his heroic actions.*

Citation: "For extraordinary heroism in action against enemy forces on Saipan, Marianas Islands, on 8 and 9 July, 1944, while serving in a Marine infantry battalion. During the night, when the company was receiving a heavy counterattack on the beach west of Kaberra Pass, Private First Class Browner set up his machine gun on the left flank of the line within six feet of the water's edge and manned the gun during the entire night despite intense rifle and machine gun fire. An estimated two hundred Japanese soldiers occupied the caves and beaches a few yards in front of Private First Class Browner's position. As the heat of the battle grew, he was receiving fire from three directions, but he courageously and willingly held his position and accounted for thirty-five enemy dead. His skill and tenacity were material factors in protecting the left flank of the line and in repulsing the counterattack. His heroic conduct throughout was in keeping with the highest traditions of the United States Naval Service."

Sources
Navy Cross Citation.
Blakeney, Jane. *Heroes: U.S. Marine Corps 1861–1955.* Washington, D.C., Guthrie Lithograph, 1957.

Buchanan, Richard W. *Corporal, United States Marine Corps, distinguished himself heroically on May 24, 1968, and was awarded the Navy Cross for his actions.*

Citation: "For extraordinary heroism while serving as an Automatic Rifleman with Company M, Third Battalion, Twenty-seventh Marines, First Marine Division (Reinforced), in the Republic of Vietnam on 24 May, 1968. While participating in Operation ALLEN BROOK, in Quang Nam Province, Corporal Buchanan's company was serving as battalion reserve, following in trace of Company K, as the unit moved against well-entrenched North Vietnamese Army forces in the village of Le Bac (1) [Numbers were used to designate different villages having the same name.]

Advancing into the objective area, Company K was ambushed by an enemy force in a tree line and two platoons were separated from the remainder of the company. As Corporal Buchanan's platoon quickly maneuvered toward the beleaguered Marines, it suddenly came under intense small arms and automatic weapons fire from a North Vietnamese Army unit entrenched in a series of bunkers and spider holes. In the initial burst of fire, several Marines were killed or seriously wounded, including the platoon commander, platoon sergeant, all the squad leaders and the radio operator. Observing a well-hidden enemy bunker, he fearlessly assaulted the position and directed accurate rifle fire into the emplacement. Then, retrieving the platoon radio and shouting to his comrades to follow, he led the Marines to the relative safety of a nearby pagoda where he established a hasty defense. Unable to establish radio communications with his company and upon observing several medical evacuation helicopters in the vicinity, he relayed a request for armed helicopter support. As he directed numerous air strikes on the enemy positions, often within ten feet of his own position, he courageously rushed into the fire-swept area to move the casualties to a better-protected position. Upon discovering an adjacent bunker occupied by several North Vietnamese Army soldiers, Corporal Buchanan boldly assaulted it single-handedly, silencing the hostile fire. Throughout the intense three-hour battle, his superb command ability and calm presence of mind in hazardous situations undoubtedly saved numerous Marine lives and inspired all who observed him. By his outstanding leadership, intrepid fighting spirit and selfless devotion to duty Corporal Buchanan upheld the highest traditions of the Marine Corps and the United States Naval Service."

Source and Additional Reading
Navy Cross Citation.
Stevens, Paul Drew, ed. *The Navy Cross: Vietnam: Citations of Awards to Men of the United States Marine Corps, 1964–1973.* Forest Ranch, Calif.: Sharp & Dunnigan, 1987.

Buckner, Simon Bolivar (1823–1914) *General, Confederate States Army.*

The organizer of the Kentucky State Guard, which largely joined the Confederacy, Simon B. Buckner rose to the rank of lieutenant general during the war. The Kentucky West Pointer (1844) served with the infantry in Mexico, winning two brevets and suffering a wound at Churubusco. He then returned to his teaching post at his alma mater.

Feeling that mandatory presence at Sunday chapel was a violation of his rights, he quit that post and returned to infantry service in 1849. In 1852 he transferred to the commissary branch but resigned three years later to engage in the real estate business. In the remaining years before the Civil War he was adjutant general of the Illinois militia and directed the reorganization of his native state's armed forces.

His Civil War assignments included the following: major general and inspector general, Kentucky State Guard (spring 1860); brigadier general, Confederate States Army (CSA) (September 14, 1861); commander, Central Geographical Division of Kentucky, Department 2 (September 18–October 28, 1861); Commander, Second Division, Central Army of Kentucky, Department 2 (October 28, 1861–February 11, 1862); commander of division, Fort Donelson, Central Army of Kentucky, Department 2 (February 11–16, 1862); commander of the fort (February 16, 1862); major general, CSA (August 16, 1862); commander of division, Left Wing, Army of the Mississippi (ca. September–November 20, 1862); commander of division, Hardee's corps, Army of Tennessee (November 20–December 14, 1862); commander, District of the Gulf, Department 2 (December 14, 1862–April 27, 1863); commander, Department of East Tennessee (May 12–September 1863); commander of corps, Army of Tennessee (September 1863); commander of division, Cheatham's corps, Army of Tennessee (October–November 1863); commander of division, Department of East Tennessee (November 26–December 1863); commander of the department (April 12–May 2, 1864); second in command, Trans-Mississippi Department (June–August 4, 1864); commander, District of West Louisiana, Trans-Mississippi Department (August 4, 1864–April 19, 1865); commander, First Corps, Trans-Mississippi Department (September 1864–May 26, 1865); lieutenant general, CSA (September 20, 1864); commander of the department (April 19–22, 1865); and commander, District of Arkansas and West Louisiana, Trans-Mississippi Department (April 22–May 26, 1865).

As the head of the state's military forces he attempted to preserve its precarious neutrality, but in July 1861 the Unionist-controlled military board of the state ordered the State Guard, which they considered prosecessionist, to turn in its arms. Buckner resigned on July 20 and two months later was named a Confederate brigadier general; neutrality had come to an end. Initially in command in central Kentucky, he later led a division from there to reinforce Fort Donelson. He directed the attempted breakout from the encircled post on February 15, 1862, but was called back by his superiors, John B. Floyd and Gideon J. Pillow. Both of them fled across the Cumberland River rather than surrender and left the task to Buckner. He was outraged by Grant's demand for unconditional surrender, but he was somewhat mollified by later developments.

He had paid Grant's New York hotel bill when the future Union general was on his way home, having resigned from the army. Grant returned the favor in kind, knowing that Buckner would have difficulty obtaining funds as a prisoner, and put his purse at the disposal of the vanquished. Exchanged on August 27, 1862, Buckner was promoted to major general and led his division at Perryville before being ordered to take command along the Gulf Coast. The next spring he took over the Department of East Tennessee. On July 25, 1863, this command was merged into the Department of Tennessee under Braxton Bragg but was retained for administrative purposes. Thus Buckner was reporting to both Bragg and Richmond. This awkward situation later led to ill feelings.

During the buildup prior to the Battle of Chickamauga, Buckner reinforced Bragg, and his command became a corps for the battle. When Jefferson Davis visited the army shortly thereafter Buckner was one of the leading critics of Bragg's generalship. For this reason Bragg shunted Buckner back off to East Tennessee just before Chattanooga. There he served under Longstreet during the siege of Knoxville. He then held a number of special assignments until again being placed in charge of the Department of East Tennessee in the spring of 1864. During this period he spent much of his time in Richmond, where he became known as "Simon the Poet" for his penchant for writing poetry.

Later that spring he was ordered to the virtually cutoff Trans-Mississippi as E. Kirby Smith's deputy. Not allowed to return to Kentucky for three years after the war, he resided for that period in New Orleans and then resurrected his fortunes. After serving as a pallbearer at his old friend Grant's funeral, he entered politics, serving a term as governor. In 1896 he ran for the vice presidency on John M. Palmer's Gold Democrats ticket.

At the time of his death he was the only surviving Confederate officer above the rank of brigadier general.

Source

Stickles, Arndt Mathias. *Simon B. Buckner: Borderland Knight.* Bloomington: Indiana University Press, 1929.

Burke, Arleigh (1901–1996) *United States naval officer; legendary World War II destroyer skipper, and cold war naval strategist.*

Born on a farm near Boulder, Colorado, Arleigh Burke never completed high school but won appointment to the United States Naval Academy, located at Annapolis, Maryland. Graduating June 7, 1923, he married Roberta "Bobbie" Gorsuch the same day. After five years aboard the battleship USS *Arizona*, Burke chose an ordnance specialty. He earned a master's degree in chemical engineering from the University of Michigan in 1931. A skilled pre–World War II and wartime commander and tactical innovator, Burke received national attention and the nickname "31 Knot Burke" in November 1943 when his Destroyer Squadron 23 decisively defeated a Japanese naval force in the Battle of Cape St. George in the Solomon Islands. Burke subsequently served as Vice Admiral Marc A. Mitscher's chief of staff in Fast Carrier Task Force 58/38 during the Marianas, Philippine, Iwo Jima, and Okinawa operations.

After the war, Burke prepared the navy's first postwar long-range plans, helped coordinate the service's testimony before Congress during the 1949 "Admirals' Revolt" hearings on defense unification and strategy, and served on the first United Nations Truce Negotiation Team during the Korean War. Eisenhower appointed Rear Admiral Burke in 1955 over 92 more senior admirals to become the chief of naval operations (CNO). He served an unprecedented three terms through August 1961.

As CNO, Burke fought against increased unification and restriction of command authority in the armed forces and for maintenance of a balanced, flexible fleet capable of responding quickly and effectively to crises and limited wars. He also accelerated the development of innovative weapons systems, championing development of the Polaris submarine-based ballistic missile, deployed in 1960, as a national nuclear deterrent system. Admiral Burke overruled advisers concerned about Polaris's cost and feasibility because he believed that a small, relatively invulnerable force of missile submarines could deter war and ensure a controlled response to Soviet attack. Burke linked the navy's strategy of "finite deterrence, controlled retaliation," to the need to prepare for limited as well as general war. He led one of the few serious challenges to massive retaliation and nuclear buildup during the first decades of the cold war.

Sources and Additional Reading

Chambers, John Whiteclay II, ed. *American Military History,* New York: Oxford University Press, 1999.

Rosenburg, David A. "Admiral Arleigh Burke" In *Men of War: Great Naval Leaders of World War II,* edited by Stephen Howarth. New York: St. Martin's Press, 1980.

Burke, Frank (also known as Francis X. Burke), (b. 1918) *First lieutenant, United States Army, 15th Infantry, Third Infantry Division, distinguished himself heroically on the battlefield during World War II and was awarded the Medal of Honor for his actions.*

Born: September 29, 1918, New York, N.Y.; **Entered service at:** Jersey City, N.J.; **Place and date:** Nuremberg, Germany, April 17, 1945. **G.O. No.:** 4, January 9, 1946.

Citation: "He fought with extreme gallantry in the streets of war-torn Nuremberg, Germany, where the 1st Battalion, 15th Infantry, was engaged in rooting out fanatical defenders of the citadel of Nazism. As battalion transportation officer he had gone forward to select a motor-pool site, when, in a desire to perform more than his assigned duties and participate in the fight, he advanced beyond the lines of the forward riflemen. Detecting a group of about 10 Germans making preparations for a local counterattack, he rushed back to a nearby American company, secured a light machine-gun with ammunition, and daringly opened fire on this superior force, which deployed and returned his fire with machine pistols, rifles, and rocket launchers. From another angle a German machine-gun tried to blast him from his emplacement, but 1st Lt. Burke killed this guncrew and drove off the survivors of the unit he had originally attacked. Giving his next attention to enemy infantrymen in ruined buildings, he picked up a rifle, dashed more than 100 yards through intense fire and engaged the Germans from behind an abandoned tank. A sniper nearly hit him from a cellar only 20 yards away, but he dispatched this adversary by running directly to the basement window, firing a full clip into it and then plunging through the darkened aperture to complete the job. He withdrew from the fight only long enough to replace his jammed rifle and to secure grenades, then re-engaged the Germans. Finding his shots ineffective, he pulled the pins from 2 grenades, and, holding 1 in each hand, rushed the enemy-held building, hurling his missiles just as the enemy threw a potato masher grenade at him. In the triple explosion the Germans were wiped out and 1st Lt. Burke was dazed; but he emerged from the shower of debris that engulfed him, recovered his rifle, and went on to kill 3 more Germans and meet the charge of a machine pistolman, whom he cut down with 3 calmly delivered shots. He then retired toward the American lines and there assisted a platoon in a raging, 30-minute fight against formidable armed hostile forces. This enemy group was repulsed, and the intrepid fighter moved to another friendly group that broke the power of a German unit armed with a 20-mm. gun in a fierce firefight. In 4 hours of heroic action, 1st Lt. Burke single-handedly killed 11 and wounded 3 enemy soldiers and took a leading role in engagements in which an additional 29 enemy were killed or wounded. His extraordinary bravery and superb fighting skill were an inspiration to his comrades, and his entirely voluntary mission into extremely dangerous territory hastened the fall of Nuremberg, in his battalion's sector."

Source
Medal of Honor Citation.

Burke, Lloyd L. (b. 1924) *First lieutenant, United States Army, Company G, Fifth Cavalry Regiment, First Cavalry Division, so distinguished himself in combat, during the Korean War, that he was awarded the Medal of Honor for his heroic actions.*

Born: September 29, 1924, Tichnor, Ark.; **Entered service at:** Stuttgart, Ark.; **Place and date:** Near Chongdong, Korea, October 28, 1951. **G.O. No.:** 43.

Citation: "1st Lt. Burke distinguished himself by conspicuous gallantry and outstanding courage above and beyond the call of duty in action against the enemy. Intense enemy fire had pinned down leading elements of his company committed to secure commanding ground when 1st Lt. Burke left the command post to rally and urge the men to follow him toward 3 bunkers impeding the advance. Dashing to an exposed vantage point he threw several grenades at the bunkers, then, returning for an Ml rifle and adapter, he made a lone assault, wiping out the position and killing the crew. Closing on the center bunker he lobbed grenades through the opening and, with his pistol, killed 3 of its occupants attempting to surround him. Ordering his men forward he charged the third emplacement, catching several grenades in midair and hurling them back at the enemy. Inspired by his display of valor his men stormed forward, overran the hostile position, but were again pinned down by increased fire. Securing a light machine gun and 3 boxes of ammunition, 1st Lt. Burke dashed through the impact area to an open knoll, set up his gun and poured a crippling fire into the ranks of the enemy, killing approximately 75. Although wounded, he ordered more ammunition, reloading and destroying 2 mortar emplacements and a machine gun position with his accurate fire. Cradling the weapon in his arms he then led his men forward, killing some 25 more of the retreating enemy and securing the objective. 1st Lt. Burke's heroic action and daring exploits inspired his small force of 35 troops. His unflinching courage and outstanding leadership reflect the highest credit upon himself, the infantry, and the U.S. Army."

Source
Medal of Honor Citation.

Bush, George H. W. (b. 1924) *Lieutenant Junior grade, United States Navy, forty-first president of the United States.*

Upon hearing of the Pearl Harbor attack while a student at Phillips Academy in Andover, Massachusetts, George Bush decided he wanted to join the navy to become an aviator. Six months later, after graduation, he enlisted in the navy on his 18th birthday and began preflight training at the University of North Carolina at Chapel Hill. After completing the 10-month course, he was commissioned as an ensign in the United States Naval Reserve on June 9, 1943, several days before his 19th birthday, making him the youngest naval aviator at that time.

After finishing flight training, he was assigned to Torpedo Squadron (VT-51) as photographic officer in September 1943. As part of Air Group 51, his squadron was based on USS *San Jacinto* in the spring of 1944. *San Jacinto* was part of Task Force 58, which participated in operations against Marcus and Wake Islands in May, and then in the Marianas during June. On June 19, the task force triumphed in one of the largest air battles of the war. During the return of his aircraft from the mission, Ensign Bush's aircraft made a forced water landing. The destroyer USS *Clarence K. Bronson* rescued the crew, but the plane was lost. On July 25, Ensign Bush and another pilot received credit for sinking a small cargo ship. After Bush was promoted to lieutenant junior grade on August 1, aboard the USS *San Jacinto*, the ship commenced operations against the Japanese in the Bonin Islands. On September 2, 1944, Bush piloted one of four aircraft from VT-51 that attacked the Japanese installations on Chi Chi Jima. For this mission his crew included Radioman Second Class John Delaney and Lieutenant Junior Grade William White, United States Naval Reserve (USNR), who substituted for Bush's regular gunner. During their attack, four TBM Avengers from VT-51 encountered intense antiaircraft fire. While starting the attack, Bush's aircraft was hit and his engine caught fire. He completed his attack and released the bombs over his target, scoring several damaging hits. With his engine on fire, Bush flew several miles from the island, where he and one other crew member on the TBM Avenger bailed out of the aircraft. However, the other man's chute did not open, and he fell to his death. It was never determined which man bailed out with Bush. Both Delaney and White were killed in action. While Bush anxiously waited four hours in his inflated raft, several fighters circled protectively overhead until he was rescued by the lifeguard submarine USS *Finback*. For this action, Bush received the Distinguished Flying Cross. During the month he remained on *Finback*, Bush participated in the rescue of other pilots.

Bush returned to San Jacinto in November 1944 and participated in operations in the Philippines. When *San*

Jacinto returned to Guam, the squadron, which had suffered 50 percent casualties of its pilots, was replaced and sent to the United States. Throughout 1944, he had flown 58 combat missions, for which he received the Distinguished Flying Cross, three Air Medals, and the Presidential Unit Citation, awarded at San Jacinto.

Because of his valuable combat experience, Bush was reassigned to Norfolk and put in a training wing for new torpedo pilots. Later, he was assigned as a naval aviator in a new torpedo squadron, VT-153. With the surrender of Japan, he was honorably discharged in September 1945 and then entered Yale University.

Citation: "The President of the United States takes pleasure in presenting the DISTINGUISHED FLYING CROSS TO LIEUTENANT, JUNIOR GRADE, GEORGE HERBERT WALKER BUSH, UNITED STATES NAVAL RESERVE for service as set forth in the following CITATION: "For heroism and extraordinary achievement in aerial flight as Pilot of a Torpedo Plane in Torpedo Squadron FIFTY ONE, attached to the U.S.S. *San Jacinto*, in action against enemy Japanese forces in the vicinity of the Bonin Islands, on September 2, 1944. Leading one section of a four-plane division in a strike against a radio station, Lieutenant, Junior Grade, Bush pressed home an attack in the face of intense antiaircraft fire. Although his plane was hit and set afire at the beginning of his dive, he continued his plunge toward the target and succeeded in scoring damaging bomb hits before bailing out of the craft. His courage and devotion to duty were in keeping with the highest traditions of the United States Naval Reserve." For the President, the Secretary of the Navy."

Source and Additional Reading
Atkinson, Rick. *Crusade: The Untold Story of the Persian Gulf War* Boston: Houghton Mifflin, 1993.
Department of the Navy, Naval Historical Center.

Bush, Robert Eugene (b. 1926) *Hospital apprentice first class, United State Naval Reserve, serving as medical corpsman with a rifle company, Second Battalion, Fifth Marines, First Marine Division, so distinguished himself in combat that he was awarded the Medal of Honor.*

Born: October 4, 1926, Tacoma, Wash.; **Entered service at:** Wash.; **Place and date:** Okinawa Jima, Ryukyu Islands, May 2, 1945.

Citation: "For conspicuous gallantry and intrepidity at the risk of his life above and beyond the call of duty while serving as Medical Corpsman with a rifle company, in action against enemy Japanese forces on Okinawa Jima, Ryukyu Islands, 2 May 1945. Fearlessly braving the fury of artillery, mortar, and machine-gun fire from strongly entrenched hostile positions, Bush constantly and unhesitatingly moved from 1 casualty to another to attend the wounded falling under the enemy's murderous barrages. As the attack passed over a ridge top, Bush was advancing to administer blood plasma to a Marine officer lying wounded on the skyline when the Japanese launched a savage counterattack. In this perilously exposed position, he resolutely maintained the flow of life-giving plasma. With the bottle held high in 1 hand, Bush drew his pistol with the other and fired into the enemy's ranks until his ammunition was expended. Quickly seizing a discarded carbine, he trained his fire on the Japanese charging pointblank over the hill, accounting for 6 of the enemy despite his own serious wounds and the loss of 1 eye suffered during his desperate battle in defense of the helpless man. With the hostile force finally routed, he calmly disregarded his own critical condition to complete his mission, valiantly refusing medical treatment for himself until his officer patient had been evacuated, and collapsing only after attempting to walk to the battle aid station. His daring initiative, great personal valor, and heroic spirit of self-sacrifice in service of others reflect great credit upon Bush and enhance the finest traditions of the U.S. Naval Service."

Source
Medal of Honor Citation.

Butler, Smedley Darlington ("Old Gimlet Eye")
(1881–1940) *Major general, United States Marine Corps, twice awarded the Medal of Honor, for the Mexican and Haitian Campaigns.*

Born: July 30, 1881, West Chester, Pa.; **Entered service at:** Pennsylvania; **G. O. No.:** December 4, 1915. **Other United States Navy awards:** Distinguished Service Medal.

Born in West Chester, Pennsylvania, into an old Quaker family, Butler first tried to secure an enlistment in the army at the outbreak of the Spanish-American War, in April 1898. He then joined the United States Marine Corps as a second lieutenant, misstating his age. He saw no combat and was discharged in February 1899. He was recommissioned as a first lieutenant in April and was ordered to the Philippines, where he saw action against the national rebels. He served in the American contingent during the Boxer Rebellion and fought at Tientsin on July 13, 1900, and on August 14 at Peking (Beijing) where he was wounded. His heroic exploits won him a brevet captaincy in February 1901.

After service in Philadelphia and then in the Caribbean (1903), he was sent back to the Philippines and was promoted to the grade of major. As commander of the Panama battalion (1909–14), Butler led his Marines into Nicaragua several times in defense of American interests, most notably in 1912. He landed his men at Corinto on August 14, 1912, and later relieved the town of Granada, disarming the besieging rebel army of General Mena in the process. Along with Marine Col. Joseph H. Pendleton, Butler stormed the rebel-held hill-top position at Coyotope (October 2–4). Butler was then assigned to the Atlantic Fleet in January 1914. He was awarded the Medal of Honor for his role in the capture of Veracruz (April 21–22, 1914) and remained there all summer for a planned (but never executed) 1,000-man raid into Mexico City to capture President Adolfo de la Huerta and bring the Mexican civil war to a close.

Butler commanded a battalion in Col. L. W. T. Waller's Marine force sent to occupy Haiti in August 1915. He engaged in active campaigning against the Cacos (Haitian mercenaries) and won distinction in a fight near Fort Dipitie (October 24–25) and a second Medal of Honor for his capture of Fort Rivière on November 17.

Promoted to lieutenant colonel, Butler then organized the Gendarmerie d'Haiti (1915–18), a military police force. He enjoyed such success that the Haitian organization served as a model for similar units in Nicaragua and the Dominican Republic.

Sent to France (1917–18), he was promoted to temporary brigadier general and was placed in command of Camp Pontanezen, near Brest, working to make that port an efficient transit point. Promoted to colonel in March 1919 and to brigadier general in March 1921, he commanded the Marine Corps base at Quantico, Virginia, transforming it from a temporary camp to a permanent installation (1920–24). He then took a leave of absence to serve as the director of public safety for the city of Philadelphia, remodeling that city's force along paramilitary lines in a successful effort to help control organized crime. As the commanding officer of the Marine Corps Base at San Diego (1926–27), he court-martialed his second in command for public drunkenness in the famous "Cocktail Trail" in the spring of 1926.

General Butler commanded the Marine expeditionary force in China from 1927 to 1929, demonstrating remarkable talent as a diplomat in a very tense situation.

Promoted to major general on his return to the United States (July 1929), he made public speeches concerning interference in elections in Nicaragua and Haiti during the Marine occupations there that earned him the Hoover administration's intense dislike.

After he was passed over as the next Marine Corps commandant, despite his position as senior general, he retired from his beloved corps and ran unsuccessfully for the U.S. Senate from Pennsylvania in 1932. In his retirement, he made increasingly radical criticisms of American imperialism, stating at one point, "I spent most of my time

Smedley Darlington Butler

being a high-class muscle man for Big Business, Wall Street, and the bankers. In short, I was a racketeer for capitalism."

Smedley D. Butler became increasingly active in the peace movement, campaigning vigorously for such leftist organizations as the united-front League against War during America's isolationist era of the mid- and late 1930s.

Smedley D. Butler was an outstanding Marine officer. "Old Gimlet Eye," as he was called, promoted a warrior-style Marine Corps mystique of physical stridency and anti-intellectual egalitarianism, contrary to contemporary trends toward elitist, bookish professionalism. His later criticism of American foreign policies in the Caribbean and Central America showed that he also had a high sense of personal honor and a very perceptive mind. He died in Philadelphia on June 21, 1940.

First Medal of Honor Citation: "For distinguished conduct in battle, engagement of Vera Cruz, 22 April 1914. Major Butler was eminent and conspicuous in command of his battalion. He exhibited courage and skill in leading his men through the action of the 22d and in the final occupation of the city."

Second Medal of Honor Citation: "As Commanding Officer of detachments from the Fifth, Thirteenth, Twenty-third Companies and the Marine and sailor detachment from the USS *Connecticut,* Major Butler led the attack on Fort Rivière, Haiti, 17 November 1915. Following a concentrated drive, several different detachments of Marines gradually closed in on the old French bastion fort in an effort to cut off all avenues of retreat for the Caco bandits. Reaching the fort of the southern side where there was a small opening in the wall, Major Butler gave the signal to attack and Marines from the Fifteenth Company poured through the breach, engaged the Cacos in hand-to-hand combat, took the bastion and crushed the Caco resistance. Throughout this perilous action Major Butler was conspicuous for his bravery and forceful leadership."

Source and Additional Reading

Medal of Honor Citations.

Schmidt, Hans. *Marverick Marine: Gen. Smedley Butler and the Contradictions of American Military History.* Lexington: University Press of Kentucky, 1987.

Thomas, Lowell. *Old Gimlet Eye.* New York: Farrar & Rinehart, 1933.

C

Cafferata, Hector Albert, Jr. (b. 1929) *For his heroic actions on November 28, 1950, Private Cafferata, United States Marine Corps, was awarded the Medal of Honor.*

Citation: "For conspicuous gallantry and intrepidity at the risk of his life above and beyond the call to duty while serving as a Rifleman with Company F, Second Battalion, Seventh Marines, First Marine Division (Reinforced), in action against enemy aggressor forces in Korea on 28 November 1950. When all the other members of his fire team became casualties, creating a gap in the lines, during the initial phase of a vicious attack launched by a fanatical enemy of regimental strength against his company's hill position, Private Cafferata waged a lone battle with grenades and rifle fire as the attack gained momentum and the enemy threatened penetration through the gap and endangered the integrity of the entire defensive perimeter. Making a target of himself under the devastating fire from automatic weapons, rifles, grenades and mortars, he maneuvered up and down the line and delivered accurate and effective fire against the onrushing force, killing fifteen, wounding many more and forcing the others to withdraw so that reinforcements could move up and consolidate the position. Again fighting desperately against a renewed onslaught later that same morning when a hostile grenade landed in a shallow entrenchment occupied by wounded Marines, Private Cafferata rushed into the gully under fire, seized the deadly missile in his right hand and hurled it free of his comrades before it detonated, severing part of one finger and seriously wounding him in the right hand and arm. Courageously ignoring the intense pain, he staunchly fought on until he was struck by a sniper's bullet and forced to submit to evacuation for medical treatment. Stouthearted and indomitable, Private Cafferata, by his fortitude, great personal valor and dauntless perseverance in the face of almost certain death, saved the lives of several of his fellow Marines and contributed essentially to the success achieved by his company in maintaining its defensive position against tremendous odds. His extraordinary heroism throughout was in keeping with the highest traditions of the United States Naval Service.

Hector Albert Cafferata Jr.

Source and Additional Reading
Medal of Honor Citation.
Blakeney, Jane. *Heroes: U.S. Marine Corps 1861–1955*. Washington, DC: Guthrie Lithographic, 1957.

Caine, Lawrence B., III *Corporal, United States Marine Corps, was awarded the Navy Cross for his heroic actions in May 1967, in the Republic of Vietnam.*

Citation: "For extraordinary heroism while serving as a Weapons Squad Leader with Company I, Third Battalion, Fifth Marines, First Marine Division (Reinforced) in the Republic of Vietnam on 13 May 1967. During Operation UNION, Corporal Caine's squad was providing covering fire during a recovery operation of Marine dead and wounded, when he observed a large force of well-entrenched enemy forces to his front. From their positions, the enemy was able to cover an area of over 2,000 meters in width with grazing and interlocking fire. He quickly took the enemy under fire and killed 20 North Vietnamese Army soldiers in front of his position. Observing a series of caves adjacent to his position he, with complete disregard for his own personal safety, entered them and while searching them accounted for two more enemy killed. Returning to his position, he continued to employ machine-gun, rocket and small-arms fire with devastating fire on the enemy. Although painfully wounded during a mortar attack, he refused medical evacuation and continued to defend his company's front until all helicopter evacuation of dead and wounded was completed. As the numerically superior enemy force advanced on the company position, Company I was ordered to withdraw 200 meters and to call air strikes and artillery fire on their former position. He directed the fire of his squad covering the successful withdrawal of the company with automatic weapons and a 3.5-inch rocket fire from his tree-line position. Corporal Caine was wounded the second time when he was struck by a bomb fragment. As his squad withdrew, 62 enemy bodies were counted in the intermittent streambed to his front. By his intrepid fighting spirit, exceptional fortitude and gallant initiative, Corporal Caine served to inspire all who observed him and contributed in large measure to the success of his unit. His great personal valor reflected the highest credit upon himself and enhanced the finest traditions of the Marine Corps and the United States Naval Service."

Source and Additional Reading
Navy Cross Citation.
Stevens, Paul Drew, ed. *The Navy Cross: Vietnam: Citations of Awards to Men of the United States Marine Corps, 1964–1973*. Forest Ranch, Calif: Sharp Dunnigan, 1987.

Call, Donald M. (b. 1892) *Corporal, United States Army, 344th Battalion, Tank Corps, distinguished himself heroically on the battlefield and was awarded the Medal of Honor for his actions in September 1918.*

Born: November 29, 1892, New York, N.Y.; **Entered service at:** France; **Place and date:** Near Varennes, France, September 26, 1918. **G. O. No.:** 13, W.D. 1919.

Citation: "During an operation against enemy machine gun-nests west of Varennes, Corporal Call was in a tank with an officer when half of the turret was knocked off by a direct artillery hit. Choked by gas from the high-explosive shell, he left the tank and took cover in a shell-hole 30 yards away. Seeing that the officer did not follow, and thinking that he might be alive, Corporal Call returned to the tank under intense machine-gun and shell fire and carried the officer over a mile under machine-gun and sniper fire to safety."

Source
Medal of Honor Citation.

Capodanno, Vincent R. (1929–1967) *Lieutenant, United States Navy, Chaplain Corps, Third Battalion, Fifth Marines, First Marine Division (Reinforced), FMF, so distinguished himself in combat, during the Vietnam War, that he was awarded (posthumously) the Medal of Honor for his heroic actions.*

Born: February 13, 1929, Staten Island, N.Y.; **Entered service at:** Staten Island, N.Y. **Place and date:** Quang Tin Province, Republic of Vietnam, September 4, 1967.

Citation: "For conspicuous gallantry and intrepidity at the risk of his life above and beyond the call of duty as Chaplain of the 3d Battalion, in connection with operations against enemy forces. In response to reports that the 2d Platoon of M Company was in danger of being overrun by a massed enemy assaulting force, Lt. Capodanno left the relative safety of the company command post and ran through an open area raked with fire, directly to the beleaguered platoon. Disregarding the intense enemy small arms, automatic-weapons, and mortar fire, he moved about the battlefield administering last rites to the dying and giving medical aid to the wounded. When an exploding mortar round inflicted painful multiple wounds to his arms and legs, and severed a portion of his right hand, he steadfastly refused all medical aid. Instead, he directed the corpsmen to help their wounded comrades and, with calm vigor, continued to move about the battlefield as he provided encouragement by voice and example to the valiant Marines. Upon encountering a wounded corpsman in the direct line of fire of an enemy machine gunner positioned approximately 15 yards away, Lt. Capodanno rushed a daring attempt to aid and assist the mortally wounded corpsman. At that instant, only inches from his goal, he was struck down by a burst of machine gun fire. By his heroic conduct on the battlefield, and his inspiring example, Lt. Capodanno upheld the finest traditions of the U.S. Naval Service. He gallantly gave his life in the cause of freedom."

Source
Medal of Honor Citation.

Carlson, Evans Fordyce (1896–1947) Brigadier General, United States Marine Corps.

Born February 26, 1896, in Sidney, New York, Carlson enlisted in the army in 1912, at the age of 16, and served in the Philippines and Hawaii from 1912 to 1915. Discharged in 1915, he was recalled for duty on the Mexican border in 1916. During World War I he was promoted to captain and served on General John Pershing's staff as assistant adjutant general (1917–19). He resigned his commission after the war to work as a salesman.

Carlson enlisted in the United States Marine Corps, as a private, in 1922 and was commissioned a second lieutenant in 1923. He served as an intelligence and operations officer in Shanghai from 1927 to 1929 and in Nicaragua in 1930. He returned to China and served in Peking from 1933 to 1935 and was promoted to captain. He formed a close friendship with President Franklin D. Roosevelt while serving with the president's military guard at Warm Springs, Georgia, from 1935 to 1937.

Carlson again returned to duty in China and was an observer with Chinese forces during their war with Japan (1937–39). He went on two long marches with the Communist Eighth Route Army and was very impressed by its rigorous training, discipline, and morale. His praise for the Communist troops generated censure from his superiors and resulted in his resignation in April 1939.

Carlson returned to the United States, traveled, lectured, and wrote two books about the Chinese army. He then joined the Marine Corps Reserves as a major in April 1941. He transferred to active duty in May of that year, was promoted to lieutenant colonel, and took command of the second Marine Raider Battalion (early 1942). Using innovative methods of training and discipline he had learned from the Chinese, he organized the battalion into an elite fighting force known as Carlson's Raiders. He led two companies of Raiders on a surprise raid against Japanese installations on Makin Island (August 17–18, 1942). During the invasion of Guadalcanal, in November, he led operations behind enemy lines; served as an observer in the Tarawa (November 22–24, 1943) and Saipan (June 15–July 13, 1944) landings; and was severely wounded in combat on Saipan. Colonel Carlson was promoted to brigadier general and was forced to retire as a result of his wounds in July 1946.

After his retirement, Carlson worked diligently to improve U.S.-Chinese relations until his death on May 27, 1947, at Portland, Oregon.

Evans Carlson was an intelligent, heroic, and innovative Marine Corps officer. The valuable lessons he learned from the Chinese military enabled him to train elite units, like the Raiders, skilled in jungle warfare. This effective training undoubtedly helped save many Marines' lives.

Additional Reading

Carlson, Evans F. *The Chinese Army: Its Organization and Military Efficiency.* New York: Institute of Pacific Relations, 1940.
Schuon, Karl. *U.S. Marine Corps Biographical Dictionary.* New York: Franklin Watts, 1963.
United States Marine Corps. *U.S. Marine Corps Historical Branch, G-3, History of the U.S. Marine Corps Operations in World War II.* Vol. I. Washington, D. C., 1958.

Carswell, Horace S., Jr. (d. 1944) Major, 308th Bombardment Group, United States Army Air Corps, so distinguished himself in aerial combat, during World War II, that he was awarded (posthumously) the Medal of Honor for his heroic actions.

Born: Fort Worth, Tex.; **Entered service at:** San Angelo, Tex.; **Place and date:** Over South China Sea, October 26, 1944. G.O. No.: 14, February 4, 1946.

Citation: "He piloted a B-24 bomber in a one-plane strike against a Japanese convoy in the South China Sea on the night of 26 October 1944. Taking the enemy force of 12 ships escorted by at least 2 destroyers by surprise, he made 1 bombing run at 600 feet, scoring a near miss on 1 warship and escaping without drawing fire. He circled and fully realizing that the convoy was thoroughly alerted and would meet his next attack with a barrage of antiaircraft fire, began a second low-level run which culminated in 2 direct hits on a large tanker. A hail of steel from Japanese guns riddled the bomber, knocking out 2 engines, damaging a third, crippling the hydraulic system, puncturing 1 gasoline tank, ripping uncounted holes in the aircraft, and wounding the copilot; but by magnificent display of flying skill, Maj. Carswell controlled the plane's plunge toward the sea and carefully forced it into a halting climb in the direction of the China shore. On reaching land, where it would have been possible to abandon the staggering bomber, one of the crew discovered that his parachute had been ripped by flak and rendered useless; the pilot, hoping to cross mountainous terrain and reach a base, continued onward until the third engine failed. He ordered the crew to bail out while he struggled to maintain altitude and, refusing to save himself, chose to remain with his comrade and attempt a crash landing. He died when the airplane struck a mountainside and burned. With consummate gallantry and intrepidity, Maj. Carswell gave his life in a supreme effort to save all members of his crew. His sacrifice, far beyond that required of him, was in keeping with the traditional bravery of America's war heroes."

Source
Medal of Honor Citation.

Casebolt, Henry C. *Corporal, United States Marine Corps, was awarded the Navy Cross for his heroic actions on February 28, 1966, while serving in the Republic of Vietnam.*

Citation: "For extraordinary heroism as Second Squad Leader, Third Rifle Platoon, Company F, Second Battalion, First Marines, in the Thua Thien Province, Republic of Vietnam, on February 28, 1966. While his company was engaged in a search and destroy operation it was taken under heavy machine-gun and mortar fire by an entrenched Viet Cong battalion. Without hesitation, Corporal Casebolt maneuvered his squad through intense hostile fire in order to position them in a location where they could block the enemy's retreat. His skillful deployment of his squad enabled his men to kill approximately twenty-five Viet Cong and successfully stop the retreat of many others. When an enemy squad attempted to envelop his squad from the left, Corporal Casebolt and two other Marines assaulted the Viet Cong squad, killing them all. Without stopping to catch his breath, he gave orders to his squad to cover him while he crossed a seventy-meter rice paddy in an attempt to destroy an enemy mortar position that he had detected. With complete disregard for his own safety, he aggressively ran across the open rice paddy toward the enemy shouting instructions to his squad and directing their fire. When he was almost across the open area, the heavy enemy fire knocked him into the rice paddy. Although mortally wounded, he crawled to a mound of earth where he could observe the enemy. From this position, and still the object of intense enemy fire, Corporal Casebolt continued to direct his squad's fire by pinpointing the enemy positions for them and ordering them to deploy to positions where he could better block the Viet Cong retreat. By his tremendous devotion to duty, professional ability, and inspiring leadership, Corporal Casebolt upheld the highest traditions of the Marine Corps and the United

States Naval Service. He gallantly gave his life in the cause of freedom."

Source and Additional Reading
Navy Cross Citation.
Stevens, Paul Drew, ed. *The Navy Cross: Vietnam: Citations of Awards to Men of the United States Marine Corps, 1964–1973.* Forest Ranch, Calif: Sharp & Dunnigan, 1987.

Castillo, William *Private first class, United States Marine Corps, was awarded the Navy Cross for his heroic actions on February 25, 1969.*

Citation: "For extraordinary heroism while serving as an Ammunition Man with Company E, Second Battalion, Fourth Marines, Third Marine Division, in connection with combat operations against the enemy in the Republic of Vietnam. On 25 February 1969, Company E was occupying a defensive position at Fire Support Base Russell, northwest of the Vandergrift Combat Base, in Quang Tri Province. Suddenly, the Marines came under a vicious ground attack by a North Vietnamese Army sapper unit strongly supported by mortars and rocket-propelled grenades. During the initial moments of the attack, several Marines were trapped inside demolished bunkers and Private First Class Castillo worked feverishly to free the men. Then, diving into his gun pit, he commenced single-handedly firing his mortar at the invaders, and although blown from his emplacement on two occasions by the concussion of hostile rounds impacting nearby, resolutely continued his efforts until relieved by some of the men he had freed. Observing a bunker that was struck by enemy fire and was ejecting thick clouds of smoke, he investigated the interior, and discovering five men blinded by smoke and in a state of shock, led them all to safety. Maneuvering across the fire-swept terrain to the command post, he made repeated trips through the hazardous area to carry messages and directions from his commanding officer, then procured a machine gun and provided security for a landing zone until harassing hostile emplacements were destroyed. Steadfastly determined to be of assistance to his wounded comrades, he carried the casualties to waiting evacuation helicopters until he collapsed from exhaustion. By his courage, bold initiative, and unwavering devotion to duty in the face of grave personal danger, Private First Class Castillo contributed significantly to the accomplishment of his unit's mission and upheld the highest traditions of the Marine Corps and the United States Naval Service."

Source
Navy Cross Citation.

Cavaiani, Jon R. (b. 1943) *Staff sergeant, United States Army, Vietnam Training Advisory Group, so distinguished himself in combat in the Republic of Vietnam that he was awarded the Medal of Honor for his heroic actions.*

Born: August 2, 1943, Royston, England; **Entered service at:** Fresno, Calif.; **Place and date:** Republic of Vietnam, June 4 and 5, 1971.

Citation: "S/Sgt. Cavaiani distinguished himself by conspicuous gallantry and intrepidity at the risk of life above and beyond the call of duty in action in the Republic of Vietnam on 4 and 5 June 1971 while serving as a platoon leader to a security platoon providing security for an isolated radio relay site located within enemy-held territory. On the morning of 4 June 1971, the entire camp came under an intense barrage of enemy small arms, automatic weapons, rocket-propelled grenade and mortar fire from a superior size enemy force. S/Sgt. Cavaiani acted with complete disregard for his personal safety as he repeatedly exposed himself to heavy enemy fire in order to move about the camp's perimeter directing the platoon's fire and rallying the platoon in a desperate fight for survival. S/Sgt. Cavaiani also returned heavy suppressive fire upon the assaulting enemy force during this period with a variety of weapons. When the entire platoon was to be evacuated, S/Sgt. Cavaiani unhesitatingly volunteered to remain on the ground and direct the helicopters into the landing zone. S/Sgt. Cavaiani was able to direct the first three helicopters in evacuating a major portion of the platoon. Due to intense increase in enemy fire, S/Sgt. Cavaiani was forced to remain at the camp overnight where he calmly directed the remaining platoon members in strengthening their defenses. On the morning of 5 June, a heavy ground fog restricted visibility. The superior size enemy force launched a major ground attack in an attempt to completely annihilate the remaining small force. The enemy force advanced in two ranks, the first firing a heavy volume of small arms automatic weapons and rocket-propelled grenade fire while the second rank continuously threw a steady barrage of hand grenades at the beleaguered force. S/Sgt. Cavaiani returned a heavy barrage of small arms and hand grenade fire on the assaulting enemy force but was unable to slow them down. He ordered the remaining platoon members to attempt to escape while he provided them with cover fire. With 1 last courageous exertion, S/Sgt. Cavaiani recovered a machine gun, stood up, completely exposing himself to the heavy enemy fire directed at him, and began firing the machine gun in a sweeping motion along the 2 ranks of advancing enemy soldiers. Through S/Sgt. Cavaiani's valiant efforts with complete disregard for his safety, the majority of the remaining platoon members were able to escape. While inflicting severe losses on the advancing enemy force, S/Sgt. Cavaiani was wounded numerous times. S/Sgt. Cavaiani's conspicuous gallantry, extraordinary heroism

and intrepidity at the risk of his life, above and beyond the call of duty, were in keeping with the highest traditions of the military service and reflect great credit upon himself and the U.S. Army."

Source
Medal of Honor Citation

Chamberlain, Joshua Lawrence (1828–1914)
Union general officer, educator, governor of Maine 1866–1871.

"Colonel Joshua Chamberlain moved his 20th Maine Volunteer Infantry Regiment on the double-quick. Men ran into the dark woods, passing boulders and the stumps of trees newly shattered by Lieutenant General James A. Longstreet's artillery batteries.

"It was the second day of the Battle of Gettysburg. After smashing Maj. gen. Daniel Sickle's III Corps in the Peach Orchard, pushing the Yankees back through the Wheat Field and Devil's Den, General Robert E. Lee's Army of Northern Virginia was on its way to turning the left flank of Maj. Gen. George G. Meade's Army of the Potomac.

Joshua Lawrence Chamberlain

"Chamberlain's soldiers reached the crest of Little Round Top in the nick of time. No troops, other than a few signalmen, had been posted in that key position before Sickles' ill-fated advance. Chamberlain told his men to dig in and to pile up rocks to make a defensive position. He remembered Fredericksburg, where on December 13, 1862, he and his regiment had been on the receiving end of intense defensive fire delivered by well-entrenched Confederate troops.

"The remainder of Colonel Strong Vincent's 3rd Brigade hurried up to Little Round Top and came on line next to the 20th Maine. The 83rd Pennsylvania deployed to the right of Chamberlain's down-easters, with the 44th New York and 16th Michigan following to complete the defensive formation. Vincent told Chamberlain: 'I place you here! This is the left of the Union line. You understand, you are to hold this ground at all costs.'

"The Maine colonel summoned his company commanders. The 50 men of Captain Walter G. Morill's B Company were sent to protect the gap between Little Round Top and Big Round Top. That left Chamberlain with 308 enlisted men. Morill was later joined by 14 survivors of Major Homer R. Staughton's 2nd U.S. (Berdan's) Sharpshooters, who had been driven back from Big Round Top.

"Gray smoke drifted into Chamberlain's position. Red battle flags appeared above the smoke, moving toward Little Round Top. Suddenly, a crackling volley of rifle fire opened against the other side of the hill. Enemy soldiers appeared in front of the 20th Maine. This force was the 47th Alabama, close to 350 men. A terrible scream, the Rebel yell, preceded the determined attack on the thin blue line. Men in gray and butternut uniforms emerged out of the dark woods.

"The Union soldiers frantically tore cartridges out of boxes, bit caps, rammed balls home in hot gun barrels and squeezed triggers. The Alabamians recoiled, then re-formed and charged again and again. Blood lay in puddles on the rocks in front of the Federal line. When Chamberlain saw Confederate troops moving toward his left flank and rear, he ordered his troops to refuse the flank—to swing a portion of the left flank back at a right angle to face the threat—a maneuver almost impossible to accomplish while under fire.

"Combat became hand-to-hand. The 15th Alabama, nearly 500 men strong, reinforced the Southern charge. The center of the 20th Maine's position was almost shot away, leaving only two men from the color guard, fighting desperately to close the breach. Chamberlain sent his adjutant—his brother Tom—and a sergeant to fill the gap by pulling men from neighboring companies. In the melee, Colonel William C. Oates, commanding the 15th Alabama, fired his pistol at Yankees only a few feet away. Oates watched Sergeant Pat O'Connor jab his bayonet into the brave Federal's head.

"Chamberlain was wounded in the right foot, dripping blood where a rock splinter or shell fragment had penetrated. No reinforcements were available, and his men were running low on ammunition as the 15th and 47th Alabama Regiments re-formed for another charge. Each man in the 20th Maine had started the fight with 60 cartridges. Together they had expended more than 20,000 rounds. One-third of Chamberlain's men were down, and there were no reserves.

"Chamberlain summoned his remaining officers. 'Bayonet!' he yelled. Socket bayonets came out and were rammed onto musket barrels. The 20th Maine charged down Little Round Top in a right-wheel forward. Men on the left crimped toward the right, pushing Southerners toward the adjoining Union troops. Most Confederates fell back, but some wheeled and fired. At the start of the bayonet charge, a Confederate officer tried to fire a Colt Navy revolver at Chamberlain's face, but the gun clicked uselessly—empty. He then handed over his sword as Chamberlain's sword pointed at his throat.

"Chamberlain gave the surrendered sword to a sergeant next to him but kept the pistol. Many Confederate soldiers tossed their weapons on the ground and threw up their hands. Others were swept away by the ferocity of the Yankee onslaught. At that crucial juncture, Captain Morill's Company B, together with Berdan's Sharpshooters, stuck their heads up over a stone wall and delivered a volley into the Confederate rear.

"Alabama's Colonel Oates later said, 'We ran like a herd of wild cattle.' Lieutenant Colonel Bulger of the 47th Alabama and Colonel Powell of the 5th Texas were taken prisoner along with some 400 other Rebel troops. With great difficulty, the limping Chamberlain halted his men when they reached the front of the 44th New York. Many troops yelling that they were 'on the road to Richmond,' had to be reined in. Chamberlain and his 20th Maine played a key role in saving Little Round Top. They also saved the Army of the Potomac from a flank attack that could have completely rolled up the Federal left. In 1893, Chamberlain was awarded the Medal of Honor for his distinguished gallantry at Gettysburg on July 2, 1863."

Joshua Lawrence Chamberlain was born in Brewer, Maine, on September 8, 1828, and grew up on a farm. His father directed him toward West Point, but his mother, a deeply religious woman, insisted that he become a minister, not a soldier. Chamberlain attended Bowdoin College from 1848 to 1952, graduating with the highest honors. Plagued with a propensity to stammer, Chamberlain taught himself to speak in a rhythmic style that made his impediment undetectable to listeners. He used that system so skillfully that he became a public speaker of great eloquence. Chamberlain's supposed natural gift for soldiering and his tenacity and ability to master any subject he wished perhaps better explain leadership.

After graduation, Chamberlain studied for three years at the Bangor Theological Seminary and then earned a master's degree at Bowdoin. His quiet life as a college professor and family man ended when he declined a paid two-year sabbatical in Europe during the summer of 1862 and instead enlisted with the 20th Maine Infantry as its lieutenant colonel. Chamberlain strongly disapproved of slavery on moral and religious grounds and was convinced that session violated the Constitution.

The 20th Maine missed the bloodletting at Antietam, but on December 13, 1862, the regiment was hurled at the stone wall on Marye's Heights at Fredericksburg. Luckily, casualties were light, and Chamberlain learned the value of defensive positions anchored in stone.

One month after Gettysburg, Chamberlain succeeded Colonel Vincent, who had died at Little Round Top, as commander of the 3rd Brigade, 1st Division, V Corps, which he led during the Mine Run campaign. Taking over a brigade of Pennsylvanians early in June 1864, Chamberlain led them on June 18 in a series of attacks against heavily fortified Confederate works at Petersburg, Virginia.

Defensive fire from the Southerners was intense. When his brigade color-bearer was shot dead at his side during the first Federal assault, Chamberlain picked up the V Corps flag—a red Maltese cross on a field of white—and raced forward. His soldiers forced a Rebel battery and supporting infantry to retreat, and later that day Chamberlain stepped off with his men to assail River's Salient, another well-defended Rebel fortification. The assaulting Union troops literally fell in piles. Chamberlain turned and beckoned the Pennsylvanians to move up. As he did so, a Minie bullet slammed into his right hip joint and passed out through his left hip. Supporting himself by leaning on his saber, he urged his men forward before loss of blood finally caused him to collapse.

The attack failed within 20 feet of the Rebel entrenchments. Chamberlain was carried to the rear. General Ulysses S. Grant, affected deeply by Chamberlain's heroism, immediately promoted him to brigadier general—the only such field promotion made by Grant during the war.

Chamberlain lingered near death for weeks. By August 1864, however, he had recuperated so remarkably that he spoke about returning to duty. In November 1864, he rejoined V Corps and, despite pain and further hospitalization, he led troops in the last campaigns against the South. In March 1865, Chamberlain's bravery earned his command the honor of leading the attack against Lee's retreating Army of Northern Virginia.

At daylight on March 29, Chamberlain's men hit Lee's divisions at the intersection of Boydton Plank and Quaker Roads, not far from Petersburg. After initial success, the Federals were stopped in front of a Confederate breastwork of logs and earth. Regrouping his men, Chamberlain led a new charge. His horse reared. A bullet aimed at Chamber-

lain ripped through his horse's neck and a leather case filled with field orders, tore his sleeve to the elbow, bruised his left arm and hit him below the heart. The round then smashed the holstered pistol of one of his officers and knocked the man out of his saddle. After regaining consciousness from the blow, Chamberlain, covered with blood, rallied his troops. Chamberlain's force, supported by artillery, smashed through the Confederate works.

Chamberlain led a new attack on Lee's retreating army on March 31 at White Oak Road. Once again confronting a breastwork heavily defended by Southern infantry, he spaced his troops in a loose-order arrangement to keep casualties low. His soldiers then swarmed over the defending Confederates. Chamberlain's leadership in these last two actions resulted in his promotion to brevet major general "for conspicuous gallantry and meritorious service."

The professor from Maine further distinguished himself at the fight for Five Forks on April 1, 1865. After General Lee's surrender on April 9, Chamberlain learned that he had been designated by General Grant to accept the formal capitulation of Confederate arms and colors at Appomattox Court House. On April 12, he startled the nation by calling his troops to attention to salute the defeated Southerners. At the Grand Review of the Union Armies in Washington, D.C., on May 23, 1865, the new president, Andrew Johnson, asked Chamberlain to sit with other dignitaries to watch the final mustering of Grant's and General William T. Sherman's troops.

During the war, Chamberlain had participated in 24 battles large and small. Troops under his command captured 2,700 prisoners and eight battle flags. At least five horses were shot from under him, and he was wounded six times.

Chamberlain's postwar career was equally remarkable. In Maine, he was elected governor four times. He then became president of Bowdoin College. Modernizing the school, he introduced science courses, de-emphasized religion, and faced student demonstrations over the issue of the Reserve Officers Training Corps. The old soldier was honored in Paris, France, for his international educational efforts. In 1898, Chamberlain volunteered to serve in the Spanish-American War, but he was instead appointed to serve as surveyor of the port of Portland, Maine.

Joshua Chamberlain died from a reinfection of his old Civil War hip wound on February 24, 1914, at the age of 85. His words on the significance of Gettysburg still resound:

In great deeds something abides. On great fields something stays. Forms change and pass; bodies disappear; but spirits linger, to consecrate ground for the vision-place souls. And reverent men and women from afar, and generations that know us not and that we know not of, heart-drawn to see where and by whom great things were suffered and done for them, shall come to see this deathless field, to ponder and dream; and lo! The shadow of a mighty presence shall wrap them in its bosom, and the power of the vision pass into their souls.

Source and Additional Reading

Trulock, Alice Rains. *In the Hands of Providence: Joshua L. Chamberlain and the American Civil War.* Chapel Hill,: University of North Carolina Press, 1992.

Chamberlain, Reid C. (1919–1995) *Corporal, United States Marine Corps.*

Reid Carles Chamberlain, born in Arkansas in 1919, enlisted in the Marine Corps on June 21, 1938, and acquired his boot camp training at the Marine Corps Base, San Diego, California. On April 4, 1939, he received a "dependency discharge" because of ill parents who were unable to work, however, the following day, he enlisted in the Marine Corps Reserve (inactive status) and was promoted to private first class the same day.

After a one-month's course of instruction in aircraft welding, he went to work for the Consolidated Aircraft Corporation at San Diego's Lindbergh Field. As the nation's defense program moved into high gear, Chamberlain was working on the newest designs of army and navy planes. He was recalled to active duty in the Marine Corps on June 26, 1941, and again reported for duty at San Diego. His special request to be transferred to duty in the Pacific was granted on August 9, 1941, when he left the United States for the Marine Barracks at Cavite, Philippine Islands, where he joined Company C, First Separate Marine Brigade.

Then came the Japanese surprise attack on Pearl Harbor, on December 7, 1941. On December 10, 1941, Private First Class Chamberlain was on duty at Binekayan, in the province of Cavite, where he received a damaged eardrum from gun detonations while repelling the enemy planes during their bombing of the Cavite Navy Yard. His last letter to his mother, in February 1942, stated that he had "some close calls but nothing to worry about." He was a member of Battery C of the anti-aircraft defenses when the Japanese landed on the west coast of Bataan. On February 25, he took a patrol of 30 men to Pucet Hill, where about five hundred Japanese troops ambushed them.

A safe withdrawal was made possible by Chamberlain's silencing of an enemy machine gun with his Browning automatic rifle. For his heroism, he was recommended for the Silver Star. Two days later he was wounded in the right forearm by a bullet from a Japanese machine gun. The following month he was promoted to the rank of corporal and was transferred to the Third Battalion, Fourth Marines.

On May, 6 1942, United States Army Gen. Jonathan M. Wainwright was ordered to surrender all U.S. forces in the Philippines. That same night Corporal Chamberlain, with a party of 16 men, attempted to escape from the island of Corregidor in a small motor launch. That was the last that was seen of him by those less fortunate Americans who became prisoners of the Japanese. He was carried on the rolls as "missing in action" as of May 6, 1942.

After many days of drifting, and suffering from the extreme hardships of thirst and hunger, he landed on the island of Mindanao and reported to Army Col. Wendell W. Fertig, in command of the United States Army forces. On January 15, 1943, he was commissioned a second lieutenant in the army of the United States and became a liaison officer for Colonel Fertig's headquarters. He served with various divisions of guerrillas operating in the islands and continuously passed through situations of great danger in areas held by the Japanese. His detachment was instrumental in obtaining supplies, in addition to getting important papers through the enemy's blockade and relaying valuable information back to the army's headquarters. Because of his ability to command, he was promoted to first lieutenant in the army on October 1, 1943.

Because of ill health and his desire to rejoin the Marine Corps, he left the Philippines on about October 15 and arrived on November 23 in Australia, where he sailed via the USS *Gripsholm* for the United States. He arrived at Headquarters Marine Corps in Washington, D.C., on December 13, 1943.

Then began the problem of straightening out of Chamberlain's active service status. Was he a Marine or was he a soldier? The affair was settled by discharging him from the Marine Corps Reserve on January 14, 1943, the day prior to his acceptance of a commission in the army. The army, likewise, discharged him on December 21, 1943, so that he might be reenlisted in the Marine Corps. On December 23, he reenlisted as a corporal in the regular Marine Corps. On February 28, 1944, Lt. Gen. Alexander A. Vandergrift, commandant of the Marine Corps, pinned the army's Distinguished Service Medal on Chamberlain's blouse. The citation related the young Marine's extraordinary heroism in action during the period he served with Colonel Fertig's soldiers on Mindanao. The decoration was awarded by order of General Douglas MacArthur.

Because of his outstanding service as a commissioned officer in the army, Corporal Chamberlain was recommended for appointment to the Marine's Officers' Candidate's School (OSC) Class at Marine Corps Schools, Quantico, Virginia. However, Chamberlain felt that he needed more time for readjustment in the ways of normal living and requested a discharge from the Marine Corps OCS Class to resume enlisted man's duties as an orderly at San Diego, where he could be near his family.

In April 1944, he requested assignment to the Pacific area. On May 26 he joined the Fifth Marine Amphibious

Corps's Replacement Battalion, at Pearl Harbor, Hawaii. In August he left Pearl Harbor en route to Guam; he arrived on September 21, 1944, when he was assigned to Company A, 21st Marines. At last he had achieved his wish of again joining a combat unit.

On February 16, 1945, his unit left Guam via the USS *President Adams* for Iwo Jima. There he participated in the bitter fighting until March 1, 1945, when he was killed in action.

Maj. Gen. Allen H. Turnage, director of personnel of the Marine Corps, sent the following letter to Corporal Chamberlain's mother:

> Your son's record was illustrious and outstanding. He was proud to serve his country as a member of the Corps he loved so well. He and his comrades, who, by their bravery and determination, are defeating the enemy on the islands of the Pacific, will always remain an inspiration with the members of the Corps and to all the people of our Nation.

Sergeant Chamberlain's decorations and medals included the following: Distinguished Service Cross (army) for his duty in the Philippines; Purple Heart with two Gold Stars (Philippines and Iwo Jima); Distinguished Unit Badge with one Oak Leaf Cluster (army); Presidential Unit Citation with one Bronze Star; American Defense Service Medal with base clasp; Philippine Defense Ribbon with one Bronze Star; Asiatic-Pacific Area Campaign Medal with two Bronze Stars; and World War II Victory Medal.

Source
Headquarters Marine Corps, Historical Foundation.

The Chaplain's Medal for Heroism

During the Second World War, four chaplains showed extreme heroism and made great sacrifice after the torpedoing of their transport ship in the North Atlantic. The four lieutenants, the Reverend George L. Fox, Methodist; Rabbi Alexander D. Goode, Jewish; Father John P. Washington, Roman Catholic; and the Reverend Clark V. Poling, Dutch Reformed, quickly and quietly spread out among the soldiers. They tried to calm the frightened, tend the wounded, and guide the disoriented to safety. When there were no more lifejackets in the storage room, the chaplains removed theirs and gave them to four frightened young men. As the ship went down, survivors in nearby rafts could see the four chaplains—arms linked and braced against the slanting deck. Their voices could also be heard offering prayers.

That night the Reverend Fox, Rabbi Goode, the Reverend Poling, and Father Washington passed life's ultimate test. In doing so, they became an enduring example of extraordinary faith, courage, and selflessness.

The Distinguished Service Cross and Purple Heart were awarded posthumously December 19, 1944, to the next of kin by Lt. Gen. Brehon B. Somervell, commanding general of the Army Service Forces, in a ceremony at the post chapel at Fort Meyer, Virginia. A posthumous Special Medal for Heroism, never before given and never to be given again, was authorized by Congress and awarded by the president January 18, 1961. Congress wished to confer the Medal of Honor but was blocked by the stringent requirement of heroism performed under fire. The special medal was intended to have the same weight and importance as the Medal of Honor.

Source
United States Naval History Foundation.

Charette, William R. *Hospital corpsman third class, United States Navy Medical Corps, serving with a Marine rifle company, so distinguished himself in combat that he was awarded the Medal of Honor for his heroic actions.*

Born: Ludington, Mich.; **Entered service at:** Ludington, Mich.; **Place and date:** Korea, March 27, 1953.

Citation: "For conspicuous gallantry and intrepidity at the risk of his life above and beyond the call of duty in action against enemy aggressor forces during the early morning hours. Participating in a fierce encounter with a cleverly concealed and well-entrenched enemy force occupying positions on a vital and bitterly contested outpost far in advance of the main line of resistance, HM3 Charette repeatedly and unhesitatingly moved about through a murderous barrage of hostile small-arms and mortar fire to render assistance to his wounded comrades. When an enemy grenade landed within a few feet of a Marine he was attending, he immediately threw himself upon the stricken man and absorbed the entire concussion of the deadly missile with his body. Although sustaining painful facial wounds, and undergoing shock from the intensity of the blast which ripped the helmet and medical aid kit from his person, HM3 Charette resourcefully improvised emergency bandages by tearing off part of his clothing, and gallantly continued to administer medical aid to the wounded in his own unit and to those in adjacent platoon areas as well. Observing a seriously wounded comrade whose armored vest had been torn from his body by the blast from an exploding shell, he selflessly removed his own battle vest and placed it upon the helpless man although fully aware of the added jeopardy to himself. Moving to the side of another casualty who was suffering excruciating pain from a serious leg wound, HM3 Charette stood upright

William R. Charette

in the trench line and exposed himself to a deadly hail of enemy fire in order to lend more effective aid to the victim and to alleviate his anguish while being removed to a position of safety. By his indomitable courage and inspiring efforts in behalf of his wounded comrades, HM3 Charette was directly responsible for saving many lives. His great personal valor reflects the highest credit upon himself and enhances the finest traditions of the U.S. Naval Service."

Source
Medal of Honor Citation.

Charlton, Cornelius H. (1929–1951) *Sergeant, United States Army, Company C, 24th Infantry Regiment, 25th Infantry Division, so distinguished himself in combat, during the Korean War, that he was awarded (posthumously) the Medal of Honor for his heroic actions.*

Born: 1929, East Gulf, W. Va. **Entered service at:** Bronx, N.Y.; **Place and date:** Near Chipo-ri, Korea, June 2, 1951. **G.O. No.:** 30, March 19, 1952.

Citation: "Sergeant Cornelius H. Charlton, Infantry, United States Army, a member of Company C 24th

Infantry Regiment, 25th Infantry Division, distinguished himself by conspicuous gallantry and intrepidity above and beyond the call of duty in action against the enemy on 2 June 1951, near Chipo-ri, Korea. His platoon was attacking heavily defended hostile positions on commanding ground when the leader was wounded and evacuated. Sergeant Charlton assumed command, rallied the men, and spearheaded the assault against the hill. Personally eliminating two hostile positions and killing six of the enemy with his rifle fire and grenades, he continued up the slope until the unit suffered heavy casualties and became pinned down. Regrouping the men he led them forward only to be again hurled back by a shower of grenades. Despite a severe chest wound, Sergeant Charlton refused medical attention and led a third daring charge, which carried to the crest of the ridge. Observing that the remaining emplacement which had retarded the advance was situated on the reverse slope, he charged it alone, was again hit by a grenade but raked the position with a devastating fire which eliminated it and routed the defenders. The wounds received during his daring exploits resulted in his death but his indomitable courage, superb leadership, and gallant self-sacrifice reflect the highest credit upon himself, the infantry, and the military service."

Source
Medal of Honor Citation.

Cheatham, Ernest C., Jr. *Colonel, United States Marine Corps, distinguished himself heroically during the Battle of Hue City, 1968, and was awarded the Navy Cross.*

Citation: "For extraordinary heroism while serving as Commanding Officer of the Second Battalion, Fifth Marines, First Marine Division (reinforced), in the Republic of Vietnam from 3 February to 3 March 1968. During Operation HUE CITY, Colonel Cheatham led his battalion in extreme heavy house-to-house fighting against a numerically superior North Vietnamese Army force. Advancing through the city on 4 February to assault the well-fortified Treasury Building/Post Office complex, his unit came under intense fire from concealed enemy positions. The enemy resistance halted the Marines' advance during two days of bitter fighting. Nevertheless, Colonel Cheatham remained steadfast in his determination to secure the enemy stronghold. Skillfully deploying a 106-mm recoilless rifle squad into advantageous firing positions, he personally pinpointed the targets with M-16 tracer rounds and directed accurate fire on the enemy, which significantly reduced the pressure on his assaulting force. Completely disregarding his own safety, he joined the assaulting unit and aggressively led his men in routing the North Vietnamese from their entrenched positions. While proceeding through the city on 6 February, he organized his battalion for an assault on the enemy-held Provincial Headquarters Building. Ignoring the hostile fire all around him, he directed his men to covered positions while he fearlessly advanced to an exposed position from which he could locate the sources of enemy fire. Calling an Ontos forward, he directed effective suppressive fire on the enemy and then courageously led his unit as it continued in the assault. Colonel Cheatham's dynamic and heroic leadership and his unflagging example inspired all who observed him and contributed greatly to the defeat of the enemy and to their subsequent withdrawal from the city. His dauntless courage and unfaltering devotion to duty upheld the highest traditions of the Marine Corps and the United States Naval Service."

Source and Additional Reading

Navy Cross Citation.

Stevens, Paul Drew, ed. *The Navy Cross: Vietnam: Citations of Awards to Men of the United States Marine Corps, 1964–1973.* Forest Ranch Calif: Sharp & Dunnigan, 1987.

Christian, Herbert F. (d. 1944) *Private, U.S. Army, 15th Infantry, Third Infantry Division, so distinguished himself in combat during World War II that he was awarded (posthumously) the Medal of Honor for his actions.*

Born: Byersville, Ohio; **Entered service at:** Steubenville, Ohio; **Place and date:** Near Valmontone, Italy, June 2–3, 1944. **G.O. No.:** 43, May 30, 1945.

Citation: "For conspicuous gallantry and intrepidity at risk of life above and beyond the call of duty. On 2–3 June 1944, at 1 a.m., Pvt. Christian elected to sacrifice his life in order that his comrades might extricate themselves from an ambush. Braving massed fire of about 60 riflemen, 3 machine-guns, and 3 tanks from positions only 30 yards distant, he stood erect and signaled to the patrol to withdraw. The whole area was brightly illuminated by enemy flares. Although his right leg was severed above the knee by cannon fire, Pvt. Christian advanced on his left knee and the bloody stump of his right thigh, firing his sub-machine-gun. Despite excruciating pain, Pvt. Christian continued on his self-assigned mission. He succeeded in distracting the enemy and enabled his 12 comrades to escape. He killed 3 enemy soldiers almost at once. Leaving a trail of blood behind him, he made his way forward 20 yards, halted at a point within 10 yards of the enemy, and despite intense fire killed a machine-pistol man. Reloading his weapon, he fired directly into the enemy position. The enemy appeared enraged at the success of his ruse,

concentrated 20-mm. machine-gun, machine-pistol and rifle fire on him, yet he refused to seek cover. Maintaining his erect position, Pvt. Christian fired his weapon to the very last. Just as he emptied his submachinegun, the enemy bullets found their mark and Pvt. Christian slumped forward dead. The courage and spirit of self-sacrifice displayed by this soldier were an inspiration to his comrades and are in keeping with the highest traditions of the armed forces."

Source

Medal of Honor Citation.

Christmas, George R. *Captain, United States Marine Corps, distinguished himself heroically in Hue City, Republic of Vietnam, on February 5, 1968, and was awarded the Navy Cross.*

Citation: "For extraordinary heroism while serving as the Commanding Officer of Company H, Second Battalion, Fifth Marines, First Marine Division in connection with operations against the enemy in the Republic of Vietnam. On the afternoon of 5 February 1968, during Operation HUE CITY, Company H was attacking a complex of

George R. Christmas

buildings known to be an enemy strong point consisting of mutually supporting bunkers, fighting holes, and trench lines. During the ensuing fire fight, two platoons seized the corner building of a city block, but intense hostile small-arms, automatic weapons, and B-40 rocket fire temporarily halted the advance. Realizing the seriousness of the situation and the urgent need to sustain the momentum of the attack, Captain Christmas, undaunted by the heavy volume of enemy fire, completely disregarded his own safety as he moved across thirty-five meters of open area to join the lead element and assess the situation. Returning across the fire-swept area, he rejoined the remaining platoon, issued an attack order, and then ran seventy meters across open terrain, ignoring automatic weapons fire, hand grenades, and satchel charges striking around him to reach a tank he had requested. Braving enemy fire and two B-40 rockets that hit the tank, he fearlessly stood atop the vehicle to direct accurate fire against the hostile positions until the intensity of enemy fire diminished. Immediately realizing the tactical advantage, he jumped from the tank, and directed his company in an aggressive assault on the hostile positions, personally leading his men in room-to-room fighting until the building complex was secured. In a large measure due to his bold initiative and courageous actions, he provided the impetus which inspired his men to aggressive action and enabled them to successfully accomplish the mission. By his dynamic leadership, unfaltering determination and selfless devotion to duty in the face of extreme personal danger, Captain Christmas upheld the highest traditions of the Marine Corps and the United States Naval Service."

Source and Additional Reading
Navy Cross Citation.
Stevens, Paul Drew, ed. *The Navy Cross: Vietnam: Citations of Awards to Men of the United States Marine Corps, 1964–1973.* Forest Ranch, Calif: Sharp & Dunnigan, 1987.

Chief Joseph (1840–1904) *A chief of the Nez Percé Native American tribe.*

He is remembered principally for his leadership during the hostilities that broke out between the United States Army and the Nez Percé in 1877. Friendly with the whites until then, the Nez Percé had once occupied much territory in the region where Washington, Oregon, and Idaho adjoin. Under the terms of the Stevens Treaty of 1855, the Nez Percé agreed to cede much of their land to the U.S. government in return for the guarantee of a large reservation in Oregon and Idaho.

When gold was discovered (1863) in Oregon, however, the government demanded that the Nez Percé also relinquish that part of the reservation. Chief Joseph resisted but later agreed to move peacefully with his people to the Lapwai Reservation in Idaho.

Fighting broke out in 1877 when young Nez Percé warriors retaliated for what they considered outrageous acts by the white settlers. In the war that followed, Joseph showed remarkable skill in military tactics by defeating larger U.S. forces in several battles. He then led his people on a retreat of more than a thousand miles over mountainous terrain in an effort to reach Canada. On September 30, 1877, however, federal troops overtook the Nez Percé only 48 kilometers (30 miles) from the border. Because most of his warriors were dead or wounded and his people were starving, Chief Joseph surrendered, saying, "I will fight no more forever."

Sent to Indian Territory in Oklahoma, the Nez Percé were allowed to return to Idaho in 1883–84. Chief Joseph died on the Colville Indian Reservation in the state of Washington.

Source and Additional Reading
Beal, Merrill D. *I Will Fight No More Forever.* Seattle, Wash.: University of Washington Press, 1963.
Gidley, M. K. *A Documentary Narrative of Chief Joseph's Last Years.* Seattle, Wash.: University of Washington Press, 1981.

Choate, Clyde L. (1920–1944) *Staff sergeant United States Army, Company C, 601st Tank Destroyer Battalion, so distinguished himself in battle that he was awarded (posthumously) the Medal of Honor.*

Born: June 28, 1920, West Frankfort, Ill. **Entered service at:** Anna, Ill.; **Place and date:** Near Bruyeres, France, October 25, 1944. **G.O. No.:** 75, September 5, 1945.

Citation: "He commanded a tank destroyer near Bruyeres, France, on 25 October 1944. Our infantry occupied a position on a wooded hill when, at dusk, an enemy Mark IV tank and a company of infantry attacked, threatening to overrun the American position and capture a command post 400 yards to the rear. S/Sgt. Choate's tank destroyer, the only weapon available to oppose the German armor, was set afire by 2 hits. Ordering his men to abandon the destroyer, S/Sgt. Choate reached comparative safety. He returned to the burning destroyer to search for comrades possibly trapped in the vehicle risking instant death in an explosion which was imminent and braving enemy fire which ripped his jacket and tore the helmet from his head. Completing the search and seeing the tank and its supporting infantry overrunning our infantry in their shallow foxholes, he secured a bazooka and ran after the tank, dodging from tree to tree and passing through the enemy's loose skirmish line. He fired a rocket from a distance of 20 yards, immobilizing the tank but leaving it able to spray the area with cannon and machine-gun fire. Running back to our infantry through vicious fire, he secured another rocket, and, advancing against a hail of machine-gun and small arms fire reached a position 10 yards from the tank. His second shot shattered the turret. With his pistol he killed 2 of the crew as they emerged from the tank; and then running to the crippled Mark IV while enemy infantry sniped at him, he dropped a grenade inside the tank and completed its destruction. With their armor gone, the enemy infantry became disorganized and was driven back. S/Sgt. Choate's great daring in assaulting an enemy tank single-handed, his determination to follow the vehicle after it had passed his position, and his skill and crushing thoroughness in the attack prevented the enemy from capturing a battalion command post and turned a probable defeat into a tactical success."

Source
Medal of Honor Citation.

Church, Benjamin (1639–1718) *Colonial soldier.*

A farmer in the Plymouth Colony, Benjamin Church soldiered in three wars. He was the son of a veteran of the Pequot War and served as a provincial captain during King Philip's War. In December 1675, Church was a member of a New England army, which struck a fortified Narragansett settlement in the Great Swamp in Rhode Island. The surprise attack succeeded, killing more than 600 Narragansetts and destroying the entire village. Church was wounded in the engagement. The following summer, he led a force into the Mount Hope swamp in Rhode Island, where the Wampanoag chieftain Metacom dwelled. The raid caught Metacom by surprise, and he was killed in the brief battle. Church emerged as a New England hero for having destroyed the settlers' adversary. He additionally achieved a reputation as a skilled fighter, a soldier who learned from the tactics of his foe and who refused to be bound by European-style warfare. In King William's War, in the 1690s, Church led expeditions against the Abenaki people in Maine and the French in Acadia. In 1704, during Queen Anne's War, he commanded a Massachusetts invasion of Acadia, which failed in the absence of naval assistance.

Source and Additional Reading
Chambers, John Whiteclay II. *The Oxford Companion to American Military History.* New York: Oxford University Press, 1999.

Clark, Mark Wayne (1896–1984) *World War II and Korean War general. Commanded the Fifth Army (1943–1944) in Italy; UN commander in Korea, 1952–1953.*

Dubbed the "American Eagle" by Sir Winston Churchill— a possible tribute to his fighting qualities or a comment on his prominent, beaked nose—Mark Clark first received public attention in late 1942. In October of that year the 46-year-old West Point graduate (class of 1917) led a secret mission to French North Africa to pave the way for the forthcoming American invasion.

Born in New York state to an old army family, Clark was wounded in battle during World War I. Between wars he rose slowly in rank but caught the eye of the United States Army chief of staff, General George C. Marshall, and in 1940 he became a member of the army's General Headquarters Staff, responsible to Marshall. After the United States entered World War II, Clark was one of the officers who recommended Dwight D. Eisenhower as Allied commander in Europe, and in June 1942, he became Eisenhower's deputy.

Prior to the American invasion of North Africa, Clark made a secret trip to Algeria (French North Africa) aboard the British submarine *Seraph* to gather intelligence for the landings. After the American landings, Clark took command of the Fifth Army, which he led through the Italian campaign in 1943 and 1944.

According to several historical accounts, the campaign in Italy turned into a bloody battle with the Germans. With his daredevil inspection tours on the front lines, Clark won the respect of his troops. He was promoted to full general in 1945. After the war Clark held a variety of political and military posts, including U.S. high commissioner for Austria (1945) and commander of United Nations (UN) forces in Korea (1952–53). In 1953, he signed a military armistice among the UN Command, the North Korean army, and the Chinese People's Volunteers in Korea.

General Clark retired from the army in 1953 and, from 1954 to 1966, served as president of the Citadel, the Military College of South Carolina. After his retirement, he was named president emeritus. He is buried on the Citadel campus beside Mark Clark Hall.

Source
Archives, Daniel Library, The Citadel, Charleston, South Carolina.

Cleburne, Patrick Ronayne (1828–1864) *General, Confederate States Army.*

The most popular Confederate division commander was the "Stonewall of the West," Patrick R. Cleburne. Appropriately, the native of County Cork was born on St.

Patrick's Day and became the only product of the Emerald Isle to become a Confederate major general. Failing the language requirements for a druggist's degree, he served with the British 41st Regiment of Foot as an officer for a number of years before purchasing his way out. Immigrating to America, he became a druggist and then a highly successful property attorney.

He joined the Confederacy. His military assignments included the following: captain, Company F, First Arkansas State Troops (early 1861); colonel, First Arkansas State Troops (early 1861); colonel, 15th Arkansas (designation change July 23, 1861); commander, Second Brigade, First (Hardee's). Division, Army of Central Kentucky, Department 2 (fall 1861–March 29, 1862); commander, Second Brigade, Hardee's division, Army of the Mississippi (July 2–August 15, 1862); commander, Second Brigade, Buckner's division, Left Wing, Army of the Mississippi (August 15–30, October1–October 8, and October 20–November 20, 1862); commander, Second Brigade, Buckner's division, Hardee's-Breckinridge's corps, Army of Tennessee (November 20–December 1862); major general Confederate States Army (CSA) (December 20, 1862, to rank from December 13); commander, of the division (December 1862–November 30, 1863); commander of the division, Hardee's (Polk's old)–Cheatham's corps, Army of Tennessee (November 30, 1863–January 1864, January–August 31, and September 2–November 30, 1864); and commander of the corps (August 31–September 2, 1864).

At the head of the Yell Rifles, he served in Arkansas before being named as commander of the state unit. Transferred with William J. Hardee to central Kentucky, he was promoted to brigadier general and fought at Shiloh and during the siege of Corinth. Taking part in the Kentucky Campaign, he was wounded at both Richmond and Perryville. Promoted to major general, he commanded a division at Murfreesboro, during the Tullahoma Campaign, and at Chickamauga. A favorite of Jefferson Davis, he is credited with covering the retreat from Chattanooga after his splendid defense of Tunnel Hill. That winter he proposed that in order to reinforce the Confederate armies, slavery would have to be abolished in a "reasonable time" and blacks be recruited for military service on the promise of their freedom. The proposal was rejected by the Richmond authorities and would not be passed by the Confederate Congress until a couple of months after Cleburne's death. Cleburne went on to command his division, and briefly the corps, through the Atlanta Campaign and then with Hood into middle Tennessee.

At the battle of Franklin on November 20, 1864, he became the senior of six Confederate generals to die in this fight, which did little more than commit mass suicide against the Union works. His death was a calamity to the Confederate cause, perhaps only exceeded by the death of Stonewall Jackson. First buried near Franklin, Cleburne's remains were later removed to Helena, Arkansas.

Source

Purdue, Howell, and Elizabeth Purdue. *Pat Cleburne, Confederate General. A Definitive Biography.* Hillsboro, Tex.: Hillsboro Junior College Press, 1973.

Cochise (c. 1823–1874) *Chiracahua Apache chief.*

Although his name was to become synonymous with terror along the southwestern frontier, Cochise, the Chiracahua Apache chief, was, until his late 30s, quite friendly toward whites. Then, in 1861, a young cavalry officer wrongly accused him of having kidnapped a rancher's son and tried to hold Cochise hostage to obtain the boy's return. Infuriated, Cochise escaped from the tent where he was being held, leaving several Native American companions behind. Seizing white hostages to secure the release of his friends, Cochise killed several of them when his comrades were not let go. The whites retaliated in kind, and an 11-year war without quarter began. Hiding with his Apache warriors in the Arizona mountains, Cochise led them in deadly raids on settlements and isolated ranches. Brutality, deceit, and slaughter of women and children were common on both sides. During the Civil War there were too few troops available to subdue the warrior and his band, but after the war the power of the federal forces slowly began to tell, and in 1872 Cochise finally surrendered to Gen. Oliver O. Howard. The great war chief agreed to live in peace only if Thomas Jeffords (1832–1914), a remarkable white army scout who had secured Cochise's friendship, became the Indian agent. And it was in Jeffords's care that the Apache warrior peacefully died at the Chiracahua Apache Reservation in New Mexico in 1874.

Source

Lummis, Charles F. *General Cook and the Apache Wars.* Flagstaff, Ariz.: Northland Press, 1966.

Coffman, Clovis C., Jr. *Sergeant, United States Marine Corps, distinguished himself heroically in hand-to-hand combat on October 10, 1966, and was awarded the Navy Cross for his actions.*

Citation: "For extraordinary heroism in action against Communist Forces while serving as a Platoon Leader with Company C, First Reconnaissance Battalion, First Marine Division in the Republic of Vietnam on 10 October 1966. Sergeant Coffman was leading a thirteen-man patrol assigned the mission of observing a valley near Long Bihn, Quang Ngai Province for enemy activity. Early in the afternoon, while leading his unit from their observation post to a helicopter landing zone, the patrol came under a heavy small arms and grenade attack from an estimated thirty-five to fifty man enemy force. Reacting immediately, Sergeant Coffman skillfully organized and directed the return fire of his outnumbered unit. Fearlessly disregarding his own safety, he repeatedly exposed himself in order to deploy his forces and deliver maximum fire power against the attackers. Courageously he went to his stricken comrade's aid. Although wounded himself, he killed three of the enemy at point blank range in order to reach the stricken Marine. Sergeant Coffman was successful in his efforts to return his stricken comrade to friendly lines. When wounds disabled the patrol's medical corpsman, he skillfully administered first aid to four seriously wounded Marines. Sergeant Coffman directed fixed wing and armed helicopter attacks against the enemy with devastating accuracy, with the result that helicopters were able to land and extract the force. Although wounded, he remained until all of his men were safely embarked, resolutely defending the landing zone. As the last rescue helicopter was loading, he and another Marine held the landing zone alone, killing four of the enemy in close combat. Only after all of his patrol were embarked, did he board the aircraft and depart the embattled area. By his courageous devotion to duty, and extraordinary leadership, Sergeant Coffman reflected great credit upon himself and the Marine Corps and upheld the highest traditions of the United States Naval Service."

Source and Additional Reading
Navy Cross Citation.
Norton, Maj. Bruce H. *Force Recon Diary, 1969.* New York: Norton, 1992.
——— *Stingray.* New York: Ballantine, 2000.
Stevens, Paul Drew, ed. *The Navy Cross: Vietnam: Citations of Awards to Men of the United States Marine Corps, 1964–1973.* Forest Ranch, Calif.: Sharp & Dunnigan, 1987.

Collier, Gilbert G. (1930–1953) *Sergeant (then corporal), United States Army, Company F, 223d Infantry Regiment, 40th Infantry Division, so distinguished himself in combat, during the Korean War, that he was awarded (posthumously) the Medal of Honor for his heroic actions.*

Born: 1930, Hunter, Ark, **Entered service at:** Tichnor, Ark: **Place and date:** Near Tutayon, Korea, July 19–20, 1953. **G.O. No.:** 3, January 12, 1955.

Citation: "Sergeant Gilbert G. Collier, Infantry, United States Army, a member of Company F, 223d Infantry Regiment, 40th Infantry Division, distinguished himself by conspicuous gallantry and indomitable courage above and beyond the call of duty in action against the enemy on 19

and 20 July 1953, near Tutayon, Korea. Sergeant Collier was point man and assistant leader of a combat patrol committed to make contact with the enemy. As the patrol moved forward through the darkness, he and his commanding officer slipped and fell from a steep, 60-foot cliff and were injured. Incapacitated by a badly sprained ankle that prevented immediate movement, the officer ordered the patrol to return to the safety of friendly lines. Although suffering from a painful back injury, Sergeant Collier elected to remain with his leader, and before daylight they managed to crawl back up and over the mountainous terrain to the opposite valley where they concealed themselves in the brush until nightfall, then edged toward their company positions. Shortly after leaving the daylight retreat they were ambushed and, in the ensuing firefight, Sergeant Collier killed two hostile soldiers, received painful wounds, and was separated from his companion. Then, ammunition expended, he closed in hand-to-hand combat with four attacking hostile infantrymen, killing, wounding, and routing the foe with his bayonet. He was mortally wounded during this action, but made a valiant attempt to reach and assist his leader in a desperate effort to save his comrade's life without regard for his own personal safety. Sergeant Collier's unflinching courage, consummate devotion to duty, and gallant self-sacrifice reflect lasting glory upon himself and uphold the noble traditions of the military service."

Source
Medal of Honor Citation.

Commiskey, Henry Alfred (b. 1927) *First lieutenant, United States Marine Corps, was awarded the Medal of Honor. He was the first Marine to be awarded the nation's highest decoration during the Korean War.*

Citation: "For conspicuous gallantry and intrepidity at the risk of his life, above and beyond the call of duty, while serving as a Platoon Leader in Company C, First Battalion, First Marines, First Marine Division (Reinforced), in action against enemy aggressor forces near Yongdungp'o, Korea, on 20 September 1950. Directed to attack hostile forces well dug in on Hill 85, First Lieutenant Commiskey, then Second Lieutenant, spearheaded the assault, charging up the steep slopes on the run. Coolly disregarding the heavy enemy machine-gun and small arms fire, he plunged on well forward to the rest of his platoon and was the first man to reach the crest of the objective. Armed only with a pistol, he jumped into a hostile machine-gun emplacement occupied by five enemy troops and quickly disposed of four of the soldiers with his automatic pistol. Grappling with the fifth, First Lieutenant Commiskey knocked him to the ground and held him until he could obtain a weapon from another member of his platoon and kill the last of the enemy gun crew. Continuing his bold assault, he moved to the next emplacement, killed two more of the enemy and then led his platoon toward the rear nose of the hill to rout the remainder of the hostile troops and destroy them as they fled from their positions. His valiant leadership and courageous fighting spirit served to inspire the men of his company to heroic endeavor in seizing the objective and reflect the highest credit upon First Lieutenant Commiskey and the United States Naval Service."

Source and Additional Reading

Blakeney, Jane. *Heroes: U.S. Marine Corps 1861–1955*. Washington, D.C.: Guthrie Lithographic, 1957.
Medal of Honor Citation.

Connor, James P. *Sergeant, United States Army, Seventh Infantry, Third Infantry Division, so distinguished himself on the battlefield that he was awarded the Medal of Honor.*

Born: Wilmington, Del.; **Entered service at:** Wilmington, Del.; **Place and date:** Cape Cavalaire, southern France, August 15, 1944. **G.O. No.:** 18, March 15, 1945.

Citation: "For conspicuous gallantry and intrepidity at risk of life above and beyond the call of duty. On 15 August 1944, Sgt. Connor, through sheer gift and determination, led his platoon in clearing an enemy vastly superior in numbers and firepower from strongly entrenched positions on Cape Cavalaire, removing a grave enemy threat to his division during the amphibious landing in southern France, and thereby insured safe and uninterrupted landings for the huge volume of men and materiel which followed. His battle patrol landed on "Red Beach" with the mission of destroying the strongly fortified enemy positions on Cape Cavalaire with utmost speed. From the peninsula the enemy had commanding observation and seriously menaced the vast landing operations taking place. Though knocked down and seriously wounded in the neck by a hanging mine which killed his platoon lieutenant, Sgt. Connor refused medical aid and with his driving spirit practically carried the platoon across several thousand yards of mine-saturated beach through intense fire from mortars, 20-mm. flak guns, machine-guns, and snipers. En route to the Cape he personally shot and killed 2 snipers. The platoon sergeant was killed and Sgt. Connor became platoon leader. Receiving a second wound, which lacerated his shoulder and back, he again refused evacuation, expressing determination to carry on until physically unable to continue. He reassured and prodded the hesitating men of his decimated platoon forward through almost impregnable mortar concentrations. Again emphasizing the prevalent urgency of their mission, he impelled his men toward a group of buildings honeycombed with enemy snipers and machine-guns. Here he received his third grave wound, this time in the leg, felling him in his tracks. Still resolved to carry on, he relinquished command only after his attempts proved that it was physically impossible to stand. Nevertheless, from his prone position, he gave the orders and directed his men in assaulting the enemy. Infused with Sgt. Connor's dogged determination, the platoon, though reduced to less than one-third of its original 36 men, outflanked and rushed the enemy with such furiousness that they killed 7, captured 40, seized 3 machine-guns and considerable other materiel, and took all their assigned objectives, successfully completing their mission. By his repeated examples of tenaciousness and indomitable spirit Sgt. Connor transmitted his heroism to his men until they became a fighting team which could not be stopped."

Source

Medal of Honor Citation.

Conran, Philip J. *Colonel (then major), United States Air Force.*

Citation: "For extraordinary heroism in military operations against an opposing armed force as Aircraft Commander of a CH-3E helicopter at a classified location in Southeast Asia on 6 October 1969. On that date, while attempting to rescue the crew of a downed helicopter, Major Conran's aircraft was hit by intense hostile round fire and he was forced to make a crash landing in the vicinity of the other aircraft. Once on the ground, he successfully evacuated his aircraft and assumed a major role in defending the crash site against an overwhelming hostile force until rescue was possible six hours later. Through his extraordinary heroism, superb airmanship, and aggressiveness in the face of hostile fire, Major Conran reflected the highest credit upon himself and the United States Air Force."

Source

Air Force Cross Citation.

Corey, Russell E. *Captain, United States Marine Corps.*

As the commanding officer of Company B, Amphibious Reconnaissance Battalion, Fleet Marine Force, during World War II, then-First Lieutenant Corey was awarded two Bronze Stars for his actions during the Battle of Okinawa, May and June 1945.

First Award Citation: "On the night of 20–21 May 1945, 1st Lt. Corey was directed by the Tenth Army

(Senior Command for Okinawa) to conduct a nighttime reconnaissance offshore of Okinawa to determine if the island was defended by the Japanese. His unit landed in rubber boats, and shortly afterward moved inland, approximately 600 yards. At that time, mortar fire began falling in on the beach site. It was obvious that the island was heavily defended and the unit quickly returned to their boats that had been secured in the brush near the beach. By the time the reconnaissance patrol had paddled several hundred yards seaward, the Japanese had emplaced light machine guns on the beach and began firing seaward. Luckily, the night was very dark and their seaward firing was random. Lines of enemy tracer rounds came from the shore, but no casualties were suffered by the patrol. The U.S. Army later sent in a landing force and killed more than 20 Japanese defenders."

Second Award Citation: "For heroic achievement as Commanding Officer of Company B, Amphibious Reconnaissance Battalion, Fleet Marine Force, in connection with operations against enemy Japanese forces on Kume Shima, Ryukyu Islands, during the night of 13 and 14 June 1945. Assigned the mission of leading a large portion of his company on an amphibious reconnaissance and prisoner-of-war raid along the north coast of enemy-held Kume Shima, 1st Lieutenant Corey landed undetected at night and, after establishing a small beachhead to cover his withdrawal, dispatched patrols over various routes through hostile territory. Taking personal charge of the patrol assigned the most hazardous mission, he skillfully led it along the selected route and avoided enemy patrols known to be operating in the vicinity. Upon capturing a Japanese prisoner and completing his mission, he returned to the beachhead, assembled the other patrols, and conducted an efficient and undetected withdrawal. By his leadership and courageous devotion to duty, he contributed materially to the attaining of information vital to the success of this operation and upheld the highest traditions of the United States Naval Service."

Source
Bronze Star Citations.

Craft, Clarence B. *Private, first class, United States Army, Company G, 382d Infantry, 96th Infantry Division, so distinguished himself in combat, during World War II, that he was awarded the Medal of Honor for his actions.*

Born: San Bernardino, Calif.; **Entered service at:** Santa Ana, Calif.; **Place and date:** Hen Hill, Okinawa, Ryukyu Islands, May 31, 1945. **G.O. No.:** 97, November 1, 1945.

Citation: "He was a rifleman when his platoon spearheaded an attack on Hen Hill, the tactical position on which the entire Naha-Shuri-Yonaburu line of Japanese defense on Okinawa, Ryukyu Islands, was hinged. For 12 days our forces had been stalled, and repeated, heavy assaults by 1 battalion and then another had been thrown back by the enemy with serious casualties. With 5 comrades, Pfc. Craft was dispatched in advance of Company G to feel out the enemy resistance. The group had proceeded only a short distance up the slope when rifle and machine-gun fire, coupled with a terrific barrage of grenades, wounded 3 and pinned down the others. Against odds that appeared suicidal, Pfc. Craft launched a remarkable 1-man attack. He stood up in full view of the enemy and began shooting with deadly marksmanship wherever he saw a hostile movement. He steadily advanced up the hill, killing Japanese soldiers with rapid fire, driving others to cover in their strongly disposed trenches, unhesitatingly facing alone the strength that had previously beaten back attacks in battalion strength. He reached the crest of the hill, where he stood silhouetted against the sky while quickly throwing grenades at extremely short range into the enemy positions. His extraordinary assault lifted the pressure from his company for the moment, allowing members of his platoon to comply with his motions to advance and pass him more grenades. With a chain of his comrades supplying him while he stood atop the hill, he furiously hurled a total of 2 cases of grenades into a main trench and other positions on the reverse slope of Hen Hill, meanwhile directing the aim of his fellow soldiers who threw grenades from the slope below him. He left his position, where grenades from both sides were passing over his head and bursting on either slope, to attack the main enemy trench as confusion and panic seized the defenders. Straddling the excavation, he pumped rifle fire into the Japanese at pointblank range, killing many and causing the others to flee down the trench. Pursuing them, he came upon a heavy machine-gun, which was still creating havoc in the American ranks. With rifle fire and a grenade he wiped out this position. By this time the Japanese were in complete rout and American forces were swarming over the hill. Pfc. Craft continued down the central trench to the mouth of a cave where many of the enemy had taken cover. A satchel charge was brought to him, and he tossed it into the cave. It failed to explode. With great daring, the intrepid fighter retrieved the charge from the cave, relighted the fuse and threw it back, sealing up the Japs in a tomb. In the local action, against tremendously superior forces heavily armed with rifles, machine-guns, mortars, and grenades, Pfc. Craft killed at least 25 of the enemy; but his contribution to the campaign on Okinawa was of much more far-reaching consequence for Hen Hill was the key to the entire defense line, which rapidly crumbled after his utterly fearless and heroic attack."

Source
Medal of Honor Citation.

Crazy Horse (Tashunca-Uitco) (1849–1877) *Oglala Sioux war chief.*

Born about 1849 into the Oglala Sioux tribe, Crazy Horse fought in the Indian Wars (1865–68 and 1875–77). His principal battles are Fetterman Fight (1866); Wagon Box Fight (1867); Rosebud Creek, Slim Buttes and Little Bighorn (1876); and Wolf Mountain (1877). As a young man he won a reputation as a brave and skillful warrior. He was present on August 19, 1854, at the Grattan massacre near Fort Laramie, Wyoming, and the first military clash between the Sioux and the Americans. Crazy Horse was absent from the Oglala village near Ash Hollow, Nebraska, on September 3, 1855, when it was destroyed by U.S. forces in retaliation for the massacre, but after his return to the scene of the carnage, his animosity toward whites was intensified.

He fought with Chief Red Cloud against the construction of the Powder River army road, later known as the Bozeman Trail, through Sioux lands, participating in the Fetterman Fight (December 21, 1866) and the Wagon Box Fight on August 2, 1867, both near Fort Phil Kearney, near Banner, Wyoming. Refusing to live on a reservation as dictated by the Fort Laramie Treaty, in 1868, he led his band of warriors to join forces with Chief Sitting Bull's Hunkpapas Sioux. He then led the Sioux against the invasion of their sacred Black Hills (1875–77). He defeated United States Army General George Cooks's expedition at Rosebud Creek in June 1876, and, with the support of Chief Gall, he annihilated Lt. Col. George A. Custer and his command at the Little Bighorn on June 25, 1876.

Defeated by General Cook at the Battle of Slim Buttes in September, he was pursued vigorously by General Miles, who destroyed his village at Wolf Mountain on January 7, 1876. He was forced to surrender at the Red Cloud Agency near Fort Robinson, Nebraska, on May 6, 1877. Crazy Horse was charged with attempting to lead another Sioux rebellion and was arrested in September 1877. Although he was promised limited freedom, he was threatened with imprisonment after he sought permission to resume his nomadic ways. This led to a misunderstanding, possibly due to a false translation by a perfidious former associate acting as an interpreter. Chief Crazy Horse tried to escape on September 5, 1877, and was stabbed in the back and fatally wounded by one of the guards.

Chief Crazy Horse was a fearless, daring, and brilliant commander. He is considered to be the greatest of the Sioux tacticians.

Source and Additional Reading
Sandoz, Mari. *Crazy Horse, Strange Man of the Oglalas.* New York: Knopf, 1942.

Crockett, Joseph R., Jr. *Sergeant, United States Marine Corps, so distinguished himself in combat, in the Republic of Vietnam, that he was awarded the Navy Cross for his heroic actions.*

Citation: "For extraordinary heroism while serving as a team leader with First Force Reconnaissance Company, First Reconnaissance Battalion, First Marine Division, in connection with operations against the enemy in the Republic of Vietnam. On 23 April 1969, Sergeant Crockett's team was clandestinely observing a major North Vietnamese Army supply route west of An Hoa, in Quang Nam Province, when the Marines came under a ground assault by an estimated hostile platoon supported by a heavy volume of automatic weapons fire, and in the initial moments of the attack sustained several casualties. Sergeant Crockett seized a grenade launcher from one of his wounded men and moved across 50 meters of exposed terrain to deliver fire upon the enemy. As a group of North Vietnamese soldiers approached his team's defensive perimeter, he quickly killed one and wounded four others; then having exhausted his ammunition, utilized a radio to adjust supporting artillery fire to within 50 meters of his men. He then ran from one Marine position to another gathering grenades, which he hurled at the hostile soldiers, forcing them to regroup and withdraw. As the enemy soldiers retreated they lighted several brush fires that rapidly spread toward the team's emplacement. Unable to extinguish the flames with his jacket, Sergeant Crockett repeatedly assisted in moving his injured Marines to safety, stopping only to render first aid and to deliver suppressive fire upon the North Vietnamese force. In order to expedite evacuation of his critically injured men, he tied an air panel to his back and boldly moved into an open clearing where he stood in full view of the enemy to mark the landing zone for the helicopters and gunships as they arrived on station. Although nearly exhausted, Sergeant Crockett refused to be extracted, and assisted in a search of the vicinity. By his courage, aggressive fighting spirit, and selfless devotion to duty in the face of grave personal danger, Sergeant Crockett upheld the highest traditions of the Marine Corps and the U.S. Naval Service."

Sources
Navy Cross Citation.
Norton, Maj. Bruce H. *Force Recon Diary, 1970.* New York: Norton, 1992.

Cromwell, John Philip (1901–1943) *Captain, United States Navy, so distinguished himself in naval combat during World War II, that he was awarded (posthumously) the Medal of Honor for his actions.*

Born: September 11, 1901, Henry, Ill.; **Entered service at:** Illinois. **Other United States Navy award:** Legion of Merit.

Citation: "For conspicuous gallantry and intrepidity at the risk of his life above and beyond the call of duty as Commander of a Submarine Coordinated Attack Group with Flag in the U.S.S. *Sculpin,* during the 9th War Patrol of that vessel in enemy-controlled waters off Truk Island, 19 November 1943. Undertaking this patrol prior to the launching of our first large-scale offensive in the Pacific, Capt. Cromwell, alone of the entire Task Group, possessed secret intelligence information of our submarine strategy and tactics, scheduled Fleet movements and specific attack plans. Constantly vigilant and precise in carrying out his secret orders, he moved his undersea flotilla inexorably forward despite savage opposition and established a line of submarines to southeastward of the main Japanese stronghold at Truk. Cool and undaunted as the submarine, rocked and battered by Japanese depth charges, sustained terrific battle damage and sank to an excessive depth, he authorized the *Sculpin* to surface and engage the enemy in a gunfight, thereby providing an opportunity for the crew to abandon ship. Determined to sacrifice himself rather than risk capture and subsequent danger of revealing plans under Japanese torture or use of drugs, he stoically remained aboard the mortally wounded vessel as she plunged to her death. Preserving the security of his mission, at the cost of his own life, he had served his country as he had served the Navy, with deep integrity and an uncompromising devotion to duty. His great moral courage in the face of certain death adds new luster to the traditions of the U.S. Naval Service. He gallantly gave his life for his country."

Source
Medal of Honor Citation.

Crook, George "Grey Fox" (1829–1890) *Union general officer who fought in the Indian Wars*

Born near Dayton, Ohio, on September 23, 1829, Crook graduated from the U.S. Military Academy, at West Point, and was commissioned in the infantry in 1852. He served as a captain in the Indians Wars prior to the Civil War and as a colonel of volunteers commanded the 36th Ohio Infantry in September 1861. He served in West Virginia in 1862 and was breveted a major of regulars in May, and a brigadier general of volunteers in August. He fought at the Battles of South Mountain, on September 14, and at Antietam on September 17, 1861, and was breveted a lieutenant colonel of regulars at that time.

As a commander of a cavalry division, Army of the Cumberland, he fought at Chickamauga (September 18–20, 1863) and at Farmington, against General Wheeler's marauding cavalry in October 1863. He was afterward breveted a colonel of regulars and served briefly as commander, Army of West Virginia, in early 1864. As a

major general of volunteers, Crook served under General Philip Sheridan in the Shanandoah Valley (August 1864–March 1865) and fought at the Battles of Winchester, Fisher's Hill, and Cedar Creek. He then commanded a division in Sheridan's cavalry corps in operations around Petersburg, Virginia (March–April 1865) and fought in the Battles of Dinwiddie Courthouse and Five Forks in April 1865.

At the end of the Civil War he reverted to lieutenant colonel, 32d Infantry, and was transferred to Idaho in 1866 to suppress uprisings of Cochise's Apaches in the Arizona Territory from 1871 to 1873. Promoted to brigadier general in 1873, Crook commanded the Department of the Platte in 1875 and served under Gen. Alfred H. Terry against Crazy Horse's Sioux and Cheyenne from 1876 to 1877. He was bested by Crazy Horse and overwhelming superior Native American numbers at the Battle of Rosebud Creek in June 1876. He moved on to destroy the Sioux village at Slim Buttes on September 9. He returned to Arizona to help quell Geronimo's uprising; there he enjoyed some success, achieved in part by basing his logistics on mule trains (1882–83), and fought in the second expedition against Geronimo until replaced by General Nelson Miles in 1885. Promoted to major general and given command of the Department of the Missouri in 1888, General Crook died at his headquarters in Chicago, Illinois, on March 21, 1890.

General Crook was an intelligent, brave, and resourceful commander and administrator. In his many campaigns against the Sioux and the Apaches he demonstrated his ability as perhaps the best Indian fighter in American military history.

Source and Additional Reading
Bourke, John G. *On the Border with Crook.* New York: Scribner, 1892.
Crook, George. *His Autobiography.* Norman: University of Oklahoma Press, 1960.
Dupuy, Trevor N. *The Harper Encyclopedia of Military Biography.* New York: HarperCollins, 1992.

Cukela, Louis (1888–1956) *Major, United States Marine Corps who was awarded both the Navy Medal of Honor and the Army Medal of Honor for extraordinary heroism in France during World War I.*

For that heroism he was also awarded decorations by France, Italy, and his native Yugoslavia.

Cukela was born at Spalato, Serbia, on May 1, 1888, the son of George and Johanna (Burbrich) Cukela. He was educated in the grade schools of Spalato then attended the Merchant Academy and later the Royal Gymnasium, both for two-year courses. His mother died in 1900. In 1913,

Louis Cukela

Cukela immigrated to the United States, and he and his brother settled in Minneapolis, Minnesota. His father and three sisters remained in Serbia.

On September 21, 1914, he enlisted in the United State Army. He was serving as a corporal in Company H, 13th Infantry, when he was honorably discharged on June 12, 1916.

Seven months later, on January 31, 1917, with war raging in Europe from a spark touched off in the major's native Serbia; he enlisted in the Marine Corps. After the United States's entry into the conflict, he went to France and took part in all the engagements in which the Fifth Marine Regiment fought.

He was awarded both Medals of Honor for the same action near Villers-Cotterets, France, on the morning of July 18, 1918, during the Soissons engagement. The 66th Company, Fifth Marines, in which Major Cukela was then a gunnery sergeant, was advancing through the Forest de Retz when it was held up by an enemy strong point. Despite the warnings of his Marines, the gunnery sergeant crawled out from the flank and advanced alone toward the German lines. Getting beyond the strong point despite heavy fire, "Gunny" Cukela captured one gun by bayoneting its crew. Picking up their hand grenades, he then demolished the remaining portions of the strong point from the shelter of a nearby gun pit. The Marine took four prisoners and captured two undamaged machine guns.

The famous Marine was wounded in action twice, but since there is no record of either wound at the United States Navy's Bureau of Medicine and Surgery, he was never awarded the Purple Heart. The first wound was suffered at Jaulny, France, on September 16, 1918, during the St. Mihiel engagement. Major Cukela was wounded again during the fighting in the Champagne sector. Neither wound was serious.

In addition to the two Medals of Honor, Major Cukela was awarded the Silver Star by the army; the Medaille Militaire (he was the first Marine officer ever to receive this medal); the Legion d'Honneur in the rank of chevalier; the croix de geurre with Silver Star, all by France; the Croce al Merito di Guerra, from Italy; and the Commander's Cross of the Royal Order of the Crown of Yugoslavia. He also received three Second Division Citations.

Major Cukela received a field appointment to the rank of second lieutenant in the Marine Corps Reserve on September 26, 1918, and was selected for a commission in the regular Marine Corps on March 31, 1919. Promoted to first lieutenant on July 17, 1919, he was advanced to the rank of captain on September 15, 1921. His promotion to major was effected on the day of his retirement, June 30, 1940.

After the war, Major Cukela served at overseas bases in Haiti, Santo Domingo, the Philippines, and China, and at domestic stations in Quantico, Virginia; Philadelphia, Pennsylvania; Norfolk, Virginia; Hampton Roads, Virginia; Mare Island, California; Washington, D.C.; and Fort Knox, Kentucky.

From June 1933 to January 1934, the major served as a company commander with the Civilian Conservation Corps. His last years in the Marine Corps were spent at Norfolk, where he served as the post quartermaster. Retired as a major on June 30, 1940, he was recalled to active duty on July 30 of the same year. During World War II, the major served at Norfolk and Philadelphia. He finally returned to the inactive retired list on May 17, 1946, after 32 years of active duty.

The Marine hero was married to Minnie Myrtle Strayer of Mifflintown, Pennsylvania, at Washington, D.C., on December 22, 1923. On March 19, 1956, Major Cukela died at the U.S. Naval Hospital, Bethesda, Maryland. After services at St. Jane Frances de Chantel Church, in Bethesda, he was buried with full military honors in Arlington National Cemetery, March 22, 1956.

Citation: "For extraordinary heroism while serving with the 66th Company, 5th Regiment, during action in the Forest de Retz, near Viller-Cottertes, France, 18 July 1918. Sergeant Cukela advanced alone against an enemy strong point that was holding up his line. Disregarding the warnings of his comrades, he crawled out from the flank in the face of heavy enemy fire and worked his way to the rear of the enemy position. Rushing a machine-gun emplacement, he killed or drove off the crew with his bayonet, bombed out the remaining part of the strong point with German hand grenades and captured 2 machine-guns and 4 men."

Source
Headquarters Marine Corps.
Medal of Honor Citations.

Custer, George Armstrong (1839–1876) *Union general officer, who also fought in the Indian War.*

Born in New Rumley, Ohio, and an 1861 West Point graduate, Custer rose to fame and high rank during the Civil War as a flamboyant and successful cavalry officer. He ended the war as a major general at the age of 25, becoming the youngest general, at age 23, who ever served in the United States Army. During the Civil War he had 11 horses killed under him, although he was wounded only once himself.

In the postwar regular army he was a lieutenant colonel in command of the Seventh Cavalry. His introduction to the Plains Indians Wars occurred in Kansas in 1867. The campaign ended in failure and court-martial on charges of misconduct. Sentenced to a year's suspension, Custer was recalled in the fall of 1868 by Maj. Gen. Philip H. Sheridan to lead his regiment in a winter campaign against the southern Plains tribes. At the Battle of the Washita, November 27, 1868, Custer surprised and destroyed Black Kettle's Cheyenne village and laid the groundwork for his Indian Wars reputation.

Assigned to Fort Abraham Lincoln in the Dakota Territory, Custer led the Seventh Cavalry in the Yellowstone Expedition of 1873, protecting surveyors of the Northern Pacific Railroad; he fought two actions with Sitting Bull's Sioux. In 1874, Custer's Black Hills Expedition discovered gold. The rush to the hills, part of the Great Sioux Reservation, inflamed the Sioux and led to the Sioux War of 1876. The Seventh Cavalry formed part of Brig. Gen. Alfred H. Terry's column, one of three converging on the Sioux. On June 25, Custer attacked a large camp of Sioux and Cheyennes at the Battle of the Little Big Horn. He and five companies under his immediate command, about 225 men, were wiped out. The other seven companies, under the command of Maj. Marcus A. Reno, held out on a hilltop four miles away until relieved two days later. Custer's actions at the Little Big Horn were and remain bitterly controversial, but he and his "last stand" gained lasting renown.

Our history notes that George Armstrong Custer is remembered for his "last stand" and the subsequent destruction of the seventh Cavalry in 1876. However, few Americans realize that, in fact, *five members of the extended Custer family died in that one engagement:* L. Col George A. Custer was accompanied by his brother, Thomas, the first American soldier to receive two Medals of Honor for his heroic actions during the Civil War; their brother, Boston Custer, not a soldier with the seventh Cavalry, but there as a "forage master" for the regiment; the Custers' teenage nephew, Autie Reed, who was assigned to help drive the regiment's accompanying beef herd and Custer's brother-in-law, 1st Lt. James Calhoun, from Company L, Seventh Cavalry.

Eventually Custer saw his prey, who had in truth ambushed him along the banks of the river. Custer tried to charge and was repelled, forced to seek the high ground. There surrounded by his gallant if foolish brothers and friends he put up a superb battle. As one Sioux, Yellow Horse, said of him, 'I never saw a man fight as Custer did.' His brothers were beside him, just as brave, just as dead. After a few minutes, fifteen at most, Custer and his 225 soldiers were shot through, gone from the living. Where Custer lay, so did Tom, Boston, and Autie Reed.

It was brothers' friendship that had gone to the extreme, even beyond it. George Custer had the presidency to gain if he had won the battle, but Tom and Boston had nothing except credit for loyalty to their older brother, who had never done anything of note for them. Their worship of him, like that of many citizens of their nation, then and later, was based not so much on what he had done as on what he chose to represent and stand for. As he became famous, they had become known as the general's brother, which isn't much. Still, by sticking to Custer they had a chance, not much of one to be sure, but still a chance to be there for the ride. Now they were stretched out beside him, not yet forty years old, never married, completely mutilated. They had given their life to their brother, their closest friend, now lying beside them.

Source and Additional Reading
Ambrose, Stephen E. *Comrades.* New York: Simon & Schuster, 1999.

Boatner, Mark M. *The Civil War Dictionary.* Rev. ed. New York: McKay, 1988.

Chambers, John Whiteclay II., ed. *Oxford Companion to American Military History.* New York: Oxford University Press, 1999.

Hutton, Paul A., ed. *The Custer Reader.* Lincoln: University of Nebraska Press, 1992.

Utley, Robert M. *Cavalier in Buckskin: George Armstrong Custer and the Western Military Frontier.* Norman: University of Oklahoma Press, 1988.

Custer, Thomas Ward (1845–1876) *Union lieutenant colonel, the first and only soldier to win two Medals of Honor during the Civil War.*

The brother of Gen. George A. Custer, only 16 years old, Thomas W. Custer enlisted as a private in Company H, 21st Ohio, on September 2, 1861. He saw action at Stones River, Chickamauga, Chattanooga, and the Atlanta Campaign, before being mustered out of the service at the completion of his three-year enlistment term on October 10, 1864.

Appointed a second lieutenant in the Sixth Michigan Cavalry, on November 8, 1864, Custer was promptly assigned to the staff of his brother in the Shanandoah Valley. He moved with Custer's division to the lines around Petersburg, Virginia, and participated in the final victory at that place and in the campaign to Appomattox.

On April 3, 1865, he captured a rebel flag in a fight at Namozine Church. Later that month he was given the Medal of Honor for this exploit. Three days after his first heroic display, he earned a second Medal of Honor at the Battle of Sayler's Creek. In this action, according to Gen. Philip H. Sheridan, "he leaped his horse over the enemy's works, being one of the first to enter them, and captured two stand of colors, having his horse shot under him and received a severe wound." In this charge, with the Second Ohio Cavalry, Thomas Custer was wounded in the face, but after turning the captured colors over to his brother, he wanted to return to the fray. General Custer had to threaten to place his younger brother under arrest to get him needed medical attention. Lieutenant Custer was also honored by being brevetted through grades major of volunteers and was later promoted to the grade of lieutenant colonel in the regulars.

After the war he was commissioned directly into the regular army and soon joined his brother's regiment, the Seventh Cavalry, with which he went to his death, along with his brother, Boston Custer, at the Battle of the Little Big Horn.

Source

Mitchell, Joseph B. *The Badge of Gallantry: Recollections of Civil War Medal of Honor Winners.* Shippensburg; Pa.: White Mane Publishing, 1960.

D

Dalessondro, Peter J.

Dalessondro, Peter J. (b. 1918) *Technical Sergeant, United States Army, Company E, 39th Infantry, Ninth Infantry Division, so distinguished himself in combat, during World War II, that he was awarded the Medal of Honor for his heroic actions.*

Born: May 19, 1918, Watervliet, N.Y.; **Entered service at:** Watervliet, N.Y.; **Place and date:** Near Kalterherberg, Germany, December 22, 1944. **G.O. No.:** 73, August 30, 1945.

Citation: "He was with the 1st Platoon holding an important road junction on high ground near Kalterherberg, Germany, on 22 December 1944. In the early morning hours, the enemy after laying down an intense artillery and mortar barrage, followed through with an all-out attack that threatened to overwhelm the position. T/Sgt. Dalessondro, seeing that his men were becoming disorganized, braved the intense fire to move among them with words of encouragement. Advancing to a fully exposed observation post, he adjusted mortar fire upon the attackers, meanwhile firing upon them with his rifle and encouraging his men in halting and repulsing the attack. Later in the day the enemy launched a second determined attack. Once again, T/Sgt. Dalessondro, in the face of imminent death, rushed to his forward position and immediately called for mortar fire. After exhausting his rifle ammunition, he crawled 30 yards over exposed ground to secure a light machinegun, returned to his position, and fired upon the enemy at almost pointblank range until the gun jammed. He managed to get the gun to fire 1 more burst, which used up his last round, but with these bullets he killed 4 German soldiers who were on the verge of murdering an aid man and 2 wounded soldiers in a nearby foxhole. When the enemy had almost surrounded him, he remained alone, steadfastly facing almost certain death or capture, hurling grenades and calling for mortar fire closer and closer to his outpost as he covered the withdrawal of his platoon to a second line of defense. As the German hordes swarmed about him, he was last heard calling for a barrage, saying, 'OK, mortars, let me have it—right in this position!' The gallantry and intrepidity shown by T/Sgt. Dalessondro against an overwhelming enemy attack saved his company from complete rout.

Source
Medal of Honor Citation.

Daly, Daniel "Dan" Joseph

Daly, Daniel "Dan" Joseph (1873–1937) *Sergeant major, United States Marine Corps, one of the two Marines who received the nation's highest military award—the Medal of Honor—twice for separate acts of extraordinary heroism.*

Daly was once acclaimed by Maj. Gen. John A. Lejeune, former commandant of the Marine Corps, as "the outstanding Marine of all time." Gen. Smedley D. Butler, the other Marine awarded two Medals of Honor, called him "the fightinest Marine I ever knew" and wrote that "it was an object lesson to have served with him." Marine officers and enlisted men alike generally expressed this kind of praise and, according to the record, "Dan" Daly deserved it.

A small man (five feet, six inches in height and weighing only 132 pounds), Daly nevertheless was a fine military figure, erect and well proportioned. His keen gray eyes looked upon danger without fear. Although a "natural" for publicity, he disdained it and disliked all the fuss made over him. He termed medals "a lot of foolishness." Personally he enjoyed a pipe, crammed with cut plug tobacco, but did not drink.

Daly was a strict disciplinarian, yet fair-minded and very popular among both officers and enlisted men. He was noted not only for his reckless daring, but also for his constant attention to the needs of his Marines. Offered a commission on several occasions, he is said to have declined on the grounds that he would rather be "an outstanding sergeant than just another officer."

Dan Daly is perhaps best remembered for a famous battle cry delivered during the desperate fighting in Belleau Wood in June 1918. Marines took a terrific pounding on the outskirts of Lucy le Bocage ("Lucy Birdcage" to the American Expeditionary Force) at the fringe of Belleau Wood. They were outnumbered, outgunned, and pinned down. Then Daly made history; he ordered an attack. Leaping forward, he yelled to his tired men, "Come on, you sons of bitches, do you want to live forever?"

Very little is known about Daly's early life other than the fact of his birth in Glen Cove, Long Island, New York, on November 11, 1873, and the fact that he was a newsboy and something of a fighter for his weight and size.

With the hope of getting into the Spanish-American War, Daly enlisted in the Marine Corps on January 10, 1899, but before he had finished boot camp training, the war had ended and he was ordered aboard ship and sent to the Asiatic Fleet.

In May 1900, he shipped aboard the USS *Newark* for Taku Bay, China, where he landed with other Marines and entrained for Peking. The American Marines and Germans had been stationed on Tartar Wall, south of the American Legation, but intense enemy fire had driven them from the position. With Captain Hall, Daly mounted the wall bastion, bayoneted rifle in hand. On August 14, Captain Hall left to bring up reinforcements and Daly remained to defend the position single-handed. Chinese snipers fired at him and stormed the bastion, but he fought them off until reinforcements arrived. For this gallantry he was awarded his first Medal of Honor.

Citation: "In the presence of the enemy during the battle of Peking, China, 14 August 1900, DALY distinguished himself by meritorious conduct."

Fifteen years later, in action against Haitian bandits, Sergeant Daly earned the rare distinction of being awarded a second Medal of Honor.

Citation: "Serving with the Fifteenth Company of Marines on 22 October 1915, Gunnery Sergeant Daly was one of the company to leave Fort Liberté", Haiti, for a 6-day reconnaissance. After dark on the evening of 24 October, while crossing the river in a deep ravine, the detachment was suddenly fired upon from three sides by about 400 Cacos concealed in bushes about 100 yards from the fort. The Marine detachment fought its way forward to a good position, which it maintained during the night, although subjected to a continuous fire from the Cacos. At daybreak the Marines, in three squads, advanced in three different directions, surprising and scattering the Cacos in all directions. Gunnery Sergeant Daly

fought with exceptional gallantry against heavy odds throughout this action."

Dan Daly's service was varied; it included sea duty aboard the USS *Newark, Panther, Cleveland, Marietta, Mississippi, Ohio,* and *Machias.* In addition to combat in China, Haiti, and France, he served in Panama, Cuba, Veracruz, Mexico, and Puerto Rico, and on eight United States posts.

During World War I, Daly served from November 4, 1917, to April 21, 1919, participating in combat in the Toulon Sector (March–May 1918); Aisne Operations (June 1918); and the Château-Thierry Sector (Belleau Wood, June 1918). During this operation, on June 5 and at the risk of his life, he extinguished a fire in the ammunition dump at Lucy le Bocage. Two days later, while the same sector was under one of its heaviest bombardments, he visited all machine gun crews of his company, then posted over a wide section of the front, cheering his men. On June 10, single-handed, he attacked an enemy machine gun emplacement, capturing it by use of hand grenades and an automatic pistol. On the same date, during an enemy attack on the village of Bouresches, he carried in wounded under heavy enemy fire.

Sergeant Daly also served in the St. Mihiel Offensive (September 1918) and the Champagne Offensive (Blanc Mont, September–October 1918). He was wounded in action on June 21 and twice on October 8, 1918. He then served with the American Army of Occupation in Germany after the Armistice, which he considered as "not a bad birthday present."

A complete list of Sergeant Major Dan Daly's decorations and medals includes the Medal of Honor (Navy) (1900, Peking, China); Medal of Honor (Navy) (1915, Haiti); Navy Cross (1918, Belleau Woods); Distinguished Service Cross; Letter of Commendation (secretary of the navy); Letter of Commendation; Good Conduct Medal with two Bronze Stars; China Relief Expedition Medal; Philippine Campaign Medal; Expeditionary Medal with one Bronze Star; Mexican Service Medal; Haitian Campaign Medal; World War I Victory Medal with Aisne, St. Mihiel, Meuse-Argonne, and Defensive-Sector clasps; Medaille Militarie; croix de geurre with palm; and the Fourragere (the last three awards from the French government).

Dan Daly remained unmarried all his life. In 1919, he was reported as saying, "I can't see how a single man could spend his time to better advantage than in the Marines." Soon thereafter he was placed on the retainer list of the Fleet Marine Corps Reserve, awaiting retirement. He accepted a job as a security guard on Wall Street, New York City, and held that position for 17 years.

Retired officially on February 6, 1929, Sg. Maj. Daniel J. Daly died at Glendale, New York, on April 28, 1937. His remains were buried in Cypress Hills.

Today a United States Navy destroyer bears Daly's name. His record as a fighting man remains unequaled in the annals of Marine Corps history.

Source and Additional Reading
Marine Historical Center.
Medal of Honor Citation.
Blakeney, Jane. *Heroes: U.S. Marine Corps 1861–1955*. Washington, D.C.: Guthrie Lithographic, 1956.

Danner, David J. *Sergeant, United States Marine Corps, distinguished himself heroically in combat on May 8, 1967, and awarded the Navy Cross for his actions.*

Citation: "For extraordinary heroism as a Tank Maintenance Man and Crewman with Company A, Third Tank Battalion, Third Marine Division, in connection with operations against the enemy in the Republic of Vietnam on 8 May 1967. While operating in support of the First Battalion, Fourth Marines, Sergeant Danner's tank was hit and heavily damaged by enemy fire during a savage mortar and infantry attack on the battalion's positions at Gio Linh by a 400-man North Vietnamese Army force. Although wounded himself, Sergeant Danner helped his dazed and wounded fellow crewman from the wreckage to the medical aid station. Realizing that enemy soldiers were in the Command Post area, having penetrated the defensive perimeter during the initial assault, he refused first aid and resolutely returned to his disabled tank to retrieve a .30-caliber machine gun. Mounting the weapon on the ground, he commenced delivering a heavy volume of fire on the attackers. With complete disregard for his own safety, he repeatedly left his position to deliver badly needed ammunition to the infantrymen in the fighting holes and to assist in moving casualties to safer positions. On one of these occasions, observing a seriously wounded Marine in need of immediate medical treatment, Sergeant Danner carried the man through intense enemy fire to the corpsman's bunker where he could receive lifesaving first aid, which prevented him from bleeding to death. Demonstrating uncommon courage and tenacity, he then returned to his machine gun where he continued to provide covering fire for his comrades, moving his weapon to alternate positions in order to deliver maximum fire on the enemy. Although in extreme pain from fragment wounds in his arms and back and suffering from severe burns and a loss of hearing as a result of an explosion, he selflessly disregarded his own welfare throughout the vicious fire fight in order to assist his comrades in repulsing the North Vietnamese attack. By his exceptional professional skill and bold initiative, he personally killed fifteen enemy soldiers and undoubtedly wounded many more. Sergeant Danner's daring and heroic actions at great personal risk, inspiring leadership, and

unwavering devotion to duty reflected great credit upon himself and were in keeping with the highest traditions of the Marine Corps and of the United States Naval Service."

Sources
Navy Cross Citation.
Stevens, Paul Drew, ed. *The Navy Cross: Vietnam: Citations of Awards to Men of the United States Marine Corps, 1964–1973*. Forest Ranch, Calif.: Sharp & Dunnigan, 1987.

Davis, Benjamin O., Jr. (1912–2002) *First black lieutenant general: "A Cadet Who Was Shunned at West Point Led Tuskegee Airmen to Legendary Heights."*

On December 9, 1998, Air Force Lt. Gen. Benjamin O. Davis Jr. was awarded his fourth star, making him a member of that service's small circle of highest-ranking officers. However, as the first African-American officer to receive this honor in retirement, Gen. Benjamin O. Davis Jr. is a member of an even smaller group.

Founder and commander of the Tuskegee Airmen, 33-year veteran of three wars, and son of the army's first black general, Davis was "a great warrior, a great officer, and a great American," as Secretary of Defense William S. Cohen said when Davis received his fourth star.

Benjamin O. Davis Jr. was born on December 18, 1912, to a career army officer, Benjamin Davis Sr., and his wife, Elnora. Davis Sr., whose career was hampered by prejudice, not only taught his son the evils of segregation but instilled in him a determination to see it abolished. Davis Jr. earned a 1932 nomination to the United States Military Academy from Rep. Oscar S. De Priest (Republican of Illinois), then America's only black congressman.

He was the first African-American to be admitted to the academy since Reconstruction. Davis Jr. was determined to fly, but after four years of being "shunned" (spoken to only for official reasons) as West Point's only black cadet, he found that even his standing as 35th in the 276-member class of 1936 could not convince the Army Air Corps to allow him to enter flight training.

However, after President Franklin D. Roosevelt promoted the elder Davis to brigadier general, he ordered the Army Air Corps to create a flying organization for black troops. Davis Jr., the only living black West Point graduate, was ordered from Fort Benning, Georgia, to Tuskegee Army Air Field in Alabama. From the day he first pinned wings on black pilots, Davis would see his Tuskegee Airmen swell in ranks to 1,000 and form the 99th Pursuit Squadron, later the 332d Fighter Squadron.

Although critics and early reviews reported that "the Negro type has not the proper reflexes to make a first-class fighter pilot," Davis used a combination of political diplomacy and professional action to convince detractors that his men were more qualified than some and braver than most. Their March 24, 1945, escort mission to Berlin, resulting in three direct kills and no loss of friendly bombers, is legendary.

General Davis's subsequent assignments and commands were a mixed bag of personal success and cultural misunderstanding. For example, while attending the Air War College in Montgomery, Alabama, Davis and his wife, Agatha, were barred by the Color Laws from eating at most of the area restaurants. In commands in Korea and Germany, Davis's performance was so exemplary that he ended his career as deputy commander in chief of the United States Air Force.

After retiring in 1970, he served as an assistant secretary at the Department of Transportation under President Richard M. Nixon. He died in 2002.

Additional Reading

Davis, Benjamin O., Jr. *Benjamin O. Davis, Jr., American: An Autobiography.* New York: Plume, 1992.

George Andrew Davis Jr.

Davis, George Andrew, Jr. (1920–1952) *Major, United States Air Force, Commander, 334th Fighter Squadron, Fourth Fighter Group, Fifth Air Force, so distinguished himself in aerial combat during the Korean War that he was awarded (posthumously) the Medal of Honor for his heroic actions.*

Born: 1920, Dublin, Tex.; **Entered service at:** Lubbock, Tex.; **Place and date:** Near Sinuiju-Yalu River area, Korea, February 10, 1952.

Citation: "Major. George Andrew Davis, Jr., United States Air Force, 334th Fighter Squadron, 4th Fighter Group, 5th Air Force, distinguished himself by conspicuous gallantry and intrepidity at the risk of his life above and beyond the call of duty on 10 February 1952, near Sinuiju-Yalu River area, Korea. While leading a flight of four F-86 Saberjets on a combat aerial patrol mission near the Manchurian border, Major Davis' element leader ran out of oxygen and was forced to retire from the flight with his wingman accompanying him. Major Davis and the remaining F-86's continued the mission and sighted a formation of approximately 12 enemy MiG-15 aircraft speeding southward toward an area where friendly fighter-bombers were conducting low level operations against the Communist lines of communications. With selfless disregard for the numerical superiority of the enemy, Major Davis positioned his two aircraft, then dove at the MiG formation. While speeding through the formation from the rear he singled out a MiG-15 and destroyed it with a concentrated burst of fire. Although he was now under continuous fire from

the enemy fighters to his rear, Major Davis sustained his attack. He fired at another MiG-15 which, bursting into smoke and flames went into a vertical dive. Rather than maintain his superior speed and evade the enemy fire being concentrated on him, he elected to reduce his speed and sought out still a third MiG-15. During this latest attack his aircraft sustained a direct hit, went out of control, then crashed into a mountain 30 miles south of the Yalu River. Major Davis' bold attack completely disrupted the enemy formation, permitting the friendly fighter-bombers to successfully complete their interdiction mission. Major Davis, by his indomitable fighting spirit, heroic aggressiveness, and superb courage in engaging the enemy against formidable odds exemplified valor at its highest."

Source

Medal of Honor Citation.

Davis, Raymond G. *Major general, United States Marine Corps, who as a lieutenant colonel, commanding officer of First Battalion, Seventh Marines, was awarded the*

Medal of Honor for his heroic actions in Korea, December 1–4, 1950.

Citation: "For conspicuous gallantry and intrepidity at the risk of his life and beyond the call of duty as Commanding Officer of the First Battalion, Seventh Marines, First Marine Division (Reinforced), in action against enemy aggressor forces in Korea from 1 through 4 December 1950. Although keenly aware that the operation involved breaking through a surrounding enemy and advancing eight miles along primitive icy trails in the bitter cold with every passage disputed by a savage and determined foe, Lieutenant Colonel Davis boldly led his battalion into the attack in a daring attempt to relieve a beleaguered rifle company and to seize, hold and defend a vital mountain pass controlling the only route available for two Marine regiments in danger of being cut off by numerically superior hostile forces during their redeployment to the port of Hungnam. When the battalion immediately encountered strong opposition from entrenched enemy forces commanding high ground in the path of the advance, he promptly spearheaded his unit in a fierce attack up the steep, ice-covered slopes in the face of withering fire and, personally leading the assault groups in a hand-to-hand encounter, drove the hostile troops from their positions, rested his men and reconnoitered the area under enemy fire to determine the best route for continuing the mission. Always in the thick of the fighting, Lieutenant Colonel Davis led his battalion over three successive ridges in the deep snow in continuous attacks against the enemy and, constantly inspiring and encouraging his men throughout the night, brought his unit to a point within 1500 yards of the surrounded rifle company by daybreak. Although knocked to the ground when a shell fragment struck his helmet and two bullets pierced his clothing, he arose and fought his way forward at the head of his men until he reached the isolated Marines. On the following morning, he bravely led his battalion in securing the vital mountain pass from a strongly entrenched numerically superior hostile force, carrying all his wounded with him, including 22 litter cases and numerous ambulatory patients. Despite repeated savage and heavy assaults by the enemy, he stubbornly held the vital terrain until two regiments of the division had deployed through the pass and, on the morning of 4 December, led his battalion into Hagaru-ri intact. By his superb leadership, outstanding courage and brilliant tactical ability, Lieutenant Colonel Davis was directly instrumental in saving the beleaguered rifle company from complete annihilation and enabled the two Marine regiments to escape possible destruction. His valiant devotion to duty and unyielding fighting spirit in the face of almost insurmountable odds enhance and sustain the highest traditions of the United States Naval Service."

Source and Additional Reading
Medal of Honor Citation.
Blakeney, Jane. *Heroes: U.S. Marine Corps 1861–1955.* Washington, D.C.: Guthrie Lithographic, 1956.
Davis, Raymond. *The Story of Ray Davis.* Fuquay Varina, N.C.: Research Triangle Publishers, 1995.

Raymond G. Davis

Davis, Stephen Winfield (d. 1967) *First lieutenant, United States Army (1943–1967).*

Stephen Winfield Davis was born at Camp Cook, California, now Vandenburg Air Force Base, on November 6, 1943. His father, United States Army Maj. Franklin M. Davis Jr., and his mother, Erma A. Davis, were both from Massachusetts.

As an "army brat" he lived on many different posts in the United States and in Germany. Davis and his mother sailed to Germany in 1946 on the first boat of military dependents to go to Europe after World War II. As a boy, Stephen always liked military vehicles, tanks, jeeps, and parades. In the States he was active in the Boy

Scouts and became an Eagle Scout. An accident damaged the nerves of one arm, and he built up the arm by taking up wrestling and track exercises. Davis attended schools in Arlington, Virginia, and Carlisle, Pennsylvania. After graduation from Carlisle High School, in 1961, he entered the University of Maine for one year and then transferred to the Citadel, class of 1966. There he was a member of the Summerall Guards, the college's prestigious drill team.

After graduation in 1966, he was posted at Fort Jackson, South Carolina. In June 1967, Davis received orders for Vietnam. At that time his father was stationed in Saigon. Stephen was with the 101st Airborne, First Brigade, 327th Infantry, First Battalion, Company C. He was promoted to First lieutenant, on August 18, 1967, he was killed in action in Tam Ky, Quang Tin Province, near the Demilitarized Zone (DMZ).

For his actions in combat he received the Silver Star and the Purple Heart. Davis was buried at Arlington National Cemetery with full military honors—horses, caisson, band, and salutes. His medals and Citadel class ring were given to the Citadel Museum by his parents at a special parade in October 1968.

Davis loved the military. He wanted to go to Vietnam, and he died for a cause he believed in. He died a hero's death—mourned by his parents, his brother, Nathaniel A. Davis (Citadel, 1969), and his Citadel classmates of 1966.

Narrative summary of the immediate events surrounding the death in action in the Republic of Vietnam of 1st Lieutenant Stephen W. Davis, 0-5329061, Infantry, Platoon Leader, Third Platoon, Company C, 1st Battalion (Airborne), 327th Infantry, 1st Brigade, 101st Airborne Division on 18 August 1967.

This narrative was compiled from eye-witness accounts of members of Third Platoon, Company C, 1st Battalion, 327th Infantry, 1st Brigade, and Mr. Dennis Suit, of United Press International, who were present during Operation Benton of Task Force Oregon, US Army Vietnam, when the action in which Lieutenant Davis was killed took place.

Third Platoon, Lieutenant Davis commanding, was inserted into Operation Benton, a search and destroy mission of Task Force Oregon, by helicopter from the battalion base camp near Chu Lai, to a landing zone south of Tam Ky, Quang Tin Province, on Friday, 18 August 1967, and immediately moved out with its parent Company C in its zone of operations, under company control. The area was known to be "Charlie country" or territory under enemy control.

A native village looked suspicious, so the company commander of Company C brought a close-support airstrike in on the village, but no contact was raised. The company commander then dispatched Lieutenant Davis and Third Platoon cross-country to take a fairly deep objective about ten kilometers away, a rather dominant hill accessible only by a spiral trail winding up its sides.

Third Platoon reached the trail and the lower slope of the objective hill by about 1600 hours, Friday, 18 August 1967 without contact.

Lieutenant Davis deployed Third Platoon into a hasty trail halt formation and moved forward up the trail with his first squad to reconnoiter. At that point platoon strength was one officer and 33 men, but since Third Platoon's normal present-for-operations strength was on the order of 22 to 24 men, it had been reinforced with part of Second Platoon for this operation away from the parent company.

Moving up the trail in normal squad trail formation, Lieutenant Davis spotted a bunker near the peak of the hill that showed signs of recent occupancy. While reconnoitering this discreetly, the squad received light sniper fire and then a concealed machine gun opened up at fairly close range, less than two hundred yards. The terrain was fairly steep on the sides of the trail, with some concealment offered by waist-high grass. Lieutenant Davis spent some time deploying his lead squad to reduce the machine gun without success, then called in supporting artillery fire, then brought the balance of the platoon up the trail under cover this fire. At the same time the North Vietnamese Army enemy, which had slipped an estimated two platoons in a rough-shaped crescent close to the trail, opened up with what was later identified as six machine guns and three mortars and a very brisk fire fight started at once.

This action cut off the lead squad and Lieutenant Davis immediately deployed the lead squad behind a low stonewall and endeavored to bring the balance of the platoon on in to this firing position. He moved around the battle area pointing out targets and giving instructions to his men. As the hostile fire increased, Lieutenant Davis moved forward over the stone wall in order to get a better vantage-point and to evaluate the situation.

Recognizing that he was outnumbered and outgunned, he ordered a withdrawal of the platoon to a more defendable position. At this juncture, as an effective withdrawal covered by fire was initiated, Lieutenant Davis was wounded in the chest and stomach by a burst of small arms fire and knocked down. He immediately got up off the ground, firing the M-16 he carried, and continued to provide accurate suppressive fire for the withdrawal. The enemy, advancing by fire and movement, increased its fire and Lieutenant Davis was wounded a second time, hit in the face and partially blinded. He stayed in command, and as yet a new enemy element—a reinforced squad—charged the stonewall position, he moved to his radio to call in artillery support. One of the charging enemy threw a grenade, killing Lieutenant Davis and two other men. The time was 1700 hours Friday, 18 August 1967.

Third Platoon, reinforced by elements of Second Platoon and Company C, who closed in on the hill, restored the situation by daylight on Saturday, 19 August, at a cost in Company C casualties of nine U.S. dead, including Lieutenant Davis, and 15 wounded. There were 28 enemy dead counted, identified as members of the 21st North Vietnamese Army Regiment. At the time of his death, Lieutenant Davis had been in the U.S. Army one year and three days, and had been a 1st Lieutenant for three days. In Vietnam as a volunteer, three different eyewitnesses reliably reported that as Lieutenant Davis died, he was smiling. He was still smiling when his body was removed from the hill early in the morning of Saturday, 19 August 1967.

His father, Brigadier General Franklin M. Davis, Jr., U.S. Army, escorted him to the United States from Vietnam, and he was buried with full military honors in Arlington National Cemetery, on Wednesday, 23 August 1967. General William C. Westmoreland, USA, Commander, US Military Assistance Command, Vietnam, when he heard of the circumstances of Lieutenant Davis' death in action, said, "he died a soldier's death; he was a brave man." Lieutenant General William R. Rosson, Commanding General of I Field Force, Vietnam, who commanded Task Force Oregon in Operation Benton said of Lieutenant Davis and the circumstances of his death, "the best go first."

Perhaps the finest tribute of all came from Third Platoon itself. Third Platoon presented a North Vietnamese Army Type 56 Chinese Communist–manufactured 7.62 mm rifle, captured by Third Platoon in the 18 August 1967 action, to Lieutenant Davis' father with these words engraved on a plate on the stock regarding Lieutenant Davis, "Served a Gentleman, Died a Hero." This weapon has since been presented to the Citadel and is now displayed as a Citadel War Trophy at the Citadel Museum.

Source
Mrs. Erma A. Davis.

Day, George "Bud" Everett (b. 1925) *Colonel, United States Air Force, Vietnam War prisoner of war (POW), and Medal of Honor recipient.*

Born: February 24, 1925, Sioux City, Iowa; **Entered service at:** Sioux City, Iowa; **Place and date:** North Vietnam, August 26, 1967. **Unit:** 37th TFW Misty FAC (Commando Sabre Super FACs). February 24, 1925. **Home City of Record:** Niagara Falls, N.Y. **Date of Loss:** August 26, 1967. **Country of Loss:** North Vietnam. **Status** (in 1973): Returnee. **Category:** Aircraft/Vehicle/Ground: F-100F,

#3954 Missions: 139. PFC/Corp in WWII—30 months South and Central Pacific April 42–Nov 45 2 Tours Air Defense F-84's—Radar tracking missions vs. Soviet radar Vladivostok Bay and Soviet coast. **Other Personnel in Incident:** Capt. Corwin Kippenham, escaped, evaded, rescued, pilot.

Major George Day was the forward Air Control Pilot in the F-105 on a strike mission over a missile site near the DMZ when he was hit. B-52s were bombing along the southern edge of the DMZ. He started a pass coming in from the southeast to the northwest. He was doing about five hundred and was full of fuel when the plane was hit in the aft section.

The GIF (guy in front) was on his first mission. The sequence for ejection was that the back seat had to go first. Day fired the canopy and punched out. The GIF followed almost immediately and landed about a mile and half away, a little south, between twenty-five and forty miles north of the DMZ. A rescue helicopter picked him up as the Vietcong got to Day. By the time the helicopter attempted Day's rescue, the Vietcong had stripped Day and had moved about a quarter mile.

In the ejection, Day's left arm was broken in three places, twice in the forearm and once in the upper arm. He was blinded in the left eye for a long time due to a blood clot or a bruise. His left knee was dislocated, as he hit the ground unconscious. The militia group that captured Day was undisciplined untrained "kids" between sixteen and twenty years old. That did not prevent them from establishing a brutal torture regimen. Day recalls,

> They would tie up my feet with about twenty-five feet of a cotton clothesline rope. It was one of the funniest things you ever saw. They would wrap it around my legs about twenty times and then tie up to sixty granny knots in the rope. Damendest exercise I had ever seen. It was really kind of funny. After they stopped tying my hand to the ceiling, I started practicing and after a while I could untie the whole strand of rope around my feet in twenty or thirty minutes—it was a piece of cake.

Early in his captivity he was able to escape. At the time, Major Day was about forty miles north of the DMZ, and from visual sightings during previous flights, he believed that the region consisted entirely of rice paddies all the way down to the DMZ. However, four or five miles south of the camp, the paddies changed to hard, cleared land. After traversing the rice paddies, Day continued for about ten miles until he hit an area of light forestation at dawn. After making about twenty miles that first night, he stopped to rest near a North Vietnamese artillery position that was firing.

After staying awake more than 24 hours, Day lost all reference to the sky in a cloudy mist. He slid under some bushes and went to sleep. After it stopped raining, something landed very close to me, and I took a hit in the leg. The concussion picked me up off the ground and then crunch back down. My sinuses and eardrums were ruptured and I was really nauseated. I barfed and barfed and barfed and barfed until I thought I'd barfed my kidneys out. I lost my equilibrium and couldn't even stand up. I was bleeding out of the nose and some of the vomit was bloody. A couple days later when I felt better I took off and was walking fairly well although my leg began to swell because of the shrapnel I'd taken in it. That day I lost about a mile because I started walking in circles. Somewhere about the tenth day I started running out of control. I began to hallucinate and talk out loud. I didn't realize what happens after you starve yourself. It would frighten me to hear myself talking out loud and the hallucinations were just wild.

The hallucinations drove Day right into the path of the Vietcong. He tried to take off running, but after the fourth or fifth step, they started firing. He was hit in the leg and hand, but he continued down the trail for about thirty feet before veering off and passing out. He was unconscious somewhere between eleven and fifteen days. They took him back to the same camp he had escaped from, with the trip lasting thirty-seven hours. That October he had the first interrogator who spoke English. Day could barely understand him—but the brutality from him was loud and clear. The arm that had partly healed, was broken again.

They had hung me up from the ceiling and paralyzed this [left] hand for about a year and a half. I could barely move my right hand. My wrist curled up and my fingers were curling. I could just barely move my [right] thumb and forefinger.

In some of the torture sessions, they were trying to make you surrender. The name of the game was to take as much brutality as you could until you got to the point that you could hardly control yourself and then surrender. The next day they'd start all over again.

I knew what he was—he was obviously Cuban and had either been raised at or near the U.S. Naval base at Guantanamo. He knew every piece of American slang and every bit of American vulgarity, and he knew how to use them perfectly. He knew Americans and understood Americans. He was the only one in Hanoi who did.

I had gotten to the Zoo on April 30, 1968, and he had already pounded Earl Cobiel out of his senses. No one knows exactly what happened. A young gook, whose name escapes me, and two other beaters beat him all night. They brought him out after a fourteen or fifteen-hour session, and he obviously didn't have a clue as to what was going on. He was totally bewildered and he never came unbewildered.

The gooks kept thinking he was putting on, so they would keep torturing him. The crowning blow came when one of the guards some people called Goose struck him across the face with a fan belt under his eye, and the eyeball popped out.

The guy never flinched, and that was the first time the gooks finally got the picture that maybe they'd scrambled his brains. It sounds so savage you have trouble picturing it.

Bud Day dropped out of high school in 1942 to join the Marine Corps, where he spent thirty months overseas in the Pacific Theatre, leaving active service in 1945. He joined the Army Reserve, acquired a Juris Doctor from the University of South Dakota in 1949, and a B.S. and Doctor of Humane Letters from Morningside College, Sioux City, Iowa.

The "smartest move of my life," says Bud, was his marrying Doris Marlene Sorensen in 1949. Bud was recalled by the USAF as a second lieutenant in 1951 and he attended jet pilot training followed by two tours in Korea and four years flying fighters in England. (He made Air Force history with the first no-chute bailout from an F-84-F in 1957!)

The Days adopted their first son, Steven, and were soon reassigned as commandant of cadets, St. Louis University, Missouri. Bud acquired a Master of Arts in political science. They adopted a second son, George E. Jr., in 1963 and the family spent three years in Niagara Falls, N.Y., where Colonel Day flew fighters. Twin adopted girls, Sandra M. and Sonja M., increased the family, just before Bud was assigned to fly an F-100 fighter-bomber in South Vietnam. After seventy-two missions, he was reassigned as Commander of MISTY, the first jet FAC unit flying in North Vietnam. He was shot down on the sixty-seventh mission while striking a missile site.

Colonel Day was the Commander of several Vietnamese prisons, the Zoo, Heartbreak Hotel, Skidrow, and Misty and Eagle Squadrons. He was incarcerated for sixty-seven months, and executed the only successful escape from North Vietnam into the South. He was recaptured near Quang Tri City, South Vietnam, after about two weeks of freedom. He was shot in the left leg and hand and had shrapnel wounds in his right leg. For this he was heavily tortured, since he was labeled as having a "bad attitude." He was "hung"; his arms were broken and paralyzed.

As Commander of the Barn in the Zoo, he was the last of the "Old Heads" tortured—a four-month stretch in irons, solo, and massive beatings with the fan belt and "rope." Of six, he was one of three who survived from Heartbreak Hotel in 1970.

Asked many times what sustained Americans in this environment, Colonel Day answers:

I am, and have been all my life, a loyal American. I have faith in may country, and am secure in the knowledge that my country is a good nation, responsible to the people of the United States and responsible to the world community of nations. I believed in my wife and children and rested secure in the knowledge that they backed both me and my country. I believe in God and that he will guide me and my country in paths of honorable conduct. I believe in the Code of Conduct of the U.S. fighting man. I believe the most important thing in my life was to return from North Vietnam with honor, not just to return. If I could not return with my honor, I did not care to return at all. I believe that in being loyal to my country that my country will be loyal to me. My support of our noble objectives will make the world a better place in which to live.

Note: Colonel Day has written a book telling of his experiences in more detail. It is entitled *Return with Honor.*

Colonel Day's decorations include the nation's highest—the Medal of Honor, Silver Star, Legion of Merit, Distinguished Flying Cross, Bronze Star, Air Medal, Purple Heart, POW Medal, and other Vietnam service awards and medals. He has numerous awards and medals from his service prior to Vietnam.

George "Bud" Day retired from the United States Air Force as a colonel in 1977. He was awarded the Medal of Honor and is the most decorated officer since MacArthur. Reflecting on his time in captivity, Day says, "Freedom has a special taste!"

Day and his wife, Doris, have been married 48 years. They reside in Florida, where he is a practicing attorney. He is involved with litigation protecting veterans' health care benefits. In his spare time he enjoys hunting. Bud and Doris have 4 children and 10 grandchildren.

Citation: "On 26 August 1967, Col. Day was forced to eject from his aircraft over North Vietnam when it was hit by ground fire. His right arm was broken in 3 places, and his left knee was badly sprained. He was immediately captured by hostile forces and taken to a prison camp where he was interrogated and severely tortured. After causing the guards to relax their vigilance, Col. Day escaped into the jungle and began the trek toward South Vietnam. Despite injuries inflicted by fragments of a bomb or rocket, he continued southward surviving only on a few berries and uncooked frogs. He successfully evaded enemy patrols and reached the Ben Hai River, where he encountered U.S. artillery barrages. With the aid of a bamboo log float, Col. Day swam across the river and entered the demilitarized zone. Due to delirium, he lost his sense of direction and wandered aimlessly for several days. After several unsuccessful attempts to signal U.S. aircraft, he was ambushed and recaptured by the Viet Cong, sustaining gunshot wounds to his left hand and thigh. He was returned to the prison from which he had escaped and later was moved to Hanoi after giving his captors false information to questions put before him. Physically, Col. Day was totally debilitated and unable to perform even the simplest task for himself. Despite his many injuries, he continued to offer maximum resistance. His personal bravery in the face of deadly enemy pressure was significant in saving the lives of fellow aviators who were still flying against the enemy. Col. Day's conspicuous gallantry and intrepidity at the risk of his life above and beyond the call of duty are in keeping with the highest traditions of the U.S. Air Force and reflect great credit upon himself and the U.S. Armed Forces."

Source and Additional Reading

Medal of Honor Citation.

Compiled by P.O.W. NETWORK March 9, 1997, from one or more of the following: raw data from U.S. Government agency sources, correspondence with POW/MIA families, published sources, interviews, quotes from *And Brave Men, Too,* by Timothy Lowry.

We Came Home. By Captain and Mrs. Frederic A Wyatt (USNR Ret), Barbara Powers Wyatt, Editor P.O.W. Publications, CA. 1977. Text is reproduced as found in the original publication (including date and spelling errors).

Day, James L. (1925–2000) *Major general, United States Marine Corps, who so distinguished himself in combat, during World War II, that he was awarded the Medal of Honor.*

Born: October 5, 1925, East St. Louis, Ill.

Major General Day enlisted in the Marine Corps in 1943. He was commissioned a second lieutenant and completed the Basic School at Quantico, Virginia, in September 1952. He was promoted to brigadier general in April 1976 and to major general in August 1980.

Major General Day is believed to be the only Marine to fight as an infantryman and be wounded and decorated for valor in three wars. He saw combat as an enlisted man during World War II on Guam and Okinawa. He served with the First Battalion, seventh Marines, and the First Reconnaissance Company during the Korean War. He completed two tours in Vietnam: in 1966 and 1972, as commander of the First Battalion, Ninth Marines, Third Marine Division, and then as operations officer with the Ninth Marine Amphibious Brigade, Third Marine Amphibious Force. He was named commanding general (CG) of the First Marine Division in August 1980 and a year later assumed the added responsibility of the CG, First Marine Amphibious Force (I MAF). He retired December 1, 1986. His personal decorations include the Medal of Honor, the Distinguished Service Medal, three

James L. Day

four seriously wounded Marines, one at a time, to safety. Corporal Day then manned a light machine gun, assisted by a wounded Marine, and halted another night attack. In the ferocious action, his machine gun was destroyed, and he suffered multiple white phosphorus and fragmentation wounds. He reorganized his defensive position in time to halt a fifth enemy attack with devastating small arms fire. On three separate occasions, Japanese soldiers closed to within a few feet of his foxhole, but were killed by Corporal Day. During the second day, the enemy conducted numerous unsuccessful swarming attacks against his exposed position. When the attacks momentarily subsided, over 70 enemy dead were counted around his position. On the third day, a wounded and exhausted Corporal Day repulsed the enemy's final attack, killing a dozen enemy soldiers at close range. Having yielded no ground and with more than 100 enemy dead around his position, Corporal Day preserved the lives of his fellow Marines and made a significant contribution to the success of the Okinawa campaign. By his extraordinary heroism, repeated acts of valor, and quintessential battlefield leadership, Corporal Day inspired the efforts of his outnumbered Marines to defeat a much larger enemy force, reflecting great credit upon himself and upholding the highest traditions of the Marine Corps and the United States Naval Service."

Source and Additional Reading
Marine Historical Center.
MCRD Historical Society, *History of MCRD*. CA, 1997.
Medal of Honor Citation.

Silver Stars, Defense Superior Service Medal, Legion of Merit with Combat "V" (denoting valor), the Bronze Star Medal with Combat V, two Navy Commendation Medals with Combat V, and six Purple Hearts.

Citation: "For conspicuous gallantry and intrepidity at the risk of his life above and beyond the call of duty as a squad leader serving with the Second Battalion, Twenty-second Marines, Sixth Marine Division, in sustained combat operations against Japanese forces on Okinawa, Ryukyu Islands from 14 to 17 May 1945. On the first day, Corporal Day rallied his squad and the remnants of another unit and led them to a critical position forward of the front lines of Sugar Loaf Hill. Soon thereafter, they came under an intense mortar and artillery barrage that was quickly followed by a ferocious ground attack by some forty Japanese soldiers. Despite the loss of one-half of his men, Corporal Day remained at the forefront, shouting encouragement, hurling hand grenades, and directing deadly fire, thereby repelling the determined enemy. Reinforced by six men, he led his squad in repelling three fierce night attacks but suffered five additional Marines killed and one wounded whom he assisted to safety. Upon hearing nearby calls for corpsman assistance, Corporal Day braved heavy enemy fire to escort

Dealey, Samuel David (b. 1906) *Commander, United States Navy, so distinguished himself in subsurface naval combat, during World War II, that he was awarded (posthumously) the Medal of Honor for his heroic actions.*

Born: September 13, 1906, Dallas, Tex.; **Entered service at:** Texas. **Other United States Navy awards:** Navy Cross with three Gold Stars, Silver Star Medal.

Citation: "For conspicuous gallantry and intrepidity at the risk of his life above and beyond the call of duty as Commanding Officer of the USS *Harder* during her Fifth war patrol in Japanese-controlled waters. Floodlighted by a bright moon and disclosed to an enemy destroyer escort which bore down with intent to attack, Comdr. Dealey quickly dived to periscope depth and waited for the pursuer to close range, then opened fire, sending the target and all aboard down in flames with his third torpedo. Plunging deep to avoid fierce depth charges, he again surfaced and, within 9 minutes after sighting another destroyer, had sent the enemy down tail first with a hit directly amidships. Evading detection, he penetrated the confined waters off Tawi Tawi with the Japanese Fleet base 6 miles away and scored death blows on 2 patrolling destroyers in quick succession. With his ship heeled over by concussion from the first exploding target and the second vessel nose-diving in a blinding detonation, he cleared the area at high speed. Sighted by a large hostile fleet force on the following day, he swung his bow toward the lead destroyer for another "down-the-throat" shot, fired 3 bow tubes and promptly crash-dived to be terrifically rocked seconds later by the exploding ship as the Harder passed beneath. This remarkable record of 5 vital Japanese destroyers sunk in 5 short-range torpedo attacks attests the valiant fighting spirit of Comdr. Dealey and his indomitable command."

Source
Medal of Honor Citation.

Dean, William F. (b. 1899) *Major general, United States Army, commanding general, 24th Infantry Division at Taejon, Korea, July 20–21, 1950, so distinguished himself heroically that he was awarded the Medal of Honor for his actions.*

Born: 1899, Carlyle, Ill. **Entered service at:** Calif. **G.O. No.:** 7, February 16, 1951.

Citation: "Major General William F. Dean, Commanding General, United States Army, 24th Infantry Division, distinguished himself by conspicuous gallantry and intrepidity at the repeated risk of his life above and beyond the call of duty on 20 and 21 July 1950, at Taejon, Korea. In command of a unit suddenly relieved from occupation duties in Japan and as yet untried in combat, faced with a ruthless and determined enemy, highly trained and overwhelmingly superior in numbers, he felt it his duty to take action which to a man of his military experience and knowledge was clearly apt to result in his death. He personally and alone attacked an enemy tank while armed only with a hand grenade. He also directed the fire of his tanks from an exposed position with neither cover nor concealment while under observed artillery and small-arm fire. When the town of Taejon was finally overrun he refused to insure his own safety by leaving with the leading elements but remained behind organizing his retreating forces, directing stragglers, and was last seen assisting the wounded to a place of safety. These actions indicate that General Dean felt it necessary to sustain the courage and resolution of his troops by examples of excessive gallantry committed always at the threatened portions of his frontlines. The magnificent response of his unit to this willing and cheerful sacrifice, made with full knowledge of its certain cost, is history. The success of this phase of the campaign is in large measure due to General Dean's

heroic leadership, courageous and loyal devotion to his men, and his complete disregard for personal safety."

Source
Medal of Honor Citation.

De Bona, Andrew D. *Captain, United States Marine Corps, distinguished himself heroically on the battlefield and was awarded the Navy Cross for his actions in the Republic of Vietnam in 1967.*

Citation: "For extraordinary heroism while serving as Commanding Officer, Company M, Third Battalion, Twenty-sixth Marines, Third Marine Division (Reinforced), in the Republic of Vietnam on 10 September 1967. During a search and destroy operation in the vicinity of Con Thien, Company M was providing flank security for the battalion, when the enemy commenced a heavy and accurate artillery, rocket, and mortar barrage, followed by an assault by an estimated North Vietnamese Army regiment. The second and third platoons absorbed the brunt of the preliminary attack with their commanders and platoon sergeants becoming casualties during the action. Quickly grasping the situation, Captain De Bona unhesitatingly, and with full knowledge of the risks involved, moved among his men, rallying them to drive off the enemy assault. After supervising the evacuation of his wounded to a secure area to await med-evac helicopters, he conducted an orderly withdrawal of his troops and casualties toward prepared positions on the ridge line. Constantly exposing himself to the enemy while repulsing another enemy assault and concurrently organizing a defensive perimeter, he displayed a tremendous degree of composure and calm, inspiring his Marines by his presence of mind and outstanding courage. Shortly after dusk approximately 20 Marines became pinned down in a bomb crater 25 meters in front of the lines. Moving swiftly, Captain De Bona gathered a small reaction force and led it, under intense fire, to the bomb crater. Upon reaching the crater, he effectively organized his men into casualty bearers and a covering party. The volume of fire laid down by the covering party allowed the removal of all of the casualties. Captain De Bona ordered his men to withdraw, remaining behind to cover the withdrawal. His bravery and determination throughout the bitter action were instrumental in driving back three waves of enemy assault and inspired all who observed him. By his intrepid fighting spirit, daring initiative and unwavering devotion to duty, Captain De Bona reflected great upon himself and the Marine Corps and upheld the highest traditions of the United States Naval Service."

Source and Additional Reading
Navy Cross Citation.

Camp, Col. Richard D. Jr., with Eric Hammel. *Lima-6: A Marine Company Commander in Vietnam, June 6, 1967–January 1968.* New York: Macmillan, 1989.

Stevens, Paul Drew, ed., *The Navy Cross: Vietnam: Citation of Awards to Men of the United States Marine Corps, 1964–1973.* Forest Ranch, Calif: Sharp & Dunnigan, 1987.

Decatur, Stephen (1779–1820) *United States Navy hero of the Barbary Wars and the War of 1812.*

Born on January 5, 1779, in Sinepuxent on the Eastern Shore of Maryland and raised in a seafaring and naval family, Stephan Decatur attended the University of Pennsylvania and served as a midshipman and acting lieutenant during the Undeclared Naval War with France (1798–1800) and as a first lieutenant and captain during the Tripolitan War (1801–5). In 1804, he commanded the party that burned the USS *Philadelphia*, which had fallen into enemy hands; then he led attacks on several Tripolitan vessels. Decatur's heroic exploits, which entailed fierce hand-to-hand combat, won him great acclaim. After the Tripolitan Wars, he helped enforce the embargo. During the War of 1812, he took part in two notable engagements: the celebrated victory of USS *United States* over HMS *Macedonia* in 1812 and the surrender of USS *President* to a British squadron. He commanded the flagship *Guerrière* in the Algerian War (1815), capturing or destroying several enemy vessels before extracting treaties from Algiers, Tripoli, and Tunis. On returning to the United States, he served on the Board of Navy Commissioners.

Decatur had served on the court-martial of James Barron after the Chesapeake affair of 1807, and enmity between the two led to a duel in 1820 in which Decatur was killed. A symbol of the reckless bravery and bold nationalism of the young republic, Decatur was particularly remembered for his toast "Our Country! In her intercourse with foreign nations, may she always be right, but [I drink to] our country, right or wrong!"

Stephen Decatur was a fearless, resourceful, and intelligent commander. He was the youngest man ever to hold the rank of captain in the United States Navy, at age twenty-five.

Source and Additional Reading

Allen, Gardner W. *Our Navy and the Barbary Corsairs.* Boston: Houghton Mifflin, 1905.

Lewis, Charles L. *Romantic Decatur.* 1937. Reprint, Freeport, N.Y.: Books for Libraries Press, 1971.

Mackenzie, Alexander S. *Life of Stephen Decatur, A Commodore in the Navy of the United States.* 1846. Freeport, N.Y.: Books for Libraries Press, 1971.

Deibert, Charles L. *(then Captain), Infantry, United States Army, 220th Reconnaissance Airplane Company, 212th Combat Support Aviation Battalion, 17th Combat Aviation Group, First Aviation Brigade, so distinguished himself in aerial combat, during the Vietnam War, that he was awarded the Distinguished Service Cross for his heroic actions.*

Citation: "For extraordinary heroism in connection with military operations involving conflict with an armed hostile force in the Republic of Vietnam. Captain Deibert distinguished himself by exceptionally valorous actions on 10 September 1967 while serving as pilot of a reconnaissance aircraft on a mission near Con Thien. While flying a routine surveillance mission, Captain Deibert was called to support a Marine battalion engaged in battle with an estimated two-regiment North Vietnamese Army force. At the time he approached the beleaguered force, enemy fire was so intense that badly needed resupply and medical evacuation helicopters could not reach their landing zones. Despite the extreme dangers of being shot down by friendly artillery barrages and hostile antiaircraft fire, Captain Deibert flew into the area. He made several low passes through a curtain of fire to locate enemy troop concentrations and routes of movement. After advising the Marines of the enemy situation, he called for tactical air support and continued making low level flights over enemy strongpoints. Ignoring warnings from the ground to leave the area, Captain Deibert marked targets for the strike planes. One of his marking rounds was so accurate that it detonated in the center of three North Vietnamese machine gun positions and caused heavy casualties to the gun crews. When air support for the operation arrived, he continued to face concentrated enemy fire to direct ravaging bombing runs on enemy positions. Captain Deibert then discovered a route to the helicopter landing zones that was in defilade to the murderous enemy barrage and directed the resupply and medical evacuation helicopters to safe landings near the besieged battalion. His fearless actions in the face of grave danger turned a possible defeat into a rout of the enemy and prevented numerous casualties to the Marines Captain Deibert's extraordinary heroism and devotion to duty were in keeping with the highest traditions of the military service and reflect great credit upon himself, his unit, and the United States Army."

Source
Distinguished Service Cross Citation.

Dervishian, Ernest H. *Second lieutenant, United States Army, 34th Infantry Division, so distinguished himself in combat, during World War II, that he was awarded the Medal of Honor for his heroic actions.*

Born: Richmond, Va.; **Entered service at:** Richmond, Va.; **Place and date:** Near Cisterna, Italy, May 23, 1944. **G.O. No.:** 3, January 8, 1945.

Citation: "For conspicuous gallantry and intrepidity at risk of life above and beyond the call of duty on 23 May 1944, in the vicinity of Cisterna, Italy, 2d Lt. Dervishian (then Tech. Sgt.) and 4 members of his platoon found themselves far ahead of their company after an aggressive advance in the face of enemy artillery and sniper fire. Approaching a railroad embankment, they observed a force of German soldiers hiding in dugouts. 2d Lt. Dervishian, directing his men to cover him, boldly moved forward and firing his carbine forced 10 Germans to surrender. His men then advanced and captured 15 more Germans occupying adjacent dugouts. The prisoners were returned to the rear to be picked up by advancing units. From the railroad embankment, 2d Lt. Dervishian and his men then observed 9 Germans who were fleeing across a ridge. He and his men opened fire and 3 of the enemy were wounded. As his men were firing, 2d Lt. Dervishian, unnoticed, fearlessly dashed forward alone and captured all of the fleeing enemy before his companions joined him on the ridge. At this point 4 other men joined 2d Lt. Dervishian's group. An attempt was made to send the 4 newly arrived men along the left flank of a large, dense vineyard that lay ahead, but murderous machinegun fire forced them back. Deploying his men, 2d Lt. Dervishian moved to the front of his group and led the advance into the vineyard. He and his men suddenly became pinned down by a machinegun firing at them at a distance of 15 yards. Feigning death while the hostile weapon blazed away at him, 2d Lt. Dervishian assaulted the position during a halt in the firing, using a hand grenade and carbine fire, and forced the 4 German crewmembers to surrender. The 4 men on the left flank were now ordered to enter the vineyard but encountered machinegun fire which killed 1 soldier and wounded another. At this moment the enemy intensified the fight by throwing potato-masher grenades at the valiant band of American soldiers within the vineyard. 2d Lt. Dervishian ordered his men to withdraw; but instead of following, jumped into the machinegun position he had just captured and opened fire with the enemy weapon in the direction of the second hostile machinegun nest. Observing movement in a dugout 2 or 3 yards to the rear, 2d Lt. Dervishian seized a machine pistol. Simultaneously blazing away at the entrance to the dugout to prevent its occupants from firing and firing his machinegun at the other German nest, he forced 5 Germans in each position to surrender. Determined to rid the area of all Germans, 2d Lt. Dervishian continued his advance alone. Noticing another machinegun position beside a house, he picked up an abandoned machine pistol and forced 6 more Germans to surrender by spraying their position with fire. Unable to locate additional targets in the vicinity, 2d Lt. Dervishian conducted

these prisoners to the rear. The prodigious courage and combat skill exhibited by 2d Lt. Dervishian are exemplary of the finest traditions of the U.S. Armed Forces."

Source
Medal of Honor Citation.

Dewert, Richard David (d. 1951) *United States Navy hospital corpsman attached to a Marine Infantry Company, First Marine Division, so distinguished himself in combat, during the Korean War, that he was awarded (posthumously) the Medal of Honor for his heroic actions.*

Born: Taunton, Mass.; **Entered service at:** Taunton, Mass.: **Place and date:** Korea, April 5, 1951.

Citation: "For conspicuous gallantry and intrepidity at the risk of his life above and beyond the call of duty while serving as a Medical Corpsman attached to a Marine Infantry Company, First Marine Division, in action against enemy aggressor forces on April 5, 1951. When a fire team from the point platoon of his company was pinned down by a deadly barrage of hostile automatic weapons, fired and suffered many casualties, Hospitalman Dewert rushed to the assistance of one of the more seriously wounded and, despite a painful leg wound sustained while dragging the stricken Marine to safety, steadfastly refused medical treatment for himself and immediately dashed back through the fire-swept area to carry a second wounded man out of the line of fire. Undaunted by the mounting hail of devastating enemy fire, he bravely moved forward a third time and received another serious wound in the shoulder after discovering that a wounded Marine had already died. Still persistent in his refusal to submit to first aid, he resolutely answered the call of a fourth stricken comrade and, while rendering medical assistance, was himself mortally wounded by a burst of enemy fire. His courageous initiative, great personal valor, and heroic spirit of self-sacrifice in the face of overwhelming odds reflect the highest credit upon Hospitalman Dewert and enhance the finest traditions of the U.S. Naval Service. He gallantly gave his life for his country."

Source
Medal of Honor Citation.

Dewey, George (1837–1917) *American admiral and naval hero who destroyed the Spanish fleet in Manila Bay, 1898.*

Dewey was born in Montpelier, Vermont, on December 26, 1837. He studied at Norwich University and graduated from the United States Naval Academy in 1858. Promoted early in the Civil War, he served aboard the steam sloop *Mississippi* under Farragut, "with distinction at the battles of New Orleans and Port Hudson." He ended the war as a lieutenant commander. He served in various peacetime assignments, including command of sloops *Pensacola* and *Narragansett*. Dewey spent the 1890s in Washington, D.C., as chief of the Bureau of Equipment, president of the Lighthouse Board, and president of the Board of Inspection and Survey. In 1897, with the support of his Vermont senator, Redfield Proctor, and Assistant Secretary of the Navy Theodore Roosevelt, Dewey was appointed to command the Asiatic Squadron, based in the Far East.

Dewey's squadron was at Hong Kong when the Spanish-American War began in April 1898. The United States Navy had long-standing plans to attack the Philippines in the event of a war with Spain, and on May 1, 1898, Dewey led his squadron boldly into Manila Bay at night, disregarding reports of sea mines at its narrow entrance. In just a few hours Dewey, with four cruisers, two gunboats, and one revenue cutter, had destroyed the antiquated Spanish squadron of seven smaller ships and blockaded Manila. He had opened the battle at 05:40 A.M. by telling his flag captain, Charles V. Gridley, "You may fire when ready, Gridley"; the Spanish vessels were all either sunk or abandoned by noon at a cost to the Americans of only seven men wounded.

News of the dramatic victory in the Battle of Manila Bay, achieved without the loss of a single American life, made Dewey a popular hero and set in motion a chain of events leading to the U.S. annexation of the Philippines.

After his return to the United States, Dewey, now promoted to the rank of admiral of the navy, flirted briefly with a run for the presidency then settled down to preside over the General Board, the navy's first military planning organization. Under Admiral Dewey's stewardship, the board prepared plans for possible war with Germany and Japan and dealt with such questions as the location of naval bases in the Pacific, ship characteristics, and navy department organization. Admiral George Dewey died on January 16, 1917, having served as a trusted naval adviser to three presidents.

An intelligent, conscientious, careful, and aggressive commander, Dewey had prepared thoroughly for operations against Spain in the Philippines, and much of his success at Manila Bay was due to such measures.

Source and Additional Reading
Dewey, George. *Autobiography of George Dewey, Admiral of the Navy*. New York, 1913. Reprint, Annapolis, Md.: Naval Institute Press, 1987.
Dupuy, Trevor N., Curt Johnson, and David L. Bongard. *The Harper Encyclopedia of Military Biographies*, New York: HarperCollins, 1992.

Sargant, Nathan. *Admiral Dewey and the Manila Campaign.* Washington, D.C.: Naval Historical Foundation, 1947.

Dillard, Henry C. *Corporal, United States Marine Corps, distinguished himself heroically in combat and was awarded the Navy Cross for his actions in the Republic of Vietnam in May 1967.*

Citation: "For extraordinary heroism while serving as a 3.5 inch Rocket Gunner with Company M, Third Battalion, Fourth Marines, Third Marine Division (Reinforced) in the Republic of Vietnam on 29 May 1967. During Operation *PRAIRE IV*, in Quang Tri Province, Company M was assigned the mission of attacking a well-camouflaged and heavily fortified enemy bunker complex defending Hill 174. The unseen enemy opened devastating automatic weapons fire on the advancing Marines, inflicting numerous casualties. As rifle fire was virtually ineffective against the enemy fortification, Corporal (then Private First Class) Dillard, with complete disregard for his own safety, moved his rocket launcher, through the devastating enemy fire, to the main point of the ensuing battle and although completely exposed to the intense fire, he single-handedly assaulted the enemy stronghold. Stopping momentarily, only ten meters in front of the enemy stronghold, he fired his rockets with deadly accuracy at the position. As the exploding rockets threw him to the ground, he quickly rallied and regained his position. Expending all his rocket rounds, he continued his daring one-man assault with hand grenades and rifle fire, silencing the enemy position and killing six enemy soldiers. By his aggressive fighting spirit and initiative, Corporal Dillard served to inspire all who observed him and contributed directly to the security of his company. His great personal valor reflected the highest credit upon himself and enhanced the finest traditions of the Marine Corps and the United States Naval Service."

Source
Stevens, Paul Drew, ed. *The Navy Cross: Vietnam: Citations of Awards to Men of the United States Marine Corps, 1964–1973.* Forest Ranch, Calif: Sharp & Dunnigan, 1987.

Dix, Drew Dennis (b. 1944) *United States Army staff sergeant who distinguished himself heroically, January 31–February 1, 1968, in Chau Doc Province, the Republic of Vietnam, while serving in the United States Senior Advisor Group, Fourth Corps, Military Assistance Command. For his heroic actions, he was awarded the Medal of Honor.*
Born: West Point, N.Y.

Citation: "For conspicuous gallantry and intrepidity in action at the risk of his life above and beyond the call of duty. S/Sgt. Dix distinguished himself by exceptional heroism while serving as a unit adviser. Two heavily armed Viet Cong battalions attacked the province capital city of Chau Phu resulting in the complete breakdown and fragmentation of the defenses of the city. Staff Sergeant Dix, with a patrol of Vietnamese soldiers, was recalled to assist in the defense of Chau Phu. Learning that a nurse was trapped in a house near the center of the city, S/Sgt. Dix organized a relief force, successfully rescued the nurse, and returned her to the safety of the Tactical Operations Center. Being informed of other trapped civilian employees located in a building, which was under heavy mortar and small arms fire, S/Sgt. Dix then returned to the center of the city. Upon approaching a building, he was subjected to intense automatic rifle and machine-gun fire from an unknown number of Viet Cong. He personally assaulted the building, killing 6 Viet Cong and rescuing 2 Filipinos. The following day S/Sgt. Dix, still on his own volition, assembled a 20-man force and, though under intense enemy fire, cleared the Viet Cong out of the hotel, theater, and other adjacent buildings within the city. During this portion of the attack, Army Republic of Vietnam soldiers, inspired by the heroism and success of S/Sgt. Dix, rallied and commenced firing upon the Viet Cong. S/Sgt. Dix captured 20 prisoners, including a high ranking Viet Cong official. He then attacked enemy troops who had entered the residence of the Deputy Province Chief and was successful in rescuing the official's wife and children. S/Sgt. Dix's personal heroic actions resulted in 14 confirmed Viet Cong killed in action and possibly 25 more, the capture of 20 prisoners, 15 weapons, and the rescue of the 14 United States and free world citizens. The heroism of S/Sgt. Dix was in the highest tradition and reflects great credit upon himself and the U.S. Army."

Source
Medal of Honor Citation.

Dixon, George E. *Lieutenant, Confederate States Army, captain of the Confederate submarine CSS* H. L. Hunley.

Onetime company commander John Cothran described the final commander of the *H. L. Hunley:* "Dixon was very handsome, fair, nearly six feet tall and of most attractive presence. I never knew a better man; and there never was a braver man in any service of any army."

More is known about Lieutenant George Dixon than any other member of the Hunley's crew. Lieutenant Dixon was assigned to the Confederacy's 21st Alabama Infantry Regiment when the war broke out and was wounded in western Tennessee, at the Battle of Shiloh in 1862. His life was spared when a Union bullet hit a gold coin, that Dixon carried in his pocket, preventing serious injury. Early in the war, in Mobile, Alabama, Queenie Bennett (Dixon's fiancée) had presented him with a $20 gold piece, on April 6, 1862, a Union bullet penetrated his trouser pocket and struck the coin. The impact left the gold piece in the shape of a bell. But for that coin, he probably would have died on the battlefield—and the *Hunley* might never have made history. He would carry that coin for the rest of his life and could be seen from time to time fingering his "good luck" piece. Dixon had the gold coin engraved with the following words:

> *Shiloh*
> *April 6, 1862*
> *My life Preserver*
> *G.E.D.*

Lieutenant Dixon had joined the *Hunley* project in Mobile after his recuperation. The submarine *Hunley* weighed 7.6 tons, was 39 feet, 6 inches long, and had a width of 3 feet, 10 inches. Its hull was just 4 feet, 3 inches high. With a crew of nine men turning a propeller shaft by hand, sitting on benches opposite each other, it could reach a surface speed of four knots, or 4.6 mph. The 40-foot, steel boiler-plate vessel sank after its attack on the Union ship *Housatonic,* on the night of February 17, 1864.

With its low silhouette, the *Hunley* had approached the *Housatonic* under the cover of darkness. Using a canister of black powder explosive attached to the end of a long spar, the end of which had a sharp barb designed to implant itself inextricably in the wood side of a Yankee ship, the crew struck the *Housatonic.* They backed the submarine off before pulling on a detonation long cord. The cord pulled twisted wires through a copper tube filled with fulminate of mercury, sparking the explosion. Five Union crewmen aboard the *Housatonic* were killed, and the Union ship sank as a result of the *Hunley's* efforts.

Historians say the *Hunley* crew then signaled to shore with a special calcium blue lantern that it had been successful. This light signal also meant the small submarine was headed home. But the *Hunley* never made it home. This was the third crew to die in the Confederate efforts to stop the Union blockade. The cost in human life was now a loss of 23 men. (The bodies of one crew were found under a soccer field at The Citadel, then later reburied in formal ceremonies with Confederate reenactors, including veiled "widows" in period dress.)

The last submarine financed by the wealthy New Orleans attorney for whom it was named, *H. L. Hunley,* was tangible evidence of Southern frustration at the Yankee blockade of the key southern port of Charleston. The recovered submarine now serves as a visible symbol of southern futility, the lost cause, the daring stubbornness of a region, the kamikaze nature of the waning months of the Civil War, and as a monument to desperation and to the personal sacrifice of its crew.

The wreck of the *H. L. Hunley* was discovered early in May 1995, off Sullivan's Island, near Charleston, South Carolina. It was raised to the surface amid a festive fanfare in August 2000, as hundreds in a large flotilla of private boats and even larger yachts looked on.

The remains inside the *Hunley,* according to Confederate records, are those of Lt. George E. Dixon, commander, Confederate States Army (CSA); Cpl. C.F. Carlson, CSA; James A. Wicks, CSN; Arnold Becker, CSN; Frank Collins, CSN, C. Simpkins, CSN; Joseph Ridgeway, CSN; and White and Miller (no first names or affiliation known).

Source

Friends of the *Hunley.*

Hicks, Brian, and Schuyler Kropf. "Dixon's Coin Found," *The Post and Courier* [Charleston, SC] May 25, 2001, p. 1.

Donlon, Roger Hugh C. (b. 1934) *Captain, United States Army, so distinguished himself in combat, in the Republic of Vietnam, that he was awarded the Medal of Honor for his heroic actions.*

Born: January 30, 1934, Saugerties, N.Y.: **Entered service at:** Fort Chaffee, Ark; **Place and date:** Near Nam Dong, Republic of Vietnam, July 6, 1964. **G.O. No.:** 41, December 17, 1964.

Citation: "For conspicuous gallantry and intrepidity at the risk of his life above and beyond the call of duty while defending a U.S. military installation against a fierce attack by hostile forces. Capt. Donlon was serving as the commanding officer of the U.S. Army Special Forces Detachment A-726 at Camp Nam Dong when a reinforced Viet Cong battalion suddenly launched a full-scale, predawn attack on the camp. During the violent battle that ensued, lasting 5 hours and resulting in heavy casualties on both sides, Capt. Donlon directed the defense operations in the midst of an enemy barrage of mortar shells, falling grenades, and extremely heavy gunfire. Upon the initial onslaught, he swiftly marshaled his forces and ordered the removal of the needed ammunition from a blazing building. He then dashed through a hail of small arms and exploding hand grenades to abort a breach of the main gate. En route to this position he detected an enemy demolition team of 3 in the proximity of the main gate and quickly annihilated them. Although exposed to the intense grenade attack, he then succeeded in reaching a 60 mm mortar position despite sustaining a severe stomach wound as he was within 5 yards of the gun pit. When he discovered that most of the men in this gunpit were also wounded, he completely disregarded his own injury, directed their withdrawal to a location 30 meters away, and again risked his life by remaining behind and covering the movement with the utmost effectiveness. Noticing that his team sergeant was unable to evacuate the gun pit he crawled toward him and, while dragging the fallen soldier out of the gunpit, an enemy mortar exploded and inflicted a wound in Capt. Donlon's left shoulder. Although suffering from multiple wounds, he carried the abandoned 60 mm mortar weapon to a new location 30 meters away where he found 3 wounded defenders. After administering first aid and encouragement to these men, he left the weapon with them, headed toward another position, and retrieved a 57 mm recoilless rifle. Then with great courage and coolness under fire, he returned to the abandoned gun pit, evacuated ammunition for the 2 weapons, and while crawling and dragging the urgently needed ammunition, received a third wound on his leg by an enemy hand grenade. Despite his critical physical condition, he again crawled 175 meters to an 81 mm mortar position and directed firing operations which protected the seriously threatened east sector of the camp. He then moved to an eastern 60 mm mortar position and upon determining that the vicious enemy assault had weakened, crawled back to the gun pit with the 60 mm mortar, set it up for defensive operations, and turned it over to 2 defenders with minor wounds. Without hesitation, he left this sheltered position, and moved from position to position around the beleaguered perimeter while hurling hand grenades at the enemy and inspiring his men to superhuman effort. As he bravely continued to move around the perimeter, a mortar shell exploded, wounding him in the face and body. As the long awaited daylight brought defeat to the enemy forces and their retreat back to the jungle leaving behind 54 of their dead, many weapons, and grenades, Capt. Donlon immediately reorganized his defenses and administered first aid to the wounded. His dynamic leadership, fortitude, and valiant efforts inspired not only the American personnel but the friendly Vietnamese defenders as well and resulted in the successful defense of the camp. Capt. Donlon's extraordinary heroism, at the risk of his life above and beyond the call of duty are in the highest traditions of the U.S. Army and reflect great credit upon himself and the Armed Forces of his country."

Source and Additional Reading

Medal of Honor Citation.

Stanton Shelby L. *Special Forces at War.* Charlottesville, Va.: Howell Press, 1990.

Donovan, Joseph P. *First lieutenant, United States Marine Corps, distinguished himself heroically as a pilot, flying a CH-46 helicopter, in the Republic of Vietnam and was twice awarded the Navy Cross.*

Citation: "For extraordinary heroism while serving as a Pilot with Marine Medium Helicopter Squadron 364 in the Republic of Vietnam on 22 February 1969. First Lieutenant Donovan launched as Wingman in a flight of two CH-46 transport helicopters assigned the emergency medical evacuation of a seriously wounded Marine from an area north of the Nam O Bridge in Quang Nam Province. When the section leader's aircraft experienced mechanical difficulties and returned to its base, First Lieutenant Donovan resolutely elected to continue the mission. Approaching the designated area, he observed a hostile rocket-launching site and dispatched his gunships to destroy the emplacement. When informed that the injured Marine was in a critical condition, First Lieutenant Donovan, undaunted by the extremely heavy volume of enemy fire and lacking gunship support, fearlessly maneuvered to a landing on the fire-swept area and embarked the casualty. Wounded by fragments from hostile grenades and mortar rounds which also severely damaged his helicopter, and caused it to vibrate violently as it lifted out of the zone, he ignored his painful injuries as he fought to regain control of the CH-46 and then skillfully maneuvered it to the nearest medical facility. After receiving medical attention and ascertaining that his aircraft was operable, he boldly launched on a second emergency medical evacuation mission and again entered an extremely hazardous area, without gunship support, to take the wounded to a medical facility. Informed that eight seriously wounded Marines in another area required immediate evacuation, First Lieutenant Donovan unhesitatingly proceeded to the site, coordinated his approach with gunship fire, and landed in the perilous zone. He resolutely remained in his dangerously exposed position until all the casualties were embarked, and then lifted out of that area. As he began to depart, he learned that additional casualties had been brought to the landing zone, two of whom were in critical condition. With complete disregard for his own safety, he again braved the heavy volume of enemy fire and landed in the fire-swept area, embarked the wounded Marines, and departed to the nearest medical facility. By his courage, superior airmanship and unwavering devotion to duty in the face of great personal danger, First Lieutenant Donovan was instrumental in the accomplishment of the hazardous mission and upheld the highest traditions of the Marine Corps and the United States Naval Service."

Gold Star Citation: "For extraordinary heroism while serving with Marine Medium Helicopter Squadron 364, Marine Aircraft Group Sixteen, First Marine Aircraft Wing during combat operations against the enemy in the Republic of Vietnam. On 21 April 1969, First Lieutenant Donovan, launched as pilot of a transport helicopter assigned the mission of medically evacuating seriously wounded Marines from an open rice paddy northwest of Liberty Bridge in Quang Nam Province. Arriving over the designated area, he commenced a high-speed, low-altitude approach toward a tree line north of the site, and immediately came under intense machine-gun fire, which damaged the forward section of his transport. Undaunted by the hostile fire, he maneuvered the helicopter in a hover while the wounded men were embarked. Still taking a heavy volume of enemy fire, First Lieutenant Donovan departed the area and delivered his patients to the hospital at Da Nang. After an inspection of the battle damage revealed that the helicopter was no longer airworthy, he took commend of a second aircraft and immediately received a request for another medical evacuation mission from the same area. Proceeding at once to the site, he commenced his second approach into the hazardous zone, again flying through intense enemy fire. As he awaited the embarkation of the casualties, additional enemy fire erupted which prevented the Marines on the ground from embarking the remainder of the casualties. When informed that his starboard gunner had been wounded, First Lieutenant Donovan lifted from the zone to evaluate the man's wounds and to appraise the damage to his aircraft. Determining that the gunner was not seriously wounded, he advised the ground unit that he was again ready to enter the hazardous zone, but was informed that another helicopter had been designated to complete the mission. By his courage, superior aeronautical ability, and unwavering devotion to duty in the face of grave personal danger, First Lieutenant Donovan was directly instrumental in saving the lives of several fellow Marines and upheld the highest traditions of the Marine Corps and of the United States Naval Service."

Source and Additional Reading
Navy Cross Citation.

Stevens, Paul Drew, ed. *The Navy Cross: Vietnam: Citations of Awards to Men of the United States Marine Corps, 1964–1973.* Forest Ranch, Calif.: Sharp & Dunnigan 1987.

Doolittle, James Harold "Jimmy" (1896–1993)
General, Army Air Corps.

Born in Alameda, California, on December 14, 1896, Doolittle was educated at Los Angeles Junior College and the University of California. After joining the air service, enlisting in the Army Reserve Corps, in October 1917, he was assigned to the Signal Corps. He served as a flight instructor during World War I (1917–19) and was commissioned a first lieutenant in the Army Air Service in July 1920. He made the first transcontinental flight in less than 14 hours on September 4, 1922. He then attended the Massachusetts Institute of Technology and received one of the first doctorates in aeronautical engineering in 1925. Assigned to a series of testing stations, he was involved in racing and demonstrating aircraft capabilities from 1925 to 1930; he made the first blind instrument landing in September 1929. He resigned his commission in February 1930 and became aviation manager for Shell Oil Corporation, helping to develop new aviation fuels, which permitted the creation of advanced piston engines that would power World War II U.S. combat aircraft. He continued to race his aircraft, pioneered instrument flying, and won the Harmon and Bendix Trophies in 1930 and 1931, respectively. Doolittle set a world speed record in 1932 and returned to active duty as a major with the Army Air Corps in July 1940.

"Jimmy" Doolittle planned and executed his famous raid on Tokyo, leading 16 B-25 bombers from the deck of the USS *Hornet* (CV-8) in a daring raid on the Japanese homeland, landing safely in China after the raid, and scoring a huge success for American morale on April 18, 1942. His heroic achievement earned him an immediate jump in rank to brigadier general and the Medal of Honor, presented by President Franklin D. Roosevelt.

Doolittle was sent to England, where he helped organize the 12th Air Force, and as a temporary major general, he commanded the 12th during Operation Torch, the invasion of French North Africa. He later directed strategic air operations against Germany, in the Mediterranean theater, from March 1943 to January 1944. Promoted to lieutenant general in March 1944, he led the Eighth Air Force's strategic operations against Germany from English air bases from January 1944 to May 1945. His promotion of aggressive fighter escort tactics gained the Americans air superiority over Germany.

Transferred with the Eighth Air Force to the Pacific theater after Germany surrendered, he saw further combat action in the battle for Okinawa (April–July 1945) and the bombardment of the Japanese home islands. He returned to reserve status and rejoined Shell Oil in a senior executive position in May 1946. "Jimmy" Doolittle served on a series of important advisory commissions on science and aeronautics from 1948 to 1957. He retired from Shell Oil and the Air Force Reserve in 1959 but continued to work with advisory committees and boards in scientific, aeronautical, and national security matters.

A man of aggressive and energetic character, Doolittle was also a shrewd and skillful tactician and one of the most flexible and adaptable figures of American military aviation in World War II.

Citation: "For conspicuous leadership above and beyond the call of duty, involving personal valor and intrepidity at an extreme hazard to life. With the apparent certainty of being forced to land in enemy territory or to perish at sea, General Doolittle personally led a squadron of Army bombers, manned by volunteer crews, in a highly destructive raid on the Japanese mainland."

Source and Additional Reading
Medal of Honor Citation.
Craven, Wesley F., and James L. Cate, eds. *The Army Air Forces in World War II.* 6 vols. Washington, D.C.: Government Printing Office, 1948–55.
Dupuy, Trevor N., Curt Johnson, and David Bongard. *The Harper Encyclopedia of Military Biography.* New York: HarperCollins, 1992.

Doss, Desmond T. *Private first class, United States Army, Medical Detachment, 307th Infantry, 77th Infantry Division, so distinguished himself in combat during World War II that he was awarded the Medal of Honor for his heroic actions.*

Born: Lynchburg, Va.; **Entered service at:** Lynchburg, Va.; **Place and date:** Near Urasoe Mura, Okinawa, Ryukyu Island, April 29–May 21, 1945. **G.O. No.:** 97, November 1, 1945.

Citation: "He was a company aid man when the 1st Battalion assaulted a jagged escarpment 400 feet high. As our troops gained the summit, a heavy concentration of artillery, mortar and machine-gun fire crashed into them, inflicting approximately 75 casualties and driving the others back. Pfc. Doss refused to seek cover and remained in the fire-swept area with the many stricken, carrying them 1 by 1 to the edge of the escarpment and there lowering them on a rope-supported litter down the face of a cliff to friendly hands. On 2 May, he exposed himself to heavy rifle and mortar fire in rescuing a wounded man 200 yards forward of the lines on the same escarpment; and 2 days later he treated 4 men who had been cut down while assaulting a strongly defended cave, advancing through a shower of grenades to within 8 yards of enemy forces in a cave's mouth, where he dressed his comrades' wounds before making 4 separate trips under fire to evacuate them to safety. On 5 May, he unhesitatingly braved enemy shelling and small arms fire to assist an artillery officer. He applied bandages, moved his patient to a spot that offered protection from small arms fire and, while artillery and mortar shells fell close by, painstakingly administered plasma. Later that day, when an American was severely wounded by fire from a cave, Pfc. Doss crawled to him where he had fallen 25 feet from the enemy position, rendered aid, and carried him 100 yards to safety while continually exposed to enemy fire. On 21 May, in a night attack on high ground near Shuri, he remained in exposed territory while the rest of his company took cover, fearlessly risking the chance that he would be mistaken for an infiltrating Japanese and giving aid to the injured until he was himself seriously wounded in the legs by the explosion of a grenade. Rather than call another aid man from cover, he cared for his own injuries and waited 5 hours before litter bearers reached him and started carrying him to cover. The trio was caught in an enemy tank attack and Pfc. Doss, seeing a more critically wounded man nearby, crawled off the litter; and directed the bearers to give their first attention to the other man. Awaiting the litter bearers' return, he was again struck, this time suffering a compound fracture of 1 arm. With magnificent fortitude he bound a rifle stock to his shattered arm as a splint and then crawled 300 yards over rough terrain to the aid station. Through his outstanding bravery and unflinching determination in the face of desperately dangerous conditions Pfc. Doss saved the lives of many soldiers. His name became a symbol throughout the 77th Infantry Division for outstanding gallantry far above and beyond the call of duty."

Source
Medal of Honor Citation.

Dunham, Russell E. (b. 1920) *Technical sergeant, United States Army, Company One, 30th Infantry, Third Infantry Division, so distinguished himself in combat, during World War II, that he was awarded the Medal of Honor for his heroic actions.*

Born: February 23, 1920, East Carondelet, Ill., **Entered service at:** Brighton, Ill.; **Place and date:** Near Kayserberg, France, January 8, 1945. **G.O. No.:** 37, May 11, 1945.

Citation: "For conspicuous gallantry and intrepidity at risk of life above and beyond the call of duty. At about 1430 hours on 8 January 1945, during an attack on Hill 616, near Kayserberg, France, T/Sgt. Dunham single-handedly assaulted 3 enemy machine-guns. Wearing a white robe made of a mattress cover, carrying 12 carbine magazines and with a dozen hand grenades snagged in his belt, suspenders, and buttonholes, T/Sgt. Dunham advanced in the attack up a snow-covered hill under fire from 2 machineguns and supporting riflemen. His platoon 35 yards behind him, T/Sgt. Dunham crawled 75 yards under heavy direct fire toward the timbered emplacement shielding the left machinegun. As he jumped to his feet 10 yards from the gun and charged forward, machinegun fire tore through his camouflage robe and a rifle bullet seared a 10-inch gash across his back sending him spinning 15 yards downhill into the snow. When the indomitable sergeant sprang to his feet to renew his 1-man assault, a German egg grenade landed beside him. He kicked it aside, and as it exploded 5 yards away, shot and killed the German machine gunner and assistant gunner. His carbine empty, he jumped into the emplacement and hauled out the third member of the gun crew by the collar. Although his back wound

was causing him excruciating pain and blood was seeping through his white coat, T/Sgt. Dunham proceeded 50 yards through a storm of automatic and rifle fire to attack the second machinegun. Twenty-five yards from the emplacement he hurled 2 grenades, destroying the gun and its crew; then fired down into the supporting foxholes with his carbine dispatching and dispersing the enemy riflemen. Although his coat was so thoroughly blood-soaked that he was a conspicuous target against the white landscape, T/Sgt. Dunham again advanced ahead of his platoon in an assault on enemy positions farther up the hill. Coming under machinegun fire from 65 yards to his front, while rifle grenades exploded 10 yards from his position, he hit the ground and crawled forward. At 15 yards range, he jumped to his feet, stagged a few paces toward the timbered machinegun emplacement and killed the crew with hand grenades. An enemy rifleman fired at pointblank range, but missed him. After killing the rifleman, T/Sgt. Dunham drove others from their foxholes with grenades and carbine fire. Killing 9 Germans, wounding 7, and capturing 2, firing about 175 rounds of carbine ammunition, and expending 11 grenades, T/Sgt. Dunham, despite a painful wound, spearheaded a spectacular and successful diversionary attack."

Source
Medal of Honor Citation.

Dunn, John F. (b. 1934) *Captain, United States Marine Corps, who received several awards for his actions during two tours of combat duty in the Republic of Vietnam.*

Born in Providence, Rhode Island, in 1934, John was one of nine children (eight brothers and one sister). He enlisted in the Marine Corps in July 1952. During his two tours of combat duty in Vietnam he was awarded the Silver Star, three Bronze Stars with Combat V device, the Army Commendation Medal with Oak Leaf Cluster, two Vietnamese crosses of gallantry, and the Purple Heart.

Silver Star Citation: "For conspicuous gallantry and intrepidity in action on 18 August 1969, while serving as Senior Advisor to the 1st Battalion, 6th Regiment, 2d Infantry Division, Army of the Republic of Vietnam. The battalion was conducting a combat sweep operation south of Quang Ngai City when contact was made with an estimated two companies of North Vietnamese main force troops. First Lieutenant Dunn immediately positioned himself with the ARVN Battalion Commander to offer his assistance in conducting the operation. Throughout the battle First Lieutenant Dunn directed air strikes and gun ships on enemy automatic weapons positions with great accuracy in spite of constant exposure to intense enemy small arms fire. While directing the supporting arms, he and the Vietnamese Battalion Commander were taken under heavy enemy fire from a creek bed approximately 50 meters from their position. Without hesitation, and in complete disregard for his personnel safety, First Lieutenant Dunn charged directly toward the enemy, firing as he ran. His selfless example of courage and valor was an inspiration to the Vietnamese soldiers and contributed significantly to their efforts to rout the enemy. First Lieutenant Dunn's conspicuous gallantry in action was in keeping with the highest traditions of the United States Naval Service."

First Bronze Star Citation: "For meritorious service in connection with operations against the insurgent communist (Viet Cong) forces in the Republic of Vietnam while serving as a Platoon Commander with Company and subsequently as Commanding Officer of Headquarters and Service Company, First Reconnaissance Battalion, First Marine Division, from 27 August 1966 to 19 August 1967. During this period, Second Lieutenant Dunn consistently performed his duties in an exemplary and highly professional manner. As a Reconnaissance Platoon Commander, he planned, organized and led thirty-one highly successful reconnaissance patrols deep into enemy controlled territory in support of numerous combat operations, including Operations MISSISSIPPI and UNION. Due to his diligent patrolling activities and sound judgment, intelligence information concerning the Viet Cong troop movements, supply routes, and defensive positions was gathered which proved invaluable in the planning and conduct of future operations. On several occasions, he displayed exceptional tactical skill and proficiency as he directed air strikes and accurately adjusted artillery fire upon the enemy while deploying his men in combat. One evening in January 1967, a numerically superior Viet Cong force suddenly attacked his twelve-man patrol. As the enemy attempted to close with the patrol, an artillery round exploded in the midst of the Marines, killing one and wounding Second Lieutenant Dunn and two others. With complete disregard for his own safety, he calmly regrouped his men, established an effective defensive perimeter and called in artillery fire and armed helicopter strikes that succeeded in repulsing the enemy. Reassigned on 22 May 1967 as the Commanding Officer of Headquarters and Service Company, he worked tirelessly in accomplishing the myriad tasks required to coordinate various functions of his command. During July, Second Lieutenant Dunn, having had no previous embarkation experience, exhibited outstanding resourcefulness and skill in relocating the company headquarters and elements of motor transport, mess, battalion supply and communications from Chu Lai to Da Nang. Through his diligent efforts the move was accomplished insertion operations in adverse terrain, he initiated rappelling training for reconnaissance personnel. The pro-

gram's effectiveness was clearly demonstrated when on one occasion, while acting as jump master, he successfully inserted a Landing Zone Clearing Team by rappelling them into the area from a height of over 100 feet, thus contributing materially to the development of a new technique for clearing helicopter landing zones in difficult terrain. Second Lieutenant Dunn's superior professionalism, inspiring leadership and unwavering devotion to duty throughout contributed significantly to the accomplishment of his unit's missions and were in keeping with the highest traditions of the Marine Corps and of the United States Naval Service."

Second Bronze Star Medal Citation: "For heroism as Senior Advisor, 1st Battalion, 6th Regiment, 2d Infantry Division, Army of the Republic of Vietnam, on 14 October 1969. Captain Dunn volunteered to serve as advisor to the regimental Reconnaissance Company on an Eagle Flight operation. The company assaulted the objective village and met and enemy force that was superior in number. The helicopter on which he was inserted received numerous automatic weapon hits which killed three soldiers and wounded one other as they off-loaded. Captain Dunn assumed control of the situation and directed gunship fire on the enemy positions as he carried the dead and wounded to a more secure area for evacuation. He repeatedly exposed himself as he traversed open terrain under heavy fire and directed the assault on the enemy position. When the position could not be breached, he directed the orderly withdrawal to a safe distance and then directed tactical air on the target, just 300 meters from his position. He then led the attack on a demoralized enemy that had abandoned their positions, leaving behind 28 dead and 14 captured along with weapons and documents."

Today, John Dunn serves as the state of Rhode Island's director, U.S. Department of Labor for Veteran's Employment and Training.

Sources
Headquarters, Marine Corps.
Official Citation United States Army Headquarters.
Personal biography.

Dusenbury, Julian D. (d. 1976) *Captain, United States Marine Corps, winner of the Navy Cross and the Silver Star in World War II.*

"Okinawa, the closest of all the major islands off the Japanese mainland coast, was the site of the Far East Japanese Headquarters, commanded by Lt. Gen. Mitsuru.

"Four divisions of the U.S. Army and two divisions of the U.S. Marines invaded Okinawa after intensive bombardment by Navy ships. A total of 170,000 U.S. servicemen took part in this battle. America had some 7,600 men killed and over 31,000 wounded on Okinawa.

"Army troops had taken devastating losses, as had the Marines. But the Army units were scheduled to take the last major positions, the historic Ryukyu "Shuri Castle" on Shuri Ridge. Army units, however, were unable to break through and deliver the final blow to capture this maximum position.

"A Marine infantry company, Company A, 1st Battalion, 5th Marine Regiment, 1st Marine Division, led by Clemson alumnus Capt. Julian Dusenbury '42, was in reserve. The unit had recently fought savagely and lost all but 40 of its original troop strength. Dusenbury called his battalion commander to report that his company had been cut off. But he could see the Shuri Castle position and felt that his unit was in an ideal spot to move into the area and take Shuri Castle and the entire Shuri Ridge.

"The battalion commander gave Capt. Dusenbury and his company permission to attack. And attack they did with everything they had. Unfortunately, by nightfall their company was rapidly running out of ammunition, and because they were cut off from their fellow units, they would soon be annihilated. The enemy sensed their plight and began coming at them from all directions, including underground tunnels. Dusenbury gave survival orders to his platoon commanders and set out alone through enemy lines to get ammunition. He knew the location where his fellow Company C unit had been before they became separated. He crawled 1,000 yards, right through the Japanese lines with their troops staring point blank at him through the dark night, evidently misjudging him as one of their own soldiers.

"The cold rain was coming down on the muddy hillside of the treacherous terrain of Shuri Ridge causing slippery footing. Three times during that long night, Dusenbury slithered back and forth through the enemy lines dragging boxes of ammunition. All night long he defied death to find enough ammunition for his troops to survive and to take the assigned prize position the next morning.

"In retrospect, his bravery in facing the enemy so close by in their own dug-in positions didn't surprise any of his men. They had seen him do incredibly brave acts before when he won the Silver Star at Peleliu Island and

the Navy Cross during their initial landings on Okinawa. What they couldn't figure out was how one man could have dragged back so much ammunition in just three trips without getting a hernia! There was no way he could have done it if the hillsides leading up to their position on Shuri Ridge hadn't been so muddy.

"At first light, the Japanese kamikazes came at Company A with a fury. They knew they were fighting to protect the final, most valuable piece of real estate in the Pacific, short of their own homeland islands. Their Lt. Gen. Mitsuru had ordered them to fight to the death.

"The Marines had been accustomed by now to fanatical enemy infantry charges. They had fought their way across the Pacific and had learned much from their battle-trained enemies. Company A's ranks had been badly depleted. But they could "smell" the end of the battle for Okinawa. They would not fail.

"Company A fought with intensity and won the battle for Shuri Castle on the famous old Shuri Ridge the next day. Dusenbury could have been relieved immediately after the battle; however, he chose to stay with his men until the entire sector was secured.

"This nearly cost him his life. The mopping-up phase lasted for a few weeks. Soon after the Shuri Battle, while American forces secured the castle area with its underground tunnels, a hidden Japanese sniper shot Dusenbury in the back, severing his spinal cord and damaging his liver and kidneys.

"After a long recovery, Dusenbury returned to his home in Florence, South Carolina. He had helped end the war, but his valor had cost him dearly. He had to spend the rest of his days in a wheelchair.

"He remained active, however, both as a farmer and as a South Carolina legislator. He also received Clemson's Alumni Distinguished Service Award and other honors along the way. In 1976, Julian D. Dusenbury died from complications of the long-endured injury he received serving his country."

Source

Laffoday, Bill. "Captain Julian D. Dusenbury, USMC, Distinguished Alumni." *Clemson World Magazine.* Summer 1999, pp. 41–43.

E

Eadie, Thomas (b. 1887) *Chief gunner's mate, United States Navy, awarded the Medal of Honor.*

Born: April 7, 1887, Scotland; **Entered service at:** Rhode Island; **Place and date:** Off Provincetown, Mass., December 18, 1927. **Other United States Navy Award:** Navy Cross.

Citation: "For display of extraordinary heroism in the line of his profession above and beyond the call of duty on 18 December 1927, during the diving operations in connection with the sinking of the U.S.S. S-4 with all on board, as a result of a collision off Provincetown, Mass. On this occasion when Michels, Chief Torpedoman, U.S. Navy, while attempting to connect an airline to the submarine at a depth of 102 feet became seriously fouled, Eadie, under the most adverse diving conditions, deliberately, knowingly, and willingly took his own life in his hands by promptly descending to the rescue in response to the desperate need of his companion diver. After 2 hours of extremely dangerous and heartbreaking work, by his cool, calculating, and skillful labors, he succeeded in his mission and brought Michels safely to the surface."

Source
Medal of Honor Citation.

Early, Jubal Anderson (1816–1894) *General, Confederate States Army.*

Always an irascible officer, Jubal A. Early suffered overwhelming defeats in the Shenandoah Valley and went on after the conflict to wage a literary war with a fellow Confederate corps commander. A West Pointer (1837) from Virginia, Early had served one year in the artillery and later in the Mexican War as a major of volunteers, before taking up law. Also involved in politics, he served in the legislature.

Although he voted against secession at the convention, he entered the military. His assignments included the following: colonel, 24th Virginia (early 1861); commander, Sixth Brigade (in First Corps from July 20), Army of the Potomac (June 20–October 22, 1861); brigadier general, Confederate States Army (CSA) July 21, 1861); commander of brigade, Van Dorn's–D.H. Hill's division (in Potomac District until March), Department of Northern Virginia (October 22, 1861–May 5, 1862); commander of Eizey's brigade, Ewell's division, Second Corps, Army of Northern Virginia (July 1–September 17, 1862); commander of the division (September 17, 1862–November 1863; ca. December 4–15, 1863; February–May 7; and May 21–27, 1864); major general, CSA (April 23, to rank from January 17, 1863); commander of the corps (November–ca. December 4, 1863, and May 27–June 13, 1864); commander of Valley District, Department of Northern Virginia (December 15, 1863–February 1864 and June 13, 1864–March 29, 1865); commander of Third Corps, Army of Northern Virginia (May 7–21, 1864); and lieutenant general, CSA (May 31, 1864).

Leading a brigade at First Bull Run and Williamsburg, he was wounded at the latter. Returning to duty, he was given another command on the day of Malvern Hill. At Cedar Mountain and Second Bull Run he directed this unit and continued until he succeeded to division level at Antietam. He went on to Fredericksburg, Chancellorsville, and Gettysburg and commanded the corps in the Mine Run operations. Detached, he commanded in the Shenandoah during the winter of 1863–64. After the battle of the Wilderness he took over temporary control of Hill's corps during the operations at Spotsylvania. He directed his division at the North Anna and took over Ewell's corps before Cold Harbor.

Several weeks later this command was sent back to the Valley and Early invaded Maryland, fighting at Monocacy and on the outskirts of Washington. Falling back to Virginia, he dispatched part of his cavalry to burn Chambersburg, Pennsylvania, in retaliation for Union devastation. In September and October he was defeated in a series of disasters at the hands of Sheridan. The reverses at Third Winchester, Fisher's Hill, and Cedar Creek ended his power in the Valley and the old Second Corps and was recalled to Lee in December. However, Early remained with a small force that was destroyed at Waynesborough the following March. Lee then removed him, explaining that he was forced to do so by public reaction and the fact that he could not defend his subordinate without revealing how weak the Confederacy was. Early fled to Mexico but soon returned to practice law. He was connected with the Louisiana Lottery and was president of the Southern Historical Society. Becoming a defender of Lee, he feuded with the Republican convert James Longstreet until his death.

Source
Bushong, Millard K. *Old Jube: A Biography of General Jubal A. Early.* Reprint, Shippensburg, Pa.: Beidel, 1955.

Ebbert, Terry J. *First lieutenant, United States Marine Corps, so distinguished himself in combat, during the Vietnam War, that he was awarded the Navy Cross for his heroic actions in December 1966.*

Citation: "For extraordinary heroism while serving as Commanding Officer of Company E, Second Battalion, Fifth Marines, First Marine Division, in the Republic of Vietnam, on 24 December 1966. When Company G was encircled by a Viet Cong force near the village of Phu Tay, (1), First Lieutenant Ebbert's company was assigned the mission of conducting a relief operation to assist the beleaguered unit. After landing on the beach by assault boats, his company was entering the village when the point platoon came under heavy enemy machine gun, mortar, and recoilless rifle and small arms fire. The platoon sustained several casualties and was unable to advance due to the intense enemy fire. With complete disregard for his own safety, First Lieutenant Ebbert courageously moved forward, under the observation and fire of the enemy, to evaluate the situation and lead the attack. Under his inspiring leadership, his unit quickly gained fire superiority and forced the enemy to withdraw from the area. He directed his company to resume its advance, but almost immediately, the point platoon was halted by intense automatic weapons fire and mortars from elements of a Viet Cong battalion. Once more, First Lieutenant Ebbert daringly moved to the front of his unit,

directing return fire, rallying and encouraging his men, and supervising the evacuation of the wounded to a position of safety. Observing an opportunity to envelop the well-entrenched enemy force, he aggressively led a squad of Marines across fifty meters of fire-swept, open terrain and flanked the enemy positions, forcing them to halt their firing and to retreat. As he directed artillery fire on the Viet Cong force, First Lieutenant Ebbert was seriously wounded in the chest by enemy fire. But he steadfastly remained at his exposed vantage point, continuing to direct his company's efforts in inflicting heavy losses on the enemy, until he fell unconscious from his wounds. First Lieutenant Ebbert's daring initiative, indomitable fighting spirit, and loyal devotion to duty at great personal risk reflected great credit upon himself and were in keeping with the highest traditions of the Marine Corps and the United States Naval Service."

Source
Navy Cross Citation.

Edmonds, Sarah Emma (1842–1898) *Emma Edmonds, one of approximately 400 women who enlisted in the Union or Confederate army during the Civil War, who not only remained in the army for several years, but was an eminently successful Union spy—all the while impersonating a man.*

Born in Nova Scotia, Emma had a very difficult early life. Her father greatly resented the fact that she was not born a boy and treated her badly in her early life. To counter his temper Emma did all she could to act like a boy. Finally the father's treatment was so abusive that Emma fled from her home to the United States, where she quickly adapted to a new life. The United States became her country, and it was natural for her to want to defend it when the war began.

Emma was living in Flint, Michigan, when the first call for Union enlistments went out. She wanted to answer the call. So she cropped her hair, got a man's suit of clothing, took the name of Frank Thompson, and tried to enlist. After four tries she finally was sworn into the Union army (at that time the physical examination consisted merely of asking questions and no medical examination). On April 25, 1861, Emma Edmonds alias Frank Thompson became a male nurse in the Second Volunteers of the United States Army.

After training in Washington, D.C., Emma's unit was sent south to be part of McClellan's campaign in Virginia. Private Thompson (Emma) was assigned as a male nurse to the hospital unit of the Second Michigan Volunteers and had no trouble in maintaining her masculine masquerade. Even before the hostilities erupted on a full scale, two events occurred that changed Private Thompson's life forever: A Union agent working in Richmond for McClellan was caught and faced a firing squad. This left a void in the intelligence gathering for McClellan. A young officer, James Vesey, whom Emma had known in Canada, was killed on a patrol. Emma, not knowing this, went to see him and arrived at his unit just as his funeral was about to begin. As a result of these events, when the word went out that McClellan's staff was looking for a person to act as a spy prior to the campaign, Private Frank Thompson volunteered. She studied all she could find on weapons, tactics, local geography, and military personalities; when interviewed for the position, Private Thompson so impressed the staff that the position was his (hers).

Before her first mission, Private Thompson had to devise a disguise that would not alert the Confederates to her real mission, and she decided to enter the Confederacy as a black man. Assisted by the wife of the local chaplain, the only person who knew her true identity, she used silver nitrate to darken her skin to the point that the doctor she worked for in the hospital did not recognize her. She donned men's clothing along with a black minstrel wig, assumed the name "Cuff," and departed on her first mission.

Once on the Confederate front she was soon assigned to work on the ramparts being built by the local slaves to counter McClellan. Her hands were so blistered after the first day that she convinced a fellow slave to swap jobs with her, and the second day she worked in the kitchen and all the time kept her eyes and ears open. She learned a great deal about the morale of the troops, the size of the army, and weapons available and even discovered the "Quaker guns" (logs painted black to look like cannons from afar) that were to be used at Yorktown.

After the second day, she was luckily assigned as a Confederate picket, a post that allowed her to escape and return to the Union side. The information she delivered was well received, and she even had a personal interview with McClellan, after which she returned to duty as a male nurse in the hospital unit, but not for long.

About two months later, she once again was ordered to infiltrate the Confederate lines. She did not want to return as Cuff, so she posed as a fat Irish peddler woman with the name Bridgett O'Shea. Once again she successfully gained admittance to the Confederate camps, sold some of her wares, and garnered as much information as she could. She returned to the Union camp not only with the information but with a beautiful horse from the Confederate camp, which she named Rebel. In the process of returning on this trip, Private Frank Thompson was wounded in the arm, but she managed to stay in the saddle and elude the Confederates in the chase. With the battle in Virginia slowing, the Second Michigan was transferred to the Shenandoah Valley, in Virginia, to sup-

port the efforts of General Philip Sheridan. Private Thompson's reputation as a nurse and also as a spy preceded the transfer and Private Thompson soon found new territory for spying. On several occasions Emma went behind the Confederate lines as Cuff, a fellow of whom Emma herself said, "I truly admire the little fellow—he's a plucky one; got his share of grit."

In August 1862, Private Thompson again went behind enemy lines, this time as a black woman with a black face and a bandanna. On this trip she became a laundress in the camp, while she was cleaning an officer's coat, a packet of official papers fell out of his pocket. Emma quickly picked them up and decided it was time to return to the Union side with the packet. She did and the officers were delighted with the information she had garnered.

At the end of 1862, her unit was sent to the Ninth Corps, commanded by General Ambrose Burnside, near Louisville, Kentucky. As before, the reputation of Private Thompson preceded the transfer and his secret missions continued in the new area. Here he was asked to assume the role of a young man with southern sympathies, Charles Mayberry, and go to Louisville to assist in identifying the southern spy network in the town. Once again, Private Thompson succeeded in his mission, this time just prior to the unit's transfer to the army of General Grant in preparation for the Battle of Vicksburg. Under General Grant, Private Thompson worked long hours in the military hospital until a real dilemma arose. She became ill with malaria and could not admit herself to the hospital, where her true identity would be discovered. After much soul-searching Emma decided that she had to leave camp for a while and recover in a private hospital. Arriving in Cairo, Illinois, she again became a woman and checked herself into a hospital for treatment of malaria. Once recovered, Emma planned to don her uniform and rejoin her unit—that is, until she read the army bulletins posted in the window of the Cairo newspaper office. There on the list of deserters from the Union army was the name Private Frank Thompson.

With the last of her funds, Emma Edmonds bought a train ticket to Washington, where she worked as a nurse until the end of the war. There would be no more secret missions for Private Frank Thompson to add to the 11 successful missions in his career.

After the war Emma wrote her memoirs, *Nurse and Spy in the Union Army,* which became a very popular book, selling thousands of copies. Emma gave all of her profits from the book to the U.S. war relief fund. Once the book was completed, Emma became homesick for her native Canada and returned. In 1867 Emma married Linus Seeyle and went back to the United States, initially to Cleveland, Ohio. The marriage was happy, and Emma raised three sons, one of whom enlisted in the army "just like Mama did."

Although happy in her family life, Emma continued to brood over being branded a deserter in the Civil War. With the encouragement of her friends she petitioned the War Department for a full review of her case. The case was debated, and on March 28, 1884, the House of Representatives passed House Bill Number 5335, validating Mrs. Seelye's case. The House Bill includes the following statements:

> Truth is oftentimes stranger than fiction, and now comes the sequel, Sarah E. Edmonds, now Sarah E. Seelye, alias Franklin Thompson, is now asking this Congress to grant her relief by way of a pension on account of fading health, which she avers had its incurrence and is the sequence of the days and nights she spent in the swamps of the Chickahominy in the days she spent soldiering. That Franklin Thompson and Mrs. Sarah E. E. Seelye are one and the same person is established by abundance of proof and beyond a doubt. She submits a statement . . . and also the testimony of ten credible witnesses, men of intelligence, holding places of high honor and trust, who positively swear she is the identical Franklin Thompson.

On July 5, 1884, a special act of Congress granted Emma Edmonds alias Frank Thompson an honorable discharge from the army, plus a bonus and a veteran's pension of 12 dollars a month. The resulting Special Act of Congress read as follows:

> Be it enacted by the Senate and House of Representatives of the United States of America in Congress assembled, That the Secretary of Interior is hereby authorized and directed to place on the pension roll, the name of Sarah E. E. Seelye, alias Frank Thompson, who was late a private in Company E, Second Regiment of Michigan Infantry Volunteers, at the rate of twelve dollars per month. Approved, July 5, 1884.

Now satisfied, Emma lived out the rest of her life in La Porte, Texas, where she died on September 5, 1898. She is buried in the military section of Washington Cemetery in Houston, Texas. In honor of her duty and devotion to her country, she is the only female member of the organization formed after the Civil War by Union veterans—the Grand Army of the Republic (GAR). In her own words Emma Edmonds said of her adventures, "I am naturally fond of adventure, a little ambitious, and a good deal romantic—but patriotism was the true secret of my success."

Source

Markle, Donald E: *Spies and Spymasters of the Civil War.* New York: Hippocrene Books, 1994.

Edson, Merritt Austin "Red Mike" (b. 1897)

General, United States Marine Corps, awarded the Navy Cross for the Nicaraguan Campaign and the Medal of Honor for his service in the Solomon Islands in World War II.

Born: April 25, 1897, Rutland Township, Vt; **Entered service at:** Burlington, Vt., June 26, 1917.

"Red Mike" Edson, born on a farm in the Cheney Hill District, Rutland Township, Vermont, on April 25, 1897, moved when he was about a year old with his family from Rutland Township to their hometown, Chester, and lived there from that time. Edson attended high school at Chester and then went on to study at the University of Vermont, at Burlington. He married Ethel Robbins of Burlington, and they had two sons, Merritt Jr. and Herbert Robbins Edson.

Edson began his active military service during the Mexican border forays of 1914, when he was a private in the National Guard, First Vermont Infantry. On June 26, 1917, he enlisted in the United States Marine Corps Reserve and received his second lieutenancy in October 1917. He served in France in 1918, when he was intelligence officer, commanding the scouting and sniping detachments of the 11th Marines. After returning to the United States in 1919, he was on duty at the Marine Barracks, Quantico, Virginia, until 1921. That duty was followed by service in Louisiana with a detachment of Leathernecks guarding the mail.

General Edson is unusual among Marine officers in that, in the words of the "Marines' Hymn," he served "in the air, on land, and sea." He entered flight training at the Naval Air Station, Pensacola, Florida, and was designated as a naval aviator in July 1922, transferring to the air detachment at Quantico. He served in an aviation unit on the island of Guam from 1923 until 1925. After his return to the mainland, he had a tour of duty at Quantico, followed by instruction in advanced flight tactics at Kelly Field, Texas, and duty as ordnance officer at the Marine Barracks of the Philadelphia Navy Yard.

After sea duty in 1927 and the Nicaraguan Campaign of 1928, "Red Mike" returned to Philadelphia as an instructor at the Marine Corps Basic School, from 1929 until 1935. It was during the second Nicaraguan Campaign that Edson first commanded, as a captain, the Marine guard attached to the USS *Denver,* and later aboard the USS *Rochester.* In this assignment, he saw combat ashore with landing parties. His performance was evaluated by his commanding officer as follows:

> Captain Edson has demonstrated that when properly led, Marines can travel in the dry and rainy season wherever bandits operate. This has been done in the face of almost insurmountable obstacles and far beyond the reach of supporting troops. Through his efforts the valley of Coco and Poteca Rivers have been denied to outlaws and the confidence of peace-

ful Nicaraguans in these sections restored. During the thirteen months that Captain Edson had served in Nicaragua he has spent ten months in the interior actively patrolling on trails and rivers against outlaws which resulted in twelve separate and distinct contacts.

"Red Mike" was awarded the Nicaraguan Medal of Merit with Silver Star for his services to the legitimate government of the little republic, as well as America's Navy Cross with the following citation:

Citation: "For distinguishing himself by display of extraordinary acts of heroism on August 7, 1928, while in command of a Marine patrol on the Coco River, en route to Poteca, Captain Edson, upon encountering a force of bandits entrenched upon both sides of the river, personally led his advance guard against the enemy engaging in hand-to-hand conflict with them, and by his exhibition of coolness, intrepidity and dash, so inspired his men that the [numerically] superior force of bandits were driven from their prepared positions, and severe losses inflicted upon them."

Thereafter, he had short tours of duty at Parris Island, South Carolina, and at Marine Corps Headquarters in Washington, D.C., as well as instruction in the senior course at the Marine Corps School, Quantico.

He served in China, at Shanghai, from the spring of 1937 until May 1939, when he was ordered to Marine Corps Headquarters in Washington for duty as officer in charge of the target-practice section and inspector of target practice. In addition to his naval aviator's wing, Edson was classified as an ordnance expert and distinguished rifleman. He took command of the First Battalion, Fifth Marine Regiment, at Quantico, in 1941. From that nucleus the famous "Marine Raiders" of World War II were developed.

Citation: "For extraordinary heroism and conspicuous intrepidity above and beyond the call of duty as Commanding Officer of the 1st Marine Raider Battalion, with Parachute Battalion attached, during action against enemy Japanese forces in the Solomon Islands on the night of 13–14 September 1942. After the airfield on Guadalcanal had been seized from the enemy on 8 August, Col. Edson, with a force of 800 men, was assigned to the occupation and defense of a ridge dominating the jungle on either side of the airport. Facing a formidable Japanese attack which, augmented by infiltration, had crashed through our front lines, he, by skillful handling of his troops, successfully withdrew his forward units to a reserve line with minimum casualties. When the enemy, in a subsequent series of violent assaults, engaged our force in desperate hand-to-hand combat with bayonets, rifles, pistols, grenades, and knives, Col. Edson, although continuously exposed to hostile fire throughout the night, personally directed defense of the reserve position against a fanatical

foe of greatly superior numbers. By his astute leadership and gallant devotion to duty, he enabled his men, despite severe losses, to cling tenaciously to their position on the vital ridge, thereby retaining command not only of the Guadalcanal airfield, but also of the 1st Division's entire offensive installations in the surrounding area."

Source and Additional Reading
Medal of Honor Citation.
Boswell, Rolfe. *Medals for Marines.* New York: Crowell, 1945.
Hoffiman, Jon T. *Once a Legend.* Novato, Calif.: Presidio Press, 1994.

Edwards, Daniel R. (b. 1897) *Private first class, United States Army, Company C, Third Machine Gun Battalion, First Division, distinguished himself heroically on the battlefield in France, in 1918, and was awarded the Medal of Honor for his actions.*

Born: April 9, 1897, Moorville, Tex. **Entered service at:** Bruceville, Tex.; **Place and date:** Near Soissons, France, July 18, 1918. **G.O. No.:** 14, W.D., 1923.

Citation: "Reporting for duty from hospital where he had been for several weeks under treatment for numerous and serious wounds and although suffering intense pain from a shattered arm, he crawled alone into an enemy trench for the purpose of capturing or killing enemy soldiers known to be concealed therein. He killed 4 of the men and took the remaining 4 men prisoners: while conducting them to the rear one of the enemy was killed by a high-explosive enemy shell which also completely shattered one of Pfc. Edward's legs, causing him to be immediately evacuated to the hospital. The bravery of Pfc. Edwards, now a tradition in his battalion because of his previous gallant acts, again caused the morale of his comrades to be raised to high pitch."

Source
Medal of Honor Citation.

Ellis, "Pete" Earl Hancock (1880–1923) *Marine officer and amphibious warfare specialist.*

Ellis was a prophetic strategist and tactician whose 1921 plan anticipated the United States Navy's Central Pacific campaign of World War II. He enlisted as a private in the Marine Corps in 1900 and was commissioned a year later. Five years' service in the Philippines and 18 months with the Asiatic Fleet acquainted him with the Far East and with the defense of Subic Bay. While at the Naval War College from 1911 to 1913, as a student and as a faculty member, Ellis developed his vision of amphibious assault operations and prepared studies for the defense of such Pacific islands as Guam, Peleliu, and Samoa. In 1914, after participating in the first advanced base exercise, he reported to Guam to help plan its defense. He joined the staff of United States Marines Gen. John A. Lejeune in Washington and later accompanied Lejeune to France in 1917–18. In 1920, Major Ellis was assigned to United States Marine Corps (USMC) headquarters, under then Commandant Lejeune. There Ellis prepared his major work, a seminal report, "Advanced Base Operations in Micronesia," in which he prescribed amphibious assault operations to seize islands needed as advanced bases to support the naval campaign against Japan. In 1922, Lejeune granted Ellis permission for a covert mission to Micronesia to ascertain whether any of the bases had been fortified. Ellis died on the trip in 1923 under mysterious circumstances. Despite rumors, no evidence exists of Japanese involvement in his death, which was instead consistent with Ellis's accelerating alcoholism.

Source and Additional Reading

Ballendorf, Dirk A. *Pete Ellis, an Amphibious Warfare Prophet.* Annapolis, Md.: Naval Institute Press, 1997.

Chambers, John Whiteclay II. *The Oxford Companion to American Military History.* New York: Oxford University Press, 1999.

Evans, Andrew J. (1918–2001) *Major general, United States Air Force.*

General Evans was born on November 11, 1918, in Charleston South Carolina. He graduated from Columbus High School in Columbus, Georgia, and attended The Citadel in Charleston. In 1937, he entered the United States Military Academy at West Point, New York, from which he graduated in 1941 with a bachelor of science degree and was commissioned a second lieutenant. He then attended pilot training at Randolph Field, Texas.

During World War II, he served with fighter squadrons in the United States, Iceland, and the European theater of operations and attended the Command and General Staff School at Fort Leavenworth, Kansas. He completed two combat tours of duty and is credited with 129 fighter combat missions with eight enemy aircraft destroyed in aerial combat. He is also credited with having destroyed four enemy aircraft during one mission. At the cessation of hostilities in Europe, he was commander of the 357th Fighter Group, headquartered in Neubiberg, Germany.

He returned to the United States in 1946 and served until 1952 in various assignments, including the staff of the Air University, Maxwell Air Force Base, Alabama,

(March 1946–August 1947), Air Command and Staff School (August 1847–June 1948), Joint Staff, Organization of the Joint Chiefs of Staff, United States Air Force (July 1950–July 1951); and Air War College, Maxwell Air Force Base (August 1951–June 1952).

General Evans again went overseas in June 1952 for a third combat tour of duty. He served as deputy commander of the 49th Fighter-Bomber Wing in Korea and completed 67 combat missions.

On his 67th mission his aircraft was hit by enemy ground fire while he was bombing enemy front line positions. He bailed out and was captured by Chinese Communist forces, ending his further active participation in the Korean War. General Evans was, in fact, the senior ranking Air Force Prisoner of War (POW) during the Korean War, and arguably one of the most mistreated. Listed as missing in action (MIA), Evans was not reported as captured by the Communists. After enduring torture, including more than eight months in solitary confinement, he was finally released from captivity in September 1953, two months after hostilities had ceased.

Forced to sign a false statement acknowledging the use of chemical agents against Chinese Communist forces, Evans was subsequently court-martialed by the Air Force for alleged violations of the Uniform Code of Military Justice (UCMJ), while being held as a POW. He was found to be not guilty of any form of collaboration. The horrendous treatment of General Evans, and of other POWs, at the hands of the Chinese Communists was instrumental in the United States Armed Forces' rewriting its Code of Conduct.

In 1960, General Evans was assigned as Commander of the 65th Air Division at Torrejon Air Base, in Spain. In this position he was responsible for joint air defense and training with the Spanish air defense commander.

General Evans returned to the United States in October 1963 and was assigned to the Office of the Deputy Chief of Staff, Research and Development, Headquarters, United States Air Force, as director of development planning. In June 1964, he became director of development with additional duty as special assistant to the deputy chief of staff for counterinsurgency (COIN). In August 1968, he was assigned as commander of the United States Air Force Tactical Air Warfare Center, at Eglin Air Force Base, Florida.

In October 1970, he assumed duties as deputy commander, 7th Air Force/13th Air Force, headquartered at Udorn Royal Thai Air Force Base, Thailand. General Evans was later appointed commander of the United States Military Assistance Command, Thailand, and chief of the Joint United States Military Advisory Group, Thailand, in July 1971.

His military decorations and awards include the Distinguished Service Medal, Silver Star, Legion of Merit, Distinguished Flying Cross with 2 Oak Leaf Clusters, Air

Medal with 12 Oak Leaf Clusters, Army Commendation Medal, Purple Heart, Distinguished Unit Citation, French croix de guerre, and Korean Ulchi Medal with Silver Star.

Source

Air Force, News Agency. "Major General Andrew R. Evans, Jr." *Biography*. Retrieved on line: http://www.af.mil/news/biographies/evans-aj.html.

Ewell, Richard Stoddert (1817–1872) *General, Confederate States Army.*

As Stonewall Jackson's successor, the gallant Richard S. Ewell proved to be a disappointment, and the argument as to why is still around today. Some claim it was the loss of a leg, others that it was the influence of the "Widow Brown," whom he married during his recovery. But the fact of the matter is that he was ill prepared by Jackson for the loose style of command practiced by Robert E. Lee.

A West Pointer (1840) and veteran of two decades as a company officer, he never quite made the adjustment to commanding large-scale units. He once went out foraging for his division and returned—with a single steer—as if he was still commanding a company of dragoons. Resigning his captaincy on May 7, 1861, to serve the South, he held the following assignments: colonel, cavalry (1861); brigadier general, Confederate States Army (CSA) (June 17, 1861); commander of brigade (in First Corps after July 20), Army of the Potomac (June 20–October 22, 1861); commander of brigade, Longstreet's division, Potomac District, Department of Northern Virginia (October 22, 1861–February 21, 1862); major general, CSA (January 23, 1862); commander E. K. Smith's (old) division, Potomac District, Department of Northern Virginia (February 21–May 17, 1862); commander E. K. Smith's division, Valley District, Department of Northern Virginia (May 17–June 26, 1862); commander of division, Second Corps, Army of Northern Virginia (June 26–August 28, 1862); commander of the corps (May 30, 1863–May 27, 1864); lieutenant general, CSA (May 23, 1863); and commander Department of Richmond (June 13, 1864–April 6, 1865).

After serving at First Bull Run he commanded a division under Jackson in the Shenandoah Valley Campaign, where he complained bitterly about being left in the dark about plans. Jackson's style of leadership was to prove the undoing of Ewell once Jackson was gone. Ewell fought through the Seven Days and at Cedar Mountain before being severely wounded and losing a leg at Groveton, in the beginning of the battle of Second Bull Run. After a long recovery, he returned to duty in May 1863 and was promoted to command part of Jackson's old corps. At Second Winchester he won a stunning victory, and for a moment he appeared to be a second Stonewall. However, at Gettysburg he failed to take advantage of the situation on the evening of the first day when given discretionary orders by Lee. He required exact instructions, unlike his predecessor. After serving through the fall campaigns he fought at the Wilderness, where the same problem developed. At Spotsylvania one of his divisions was all but destroyed. After the actions along the North Anna he was forced by illness to relinquish command temporarily but Lee made it permanent. He was given command in Richmond and was captured at Sayler's Creek on April 6, 1865, during the retreat to Appomattox. After his release from Fort Warren in July, "Old Baldy" retired to a farm near Spring Hill, Tennessee, where he died on January 25, 1872. He is buried in the Old City Cemetery, Nashville, Tennessee.

Source and Additional Reading

Hamlin, Percy Gatling, *"Old Bald Head": The Portrait of a Soldier.* Strasburg, Va.: Shenandoah Publishing House, 1940.

Faith, Don C., Jr.

Faith, Don C., Jr. (1918–1950) *Lieutenant colonel, United States Army, commanding officer, First Battalion, 32d Infantry Regiment, Seventh Infantry Division, so distinguished himself in combat, during the Korean War, that he was awarded (posthumously) the Medal of Honor for his heroic actions.*

Born: 1918, Washington, Ind.; **Entered service at:** Washington, Ind.; **Place and date:** Vicinity Hagaru-ri, North Korea, November 27 to December 1, 1950. **G.O. No.:** 59, August 2, 1951.

Citation: "Lieutenant Colonel Don C. Faith Jr., Infantry, United States Army, Commanding 1st Battalion, 32d Infantry Regiment, 7th Infantry Division, distinguished himself conspicuously by gallantry and intrepidity in action above and beyond the call of duty 27 November to 1 December 1950, in the area of the Chosin Reservoir. When the enemy launched a fanatical attack against his battalion, Colonel Faith unhesitatingly exposed himself to heavy enemy fire as he moved about directing the action. When the enemy penetrated the positions, Colonel Faith personally led counterattacks to restore the position. During an attack by his battalion to effect a junction with another U.S. unit, Colonel Faith reconnoitered the route for, and personally directed the first elements of, his command across the ice-covered reservoir and then directed the movement of his vehicles, which were loaded with wounded until all of his command had passed through the enemy fire. Having completed this he crossed the reservoir himself. Assuming command of the force his unit had joined he was given the mission of attacking to join friendly elements to the south. Colonel Faith, although physically exhausted in the bitter cold, organized and launched an attack, which was soon stopped by enemy fire. He ran forward under enemy small arms and automatic weapons fire, got his men on their feet and personally led the fire attack as it blasted its way through the enemy ring. As they came to a hairpin curve, enemy fire from a roadblock again pinned the column down. Colonel Faith organized a group of men and directed their attack on the enemy positions on the right flank. He then placed himself at the head of another group of men and in the face of direct enemy fire led an attack on the enemy roadblock, firing his pistol and throwing grenades. When he had reached a position approximately 30 yards from the roadblock he was mortally wounded, but continued to direct the attack until the roadblock was overrun. Throughout the five days of action Colonel Faith gave no thought to his safety and did not spare himself. His presence each time in the position of greatest danger was an inspiration to his men. Also, the damage he personally inflicted firing from his position at the head of his men was of material assistance on several occasions. Colonel Faith's outstanding gallantry and noble self-sacrifice above and beyond the call of duty reflect the highest honor on him and are in keeping with the highest traditions of the U.S. Army. (This award supersedes the prior award of the Silver Star [First Oak Leaf Cluster] as announced in General Order No. 32, Headquarters X Corps, dated Feb. 23, 1951, for gallantry in action Nov. 27, 1950.)

Source
Medal of Honor Citation.

Farragut, David Glasgow

Farragut, David Glasgow (1801–1870) *Union admiral in the Civil War; seized New Orleans in 1862, captured Mobile Bay in 1864, and was the United States Navy's first admiral.*

Adopted by David Porter after the death of his parents, Farragut served as a midshipman at the age of nine. He served under Porter on the frigate *Essex* in the War of 1812 and was made prize master of a captured ship. From 1815 until 1861, Farragut alternated between routine sea duty and shore duty, with periods of leave. At the outbreak of the Civil War he was a senior officer with a long but undistinguished record of service.

A resident of Norfolk, Virginia, Farragut left for New York on April 18, 1861, the day after Virginia seceded from the Union. Once satisfied with Farragut's loyalty to the Union, the Navy Department chose him to capture New Orleans, a major northern objective. Farragut boldly led his ships past Forts Jackson and St. Philip, the principal obstacles on the Mississippi River below New Orleans. He arrived at the city on April 25, 1862, and the army occupied it on May 1. Farragut's heroic feat electrified the North, opened the lower Mississippi to federal forces, and discouraged European intervention on behalf of the Confederacy. It also earned Farragut promotion to rear admiral; he was the first to hold that rank in the United States Navy.

On August 5, 1864, Farragut similarly bypassed strongly defended forts in Mobile Bay to attack and destroy the Confederate warships defending Mobile, Alabama. Although the city itself was not captured until April 1865, Farragut effectively closed the Confederacy's last major Gulf port. During a critical moment of this assault, when one ship's captain hesitated because of fear of Confederate mines, then called torpedoes, Farragut shouted, "Damn the torpedoes, full speed ahead!" Between 1865 and 1870, Farragut was twice promoted and became the United States Navy's first four-star admiral.

Sources and Additional Reading

Farragut, Loyall, *The Life of David Glasgow Farragut, First Admiral of the United States Navy, Embodying His Journal and Letters.* New York: Appleton, 1879.

Hagan, Kenneth J. and Duffy, James P. *Lincoln's Admiral: The Civil War Campaigns of David Farragut.* New York: Wiley, 1997.

Hearn, Chester G. *Admiral David Glasgow Farragut: The Civil War Years.* Annapolis, Md.: Naval Institute Press, 1998.

Lewis, Charles L. *David Glasgow Farragut,* 2 vols. 1941–43. Reprint, Annapolis, Md.: Naval Institute Press, 1980.

Mahan, Alfred T. *Admiral Farragut.* Reprint. New York: Appleton, 1892.

Fisher, Almond E. *Second lieutenant, United States Army, Company E, 157th Infantry, 45th Infantry Division, so distinguished himself in combat, during World War II, that he was awarded the Medal of Honor for his heroic actions.*

Born: Hume, N.Y.; **Entered service at:** Brooklyn, N.Y.; **Place and date:** Near Grammont, France, September 12–13, 1944. **G.O. No:** 32, April 23, 1945.

Citation: "For conspicuous gallantry and intrepidity at the risk of his life above and beyond the call of duty on the night of 12–13 September 1944, near Grammont, France. In the darkness of early morning, 2d Lt. Fisher was leading a platoon of Company E, 157th Infantry, in single column to the attack of a strongly defended hill position. At 2:30 A.M., the forward elements were brought under enemy machinegun fire from a distance of not more than 20 yards. Working his way alone to within 20 feet of the gun emplacement, he opened fire with his carbine and killed the entire guncrew. A few minutes after the advance was resumed, heavy machinegun fire was encountered from the left flank. Again crawling forward alone under withering fire, he blasted the gun and crew from their positions with hand grenades. After a halt to replenish ammunition, the advance was again resumed and continued for 1 hour before being stopped by intense machinegun and rifle fire. Through the courageous and skillful leadership of 2d Lt. Fisher, the pocket of determined enemy resistance was rapidly obliterated. Spotting an emplaced machine pistol a short time later, with 1 of his men he moved forward and destroyed the position. As the advance continued the firefight became more intense. When a bypassed German climbed from his foxhole and attempted to tear an M1 rifle from the hands of one of his men, 2d Lt. Fisher whirled and killed the enemy with a burst from his carbine. About 30 minutes later the platoon came under the heavy fire of machineguns from across an open field. 2d Lt. Fisher, disregarding the terrific fire, moved across the field with no cover or concealment to within range, knocked the gun from the position and killed or wounded the crew. Still under heavy fire he returned to his platoon and continued the advance. Once again heavy fire was encountered from a machinegun directly in front. Calling for hand grenades, he found only 2 remaining in the entire platoon. Pulling the pins and carrying a grenade in each hand, he crawled toward the gun emplacement, moving across areas devoid of cover and under intense fire to within 15 yards when he threw the grenades, demolished the gun and killed the guncrew. With ammunition low and daybreak near, he ordered his men to dig in and hold the ground already won. Under constant fire from the front and from both flanks, he moved among them directing the preparations for the defense. Shortly after the ammunition supply was replenished, the Germans launched a last determined effort against the depleted group. Attacked by superior numbers from the front, right, and left flank, and even from the rear, the platoon, in bitter hand-to-hand engagements drove back the enemy at every point. Wounded in both feet by close-range machine pistol fire early in the battle, 2d Lt. Fisher refused medical attention. Unable to walk, he crawled from man to man encouraging them and checking each position. Only after the fighting had subsided did 2d Lt. Fisher crawl 300 yards to the aid station from which he was evacuated. His extraordinary heroism, magnificent valor, and aggressive determination in the face of point-blank enemy fire is an inspiration to his organization and reflects the finest traditions of the U.S. Armed Forces."

Source
Medal of Honor Citation.

Fluckey, Eugene Bennett (b. 1913) *Commander, United States Navy, commanding U.S.S.* Barb, *so distinguished himself in subsurface naval combat, during World War II, that he was awarded the Medal of Honor for his heroic actions.*

Born: October 5, 1913, Washington, D.C.; **Entered service at:** Illinois; **Place and date:** Along coast of China, December 19, 1944, to February 15, 1945. **Other United States Navy award:** Navy Cross with Three Gold Stars.

Citation: "For conspicuous gallantry and intrepidity at the risk of his life above and beyond the call of duty as commanding officer of the U.S.S. *Barb* during her 11th war patrol along the east coast of China from 19 December 1944 to 15 February 1945. After sinking a large enemy ammunition ship and damaging additional tonnage during a running 2-hour night battle on 8 January, Comdr. Fluckey, in an exceptional feat of brilliant deduction and bold tracking on 25 January, located a concentration of more than 30 enemy ships in the lower reaches of Nankuan Chiang (Mamkwan Harbor). Fully aware that a safe retirement would necessitate an hour's run at full speed through the uncharted, mined, and rock-obstructed waters, he bravely ordered, "Battle station—torpedoes!" In a daring penetration of the heavy enemy screen, and riding in 5 fathoms of water, he launched the *Barb's* last forward torpedoes at 3,000-yard range. Quickly bringing the ship's stern tubes to bear, he turned loose 4 more torpedoes into the enemy, obtaining 8 direct hits on 6 of the main targets to explode a large ammunition ship and cause inestimable damage by the resultant flying shells and other pyrotechnics. Clearning the treacherous area at high speed, he brought the *Barb* through to safety and 4 days later sank a large Japanese freighter to complete a record of heroic combat achievement, reflecting the highest credit upon Comdr. Fluckey, his gallant officers and men, and the U.S. Naval Service."

Source
Medal of Honor Citation.

Forrest, Nathan Bedford (1821–1877) *Civil War general, slave trader, planter.*

Born in Bedford County, Tennessee, Forrest received little formal education but learned to hold his own—and then some—in a violent frontier society. By ruthless drive and intelligence he made himself a planter and a slave trader.

At the outset of the Civil War, Forrest raised a cavalry battalion in the Confederate army. He led his men out of Fort Donelson just before its February 16, 1862, surrender and at the April 6–7 Battle of Shiloh was conspicuously aggressive, being severely wounded covering the Confederate retreat. That summer he led a cavalry brigade in a spectacular raid through middle Tennessee. Promoted to brigadier general July 21, he again raided behind federal lines in December, helping to defeat Gen. Ulysses S. Grant's first drive on Vicksburg.

In Alabama, in April 1863, he captured Col. Abel D. Streight's superior Union raiding force by bluff. At the Battle of Chickamauga, September 19–20, Forrest's troops opened the fighting. Afterward, he fell out with his army commander, General Braxton Bragg, was transferred to Mississippi, and was promoted to major general on December 4, 1863.

In April 1864 his troops at the Battle of Fort Pillow, Tennessee, stormed the fort, killing black Union soldiers as they attempted to surrender. In June, he routed a superior force under Samuel D. Sturgis at Brice's Cross Roads, Mississippi, but suffered defeat at Tupelo the following month. In November and December, Forrest commanded all the cavalry accompanying General John Bell Hood's ill-fated offensive into Tennessee and skillfully covered the Confederate retreat.

On February 28, 1865, Forrest was promoted to lieutenant general, but he and his command were worn out, and they faced a powerful federal mounted force under Gen. James H. Wilson driving into Alabama. Wilson defeated Forrest at Selma in April. After the war, Forrest returned to planting and served as the first grand wizard of the Ku Klux Klan.

His military usefulness in the Civil War was marred by his hot temper; he virtually required autonomy. Nevertheless, as the leader of a semi-independent mobile striking force, he has had few equals. He is also remembered for his alleged advice to commanders to "get there 'firstest' with the 'mostest.'"

Source and Additional Reading
Chambers, John Whiteclay II. *The Oxford Companion to American Military History.* New York: Oxford University Press, 1999.

Warner, Ezra J. *Generals in Gray: Lines of the Confederate Commanders.* Baton Rouge: Louisiana State University Press, 1959.

Wills, Brian Steel. *A Battle from the Start: The Life of Nathan Bedford Forrest.* New York: HarperCollins, 1992.

Wyeth, John Allan. *That Devil Forrest.* 1899. Reprint, Baton Rouge: Louisiana State University Press, 1989.

Fox, John R. (d. 1944) *First lieutenant, United States Army, so distinguished himself in combat, during World War II, that he was awarded the Medal of Honor for his heroic actions.*

Citation: "For extraordinary heroism against an armed enemy in the vicinity of Sommocolonia, Italy on 26 December 1944, while serving as a member of Cannon Company, 366th Infantry Regiment, 92d Infantry Division. During the proceeding few weeks, Lieutenant Fox served with the 598th Field Artillery Battalion as a forward observer. On Christmas night, enemy soldiers gradually infiltrated the town of Sommocolonia in civilian clothes, and by early morning the town was largely in hostile hands. Commencing with a heavy barrage of enemy artillery at 0400 hours on 26 December 1944, an organized attack by uniformed German units began. Being greatly outnumbered, most of the United States Infantry forces were forced to withdraw from the town, but Lieutenant Fox and some other members of his observer party voluntarily remained on the second floor of a house to direct defensive artillery fire. At 0800 hours, Lieutenant Fox reported that the Germans were in the streets and attacking in strength. He then called for defensive artillery fire to slow the enemy advance. As the Germans continued to press the attack towards the area that Lieutenant Fox occupied, he adjusted the artillery fire closer to his position. Finally he was warned that the next adjustment would bring the deadly artillery right on top of his position. After acknowledging the danger, Lieutenant Fox insisted that the last adjustment be fired as this was the only way to defeat the attacking soldiers. Later, when a counterattack retook the position from the Germans, Lieutenant Fox's body was found with the bodies of approximately 100 German soldiers. Lieutenant Fox's gallant and courageous actions, at the supreme sacrifice of his own life, contributed greatly to delaying the enemy advance until other infantry and artillery units could reorganize to repel the attack. His extraordinary valorous actions were in keeping with the most cherished traditions of military service, and reflect the utmost credit on him, his unit, and the United States Army."

Source
Medal of Honor Citation.

Fox, Wesley L. *Captain, United States Marine Corps, was the 48th Marine to be awarded the Medal of Honor for extraordinary heroism, while serving as commanding officer, Company A, First Battalion, Ninth Marines, Third Marine Division, in action against the enemy in the Republic of Vietnam, on February 22, 1969.*

Citation: "For conspicuous gallantry and intrepidity at the risk of his life above and beyond the call of duty while serving as commanding officer of Company A, in action against the enemy in the northern A Shau Valley. Capt. (then 1st Lt.) Fox's company came under intense fire from a large well-concealed enemy force. Capt. Fox maneuvered to a position from which he could assess the situation and confer with his platoon leaders. As they departed to execute the plan he had devised, the enemy attacked and Capt. Fox was wounded along with all of the other members of the command group, except the executive officer. Capt. Fox continued to direct the activity of his company. Advancing through heavy enemy fire, he personally neutralized 1 enemy position and calmly ordered an assault against the hostile emplacements. He then moved through the hazardous area coordinating aircraft

Wesley L. Fox

support with the activities of his men. When his executive officer was mortally wounded, Capt. Fox reorganized the company and directed the fire of his men as they hurled grenades against the enemy and drove the hostile forces into retreat. Wounded again in the final assault, Capt. Fox refused medical attention, established a defensive posture, and supervised the preparation of casualties for medical evacuation. His indomitable courage, inspiring initiative, and unwavering devotion to duty in the face of grave personal danger inspired his Marines to such aggressive action that they overcame all enemy resistance and destroyed a large bunker complex. Capt. Fox's heroic actions reflect great credit upon himself and the Marine Corps, and uphold the highest traditions of the U.S. Naval Service."

Sources
Headquarters Marine Corps, Historical Center.
Medal of Honor Citation.

Frémont, John Charles (1813–1890) *Union general officer.*

Born in Savannah, Georgia, on January 21, 1813, Frémont was one four major generals appointed by President Lincoln, certainly the most celebrated. Frémont's major Civil War contribution as a Union general was more political than military when he focused Union attention on the role emancipation should play in the North's war policy.

The magnetic and legendary "Pathfinder" became a national hero early in life for his trail-blazing exploits in the Far West. A leader in wresting California from Mexico, he served as one of the state's first senators and got rich in the gold rush. Frémont's popularity and his antislavery position were equally instrumental in his being chosen the Republican Party's first presidential nominee in 1856, the youngest man yet to run for the office. With southern states' threatening secession if he were elected, Frémont's loss to James Buchanan forestalled dissolution of the union for another four years.

In Europe at the outbreak of the Civil War, he purchased a cache of arms in England for the North on his own initiative and returned to America. Abraham Lincoln, mainly for political reasons, appointed him major general in May 1861, placing him in command of the precarious Department of the West. Based in St. Louis, Fremont spent more energy fortifying the city and developing flashy guard units than equipping the troops in the field. His forces suffered several losses, particularly a major defeat at Wilson's Creek that August. Attempting to gain a political advantage in the absence of a military one, Fremont, in an unprecedented and unauthorized move, issued a startling proclamation at the end of the month declaring martial law in Missouri and ordering that secessionists' property be confiscated and their slaves emancipated. The action was cheered by antislavery Republicans, but Lincoln, concerned that linking abolition to the war effort would destroy Union support throughout the slave-holding border states, asked Fremont at the very least to modify the order.

The Pathfinder refused, sending his wife, the politically influential daughter of the former Senate leader Thomas Hart Benton, to Washington to talk to the president. Displeased with Frémont's effrontery, Lincoln revoked the proclamation altogether and removed him from command. Pressure from his fellow Republicans forced Lincoln to give the popular Frémont another appointment, and in March 1862 he was named head of the army's new Mountain Department, serving in Western Virginia. Over the following two months, he endured several crushing losses against Thomas "Stonewall" Jackson during the Confederate general's brilliantly successful Shenandoah Valley Campaign. After a military reorganization placed him under the command of a former subordinate, John Pope, Frémont angrily resigned his post, never to receive another Civil War appointment.

In 1864, however, he began another presidential bid with the backing of a cadre of Radical Republicans but withdrew from the race in September and threw his support to Lincoln after a rapprochement in the party. When he lost most of his fortune by the end of the war, Frémont tried the railroad industry. His reputation damaged by an 1873 conviction for his role in a swindle, he nevertheless resumed his political career, and later in the decade he began serving as territorial governor of Arizona but depended on his wife's income from writing during most of his later years. He died in New York City, July 13, 1890.

Source and Additional Reading
Frémont, John Charles. "The Conquest of California." *Century Magazine,* April 1890.
———. *Memoirs of My Life.* New York: Belford, Clarke & Co., 1887.
Goodwin, Cardinal. *John C. Frémont, An Explanation of His Career.* New York: Macmillan, 1930.

Funk, Leonard A., Jr. *First sergeant, United States Army, Company C, 508th Parachute Infantry, 82d Airborne Division, so distinguished himself in combat during World War II that he was awarded the Medal of Honor for his heroic actions.*

Born: Braddock Township, Pa.; **Entered service at:** Wilkinsburg, Pa.; **Place and date:** Holzheim, Belgium, January 29, 1945. **G.O. No.:** 75, September 5, 1945.

Citation: "He distinguished himself by gallant, intrepid actions against the enemy. After advancing 15 miles in a

Leonard A. Funk Jr.

driving snowstorm, the American force prepared to attack through waist-deep drifts. The company executive officer became a casualty, and 1st Sgt. Funk immediately assumed his duties, forming headquarters soldiers into a combat unit for an assault in the face of direct artillery shelling and harassing fire from the right flank. Under his skillful and courageous leadership, this miscellaneous group and the 3d Platoon attacked 15 houses, cleared them, and took 30 prisoners without suffering a casualty. The fierce drive of Company C quickly overran Holzheim, netting some 80 prisoners, who were placed under a 4-man guard, all that could be spared, while the rest of the understrength unit went about mopping up isolated points of resistance. An enemy patrol, by means of a ruse, succeeded in capturing the guards and freeing the prisoners, and had begun preparations to attack Company C from the rear when 1st Sgt. Funk walked around the building and into their midst. He was ordered to surrender by a German officer who pushed a machine pistol into his stomach. Although overwhelmingly outnumbered and facing almost certain death, 1st Sgt. Funk, pretending to comply with the order, began slowly to unsling his submachine gun from his shoulder and then, with lightning motion, brought the muzzle into line and riddled the German officer. He turned upon the other Germans, firing and shouting to the other Americans to seize the enemy's weapons. In the ensuing fight 21 Germans were killed, many wounded, and the remainder captured. 1st Sgt. Funk's bold action and heroic disregard for his own safety were directly responsible for the recapture of a vastly superior enemy force, which, if allowed to remain free, could have taken the widespread units of Company C by surprise and endangered the entire attack plan."

Source
Medal of Honor Citation.

G

★ ✫ ★ ✫

Gaffney, Frank *Private first class, United States Army, Company G, 108th Infantry, 27th Division, distinguished himself in combat in September 1918 and was awarded the Medal of Honor for his heroic actions.*

Born: Buffalo, N.Y.; **Entered service at:** Niagara Falls, N.Y.; **Place and date:** Near Ronssoy, France, September 29, 1918. **G.O. No.:** 20, W.D., 1919.

Citation: "Pfc. Gaffney, an automatic rifleman, pushing forward, alone, after all the other members of his squad had been killed, discovered several Germans placing a heavy machine-gun in position. He killed the crew, captured the gun, bombed several dugouts, and, after killing 4 more of the enemy with his pistol, held the position until reinforcements came up, when 80 prisoners were captured."

Source
Medal of Honor Citation.

Gall (Pizi) (1840–1894)

Chief Gall was a famous Lakota Sioux warrior who fought in the Battle of the Little Bighorn (1876), in which Gen. George Armstrong Custer and the entire Seventh Cavalry were killed. He was a leader in the Hunkpapa section of the Sioux encampment, which was the focal point of Custer's attack. Gall had played a vital role in the forced retreat of 1868, which confined the Native Americans to a reservation, and with Sitting Bull and Crazy Horse led Indian attempts to thwart the construction of forts and roads through the Lakota Sioux buffalo country. After Little Bighorn, Gall and Sitting Bull retreated into Canada. After a dispute with Sitting Bull, Gall returned to the United States with part of the Hunkpapa band in early 1881. After a brief battle with Gen. Nelson A. Miles he was taken as a prisoner to Fort Buford.

He was released (June 1881) to the Standing Rock Indian Reservation in South Dakota, where he cultivated land and attempted to live up to treaty agreements. He converted to Christianity and is said to have attended church carrying his weapons and painted as if for a war council.

Source and Additional Reading
Fox, R.A. Jr. *Archaeology, History, and Custer's Last Battle.* Norman; University of Oklahoma Press, 1993.
Marquis, Thomas. *Sitting Bull and Gall.* Scottsdale, Ariz.: Cactus Pony; 1934.

Garman, Harold A. (b. 1918) *Private United States Army, Company B, Fifth Medical Battalion, Fifth Infantry Division, so distinguished himself in combat, during World War II, that he was awarded the Medal of Honor for his heroic actions.*

Born: February 26, 1918, Fairfield, Ill.; **Entered service at:** Albion, Ill.; **Place and date:** Near Montereau, France, August 25, 1944. **G.O. No.:** March 29, 1945.

Citation: "For conspicuous gallantry and intrepidity at the risk of his life above and beyond the call of duty. On 25 August 1944, in the vicinity of Montereau, France, the enemy was sharply contesting any enlargement of the bridgehead that our forces had established on the northern bank of the Seine River in this sector. Casualties were being evacuated to the southern shore in assault boats paddled by litter bearers from a medical battalion. Pvt. Garman, also a litter bearer in this battalion, was working on the friendly shore carrying the wounded from the boats to waiting ambulances. As 1 boatload of wounded reached midstream, a German machinegun suddenly opened fire upon it from a commanding position on the northern bank 100 yards away. All of the men in the boat immediately took to the water except 1 man who was so badly wounded he could not rise from his litter. Two other patients who were unable to swim because of their wounds clung to the sides of the boat. Seeing the extreme danger of these patients, Pvt. Garman without a moment's hesitation plunged into the Seine. Swimming directly into a hail of machinegun bullets, he rapidly reached the assault boat and then while still under accurately aimed fire towed the boat with great effort to the southern shore. This soldier's moving heroism not only saved the lives of the three patients but so inspired his comrades that additional assault boats were immediately procured and the evacuation of the wounded resumed. Pvt. Garman's great courage and his heroic devotion to the highest tenets of the Medical Corps may be written with great pride in the annals of the corps."

Source
Medal of Honor Citation.

Gates, Horatio (1727–1806) *Revolutionary War general.*

Horatio Gates was an American general who won the Battle of Saratoga, perhaps the most significant engagement of the American Revolution.

Born in England on July 26, 1727, he entered the British army and served in America during the French and Indian War (1754–63). Retiring on half-pay, he immigrated to America in 1772 and bought a Virginia plantation. Gates became adjutant general of the Continental Army in 1775. Promoted to major general in 1776, he was placed in command of the northern army. On October 17, 1777, General John Burgoyne surrendered his army to Gates at Saratoga after two fierce battles. Saratoga proved to be a turning point in the war, for it convinced France to become America's ally.

Gates was appointed president of the Board of War in 1777. The alleged object of the Conway Cabal of that year was to replace George Washington with Gates as commander in chief, but there is little evidence of a real conspiracy.

Taking command of the southern army in 1780, Gates was disastrously defeated at Camden, South Carolina on August 16, by General Charles Cornwallis. Retiring to his Virginia plantation, Gates returned to active duty in 1782 at Newburgh, New York. Leaving the army in 1783, he eventually moved to Manhattan Island, where he died on April 10, 1806.

Source and Additional Reading
Mintz, Max M. *Generals of Saratoga: John Burgoyne and Horatio Gates.* New Haven, Conn.: Yale University Press, 1990.

Nelson, Paul D. *Horatio Gates.* Baton Rouge: Louisiana State University Press, 1976.

Geiger, Roy S. (1885–1947) *General officer, United States Marine Corps.*

Born in Middleburg, Florida, on January 25, 1885, Geiger graduated from John B. Stetson University in 1907. He briefly practiced law before enlisting in the Marine Corps in November 1907. Commissioned a Second lieutenant in 1909, he was promoted to First lieutenant after service at sea and in the Caribbean area, the Philippines, and China in 1915.

As a captain, he was the fifth Marine Corps officer to complete pilot training in 1917, and as a major he commanded a squadron in the First Marine Aviation Force in France, flying numerous bombing mission from July to November 1918. Stationed in Haiti from 1919 to 1921, he commanded the First Aviation Group, Third Marine Brigade, at Quantico, Virginia, from 1921 to 1924. Geiger graduated from the army's Command and General Staff School in 1925 and entered the Army War College in 1929. Promoted to lieutenant colonel in 1934, Geiger commanded Marine Air Group One, First Marine Brigade, from 1931 to 1935. Promoted to brigadier later that year, he was placed in command of the First Marine Air Wing, Fleet Marine Force, and led the Air Wing on Guadalcanal, headquartered at Henderson Field, from September 1942 to February 1943. Promoted to major general, he returned to Washington, D.C., and was assigned as director, Division of Aviation, until November 1943.

General Geiger succeeded Gen. Alexander A. Vandegrift as commander of First Amphibious Corps and led that unit in the invasion of Guam. He directed the Battle of Peleliu and led his corps on Okinawa as part of Gen. Simon B. Buckner's 10th Army. He briefly commanded the 10th Army after General Buckner was killed and before United States Army Gen. Joseph W. Stilwell took over, thus becoming the first, and only, Marine officer to command a field army.

General Geiger returned to Washington, D.C., in November 1946 and fell seriously ill before his scheduled retirement. He died at Bethesda Naval Hospital on January 23, 1947.

Congress posthumously gave him the honorary rank of general in July 1947.

A brave, tenacious, and aggressive commander, Geiger directed some of the fiercest fighting of World War II on Peleliu and Okinawa.

Source and Additional Reading
Frank, Benis M., and Henry I. Shaw. *History of the United States Marine Corps in World War II.* 5 vols. Washington, D.C., 1958–68.

Geronimo (1829–1909) (Jerome, Goyathlay, "One Who Yawns") *Apache leader, who led Native American raids in Mexico and the United States.*

To North Americans and to Mexicans of the 1870s and 1880s, Geronimo personalized the horrors of Apache warfare. Never a chief, and despised by many of his own people, he nonetheless attained leadership through mastery of the partisan fighting style that baffled U.S. and Mexican troops. In cunning, stealth, endurance, perseverance, ruthlessness, fortitude, fighting skill, and command of the harsh conditions of his homeland he excelled.

Geronimo was born in June 1829, into the Nednis Apache tribe at Nodoyohn Canyon, Arizona. After Mexicans killed his mother, wife, and children, he led reprisal raids into Mexican territory. With small followings, he alternated between reservation life in Arizona and raids from Mexico's Sierra Madre. In 1882, Brigadier General George Crook, relying heavily on Apache scouts and pack mules, penetrated the Sierra Madre and obtained Geronimo's surrender. In 1885, however, Geronimo again took refuge in Mexico. Again Crook and his scouts pursued, and again Geronimo surrendered. But he had second thoughts and fled into the mountains.

Crook, his methods under fire from Washington, D.C., asked to be relieved. Brig. Gen. Nelson A. Miles, along with 5,000 U.S. troops and 500 Native American scouts, took up the chase but eventually had to adopt Crook's unorthodox approach.

With only 35 warriors and over 100 women and children, Geronimo kept the United States Army at bay for over five months. He outfought and outmaneuvered General Miles and his men through Arizona and New Mexico.

Geronimo finally surrendered to Miles at Skeleton Canyon, Arizona, on September 4, 1886. Confined in Florida, Alabama, and finally near Fort Sill, Oklahoma, he became a celebrity in parades and expositions, appearing at the Louisiana Purchase Exposition in St. Louis in 1904 and in Theodore Roosevelt's inaugural parade in 1905. Geronimo became a Christian and took up farming. He dictated his autobiography in 1906. He died of pneumonia on February 17, 1909, at Fort Sill.

Geronimo was a courageous, resolute, intelligent, and skilled leader and an excellent strategist and tactician. His campaigns serve as classic examples of highly mobile, hit-and-run guerrilla tactics.

Source

Debo, Angie. *Geronimo: The Man, His Time, His Place.* Norman: University of Oklahoma Press, 1976.

Gibson, Eric G. (d. 1944) *Technician fifth grade, United States Army, Third Infantry Division, so distinguished*

himself in combat during World War II that he was awarded (posthumously) the Medal of Honor for his heroic actions.

Born: Nysund, Sweden; **Entered service at:** Chicago, Ill., **Place and date:** Near Isola Bella, Italy, January 28, 1944. **G.O. No.:** 74, September 11, 1944.

Citation: "For conspicuous gallantry and intrepidity at risk of life above and beyond the call of duty. On 28 January 1944, near Isola Bella, Italy, Tech. 5th Grade Gibson, company cook, led a squad of replacements through their initial baptism of fire, and destroyed four enemy positions, killed 5 and captured 2 German soldiers, and secured the left flank of his company during an attack on a strongpoint. Placing himself 50 yards in front of his new men, Gibson advanced down the wide stream ditch known as the Fossa Femminamorta, keeping pace with the advance of his company. An enemy soldier allowed Tech. 5th Grade Gibson to come within 20 yards of his concealed position and then opened fire on him with a machine pistol. Despite the stream of automatic fire which barely missed him, Gibson charged the position, firing his submachine gun every few steps. Reaching the position, Gibson fired pointblank at his opponent, killing him. An artillery concentration fell in and around the ditch; the concussion from one shell knocked him flat. As he got to his feet Gibson was fired on by two soldiers armed with a machine pistol and a rifle from a position only 75 yards distant. Gibson immediately raced toward the foe. Halfway to the position a machinegun opened fire on him. Bullets came within inches of his body, yet Gibson never paused in his forward movement. He killed one and captured the other soldier. Shortly after, when a heavy machinegun 200 yards down the ditch fired him upon, Gibson crawled back to his squad and ordered it to lay down a base of fire while he flanked the emplacement. Despite all warning, Gibson crawled 125 yards through an artillery concentration and the cross fire of 2 machineguns which showered dirt over his body, threw 2 hand grenades into the emplacement and charged it with his submachine gun, killing 2 of the enemy and capturing a third. Before leading his men around a bend in the stream ditch, Gibson went forward alone to reconnoiter. Hearing an exchange of machine pistol and submachine gun fire, Gibson's squad went forward to find that its leader had run 35 yards toward an outpost, killed the machine pistol man, and had himself been killed while firing at the Germans."

Source

Medal of Honor Citation.

Gilmore, Howard Walter (1902–1943) *Commander, United States Navy, so distinguished himself in subsurface* *naval combat, during World War II, that he was awarded (posthumously) the Medal of Honor for his heroic actions.*

Born: September 29, 1902, Selma, Ala.; **Entered service at:** Louisiana. **Other United States Navy award:** Navy Cross with one gold star.

Citation: "For distinguished gallantry and valor above and beyond the call of duty as commanding officer of the U.S.S. *Growler* during her Fourth War Patrol in the Southwest Pacific from 10 January to 7 February 1943. Boldly striking at the enemy in spite of continuous hostile air and antisubmarine patrols, Comdr. Gilmore sank one Japanese freighter and damaged another by torpedo fire, successfully evading severe depth charges following each attack. In the darkness of night on 7 February, an enemy gunboat closed range and prepared to ram the *Growler*. Comdr. Gilmore daringly maneuvered to avoid the crash and rammed the attacker instead, ripping into her port side at 11 knots and bursting wide her plates. In the terrific fire of the sinking gunboat's heavy machine-guns, Comdr. Gilmore calmly gave the order to clear the bridge, and refusing safety for himself, remained on deck while his men preceded him below. Struck down by the fusillade of bullets and having done his utmost against the enemy, in his final living moments, Comdr. Gilmore gave his last order to the officer of the deck, "Take her down." The *Growler* dived; seriously damaged but under control, she was brought safely to port by her welltrained crew inspired by the courageous fighting spirit of their dead captain."

Source
Medal of Honor Citation.

Gordon, Gary I. (d. 1993) *Master sergeant, United States Army, so distinguished himself in combat in Somalia, in 1993, that he was awarded (posthumously) the Medal of Honor for his heroic actions.*

Born: Lincoln, Maine; **Place and date:** October 3, 1993, Mogadishu, Somalia.

Citation: "Master Sergeant Gordon, United States Army, distinguished himself by actions above and beyond the call of duty on 3 October 1993, while serving as Sniper Team Leader, United States Army Special Operations Command with Task Force Ranger in Mogadishu, Somalia. Master Sergeant Gordon's sniper team provided precision fires from the lead helicopter during an assault and at two helicopter crash sites, while subjected to intense automatic weapons and rocket propelled grenade fires. When Master Sergeant Gordon learned that ground forces were not immediately available to secure the second crash site, he and another sniper unhesitatingly volunteered to be

inserted to protect the four critically wounded personnel, despite being well aware of the growing number of enemy personnel closing in on the site. After his third request to be inserted, Master Sergeant Gordon received permission to perform his volunteer mission. When debris and enemy ground fires at the site caused them to abort the first attempt, Master Sergeant Gordon was inserted one hundred meters south of the crash site. Equipped with only his sniper rifle and a pistol, Master Sergeant Gordon and his fellow sniper, while under intense small arms fire from the enemy, fought their way through a dense maze of shanties and shacks to reach the critically injured crewmembers. Master Sergeant Gordon immediately pulled the pilot and the other crewmembers from the aircraft, establishing a perimeter, which placed him and his fellow sniper in the most vulnerable position. Master Sergeant Gordon used his long-range rifle and side arm to kill an undetermined number of attackers until he depleted his ammunition. Master Sergeant Gordon then went back to the wreckage, recovering some of the crew's weapons and ammunition. Despite the fact that he was critically low on ammunition, he provided some of it to the dazed pilot and then radioed for help. Master Sergeant Gordon continued to travel the perimeter, protecting the downed crew. After his team member was fatally wounded and his own rifle ammunition exhausted, Master Sergeant Gordon returned to the wreckage, recovering a rifle with the last five rounds of ammunition and gave it to the pilot with the words, "good luck." Then, armed only with his pistol, Master Sergeant Gordon continued to fight until he was fatally wounded. His actions saved the pilot's life. Master Sergeant Gordon's extraordinary heroism and devotion to duty were in keeping with the highest standards of military service and reflect great credit upon him, his unit and the United States Army."

Source
Medal of Honor Citation.

Gordon, John Brown (1832–1904) *General, Confederate States Army.*

Born in Upson City, Georgia, February 6, 1832, he attended the University of Georgia but dropped out to study law and become a member of the Atlanta Bar. A civilian turned soldier, John B. Gordon became a trusted corps commander under Lee in the final days of the Confederacy. Involved in the coal industry in his native Georgia, Gordon raised the Raccoon Roughs (a state militia) for the southern cause.

His assignments included captain, Company One, Sixth Alabama (May 1861); major Sixth Alabama (ca. May 14, 1861); colonel, Sixth Alabama (April 28, 1862); commander, Rodes's brigade, D.H. Hill's division, Department of the Virginia (May 31–June and July 1862); brigadier general, Confederates States Army (CSA) (November 1, 1862; not confirmed and reappointed May 7, 1863); commander Lawton's (old) brigade, Early's division, Second Corps, Army of Northern Virginia (April 11, 1863–May 8, 1864); commander of the division (May 8–21, 1864); major general, CSA (May 14, 1864); commander Johnson's (old) division, Second Crops, Army of Northern Virginia (May 21–June 13, 1864); commander, Johnson's (old) division, Valley District, Department of Northern Virginia (June 13–December 1864); and commander, Second Corps, Army of Northern Virginia (December 1864–April 9, 1865).

Having fought at First Bull Run, he was elected colonel on the regiment's reorganization and led it at Williamsburg. At Seven Pines he distinguished himself when he assumed command of the brigade. He fought through the Seven Days, part of the time in brigade command. He led the regiment at Antietam, where he was wounded in the head and lived to relate how a hole in his cap from a bullet earlier in the day had saved him from drowning in his own blood, which had accumulated in it. Recovering, he was given command of a Georgia brigade with which he fought at Chancellorsville and Gettysburg. At the latter he aided a wounded Union general, Francis C. Barlow, whom he met, decades later, each thinking the other had died in the war. They were friends until Barlow's death. Gordon received Lee's praise for planning a successful attack on the Union at the Wilderness, and two days later Lee juggled a number of commands so that Gordon could lead Early's division. At Spotsylvania, Gordon earned permanent promotion to major general and was soon given the remnants of Johnson's former division plus his own Georgia brigade. This unit he led at Cold Harbor and in the Shenandoah Valley Campaign, during which he was sometimes in charge of an informal corps. He saw action at Monocacy, on the outskirts of Washington, at Third Winchester, Fisher's Hill, and Cedar Creek. Rejoining Lee in the trenches at Petersburg, he directed the corps and planned the attack on Fort Stedman. At Appomattox his men made the last charge of the Army of Northern Virginia.

It is often claimed that he was a lieutenant general, but Gordon himself is silent on the matter in his *Reminiscences of the Civil War,* in which he recounts each of his other promotions. He went on to a distinguished career in politics, serving as governor and senator and was active in veterans' affairs. He died in Miami, Florida, January 9, 1904, and was buried in Oakland Cemetery, Atlanta, Georgia.

Sources

Tankersley, Allen P. *John B. Gordon: A Study in Gallantry.* Atlanta, Ga.: Whitehall Press, 1955.

Gordon, Nathan Green (1916–1944) *Lieutenant, United States Navy, commander of Catalina patrol plane, so distinguished himself in aerial combat, during World War II, that he was awarded the Medal of Honor for his heroic actions.*

Born: September 4, 1916, Morrilton, Ark.; **Entered service at:** Arkansas; **Place and date:** Bismarck Sea, February 15, 1944.

Citation: "For extraordinary heroism above and beyond the call of duty as commander of a Catalina patrol plane in rescuing personnel of the U.S. Army 5th Air Force shot down in combat over Kavieng Harbor in the Bismarck Sea, 15 February 1944. On air alert in the vicinity of Vitu Islands, Lt. (then Lt. jg.) Gordon unhesitatingly responded to a report of the crash and flew boldly into the harbor, defying close-range fire from enemy shore guns to make 3 separate landings in full view of the Japanese and pick up 9 men, several of them injured. With his cumbersome flying boat dangerously overloaded, he made a brilliant takeoff despite heavy swells and almost total absence of wind and set a course for base, only to receive the report of another group stranded in a rubber life raft 600 yards from the enemy shore. Promptly turning back, he again risked his life to set his plane down under direct fire of the heaviest defenses of Kavieng and take aboard 6 more survivors, coolly making his fourth dexterous takeoff with 15 rescued officers and men. By his exceptional daring, personal valor, and incomparable airmanship under most perilous conditions, Lt. Gordon prevented certain death or capture of our airmen by the Japanese."

Source
Medal of Honor Citation.

Grant, Ulysses Simpson (1822–1885) *General, United States Army.*

The best evidence of the changes that had occurred in warfare from Jomini to Clausewitz can be found in the campaigns of Robert E. Lee and Ulysses S. Grant. The latter was born Hiram Ulysses Grant in Ohio, but through confusion at West Point he became Ulysses Simpson Grant. Appointed to the military academy, he found it distasteful and hoped that Congress would abolish the institution, freeing him. He excelled only in horsemanship, for which he had displayed a capability early in life and graduated in 1843, 21st of 39 graduates. Posted to the Fourth, Infantry, since there were no vacancies in the dragoons, he served as regimental quartermaster during most of the Mexican War. Nonetheless he frequently led a company in combat under Zachary Taylor in northern Mexico.

He came to admire his chief greatly but was transferred with his regiment to Winfield Scott's army, operating from the coast. He received brevets for Molino del Rey and Chapultepec. With the resumption of peace he was for a time stationed in Mexico, a country that he admired then was posted to the West Coast. Separated from his wife, he tried numerous business ventures to raise enough capital to bring her to the coast but proved singularly unsuccessful. On July 31, 1854, he resigned his captaincy amid rumors of heavy drinking and warnings of possible disciplinary action by his post commander.

His return to civilian life proved unsuccessful. Farming on his father-in-law's land was a failure, as were his real estate business and attempts to gain engineering and clerk posts in St. Louis. He finally became a clerk in a family leather goods store in Galena, which was run by his two younger brothers. Before he had been there long the Civil War broke out. Offering his services to the War Department and to Gen. George B. McClellan in Ohio, he met with no success in gaining an appointment.

After organizing and mustering state volunteers and with the aid of a local congressman, Elihu B. Washburne, he got his second military career off to a start. His assignments included colonel, 21st Illinois (June 17, 1861); brigadier general, United States Volunteers (USV) (July

Ulysses Simpson Grant

31, 1861, to rank from May 17); commander, District of Ironton, Western Department (August 8–21, 1861); commander, United States Forces, Jefferson City, Western Department (August 21–28, 1861); commander, Post of Cape Girardeau, Western Department (August 30–September 1, 1861); commander, District of Southeast Missouri, Western Department (September 1–November 9, 1861); commander, District of Southeast Missouri, Department of the Missouri (November 9–December 23, 1861); commander, District of Cairo, Department of the Missouri (December 23, 1861–February 21, 1862); major general, USV (February 16, 1862); commander, District of West Tennessee, Department of the Missouri (February 21–March 11, 1862); commander, District of West Tennessee, Department of the Mississippi (March 11–April 29 and June 10–October 16, 1862); second in command, Department of the Mississippi (April 29–June 10, 1862); commander Army and Department of the Tennessee (October 16, 1862–October 24, 1863); also commander, 13th Corps, Army of the Tennessee (October 24–December 18, 1862); major general, USV (July 4, 1863); commander, Military Division of the Mississippi (October 18, 1863–March 18, 1864); lieutenant general, USA (March 2, 1864); commander in chief, United States Army (March 12, 1864–March 4, 1869); general, USA (July 25, 1866); secretary of war ad interim (August 17, 1867–January 14, 1868); and president of the United States (March 4, 1869–March 4, 1877).

When Kentucky's fragile neutrality was disintegrating, Grant moved quickly from his Cairo, Illinois, base to take Paducah, Kentucky, at the mouth of the Tennessee River. His subsequent action at Belmont, Missouri, turned into a defeat after early success. In a joint operation with the navy his land forces arrived too late to take part in the capture of Fort Henry, but at neighboring. Fort Donelson a major engagement was fought by the ground forces, defeating a Confederate breakout attempt. His reply when asked for terms earned him the nickname "Unconditional Surrender" Grant. He got in hot water with his superior, Henry W. Halleck, for reports that were not filed and his unauthorized trip to Nashville. Ordered to remain at Fort Henry while his forces advanced up the Tennessee, he was restored to field command after the injury of Gen. Charles F. Smith. Surprised by the Confederate attack at Shiloh—William T. Sherman was in charge on the field at the time—Grant recovered to score a major victory on the second day.

Again in trouble with Halleck, he was demoted to second in command of Halleck's field army in the slow advance on Corinth, Mississippi. Subsequently restored to command, he was thwarted in his attempt to reach Vicksburg by following the railroads through central Mississippi when his supply base at Holly Spring was destroyed by Confederate cavalry. Over the next months he tried various routes to get at the river city but did not launch his final thrust until late April 1863. In a brilliant manner he shifted his troops south of the city and advanced on Jackson to defeat Joseph E. Johnston before scoring two victories over Pemberton at Champion's Hill and Big Black River Bridge—and finally besieging Vicksburg. With the July 4, 1863, capitulation of the city he was awarded a major generalcy in the regular army. His return was complete.

After some minor operations in Mississippi he was given charge of all the armies in the West and raised the siege of Chattanooga and sent Sherman to raise that of Knoxville. That winter he was appointed to the recreated grade of lieutenant general and given command of all the Union armies. He also received the thanks of Congress. Making his headquarters with George G. Meade's Army of the Potomac, he hammered away at Lee—the devout follower of Jomini—in his Overland Campaign. Despite heavy losses at the Wilderness, Spotsylvania, and Cold Harbor, Grant kept going. His attack at the latter was one of two movements he wished he had never ordered (the other was at Vicksburg). Swinging south of Richmond he besieged Petersburg and after a 10-month siege took both cities. Pursuing Lee to Appomattox, he had virtually ended the war. Meanwhile, the other armies under his direction had torn the Confederacy apart.

In the postwar reorganization of the army he was promoted to full general in 1866 and oversaw the military portion of Reconstruction and the reduction of the army. During Andrew Johnson's fight with the Radical Republicans in Congress Grant was in an awkward position. He was ordered to replace the suspended Edwin M. Stanton as secretary of war, in violation of the Tenure of Office Act. He weathered the storm and became the party's nominee for president in 1868. Elected, he served two terms, during which, although he personally remained untainted, there were many scandals, especially in relation to the Whiskey Tax and the appointment of Indian agents. Despite Grant's interest in creating a peace with the Native Americans, Custer's Massacre occurred during his tenure. Also the freedmen lost much ground during his term, as the white supremacists regained control in the southern states. During his term problems with England that had arisen during the Civil War, were resolved, and an attempt to gain Santo Domingo for the United States failed. Thwarted for a third term, he embarked on a two-year tour around the world, which took on the appearance of a political campaign. Denied renomination in 1880, he was involved in a number of unsuccessful ventures, the worst of which—in the brokerage firm of Grant & Ward—wiped him out. He then wrote *Personal Memoirs of U.S. Grant,* while dying of cancer of the throat. His family realized profits on the book of almost $450,000. Shortly before his death at Mount McGregor, New York, on July 23, 1885, he had been placed on the retired list with the rank of general in order to ease his financial situation. His remains lie in a mausoleum on Riverside Drive in New York City.

Source and Additional Reading

Catton, Bruce. *Grant Moves South.* Boston: Little, Brown, 1960.

Dupuy, Trevor N., Curt Johnson, and David L. Bongard. *The Harper Encyclopedia of Military Biography.* New York HarperCollins, 1992.

Fuller, F. C. *The Generalship of Ulysses S. Grant.* IN, 1929. Reprint, New York: DaCapo, 1991.

Simon, John Y. *The Papers of Ulysses S. Grant.* 5 Vols. Carbondale and Edwardsville, Ill.: Southern Illinois University Press, 1970.

Gray, Ross Franklin (b. 1920) *Sergeant, U.S. Marine Corps Reserve, so distinguished himself in combat, on Iwo Jima, that he was awarded (posthumously) the Medal of Honor for his heroic actions.*

Born: August 1920, Marvel Valley, Ala.; **Entered service at:** Alabama.

Citation: "For conspicuous gallantry and intrepidity at the risk of his life above and beyond the call of duty as a Platoon Sergeant attached to Company A, 1st Battalion, 25th Marines, 4th Marine Division, in action against enemy Japanese forces on Iwo Jima, Volcano Islands, 21 February 1945. Shrewdly gauging the tactical situation when his platoon was held up by a sudden barrage of hostile grenades while advancing toward the high ground northeast of Airfield No. 1, Sgt. Gray promptly organized the withdrawal of his men from enemy grenade range, quickly moved forward alone to reconnoiter and discovered a heavily mined area extending along the front of a strong network of emplacements joined by covered trenches. Although assailed by furious gunfire, he cleared a path leading through the minefield to one of the fortifications, then returned to the platoon position and, informing his leader of the serious situation, volunteered to initiate an attack under cover of 3 fellow Marines. Alone and unarmed but carrying a huge satchel charge, he crept up on the Japanese emplacement, boldly hurled the short-fused explosive and sealed the entrance. Instantly taken under machinegun fire from a second entrance to the same position, he unhesitatingly braved the increasingly vicious fusillades to crawl back for another charge, returned to his objective and blasted the second opening, thereby demolishing the position. Repeatedly covering the ground between the savagely defended enemy fortifications and his platoon area, he systematically approached, attacked and withdrew under blanketing fire to destroy a total of 6 Japanese positions, more than 25 troops and a quantity of vital ordnance gear and ammunition. Stouthearted and indomitable, Sgt. Gray had single-handedly overcome a strong enemy garrison and had completely disarmed a large minefield before finally rejoining his unit. By his great personal valor, daring tactics and tenacious perseverance in the face of extreme peril, he had contributed materially to the fulfillment of his company mission. His gallant conduct throughout enhanced and sustained the highest traditions of the U.S. Naval Service."

Source

Medal of Honor Citation.

Greene, Nathanael (1742–1786) *Continental Army major general who was an aide and confidant of General George Washington.*

Greene was born in Warwick, Rhode Island, on August 7, 1742, the son of a prosperous Quaker farmer and ironmaster. His leadership in the later stages of the campaign in the South proved him to be a great general, second in ability only to Washington and in some ways at least his equal.

Greene had little formal schooling, but he was an avid reader, and under the guidance of Ezra Stiles, a clergyman, later president of Yale College, he acquired a good education.

In 1770, Greene moved to Coventry, Rhode Island, to manage his father's forge. He served in the Rhode Island Assembly from 1770 to 1772 and again in 1775. He was expelled from the Quaker meeting in 1773 for attending a military parade. In 1776 he participated in the defense of New York City, was promoted to major general, and, in December, played an important role in Washington's surprise attack on Trenton. During 1777–78 he worked closely with Washington at Morristown, Brandywine, Germantown, Valley Forge, and Monmouth. He was appointed quartermaster general in 1778 and served in that position until 1780.

Foreseeing trouble between the American colonies and Britain, Greene helped to organize a local military company in 1774. He suffered from a stiff knee, which caused a slight limp, and because of this the company felt that he should not be an officer. He served as a private.

In May 1775, after the outbreak of the Revolution, the Rhode Island Assembly authorized the raising of a force of 1,500 soldiers, and Greene was named brigadier in command. In early June the brigade joined Washington's army besieging Boston. Greene served through the siege and then was sent by Washington to take charge of the defenses of New York City pending his arrival.

After the Battle of Long Island (August 27–28, 1776), during which he was seriously ill, Greene advised that the Americans should retreat from New York to prevent being trapped on Manhattan Island by the British. His advice was not taken, and the army had a narrow escape. Washington had come to depend on Greene, and their relationship soon became confidential. Before long, Greene was virtually second in command. He took an active part in all the army's operations until March 1778, when Washington asked him to leave the fighting line and assume the duties of quartermaster general, which had been poorly handled. Greene agreed reluctantly and served for more than two years, except in a brief interval when he fought in the Battle of Monmouth (June 28, 1778). In July 1780, Greene returned to active service. In the autumn he presided at the trial of Major John André, the British spy, who was hanged.

Greene's generalship was largely responsible for the triumph of the American forces in the South. After the Americans were defeated in the Battle of Camden, South Carolina (August 16, 1780), Greene was chosen to succeed General Horatio Gates in command of the southern war theater, and in early December he took over the leadership of a shattered and destitute army. He quickly reorganized it and devised a strategy of retreat northward into North Carolina, goading Lord Cornwallis, the British commander, into following him. His strategy succeeded in dividing the British forces, making possible the victory at Cowpens in January 1781. Within eight months Greene freed most of the Carolinas from British control. At the Battle of Guilford Courthouse on March 15, 1781, Greene suffered a defeat, but his troops fell back in good order without serious loss. Cornwallis, who was far from his base, was compelled by lack of supplies to withdraw. Greene had lost the battle but won the campaign. His strategic skill thereafter brought the war in the South to a successful close. In 1785 he retired near Savannah to a plantation given to him by Georgia.

Source and Additional Reading

Greene, George Washington. *The Life of Nathanael Greene.* 3 vols. New York: Hurd & Houghton, 1867–71.

Greene, Nathanael. *The Papers of Nathanael Greene.* 6 vols. Edited by Richard K. Showman and Dennis Conrad. Chapel Hill, University of North Carolina Press for the Rhode Island Historical Society, 1976–1991.

Greenhow, Rose O'Neal (1817–1864) *Confederate spy.*

Born in Port Tobacco, Maryland, O'Neal moved as a teenager from her family's Maryland farm to her aunt's fashionable boardinghouse in Washington, D.C. Personable, intelligent, and outgoing, she adapted easily to the social scene of the capital, and people in Washington's highest circles opened their doors to her. Regarded as a beautiful, ambitious, seductive woman, she disappointed an army of suitors by marrying Dr. Robert Greenhow, an influential, learned man under whose tutelage she flourished and with whom she bore four daughters.

Among her friends were presidents, senators, high-ranking military officers, and less important people from all walks of life, many of whom played knowing or unknowing roles in the espionage ring she organized in 1861. One of her closest companions had been John C. Calhoun, whose political instruction sealed Rose's identification with and loyalty to southern interests. A widow when war broke out, Greenhow immediately used her contacts and talents to provide Gen. P. G. T. Beauregard with information that resulted in the Union rout at First Bull Run.

Suspected of espionage and imprisoned in August 1861, she continued gathering and forwarding information vital to Confederate operations. News of her activities generated publicity and tremendous popularity among southern sympathizers. After her trial in spring 1862, Greenhow was deported to Richmond, where cheering crowds greeted her. That summer Jefferson Davis sent her to Europe as a courier. She stayed there collecting diplomatic intelligence and writing her memoirs until recalled in 1864, apparently bearing dispatches urgent to the Confederacy. Sailing on the blockade runner *Condor,* she reached the mouth of the Cape Fear River just outside Wilmington, North Carolina, when a Union ship gave chase, forcing the *Condor* aground on a sandbar early on the morning of October 1, 1864. Greenhow, fearing capture and imprisonment, persuaded the captain to send her and two companions ashore in a lifeboat, but in stormy seas the small vessel overturned. Rose drowned, dragged down by the $2,000 in gold she carried. Her body was found and identified a few days later and buried with honors in Wilmington, North Carolina.

Source

Boatner, Mark M. III. *The Civil War Dictionary,* New York: David Mackay, 1959.

Gregg, Stephen R. *Second lieutenant, United States Army, 143d Infantry, 36th Infantry Division, so distinguished himself in combat, during World War II, that he was awarded the Medal of Honor for his heroic actions.*

Born: New York, N.Y.; **Entered service at:** Bayonne, N.J.; **Place and date:** Near Montelimar, France, August 27, 1944. **G.O. No.:** 31, April 17, 1945.

Citation: "For conspicuous gallantry and intrepidity at risk of life above and beyond the call of duty on 27 August 1944, in the vicinity of Montelimar, France. As his platoon advanced upon the enemy positions; the leading scout was fired upon and 2d Lt. Gregg (then a Tech. Sgt.) immediately put his machine-guns into action to cover the advance of the riflemen. The Germans, who were at close range, threw hand grenades at the riflemen, killing some and wounding 7. Each time a medical aid man attempted to reach the wounded, the Germans fired at him. Realizing the seriousness of the situation, 2d Lt. Gregg took 1 of the light .30-caliber machine-guns, and firing from the hip, started boldly up the hill with the medical aid man following him. Although the enemy was throwing hand grenades at him, 2d Lt. Gregg remained and fired into the enemy positions while the medical aid man removed the 7 wounded men to safety. When 2d Lt. Gregg had expended all his ammunition, he was covered by 4 Germans who ordered him to surrender. Since the attention of most of the Germans had been diverted by watching this action, friendly riflemen were able to maneuver into firing positions. One, seeing 2d Lt. Gregg's situation, opened fire on his captors. The 4 Germans hit the ground and hereupon 2d Lt. Gregg recovered a machine pistol from one of the Germans and managed to escape to his other machinegun positions. He manned a gun, firing at his captors, killed 1 of them and wounded the other. This action so discouraged the Germans that the platoon was able to continue its advance up the hill to achieve its objective. The following morning, just prior to daybreak, the Germans launched a strong attack, supported by tanks, in an attempt to drive Company L from the hill. As these tanks moved along the valley and their foot troops advanced up the hill, 2d Lt. Gregg immediately ordered his mortars into action. During the day by careful observation, he was able to direct effective fire on the enemy, inflicting heavy casualties. By late afternoon he had directed 600 rounds when his communication to the mortars was knocked out. Without hesitation he started checking his wires, although the area was under heavy enemy small arms and artillery fire. When he was within 100 yards of his mortar position, 1 of his men informed him that the section had been captured and the Germans were using the mortars to fire on the company. 2d Lt. Gregg with this man and another nearby rifleman started for the gun position where he could see 5 Germans firing his mortars. He ordered the 2 men to cover him, crawled up, threw a hand grenade into the position, and then charged it. The hand grenade killed 1, injured 2, 2d Lt. Gregg took the other 2 prisoners, and put his mortars back into action."

Source
Medal of Honor Citation.

Hagerty, Robert Fleming *Lieutenant, United States Naval Reserve, Medical Corps. Lt. Hagerty so distinguished himself in combat, in May 1945, with First Battalion, First Marine Regiment, as a battalion surgeon during the Battle for Okinawa that he was awarded the Silver Star for his heroic actions.*

Citation: "For conspicuous gallantry and intrepidity as Battalion Surgeon, First Battalion, First Marines, in action against enemy Japanese forces on Okinawa, Ryukyu Islands, May 11, 1945. When he and his corpsmen were subjected to large caliber enemy artillery fire at the conclusion of one of many forward displacements to maintain their position just in the rear of the advancing from lines, Lieutenant Hagerty ordered his men to remain in their covered positions and, unhesitatingly, braved the hostile barrage to go to the aid of the wounded. Undaunted by continuing shell bursts, he answered a call for medical assistance at the battalion observation post and, discovering that one of the casualties was too severely wounded to be moved immediately to a covered position, voluntarily remained with the wounded man in an unprotected area to administer blood plasma. His unselfishness in risking his life to save that of another and his courageous devotion to duty undoubtedly were responsible for saving the lives of many and reflect the highest credit on Lieutenant Hagerty and the United States Naval Service."

Source
Silver Star Citation.

Robert Fleming Hagerty

Hale, Nathan (1755–1776) *Revolutionary War hero; hanged by the British as a spy, September 22, 1776.*

Nathan Hale was born on June 6, 1755, in Coventry, Connecticut, the sixth of 10 children. His parents were strict Puritans who taught religious devotion and a work ethic in their home. His father, Richard Hale, was a successful farmer and well respected in the community. Like other mothers at that time, his mother, Elizabeth Strong, provided her children's early education. The Reverend Joseph Huntington, the minister of their church, also tutored him. Huntington encouraged him to continue his education, in 1769, when Nathan Hale was 14 years old, he attended Yale College with his brother, Enoch, who was two years older. While Nathan Hale was at Yale, he experienced a way of life that was different from his family's Puritan life-style. He joined a secret club, Linonia, whose members discussed astronomy, literature, and the ethics of slavery. He became famous for his debating talents and graduated in 1773 with honors at the age of 18.

At the time, after graduation, most men taught school a temporarily while deciding on a career. Hale first taught in East Haddam, Connecticut, but it appears that he was not happy in this town. He later received an offer to teach at Union School in New London, Connecticut, where records show he seemed more content. Here he taught 30 young men Latin, writing, mathematics, and classic literature. He taught an early morning swimming class for the young women during the summer months.

Nathan Hale enjoyed teaching and toward the end of 1774 accepted a permanent position as the master of the Union School. In 1774, the colonists were organizing local militias to protect their rights against the British soldiers in the colonies to protect the British laws of King George III. Though not of legal age, Hale joined the local militia.

When news of the Battles of Lexington and Concord reached New London, Nathan Hale spoke out at a town meeting. "Let us march immediately," he said, "and never lay down our arms until we obtain our independence." This was one of the first times that the word *independence* was used in connection with the patriots' war against the British.

Though local militias were traveling to Massachusetts to help their countrymen in the Siege of Boston and the Battle of Bunker Hill, Hale remained in New London to finish his contract with the Union School.

In July 1774, Hale received a letter from a friend, Benjamin Tallmadge. Tallmadge had gone to Massachusetts to observe the British siege. When he returned he wrote to Hale, "If I were in your condition . . . I think the more extensive Service would be my choice. Our holy Religion, the honour of our God, a glorious country, & a happy constitution is what we have to defend." Nathan Hale joined the army the day after receiving the letter and accepted a commission as first lieutenant in Colonel Charles Webb's Seventh Connecticut regiment.

During the Siege of Boston, Nathan Hale kept a detailed journal that gives historians a view of what happened. Hale appeared to enjoy military life and became committed to helping the Continentals win the war against Britain. His unit was soon sent to New York to fight against General Hale's British forces, who were planning to invade and conquer that city.

In January 1776, the Continental Army was reorganized and Hale was promoted to captain in the new 19th Connecticut Regiment. In the spring, the Continentals moved to Manhattan to prevent the British from taking New York City. Hale spent almost six months there, building fortifications and preparing for a battle against the

British. He had seen little action during the time he had been in the army.

During the Battle of Long Island on August 27, 1775, his regiment protected several forts but was never attacked. This gave him time to write in his journals and to keep detailed records of the events happening around him. During September 1776, General George Washington needed to obtain information on British locations and preparations. Washington established a group of soldiers who would obtain this information and titled them the New England Rangers. General Washington trusted Lieutenant Colonel Thomas Knowlton and placed him in command of the Rangers. Nathan Hale was given command of one of the four companies and assigned to patrol the shorelines around Hell's Gate. Later, Hale volunteered to go behind the British lines and learn of their future plans.

At the time, spying was not a respected position in the army, as it was not the occupation of any "gentleman." Captain William Hull, Hale's closet friend, tried to dissuade from conducting his reconnaissance mission, but Hale insisted that he was doing it for the good of the colonies. He crossed the Long Island Sound from Norwalk, Connecticut, disguised as a schoolmaster and carrying his Yale papers. He learned the British were going to invade Manhattan at Kip's Bay, but before he could pass on the valuable information, the British invaded and took control of Manhattan. Hale thought it necessary to go to New York City and see what was happening there. General Washington and his men were positioned behind the bluffs at Harlem Heights, when New York City was set on fire on September 20. On Nathan Hale's return to Long Island Sound, on September 21, 1776, he was stopped by Lieutenant Colonel Robert Rogers of the Queen's Rangers and arrested. The British found evidence of secret information in the possession of Nathan Hale. Historical records show that he admitted who he was and what he was doing in New York. Some historians believe that his cousin, Samuel Hale, who was working for General Howe, knew what Nathan was doing and told the British authorities. General Howe ordered that Nathan Hale be hanged as a spy the next morning.

Early on September 22, 1776, British soldiers marched Nathan Hale five and one half miles outside the city and began to prepare for the hanging. Captain Montresor, an English officer, was there to observe the execution. General Howe allowed Nathan Hale to sit in the shade of Captain Montresor's marquee; during this time he wrote two letters, one to his mother and one to his brother, Enoch. (These letters were destroyed by the British after the hanging, for fear that Hale's statement, that he would "gladly give his life for something he believed in," was not something other Continental soldiers should hear.) Hale asked for a Bible but was denied the request.

Nathan Hale was executed by hanging on September 22, 1776, at the age of 21. When asked whether he had any last words, Hale boldly stated, "I only regret I have but one life to lose to my country." This statement, a paraphrase from *Cato,* a popular play by Addison, is forever associated with the American patriot Nathan Hale.

Source

Dupuy, Trevor N., Curt Johnson, and David L. Bongard. *The Harper Encyclopedia of Military Biography.* New York: HarperCollins, 1992.

Halsey, William F. "Bull," Jr. (1882–1959)

American Fleet Admiral, who defeated the Japanese in many battles of World War II and played a vital part in securing Allied victory.

Halsey was born in Elizabeth, New Jersey on October 30, 1882, and graduated in 1904 from the United States Naval Academy. As a midshipman, Halsey began his seagoing career on the USS *Missouri,* the "Mizzy." At the end of World War II his flagship was another *Missouri,* the "Mighty Mo," on which the formal Japanese surrender was signed. During World War I, he commanded destroyers engaged in patrol and convoy escort duty and received a Navy Cross for his heroic actions. Between World Wars I and II he successively commanded groups of destroyers; the aircraft carrier *Saratoga,* the naval air station at Pensacola, Florida; groups of carriers; and groups of aircraft. He attended the Naval War College in 1933 and the Army War College in 1934. At 52 he won the wings of a naval aviator.

When the Japanese attacked Pearl Harbor, Hawaii, on December 7, 1941, Halsey, then a vice admiral with his flag in the aircraft carrier USS *Enterprise,* was sailing to Pearl Harbor after having delivered planes to Wake Island. Early in 1942 he made forays on Japanese–held islands in the Gilberts and Marshalls, attacking Wake Island in February. For valor in these two raids he received the Distinguished Service Medal. On April 18, 1942, the aircraft carrier USS *Hornet,* which launched Lt. Col. James H. Doolittle's Army B-25 bombers for the bombing of Tokyo, was escorted by Halsey's task force to within 800 miles (1,300 kilometers) of Tokyo.

Halsey was assigned as commander, South Pacific Force and South Pacific Area, in October 1942 and was promoted to admiral in November. His forces defeated the Japanese at Santa Cruz, Guadalcanal, and the Solomons attacked Japanese naval power; and invaded the Solomon Islands.

On June 16, 1944, he took command of the Third Fleet and became commander, Western Pacific Task Forces. His new forces lived up to his old motto, "Hit hard, hit fast, and hit often." Under Admiral Halsey, the Third Fleet executed the first carrier attack on land-based air forces in the central Philippines; supported attacks on Peleliu and Angaur in the Palau Islands; supported General Douglas MacArthur at Leyte, Mindoro, and Luzon; and made the first carrier attack on the island of Okinawa.

Admiral Halsey's salty, belligerent speech and generous nature made him popular with his men and the public. During the war, newspapers gave him the nickname "Bull." His captains never knew what to expect, expect that he would find and fight the enemy. As a result of faulty intelligence he chased a Japanese decoy fleet northest of the Philippines in October 1944, leaving the Seventh Fleet temporarily outnumbered at the Battle of Leyte Gulf. Nevertheless, that battle cost Japan greater damage (including four aircraft carriers and a battleship sunk by Halsey) than any fleet had ever suffered in a naval battle in history.

Thereafter, Halsey supported the final stages of the Okinawa Campaign, struck at Tokyo, attacked Honshu and Hokkaido in July 1945, and continued to hammer at the Japanese homeland until the cease-fire on August 15, 1945, which was followed by the surrender aboard his flagship on September 2, 1945.

Halsey took an oath as Fleet Admiral in December 1945 and resided in New York City until his death at Fishers Island, New York on August 16, 1959.

Source and Additional Reading

Frank, Benis. *Halsey,* New York: Ballantine, 1974.

Halsey, William F. *Admiral Halsey's Story.* New York: Whittlesey House, 1947.

Merrill, James M. *A Sailor's Admiral: A Biography of William F. Halsey.* New York: Crowell, 1976.

Halyburton, William David, Jr. (1924–1945)

Pharmacist's mate second class, United States Naval Reserve, so distinguished himself in combat, during World War II, that he was awarded (posthumously) the Medal of Honor for his heroic actions.

Born: August 2, 1924, Canton, N.C.; **Accredited to:** North Carolina.

Citation: "For conspicuous gallantry and intrepidity at the risk of his life above and beyond the call of duty while serving with a Marine Rifle Company in the 2d Battalion, 5th Marines, 1st Marine Division, during action against enemy Japanese forces on Okinawa Shima in the Ryukyu Chain, 10 May 1945. Undaunted by the deadly accuracy of Japanese counterfire as his unit pushed the attack through a strategically important draw, Halyburton unhesitatingly dashed across the draw and up the hill into an open fire-swept field where the company advance squad was suddenly pinned down under a terrific concentration of mortar, machinegun and sniper fire with resultant severe casualties. Moving steadily forward despite the enemy's merciless barrage, he reached the wounded Marine who lay farthest away and was rendering first aid when his patient was struck for the second time by a Japanese bullet. Instantly placing himself in the direct line of fire, he shielded the fallen fighter with his own body and staunchly continued his ministrations although constantly menaced by the slashing fury of shrapnel and bullets falling on all sides. Alert, determined and completely unselfish in his concern for the helpless Marine, he persevered in his efforts until he himself sustained mortal wounds and collapsed, heroically sacrificing himself that his comrade might live. By his outstanding valor and unwavering devotion to duty in the face of tremendous odds, Halyburton sustained and enhanced the highest traditions of the U.S. Naval Service. He gallantly gave his life in the service of his country."

Source
Medal of Honor Citation.

Hamblen, Donald J. "Woody" (b. 1932) *First sergeant, United States Marine Corps.*

Don Hamblen was born July 7, 1932 outside Winthrop Center, Maine. The youngest of four children, he was raised as a Quaker on his family's farm on Lake Cobbosseecontee. By the time he reached his teens he had learned enough from his father about hard work, fishing, and hunting to work as a guide in the Maine woods, taking vacationers out to the surrounding lakes and forests to catch bass and trout and to hunt the elusive white–tailed deer.

In the summer of 1949, Marine recruiters challenged Hamblen to enlist in their corps. He accepted and soon found himself at Parris Island, South Carolina, as he turned 18 years old. On graduation from "boot camp" he joined the Sixth Marine Regiment at Camp Lejeune, North Carolina, and then received orders for Camp Pendleton, California. There, he was assigned to a Replacement Draft Battalion and was assigned to the First Marine Division fighting in Korea. In November 1951, Hamblen was assigned to Company D, Second Battalion, Fifth Marine Regiment. Just before Christmas, he was sent to the division's sniper school, where he sharpened his marksmanship skills.

On May 4, 1952, Hamblen was wounded in his left leg during an enemy mortar barrage. As four-man stretcher team began to carry him back toward friendly lines, a squad of Red Chinese ambushed them. They dropped the stretcher to find cover, and as they Chinese continued their assault, Hamblen was shot.

A second rescue team finally picked him up and took him to a battalion aid station, where pieces of shrapnel were taken from his leg and a bullet removed from his right shoulder. After only 10 days of hospitalization, Hamblen returned to his company, assigned as a squad leader. He sailed home in November 1952, as a corporal.

In October 1960, Hamblen was transferred to First Force Reconnaissance Company, as assistant platoon sergeant of the Pathfinders Platoon, whose dual mission was to perform preassault and distant postassault reconnaissance and to conduct guidance of helicopter waves into designated landing zones.

To become ready for their one-year deployment to Okinawa, all Pathfinders were required to complete a number of parachute jumps, with and without equipment, from a variety of navy and Marine aircraft. On the morning of September 21, 1962, members of Hamblen's platoon were scheduled to parachute into drop zone Tank Park. Ten Marines made up the "stick," and Hamblen was the last to go.

After exiting the aircraft, Hamblen looked to make sure he had a good canopy opening He did, but at 800 feet he was being blown toward the high-tension electrical lines that crossed Camp Pendleton. "My canopy became entangled in the 69,000-volt lines, and I was hanging, swaying above a lower set of three 12,000-volt lines. My momentum caused me to swing out, and as I swung back, I felt myself drop. That was when my left foot hit the middle line, and I pushed it out against the outside line. I was the only obstacle between the humming 12,000-volt and 69,000-volt lines."

Marines in the drop zone could only stand and watch as a bluish white flame shot up from the lines and arched against Hamblen's leg. The charge of electricity traveled up and over his body and an orange ball of flame rose from the lines, causing his nylon canopy to smoke and burn.

Hamblen fell 40 feet to the ground. One of the electrical lines snapped and fell, too, causing the dry brush around him to ignite.

Hamblen watched the fire spread while trying to reach his signaling flare, but he did not have the strength to pull his flare away from his harness. "Our training had been so repetitive, that it was an instinctive reaction to get my signal flare ignited and let someone know where I was and that I was still alive," said Hamblen during a later interview.

Medevaced by helicopter to the Camp Pendleton Naval Hospital, Hamblen was told that the lower part of his left leg would have to be amputated to save his life. "Late in the afternoon, I finally awoke. I couldn't feel that part of my leg was gone, but when I focused my eyes toward the foot of the bed that place beneath the blue sheets where my leg and foot should have been was flat and empty."

A few days later, Major General Herman Nickerson Jr., his commanding general, visited Hamblen. Taken by jeep to a nearby drop zone, Hamblen and Nickerson watched as recon Marines exited from aircraft above them and made their way down to the drop zone. "The general told me we had more in common than being Marines. He reminded me that while I had been a squad leader in Korea, he had been on my right flank as regimental commander of the 7th Marines. We shook hands and he repeated his offer of personal assistance, anytime or anywhere."

By January 1963, Hamblen's condition, because of his rigid physical-therapy program, allowed him to be transferred to the Oak Knoll Naval Hospital

The navy and the Marine Corps were interested in Hamblen's prognosis, each for a different reason. The navy wanted to know only what his physical status was and whether he could return to duty. The Marine Corps wanted to know *when* he would return to a limited or full-duty status.

"I knew the key to a rapid recovery was more mental than physical, and I wanted to show those who would evaluate my condition that I could do much more than sit in a wheelchair and sew leather moccasins together," said Hamblen.

On March 28, 1963, only 58 days after his admission to Oak Knoll, Hamblen was helped by a navy nurse to load his sea bag into his car before he headed back to Camp Pendleton.

During the seven months he had spent away from his recon company, changes in personnel that affected his being considered for full-duty status had occurred. Major General Nickerson was about to leave a new general in command. Concerned that those who knew of his request for "full-duty status" were leaving, Hamblen met with the general one more time. A mutual agreement was made, to ensure that no Marine Corps standards would be lowered; Hamblen was tasked to pass the Physical Readiness Test, complete a 1,400-foot parachute jump into a body of water, then make a successful 120-foot scuba dive off the western coast. Staff Sergeant Hamblen, now affectionately known as "Woody" to his fellow Marines, completed all three tasks without difficulty. He was again placed on a jump-qualified status and participated in operations in the state of Washington, and the Philippines Islands and as a test parachutist at El Centro, California.

In late April 1964, Hamblen flew to Washington, D.C., as an honored guest of President Johnson. He met with Senators Edmund S. Muskie and Margaret Chase Smith, from Maine. Hamblen also met one of the legends of the Marine Corps, Gen. Graves B. Erskine, then the chief administrator of the President's Retraining and Reemployment Administration, who had commanded the Third Marine Division during the battle of Iwo Jima.

Returning to Camp Pendleton, Hamblen was sent to the division's Intelligence Section to study reports detailing the Marine advisory role conducted by the Military Assistance Command Vietnam/Studies and Observation Group (MACV/SOG), who were requesting volunteers for duty with the Naval Advisory Detachment in Vietnam.

Hamblen did not think that duty in Vietnam could be any more demanding than at Camp Pendleton. He volunteered for SOG Duty and was told he would not be going alone. First Lieutenant Jerome Paull, Corporal Gene Graffenstein, and Sergeant Johann Haferkamp would make up the remainder of the advisory team. After Vietnamese language school, the group loaded its gear and arrived in Saigon several days later. The team's primary mission was to conduct prisoner snatches of North Vietnamese officers, village or hamlet chiefs, or other designated "key political figures" living in villages along the North Vietnamese coastline.

Hamblen and his SOG Team, codenamed *Romulus*, participated in more than 80 SOG missions during the 30 consecutive months he served in Vietnam. When the normal length of tour had been six months, the short duration had caused problems; the Vietnamese had little regard for those American advisers less committed than to the war against the Viet Cong and North Vietnamese Army (NVA).

In October 1966, Major General Nickerson assumed command of the First Marine Division, and his presence again had an impact on Hamblen's life. In July 1966, Hamblen was promoted to gunnery sergeant, and in November he received orders to leave Vietnam for further assignment. There was no place that Hamblen, who had extended his assignment twice before, wanted to be more than with his team. In hope of getting his orders modified, he went to the general. Nickerson told "Woody" that as long as he was in Vietnam, Hamblen could stay.

In March 1966, Hamblen was wounded when a piece of shrapnel hit him in the chest. This wound required minor surgery, but it was not considered very serious and served as a reminder of how easy it was to get hit.

In March 1967, Hamblen accompanied 11 members of Team Romulus into North Vietnam to kidnap an officer. After traveling 70 miles north of the Demilitarized Zone (DMZ), the team went ashore. The snatch team was soon involved in a firefight. As the team tried to make its way back to their boat, Hamblen was struck in the left arm by a .32-caliber bullet. Three other team members were wounded seriously enough to require hospitalization.

General Nickerson heard about Hamblen's wounding at the same time that two newspaper reporters arrived to do a follow-up story on the one-legged Marine who was leading a SOG team. This caused another meeting between Hamblen and the general, who told Hamblen that the SOG operation could be compromised: having now been wounded four times, he should think about going back to the States.

"To make matters worse," said General Nickerson, "if you get yourself killed north of the DMZ, there would be hell to pay. Americans would think the Marine Corps has been forced to scrape the bottom of the barrel, allowing amputees to do its fighting. That would not look good for the Corps."

General Nickerson told Hamblen he could select any post or station for his next assignment.Hamblen departed Da Nang in November 1967, assigned to Camp Pendleton, as operations and training chief for Fifth Force Recon Company.

In May 1968, Hamblen was assigned to a joint tour at McDill Air Force Base in Florida. The Operations Division, United States Strike Command, requested his services as it prepared plans for joint airborne operations in the United States, the Caribbean, Africa, the Middle East, and Korea.

In 1969, "Woody" Hamblen was promoted to first sergeant and left again to serve with Fifth Force as that company's first sergeant. He retired from the Marine Corps on March 1, 1970.

Source and Additional Reading

Norton, Maj. Bruce H. *One Tough Marine: The Biography of First Sergeant Donald N. Hamblen, USMC.* New York: Ballantine Books, 1993.

Hammerberg, Owen Francis Patrick (b.1920)

Boatswain's mate second class, United States Navy, was awarded the Medal of Honor for his heroic actions.

Born: May 31, 1920, Daggett, Mich.; **Accredited to:** Michigan.

Citation: "For conspicuous gallantry and intrepidity at the risk of his life above and beyond the call of duty as a diver engaged in rescue operations at West Loch, Pearl Harbor, 17 February 1945. Aware of the danger when 2 fellow divers were hopelessly trapped in a cave-in of steel wreckage while tunneling with jet nozzles under an LST sunk in 40 feet of water and 20 feet of mud, Hammerberg unhesitatingly went overboard in a valiant attempt to effect their rescue despite the certain hazard of additional cave-ins and the risk of fouling his lifeline on jagged pieces of steel imbedded in the shifting mud. Washing a passage through the original excavation, he reached the first of the trapped men, freed him from the wreckage and, working desperately in pitch-black darkness, finally effected his release from fouled lines, thereby enabling him to reach the surface. Wearied but undaunted after several hours of arduous labor, Hammerberg resolved to continue his struggle to wash through the oozing submarine, subterranean mud in a determined effort to save the second diver. Venturing still farther under the buried hulk, he held tenaciously to his purpose, reaching a place immediately above the other man just as another cave-in occurred and a heavy piece of

steel pinned him crosswise over his shipmate in a position which protected the man beneath from further injury while placing the full brunt of terrific pressure on himself. Although he succumbed in agony 18 hours after he had gone to the aid of his fellow divers, Hammerberg, by his cool judgment, unfaltering professional skill and consistent disregard of all personal danger in the face of tremendous odds, had contributed effectively to the saving of his 2 comrades. His heroic spirit of self-sacrifice throughout enhanced and sustained the highest traditions of the U.S. Naval Service. He gallantly gave his life in the service of his country."

Source
Medal of Honor Citation.

Hampton, Wade (1818–1902) *General, Confederate States Army, American Civil War hero who restored southern white rule to South Carolina after Radical Reconstruction.*

Born into an aristocratic South Carolina plantation family, Hampton graduated from South Carolina College in 1836 and studied law. He never practiced, however, instead devoting himself to the management of his family's land holdings in Mississippi and South Carolina.

From 1852 to 1861 Hampton served in the South Carolina legislature. He consistently upheld a conservative position on slavery and secession. When the South seceded, Hampton gave unstintingly of himself and his fortune to the Confederacy. Though lacking military experience, he organized and commanded Hampton's Legion of South Carolina troops. He rose from colonel to lieutenant general and saw combat in many key battles.

He served as second in command to Gen. J. E. B. Stuart and after Stuart's death led the cavalry corps. Wounded three times, he survived to become a military hero to the defeated South and a symbol of the nobility and gallantry of the "lost cause."

Hampton backed President Andrew Johnson's plans for Reconstruction and sought reconciliation between North and South. But with the imposition of Radical policies, Hampton took the lead in South Carolina in the fight to restore white supremacy. With the Republicans firmly in control from 1868 to 1876, however, he devoted himself primarily to restoring his greatly depleted fortune. In 1876 he campaigned vigorously as the Democratic candidate for governor. His triumph was largely attributable to systematic efforts by his backers to prevent blacks from voting.

Reelected in 1878, Hampton resigned the following year when elected to the U.S. Senate. He served until 1891, defeated for reelection the previous year by "Pitchfork Ben" Tillman. The transition from Hampton to Tillman represented the end of rule by genteel antebellum aristocrats in the South. Hampton served as a commissioner of Pacific Railways from 1893 to 1897 before retiring to Columbia, South Carolina.

Source and Additional Reading

Snow, Capt. William P. *Lee and His Generals.* 1867. Reprint, Cambridge, Mass.: Fairfax Press, New York, 1982.

Wellman, Manly Wade. *Giant in Gray: A Biography of Wade Hampton of South Carolina.* 1949. Reprint, Dayton, Ohio: Morningside Bookshop, 1996.

Wells, Edward A. *Hampton and His Cavalry in '64.* Richmond, Va: B. F. Johnson Publishing Co., 1899.

Hancock, Winfield Scott (1824–1886) *Major general, Union army.*

Although named for America's top military hero of the day, Winfield Scott Hancock was not originally intended for a military career; nevertheless he was destined to become one of the best corps commanders in the Union army.

Born in Montgomery County, Pennsylvania, on February 14, 1824, he was an 1844 graduate of West Point and served with distinction in the infantry during the Mexican War, earning a brevet before transferring to the quartermaster's department.

His Civil War assignments included the following: captain and assistant quartermaster (from November 7, 1855); brigadier general, United States Volunteers (USV) (September 23, 1861); commander, Third Brigade, Smith's division, Army of the Potomac (October 3, 1861–March 13, 1862); commander, First Brigade, Second Division, Fourth Corps (Sixth Corps after May 18) Corps, Army of the Potomac (March 13–September 17, 1862); commander, First Division, Second Corps, Army of the Potomac (September 17, 1862–January 24, 1863 and February 20–May 22, 1863); major general, USV (November 29, 1862); commander of the corps (May 22–July 1 and July 2–3, 1863, and March 24–June 18 and July 27–November 26, 1864); major and quartermaster (November 30, 1863); bridgadier general USA (August 12, 1864); Department of West Virginia (February 28–March 1, March 7–20, and March 22–June commander, First Veteran Volunteer Corps (November 27, 1864–February 27, 1865); commander, Middle Military Division (February 27–June 27, 1865); command Department of West Virginia (February 28–March 1, March 7–20, and March 22–June 27, 1965); major general, United States Army, July 26, 1866.

Fearing that he would be left to sit in California, where he had been instrumental in frustrating the plans of local secessionists, while the war raged elsewhere, he was ordered east for quartermaster duties but arrived to receive a brigadier's star. Taking his brigade to the Peninsula, he led a critical flank attack at Williamsburg and earned the sobriquet "Superb." He continued to distinguish himself during the rest of the dismal campaign. During the Battle of Antietam, Israel B. Richardson was killed and Hancock was sent to command his division in the Second Corps, thus beginning a historic association. At Fredericksburg his division took part in the costly assaults on Marye's Heights, and at Chancellorsville he skillfully covered the Union withdrawal. With Corps Commander Couch's request for transfer accepted, Hancock stepped up to the Second Corps leadership.

With the fall of John F. Reynolds early on the first day at Gettysburg, General Meade dispatched Hancock to take over that wing of the army and decide whether the battle should be fought there or not. This was a high honor since Oliver O. Howard, a senior officer, was already on the field. Belatedly he received the Thanks of Congress for this action. On the second and third days of the battle Hancock directed the Union center until wounded by a nail and by wood fragments, possibly from his saddle, driven into his thigh by enemy fire. A long recovery followed, during which he performed some recruiting duty. Returning in time for the Overland Campaign, he fought well at the Wilderness and was brevetted major general in the regular army for his crashing through the Confederate salient at Spotsylvania. At Cold Harbor his troops were slaughtered in a futile assault ordered by Grant. Arriving on the Petersburg front, because of a lack of knowledge of the situation, he deferred command to the corps commander on the field, who failed to launch a final assault, which could very well have ended the war 10 months earlier.

Shortly afterward General Hancock's old wound broke open and he had to leave the army for a time. Returning, he was humiliated by the defeat at Reams' Station and in November was forced to give up field command, and he began recruiting the First Veteran Volunteer Corps. Results were poor, and early in 1865 he took over command in Washington, D.C., Maryland, West Virginia, and the Shanandoah Valley. After the Confederacy's collapse he came into conflict with Grant, who objected to his lenient treatment of the South. He was mustered out of the volunteer service on July 26, 1866, the same day that he received the appointment of major general in the regular establishment.

Remaining in the army, he assumed command of the Department of the East, with headquarters (HQ) at Governors Island, New York, in 1877. He was a potential Democratic candidate for the presidency in 1868; in 1880 he was the nominee but was narrowly defeated by James Garfield. On February 9, 1886, he died at Governors Island while still in command of the Department of the East. He is buried in Montgomery Cemetery, Norristown, Pennsylvania.

Source and Additional Reading
Hancock, Anne. *Reminiscences of Winfield Scott Hancock*. New York: Webster Publishing, 1887.
Tucker, Glenn. *Hancock: The Superb*. Indianapolis, Ind.: Bobbs-Merrill, 1960.
Walker, Francis A. *General Hancock*. New York: Appleton, 1897.
Warner, Ezra. *Generals in Blue*. Baton Rogue: Louisiana State University Press, 1978.

Handrich, Melvin O. (1919–1950) *Master sergeant, United States Army, Company C, Fifth Infantry Regiment, so distinguished himself in combat during the Korean War that he was awarded (posthumously) the Medal of Honor for his heroic actions.*

Born: January 26, 1919, Manawa, Wis.; **Entered service at:** Manawa, Wis.; **Place and date:** Near Sobuk San Mountain, Korea, August 25 and 26, 1950. **G.O. No.:** 60, August 2, 1951.

Citation: "M/Sgt. Handrich, Company C, distinguished himself by conspicuous gallantry and intrepidity above and beyond the call of duty in action. His company was engaged in repulsing an estimated 150 enemy who were

Melvin O. Handrich

threatening to overrun its position. Near midnight on 25 August, a hostile group over 100 strong attempted to infiltrate the company perimeter. M/Sgt. Handrich, despite the heavy enemy fire, voluntarily left the comparative safety of the defensive area and moved to a forward position where he could direct mortar and artillery fire upon the advancing enemy. He remained at this post for 8 hours directing fire against the enemy who often approached to within 50 feet of his position. Again, on the morning of 26 August, another strong hostile force made an attempt to overrun the company's position. With complete disregard for his safety, M/Sgt. Handrich rose to his feet and from this exposed position fired his rifle and directed mortar and artillery fire on the attackers. At the peak of this action he observed elements of his company preparing to withdraw. He perilously made his way across fire-swept terrain to the defense area where, by example and forceful leadership, he reorganized the men to continue the fight. During the action M/Sgt. Handrich was severely wounded. Refusing to take cover or be evacuated, he returned to his forward position and continued to direct the company's fire. Later a determined enemy attack overran M/Sgt. Handrich's position and he was mortally wounded. When the position was retaken, over 70 enemy dead were counted in the area he had so intrepidly defended. M/Sgt. Handrich's sustained personal bravery, consummate courage, and gallant self-sacrifice reflect untold glory upon himself and the heroic traditions of the military service."

Source
Medal of Honor Citation.

Hansen, Dale Merlin (b.1922) *Private, United States Marine Corps, so distinguished himself in combat, during World War II, that he was awarded (posthumously) the Medal of Honor for his heroic actions.*

Born: December 13, 1922, Wisner, Nebr.; **Entered Service at:** Nebraska.

Citation: "For conspicuous gallantry and intrepidity at the risk of his life above and beyond the call of duty while serving with Company E, 2d Battalion, 1st Marines, 1st Marine Division, in action against enemy Japanese forces on Okinawa Shima in the Ryukyu Chain, 7 May 1945. Cool and courageous in combat, Pvt. Hansen unhesitatingly took the initiative during a critical stage of the action and, armed with a rocket launcher, crawled to an exposed position where he attacked and destroyed a strategically located hostile pillbox. With his weapon subsequently destroyed by enemy fire, he seized a rifle and continued his 1-man assault. Reaching the crest of a ridge, he leaped across, opened fire on 6 Japanese and killed 4 before his rifle jammed. Attacked by the remaining 2 Japanese, he beat them off with the butt of his rifle and then climbed back to cover. Promptly returning with another weapon and supply of grenades, he fearlessly advanced, destroyed a strong mortar position and annihilated 8 more of the enemy. In the forefront of battle throughout this bitterly waged engagement, Pvt. Hansen, by his indomitable determination, bold tactics and complete disregard of all personal danger, contributed essentially to the success of his company's mission and to the ultimate capture of this fiercely defended outpost of the Japanese Empire. His great personal valor in the face of extreme peril reflects the highest credit upon himself and the United States Naval Service."

Source
Medal of Honor Citation.

Hanson, Jack G. (1930–1951) *Private first class, United States Army, Company F, 31st Infantry Regiment, so distinguished himself in combat during the Korean War that he was awarded (posthumously) the Medal of Honor for his heroic actions.*

Born: September 18, 1930, Escaptawpa, Miss.; **Entered service at:** Galveston, Tex.; **Place and date:** Near Pachi-dong, Korea, June 7, 1951. **G.O. No.:** 15, February 1, 1952.

Citation: "Pfc. Hanson, a machine gunner with the 1st Platoon, Company F, distinguished himself by conspicuous gallantry and intrepidity at the risk of his life above and beyond the call of duty in action against an armed enemy of the United Nations. The company, in defensive positions on two strategic hills separated by a wide saddle, was ruthlessly attacked at approximately 0300 hours, the brunt of which centered on the approach to the divide within range of Pfc. Hanson's machine gun. In the initial phase of the action, 4 riflemen were wounded and evacuated and the numerically superior enemy, advancing under cover of darkness, infiltrated and posed an imminent threat to the security of the command post and weapons platoon. Upon orders to move to key terrain above and to the right of Pfc. Hanson's position, he voluntarily remained to provide protective fire for the withdrawal. Subsequent to the retiring elements fighting a rearguard action to the new location, it was learned that Pfc. Hanson's assistant gunner and 3 riflemen had been wounded and had crawled to safety, and that he was maintaining a lone-man defense. After the 1st Platoon reorganized, counterattacked, and retook its original positions at approximately 0530 hours, Pfc. Hanson's body was found lying in front of his emplacement, his machine gun ammunition expended, his empty pistol in his right hand, and a machete with blood on the blade in his left hand,

and approximately 22 enemy dead lay in the wake of his action. Pfc. Hanson's consummate valor, inspirational conduct, and willing self-sacrifice enabled the company to contain the enemy and regain the commanding ground, and reflect lasting glory on himself and the noble traditions of the military service."

Source
Medal of Honor Citation.

Hardee, William Joseph (1815–1873) *General officer, Confederate States Army.*

Problems with Braxton Bragg affected only slightly the outstanding record of the premier lieutenant general to serve in the Confederate Army of Tennessee. By the time that this Georgian West Pointer (1838) resigned as lieutenant colonel, First Cavalry, on January 31, 1861, he was one of the most distinguished and well known officers in the old army. Serving in the Seminole and Mexican conflicts, he won two brevets in the latter and was wounded at La Rosia, Mexico. He returned to his alma mater as a tactics instructor and served as commandant of cadets. His textbook *Rifle and Light Infantry Tactics*, or more familiarly *Hardee's Tactics*, became the standard textbook and was widely used by both sides during the Civil War.

Joining the Confederacy, his assignments included the following: colonel, Cavalry (March 16, 1861); brigadier general, Confederate States Army (CSA) (June 16, 1861); commander, Upper District of Arkansas, Department 2 (July 22–October 1861); major general, CSA (October 7, 1861); commander, First Division, Central Army of Kentucky, Department 2 (October 28–December 5, December 18–December 30, 1861, and February 23–March 29, 1862); commander of the army (December 5–18, 1861, and December 30, 1861–February 23, 1862); commander, Third Corps, Army of the Mississippi (March 29–July 5, 1862); commander of the army (July 5–August 15, 1862); commander, Left Wing, Army of the Mississippi (August 15–November 20, 1862); lieutenant general, CSA (October 10, 1862); commander, Second Corps, Army of Tennessee (November 20, 1862–July 14, 1863); commander, Army of the Department of Mississippi and East Louisiana (July 14–November 1863); commander, First (Polk's old) Corps, Army of Tennessee (November–December 2, 1863, December 22–January 1864, early 1864–August 31, and September 2–October 5, 1864); commander of the army (December 2–22, 1863); commander of his and Lee's corps, Army of Tennessee (August 31–September 2, 1864); commander, Department of South Carolina, Georgia and Florida (October 5, 1864–February 16, 1865); commander, Hardee's corps, cooperating with Joseph E.

Johnston's forces (February 16–April 9, 1865); and commander of corps, Army of Tennessee (April 9–26, 1865).

As a brigadier general, he served in Arkansas and was then promoted to major general and assigned to central Kentucky. He commanded one of the corps in the Confederate attacks at Shiloh, where he was wounded. He led his corps during the defense of Corinth, Mississippi, and after leading the Army of Mississippi into Kentucky under Bragg, he commanded the left at Perryville.

One of the original lieutenant generals allowed under Confederate law, he led an official corps at Murfreesboro and during the Tullahoma Campaign. In order to get away from the despised army commander, Bragg, he took an assignment in Mississippi under Joseph E. Johnston but after taking part in the minor operations there was recalled to the Army of Tennessee to take over Leonidas Polk's corps at Chattanooga and during the Atlanta Campaign.

During the final stages of the latter, that is, at Jonesboro, he was in charge of two corps in the Confederate attacks. Disenchanted with Hood's leadership, he accepted transfer to command of the Atlantic coast and served there for the balance of the war. He was unable to stop Sherman's March to the Sea but successfully evacuated Savannah at the last minute. Forced to abandon Charleston as Sherman's command bypassed it, he continued to withdraw into North Carolina with his "corps" drawn from the coastal defenders. Joining Johnston's forces, he had his last fight at Bentonville. It was also the last for his only son, who was killed there. In the final reorganization and consolidation of the Army of Tennessee he retained corps command. His new corps comprised two divisions of Army of Tennessee men who had previously served under him and one from the Department of North Carolina. This force he surrendered along with Johnston's command on April 26, 1865. "Old Reliable" refused command of the army just after the disaster at Chattanooga but seems to have found his appropriate position as a top corps leader. After the war he settled on an Alabama plantation.

Sources

Hughes, Nathaniel C. *General William J. Hardee: Old Reliable.* Baton Rouge: Louisiana State University Press, 1985.

Harrell, William George (b. 1922) *Sergeant, United States Marine Corps, First Battalion, 28th Marines, Fifth Marine Division, so distinguished himself in combat during World War II that he was awarded the Medal of Honor for his heroic actions.*

Born: June 26, 1922, Rio Grande City, Tex.: **Entered service at:** Mercedes, Tex.; **Place and date:** Iwo Jima, Volcano Islands, March 3, 1945.

Citation: "For conspicuous gallantry and intrepidity at the risk of his life above and beyond the call of duty as leader of an assault group attached to the 1st Battalion, 28th Marines, 5th Marine Division during hand-to-hand combat with enemy Japanese at Iwo Jima, Volcano Islands, on 3 March 1945. Standing watch alternately with another Marine in a terrain studded with caves and ravines, Sgt. Harrell was holding a position in a perimeter defense around the company command post when Japanese troops infiltrated our lines in the early hours of dawn. Awakened by a sudden attack, he quickly opened fire with his carbine and killed 2 of the enemy as they emerged from a ravine in the light of a star-shell burst. Unmindful of his danger as hostile grenades fell closer, he waged a fierce lone battle until an exploding missile tore off his left hand and fractured his thigh. He was vainly attempting to reload the carbine when his companion returned from the command post with another weapon. Wounded again by a Japanese who rushed the foxhole wielding a saber in the darkness, Sgt. Harrell succeeded in drawing his pistol and killing his opponent and then ordered his wounded companion to a place of safety. Exhausted by profuse bleeding but still unbeaten, he fearlessly met the challenge of 2 more enemy troops who charged his position and placed a grenade near his head. Killing 1 man with his pistol, he grasped the sputtering grenade with his good right hand, and, pushing it painfully toward the crouching soldier, saw his remaining assailant destroyed but his own hand severed in the explosion. At dawn Sgt. Harrell was evacuated from a position hedged by the bodies of 12 dead Japanese, at least 5 of whom he had personally destroyed in his self-sacrificing defense of the command post. His grim fortitude, exceptional valor, and indomitable fighting spirit against almost insurmountable odds reflect the highest credit upon himself and enhance the finest traditions of the U.S. Naval Service."

Source

Medal of Honor Citation.

Harrington, Myron Charles (b. 1938) *Colonel, United States Marine Corps, awarded the Navy Cross, during the Vietnam War, for his heroic actions.*

Born in Augusta, Georgia, Harrington graduated from the Citadel, class of 1960, with a bachelor of arts in history. He was commissioned a lieutenant of Marines in May 1961. He attended the Basic School, Amphibious Warfare School, in 1968; the Armed Forces Staff College at Norfolk, Virginia, in 1977; and the Army War College at Carlisle, Pennsylvania, in 1980. He received a master's of science degree in public administration from Shippensburg State College in Shippensburg, Pennsylvania that same year.

Highlights of Harrington's Marine Corps career include service as a rifle company commander (D/1/5), in the Republic of Vietnam in 1968 during the Battle for Hue City during the infamous Tet Offensive, for which he was awarded the Navy Cross; service as the first Marine Corps assistant naval attaché at the American Embassy, Canberra, Australia (1969–72); aide-de-camp to four Marine general officers; commanding officer, Third Recruit Training Battalion, Parris Island, South Carolina, (1978–79); operations officer, Fleet Marine Forces Atlantic (1982–84); commanding officer, 24th Marine Amphibious Unit, Beirut, Lebanon (1984); and chief of staff of Marine Corps Base, Camp Lejeune, North Carolina (1986–88). Colonel Harrington retired from the Marine Corps as professor of naval science and commanding officer of the Naval Reserve Officer's Training Corps, the Citadel, in June 1991.

Since leaving the Marine Corps, Colonel Harrington has been active in independent school education. In 1992, he joined the staff of Trident Academy, Mount Pleasant, South Carolina, an independent school specializing in the education of students with learning disabilities, as headmaster. He is the vice-president of the South Carolina Independent School Association (SCISA). The association has 90 member schools throughout the state, representing 30,000 students and more than 1,500 teachers.

Colonel Harrington's military decorations include the following: the Navy Cross; Silver Star; Legion of Merit with two Gold Stars in lieu of second and third awards; the Meritorious Service Medal with Gold Star in lieu of a second award; the Navy Commendation Medal with Combat V and Gold Star in lieu of a second award; the Vietnamese Cross of Gallantry with Gold Star, and the Vietnamese Staff Honor Medal First Class. He is also the recipient of numerous service and campaign medals as well as unit commendations; the Combat Action Ribbon; Presidential Unit Citation (two awards); the Navy Unit Commendation Award; the Meritorious Unit Citation; the National Defense Medal; the Armed Forces Expeditionary Medal, and the Vietnam Service Medal.

He was honored in March 1994 by the city of Augusta, Georgia, and the Richmond County Historical Society as one of the 24 natives of Augusta who have earned one of the nations's two highest awards for heroism (the Medal of Honor, the Distinguished Service Cross, or the Navy Cross).

Citation: "For extraordinary heroism while serving as Commanding Officer for Company D, First Battalion, Fifth Marines, First Marine Division (Reinforced), in connection with operations against the enemy in the Republic of Vietnam. On the afternoon of 23 February 1968, Company D was attacking a well-entrenched North Vietnamese Army force that was occupying a fortified section of the wall surrounding the Hue Citadel. As the Marines maneuvered forward, they began receiving a heavy volume of

Myron Charles Harrington

small arms, automatic weapons, mortar and antitank rocket fire. Realizing the seriousness of the situation, Captain Harrington skillfully deployed his 3.5-inch rocket teams into advantageous firing positions. Continuously moving from one position to another, he pinpointed enemy emplacements and skillfully directed the fire of his men. After silencing four hostile positions, he requested supporting arms fire and skillfully adjusted 60-mm mortar fire to within twenty-five meters of the forward elements of his company, while simultaneously adjusting artillery fire. Disregarding his own safety, Captain Harrington then fearlessly maneuvered to the point of the heaviest contact and, rallying his men, boldly led a determined assault against the enemy soldiers. Shouting words of encouragement to his men, he skillfully maneuvered his unit forward and directed the Marines' fire upon the hostile emplacements. Largely due to his resolute determination and intrepid fighting spirit, his men overran the hostile positions and routed the North Vietnamese soldiers, accounting for twenty-five enemy soldiers confirmed killed. By his courage, superb leadership and unfaltering devotion to duty in the face of extreme personal danger,

Captain Harrington upheld the highest traditions of the Marine Corps and the United States Naval Service."

Sources
Eugene D. Foxworth III.
Navy Cross Citation.

Hawkins, William Deane (1914–1943) *First lieutenant, United States Marine Corps, so distinguished himself in combat, during the Vietnam War, that he was (posthumously) awarded the Medal of Honor for his heroic actions.*

Born: April 18, 1914, Fort Scott, Neb.; **Place and date:** Betio Island, November 21, 1943.

Lieutenant Hawkins's father was an insurance claims adjuster; his mother, the daughter of a Missouri doctor. When he was a baby, young Hawkins suffered an accident that scarred him for life. A neighbor upset a pot of scalding hot water over him, and it was a year before his mother was able to cure the muscular damage by massage and the boy could walk again.

When he was five, the family moved to El Paso, Texas; when he was eight, his father died and his mother had to seek employment outside their home. She was employed as the secretary to a high school principal and later as a teacher at the El Paso Technical Institute.

An excellent student, young Hawkins skipped the fifth grade at LaMar and Alta Vista Schools and graduated from El Paso High School when he was only 16. He won a scholarship to the Texas College of Mines, where he studied engineering. During summer vacations, he delivered magazines and sold newspapers and worked as a bellhop, ranch hand, and railroad laborer.

When he was 21, he went to Tacoma, Washington, to work. There he was married and later divorced, at 23 he was working as an engineer for a Los Angeles title-insurance company.

After the surprise attack on Pearl Harbor, he enlisted in the Marine Corps, on January 5, 1942, and was assigned to the Seventh Recruit Battalion, Recruit Depot, San Diego. He had tried unsuccessfully to enter both the army and the United States Navy Air Corps, but his scars prevented his being accepted. Now, as a Marine, he joined the Second Marines, Second Marine Division, completed Scout Sniper School at Camp Elliott, San Diego, and on July 1, 1942, embarked on board the USS *Crescent City* for the Pacific area.

A private first class when he went overseas, he was quickly promoted to corporal and then to sergeant. On November 17, 1942, he was commissioned a second lieutenant while taking part in the Guadalcanal Campaign in the battle for the Solomon Islands. On June 1, 1943, he

was promoted to first lieutenant. Less than six months later he was killed in action leading a scout-sniper platoon in the attack on Betio Island during the assault on Tarawa.

During that two-day assault, Lieutenant Hawkins led attacks on pillboxes and Japanese installations, personally initiated an assault on a hostile position fortified by five enemy machine guns, refused to withdraw after being seriously wounded, and then destroyed three more pillboxes before he was mortally wounded, November 21, 1943.

Mr. Robert Sherrod, later to become editor of *The Saturday Evening Post,* wrote the following about the Marine platoon leader:

Hawkins had told me aboard ship that he would put his platoon of Marines up against any company of soldiers on earth and guarantee to win. He was slightly wounded by shrapnel as he came ashore in the first wave, but the furthest thing from his mind was to be evacuated. He led his platoon into the forest of coconut palms. During a day and a half, he personally cleaned out six Jap machine gun nests, sometimes standing on top of a half-track and firing point blank at four or five men who fired back at him from behind blockhouses. Lieutenant Hawkins was wounded a second time, but he still refused to retire. To say that his conduct was worthy of the highest traditions of the Marine Corps is like saying the Empire State Building is moderately high.

In recognition of his leadership and daring action against enemy positions, the air strip on Betio Island was named Hawkins Field in honor of the Marine hero. With his unit Lieutenant Hawkins also shared in the two Presidential Unit Citations awarded the First Marine Division (Reinforced) for heroic action during the Guadalcanal and Tarawa Campaigns.

Citation: "For valorous and gallant conduct above and beyond the call of duty as commanding officer of a Scout Sniper Platoon attached to the Assault Regiment in action against Japanese-held Tarawa in the Gilbert Islands, 20 and 21 November 1943. The first to disembark from the jeep lighter, 1st Lt. Hawkins unhesitatingly moved forward under heavy enemy fire at the end of the Betio Pier, neutralizing emplacements in coverage of troops assaulting the main beach positions. Fearlessly leading his men on to join the forces fighting desperately to gain a beachhead, he repeatedly risked his life throughout the day and night to direct and lead attacks on pillboxes and installations with grenades and demolitions. At dawn on the following day, 1st Lt. Hawkins resumed the dangerous mission of clearing the limited beachhead of Japanese resistance, personally initiating an assault on a hostile position fortified by 5 enemy machine-guns, and, crawling forward in the face of withering fire, boldly fired pointblank into the loopholes and completed the destruction with grenades. Refusing to withdraw after being seriously wounded in the chest during this skirmish, 1st Lt. Hawkins steadfastly carried the fight to the enemy, destroying 3 more pillboxes before he was caught in a burst of Japanese shellfire and mortally wounded. His relentless fighting spirit in the face of formidable opposition and his exceptionally daring tactics served as an inspiration to his comrades during the most crucial phase of the battle and reflect the highest credit upon the U.S. Naval Service. He gallantly gave his life for his country."

Source
Marine Corps Historical Center.
Medal of Honor Citation.

Hernandez, Rodolfo P. (b.1931) *Corporal, United States Army, Company G, 187th Airborne Regimental Combat Team, so distinguished himself in combat, during the Korean War, that he was awarded the Medal of Honor for his heroic actions.*

Born: 1931, Colton, Calif.; **Entered service at:** Fowler, Calif.; **Place and date:** Near Wontong-ni, Korea, May 31, 1951. **G.O. No.:** 40, April 21, 1962.

Citation: "Corporal Rodolfo P. Hernandez, United States Army, a member of Company G 187th Airborne Regimental Combat Team, distinguished himself by conspicuous gallantry and intrepidity above and beyond the call of duty in action against the enemy near Wontong-ni, Korea on 31 May 1951. His platoon, in defensive positions on Hill 420 came under ruthless attack by a numerically superior and fanatical hostile force, accompanied by heavy artillery, mortar, and machinegun fire that inflicted numerous casualties on the platoon. His comrades were forced to withdraw due to lack of ammunition but Corporal Hernandez, although wounded in an exchange of grenades, continued to deliver deadly fire into the ranks of the onrushing assailants until a ruptured cartridge rendered his rifle inoperative. Immediately leaving his position, Corporal Hernandez rushed the enemy armed only with rifle and bayonet. Fearlessly engaging the foe, he killed six of the enemy before falling unconscious from grenade, bayonet, and bullet wounds but his heroic action momentarily halted the enemy advance and enabled his unit to counterattack and retake the lost ground. The indomitable fighting spirit, outstanding courage, and tenacious devotion to duty clearly demonstrated by Corporal Hernandez reflect the highest credit upon himself, the infantry, and the U.S. Army."

Source
Medal of Honor Citation.

Herring, Rufus G. (b. 1921) *Lieutenant, United States Naval Reserve, LCI (G) 449, so distinguished himself in combat during World War II that he was awarded the Medal of Honor for his heroic actions.*

Born: June 11, 1921, Roseboro, N.C., **Entered service at:** North Carolina; **Place and date:** Iwo Jima, February 17, 1945.

Citation: "For conspicuous gallantry and intrepidity at the risk of his life above and beyond the call of duty as commanding officer of *LCI (G) 449* operating as a unit of *LCI (G)* Group 8, during the pre-invasion attack on Iwo Jima on 17 February 1945. Boldly closing the strongly fortified shores under the devastating fire of Japanese coastal defense guns, Lt. (then Lt. [j.g.]) Herring directed shattering barrages of 40 mm. and 20 mm. gunfire against hostile beaches until struck down by the enemy's savage counterfire which blasted the *449*'s heavy guns and whipped her decks into sheets of flame. Regaining consciousness despite profuse bleeding he was again critically wounded when a Japanese mortar crashed the conning station, instantly killing or fatally wounding most of the officers and leaving the ship wallowing without navigational control. Upon recovering the second time, Lt. Herring resolutely climbed down to the pilothouse and, fighting against his rapidly waning strength, took over the helm, established communication with the engine room, and carried on valiantly until relief could be obtained. When no longer able to stand, he propped himself against empty shell cases and rallied his men to the aid of the wounded; he maintained position in the firing line with his 20 mm. guns in action in the face of sustained enemy fire, and conned his crippled ship to safety. His unwavering fortitude, aggressive perseverance, and indomitable spirit against terrific odds reflect the highest credit upon Lt. Herring and uphold the highest traditions of the U.S. Naval Service."

Source
Medal of Honor Citation.

Hill, Daniel Harvey (1821–1889) *General officer, Confederate States Army.*

Criticism of his army commander, Braxton Bragg, to Jefferson Davis cost the South Carolinian West Pointer (1842) Daniel H. Hill his corps command and his promotion to lieutenant general in the Confederate army. Posted to the artillery, he had won two brevets in the Mexican War before resigning as a first lieutenant in the Fourth Artillery in 1849. Active in education until the outbreak of the Civil War, he was superintendent of the North Carolina Military Institute in 1861.

His southern assignments included the following: colonel, First North Carolina Volunteers (May 1, 1861); commander, Department of the Peninsula (May 31–June 1861); brigadier general, Confederate States Army (CSA) (July 10, 1861); commander, Department of Fredericksburg (July 17–July 1861); commander, District of the Pamlico, Department of North Carolina (ca. October 4–November 16, 1861); commander, First Brigade, Third (Longstreet's) Division, Potomac District, Department of Northern Virginia (November 16, 1861–January 1862); commander of forces, Leesburg, Potomac District, Department of Northern Virginia (January–March 1862); major general, CSA (March 26, 1862); commander, Fourth (Van Dorn's old) Division, Department of Northern Virginia (March–July 17, 1862); commander, Department of North Carolina (July 17–August 1862 and April 1–July 1, 1863); commander of division, Jackson's corps, Army of Northern Virginia (August 1862–April 1, 1863); temporary commander, Valley District, Army of Northern Virginia (September 6, 1862); lieutenant general, CSA (July 11, 1863); commander, Second (Hardee's old) Corps, Army of Tennessee (July 24–November 8, 1863); volunteer aide-de-camp, Department of North Carolina and Southern Virginia (May 5–18 and May 21–ca. June 1864); commander of division, Department of North Carolina and Southern Virginia (May 18–21, 1864); commander, District of Georgia, Department of South Carolina, Georgia and Florida (January 21–ca. March 1865); commander of division, Lee's corps, Army of Tennessee (ca. March and late March–April 26, 1865); and commander of corps (late March 1865).

Commanding a regiment of six-month volunteers, he played a leading role in the Confederate victory at Big Bethel. Promoted to brigadier general, he served for a time in northern Virginia and then returned to the Peninsula as a division leader with the rank of major general. He saw action at Yorktown, Williamsburg, and Seven Pines and during the Seven Days. Left in southeastern Virginia during the Second Bull Run Campaign, he rejoined Lee's army for the Maryland Campaign, performing well at both South Mountain and Antietam. His last battle with the Army of Northern Virginia was at Fredericksburg. He then returned to command the Department of North Carolina until named a lieutenant general and ordered to Bragg's army. He took over Hardee's old corps, leading it at Chickamauga. Disgusted with Bragg's failure to reap the benefits of the victory, he made his view known to the president, who still supported his friend. Hill was relieved of corps command and Davis refused to submit his nomination as lieutenant general to the Senate. Thus he reverted to a major generalcy on October 15, 1863.

His next action was as a volunteer on Beauregard's staff at Drewry's Bluff and Petersburg. He was in command of a provisional division for a couple of days. Ordered to the Atlantic coast, he finished out the war with Joseph E.

Johnston's army in the Carolinas as a division commander. After the surrender he returned to education and engaged in literary and historical writing.

Source

Bridges, Leonard Hal. *Lee's Maverick General, Daniel Harvey Hill.* 1965. Reprint, Lincoln: University of Nebraska Press, 1991.

Hooker, Joseph (1814–1879) *Union general officer.*

One of the most immodest and immoral of the high Union commanders, "Fighting Joe" Hooker frequently felt slighted by his superiors and requested to be relieved of duty. The Massachusetts native and West Pointer (1837) had been posted to the artillery but was serving as a staff officer when he won three brevets in Mexico. Unfortunately for his later career he testified against Winfield Scott before a court of inquiry on the Mexican War. After a two-year leave he resigned on February 21, 1853, to settle in California, where he was in the farming and land businesses.

At the outset of the Civil War he became a colonel of the state militia but soon offered his services to Washington, where his anti-Scott testimony haunted him. As a civilian he witnessed the disaster at First Bull Run and wrote to Lincoln complaining of the mismanagement and advancing his own claim to a commission. After he was accepted, his assignments included the following: brigadier general, USV (August 3, 1861, to rank from May 17); commander of brigade, Division of the Potomac (August–October 3, 1861); commander of division, Army of the Potomac (October 3, 1861–March 13, 1862); commander, Second Division, Third Corps, Army of the Potomac (March 13–September 5, 1862); major general, USV (May 5, 1862); commander, Third Corps, Army of Virginia (September 6–12, 1862); commander, First Corps, Army of the Potomac (September 12–17, 1862); brigadier general, USA (September 20, 1862); commander, Fifth Corps, Army of the Potomac (November 10–16, 1862); commander, Center Grand Division, Army of the Potomac (November 16, 1862–January 26, 1863); commander, Department and Army of the Potomac (January 26–June 28, 1863); commander, 11th and 12th Corps, Army of the Cumberland (September 25–April 14, 1863); commander, 20th Corps, Army of the Cumberland (April 14–July 28, 1864); and commander, Northern Department (October 1, 1864–June 27, 1865).

After leading a brigade and then a division around Washington he went with McClellan's army to the Peninsula, earning a reputation for looking after his men during the siege operations at Yorktown. His other reputation as a heavy user of alcohol was not so enviable. He was particularly distinguished at Williamsburg, and although he felt slighted by his commander's report, he was named a major general of volunteers from the date of the action. Further fighting for Hooker occurred at Seven Pines and throughout the Seven Days. After its close he scored a minor success in the retaking of Malvern Hill from the Confederates. Transferred to Pope with his division, he took part in the defeat at Second Bull Run.

Given command of a corps for the Maryland Campaign, he fought at South Mountain and was wounded in the foot early in the morning fighting at Antietam. Three days later he was named a regular army brigadier general. Returning to duty, he briefly commanded the Fifth Corps before being given charge of the Center Grand Division when Burnside reorganized his army into these two-corps formations. After the defeat at Fredericksburg and the disastrous Mud March, Burnside was relieved. In a letter to the Army of the Potomac's new commander, Hooker, Lincoln praised the general's fighting abilities but strongly questioned Hooker's previous criticism of commanders and feared that it might haunt the new chief. Lincoln was also critical of the general's loose talk on the need for a military dictatorship to win the war.

Once Hooker was in charge his headquarters was roundly criticized by many as a combination of bar and brothel. When he launched his campaign against Lee, Hooker swore off liquor. This may have hurt more than it helped. After a brilliantly executed maneuver around Lee's flank and the crossing of two rivers, Hooker lost his nerve and withdrew his forces back into the Wilderness to await reinforcements from John Sedgewick's command from Fredericksburg. Here he felt convinced that Lee was in retreat but was surprised by Jackson's flank attack, which routed Oliver "oh" O. Howard's 11th Corps. To make matters worse, Hooker was dazed by the effects of a shell's striking a pillar on the porch of his headquarters. He lost control of the army and ordered a withdrawal. Kept in command, he led the army northward in the early part of the Gettysburg Campaign until he resigned on June 28, 1863, over control of the garrison at Harpers Ferry. On January 28, 1864, he received the Thanks of Congress for the beginnings of the campaign. With the Union defeat at Chickamauga, he was given charge of the Army of the Potomac's 11th and 12th Corps and sent to the relief of the Army of the Cumberland at Chattanooga. In the battles around that place in November 1863 he did well in the maintenance of open supply lines and in the taking of Lookout Mountain. However, in Grant's report his actions were overshadowed by the less distinguished role of Sherman. The next spring the two corps merged into the new 20th Corps with Hooker at their head. He fought through the Atlanta Campaign, but when McPherson was killed before the city and Howard received command of the Army of the Tennessee, he asked to be relieved. This request was granted, and he finished the war in the quiet sector of Michigan, Ohio, Indiana, and Illinois. Brevetted major general in the regular army for Chattanooga, he was mustered out of the volunteers on September 1, 1866, and two years later was retired with the increased rank of major general. Always popular with his men, he lacked the confidence of his subordinate officers and was quarrelsome with his superiors. His nickname, which he never liked, resulted from the deletion of a dash in a journalistic dispatch that was discussing the Peninsula Campaign and "Fighting" was thereafter linked to his name. Popular legend has it that his name was permanently attached to prostitutes from his Civil War actions in rounding them up in one area of Washington. He died in Garden City, New York, on October 31, 1879, and is buried in Cincinnati.

Source

Herbert, Walter H. *Fighting Joe Hooker.* 1944. Reprint, Lincoln: University of Nebraska Press/Bison Books, 1999.

Hopkins, Esek (1718–1802) *Commodore, United States Navy, First commodore of the United States Navy in the period of the American Revolution (1775–1783).*

Born on April 26, 1718, in Providence, Rhode Island, Hopkins went to sea at the age of 20, proving his ability as a seaman and trader, and a marriage into wealth put him at the head of a large merchant fleet prior to the French and Indian War (1754–63). By privateering during that war, he added to his fortune and won a considerable naval reputation. Rhode Island named him a brigadier general of its land forces at the outbreak of the Revolution, but a call from the Continental Congress, in which his brother was chairman of the naval committee, induced him to forsake the army and accept the command (December 22, 1775) of the first Continental Fleet, then outfitting at Philadelphia. Instructed to attack the British fleet under John Murray, fourth earl of Dunmore, in Chesapeake Bay, Hopkins considered his orders discretionary and the enemy too strong. He therefore sailed his fleet of eight armed vessels to the Bahamas, captured considerable war matériel at New Providence Island, and his return fought an inconclusive action with the British ship *Glasgow* (April 1776).

Dissatisfaction with the achievements of the fleet and its subsequent inactivity in Rhode Island led to an investigation by Congress. Censured for disobedience of orders, Hopkins returned to the fleet, but his continued inactivity and quarrels with his officers induced Congress to suspend him from his command in March 1777. He was dismissed from the navy in 1778 and thereafter played a prominent part in Rhode Island politics. He died February 26, 1802, in Providence, Rhode Island.

Source and Additional Reading

Field, Edward. *Esek Hopkins: Commander-in-Chief of the Continental Navy. Providence,* R.I.: Preston & Rounds, 1898.

Fowler, William M. Jr. *Rebels under Sail: The American Navy during the Revolution.* New York: Scribner, 1976.

Morgan, William J. *Captain to Northward: The New England Captains in the Continental Navy.* Barre, Mass.: Barre *Gazette*, 1959.

Houghton, Kenneth J. (b. 1920) *Major general, United States Marine Corps.*

Born August 19, 1920, in San Francisco, California, Houghton was commissioned a second lieutenant in September 1942 and first saw combat during World War II at Tarawa, in the Marshall Islands, and on Saipan. For his service with a Marine reconnaissance company during the Korean War, he received his first Silver Star and Bronze Star with Combat V and a Gold Star in lieu of a second Bronze Star. Featured on the cover of the September 4, 1950, issue of *Life* magazine, he was wounded in action the next month. From April 1964 to February 1967, he was the action officer (J-3), for the Joint Chiefs of Staff and was awarded the Legion of Merit for his service. He then took command of the Fifth Marine Regiment in Vietnam and for his heroic actions received the Navy Cross; a Gold Star in lieu of a second Silver Star, and two Gold Stars in lieu of second and third Purple Hearts. From August 1967 to February 1968, he was assistant chief of staff with the third Marine Amphibious Force (III MAF). He was promoted to brigadier general in August 1968 and to major general in April 1973. He retired on October 31, 1977, at the Marine Corps Recruit Depot (MCRD), San Diego, California.

Citation: "For extraordinary heroism as Commanding Officer, Fifth Marines, First Marine Division (Reinforced) in the Republic of Vietnam from 26 May to 5 June 1967. The Fifth Marine Regiment was launched on Operation UNION II to track down the remnants of the 21st North Vietnamese Regiment, which had been thoroughly decimated by them nine days previous. Responding to intelligence reports that the enemy was attempting to withdraw to the western mountains, Colonel Houghton committed two battalions in pursuit. The First Battalion swept overland while the Third Battalion was inserted by helicopter near Cam La. The Third Battalion met with heavy resistance, but completely overran the enemy positions, causing many casualties. He was constantly in the operational area, bravely exposing himself to all the hazards of the battlefield. Colonel Houghton revised his tactics when intelligence reports indicated a much larger force in the area, which was identified as the 3d North Vietnamese Regiment and pointed to a buildup along the Suio Cau Doi River, in the vicinity of Vinh Huy (2). Instantly reacting, he launched his attack from the east, with the First and Third Battalions abreast and the second Battalion in reserve. On 2 June the First Battalion came under intense enemy mortar, recoilless rifle and automatic weapons fire, indicating contact with the main force of the 3d North Vietnamese Army force. While the First and Third Battalions maintained heavy pressure on the enemy, he committed the Second Battalion to assault the enemy's flank. Although wounded at this time, he continued to aggressively advance on the enemy with renewed determination. Colonel Houghton launched a bold night attack, which smashed through the enemy defenses, and annihilated the large enemy force. By his outstanding leadership, gallant fighting spirit and bold initiative, he contributed materially to the success of the First Marine Division, thereby upholding the highest traditions of the Marine Corps and the United States Naval Service."

Source and Additional Reading

Marine Corps Historical Center.
Navy Cross Citation.

Howard, Jimmie E. (b. 1929) *Gunnery sergeant (then staff sergeant), United States Marine Corps, Company C, First Reconnaissance Battalion, First Marine Division, so distinguished himself in combat, during the Vietnam War, that he was awarded the Medal of Honor for his heroic actions.*

Born: July 27, 1929, Burlington, Iowa; **Entered service at:** Burlington, Iowa. **Place and date:** Republic of Vietnam, June 16, 1966.

Citation: "For conspicuous gallantry and intrepidity at the risk of his own life above and beyond the call of duty G/Sgt. Howard and his 18-man platoon were occupying an observation post deep within enemy-controlled territory. Shortly after midnight a Viet Cong force of estimated battalion size approached the Marines' position and launched a vicious attack with small arms, automatic weapons, and mortar fire. Reacting swiftly and fearlessly in the face of the overwhelming odds, G/Sgt. Howard skillfully organized his small but determined force into a tight perimeter defense and calmly moved from position to position to direct his men's fire. Throughout the night, during assault after assault, his courageous example and firm leadership inspired and motivated his men to withstand the unrelenting fury of the hostile fire in the seemingly hopeless situation. He constantly shouted encouragement to his men and exhibited imagination and resourcefulness in directing their return fire. When fragments of an exploding enemy

Jimmie E. Howard

grenade wounded him severely and prevented him from moving his legs, he distributed his ammunition to the remaining members of his platoon and proceeded to maintain radio communications and direct air strikes on the enemy with uncanny accuracy. At dawn, despite the fact that 5 men were killed and all but 1 wounded, his beleaguered platoon was still in command of its position. When evacuation helicopters approached his position, G/Sgt. Howard warned them away and called for additional air strikes and directed devastating small-arms fire and air strikes against enemy automatic weapons positions in order to make the landing zone as secure as possible. Through his extraordinary courage and resolute fighting spirit, G/Sgt. Howard was largely responsible for preventing the loss of his entire platoon. His valiant leadership and courageous fighting spirit served to inspire the men of his platoon to heroic endeavor in the face of overwhelming odds, and reflect the highest credit upon G/Sgt. Howard, the Marine Corps, and the U.S. Naval Service."

Source

Medal of Honor Citation.

Norton, Maj. Bruce H. *Sergeant Major, U.S. Marines.* New York: Ivy Books, 1995.

Howard, O. O. (1830–1909) *Union general officer in the American Civil War (1861–1865) who headed the Freedmen's Bureau (1865–1872) to help rehabilitate former slaves during the period of Reconstruction.*

Born on November 8, 1830, in Leeds, Maine, and graduate of the United States Military Academy, West Point, New York (1854), Howard resigned his regular army commission at the beginning of the war to become colonel of a Maine volunteer regiment. He was given the rank of major general (1862) after fighting in Virginia at the First Battle of Bull Run, the Peninsular Campaign, the Battle of Fair Oaks (Seven Pines)—in which he lost his right arm—and Antietam. He also took part in the Battle of Chancellorsville (May) and in the Tennessee and Atlanta Campaigns (1863–64). Promoted to command the Army of the Tennessee (July 1864), he marched with Gen. William T. Sherman through Georgia to the sea (November–December) and fought in the Carolinas Campaign (early 1865).

Unusually interested in the welfare of the nearly 4 million slaves who had been freed during the war, Howard was appointed by President Andrew Johnson as commissioner of the Bureau of Refugees, Freedmen, and Abandoned Lands (the Freedmen's Bureau). Because he was not a skilled administrator, many abuses occurred in the bureau, much of whose staff was poorly trained. Nevertheless, his agency fed millions of the indigent, built hospitals, provided direct medical aid, and negotiated thousands of labor contracts for the former slaves. Most importantly it established a multitude of schools and training institutes for blacks; Howard University, Washington, D.C. (founded 1867), was named in recognition of his work in the bureau and as one of the university's founders. He served as the university's third president (1869–74), after which he resigned to return to military service.

Howard fought against Native Americans in the West and served as superintendent at West Point (1880–82). He wrote several books on military history in addition to his autobiography, published in 1907. He died October 26, 1909, in Burlington, Vermont.

Source

Howard, Oliver O. *The Freedmen's Bureau.* Lee & Shepard, Boston: 1885.

Hulbert, Henry Louis (b. 1867) *First lieutenant, United States Marine Corps, in whose honor the destroyer USS Hulbert DD-342, was named. For his actions during his first experience in combat, in Samar Philippines, in 1899, he was awarded the Medal of Honor. In France, in 1918, he was awarded the Distinguished Service Cross, the* *croix de guerre with palm, and the Navy Cross before he was killed in action in October near Blanc Mont.*

Born: January 12, 1867, Yorkshire County, Kingston-upon Hull, England: **Entered service at:** Mare Island, Calif, March 28, 1989.

Hulbert was 31 years old and a civil engineer when he enlisted in the Marine Corps. Between 1899 and 1918 he packed 19 years of spotless enlisted service in the United States Marine Corps. When the corps made him a Marine gunner (warrant officer), in March 1917, it noted that he had advanced to the top enlisted grade without even missing a Good Conduct Medal for any enlistment period.

Within a year after his enlistment he was serving on board the U.S. fighting ship USS *Philadelphia* when the Americans and British landed a joint force in Soma to protect their consulates from warring tribes, each trying to establish its chief as the supreme ruler of the island of Upolu. During a clash with natives near the village of Faglii on April 1, 1899, Hulbert was a member of a small rear guard, which held off the natives while the remainder of the column pulled back toward the beach. Two other Marines were killed, and another portion of the rear guard withdrew when its Colt's automatic gun was disabled. Hulbert made a lone stand with his rifle until the wounded men and civilians reached safety. "His behavior throughout was worthy of all praise and honor," reported Hulbert's commanding officer, First Lieutenant Constantine Perkins.

In 1917, Hulbert, then on duty in the office of Major General Barnett, commandant of the Marine Corps, was considered too old for duty in France. But he bothered everyone until the corps relented and shipped him off to Europe. In France his superiors told him to use his engineering knowledge to help build barracks and a rifle range. He did this work and still found time to get up front in the fighting.

On June 6, 1918, Hulbert repeatedly risked enemy fire to get supplies up to the front at Chateau-Thierry, and at one point he organized an attack that charged enemy machine guns, killed several German gunners, and captured most of the guns. For this heroic action the United States Army awarded him the Distinguished Service Cross; later, an award of the Navy Cross was made for the same action. Dispatches from Belleau Wood action also cited his courage.

On July 17, 1918, he was appointed a temporary second lieutenant, and on September 6, 1918, he was promoted to the rank of first lieutenant. Less than one month later, on October 4, Hulbert was at the front with the 66th Company, Fifth Marines. He was leading an attack in the Battle of Blanc Mont, in the Meuse-Argonne, when he was killed by enemy fire. For this attack, during which he continually exposed himself to enemy fire while leading his men, Hulbert was awarded the French croix de guerre with palm. Dispatches also mentioned his gallantry in action and later gained for him the Silver Star Medal.

On July 10, 1918, Hulbert was at the front when he received word that General Pershing was going to present him with the Distinguished Service Cross, which he had won at Chateau-Thierry. The ceremony would take place back across the Marne, and since Hulbert was late leaving the trenches, he borrowed a horse from an artillery outfit. But the parade was already drawn up when Hulbert caught sight of the field. Pershing was there, and so were the president of France, Marshal Foch, and other military and civilian dignitaries. The Marne flowed between Hulbert and his proper place in the honor rank, and crossing by the nearest bridge meant an additional ride that would take several minutes. The Marine gunner reined his horse down to the river and swam across alongside the animal.

Hulbert snapped to dripping attention in front of Pershing, saluted, and said, "Sir, the order was for 2:30. It is now 2:29 and one-half." Hulbert had always prided himself on promptness.

Citation: "For distinguished conduct in the presence of the enemy at Samar, Philippine Islands, 1 April 1899."

Sources
Marine Corps Historical Center.
Medal of Honor Citation.

Hull, Isaac (1773–1843) *American naval officer in the War of 1812, who as captain of "Old Ironsides," defeated the British* Guerrière *in the War of 1812.*

Hull was born in Shelton, Connecticut, on March 9, 1773, and was adopted early in life by his uncle, General William Hull, who lived in Newton, Massachusetts. After some merchant service, Isaac was commissioned a lieutenant in the new United States Navy on March 9, 1798, serving first in the 44-gun frigate *Constitution* ("Old Ironsides"). In the Barbary Wars he commanded the brig *Argus* and skillfully assisted William Eaton in the capture of the Libyan port of Derna.

In command of the *Constitution* early in the War of 1812, through superior seamanship Hull saved his frigate from capture, escaping from a British fleet composed of a ship of the line and several frigates. A few weeks later, brilliant seamanship and gunnery enabled him in a short action that lasted less than 30 minutes to wreck and capture the British 38-gun frigate *Guerrière*, about 700 miles (1,130 kilometers) east of Boston.

Hull commanded the Pacific Squadron from 1824 to 1827, most of the time in Callao, Peru, during the liberation of Peru by Simón Bolívar, with whom he maintained good relations. He headed the Washington Navy Yard from 1829 to 1835 and commanded the Mediterranean

Squadron from 1838 to 1841. Hull became unpopular in the navy in later years, partly because he took his wife and her sister on cruises, inconveniencing his officers. Hull was twice charged with financial irregularities but was exonerated. He died in Philadelphia on February 13, 1843.

Hull was an excellent seaman, an intelligent, brave, skilled commander and administrator. His victory over the *Guerrière* grave destroyed the myth of British naval superiority and rallied the morale of the nation.

Source and Additional Reading

Allen, Gardner W., ed. *Papers of Commodore Hull.* Boston: Boston Athenaeum, 1929.

Dupuy, Trevor N., Curt Johnson, and David L. Bongard. *The Harper Encyclopedia of Military Biography.* New York: HarperCollins, 1992.

Grant, Bruce. *Isaac Hull: Captain of Old Ironsides.* Chicago: Pellegrini & Cudahy, 1947.

I

Ingman, Einar H., Jr. (b. 1929) *Sergeant (then corporal) United States Army, Company E, 17th Infantry Regiment, Seventh Infantry Division, so distinguished himself in combat, during the Korean War, that he was awarded the Medal of Honor for his heroic actions.*

Born: 1929, Milwaukee, Wis.; **Entered service at:** Tomahawk, Wis.; **Place and date:** Near Maltari, Korea, February 26, 1951. **G.O. No.:** 68, August 2, 1951.

Citation: "Sergeant Einar H. Ingman Jr., Infantry, United States Army, a member of Company E 17th Infantry Regiment, 7th Infantry Division, distinguished himself by conspicuous gallantry and intrepidity above and beyond the call of duty in action against the enemy near Maltari, Korea, on 26 February 1951. The two leading squads of the assault platoon of his company, while attacking a strongly fortified ridge held by the enemy, were pinned down by withering fire and both squad leaders and several men were wounded. Corporal Ingman assumed command, reorganized and combined the two squads, then moved from one position to another, designating fields of fire and giving advice and encouragement to the men. Locating an enemy machinegun position that was raking his men with devastating fire he charged it alone, threw a grenade into the position, and killed the remaining crew with rifle fire. Another enemy machinegun opened fire approximately 15 yards away and inflicted additional casualties to the group and stopped the attack. When Corporal Ingman charged the second position he was hit by grenade fragments and a hail of fire, which seriously wounded him about the face and neck and knocked him to the ground. With incredible courage and stamina, he arose instantly and, using only his rifle, killed the entire guncrew before falling unconscious from his wounds. As a result of the singular action by Corporal Ingman the defense of the enemy was broken, his squad secured its objective, and more than 100 hostile troops abandoned their weapons and fled in disorganized retreat. Corporal Ingman's indomitable courage, extraordinary heroism, and superb leadership reflect the highest credit on himself and are in keeping with the esteemed traditions of the infantry and the U.S. Army."

Source
Medal of Honor Citation.

Ingram, Robert R. *Hospital corpsman (HM3), United States Navy, so distinguished himself in combat that he was awarded the Medal of Honor for his heroic actions during the Vietnam War in 1966.*

Citation: "For conspicuous gallantry and intrepidity at the risk of his life above and beyond the call of duty while serving as Corpsman with Company C, First Battalion, Seventh Marines against elements of a North Vietnam Aggressor (NVA) battalion in Quang Ngai Province Republic of Vietnam on 28 March 1966. Petty Officer Ingram accompanied the point platoon as it aggressively dispatched an outpost of an NVA battalion. The momentum of the attack rolled off a ridgeline down a tree covered slope to a small paddy and a village beyond. Suddenly, the village tree line exploded with an intense hail of automatic rifle fire from approximately 100 North Vietnamese regulars. In mere moments, the platoon ranks were decimated. Oblivious to the danger, Petty Officer Ingram crawled across the bullet spattered terrain to reach a downed Marine. As he administered aid, a bullet went through the palm of his hand. Calls for "CORPSMAN" echoed across the ridge. Bleeding, he edged across the fire swept landscape, collecting ammunition from the dead and administering aid to the wounded. Receiving two more wounds before realizing the third wound was life threatening, he looked for a way off the face of the ridge, but again he heard the call for corpsman and again, he resolutely answered. Though severely wounded three times, he rendered aid to those incapable until he finally reached the right flank of the platoon. While dressing the head wound of another corpsman, he sustained his fourth bullet wound. From sixteen hundred hours until just prior to sunset, Petty Officer Ingram pushed, pulled, cajoled, and doctored his Marines. Enduring the pain from his many wounds and disregarding the probability of his demise, Petty Officer Ingram's intrepid actions saved many lives that day. By his indomitable fighting spirit, daring initiative, and unfaltering dedication to duty, Petty Officer Ingram reflected great credit upon himself and upheld the highest traditions of the United States Naval Service."

Source
Medal of Honor Citation.

Izac, Edouard Victor Michel (b. 1891) *Lieutenant, United States Navy, distinguished himself as a prisoner of war, during World War I, and was awarded the Medal of Honor for his heroic actions on May 21, 1918.*

Born: December 18, 1891, Cresco, Iowa; **Entered service at:** Illinois; **Place and date:** Aboard German submarine *U-90* as a prisoner of war, May 21, 1918.

Citation: "When the U.S.S. *President Lincoln* was attacked and sunk by the German submarine *U-90,* on 21 May 1918, Lt. Izac was captured and held as a prisoner on board *U-90* until the return of the submarine to Germany, when he was confined in the prison camp. During his stay on the *U-90,* he obtained information of the movements of German submarines, which was so important that he determined to escape, with a view of making this information available to the U.S. and Allied Naval authorities. In attempting to carry out this plan, he jumped through the window of a rapidly moving train at the imminent risk of death, not only from the nature of the act itself, but from the fire of the armed German soldiers who were guarding him. Having been recaptured and reconfined, Lt. Izac made a second and successful attempt to escape, breaking his way through barbed-wire fences and deliberately drawing the fire of the armed guards in the hope of permitting others to escape during the confusion. He made his way through the mountains of southwestern Germany, having only raw vegetables for food, and at the end, swam the River Rhine during the night in the immediate vicinity of German sentries."

Source
Medal of Honor Citation.

J

Jackson, Arthur J.

Jackson, Arthur J. (b.1924) *Private first class, United States Marine Corps, Third Battalion, Seventh Marines, First, Marine Division, so distinguished himself in combat, during World War II, that he was awarded the Medal of Honor for his heroic actions.*

Born: October 18, 1924, Cleveland, Ohio; **Entered service at:** Oregon; **Place and date:** Island of Peleliu in the Palau group, September 18, 1944.

Citation: "For conspicuous gallantry and intrepidity at the risk of his life above and beyond the call of duty while serving with the 3d Battalion, 7th Marines, 1st Marine Division, in action against enemy Japanese forces on the Island of Peleliu in the Palau group, 18 September 1944. Boldly taking the initiative when his platoon's left flank advance was held up by the fire of Japanese troops concealed in strongly fortified positions, Pfc. Jackson unhesitatingly proceeded forward of our lines and, courageously defying the heavy barrages, charged a large pillbox housing approximately 35 enemy soldiers. Pouring his automatic fire into the opening of the fixed installation to trap the occupying troops, he hurled white phosphorus grenades and explosive charges brought up by a fellow Marine, demolishing the pillbox and killing all of the enemy. Advancing alone under the continuous fire from other hostile emplacements, he employed similar means to smash 2 smaller positions in the immediate vicinity. Determined to crush the entire pocket of resistance although harassed on all sides by the shattering blasts of Japanese weapons and covered only by small rifle parties, he stormed 1 gun position after another, dealing death and destruction to the savagely fighting enemy in his inexorable drive against the remaining defenses, and succeeded in wiping out a total of 12 pillboxes and 50 Japanese soldiers. Stouthearted and indomitable, despite the terrific odds, Pfc. Jackson resolutely maintained control of the platoon's left flank movement throughout his valiant 1-man assault and, by his cool decision and relentless fighting spirit during a critical situation, contributed essentially to the complete annihilation of the enemy in the southern sector of the island. His gallant initiative and heroic conduct in the face of extreme peril reflect the highest credit upon Pfc. Jackson and the U.S. Naval Service."

Source
Medal of Honor Citation.

Jackson, Thomas Jonathan ("Stonewall")

Jackson, Thomas Jonathan ("Stonewall") (1824–1863) *General officer, Confederate States Army.*

Next to Robert E. Lee himself, Thomas J. Jackson is the most revered of all Confederate commanders. A graduate of West Point (1846), he had served in the artillery in the Mexican War, earning two brevets, before resigning to accept a professorship at the Virginia Military Institute. Thought strange by the cadets, he earned "Tom Fool Jackson" and "Old Blue Light" as nicknames. At the outbreak of the Civil War he was commissioned a colonel in the Virginia forces and dispatched to Harper's Ferry, where he was active in organizing the raw recruits until relieved by Joe Johnston. His later assignments included the following: commander, First Brigade, Army of the Shenandoah (May–July 20, 1861); brigadier general, Confederate States Army (CSA) (June 17, 1861); commander, First Brigade, Second Corps, Army of the Potomac (July 20–October 1861); major general, CSA (October 7, 1861); commander, Valley District, Department of Northern Virginia (November 4, 1861–June 26, 1862); commander, Second Corps, Army of Northern Virginia (June 26, 1862–May 2, 1863); and lieutenant general, CSA (October 10, 1862).

Leaving Harper's Ferry, his brigade moved with Johnston to join Beauregard at Manassas. In the fight at First Bull Run they were so distinguished that both the brigade and its commander were dubbed "Stonewall" by General Barnard Bee. (However, Bee may have been complaining that Jackson was not coming to his support.) The First Brigade was the only Confederate brigade to have its nickname become its official designation. That fall Jackson was given command of the Valley with a promotion to major general.

That winter he launched a dismal campaign into the western part of the state that resulted in a long feud with General William Loring and caused Jackson to submit his resignation, which he was persuaded to withdraw. In March he launched an attack on what he thought was a Union rear guard at Kernstown.

Faulty intelligence from his cavalry chief, Turner Ashby, led to a defeat. A religious man, Jackson always regretted having fought on a Sunday. But the defeat had the desired result, halting reinforcements being sent to General McClellan's army from the Valley. In May Jackson defeated Fremont's advance at McDowell, and later that month he launched a brilliant campaign that kept several Union commanders in the area off balance. He won victories at Front Royal, First Winchester, Cross Keys, and Port Republic. He then joined Lee in the defense of Richmond but displayed a lack of vigor during the Seven Days.

Detached from Lee, he swung off to the north to face John Pope's army and after a slipshod battle at Cedar Mountain, slipped behind Pope and captured his Manassas junction supply base. He then hid along an incomplete branch railroad and awaited Lee and Longstreet. Attacked before they arrived, he held on until Longstreet could launch a devastating attack that produced a second Bull Run victory.

In the invasion of Maryland, Jackson was detached to capture Harper's Ferry and was afterward distinguished at Antietam with Lee. He was promoted after this and given command of the now official Second Corps. It had been known as a wing or command before this. He was disappointed with the victory at Fredericksburg because it could not be followed up. In his greatest day he led his corps around the Union right flank at Chancellorsville and routed the 11th Corps. Reconnoitering that night, he was returning to his own lines when he was mortally wounded by some of his own men.

After the amputation of his arm, he died eight days later on May 10, 1863, of pneumonia. A superb commander, he had several faults. Personnel problems haunted him, as in the feuds with Loring and with Garnett after Kernstown. His choices for promotion were often not first rate. He did not give his subordinates enough latitude, thereby denying them the training for higher positions under Lee's loose command style. This was especially devastating in the case of his immediate successor, Richard Ewell.

"Stonewall" Jackson was a fearless, intelligent, aggressive combat commander; a brilliant tactician; and a master of rapid maneuver. His Shenandoah campaign was a strategic masterpiece and won his hard-marching men the sobriquet "Jackson's foot cavalry." A strict disciplinarian, he was idolized by his men and greatly admired by Robert E. Lee, who wrote to him after Chancellorsville, "You have lost your left arm. I have lost my right arm."

After his death at Guinea Station, Virginia, Stonewall Jackson was buried in Lexington, Virginia.

Source and Additional Reading

Henderson, G. F. R. *Stonewall Jackson and the American Civil War.* New York: Macmillan, 1997.
Robertson, James I. *Stonewall Jackson.* New York: Macmillan, 1995.

Thomas Jonathan "Stonewall" Jackson

Jackson, Willis *First lieutenant, Company F, 35th Infantry Regiment, 25th Infantry Division, United States Army, distinguished himself by extraordinary heroism in action against the enemy in the vicinity of Seoul, Korea, on May 21, 1951, and was awarded the Distinguished Service Cross.*

Citation: "On that date, Company F was assigned the mission of securing Hill 329 from a well-entrenched and fanatically determined enemy. Lieutenant Jackson was leading one of the assault platoons up the slope when a sudden burst of intense and accurate automatic-weapons fire from the enemy emplacement halted his men in an exposed area, pinning them down and painfully wounding Lieutenant Jackson. As friendly artillery began to bombard the hostile position, the platoon renewed its attack and fought fiercely for two hours until enemy fire from the crest of the hill became so intense that they were pinned down once more. In an effort to rally his men into making a final sweeping assault against the hilltop, Lieutenant Jackson single-handedly charged an enemy position and, despite his wound, wrested an enemy soldier's own weapon from him and beat him to death with it. This courageous action so inspired Lieutenant Jackson's men that they charged forward, overrunning the enemy emplacements. As the enemy fled in wild disorder down the reverse slope of the hill, Lieutenant Jackson pitched grenades after them and then succeeded in killing three more of the enemy with his rifle. Despite his painful wound, he organized his men in a defense against a counterattack and only fell back to be treated when the company commander ordered him to do so. The extraordinary heroism and completely selfless devotion to duty displayed by Lieutenant Jackson reflect great credit on himself and were in keeping with the highest traditions of the military service."

Source
Distinguished Service Cross Citation.

Douglas T. Jacobson

Jacobson, Douglas T. (b. 1925) *Private first class, United States Marine Corps Reserve, Third Battalion, 23d Marines, Fourth Marine Division, so distinguished himself in combat that he was awarded the Medal of Honor for his heroic actions.*

Born: November 25, 1925, Rochester, N.Y.; **Entered service at:** New York; **Place and date:** Iwo Jima, Volcano Islands, February 26, 1945.

Citation: "For conspicuous gallantry and intrepidity at the risk of his life above and beyond the call of duty while serving with the 3d Battalion, 23d Marines, 4th Marine Division, in combat against enemy Japanese forces during the seizure of Iwo Jima in the Volcano Islands, 26 February 1945. Promptly destroying a stubborn 20 mm antiaircraft gun and its crew after assuming the duties of a bazooka man who had been killed, Pfc. Jacobson waged a relentless battle as his unit fought desperately toward the summit of Hill 382 in an effort to penetrate the heart of Japanese cross-island defense. Employing his weapon with ready accuracy when his platoon was halted by overwhelming enemy fire on 26 February, he first destroyed 2 hostile machinegun positions, then attacked a large blockhouse, completely neutralizing the fortification before dispatching the 5-man crew of a second pillbox and exploding the installation with a terrific demolitions blast. Moving steadily forward, he wiped out an earth-covered rifle emplacement and, confronted by a cluster of similar emplacements which constituted the perimeter of enemy defenses in his assigned sector, fearlessly advanced, quickly reduced all 6 positions to a shambles, killed 10 of the enemy, and enabled our forces to occupy the strong point. Determined to widen the breach thus forced, he volunteered his services to an adjacent assault company, neutralized a pillbox holding up its advance, opened fire on a Japanese tank pouring a steady stream of bullets on 1 of our supporting tanks, and smashed the enemy tank's gun turret in a brief but furious action culminating in a single-handed assault against still another blockhouse and the subsequent neutralization of its firepower. By his dauntless skill and valor, Pfc. Jacobson destroyed a total of 16 enemy positions and annihilated approximately 75

Japanese, thereby contributing essentially to the success of his division's operations against this fanatically defended outpost of the Japanese Empire. His gallant conduct in the face of tremendous odds enhanced and sustained the highest traditions of the U.S. Naval Service."

Source and Additional Reading
Medal of Honor Citation.
Blakeney, Jane. *Heroes: U.S. Marine Corps 1861–1955.* Washington, D.C.: Guthrie Lithograhic; 1956.

Jacques, Maurice J. (1931–1997) *Sergeant major, United States Marine Corps.*

Jacques was born June 17, 1931, and enlisted in the Marine Corps from Lawrence, Massachusetts, in June 1948, at the age of 17. He distinguished himself as a model recruit at Parris Island, South Carolina, and was one of only five Marines in his series to be promoted to the rank of private first class on graduation. His first tour

Maurice J. Jacques

of duty was with Company B, First Battalion, Fifth Marine Regiment, on Guam, until March 1949. Next was duty at the Marine Barracks Pearl Harbor under the command of then Col. Lewis B. "Chesty" Puller, where Jacques he won the Hawaiian Golden Gloves Boxing Championships in 1949.

Jacques's first taste of combat occurred during the Korean War in early 1953. As a rifle squad leader during the Battle of the Nevada Cities (Marine combat outposts named Reno Block, Vegas, and Carson), Jacques saw his platoon decimated when elements of the Chinese 358th, 46th Chinese Communist Forces (CCF) army swarmed down upon them, with an enemy ratio of 20 to 1.

This action, in March 1952, developed into a five-day siege involving over 4,000 ground and air Marines and was the most bloody action Marines on the western front had yet engaged in. Marine casualties totaled 1,015: 116 killed, 441 wounded/evacuated, 360 wounded/not evacuated, and 98 missing, of whom 19 were known to be prisoners. Enemy casualties were listed conservatively as 2,221. This represented 536 killed, 654 estimated killed, 174 counted wounded, 853 estimated wounded, and 4 prisoners. The Marines of Jacques's regiment, moreover, in the five days of furious fighting had knocked out the 358th CCF Regiment, numbering between 3,000 and 3,500 men, and destroyed its effectiveness as a unit.

Jacques spent one year in combat, from early December 1952 until his departure on December 10, 1953. Those early "lessons learned" in bloody Korea would serve him well in the years ahead.

Jacques received orders to attend Drill Instructors School, and on completion of that training he served as a drill instructor at Marine Corps Recruit Depot, San Diego, California, from 1960 to 1963. Assigned to the Second Battalion of the Recruit Training Regiment, Jacques distinguished himself as a professional Marine noncommissioned officer (NCO). His training platoons won numerous drill and marksmanship competitions, which became benchmarks at the depot.

After another tour of duty with the Third Marine Division on Okinawa from 1963 to 1964, Jacques volunteered for duty with First Force Reconnaissance Company and was selected to join that company at Camp Pendleton, California in 1964. After completing jump school and scuba school, now a staff sergeant and a recon platoon sergeant, he went aboard the USS *Diachenko* (APD-123), on June 14, 1965, and headed toward combat in Vietnam. During the Vietnam War, Jacques served as a platoon sergeant and platoon leader in First Force Reconnaissance Company.

On June 14, 1966, Gunnery Sergeant Jacques helped plan and participated in the first combat parachute jump in the history of the Marine Corps. As a part of Operation KANSAS, Jacques and 12 other Marines from First Force Recon Company parachuted at night from a CV-2 Caribou into an area south of the village of Hiep Duc. Though the recon patrol lasted only one day and was compromised by a dog's alerting the enemy to hidden parachutes, history had been made.

Maurice Jacques served three combat tours in the Republic of Vietnam, for a total of 43 months in country, nearly all of that time with Marine reconnaissance units.

After his last tour in Vietnam, ending in 1970, Jacques served as First sergeant on Okinawa and then with the First Marine Brigade in Hawaii. Promoted to sergeant major, on December 2, 1971, he served as the sergeant major of Second Battalion, Third Marines and as sergeant major of the First Marine Brigade. Returning to the States, he served with distinction as the sergeant major of the First Marine Regiment. He was assigned to his last command, serving as the sergeant major of the Fifth Marine Regiment from 1977 to 1978, the same Marine regiment Jacques had first joined as a private first class in 1948.

Sergeant Major Jacques, a Marine's Marine, died on Sunday, May 11, 1997.

Source and Additional Reading

Norton, Maj. Bruce H. *Force Recon Diary, 1970.* New York: Ballantine, 1993.

———. *Sergeant Major, U.S. Marines.* New York: Ballantine 1995.

Johnson, Oscar G. *Sergeant, United States Army, Company B, 363d Infantry, 91st Infantry Division, so distinguished himself in combat during World War II that he was awarded the Medal of Honor for his heroic actions.*

Born: Foster City, Mich.; **Entered service at:** Foster City, Mich.; **Place and date:** Near Scarperia, Italy, September 16–18, 1944. G.O. No.: 58, July 19, 1945.

Citation: "He practically single-handed protected the left flank of his company's position in the offensive to break the German's gothic line. Company B was the extreme left assault unit of the corps. The advance was stopped by heavy fire from Monticelli Ridge, and the company took cover behind an embankment. Sgt. Johnson, a mortar gunner, having expended his ammunition, assumed the duties of a rifleman.

As leader of a squad of 7 men he was ordered to establish a combat post 50 yards to the left of the company to cover its exposed flank. Repeated enemy counterattacks, supported by artillery, mortar, and machinegun fire from the high ground to his front, had by the afternoon of 16 September killed or wounded all his men. Collecting weapons and ammunition from his fallen comrades, in the face of hostile fire, he held his exposed position and inflicted heavy casualties upon the enemy, who several times came close enough to throw hand grenades. On the night of 16–17 September, the enemy launched his heaviest attack on Company B, putting his greatest pressure against the lone defender of the left flank. In spite of mortar fire, which crashed about him, and machinegun bullets that whipped the crest of his shallow trench, Sgt. Johnson stood erect and repulsed the attack with grenades and small arms fire. He remained awake and on the alert throughout the night, frustrating all attempts at infiltration. On 17 September, 25 German soldiers surrendered to him. Two men, sent to reinforce him that afternoon, were caught in a devastating mortar and artillery barrage. With no thought of his own safety, Sgt. Johnson rushed to the shell hole where they lay half buried and seriously wounded, covered their position by his fire, and assisted a Medical Corpsman in rendering aid. That night he secured their removal to the rear and remained on watch until his company was relieved. Five companies of a German paratroop regiment had been repeatedly committed to the attack on Company B without success. Twenty dead Germans were found in front of his position. By his heroic stand and utter disregard for personal safety, Sgt. Johnson was in a large measure responsible for defeating the enemy's attempts to turn the exposed left flank."

Source
Medal of Honor Citation.

Johnston, Joseph Eggleston (1807–1891) *General officer, Confederate States Army.*

Petty considerations over rank and military etiquette and wounds cost the Confederacy, for lengthy periods, the services of one of its most effective top commanders, Joseph E. Johnston. The Virginia native and West Pointer (1829), rated by many as more capable than Lee, was the highest-ranking regular army officer to resign and join the Confederacy. With the staff rank of brigadier general, he had been the national army's quartermaster general for almost a year when he quit on April 22, 1861.

His earlier career had included eight years in the artillery before he was transferred to the topographical engineers in 1838, when he rejoined the army a year after his resignation. During the Mexican War he won two brevets and was wounded at both Cerro Gordo and Chapultepec. He had also been brevetted for earlier heroic service against the Seminoles in Florida. Having been appointed quartermaster general on June 28, 1860, he remained in the service until after the secession of his native state.

His Virginia and Confederate assignments included the following: major general, Virginia Volunteers (April 1861); brigadier general, Confederate States Army (CSA) (May 14, 1861); commander, Army of the Shenandoah

(June 30–July 20, 1861); commander, Army of the Potomac (July 20–October 22, 1861); general, CSA (August 31, 1861, to rank from July 21); commander, Department of Northern Virginia (October 22, 1861–May 31, 1862); commander, Department of the West (December 4, 1862–December 1863); commander, Army of Tennessee (December 27, 1863–July 18, 1864); commander, Army of Tennessee and Department of Tennessee and Georgia (February 25–April 26, 1865); also commander, Department of South Carolina, Georgia and Florida (February 25–April 26, 1865); and commander, Department of North Carolina (March 16–April 26, 1865).

Initially commissioned in the Virginia forces, he relieved Thomas J. (later "Stonewall") Jackson in command at Harper's Ferry and continued the organization of the Army of the Shanandoah. When the Virginia forces were absorbed into the Confederate army he was reduced to a brigadier generalship.

When the Union army under Irvin McDowell moved out of Washington and Alexandria to attack Pierre G. T. Beauregard at Manassas, Johnston managed to fool the Pennsylvania general Robert Patterson totally with a small force in the Shanandoah Valley and move the bulk of his forces to Beauregard's support. During the battle of First Bull Run, Johnston, although senior to Beauregard, left the general direction of the battle to the junior officer because of lack of familiarity with the terrain. Johnston was basically engaged in forwarding freshly arrived Valley troops to the threatened sectors.

The two generals shared the glory and were critical of supply problems, which they felt prevented a march on Washington. The next month Johnston became one of five men advanced to the grade of full general—all Confederate generals wore the same insignia of rank, three stars in a wreath—but was not pleased with the relative ranking of the five. He felt that since he was the senior officer to leave the "old" service and join the Confederacy, he should not be ranked behind Samuel Cooper, Albert Sidney Johnston, and Robert E. Lee. Only Beauregard was placed behind Johnston on the list. This led to much bad blood between Johnston and Jefferson Davis. There would be more.

With his increased rank, Johnston was given command of the Department of Northern Virginia and became engaged in what was virtually a phony war with the Washington-based army of George B. McClellan. Throughout the winter of 1861–62 he maintained his position at Manassas junction and then withdrew just as McClellan's superior force advanced. In the meantime he had engaged in a dispute with his president over a policy of brigading troops from the same state together. Johnston argued that a recognization could not with propriety be carried out in the face of an active enemy.

When he withdrew his army from the line of Bull Run he reinforced John B. Magruder on the Peninsula east of Richmond and took command there. With McClellan again facing him, he held Yorktown for a month before pulling back just before his opponent again advanced. His forces fought a rearguard action at Williamsburg and were then encamped on the very outskirts of the new nation's capital. In an effort to drive off McClellan, Johnston launched an attack south of the Chickahominy River at the end of May 1862. The Battle of Seven Pines, or Fair Oaks, turned out to be an accumulation of errors in the confusing terrain. For years afterward there was acrimonious debate among various Confederate generals over who was to blame for the limited success.

On the first day of the battle Johnston reexhibited his tendency to attract enemy bullets and was succeeded the next day by Robert E. Lee, who was to lead the Army of Northern Virginia for the balance of the war. On his recovery he was given charge of a largely supervisory command, entitled the Department of the West. He was in charge of Braxton Bragg's Army of Tennessee and John C. Pemberton's Department of Mississippi and East Louisiana. With few troops under his immediate command he proved powerless in attempting to relieve the besieged garrison of Vicksburg under Pemberton.

After the river city's fall, he made a feeble attempt to hold Jackson, Mississippi, against the advance of William T. Sherman. After Bragg's disastrous defeat at Chattanooga, Johnston was given immediate command of his army and the next spring and summer directed a masterful delaying campaign against Sherman during his advance on Atlanta. However, his continued withdrawals raised the ire of Jefferson Davis, and he was relieved in front of the city.

His successor, John B. Hood, then began his destruction of the Army of Tennessee with reckless tactics. After Sherman had marched clear through Georgia and begun his drive through the Carolinas, a clamor arose in the Confederate Congress for Johnston's resumption of command. Davis finally relented in early 1865, and the general took eventual command of three departments. Unfortunately for the Confederacy his forces were heavy on generals but weak on men. He could do little but hope for a linkup with Lee's army so that they could turn on either Grant or Sherman and then on the other. It never came off, and he surrendered his forces after some difficulties over terms, bordering on the political, on April 26, 1865, at the Bennett House near Durham Station, North Carolina. He had been one of the most effective Confederate commanders when directives from the president did not hamper him.

After the war he sat in Congress and was a federal railroad commissioner. Engaged in much debate over the causes of the Confederate defeat, he wrote his *Narrative of Military Operations,* which was highly critical of Davis and many of his fellow generals. In an example of the civil relationships of former wartime opponents, Johnston died of a cold caught while attending the funeral of his archopponent, William T. Sherman.

Source and Additional Reading

Govan, Gilbert E., and Livingood, James W. *A Different Valor: The Story of General Joseph E. Johnston.* Indianapolis Ind.: Bobbs Merrill, 1956.

Jones, John Paul (1747–1792) *American Revolutionary War naval hero and "Father of the American Navy." John Paul Jones was born in Kirkbean, Kirkcudbright county, Scotland, on July 6, 1747.*

As the strains of "The Star Spangled Banner" died, Secretary of the Navy Charles J. Bonaparte rose, walked to the lecturn, and began to speak. "We have met to honor the memory of that man who gave our Navy its earliest traditions of heroism and victory." With these words, the secretary began his introduction of the president of the United States, Theodore Roosevelt, at commemorative ceremonies and entombment exercises held in honor of John Paul Jones at the United States Naval Academy, Annapolis, Maryland.

Before the podium stood a star-draped casket containing the body of Jones, recently returned to the United States after lying for over a century in an unmarked grave in France. Upon the casket lay a wreath of laurel, a spray of palm, and the sword presented to Jones by Louis XVI of France in honor of his victory over the *Serapis.* The ceremony's date, April 24, 1906, the 128th anniversary of Jones's capture of the *Drake* had been selected by President Roosevelt and the observance in Annapolis capped a series of activities that included a White House reception and an official visit by a French naval squadron.

Named John Paul, he inherited from his parents, John Paul Sr., and Jean McDuff, the independence of the Scottish Lowlander and the fighting instincts of the Highlander. When only 12 years old, he sailed as a shipboy on a merchantman to Virginia, where his older brother William was in business. "America," he was to declare, "has been my favorite country from the age of thirteen when I first saw it."

He served at an early age in merchant vessels, armed ships, perhaps ships of war, and slavers. In practice of his own maxim, "A warrior is always ready," his resourcefulness and skill won him the position as master of a merchantman, the *John,* at the age of 21. In command of this vessel in Tobago in the West Indies in 1770, he punished with the cat-o'-nine-tails a negligent carpenter, Mungo Maxwell, who later died from malaria aboard another ship. Jones proved his innocence of the death of Maxwell, but suffered widespread criticism. Several years later, on a different ship, when a mutineer swung a bludgeon at him, Jones killed him. As an admiralty court was not in session at the time in Tobago, he left the island at the close of 1773, intending to return for trail. He took, temporarily, an assumed name.

Jones passed 20 months in obscurity in America, chiefly in Fredericksburg, Virginia. A tradition assumes he changed his name during this period from John Paul to Paul Jones and John Paul Jones in gratitude to two brothers, Willie and Allen Jones of North Carolina. But no authentic record proves that he ever met either of them or that they served him in any way. What is known with certainty is that Joseph Hewes, shipowner and signer of the Declaration of Independence, was his greatest early benefactor.

Jones was among the foremost in service at the founding of the Continental Navy. He was commissioned in December 1775 as the first lieutenant on the frigate *Alfred,* on which he hoisted the Continental flag, the old Grand Union. As captain of the sloop of war *Providence* and as commander of both the *Alfred* and the *Providence,* he captured valuable British merchantmen and destroyed important fisheries and many vessels. His skill in harrying the enemy was widely noted, and in February 1777, the Marine Committee directed its secretary, Robert Morris, to place the Continental fleet in his hands. But the jealousy of others thwarted these orders.

Superseded by many officers, he became, unfairly, the 18th captain in naval rank. But John Hancock, president of Congress, as well as Robert Morris recognized his abilities. Accordingly, on June 14, 1777, he received the command of the new sloop of war *Ranger,* one of the first naval vessels to fly the Stars and Stripes, and sailed to France.

Jones sailed the *Ranger* to the very shores of England, and tried to burn the shipping at Whitehaven. At Saint Mary's Isle he attempted, unsuccessfully, to take the earl of Belkirk as a hostage for the exchange of prisoners. On April 24, 1778, he captured the *Drake,* the first victory of a Continental vessel over a British warship.

Upon his return to the French port of Brest, Jones was eager to undertake more ambitious enterprises in larger ships. At every turn, however, he found political and naval intrigues, both French and American. The ship he eventually received (a merchantmen renamed the *Bonhomme Richard* in honor of Benjamin Franklin) was old and slow, armed with 42 guns, and ill suited to fight or escape.

Off Flamborough Head, however, the *Richard* pursued and challenged to battle two British ships of war—the *Serapis,* carrying 50 guns, and the *Countess of Scarborough,* with 22 guns. In the grim struggle on September 23, 1779, Jones had to fight not only against the superior crew, armament, speed, and maneuvering ability of the *Serapis,* as well as the *Countess of Scarborough,* but also against a grave and almost fatal accident. Two of the six old 18-pounders of the Richard burst at their first broadside and killed or wounded many men. It became imperative for Jones to outwit Richard Pearson, the captain of the *Serapis*. An initial attempt to board the British frigate and win by sheer desperate fighting failed. In a second effort he managed to lock the two ships together. The *Serapis* was beating in one of the *Richard*'s sides and blowing out the other. Most of the guns of the American ship were broken and silenced. The *Richard* with its dry old timbers was afire again and again, and the water in the hold rose ominously. A gunner, crediting a report that Jones had been killed, called to offer surrender of the *Richard,* and Pearson loudly responded, "Do you ask for quarter?" Jones then made his memorable reply, emphasizing it by hurling his two pistols at the head of the gunner: "I have not yet begun to fight!"

A grenade thrown from the *Richard* caused a disastrous explosion of ammunition on board the *Serapis*. After three and one-half hours of heroic battle in full moonlight, the *Serapis* struck its flag. Then Jones and his crew boarded the British ship and saw the *Bonhomme Richard* sink stern uppermost and with its colors flying.

Jones escaped in the *Serapis* to Holland, accompanied by the captured *Countess of Scarborough*. He later went to Paris, where he was acclaimed by the populace, honored by the king, and feted and lionized by society. His dalliance in the French capital, his verse writing, and several romantic attachments made an unusual interlude in Jones's career. Jones returned to America in February 1781 in the *Ariel*. Congress passed resolutions in his honor, recommended the award of a gold medal, and gave him command of the ship of the line *America*, which, in essence, conferred the rank of rear admiral. The war ending soon, he urged, "In time of peace . . . prepare . . . for war."

The prospect of service in the Russian Navy as a rear admiral now arose. Jones asserted that he would never renounce the glorious title of citizen of the United States. But men no less astute than Thomas Jefferson and George Washington seemed to think that employment in Russia, in the absence of any at home, would qualify him, in case of need, for still higher professional duties. Arriving in Russia in April 1788, Jones was given command of a squadron in the Black Sea for a campaign against the Turks. Jones's grim dedication to his professional duties resulted in victories scarcely less daring and strategic than those in the American Revolution. It was primarily his operations that saved Kherson and the Crimea and decided the successful outcome of the war. While he won the battles, however, his colleagues usurped the honors. "The first duty of a gentleman is to respect his own character," he wrote in explanation of his aloofness from the deceit that surrounded him. "I saw that I must conquer or die," he stated on his early recognition of the ineptitude as well as the villainy to which he was exposed. The intrigue against him grew, both professional and personal, including a baseless charge of moral turpitude, and Jones left Russia for

France. Becoming progressively ill in Paris, Jones died there on July 18, 1792.

Moral courage inspired by reverence for his country, physical boldness derived from a nature inured from youth to hardship and danger, and zeal for perfection in his profession were the qualities that combined to raise Jones from obscurity to international eminence. He was outstanding among his fellow officers for never losing a ship. He was unequaled by any of them for vision and resourcefulness, and his urgent recommendations for an unmatched American Navy showed remarkable foresight and devotion. After lying for a hundred years in an unmarked Paris grave, his remains were moved in 1906 to the chapel of the U.S. Naval Academy in Annapolis, Maryland.

Jones's life paralleled that of the Continental Navy. Both rose from humble origins, appeared briefly on the world scene, and then passed with few mourners. Jones gave to it some of its brightest moments, including the capture of the two largest Royal Navy ships to strike their flags to Americans during the Revolution. He always made the most of the limited resources available to him. In the battle against *Serapis,* he left a legacy of dauntless courage and unconquerable persistence in the most desperate of circumstances. Every fighting service needs a tradition of refusal to surrender in the face of seemingly overwhelming odds. "It was [John Paul Jones] who . . . created the spirit of my country's infant Navy," wrote a mid-nineteenth-century naval officer.

At the start of the twentieth century when the U.S. Navy took its place among leaders of the world, the image of Jones held by the general public and by naval officers began to change. The Navy's rising professionalism led it to value Jones not simply as a courageous leader in time of battle but as a complete naval officer. Jones understood the basics of his vocation. His grasp of naval architecture was demonstrated by his supervision of the construction of the *Ranger* and the *America,* the virtual reconstruction of the *Bonhomme Richard,* and alterations to the masts and rigging of almost every ship he commanded.

His victories were not won by courage and superior tactics alone, but were the result of careful preparation. His letters and actions show the respect he had for his subordinates, though he often failed to give enough credit to the officers who served under him.

His desire to establish boards to evaluate officers for promotion was visionary for his time. His proposals for a fleet of evolution and naval academies predated the establishment of such institutions in the United States by over a half a century. Consequently, quotations from his writings, sometimes imaginary, appeared on the fitness report forms of the Navy's Bureau of Personnel and on examination books at the U.S. Naval Academy in the early twentieth century.

Jones's strategic ideals were equally sound. As clearly as anyone, he understood the limitation of the Continental Navy and advocated operations congruent with its capabilities. The need for French assistance in ejecting the British army from America was apparent to Jones. It is not surprising that Admiral DeGrasse's biographer credits Jones with suggesting the strategy that ultimately brought victory at Yorktown.

That he was a man of talent cannot be denied, nor can his patriotism. His disappointments in terms of recognition and command rivaled those of Benedict Arnold, but their reactions differed sharply. Jones's reputation rests on his exploits of 1778 and 1779, when he took the war to the British people and strengthened American morale at times when it was sinking. Sadly, he was never destined to test his talents on a broad scale. With the end of the war, America thought it no longer needed a navy and thus had no use for Jones as a naval officer.

But Jones never fully adapted to peace. His success as a diplomat was no compensation for his disappointment when his plans for an American navy were rejected. Throughout the Revolution, he had remained optimistic, convinced that the Continental Navy, no matter how low its fortunes, could win respect from Europe for the new United States. That he sought personal fame at the same time is not surprising. His pursuit of glory as a reward for self-sacrifice and service to the nation was fully in keeping with the spirit of the time.

In the end, John Paul Jones's legacy rests not so much on what he accomplished as on how he did it. As the inscription on his tomb reads:

"He Gave to Our Navy Its Earliest Traditions of Heroism and Victory." His remains are entombed beneath the United States Naval Academy Chapel's Rotunda, Annapolis, Maryland, where United States Marines guard his crypt 24 hours a day.

Source and Additional Reading

Abbazia, Patrick. *John Paul Jones, America's First Naval Hero.* Charlotteville, N.Y.: SamHar Press, 1976.

Bradford, James C. "John Paul Jones: Honor and Professionalism" in *Command Under Sail—Makers of the American Naval Tradition 1775–1850.* Annapolis, Md.: Naval Institute Press, 1985.

De Koven, Anna, ed. *Life and Letters of John Paul Jones.* 2 vols. New York: Charles Scribner's Sons, 1913.

Gilkerson, William. *The Ships of John Paul Jones.* Annapolis, Md.: Naval Institute Press, 1987.

Jones, John Paul. *Memoirs of Rear Admiral John Paul Jones.* 1830. Reprint, New York: Da Capo, 1972.

Lorenz, Lincoln. *John Paul Jones, Fighter for Freedom and Glory.* Annapolis, Md.: Naval Institute Press, 1943.

Morison, Samuel E. *John Paul Jones: A Sailor's Biography.* 1959. Reprint, Annapolis, Md.: Naval Institute Press, 1990.

K

★ ★ ★ ★

Kandle, Victor L. (d. 1944) *First lieutenant, United States Army, 15th Infantry, Third Infantry Division, so distinguished himself in combat, during World War ll, that he was awarded (posthumously) the Medal of Honor.*

Born: Roy, Wash.; **Entered service at:** Redwood City, Calif.; **Place and date:** Near La Forge, France, October 9, 1944. **G.O. No.:** 37, May 11, 1945.

Citation: "For conspicuous gallantry and intrepidity at risk of his life above and beyond the call of duty. On 9 October 1944, at about noon, near La Forge, France, 1st Lt. Kandle, while leading a reconnaissance patrol into enemy territory, engaged in a duel at pointblank range with a German field officer and killed him. Having already taken 5 enemy prisoners that morning, he led a skeleton platoon of 16 men, reinforced with a light machinegun squad, through fog and over precipitous mountain terrain to fall on the rear of a German quarry stronghold which had checked the advance of an infantry battalion for 2 days. Rushing forward, several yards ahead of his assault elements, 1st Lt. Kandle fought his way into the heart of the enemy strongpoint, and, by his boldness and audacity, forced the Germans to surrender. Harassed by machinegun fire from a position which he had bypassed in the dense fog, he moved to within 15 yards of the enemy, killed a German machinegunner with accurate rifle fire and led his men in the destruction of another machinegun crew and its rifle security elements. Finally, he led his small force against a fortified house held by 2 German officers and 30 enlisted men. After establishing a base of fire, he rushed forward alone through an open clearing in full view of the enemy, smashed through a barricaded door, and forced all 32 Germans to surrender. His intrepidity and bold leadership resulted in the capture or killing of 3 enemy officers and 54 enlisted men, the destruction of 3 enemy strong-points, and the seizure of enemy positions which had halted a battalion attack."

Source
Medal of Honor Citation.

Kearny, Philip (1815–1862) *American general officer.*

Kearny was born in New York City, on June 2, 1815. After his mother died, when he was just nine years old, he spent his childhood and youth with his maternal grandfather, a man of wealth and high social position. Kearny's uncle, Gen. Stephen Watts Kearny, was a United States Dragoon and Phillip favored a military life, but his grandfather, who had lost all of his sons, persuaded him to attend Columbia University.

After graduating in 1833, Kearny traveled widely. When his grandfather died, leaving him $1 million, he returned home and in 1837 obtained a commission as a Second lieutenant in the United States Dragoons. After two years of service with them, he was sent by the secretary of war to the French Cavalry School at Saumur Chasseurs d'Afrique. On his return to the United States, he served as aide-de-camp to General's Alexander Macomb and Winfield Scott, successively generals in chief of the army.

During the Mexican War, Kearny accompanied Scott to Mexico City and at the Battle of Churubusco was wounded so severely that his left arm had to be amputated. He was brevetted major for his gallantry and, after service in California, resigned from the army, married, and made his home in New Jersey.

The military attracted him once again in 1859, when he served in Napoleon's III's Imperial Guard in the Italian War, winning the French Legion of Honor for bravery at

Solferino. When the Civil War began, Kearny was appointed brigadier general of volunteers, commanding a brigade of New Jersey regiments in Brig. Gen. William B. Franklin's division. One of the best known and most respected soldiers in the army, he distinguished himself during the Peninsular Campaign, rising to major general and command of the First Division of Maj. Gen. Samuel P. Heitzelman's Third Corps. After Second Bull Run, he accidentally rode into the enemy lines during the indecisive Battle of Chantilly, September 1, 1862, and was killed instantly. He was buried in Trinity Churchyard in New York City but was later moved to the National Cemetery at Arlington, Virginia. The New Jersey town in which he had resided was renamed in his honor.

Kearny was a fearless, intelligent, and skillful commander and an excellent cavalry officer. His daring and chivalrous bearing won him the admiration and the respect of his men and fellow officers. General Winfield Scott referred to Kearny as a "perfect soldier" and "the bravest man I ever knew."

Source and Additional Reading

De Peyster, John Watts. *Personal and Military History of Philip Kearny, Major General, United States Volunteers*. New York, Rice & Gage, 1869.

Dupuy, T. N., Johnson, Curt, and Bongard, David L. *The Harper Encyclopedia of Military Biography*. New York: HarperCollins, 1995.

Kearny, Philip. *Service with the French Troops in Africa*. New York: n.p., 1844.

Kearny, Thomas. *General Philip Kearny*. New York: Putnam, 1937.

Keathley, George D. (d. 1944) *Staff Sergeant, United States Army, 85th Infantry Division, so distinguished himself in combat during World War II that he was awarded (posthumously) the Medal of Honor.*

Born: Olney, Tex.; **Entered service at:** Lamesa, Tex.; **Place and date:** Mt. Altuzzo, Italy, September 14, 1944. G.O. No.: 20, March 29, 1945.

Citation: "For conspicuous gallantry and intrepidity at risk of life above and beyond the call of duty, in action on the western ridge of Mount Altuzzo, Italy. After bitter fighting his company had advanced to within 50 yards of the objective, where it was held up due to intense enemy sniper, automatic, small arms, and mortar fire. The enemy launched 3 desperate counterattacks in an effort to regain their former positions, but all 3 were repulsed with heavy casualties on both sides. All officers and noncommissioned officers of the 2d and 3d platoons of Company B had become casualties, and S/Sgt. Keathley, guide of the 1st platoon, moved up and assumed command of both the 2d and 3d platoons, reduced to 20 men. The remnants of the 2 platoons were dangerously low on ammunition, so S/Sgt. Keathley, under deadly small arms and mortar fire, crawled from 1 casualty to another, collecting their ammunition and administering first aid. He then visited each man of his 2 platoons, issuing the precious ammunition he had collected from the dead and wounded, and giving them words of encouragement. The enemy now delivered their fourth counterattack, which was approximately 2 companies in strength. In a furious charge they attacked from the front and both flanks, throwing hand grenades, firing automatic weapons, and assisted by a terrific mortar barrage. So strong was the enemy counterattack that the company was given up for lost. The remnants of the 2d and 3d platoons of Company B were now looking to S/Sgt. Keathley for leadership. He shouted his orders precisely and with determination and the men responded with all that was in them. Time after time the enemy tried to drive a wedge into S/Sgt. Keathley's position and each time they were driven back, suffering huge casualties. Suddenly an enemy hand grenade hit and exploded near S/Sgt. Keathley, inflicting a mortal wound in his left side. However, hurling defiance at the enemy, he rose to his feet. Taking his left hand away from his wound and using it to steady his rifle, he fired and killed an attacking enemy soldier, and continued shouting orders to his men. His heroic and intrepid action so inspired his men that they fought with incomparable determination and viciousness. For 15 minutes S/Sgt. Keathley continued leading his men and effectively firing his rifle. He could have sought a sheltered spot and perhaps saved his life, but instead he elected to set an example for his men and make every possible effort to hold his position. Finally, friendly artillery fire helped to force the enemy to withdraw, leaving behind many of their number either dead or seriously wounded. S/Sgt. Keathley died a few moments later. Had it not been for his indomitable courage and incomparable heroism, the remnants of 3 rifle platoons of Company B might well have been annihilated by the overwhelming enemy attacking force. His actions were in keeping with the highest traditions of the military service."

Source

Medal of Honor Citation.

Keaveney, Paul S. (b. 1942) *Lance corporal, United States Marine Corps, so distinguished himself in close combat in 1970 that he was awarded the Silver Star for his heroic actions, February 7, 1970.*

Born in Boston, Massachusetts, on June 29, 1942, Paul S. Keaveney enlisted in the United States Marine Corps in July 1967 and served as a long-range reconnaissance team member in Third Force Reconnaissance Company.

Paul S. Keaveney

Citation: "For conspicuous gallantry and intrepidity in action while serving as a Reconnaissance Man with the Third Force Reconnaissance Company, First Marine Division in connection with combat operations against the enemy in the Republic of Vietnam. On 7 February 1970, Lance Corporal Keaveney was a member of a reconnaissance team which was conducting a patrol within the A Shau Valley in Thua Thein Province when the Marines came under intense fire from a numerically superior North Vietnamese Army force, pinning down the team and wounding four Marines, including Lance Corporal Keaveney. Despite his painful wounds, he moved to a vantagepoint along the trail from which he could more clearly observe the movements of the enemy and from which he could more accurately deliver fire with his grenade launcher. With complete disregard for his own safety, Lance Corporal Keaveney boldly stood in full view of the hostile force on three separate occasions, and fearlessly remained in his precarious position while the enemy concentrated their fire on him, and delivered his grenade launcher fire with such devastating effectiveness that the North Vietnamese were prevented from advancing down the trail toward the Marines' position. Each time he stood, he was struck by hostile small arms fire, but undeterred by

his serious wounds, he would again resolutely stand to deliver fire. When the nature of his wounds finally rendered him unable to fire his weapon, Lance Corporal Keaveney obtained the radio from the operator, thereby freeing a fellow recon team member to more actively engage the enemy while he requested helicopter gunship support and medical evacuation helicopters. His aggressive fighting spirit and valiant actions inspired all who observed him and were instrumental in a defeat of a numerically superior North Vietnamese Army force. By his dauntless courage, bold initiative, and unwavering devotion to duty in the face of great personal danger, Lance Corporal Keaveney upheld the highest traditions of the Marine Corps and of the United States Naval Service."

Source and Additional Reading
Silver Star Citation.
Norton, Maj. Bruce H. *Force Recon Diary, 1969.* New York: Ballantine, 1990.
———. *Force Recon Diary, 1970.* New York: Ballantine, 1992.

Kennedy, John F. (1917–1963) *Lieutenant, United States Navy, and 35th president of the United States.*

"Any man who may be asked in this century what he did to make his life worthwhile, I think can respond with a good deal of pride and satisfaction, 'I served in the United States Navy,'" wrote President John F. Kennedy in August 1963. A former naval officer, Kennedy was born in Brookline, Massachusetts, on May 29, 1917, to Rose and Joseph P. Kennedy. After attending public schools in Brookline, Kennedy went on to the Choate School in Wallingford, Connecticut, and attended the London School of Economics from 1935 to 1936. Kennedy graduated cum laude from Harvard University in 1940 and began graduate school at Stanford University.

Despite having a bad back, Kennedy was able to join the United States Navy through the assistance of Captain Alan Kirk, the director, Office of Naval Intelligence (ONI), who had been the naval attaché in London when Joseph Kennedy was the American ambassador to Great Britain. In October 1941, Kennedy was appointed an ensign in the United States Naval Reserve and joined the staff of the Office of Naval Intelligence. The office for which Kennedy worked prepared intelligence bulletins and briefing information for the secretary of the navy and other top officials. On January 15, 1942, he was assigned to an ONI field office at the Sixth Naval District in Charleston, South Carolina. After spending most of April and May at naval hospitals at Charleston and at Chelsea, Massachusetts, Kennedy attended Naval Reserve Officers Training School at Northwestern University in Chicago, Illinois, July 27 through September 27. After completing this training, Kennedy entered the Motor Torpedo Boat Squadron Training Center, at Melville, Rhode Island. On October 10, he was promoted to the rank of lieutenant, junior grade. On completing his training, on December 2, he was ordered to the training squadron, Motor Torpedo Squadron Four, for duty as the commanding officer of a motor torpedo boat, *PT 101*, a 78-foot Higgins boat. In January 1943, *PT 101* along with four other boats was ordered to Motor Torpedo Boat Squadron 14, which was assigned to Panama.

Seeking combat duty, Kennedy transferred on February 23 as a replacement officer to Motor Torpedo Boat Squadron Two, which was based at Tulagi Island in the Solomons. Traveling to the Pacific aboard the USS *Rochambeau*, Kennedy arrived at Tulagi on April 14 and took command of *PT 109* on April 23, 1943. On May 30, several PT boats, including *PT 109*, were ordered to the Russell Islands, in preparation for the invasion of New Georgia. After the invasion of Rendova, *PT 109* moved to Lumbari. From that base PT boats conducted nightly operations to interdict the heavy Japanese barge traffic resupplying the Japanese garrisons in New Georgia and to patrol the Ferguson and Blackett Straits near the islands of Kolumbangara, Gizo, and Vella-Lavella, in order to sight and to give warning when the Japanese Tokyo Express warships entered the straits to assault United States forces in the New Georgia–Rendova area.

PT 109, commanded by Kennedy with executive officer Ens. Leonard Jay Thom and 10 enlisted men, was one of the 15 boats sent out on patrol on the night of August 1–2, 1943, to intercept Japanese warships in the straits. A friend of Kennedy, Ens. George H. R. Ross, whose ship was damaged, joined Kennedy's crew that night. The PT boat was creeping along to keep the wake and noise at a minimum in order to prevent detection. Around 0200, with Kennedy at the helm, the Japanese destroyer *Amagiri* traveling at 40 knots cut *PT 109* in two in 10 seconds. Although the Japanese destroyer had not realized that their ship had struck an enemy vessel, the damage to *PT 109* was severe. At the time of impact, Kennedy was thrown into the cockpit, where he landed on his bad back. As *Amagiri* steamed away, its wake doused the flames on the floating section of *PT 109* to which five Americans clung: Kennedy, Thom, and three enlisted men, Sl/c Raymond Albert, RM2/c John E. Maguire, and QM3/c Edman Edgar Mauer. Kennedy yelled out for others in the water and heard replies from Ross and five members of the crew, two of who were injured. GM3/c Charles A. Harris had an injured leg and MoMM1/c Patrick Henry McMahon, the engineer, was badly burned. Kennedy swam to these men as Ross and Thom helped the others, MoMM2/c William Johnston, TM2/c Ray L. Starkey, and MoMM1/c Gerald E. Zinser, onto the floating remnant of *PT 109*. Although they were only 100 yards from the floating pieces, in the darkness it took Kennedy three hours to tow McMahon

and help Harris back to the *PT 109* hulk. TM2/c Andrew Jackson Kirksey and MoMM2/c Harold W. Marney had been killed in the collision with the *Amagiri*.

Because the remnant (hull) was listing badly and starting to swamp, Kennedy decided to swim for a small island barely visible (actually three miles) to the southeast. Five hours later, all 11 survivors had made it to the island after having spent a total of 15 hours in the water. Kennedy had given McMahon a life jacket and had towed him all three miles with the strap of the device held in his teeth. After finding no food or water on the island, Kennedy concluded that he should swim the route the PT boats took through Ferguson Passage in hope of sighting another ship. Ross and Kennedy had spotted another, slightly larger island with coconuts to eat and all the men swam there, Kennedy again towing McMahon. Now at their fourth day, Kennedy and Ross made it to Nauru Island and found several natives. Kennedy cut a message on a coconut that read, "11 alive native knows posit and reef Nauru Island Kennedy." He purportedly handed the coconut to one of the natives and said, "Rendova, Rendova!," indicating that the coconut should be taken to the PT base on Rendova.

Kennedy and Ross again attempted to look for boats that night without any luck. The next morning the natives returned with food and supplies, as well as a letter from the coast-watcher commander of the New Zealand camp, Lt. Arthur Reginald Evans. The message indicated that the natives should return with the American commander, and Kennedy complied immediately. He was greeted warmly and then taken to meet *PT 157*, which returned to the island and finally rescued the survivors on August 8.

Kennedy was later awarded the Navy and Marine Corps Medal for his heroics in the rescue of the crew of the *PT 109*, as well as the Purple Heart for the injuries sustained in the accident on the night of August 1, 1943. An official account of the entire incident was written by intelligence officers in August 1943 and subsequently declassified in 1959. As president, Kennedy met once again with his rescuers and was toasted by members of the Japanese destroyer crew.

In September, Kennedy went to Tulagi and accepted the command of *PT 59*, which was scheduled to be converted to a gunboat. In October 1943, Kennedy was promoted to lieutenant and continued to command the motor torpedo boat when the squadron moved to Vella-Lavella, until a navy doctor ordered him to leave *PT 59* on November 18. Kennedy left the Solomons on December 21 and returned to the United States in early January 1944.

On February 15, Kennedy reported to the Motor Torpedo Boat Squadron Training Center, Melville, Rhode Island. As a result of the reinjury of his back during the sinking of *PT 109*, Kennedy entered a hospital for treatment. In March, Kennedy went to the Submarine Chaser Training Center, Miami, Florida. In May, while still assigned to the center, Kennedy entered the Naval Hospital, Chelsea, Massachusetts, for further treatment as an outpatient. At the navy hospital, in June, he received his Navy and Marine Corps Medals. Under treatment as an outpatient, Kennedy was released from all active duty and finally retired from the United States Naval Reserve on physical disability in March 1945.

Citation: "For heroism in the rescue of three men following the ramming and sinking of his motor torpedo boat while attempting a torpedo attack on a Japanese destroyer in the Solomon Islands area on the night of August 1–2, 1943. Lt. Kennedy, Captain of the boat, directed the rescue of the crew and personally rescued three men, one of whom was seriously injured. During the following six days, he succeeded in getting his crew ashore, and after swimming many hours attempting to secure aid and food, finally effected the rescue of his men. His courage, endurance and excellent leadership contributed to the saving of several lives and was in keeping with the highest traditions of the United States Naval Service."

Source and Additional Reading
Official United States Naval Citation.
United States Naval Historical Center, 1999.

Keys, William M.   *Lieutenant general, United States Marine Corps, as a captain, so distinguished himself in combat, in the Republic of Vietnam that he was awarded the Navy Cross for his heroic actions in 1967.*

A native of Fredericktown, Pennsylvania, General Keys was commissioned a second lieutenant in the United States Marine Corps on his graduation from the United States Naval Academy with a B.S. in June 1960. His professional military education includes the Basic School, Amphibious Warfare School, and Command and Staff College, all at Quantico, Virginia. General Keys is also a graduate of the National War College in Washington, D.C., and holds an M.S. degree from American University and an honorary Ph.D. in public service from Washington and Jefferson College.

Designated an infantry officer, General Keys has served at every level of operational command: initially as a platoon leader with Third Battalion, Second Marine Regiment; as a company commander with First Battalion, Ninth Marine Regiment in Vietnam; as commanding officer, Third Battalion, Fifth Marine Regiment; as regimental commander, Sixth Marines; and as commanding general, Second Marine Division, during Desert Storm combat operations in Southwest Asia. There he led the division in its successful assault across the Kuwaiti border, breaching Iraqi barriers and minefields, and into Kuwait City. He also served an early tour with the Marine Detachment abroad the USS *Long Beach* and a second tour in Vietnam as an adviser to the Vietnamese Marine Corps.

He held the following principal staff assignments: infantry officers' monitor, Personnel Management Division, Headquarters Marine Corps; Marine Corps liaison officer to the U.S. Senate; special projects director, Office of the Commandant; aide de camp, assistant commandant of the Marine Corps; deputy director then director, Personnel Management Division, Manpower and Reserve Affairs Department, Marine Corps Headquarters (HQMC); and deputy, Joint Secretariat, Joint Chiefs of Staff, Washington, D.C.

General Keys's decorations and medals include the Navy Cross; Distinguished Service Medal; Silver Star; Legion of Merit with Combat V; Bronze Star with Combat V; Defense Meritorious Service Medal; Combat Action Ribbon; Presidential Unit Citation; Navy Unit Commendation; Meritorious Unit Commendation; and National Defense Medal.

General Keys retired from the Marine Corps on September 1, 1994. His last active duty assignment was as the commander, U.S. Marine Corps Forces, Atlantic; commanding general, Fleet Marine Force, Atlantic; commanding general, Second Marine Expeditionary Force; commander, Marine Striking Force, Atlantic; commander, U.S. Marine Corps Forces, South (Designate); and commander, U.S. Marine Corps Forces, Europe (Designate).

Citation: "For extraordinary heroism as Commanding Officer Company D, First Battalion, Ninth Marines, while engaged in action against elements of the North Vietnamese Army and insurgent communist (Viet Cong) forces during Operation PRAIRE II in the Cam Lo district of the Republic of Vietnam on 2 March 1967. While on a search and destroy mission, Captain Keys's company made contact with a large enemy force estimated to be two companies in strength. During this contact, the company command post group received heavy automatic-weapons fire and mortar fire from the rear. Realizing that his rifle platoons were heavily engaged, Captain Keys organized his command group into an assault element and led them against the enemy, who were firing into his position. Personally leading this small group against a numerically superior force, he succeeded in completely overrunning the North Vietnamese, personally killing six and destroying a machine gun position. Immediately following this firefight he rushed to the rear of his center platoon where he could best direct the deployment of his company. During the next four hours his company repelled attack after attack by a determined enemy. This period found Captain Keys along the entire line of his company, shouting encouragement, shifting force to meet each new attack, and successfully directing all aspects of his company's firepower and supporting arms. Following the enemy's last attack, Captain Keys immediately reorganized his company and attacked the enemy before they could withdraw to a safe area. While completely overrunning the enemy camp, his company succeeded in killing 183 North Vietnamese soldiers and capturing eight prisoners and nearly 200 weapons. Realizing that the surviving enemy would attempt to circumvent his company during the oncoming darkness and escape to the north, Captain Keys placed his company in a blocking position, thereby forcing the enemy to withdraw onto a prearranged zone where they were pounded by air and artillery resulting in 44 more enemy killed. As a result of his professional skill and stirring example, the enemy forces in his area of operations were completely routed. By his daring performance and loyal devotion to duty in the face of great personal risk, Captain Keys reflected great credit upon himself and the Marine Corps and upheld the highest traditions of the United States Naval Service."

Source and Additional Reading
Marine Corps Historical Center.
Navy Cross Citation.
Stevens, Paul D., ed. *The Navy Cross: Citations of Awards to Men of the United States Marine Corps, Vietnam 1964–1973.* Forest Ranch, Calif.: Sharp & Dunnigan, 1987.

Knight, Noah O. (1929–1951) *Private first class, United States Army, Company F, Seventh Infantry Regiment, Third Infantry Division, so distinguished himself in combat, during the Korean War, that he was awarded (posthumously) the Medal of Honor.*

Born: October 27, 1929, Chesterfield Country, S.C. **Entered service at:** Jefferson, S.C., **Place and date:** Near Kowang-San, Korea, November 23 and 24, 1951. G.O. No.: 2, January 7, 1953.

Citation: "Pfc. Knight, a member of Company F, distinguished himself by conspicuous gallantry and indomitable courage above and beyond the call of duty in action against the enemy. He occupied a key position in the defense perimeter when waves of enemy troops passed through their own artillery and mortar concentrations and charged the company position. Two direct hits from an enemy emplacement demolished his bunker and wounded him. Disregarding personal safety, he moved to a shallow depression for a better firing vantage. Unable to deliver effective fire from his defilade position, he left his shelter, moved through heavy fire in full view of the enemy and, firing into the ranks of the relentless assailants, inflicted numerous casualties, momentarily stemming the attack. Later during another vicious onslaught, he observed an enemy squad infiltrating the position and, counterattacking, killed or wounded the entire group. Expending the last of his ammunition, he

discovered 3 enemy soldiers entering the friendly position with demolition charges. Realizing the explosives would enable the enemy to exploit the breach, he fearlessly rushed forward and disabled 2 assailants with the butt of his rifle when the third exploded a demolition charge killing the 3 enemy soldiers and mortally wounding Pfc. Knight. Pfc. Knight's supreme sacrifice and consummate devotion to duty reflect lasting glory on himself and uphold the noble traditions of the military service."

Source
Medal of Honor Citation.

Knox, Henry (1750–1806) *Revolutionary War general and George Washington's first secretary of war.*

Born in Boston, July 25, 1750, Knox was employed by a Boston bookseller at the age of 12 and in 1771 opened his own shop, the London Bookstore, which became a gathering place for British officers. Knox spent much of his spare time studying military science. He had joined a local military company when he was 18, and in 1772 he became second in command of the newly formed Boston Grenadier Corps. He served with distinction as an artillery officer in the American Revolution and later became secretary of war.

Knox joined the American colonial army in 1775 and participated in nearly every important military engagement throughout the Revolution. In November 1775 he was commissioned colonel of artillery. In 1775, Knox helped save Boston from capture by the British when, with the sanction of General George Washington, he went to Fort Ticonderoga near the Canadian frontier to transport to Boston 55 pieces of badly needed artillery captured by Ethan Allen.

Using oxen and horses, he transported the guns 300 miles (480 kilometers) overland to the besieged city under difficult winter conditions. The fortification of Dorchester Heights with these 55 captured guns compelled the British evacuation of Boston on March 17, 1776.

Knox became Washington's trusted adviser and friend. He organized the American artillery and fought in the battles in and around New York in 1776. It was under his supervision that Washington's troops crossed the Delaware River on Christmas night, 1776, to attack the Hessian soldiers in Trenton. For this he was rewarded with a commission as brigadier general. Under his direction the artillery was effective in the Battles of Princeton (January 3, 1777), Brandywine (September 11, 1777), Germantown (October 4, 1777), and Monmouth (June 28, 1778), and in the siege of Yorktown (October 1781). Knox had been with Washington during the cruel winter of 1777 in Valley Forge, and, while in winter quarters in New Jersey in

1779, he organized a temporary military academy at Pluckemin, New Jersey. Knox served on the court-martial that condemned Major John André as a spy in 1780.

After the British surrender at Yorktown, Knox was made a major general. In 1782 he was placed in command of West Point. At his urging a group of Revolutionary officers founded the Society of the Cincinnati in 1783 to perpetuate their mutual friendships and to assist needy officers and their families. He served (1785–94) as secretary of war under the Articles of Confederation and also, in George Washington's administration, under the U.S. Constitution.

Knox was a firm believer in a strong federal government and welcomed the new Constitution. A plan for a national militia advanced by Knox in 1790 failed to win congressional approval. He retired from public life in 1794 and in 1796 settled on his estate, Montpelier, in Thomaston, Maine, where he died on October 25, 1806.

Source
Callahan, North. *Henry Knox: General Washington's General.* New York: Rinehart, 1958.

Kouma, Ernest R. (b. 1919) *Master sergeant (then sergeant first class), United States Army, Company A, 72d Tank Battalion, so distinguished himself in combat, during the Korean War, that he was awarded the Medal of Honor for his heroic actions.*

Born: November 23, 1919, Dwight, Nebr.; **Entered service at:** Dwight, Nebr.; **Place and date:** Vicinity of Agok, Korea, August 31, and September 1, 1950. **G.O. No.:** 38, June 4, 1951.

Citation: "M/Sgt. Kouma, a tank commander in Company A, distinguished himself by conspicuous gallantry and intrepidity at the risk of his life above and beyond the call of duty in action against the enemy. His unit was engaged in supporting infantry elements on the Naktong River front. Near midnight on 31 August, a hostile force estimated at 500 crossed the river and launched a fierce attack against the infantry positions, inflicting heavy casualties. A withdrawal was ordered and his armored unit was given the mission of covering the movement until a secondary position could be established. The enemy assault overran 2 tanks, destroyed 1 and forced another to withdraw. Suddenly M/Sgt. Kouma discovered that his tank was the only obstacle in the path of the hostile onslaught. Holding his ground, he gave fire orders to his crew and remained in position throughout the night, fighting off repeated enemy attacks. During 1 fierce assault, the enemy surrounded his tank and he leaped from the armored turret, exposing himself to a hail of hostile fire, manned the .50 caliber machine gun mounted on the rear deck, and delivered pointblank fire into the fanatical foe. His machine-gun emptied, he fired his pistol and threw grenades to keep the enemy from his tank. After more than 9 hours of constant combat and close-in fighting, he withdrew his vehicle to friendly lines. During the withdrawal through 8 miles of hostile territory, M/Sgt. Kouma continued to inflict casualties upon the enemy and exhausted his ammunition in destroying 3 hostile machine gun positions. During this action, M/Sgt. Kouma killed an estimated 250 enemy soldiers. His magnificent stand allowed the infantry sufficient time to reestablish defensive positions. Rejoining his company, although suffering intensely from his wounds, he attempted to resupply his tank and return to the battle area. While being evacuated for medical treatment, his courage was again displayed when he requested to return to the front. M/Sgt. Kouma's superb leadership, heroism, and intense devotion to duty reflect the highest credit on himself and uphold the esteemed traditions of the U.S. Army."

Source
Medal of Honor Citation.

L

★ ★ ★ ★

Larsen, David R. *Gunner's mate, third class (GMG3), United States Navy, so distinguished himself in combat, in the Republic of Vietnam, that he was awarded the Navy Cross for his heroic actions.*

Citation: "For extraordinary heroism on 2 August 1969 while serving with friendly foreign forces engaged in armed conflict against North Vietnamese and Viet Cong communist aggressor forces in the Republic of Vietnam. GMG3 Larsen was serving as a gunner's mater mate aboard *PBR 775,* which was part of a two-boat night waterborne guard post stationed on the upper Saigon River. Operating in conjunction with the patrol, a six-man ambush team, which was providing bank security for the guard post, engaged four enemy soldiers who were part of an estimated 35- to 50-man force that returned the contact with accurate rocket fire, killing or critically wounding all but one member of the six-man ambush team. One man from the team managed to call for the PBR crewmen's help. Armed with a machine gun and several ammunition belts, GMG3 Larsen hastened to the assistance of the ambush team. As he led his small force ashore, he saw three enemy soldiers about to overrun the friendly position. He immediately rushed toward them, firing his machine gun, and single-handedly turned back the enemy assault, killing at least one of the enemy. GMG3 Larsen then maintained a one-man perimeter defensive position and, although under continuous enemy fire, succeeded in discouraging further enemy attacks until additional help arrived. Later, armed with three different weapons, GMG3 Larsen was the first man to take his post on the perimeter established to provide security for the medical evacuation helicopter. By his extremely courageous one-man assault in the face of direct enemy fire, GMG3 Larsen was responsible for saving the lives of three fellow servicemen, and for protecting his shipmates as they administered aid to the wounded. His valiant and inspiring efforts reflect the highest credit upon himself and the United States Naval Service."

Source
Navy Cross Citation.

Lee, Henry Lee, III (Light Horse Harry) (1756–1818)
Revolutionary War hero and father of Robert E. Lee.

Henry "Light Horse Harry" Lee III, born at Leesylvania near Dumfries, Virginia, was blond, blue-eyed, and full of spirit. He graduated from Princeton in 1773 and returned home to prepare for war. His skill as a horseman, as well as his temperament, made him a natural cavalryman. He soon was commissioned as captain in the fifth group of Virginia Light Dragoons and sent north to join the Continental army.

Leading his men on lightning raids against enemy supply trains, Harry attracted the attention and admiration of General George Washington and was rapidly promoted. In a surprise attack at Paulus Hook, New Jersey, he captured 400 British soldiers with the loss of only 1 man. His adroit horsemanship soon earned him the nickname "Light Horse Harry." When the military theater shifted, he enjoyed equal success in the Southern Department.

Resigning his commission after the British surrender at Yorktown, Harry returned to Virginia to marry his cousin, the "divine Matilda" Lee. The wedding took place at Stratford, and it is said that General Washington contributed several pipes of his best Madeira to the festive occasion. Matilda had inherited Stratford in the division of her father's estate and lived there with her new husband. The dashing young cavalryman, however, was no farmer. His interests in the livelier arena of politics led to Harry's election to the new Virginia House of Delegates. After only eight years of marriage, Matilda died in 1790, leaving three young children and a husband desperate with grief. Two years later, Harry was elected governor of Virginia he served three one-year terms. While living in Richmond, he fell in love with Ann Hill Carter of nearby Shirley Plantation. In 1793 they were married. His governorship behind him, he took his bride to Stratford. Again, family life was interrupted by his appointment to the Continental Congress in Philadelphia. On the death of President George Washington, Harry was asked by Congress to deliver a tribute to his beloved general; Lee described him for posterity: "First in war, first in peace, and first in the hearts of his countrymen."

Lee was badly crippled in an antiwar riot in Baltimore, in July 1812, while trying to protect a friend. He left for the West Indies to convalesce (1813); en route back to Virginia, he died at Cumberland Island, Georgia, on March 25, 1818.

"Light Horse Harry" Lee was an intelligent, courageous, impetuous, talented commander and administrator. Like Francis Marion's, his independent guerrilla-style, combat operations were instrumental in winning the Revolutionary War in the South. Admired by George Washington and respected by the nation, he was awarded one of eight Congressional Medals for his heroic wartime service.

Source and Additional Reading

Boyd, Thomas. *Light Horse Harry Lee.* New York: Charles Scribner's Sons, 1931.

Gerson, Noel B. *Light Horse Harry: A Biography of Washington's Great Cavalryman, General Henry Lee.* Garden City, N.Y.: Doubleday, 1966.

Lee, Henry. *The Campaign of 1781 in the Carolinas, with Remarks Historical and Critical on Johnson's Life of Greene.* Philadelphia: E. Littell, 1824.

Hubert L. Lee

Lee, Hubert L. (b. 1915) *Master sergeant, United States Army, Company One, 23d Infantry Regiment, Second Infantry Division, so distinguished himself in combat, during the Korean War, that he was awarded the Medal of Honor for his heroic actions.*

Born: 1915, Arburg, Mo.; **Entered service at:** Leland, Miss.; **Place and date:** Near Ip-ori, Korea, February 1, 1951. **G.O. No.:** 21, February 5, 1952.

Citation: "Master Sergeant Hubert L. Lee, Infantry, United States Army, a member of Company I 23d Infantry Regiment, 2d Infantry Division, distinguished himself by conspicuous gallantry and intrepidity above and beyond the call of duty in action against the enemy near Ip-ori, Korea on 1 February 1951. When his platoon was forced from its position by a numerically superior enemy force, and his platoon leader wounded, Sergeant Lee assumed command, regrouped the remnants of his unit, and led them in repeated assaults to regain the position. Within 25 yards of his objective he received a leg wound from grenade fragments, but refused assistance and continued the attack. Although forced to withdraw five times, each time he regrouped his remaining men and renewed the assault. Moving forward at the head of his small group in the fifth attempt, he was struck by an exploding grenade, knocked to the ground, and seriously wounded in both legs. Still refusing assistance, he advanced by crawling, rising to his knees to fire, and urging his men to follow. While thus directing the final assault he was wounded a third time, by small-arms fire. Persistently continuing to crawl forward, he directed his men in a final and successful attack, which regained the vital objective. His intrepid leadership and determination led to the destruction of 83 of the enemy and withdrawal of the remainder, and was a vital factor in stopping the enemy attack. Sergeant Lee's indomitable courage, consummate valor, and outstanding leadership reflect the highest credit upon himself and are in keeping with the finest traditions of the infantry and the U.S. Army."

Source
Medal of Honor Citation.

Lee, Robert Edward (1807–1870) *General, Confederate States Army, son of Henry "Light Horse Harry" Lee.*

Lee wrote the following in a letter to his sister, April 20, 1861:

> With all my devotion to the Union and the feeling of loyalty and duty of an American citizen, I have not been able to make up my mind to raise my hand against my relatives, my children, my home. I have therefore resigned my commission in the Army, and save in defense of my native State, with the sincere hope that my poor services may never be needed, I hope I may never be called on to draw my sword.

The idol of the South to this day, the Virginian Robert E. Lee had some difficulty in adjusting to the new form of warfare that unfolded with the Civil War, but this did not prevent him from keeping the Union armies in Virginia at bay for almost three years. The son of the Revolutionary War hero "Light Horse Harry" Lee, who fell into disrepute in his later years, attended West Point and graduated second in his class. During his four years at the military academy he did not earn a single demerit and served as the cadet corps's adjutant. On his 1829 graduation he was posted to the engineers. Before the Mexican War he served on engineering projects in Georgia, Virginia, and New York. During the war he served on the staffs of John Wool and Winfield Scott. Particularly distinguishing himself scouting for and guiding troops, he won three brevets and was slightly wounded at Chapultepec.

After a stint in Baltimore Harbor he became superintendent of the military academy in 1852. When the mounted arm was expanded in 1855, Lee accepted the lieutenant colonelcy of the Second Cavalry in order to escape from the painfully slow promotion in the engineers. Ordered to western Texas, he served with his regiment until the 1857 death of his father-in-law forced him to ask for a series of leaves to settle the estate. In 1859 he was called on to lead a force of Marines, to join with the militia on the scene, to put an end to John Brown's Harper's Ferry Raid. Thereafter he served again in Texas until summoned to Washington in 1861 by Winfield Scott, who tried to retain Lee in the U.S. service. But the Virginian rejected the command of the Union's field forces on the day after Virginia seceded. He then accepted an invitation to visit Governor John Letcher in Virginia. His resignation as colonel, First Cavalry, to which he had recently been promoted, was accepted on April 25, 1861.

His Civil War assignments included the following: major general, Virginia's land and naval forces (April 23, 1861); commander Virginia forces (April 23–July 1861); brigadier general, Confederate States Army (CSA) (May 14, 1861); general, CSA (from June 14, 1861); commander, Department of Northwestern Virginia (late July–October 1861); commander, Department of South Carolina, Georgia and Florida (November 8, 1861–March 3, 1862); commander, Army of Northern Virginia (June 1, 1862–April 9, 1865).

In charge of Virginia's fledgling military might, he was mainly involved in organizational matters. As a Confederate brigadier general, and later a full general, he was in charge of supervising all southern forces in Virginia. In the first summer of the war he was given his first field command in western Virginia. His Cheat Mountain Campaign was a disappointing fizzle, largely as a result of the failings of his superiors. His entire tenure in the region was unpleasant, dealing with the bickering of his subordinates—William W. Loring, John B. Floyd, and Henry A. Wise. Afterward he became known throughout the South as "Granny Lee," as he was slow to move. His debut in field command had not been promising, but Jefferson Davis appointed him to command along the southern coast.

Early in 1862 he was recalled to Richmond and made an adviser to the president. From this position he had some influence over military operations, especially those of Stonewall Jackson in the Shenandoah Valley. When Joseph E. Johnston launched his attack at Seven Pines, Davis and Lee were taken by surprise and rode out to the field. In the confusion of the fight Johnston was badly

Robert Edward Lee

wounded, and that night Davis instructed Lee to take command of what he renamed the Army of Northern Virginia. He fought the second day of the battle, but the initiative had already been lost the previous day. Later in the month, in a daring move, he left a small force in front of Richmond and crossed the Chickahominy to strike the one Union corps north of the river. In what was to be called the Seven Days Battles, the individual fights—Beaver Dam Creek, Gaines' Mill, Savage Station, Glendale, White Oak Swamp, and Malvern Hill—were all tactical defeats for the Confederates. But Lee had achieved the strategic goal of removing McClellan's army from the very gates of Richmond.

This created a new opinion of Lee in the South. He gradually became "Uncle Robert" and "Marse Robert." With McClellan neutralized, a new threat developed under John Pope in northern Virginia. First Lee detached Jackson and then followed with Longstreet's command. Winning at Second Bull Run, he moved on into Maryland but suffered the misfortune of having a copy of his orders detailing the disposition of his divided forces fall into the hands of the enemy. McClellan moved with unusual speed and Lee was forced to fight a delaying action along South Mountain while waiting for Jackson to complete the capture of Harper's Ferry and rejoin him. He masterfully fought McClellan to a standstill at Antietam and two days later recrossed the Potomac.

Near the end of the year he won an easy victory over Burnside at Fredericksburg and then trounced Hooker in his most creditable victory at Chancellorsville, where he had detached Jackson with most of the army on a lengthy flank march while he remained with only two divisions in the immediate front of the Union army. Launching his second invasion of the North, he lost at Gettysburg. On the third day of the battle he displayed one of his major faults when at Malvern Hill and on other fields he ordered a massed infantry assault across a wide plain, not recognizing that the rifle, which had come into use since the Mexican War, put the charging troops under fire for too long. Another problem was his issuance of general, nonspecific orders to be executed by his subordinates.

Returning to Virginia he commanded in the inconclusive Bristoe and Mine Run Campaigns. From the Wilderness to Petersburg he fought a retiring campaign against Grant in which he made full use of entrenchments and became known as "Ace of Spades" Lee. Finally forced into a siege, he held on to Richmond and Petersburg for nearly 10 months before beginning his retreat to Appomattox, where he was forced to surrender. On January 23, 1865, he had been named as commander in chief of the Confederate armies, but he found himself too burdened in Virginia to give more than general directives to the other theaters.

Lee returned to Richmond as a paroled prisoner of war and submitted with the utmost composure to an altered destiny. He devoted the rest of his life to setting an example of conduct for other thousands of ex-Confederates. He refused a number of offers that would have secured substantial means for his family. Instead, he assumed the presidency of Washington College (now Washington and Lee University) in Lexington, Virginia, and his reputation revitalized the school after the war. Lee's enormous wartime prestige in the North and the South, and the devotion inspired by his unconscious symbolism of the "Lost Cause" made his a legendary figure even before his death, October 12, 1870, of heart disease, which had plagued him since the spring of 1863, at Lexington, Virginia, where he is buried.

Somehow his application for restoration of citizenship was mislaid, and it was not until the 1970s that it was found and citizenship granted by an act of Congress in 1975.

Lee's skill as a general rested on his ability to analyze a situation swiftly and accurately, his knack for anticipating an enemy's movements, and his abilities at improvisation and extemporization; these skills were matched by great strength of character, a high sense of duty, and genuine humility and selflessness. Lee was one of the nation's great generals.

Source and Additional Reading

Freeman, Douglas Southall. *Lee's Lieutenants.* 3 vols. New York: Charles Scribner's Sons, 1942–44.

Fuller, J. F. C. *Grant and Lee: A Study in Personality and Generalship.* 2d ed. Bloomington: University of Indiana Press, 1957.

Lindbergh, Charles ("The Lone Eagle")

(1902–1974) *Captain, United States Army Air Corps Reserve, the American aviator, who in 1927 was the first person to fly alone across the Atlantic Ocean, an achievement that earned him the Medal of Honor.*

Born: February 4, 1902, Detroit, Mich.; **Entered service at:** Little Falls, Minn.; **Place and date:** From New York City to Paris, France, May 20–21, 1927. **G.O. No.:** 5, W.D., 1928; act of Congress, December 14, 1927.

Born on February 4, 1902, in Detroit, Charles Augustus Lindbergh spent his childhood in Little Falls, Minnesota. His father served in the U.S. Congress from 1907 to 1917. The son, however, was unconcerned with politics until later in life. Lindbergh learned to fly at age 20. In 1926 he was flying a mail route between Chicago and St. Louis when he heard of a $25,000 prize offered for the first solo Atlantic flight. With the help of St. Louis businessmen he set out to accomplish this feat in a specially built plane, *The Spirit of St. Louis.* Leaving Roosevelt Field, Long Island, at 7:52 on May 20, 1927, he arrived at Le Bourget airport, Paris, at 10:22 (French time) on May 21. He had flown 3,600 miles (5,800 kilometers) in 33 $\frac{1}{2}$ hours and returned home a hero.

Lindbergh spent much of his subsequent life as a consultant to the aircraft and airline industries. In 1929 he married Anne Spencer Morrow, daughter of the U.S. ambassador to Mexico, Dwight Morrow. Their life, however, was touched by tragedy in 1932 when their infant son was kidnapped from their home in New Jersey and murdered. Soon thereafter Congress enacted the "Lindbergh law," making kidnapping a federal crime.

After a sensational trial Bruno Richard Hauptmann was convicted of the crime and executed in 1936. By 1940, Lindbergh had become politically controversial. After touring the centers of European air power in the late 1930s, he repeatedly warned of the superiority of the German air force. In 1940–41 he spoke out, his remarks tainted with anti-Semitism, in favor of American isolation as the European war intensified. Once the United States had entered World War II, however, he served as a civilian aircraft consultant and flew 50 missions against the Japanese. Lindbergh later used his influence to further U.S. space capabilities. He would also devote his energies to conservation. He died on Maui, Hawaii, on August 26, 1974.

Citation: "For displaying heroic courage and skill as a navigator, at the risk of his life, by his nonstop flight in his airplane, the *Spirit of St. Louis,* from New York City to Paris, France, 20–21 May 1927, by which Capt. Lindbergh not only achieved the greatest individual triumph of any American citizen but demonstrated that travel across the ocean by aircraft was possible."

Sources and Additional Reading

Medal of Honor Citation.
Berg, A. Scott. *Lindbergh.* New York: Putnam, 1998.
Davis, Kenneth S. *The Hero: Charles A. Lindbergh and the American Dream.* New York: Doubleday, 1959.
Lindbergh, C. *The Spirit of St. Louis.* New York: Scribner, 1953.
———. *Wartime Journals.* New York: Harcourt, 1970.
Lindbergh, Reeve. *Under a Wing: A Memoir.* New York: Simon & Schuster, 1998.
Milton, Joyce. *Loss of Eden: A Biography of Charles and Anne Morrow Lindbergh.* New York: HarperCollins, 1993.
Mosley, Leonard. *Lindbergh.* Garden City; N.Y.: Doubleday, 1976.
Ross, Walter S. *The Last Hero.* New York: Harper & Row, 1976.

Liteky, Charles (Angelo J.) (b. 1931) *Chaplain, captain, United States Army. H&S Company, 199th Infantry Brigade, so distinguished himself in combat on December 6,* 1967, *that he was awarded the Medal of Honor for his heroic actions.*

Born: February 14, 1931, Washington D.C. **Entered service at:** Fort Hamilton, N.Y.; **Place and date:** Near Phuoc-Lac, Bien Hoa Province, Republic of Vietnam.

Citation: "Chaplain Liteky distinguished himself by exceptional heroism while serving with Company A, 4th Battalion, 12th Infantry, 199th Light Infantry Brigade. He was participating in a search and destroy operation when Company A came under intense fire from a battalion size enemy force. Momentarily stunned from the immediate encounter that ensued, the men hugged the ground for cover. Observing 2 wounded men, Chaplain Liteky moved to within 15 meters of an enemy machine gun position to reach them, placing himself between the enemy and the wounded men. When there was a brief respite in the fighting, he managed to drag them to the relative safety of the landing zone. Inspired by his courageous actions, the company rallied and began placing a heavy volume of fire upon the enemy's positions. In a magnificent display of courage and leadership, Chaplain Liteky began moving upright through the enemy fire, administering last rites to the dying and evacuating the wounded. Noticing another trapped and seriously wounded man, Chaplain Liteky crawled to his aid. Realizing that the wounded man was too heavy to carry, he rolled on his back, placed the man on his chest and through sheer determination and fortitude crawled back to the landing zone using his elbows and heels to push himself along. Pausing for breath momentarily, he returned to the action and came upon a man entangled in the dense, thorny underbrush. Once more intense enemy fire was directed at him, but Chaplain Liteky stood his ground and calmly broke the vines and carried the man to the landing zone for evacuation. On several occasions when the landing zone was under small arms and rocket fire, Chaplain Liteky stood up in the face of hostile fire and personally directed the medivac helicopters into and out of the area. With the wounded safely evacuated, Chaplain Liteky returned to the perimeter, constantly encouraging and inspiring the men. Upon the unit's relief on the morning of 7 December 1967, it was discovered that despite painful wounds in the neck and foot, Chaplain Liteky had personally carried over 20 men to the landing zone for evacuation during the savage fighting. Through his indomitable inspiration and heroic actions, Chaplain Liteky saved the lives of a number of his comrades and enabled the company to repulse the enemy. Chaplain Liteky's actions reflect great credit upon himself and were in keeping with the highest traditions of the U.S. Army."

Source

Medal of Honor Citation.

Livingston, James E. (b. 1940) *Captain, United States Marine Corps, Company E, Second Battalion, Fourth Marines, Ninth Marine Amphibious Brigade, so distinguished himself in combat at Dai Do, in the Republic of Vietnam, on May 2, 1968, that he was awarded the Medal of Honor for his heroic actions.*

Born: January 12, 1940, Towns, Telfair County, Ga.; **Entered service at:** McRae, Ga.

Citation: "For conspicuous gallantry and intrepidity at the risk of his life above and beyond the call of duty while serving as Commanding Officer, Company E, in action against enemy forces. Company E launched a determined assault on the heavily fortified village of Dai Do, which had been seized by the enemy on the preceding evening isolating a Marine company from the remainder of the battalion. Skillfully employing screening agents, Capt. Livingston maneuvered his men to assault positions across 500 meters of dangerous open rice paddy while under intense enemy fire. Ignoring hostile rounds impacting near him, he fearlessly led his men in a savage assault against enemy emplacements within the village. While adjusting supporting arms fire, Capt. Livingston moved to the points of heaviest resistance, shouting words of encouragement to his Marines, directing their fire, and spurring the dwindling momentum of the attack on repeated occasions. Although twice painfully wounded by grenade fragments, he refused medical treatment and courageously led his men in the destruction of over 100 mutually supporting bunkers, driving the remaining enemy from their positions, and relieving the pressure on the stranded Marine company. As the 2 companies consolidated positions and evacuated casualties, a third company passed through the friendly lines launching an assault on the adjacent village of Dinh To, only to be halted by a furious counterattack of an enemy battalion. Swiftly assessing the situation and disregarding the heavy volume of enemy fire, Capt. Livingston boldly maneuvered the remaining effective men of his company forward, joined forces with the heavily engaged Marines, and halted the enemy's counterattack. Wounded a third time and unable to walk, he steadfastly remained in the dangerously exposed area, deploying his men to more tenable positions and supervising the evacuation of casualties. Only when assured of the safety of his men did he allow himself to be evacuated. Capt. Livingston's gallant actions uphold the highest traditions of the Marine Corps and the U.S. Naval Service."

Source
Medal of Honor Citation.

James E. Livingston

Longstreet, James ("Old Pete") (1821–1904)
General officer, Confederate States Army.

Corps Commander James Longstreet made three mistakes that have denied him his deserved place in southern posterity: He argued with Lee at Gettysburg, he was right, and he became a Republican. Born in South Carolina, he entered West Point from Alabama, graduated in 1842, and was wounded at Chapultepec in Mexico. With two brevets and the staff rank of major he resigned his commission on June 1, 1861, and joined the Confederacy.

His assignments included the following: brigadier general, Confederate States Army (CSA) (June 17, 1861); commander of brigade (in First Corps after July 20), Army of the Potomac (July 2–October 7, 1861); major general, CSA (October 7, 1861); commander of division; First Corps, Army of the Potomac (October 14–22, 1861); commander of division (in Potomac District until March 1862), Department of Northern Virginia (October 22, 1861–July 1862); commander, First Corps, Army of Northern Virginia (July 1862–February 25, 1863; May–September 9, 1863; April 12–May 6, 1864; October 19, 1864–April 9, 1865); lieutenant general, CSA (October 9, 1862); commander, Department of Virginia and North Carolina (February 25–May 1863); commander of corps, Army of Tennessee (September 19–November 5, 1863); and commander, Department of East Tennessee (November 5, 1863–April 12, 1864).

Commanding a brigade, he fought at Blackburn's Ford and First Bull Run before moving up to divisional leadership for the Peninsula Campaign. There he saw further action at Yorktown, Williamsburg, Seven Pines, and the Seven Days. In the final days of the latter he also directed A. P. Hill's men. Commanding what was variously styled a "wing," "command," or "corps" (the latter was not legally recognized until October 1862), he proved to be a capable subordinate to Lee at Second Bull Run, where he delivered a crushing attack; South Mountain; Antietam; and Fredericksburg.

By now promoted to be the Confederacy's senior lieutenant general, he led an independent expedition into southeastern Virginia, where he displayed a lack of ability when on his own. Rejoining Lee, he opposed attacking at Gettysburg in favor of maneuvering Meade out of his position. Longstreet, who had come to believe in the strategic offense and the tactical defense, was proved right when the Confederate attacks on the second and third days were repulsed. Detached to reinforce Bragg in Georgia, he commanded a wing of the army on the second day at Chickamauga. In the dispute over the follow-up of the victory he was critical of Bragg and was soon detached to operate in East Tennessee. Here again he showed an incapacity for independent operations, especially in the siege of Knoxville. Rejoining Lee at the Wilderness, he was severely wounded, in the confusion, by Confederate troops. He resumed command in October during the Petersburg operations and commanded on the north side of the James. Lee's "Old War Horse" remained with his chief through the surrender at Appomattox.

After the war he befriended Grant and became a Republican. He served as Grant's minister to Turkey. He also served as commissioner of Pacific Railroads under Mckinley and Roosevelt, from 1897 to 1904. Criticized by many former Confederates, he struck back with his book *From Manassas to Appomattox* and outlived most of his high-ranking postwar detractors. He died at Gainsville, Georgia, on January 2, 1904, the last of the high command of the Confederacy. He is buried in Gainsville, Georgia.

Source

Dupuy, Trevor. N., Curt Johnson, and David L. Bongard. *The Harper Encyclopedia of Military Biography*. New York, HarperCollins, 1992.

Lopez, Jose M. *Sergeant, United States Army, 23d Infantry, Second Infantry Division, so distinguished himself in combat, during World War II, that he was awarded the Medal of Honor for his heroic actions.*

Born: Mission, Tex; **Entered service at:** Brownsville, Tex; **Place and date:** Near Krinkelt, Belgium, December 17, 1944. **G.O. No.:** 47, June 18, 1945.

Citation: "On his own initiative, he carried his heavy machinegun from Company K's right flank to its left, in order to protect that flank which was in danger of being overrun by advancing enemy infantry supported by tanks. Occupying a shallow hole offering no protection above his waist, he cut down a group of 10 Germans. Ignoring enemy fire from an advancing tank, he held his position and cut down 25 more enemy infantry attempting to turn his flank. Glancing to his right, he saw a large number of infantry swarming in from the front. Although dazed and shaken from enemy artillery fire which had crashed into the ground only a few yards away, he realized that his position soon would be outflanked. Again, alone, he carried his machinegun to a position to the right rear of the sector; enemy tanks and infantry were forcing a withdrawal. Blown over backward by the concussion of enemy fire, he immediately reset his gun and continued his fire. Single-handed he held off the German horde until he was satisfied his company had effected its retirement. Again he loaded his gun on his back and in a hail of small arms fire he ran to a point where a few of his comrades were attempting to set up another defense against the onrushing enemy. He fired from this position until his ammunition was exhausted. Still carrying his gun, he fell back with his small group to Krinkelt. Sgt. Lopez's gallantry and intrepidity, on seemingly suicidal missions in which he killed at least 100 of the enemy, were almost solely responsible for allowing Company K to avoid being enveloped, to withdraw successfully and to give other forces coming up in support time to build a line which repelled the enemy drive."

Source

Medal of Honor Citation.

Lourim, William *Sergeant, United States Marine Corps, as a Marine combat correspondent, assigned to First Battalion, First Marine Regiment, distinguished himself in combat, during the Korean War, and was awarded (posthumously) the Navy Cross for his actions.*

Citation: "For extraordinary heroism while serving as a Combat Correspondent attached to Company A, First Battalion, First Marine Division (Reinforced), in action against enemy aggressor forces in Korea on 10 June 1951. Volunteering to accompany the point squad of the assault platoon north of Yanggu, Sergeant Lourim bravely moved forward in the face of hostile automatic weapons, small arms and grenade fire, alternately firing his rifle and taking notes of the action. When a Marine was wounded nearby, he quickly went to the aid of the helpless man despite intense close-range enemy machine-gun fire and, after moving the casualty to a safer place, gallantly shielded him with his own body until the stretcher-bearers arrived. Learning that the assault unit was heavily engaged and subjected to hostile crossfire, he hurriedly rejoined the attack and assisted in caring for the casualties during the ensuing firefight. Later, in a daring attempt to aid another stricken Marine, he dashed around in the open area swept by frontal and flanking hostile machine-gun fire and, while assisting the casualties, was himself mortally wounded by the enemy. By his outstanding courage, unselfish efforts in behalf of his comrades, and unswerving devotion to duty, Sergeant Lourim served to inspire all who observed him and upheld the highest traditions of the Marine Corps and U.S. Naval Service. He gallantly gave his life for his country."

Source

Cameron, Garry M. *Last to Know, First to Go: The Marine Corps Combat Correspondents.* Capistrano Beach, Calif.: Charger Books, 1988.

Luke, Frank, Jr. (1897–1918) *Second lieutenant, United States Army Air Corps, 27th Aero Squadron, First Pursuit Group, Air Service, distinguished himself in aerial combat in France in September 1918 and was awarded the Medal of Honor (posthumously) for his heroic action.*

Born: May 19, 1897, Phoenix, Ariz.; **Entered service at:** Phoenix, Ariz.; **Place and date:** Near Murvaux, France, September 29, 1918. **G.O. No.:** 59, W.D. 1919.

Citation: "After having previously destroyed a number of enemy aircraft within 17 days, he voluntarily started on a patrol after German observation balloons. Though pursued by 8 German planes, which were protecting the enemy balloon line, he unhesitatingly attacked and shot down in flames 3 German balloons, being himself under heavy fire from ground batteries and the hostile planes. Severely wounded, he descended to within 50 meters of the ground, and flying at this low altitude near the town of Murvaux, opened fire upon enemy troops, killing 6 and wounding as many more. Forced to make a landing and surrounded on all sides by the enemy, who called upon him to surrender, he drew his automatic pistol and defended himself gallantly until he fell dead from a wound in the chest."

Source

Medal of Honor Citation.

M

MacArthur, Arthur, Jr.
MacArthur, Arthur, Jr. (1845–1912) *Union Army officer, governor of Philippines, soldier in the Civil War and Spanish-American War, and father of General Douglas MacArthur, so distinguished himself in combat that he was awarded the Medal of Honor.*

Remembered today primarily as the father of General Douglas MacArthur, Arthur MacArthur was himself a highly distinguished soldier. Massachusetts-born MacArthur was raised in Wisconsin and at the age of 17 was commissioned a lieutenant in that state's volunteer infantry during the Civil War. Twice wounded, he rose quickly in rank and became a colonel of volunteers at age 19. His courage at the Battle of Missionary Ridge in 1863 earned him the Medal of Honor. After the Civil War MacArthur chose to remain in the army; he took more than 30 years to regain the rank he had held as a volunteer.

The Spanish-American War offered MacArthur the chance for action and promotion once more. In June 1898, as a brigadier general of volunteers, he sailed for the Philippines and the following year his troops repulsed an attack on Manila by independence-minded Filipino insurrectionists. Taking the offensive, MacArthur soon captured the rebel capital of Malolos and, as military governor of the islands, directed ongoing operations against the guerrillas. After returning to the United States in 1901, MacArthur held several commands and was promoted to lieutenant general in 1906. He retired from the army in 1909 and died three years later.

Citation: "Seized the colors of his regiment at a critical moment and planted them on the captured works on the crest of Missionary Ridge."

Source and Additional Reading
Medal of Honor Citation.

Boatner, Mark M. *Civil War Dictionary.* New York: David McKay, 1959.
Long, Gavin H. *MacArthur—as Military Commander.* London: Batsford, 1960.

MacArthur, Douglas
MacArthur, Douglas (1880–1964) *American general, commander of Allied forces in the southwest Pacific during World War II, commander of the occupation of Japan and of United Nations forces in Korea.*

Born on January 26, 1880, at the United States Army barracks in Little Rock, Arkansas, MacArthur was the son of Arthur MacArthur, a professional army officer (and a recipient of the Medal of Honor for heroic action during the Civil War) and Mary Pinkney Hardy MacArthur, the daughter of an old Virginia family. His father's assignments required the family to move from one army post to another, frequently interrupting the boy's schooling. But Douglas worked hard at his studies, because he had set his heart on attending the United States Military Academy at West Point. In 1898 he passed the competitive examination for West Point and received an appointment as a cadet.

MacArthur entered West Point in 1899. His achievements there gave rich promise of an outstanding career. First in his class, he made a scholastic record that had not been equaled for many years. He won the coveted appointment of first captain, the highest military honor at the academy. He also played varsity baseball and managed the football team. Graduating in 1903, he was commissioned a second lieutenant in the Corps of Engineers.

MacArthur's first assignment was in the Philippines as an engineer. After a year there, he was sent to work in the Army Engineer Office in San Francisco. In 1905 he traveled to East Asia as an aide to his father, who had been appointed official U.S. observer of the Russo-Japanese War.

Promotions accrued rapidly for MacArthur in the years before World War I, and by the time the United States entered the war in 1917, he had reached the rank of major.

MacArthur helped organize the famed 42d Infantry (Rainbow) Division, and the war brought him into national prominence for the first time. As the division's first chief of staff, with the rank of colonel, he sailed with his troops to France in October 1917. In August 1918, after being promoted to brigadier general, he became commander of the division's 84th Infantry Brigade.

MacArthur led his brigade with an enthusiasm and dash that earned him the loyalty and affection of his men. Twice wounded, he received many decorations for his bravery in battle. He also won recognition for his skill in tactical and strategic matters.

After the war, MacArthur was named superintendent of West Point; he began his duties in 1919. He modernized the curriculum of the academy and raised its academic standards, while placing great emphasis on athletics.

In 1922 he left West Point. From then until 1930 he held various posts in the United States and the Philippines, which he came to regard as his second home. In 1925 he was promoted to major general, and five years later he was named chief of staff of the United States Army by President Herbert Hoover. At 50, MacArthur was the youngest man to have been appointed to this post.

MacArthur took office in the worst days of the Great Depression, when the American people were bitterly disillusioned with war. He spent a great deal of time and energy trying to convince Congress to appropriate adequate funds for his plans to reorganize the army and make it more efficient. He achieved much of his program but was generally unsuccessful in his effort to strengthen air and armored units and to integrate them with the ground force.

MacArthur's most controversial action during his five-year service as chief of staff was his rout of the Bonus Army on July 28, 1932. About 15,000 men, most of whom were unemployed veterans of World War I, had streamed into Washington, D.C., to demand payment of federal war bonuses. When the police were unable to handle such a large crowd, President Hoover ordered the army to clear the veterans out of the capital. In full uniform, with his aide, Maj. Dwight D. Eisenhower, at his side, MacArthur personally carried out the order, routing the veterans and driving them from their camp. For many persons, such use of force created an image of MacArthur as a potential military dictator.

MacArthur completed his duty as chief of staff in October 1935. He was then appointed military adviser to the newly created Philippine Commonwealth. He retired from the United States Army in 1937 but continued as Philippine military adviser with the rank of field marshal. During this period he adopted the gold-braided hat, sunglasses, and corncob pipe that became his hallmark.

MacArthur was married twice, first in 1922, to Henrietta Louise Cromwell Brooks. This marriage ended in divorce by mutual consent in 1929. He married his second wife, Jean Marie Faircloth, in 1937. They had one son, Arthur, born on February 21, 1938.

On July 26, 1941, as war with Japan threatened, the 61-year-old MacArthur was recalled to active duty as commander of the newly formed United States Army Forces in the Far East. Officials hoped that MacArthur's assignment would serve notice of American determination to halt Japanese aggression.

On December 7, 1941, Japan began the Pacific war by attacking Pearl Harbor in Hawaii. About eight hours later, the Japanese bombed Clark Field, north of Manila, in the Philippines. The Japanese landed large forces north and south of Manila on December 22. Three days later, MacArthur declared Manila an open city and moved to Corregidor, an island fortress off Bataan Peninsula at the entrance to Manila Bay. During the next two weeks, under heavy Japanese pressure, American and Philippine troops withdrew to Bataan, where they continued heroically to resist the Japanese for three months.

In March 1942, President Franklin Roosevelt ordered MacArthur and his family to go to Australia. Strategists felt that MacArthur was too valuable to be lost in the hopeless defense of the Philippines, which finally fell to the Japanese in early May. On the trip to Melbourne, MacArthur made his famous statement of determination: "I came through," he declared, "and I shall return." He received the Medal of Honor on March 25 and on April 18 was formally named supreme commander of the Southwest Pacific Area.

His first task was to protect Australia's sea-lanes to the United States from the Japanese forces, who sought to capture Port Moresby on the south coast of New Guinea. After they failed to take this objective by sea, they were stopped on land in September 1942 by Australian troops under MacArthur's command. The Allies then took the offensive and began a long and difficult campaign to drive the enemy out of New Guinea. By February 1943 the Allies had won control of southeast New Guinea and eliminated the threat to the sea-lanes.

MacArthur's victory in New Guinea was one of the first steps in a campaign that took his forces westward toward the Philippines. During this campaign, South Pacific naval units led by Admiral William Halsey were placed under MacArthur's strategic command. After advancing up the chain of the Solomon Islands, MacArthur's troops seized the Admiralty Islands and neutralized the powerful Japanese base at Rabaul in early 1944. They then moved along the northern New Guinea coast, bypassing and rendering ineffective large Japanese forces along the way.

On October 20, 1944, MacArthur's forces invaded Leyte in the central Philippines. The general waded ashore with his troops, fulfilling his promise to return made more than two years earlier. On December 18, three days after his forces landed on Mindoro, he was promoted to the rank of five-star General of the Army, are of nine five-star U.S. generals. In early January 1945, MacArthur's army invaded Luzon, the main island of the Philippines, and by the end of February had recaptured Manila and Corregidor.

On August 14, 1945, after the atomic bombing of Hiroshima and Nagasaki, the Japanese accepted Allied terms of unconditional surrender. The next day, MacArthur was named supreme commander in Japan for the Allied powers. On September 2, at ceremonies aboard the battleship *Missouri* in Tokyo Bay, he received the formal surrender of the Japanese.

At an age when most men retire, the 65-year-old general began a new career as commander of the occupation of Japan. Under his guidance, Japan moved from defeat to prosperity. He disarmed the military, established a liberal government, instituted land reform, and restored the country's shattered industry. He also abolished the nobility and brought about other social changes that had an important effect on Japanese society by making it more democratic.

MacArthur was still in Japan when Communist North Korea attacked South Korea on June 25, 1950. President Harry Truman ordered MacArthur to take command of a small American military mission stationed there and to provide U.S. air and sea support for the South Korean Army. On July 8, MacArthur was named commander of a United Nations (UN) international force established to repel the Communist attack.

The 70-year-old general faced a formidable task. By the time the first American troops arrived on July 1, the North Koreans had overwhelmed South Korean defenses. By early September they had forced the defenders into a small beachhead, called the Pusan perimeter, at the southeast tip of the peninsula.

On September 15, MacArthur executed a daring outflanking maneuver by landing troops at Inchon, west of Seoul. At the same time, the United States Eighth Army launched a massive counteroffensive from within the Pusan perimeter. The North Koreans fled toward the 38th parallel, the boundary between North and South Korea. By the end of the month, UN forces had recaptured most of South Korea. On October 8, UN troops crossed the 38th parallel and moved north toward the Yalu River, the boundary between North Korea and the People's Republic of China. UN advance units reached the Yalu on October 26.

MacArthur's attempt to subdue North Korea ended in failure because of the People's Republic of China's entry into the war. The Chinese attacked in force on November 24 and forced MacArthur's army to retreat behind the 38th parallel. MacArthur began a counterattack in February

1951, but it proved indecisive and the Korean War settled into a stalemate. MacArthur proposed various new measures to achieve victory, including bombing supply centers in Manchuria and "unleashing" the Chinese Nationalists on Taiwan against the Communist-held mainland. President Truman feared that such actions might ignite a larger war, and he rejected MacArthur's proposals. The general then made public his disagreement with the president, and on April 11, 1951, Truman dismissed him from command.

MacArthur returned to the United States for the first time in 15 years. As he crossed the country from San Francisco to New York, he received a hero's welcome. On April 19 he addressed a joint session of Congress. His speech, a stirring defense of his policy, closed with a line from an old army ballad: "Old soldiers never die; they just fade away."

But the old general did not fade away. MacArthur had become a leading figure in Republican politics. He became one of the party's leading candidates for the presidential nomination in 1948. At the 1952 convention he delivered the keynote address and was again mentioned as a possible candidate. But the nomination went instead to his former aide, Dwight D. Eisenhower, whose command in Europe during World War II paralleled MacArthur's in the Pacific. MacArthur entered Walter Reed Hospital in Washington D.C. on March 2, 1964, and underwent three operations for an abdominal illness. On April 5 he lost the battle and died at the age of 84. President Lyndon Johnson declared a period of national mourning, and the general's body lay in state in the rotunda of the Capitol.On April 11, MacArthur was buried with full military honors in a memorial built for him by the city of Norfolk, Virginia, his mother's hometown.

In an age when war had grown more complex, MacArthur showed a mastery over all aspects of his profession. He combined supreme self-confidence with unflinching courage. His unusual strategic sense and intuitive understanding of the enemy led him to make insightful, often brilliant wartime decisions. Impressive in appearance and dramatic in action, he demanded and received unquestioning obedience.

But the qualities that made MacArthur great were also the sources of his weaknesses. He was extremely egotistical and tolerated no criticism. Remote and authoritarian, he seemed to lose touch with common people. Although he insisted on complete loyalty from his subordinates, he often disagreed bitterly with his superiors.

MacArthur's complex personality inspired both love and fear. His admirers gave him their wholehearted devotion. His critics seemed to find fault with almost everything he did. Few persons could be indifferent to this proud and colorful warrior. But no one could deny that he had served his country well during the period when it assumed leadership of the free world.

Source and Additional Reading

James, D. Clayton. *The Years of MacArthur.* 3 Vols. Boston: Houghton Mifflin, 1970, 1975, 1985.

MacArthur, Douglas. *Reminiscences.* 1964. Reprint, New York: Da Capo, 1985.

Manchester, William. *American Caesar: Douglas MacArthur, 1880–1964.* Boston: Little Brown, 1978.

Morton, Louis. *United States Army in World War II: The War in the Pacific Fall of the Philippines.* Washington, D.C.: Government Printing Office, 1953.

———. *The United States Army in World War II: Strategy and Command. The First Two Years.* Washington, D.C. Government Printing Office.

Rhoades, Weldon E. *Flying MacArthur to Victory.* College Station: Texas A&M University Press, 1987.

Rogers, Paul P. *The Bitter Years: MacArthur and Sutherland.* Westport, Conn.: Greenwood Press, 1990.

Schaller, Michael. *Douglas MacArthur.* New York: Oxford University Press, 1989.

McCaffrey, Barry H. *Captain, United States Army, Second Airborne Task Force, Airborne Division Advisory Detachment (Airborne), so distinguished himself in combat that he was awarded the Distinguished Service Cross for his heroic actions on October 6, 1966, in the Republic of Vietnam and the Distinguished Service Cross (First Oak Leaf Cluster) for heroic actions on March 9, 1969, in the Republic of Vietnam.*

Citation: "For extraordinary heroism in connection with military operations involving conflict with an armed hostile force in the Republic of Vietnam: Captain (then First Lieutenant) McCaffrey distinguished himself by exceptionally valorous actions on 6 October 1966 while advising a Vietnamese Airborne Battalion on a search and clear operation near Dong Ha. At 0315 hours the camp received intense mortar fire which severely wounded Captain McCaffrey in the shoulder. With complete disregard for his safety, he unhesitatingly ran through the intense automatic weapons and mortar fire to estimate the severity of the attack. He soon discovered that the senior American advisor had been killed, and all but one of the company commanders were seriously wounded. After rendering aid to the casualties, Captain McCaffrey took command and dauntlessly proceeded around the perimeter to direct the defense against the insurgent human wave assaults. Again he was wounded by mortar fragments, but ignored his own condition and quickly organized a counterattack which successfully repelled another Viet Cong attack. During the remainder of the 12-hour battle, Captain McCaffrey repeatedly exposed himself to the hostile fire and directed artillery and air strikes against the insurgent forces. Through his unremitting courage and personal example, he inspired the besieged Vietnamese unit to defeat four determined Viet Cong attacks and inflict heavy casualties on a numerically superior hostile force. Only after assuring that all the wounded had been extracted, and that a replacement advisor was with the battalion, did he permit himself to be evacuated. Captain McCaffrey's extraordinary heroism and devotion to duty were in keeping with the highest traditions of the military service and reflect great credit upon himself, his unit, and the United States Army."

Oak Leaf Cluster Citation: "For extraordinary heroism in connection with military operations involving conflict with an armed hostile force in the Republic of Vietnam. Captain McCaffrey distinguished himself by exceptionally valorous actions on 9 March 1969 as company commander during a reconnaissance-in-force mission. When elements of one of his platoons came under intense fire from a well-fortified enemy bunker complex, Captain McCaffrey immediately moved forward to assault the hostile position in order to relieve pressure on the beleaguered squad. He quickly deployed his men for an attack and led the advance through the fusillade. When he had pinpointed the source of the greatest concentration of fire, he initiated a single-handed assault on the bunker. After several attempts, he finally succeeded in destroying the machine gun bunker and its occupants. Despite being wounded in the left arm, he continued to supervise the overrunning and destruction of the hostile bunker system. After organizing the evacuation of his casualties, he called in supporting fire on the enemy. Only after he was assured that all of the wounded had been cared for and after he had organized a defensive position, did he allow himself to be evacuated for medical treatment. Captain McCaffrey's extraordinary heroism and devotion to duty were in keeping with the highest traditions of the military service and reflect great credit upon himself, his unit, and the United States Army."

Source
Distinguished Service Cross Citations.

McCain, John Sidney, III (b. 1936) *Lieutenant Commander, United States Navy, as Vietnam War prisoner of war spent 5 ½ years in captivity.*

John S. McCain III graduated from Episcopal High School, Alexandria, Virginia, in 1954. He attended the United States Naval Academy in Annapolis, Maryland. McCain was a member of a navy family. Both his father and his grandfather became navy aviators, as did John III. He graduated from the United States Naval Academy in 1958, as his father had in 1931. John III was later shipped to Vietnam, the third generation of his family to serve.

John McCain's grandfather was a gaunt, hawk-faced man known as "Slew" by his fellow officers and, affectionately, as "Popeye" by the sailors who served under him. McCain Sr. played the horses, drank bourbon and water, and rolled his own cigarettes with one hand. More significant, he was one of the navy's greatest commanders, and led the strongest aircraft carrier force of the Third Fleet in key battles during World War II.

Rear Admiral John S. McCain, II, who, as Commander Aircraft South Pacific Forces (COMAIRSOPAC), controlled all land-based aircraft in the South Pacific Area, including those of the US Army Air Forces (USAAF).

Born at Carroll County, Mississippi, August 9, 1884, the son of John Sidney and Elizabeth-Ann Young McCain. He was a student at the University of Mississippi, 1901–02 and graduated from the United States Naval Academy in 1906, from the Navy War College in 1929, from Flight Instruction School, 1936. He married Katherine Vaulx, August 9, 1909. Their children are: John Sidney, James Gordon, and Katherine Vaulx. He was commissioned an Ensign, 1906, and promoted through the grades to Rear Admiral, 1941; Vice Admiral, July 1943. He served as Chief of the Naval Bureau of Aeronautics, September 1942–July 1943; Deputy Chief of Naval Operations for Air, July 1943; Commander, Carrier Task Force 38. Planes under his command took part in action over Peleliu, Leyte Gulf, Philippine Sea, Mindoro, Luzon, Formosa, Ryukyus and the Japanese homeland. His planes once sank 49 Japanese ships in a single day. Between July 10 and August 14, 1945, his aviators located and destroyed 3,000 grounded enemy planes. He witnessed the Japanese surrender aboard the USS *Missouri* in Tokyo Bay on September 2, 1945. He died on September 6, 1945 and was buried in Section 3 (Grave 4356), Arlington National Cemetery, among other family members, including his brother, William Alexander McCain, Brigadier General, U.S. Arlington National Cemetery.

John McCain's father followed a similar path, equally distinguished by heroic service in the navy, as a submarine commander during World War II. McCain, Jr., was a slightly built man, but like his father, he earned the respect and affection of his men. He, too, rose to the rank of four-star admiral, making the McCains the first family in American history to achieve that distinction. McCains Jr.'s final assignment was as commander of all U.S. forces in the Pacific during the Vietnam War.

Admiral John S. McCain, Jr., submariner, became Commander-in-Chief of the Pacific Command (CINC-PAC) in July 1968, a position he held until 1972. As such, he directed all U.S. military operations in the vast war theater during the Vietnam War, exercising command through CINCPACFL (Commander-in-Chief of the Pacific Fleet) and CINCPACAF (Commander-in-Chief of the Pacific Air Force). He exercised command over ground and air operations in Vietnam through CONMUSMACV (Commander-in-Chief of the U.S. Military Assistance Command Vietnam), U.S. Army General Creighton Abrams. Admiral John McCain Jr. died March 24, 1981.

Lt Cdr. John S. McCain III was a pilot assigned to Attack Squadron 163 onboard the aircraft carrier USS *ORISKANY* (CVA-34). On October 26, 1967, he launched in his A4E "Skyhawk" attack aircraft as the number three aircraft in the first division of a strike group against the Hanoi Thermal Power Plant.

The flight met with considerable resistance in the form of anti-aircraft fire and surface-to-air missiles (SAM) approaching the target. As McCain rolled into his dive, his aircraft was observed by his wingman to take a direct hit from anti-aircraft fire and to burst into flames. McCain was able to eject from his crippled aircraft and made brief emergency contact before his parachute landed in a nearby lake in Hanoi. He was captured immediately and confined in the Hanoi prison system, as was verified by Radio Hanoi broadcasts and later information gathered during his years of imprisonment.

McCain was severely injured, having broken both arms and his right leg, and his strength in coping through his recuperation was inspiring to many of his fellow POWs.

On my 23rd mission, a missile the size of a telephone pole blew the right wing off the Skyhawk bomber which I was piloting. It went into an inverted, almost straight down spin. I was knocked unconscious by the force of the ejection. I did not realize it at the moment, but I had broken my right leg at the knee, my left arm and my right arm in three places. I regained consciousness as I parachuted into a lake right in the center of Hanoi. My helmet and oxygen mask had been blown off. With my fifty pounds of equipment and gear I sank to the bottom. I rose and then started sinking. I could not understand why I could not use my right arm or leg. The third time I sank I couldn't get back to the surface. With my teeth I was finally able to get the toggle released thus inflating the life preserver, which floated me to the top.

Some North Vietnamese swam out and pulled me to the side of the lake. As they stripped me of my clothes, they kicked and spit on me. I noticed my right foot was at a 90-degree position resting next to my left knee. When I said, "My God—my leg!" they became enraged. They slammed a rifle butt down on my shoulder, which smashed it pretty badly, and another stuck a bayonet in my foot. About this time a guy appeared who quieted the crowd. I was then put on a stretcher and was taken to prison. Immediately the interrogations began and when I refused to answer their questions they would knock me into unconsciousness. Finally after four days of this I agreed to give information if they would take me to a hospital. The doctor, after taking my pulse said, "It's too late." They left the room. Sometime later, the chief interrogator again returned shouting "Your father a big admiral, now we take you to hospital." I tell you this to make a point. There were hardly any amputees among the prisoners who came back because the North Vietnamese would not give medical treatment to someone badly injured. The transition to the dirt, filth and infection made it difficult for a guy to survive. In fact, the treatment in the hospital almost killed me.

The hospital was filthy and every time it rained there would be almost an inch of water on the floor. I almost never saw a doctor or a nurse. I was, however, assigned a 16-year-old kid right out of the rice fields. He delighted in hitting and slapping me. Then as I could not use my arms he was to feed me, but ate most of the food himself. I was getting from three to four tablespoons per day.

I knew that because of my father the North Vietnamese would try to obtain more than the usual propaganda. They worked on setting my right arm for an hour and a half, trying to align the three broken bones—all without any sedation. When it was over they took me into a room with a nice bed, in came the TV cameras and I was filmed with a French Communist. They wanted me to tell about the lenient and humane treatment I had received. As soon as the filming was over I was put back in my room. They gave me one operation on my leg (said I needed two but because of my bad attitude I would get one). My left arm was to heal itself.

After six weeks in the hospital I was put in prison. My weight was down to 100 from 155 and my roommates said later that they had not expected that I could live one week. George Day and Norris Overly kept me alive during those days I was incapacitated. In March 1968 I started two years of living in solitary.

They tried many designs to force me to embarrass my father and the United States. I found that prayer helped. It wasn't a question of asking for superhuman strength or for God to strike the North Vietnamese dead. It was asking for moral and physical courage, for guidance and wisdom to do the right thing. I asked for comfort when I was in pain and sometimes I received relief. I was sustained in many times of trial.

When the pressure was on you seemed to go one way or the other. Either it was easier for them to break you the next time or it was harder. In other words, if you are going to make it, you get tougher.

The Communists left no doubt in my mind that it was not a question of South Vietnam alone. Two North Vietnamese generals said to me at separate times, "After we liberate South Vietnam, we're going to liberate Cambodia. And after Cambodia we're going to liberate Laos and after we liberate Laos we're going to liberate Thailand and after we liberate Thailand we're going to liberate Malaysia and then Burma. We're going to liberate all of Southeast Asia. That is what Communism is all about—armed struggle to overthrow the capitalist countries."

I had a lot of time to think and I came to the conclusion that one of the most important things in life—along with a man's family—is to make some contribution to his country.

Years after the war, McCain returned to Hanoi and visited the site of the monument erected at the lake in Hanoi that celebrated his capture. John McCain III left the United States Navy and ultimately was elected to the U.S. House of Representatives in 1982 and again in 1984. He won the Senate seat vacated by Barry Goldwater from Arizona in 1986. During his terms in Congress, McCain has been involved in the issue of Americans still prisoner, missing, or unaccounted for in Vietnam, although prisoner of war/missing in action (POW/MIA) advocates disagree as to his helpfulness to the issue. Supporters point to a number of bills supported, speeches made, and initiatives begun (such as asking for the Tighe Commission to investigate Defense Intelligence Agency and the move for a U.S. Special Interest Section in Vietnam), whereas critics of McCain (also critics of U.S. Government policy on the issue) assert that McCain was too close to the Reagan administration to force progress on the ultimate goal of bringing home American prisoners.

In 1973 McCain returned to school and attended the National War College in Washington, D.C. He retired a captain, having served in the Navy from 1958 to 1981. During his service he was awarded the Silver Star, Bronze Star, Legion of Merit, Purple Heart, and Distinguished Flying Cross. His second marriage was to the former Cindy Hensley, and they have six children. In 1999, as a senator from Arizona, he ran as a Republican candidate for the presidential nomination.

Source and Additional Reading

Capt. and Mrs. Frederic A. Wyatt (USNR Ret.). *We Came Home*, Barbara Powers Wyatt, ed. Toluca Lake, Calif.: P.O.W. Publications, 1977.

Additional information compiled by from one or more of the following: raw data from U.S. Government agency sources; correspondence with POW/MIA families; published sources, interviews, information from John

McCain III; Arlington National Cemetery Updated by the P.O.W. NETWORK 2000.

McCarter, Lloyd G. (b. 1917) *Private, United States Army, 503d Parachute Infantry Regiment, so distinguished himself in combat, during World War II, that he was awarded the Medal of Honor for his heroic actions.*

Born: May 11, 1917, St. Maries, Idaho; **Entered service at:** Tacoma, Wash.; **Place and date:** Corregidor, Philippine Islands, February 16–19 1945. **G.O. No.:** 77, September 10, 1945.

Citation: "He was a scout with the regiment which seized the fortress of Corregidor, Philippine Islands. Shortly after the initial parachute assault on 16 February 1945, he crossed 30 yards of open ground under intense enemy fire, and at pointblank range silenced a machinegun with hand grenades. On the afternoon of 18 February he killed 6 snipers. That evening, when a large force attempted to bypass his company, he voluntarily moved to an exposed area and opened fire. The enemy attacked his position repeatedly throughout the night and was each time repulsed. By 2 o'clock in the morning, all the men about him had been wounded; but shouting encouragement to his comrades and defiance at the enemy, he continued to bear the brunt of the attack, fearlessly exposing himself to locate enemy soldiers and then pouring heavy fire on them. He repeatedly crawled back to the American line to secure more ammunition. When his submachine gun would no longer operate, he seized an automatic rifle and continued to inflict heavy casualties. This weapon, in turn, became too hot to use and, discarding it, he continued with an M-1 rifle. At dawn the enemy attacked with renewed intensity. Completely exposing himself to hostile fire, he stood erect to locate the most dangerous enemy positions. He was seriously wounded; but, though he had already killed more than 30 of the enemy, he refused to evacuate until he had pointed out immediate objectives for attack. Through his sustained and outstanding heroism in the face of grave and obvious danger, Pvt. McCarter made outstanding contributions to the success of his company and to the recapture of Corregidor."

Source
Medal of Honor Citation.

McCausland, John (1836–1927) *Brigadier general, Confederate States Army.*

John McCausland, one of the most conspicuous figures in the warfare in the valley of the Shenandoah and on the borders of Virginia, held important Confederate commands and gained a national reputation as a brilliant leader and persistent fighter. He was the son of John McCausland, a native of country Tyrone, Ireland, who immigrated to America when about 21 years of age and first made his home at Lynchburg, with David Kyle, whose daughter, Harriet, he subsequently married. He became a prominent merchant and finally resided at St. Louis, where he rendered valuable service as commissioner of taxation. His son, John McCausland, was born at St. Louis, September 13, 1837, and in 1849 went with his brother to Point Pleasant, Mason County, where he received a preparatory education. He was graduated with first honors in the class of 1857 at the Virginia Military Institute and subsequently worked as an assistant professor in that institution until 1861.

On the secession of Virginia he organized the famous Rockbridge Artillery, of which he was elected commander; but leaving Dr. Pendleton in charge of that company, he made his headquarters at Charleston, in the Kanawha Valley, under commission from Governor Letcher, with the rank of lieutenant colonel, for the organization of troops in the military department of Western Virginia. He gathered about 6,000 men for the commands of Generals Wise and Floyd, who subsequently operated in that region, and formed the 36th Regiment, Virginia Infantry, of which he took command with a commission as colonel. This regiment, made up of the best blood of the western Virginia counties, was distinguished under his leadership in the campaign of Floyd's brigade in West Virginia and in the latter part of 1861 moved to Bowling Green, Kentucky, to unite with the army of Gen. Albert Sidney Johnston.

At Fort Donelson, Colonel McCausland commanded a brigade of Floyd's division, and after having a conspicuous part in the gallant and successful battle before the fort, took away his Virginians before the surrender. After reorganizing at Nashville, he remained at Chattanooga with his command until after the Battle of Shiloh, when he moved to Wytheville, Virginia. During 1862 and 1863 he was engaged in the campaigns in southwestern and western Virginia and the Shenandoah Valley, under Generals Loring, Echols, and Sam Jones, taking a conspicuous part in the battle at Charleston, September 1862. Early in May 1864, he was ordered by Gen. A. G. Jenkins to move his brigade from Dublin to meet the federal force advancing under General Crook from the Kanawha Valley. He took position on Cloyd's farm, where he was reinforced by General Jenkins and attacked by the enemy May 9. After several hours' fighting, Jenkins was mortally wounded and the Confederate line was broken by the superior strength of the enemy. Colonel McCausland assumed command and made a gallant fight, forming two new lines successively, and finally retired in good order, repulsing the attacks of the federal cavalry and carrying with him 200 prisoners. In this battle the federals outnumbered the Confederates three to one. By his subsequent active movements, General McCausland delayed the contemplated juncture of Crook and Hunter and rendered the federal movement on Dublin a practical failure. He was immediately promoted to brigadier general and assigned to the command of Jenkins's cavalry brigade.

After the battle at Port Republic, June 5, he stubbornly contested the advance of the federals under Hunter and Crook all the way to Lynchburg, his command of about 1,800 men the only organized force in the front of the enemy. His tenacious contest saved the city, and in recognition of his services the citizens presented him an address of congratulation, accompanied by a handsome cavalry officer's outfit, horse, sword, and spurs. Early arrived from Cold Harbor in time to relieve McCausland from the pressure of the federal troops, and McCausland and his troopers were soon on their heels, intercepting Hunter at Falling Rock and capturing his artillery and wagon train.

Sweeping on down the valley, he was a conspicuous figure in the July raid through Maryland, levying $25,000 tribute from Hagerstown, winning a handsome cavalry fight at Frederick City, and making the first attack at the ford of the Monocacy, across which Gordon moved to strike the federal flank at the defeat of Wallace. Joining in the demonstration against Washington, D.C., the daring commander actually penetrated into the town of Georgetown but was compelled to retire before the federal reinforcements. He returned with Early's army to the Shenandoah Valley and soon afterward was ordered to make a raid on Chambersburg, Pennyslvania, and destroy it in retaliation for the destruction that attended the operations of the federals in the valley. This duty he faithfully performed.

In command of a brigade of Lomax's cavalry division he participated in the Valley Campaign against Sheridan and subsequently, attached to Rosser's division, fought before Petersburg, made a gallant struggle at the decisive battle of Five Forks, during the retreat was engaged in continuous fighting, and finally, cutting his way through the federal lines at Appomattox, took a number of his men to Lynchburg, where he once more saved the city from rapine by repressing the efforts of the stragglers who infested the suburbs. A few days later he disbanded his men.

Returning home, to what was now West Virginia, he had difficulties with his Unionist neighbors. He soon went into exile and spent several years in Canada, Europe, and Mexico. He was formally charged with arson in Pennsylvania, but President Grant intervened on his behalf. He increasingly felt mistreated by his neighbors and the press, who he felt never presented his case properly, and became something of a recluse on his farm at Grimm's Landing until his death. He was the next to the last Confederate general to die.

Source

Dupuy, Trevor N., Curt Johnson, and David L. Bongard. *The Harper Encyclopedia of Military Biography.* New York: HarperCollins, 1992.

McClellan, George Brinton (1826–1885) *Union general officer.*

Born in Philadelphia, Pennsylvania on December 3, 1826, after attending preparatory schools and the University of Pennsylvania, McClellan entered West Point in 1842. He graduated second in his class in 1846. As a second lieutenant in the Engineer Corps, he immediately saw service in the Mexican War and was with General Winfield Scott in the victorious campaign against Mexico City.

After the war he served from 1848 to 1851 as an assistant instructor at West Point. In 1855, as a captain, he was appointed to a board of officers to study European military systems. The board visited the principal European countries and observed the siege of Sebastopol in the Crimean War. In his report McClellan proposed, among other recommendations, a new type of saddle for the United States Army. Known as the McClellan saddle, it became standard equipment in the cavalry.

Seeking more lucrative employment, McClellan resigned his commission in 1857. He became chief engineer and later (1858) vice president of the Illinois Central Railroad and president of the eastern division of the Ohio and Mississippi Railroad (1860).

At the outbreak of the Civil War, McClellan accepted a commission as major general of Ohio volunteers and commander of Ohio's forces. Then the national government appointed him major general in the regular army, in command of the Department of the Ohio. Troops under his direction cleared western Virginia of Confederates. In July 1861, after the federal reverse at the First Battle of Bull Run, or Manassas, President Lincoln called him to Washington to command the troops being concentrated around the capital. McClellan forged these troops into the dogged fighting force known as the Army of the Potomac. Even his severest critics concede that he was a fine trainer of men. In November 1861, while retaining command of his field army, he also became general in chief of all federal armies.

During the winter of 1861–62, McClellan began to exhibit personality traits that aroused impatience in Lincoln and anger in other leaders. Insisting that he could not advance until he had properly trained and organized a large army, he refused to attack the Confederates at Manassas.

He magnified the dangers in his front and the size of the enemy forces. He associated with politicians in the Democratic Party and let it be known that he opposed emancipation of the slaves, thereby stirring the ire of the powerful Radical Republicans. To Lincoln he seemed timid and hesitant, and to some of the Radicals he appeared a southern sympathizer.

McClellan's plan for the spring campaign of 1862 involved a move against Richmond on one of the waterways from the east, either the Rappahannock or the York–James Rivers line. Although Lincoln feared that the operation might leave Washington unprotected, he permitted McClellan to execute the plan, at the same time relieving McClellan as general in chief. McClellan decided on the York River line, and in March he began to move his army to Fortress Monroe, between the York and the James. Lincoln, believing that McClellan had violated instructions to protect Washington, detained a corps of the army south of the capital. McClellan still had some 100,000 men in his command. Taking Yorktown by siege, he advanced along the York line. By June 1 he was within a few miles of Richmond.

About this time Gen. Robert E. Lee became commander of the Confederate army. With his army reinforced to 85,000, he attacked McClellan's right flank north of the York on June 26, beginning the offensive known as the Seven Days. Although McClellan was confused and convinced that he faced a superior enemy, he skillfully retired his army to the James, repulsing Lee at Malvern Hill (July 1) and reaching Harrison's Landing. The high command in Washington now decided to withdraw the army to northern Virginia, where it would be joined to a force under Major General John Pope, the whole to be commanded by McClellan.

Early in August the movement began by water. But Lee hurried north with the intention of destroying Pope before McClellan could join him. This forced the government to send McClellan's troops to Pope as they arrived. When Pope faced Lee at the Battle of Second Manassas, most of McClellan's army was with him or en route. After Pope's defeat, McClellan was placed in command of the disorganized troops and rapidly reorganized them. He then moved to meet Lee's invasion of Maryland. Believing that a part of Lee's army was occupied at Harper's Ferry, he attacked the enemy on September 17, 1862, at the Battle of Antietam. But the absent Confederate forces had returned or were returning, and Lee managed to hold his lines.

President Lincoln, convinced that McClellan had not followed up his success, replaced him on November 7 with Maj. Gen. Ambrose Everett Burnside, and McClellan's military career was ended.

In 1864 the Democratic Party made McClellan its presidential candidate. An advocate of continuing the war, he was embarrassed by the platform's call for a cessation of hostilities. He resigned his commission on Election Day.

Lincoln won 212 electoral votes to McClellan's 21, but McClellan's popular vote was only 400,000 less than Lincoln's. After his defeat he spent three years abroad. Returning to the United States, he was chief engineer of the New York City department of docks from 1870 to 1872 and served as governor of New Jersey from 1878 to 1881. He died in Orange, New Jersey, on October 29, 1885.

McClellan was an important and in some ways a unique military figure. Elevated to high command at the age of 34, he led one of the largest Northern field armies and for a time was general in chief of all armies. He was a controversial figure during the war, and he has been a center of dispute among historians ever since. Some writers contend that he was the greatest of the northern generals, denied victory by political interference. Others argue that he was temperamentally unfit for high command.

Source and Additional Reading

Sears, Stephen W. *George B. McClellan: The Young Napoleon*. New York: Ticknor & Fields, 1988.

Sears, Stephen W., ed. *The Civil War Papers of George B. McClellan*. New York: Ticknor & Fields, 1989.

Williams, Thomas Harry. *McClellan, Sherman, and Grant*. 1962. Reprint, Westport, Conn.: Greenwood Press, 1976.

McGill, Troy A. (d. 1944) *Sergeant, United States Army, Troop G, Fifth Cavalry Regiment, First Cavalry Division, so distinguished himself in combat, during World War II, that he was awarded (posthumously) the Medal of Honor for his heroic actions.*

Born: Knoxville, Tenn.; **Entered service at:** Ada, Okla.; **Place and date:** March 4, 1944, Los Negros Islands, Admiralty Group; **G.O. No.:** 74, September 11, 1944.

Citation: "For conspicuous gallantry and intrepidity above and beyond the call of duty in action with the enemy at Los Negros Island, Admiralty Group, on 4 March 1944. In the early morning hours Sgt. McGill, with a squad of 8 men, occupied a revetment which bore the brunt of a furious attack by approximately 200 drink-crazed enemy troops. Although covered by crossfire from machine-guns on the right and left flank he could receive no support from the remainder of our troops stationed at his rear. All members of the squad were killed or wounded except Sgt. McGill and another man, whom he ordered to return to the next revetment. Courageously resolved to hold his position at all cost, he fired his weapon until it ceased to function. Then, with the enemy only 5 yards away, he charged from his foxhole in the face of certain death and clubbed the enemy with his rifle in hand-to-hand combat until he was killed. At dawn 105 enemy dead were found around his position. Sgt. McGill's intrepid stand was an inspiration to his comrades and a decisive factor in the defeat of a fanatical enemy."

Source
Medal of Honor Citation.

McGinty, John J., III (b. 1940) *Second lieutenant (then staff sergeant), United States Marine Corps, so distinguished himself in combat, during the Vietnam War that he was awarded the Medal of Honor for his heroic actions.*

Born: January 21, 1940, Boston, Mass.; **Entered service at:** Louisville, Ky.;

John James McGinty III was born in Boston, Massachusetts; completed grammar school in Louisville, Kentucky, in 1955; and attended high school in Louisville for a year and a half prior to enlisting in the United States Marine Corps Reserve (USMCR) in 1957. Discharged from the Marine Corps Reserve, he then enlisted in the Regular Marine Corps, on March 3, 1958.

He completed recruit training with the Third Recruit Training Battalion, Marine Corps Recruit Depot, Parris Island, South Carolina, and Advanced Infantry Combat Training with Company M Third Battalion, First Infantry Training Regiment, Marine Corps Base, Camp Lejeune, North Carolina. He was promoted to private first class in September 1957 and was transferred to the Seventh Infantry Company, (USMCR), Louisville, Kentucky, to serve as a rifleman until March 1958.

Private First Class McGinty completed Noncommissioned Officers Leadership School, Marine Corps Base, Camp Pendleton, California, in May 1958. He was then ordered to Marine Barracks, United States Naval Station, Kodiak, Alaska, until May 1959. While stationed in Alaska, he was promoted to corporal in September 1958.

Transferred to the First Marine Division (Reinforced) Fleet Marine Force (FMF), in June 1959, he saw duty as fireteam leader, and later, squad leader with Company T, Third Battalion, Fifth Marines. On his return to the United States, he served as guard/company police sergeant, H&S (Headquarter and Service) Battalion, FMF, Atlantic, Norfolk, Virginia, until March 1962.

From there, he was ordered to Marine Corps Recruit Depot, Parris Island, South Carolina, and assigned duty as drill instructor, Second Recruit Training Battalion. He was promoted to sergeant in August 1962.

From November 1964 until December 1965, Sergeant McGinty saw duty as assistant brig warden, Marine Barracks, United States Naval Base, Norfolk, Virginia.

In April 1966, Sergeant McGinty joined Company K, Third Battalion, Fourth Marines, Third Marine Division, in the Republic of Vietnam. It was for his heroic action while serving as acting platoon leader, First Platoon, Company K, on July 18, 1966, that he was awarded the Medal of Honor.

Citation: "For conspicuous gallantry and intrepidity at the risk of his life above and beyond the call of duty. 2d Lt. McGinty's platoon, which was providing rear security to protect the withdrawal of the battalion from a position which had been under attack for 3 days, came under heavy small arms, automatic weapons and mortar fire from an estimated enemy regiment. With each successive human wave which assaulted his 32-man platoon during the 4-hour battle, 2d Lt. McGinty rallied his men to beat off the enemy. In 1 bitter assault, 2 of the squads became separated from the remainder of the platoon. With complete disregard for his safety, 2d Lt. McGinty charged through intense automatic weapons and mortar fire to their position. Finding 20 men wounded and the medical corpsman killed, he quickly reloaded ammunition magazines and weapons for the wounded men and directed their fire upon the enemy. Although he was painfully wounded as he moved to care for the disabled men, he continued to shout encouragement to his troops and to direct their fire so effectively that the attacking hordes were beaten off. When the enemy tried to out-flank his position, he killed 5 of them at point-blank range with his pistol. When they again seemed on the verge of overrunning the small force, he skillfully adjusted artillery and air strikes within 50 yards of his position. This destructive firepower routed the enemy, who left an estimated 500 bodies on the battlefield. 2d Lt. McGinty's personal heroism, indomitable leadership, selfless devotion to duty, and bold fighting spirit inspired his men to resist the repeated attacks by a fanatical enemy, reflected great credit upon himself, and upheld the highest traditions of the Marine Corps and the U.S. Naval Service."

In addition to the Medal of Honor and the Purple Heart, McGinty's medals and decorations include the Good Conduct Medal with two Bronze Stars, the National Defense Service Medal, the Vietnam Service Medal with two Bronze Stars, the Vietnamese cross of gallantry with palm, and the Republic of Vietnam campaign Medal.

Source
Marine Corps Historical Center.
Medal of Honor Citation.

McGuire, Fred Henry (b. 1890) *United States Navy Hospital apprentice, United States Navy, so distinguished himself in combat that he was awarded the Medal of Honor for his heroic actions in 1911*

Born: November 7, 1890, Gordonville, Mo.; **Entered service at:** Gordonville, Mo. **G.O. No.:** 138, December 13, 1911.

Citation: "While attached to the U.S.S. *Pampang,* McGuire was one of a shore party moving in to capture Mundang, on the island of Basilan, Philippine Islands, on the morning of 24 September 1911. Ordered to take station within 100 yards of a group of nipa huts close to the trail, McGuire advanced and stood guard as the leader and his scout party first searched the surrounding deep grasses, and then moved into the open area before the huts. Instantly enemy Moros opened point-blank fire on the exposed men and approximately 20 Moros charged the small group from inside the huts and from other concealed positions. McGuire, responding to the calls for help, was one of the first on the scene. After emptying his rifle into the attackers, he closed in with rifle, using it as a club to wage fierce battle until his comrades arrived on the field, when he rallied to the aid of his dying leader and other wounded. Although himself wounded, McGuire ministered tirelessly and efficiently to those who had been struck down, thereby saving the lives of 2 who otherwise might have succumbed to enemy-inflicted wounds."

Source
Medal of Honor Citation.

McKibben, Ray (1945–1968) *Sergeant, United States Army, Troop B, Seventh Squadron (Airmobile), 17th Cavalry, so distinguished himself in combat, during the Vietnam War, that he was awarded (posthumously) the Medal of Honor for his actions near Song Mao, Republic of Vietnam, December 8, 1968.*

Born: October 27, 1945, Felton, Ga.; **Entered service at:** Atlanta, Ga.

Citation: "For conspicuous gallantry and intrepidity in action at the risk of his life above and beyond the call of duty, Sgt. McKibben distinguished himself in action while serving as team leader of the point element of a reconnaissance patrol of Troop B, operating in enemy territory. Sgt. McKibben was leading his point element in a movement to contact along a well-traveled trail when the lead element came under heavy automatic weapons fire from a fortified bunker position, forcing the patrol to take cover. Sgt. McKibben, appraising the situation and without regard for his own safety, charged through bamboo and heavy brush to the fortified position, killed the enemy gunner, secured the weapon and directed his patrol element forward. As the patrol moved out, Sgt. McKibben observed enemy movement to the flank of the patrol. Fire support from helicopter gunships was requested and the area was effectively neutralized. The patrol again continued its mission and as the lead element rounded the bend of a river it came under heavy automatic weapons fire from camouflaged bunkers. As Sgt. McKibben was deploying his men to covered positions, he observed one of his men fall wounded. Although bullets were hitting all around the wounded man, Sgt. McKibben, with complete disregard for his safety, sprang to his comrade's side and under heavy enemy fire pulled him to safety behind the cover of a rock emplacement where he administered hasty first aid. Sgt. McKibben, seeing that his comrades were pinned down and were unable to deliver effective fire against the enemy bunkers, again undertook a single-handed assault of the enemy defenses. He charged through the brush and hail of automatic weapons fire closing on the first bunker, killing the enemy with accurate rifle fire and securing the enemy's weapon. He continued his assault against the next bunker, firing his rifle as he charged. As he approached the second bunker his rifle ran out of ammunition; however, he used the captured enemy weapon until it too was empty; at that time he silenced the bunker with well placed hand grenades. He reloaded his weapon and covered the advance of his men as they moved forward. Observing the fire of another bunker impeding the patrol's advance, Sgt. McKibben again single-handedly assaulted the new position. As he neared the bunker he was mortally wounded but was able to fire a final burst from his weapon killing the enemy and enabling the patrol to continue the assault. Sgt. McKibben's indomitable courage, extraordinary heroism, profound concern for the welfare of his fellow soldiers and disregard for his personal safety saved the lives of his comrades and enabled the patrol to accomplish its mission. Sgt. McKibben's gallantry in action at the cost of his life above and beyond the call of duty is in the highest traditions of the military service and reflects great credit upon himself, his unit, and the U.S. Army."

Source
Medal of Honor Citation.

McKinney, John R. *Sergeant (then private), United States Army, Company A, 123d Infantry, 33d Infantry Division, so distinguished himself in combat during World War II that he was awarded the Medal of Honor for his heroic actions.*

Born: Woodcliff, Ga.; **Entered service at:** Woodcliff, Ga.; **Place and date:** Tayabas Province, Luzon, Philippine Islands, May 11, 1945. **G.O. No.:** 14, February 4, 1946.

Citation: "He fought with extreme gallantry to defend the outpost which had been established near Dingalan Bay. Just before daybreak approximately 100 Japanese stealthily attacked the perimeter defense, concentrating on a light machinegun position manned by 3 Americans. Having completed a long tour of duty at this gun, Pvt. McKinney was resting a few paces away when an enemy soldier dealt him a glancing blow on the head with a saber. Although dazed by the stroke, he seized his rifle, bludgeoned his attacker, and then shot another assailant who was charging him. Meanwhile, 1 of his comrades at the machinegun had been wounded and his other companion withdrew carrying the injured man to safety. Alone, Pvt. McKinney was confronted by 10 infantrymen who had captured the machinegun with the evident intent of reversing it to fire into the perimeter. Leaping into the emplacement, he shot 7 of them at pointblank range and killed 3 more with his rifle butt. In the melee the machinegun was rendered inoperative, leaving him only his rifle with which to meet the advancing Japanese, who hurled grenades and directed knee mortar shells into the perimeter. He warily changed position, secured more ammunition, and reloading repeatedly, cut down waves of the fanatical enemy with devastating fire or clubbed them to death in hand-to-hand combat. When assistance arrived, he had thwarted the assault and was in complete control of the area. Thirty-eight dead Japanese around the machinegun and 2 more at the side of a mortar 45 yards distant was the amazing toll he had exacted single-handedly. By his indomitable spirit, extraordinary fighting ability, and unwavering courage in the face of tremendous odds, Pvt. McKinley saved his company from possible annihilation and set an example of unsurpassed intrepidity."

Source
Medal of Honor Citation.

McLaughlin, Alford L. (b. 1928) *Private first class, United States Marine Corps, Company L, Third Battalion, Fifth Marines, First Marine Division (Reinforced), so distinguished himself in combat, during the Korean War, that he was awarded the Medal of Honor for his heroic actions.*

Born: 1928, Leeds, Ala.; **Entered service at:** Leeds, Ala.; **Place and date:** Korea, September 4–5, 1952.

Citation: "For conspicuous and intrepidity at the risk, of his life above and beyond the call of duty while serving as a Machine Gunner of Company I, Third Battalion, Fifth Marines, First Marine Division (Reinforced), in action against enemy aggressor forces in Korea on the night of 4–5 September 1952. Volunteering for his second continuous tour of duty on a strategic combat outpost far in advance of the main line of resistance, Private First Class McLaughlin, although operating under a barrage of enemy artillery and mortar fire, set up plans for the defense of his platoon which proved decisive in the successful defense of the outpost. When hostile forces attacked in battalion strength during the night, he maintained a constant flow of devastating fire upon the enemy, alternating employing two machine guns, a carbine and hand grenades. Although painfully wounded, he bravely fired the machine guns from the hip until his hands became blistered by the heat from the weapons and, placing the guns on the ground to allow them to cool continued to defend the position with his carbine and grenades. Standing up in full view, he shouted words of encouragement to his comrades above the din of battle and, throughout a series of fanatical enemy attacks, sprayed the surrounding area with deadly fire accounting for an estimated one hundred and fifty enemy dead and fifty wounded. By his indomitable courage, superb leadership and valiant fighting spirit in the face of overwhelming odds, Private First Class McLaughlin served to inspire his fellow Marine in their gallant stand against the determined and numerically superior hostile force. His outstanding heroism and unwavering devotion to duty reflect the highest credit upon himself and enhance the finest traditions of the United States Naval Service."

Source
Medal of Honor Citation.

McWethy, Edgar Lee, Jr. (1944–1967) *Specialist fifth class, United States Army, Company B, First Battalion, Fifth Cavalry, First Cavalry Division (Airmobile), so distinguished himself in combat, during the Vietnam War, that he was awarded (posthumously) the Medal of Honor for his heroic actions at Binh Dinh province, Republic of Vietnam, June 21, 1967.*

Born: November 22, 1944, Leadville, Colo.; **Entered service at:** Denver, Colo.

Citation: "For conspicuous gallantry and intrepidity in action at the risk of his life above and beyond the call of duty. Serving as a medical aidman with Company B, Sp5c. McWethy accompanied his platoon to the site of a downed helicopter. Shortly after the platoon established a defensive perimeter around the aircraft, a large enemy force attacked the position from 3 sides with a heavy volume of automatic weapons fire and grenades. The platoon leader and his radio operator were wounded almost immediately, and Sp5c. McWethy rushed across the fire-swept area to their assistance. Although he could not help the mortally wounded radio operator, Sp5c. McWethy's timely first aid enabled the platoon leader to retain command during this critical period. Hearing a call for aid, Sp5c. McWethy started across the open toward the injured men, but was wounded in the head and knocked to the ground. He regained his feet and continued on but was hit again, this time in the leg. Struggling onward despite his wounds, he gained the side of his comrades and treated their injuries. Observing another fallen rifleman lying in an exposed position raked by enemy fire, Sp5c. McWethy moved toward him without hesitation. Although the enemy fire wounded him a third time, Sp5c. McWethy reached his fallen companion. Though weakened and in extreme pain, Sp5c. McWethy gave the wounded man artificial respiration but suffered a fourth and fatal wound. Through his indomitable courage, complete disregard for his safety, and demonstrated concern for his fellow soldiers, Sp5c. McWethy inspired the members of his platoon and contributed in great measure to their successful defense of the position and the ultimate rout of the enemy force. Sp5c. McWethy's profound sense of duty, bravery, and his willingness to accept extraordinary risks in order to help the men of his unit are characteristic of the highest traditions of the military service and reflect great credit upon himself and the U.S. Army."

Source
Medal of Honor Citation.

Maffioli, Leonard J. (b. 1925) *Master gunnery sergeant, United States Marine Corps, three-war-Marine veteran and 1 of only 18 Marines to have escaped from a Chinese prisoner of war camp during the Korean War.*

Len Maffioli was born in Berkeley, California, on July 1, 1925. He enlisted in the Marine Corps after graduation from high school in San Diego in 1943 and saw combat in the Pacific on the islands of Saipan, Tinian, and Iwo Jima with the Fourth Marine Division.

To supplement his family's income, because he had enjoyed his time in the corps, he joined the 11th Tank Battalion, a reserve unit in San Diego, after the war ended. On June 25, 1950, war broke out in Korea, and Maffioli reenlisted and sailed for Korea with the First Tank Battalion, First Marine Division. He participated in the Inchon landing, the capture of Seoul, and the Chosin Reservoir Campaigns. It was during this later action that Corporal Maffioli began an ordeal that changed his life.

As a member of Task Force Drysdale (named after the senior officer present; Lt. Col. Douglas B. Drysdale, commander of the Royal Marine Commando unit assigned to lead the convoy), Maffioli was among approximately 712 men who made up the relief force convoy headed for the Chosin Reservoir.

The convoy was ambushed and cut into three sections by Chinese Communist forces in a place known as Hell Fire Valley, near the town of Hagaru, on November 29, 1950. The center portion of the convoy had come under intense enemy fire and heavy casualties continued to mount. Adding to the plight was the temperature, which had dropped to 20 below zero. With casualties high, no relief available, and running out of ammunition, terms of surrender to the Chinese were considered by senior American officers.

> Major McLaughlin returned to our position and explained the situation, having determined that by surrendering we would guarantee the safety of our wounded. Reasoning that the Chinese would systematically slaughter those of us who remained, many men began saying goodbye to one another, while many other men could be heard crying softly. Not wanting to give the Chinese anything of value, we began to destroy everything that might be of use to them.
>
> Our group of prisoners consisted of 123 men: 40 Marines, 20 British Royal Marines and the remainder, U.S. Army soldiers. We were marched northwest toward the Pyongyang-Manpojin railroad and to a place called Kaggye, 60 air miles from where we had been ambushed. We walked for 11 days, mostly at night to avoid allied aircraft, and we covered a distance of approximately 150 miles.

Thus began Maffioli's time as a prisoner of war (POW), in North Korea, at the hands of the Chinese Communists.

In April 1951, Maffioli, in a group of 60 fellow POWs, was moved to a place called Chorwon, a site of a new Communist-run POW camp.

> The Chinese passed the word that they wanted 19 Marines to assemble. They called out the names of 18 of us, and the last man called was Corporal "Sam" Shimomura, a U.S. Army Nisei soldier from an intelligence group who had been assigned to the First Marine Division at the time of our capture. Despite wearing an Army uniform, the Chinese, from that point on, considered him to be a Marine.
>
> When 19 of us had finally assembled, we were marched across the valley to a separate part of the camp, where we were isolated from the rest of the prisoners. Without warning, two cargo trucks came into camp, and we were ordered to climb aboard. Instead of having to walk toward the town of Chunchon, in South Korea, as we had been

doing for the last three months, the Chinese planned that we would ride for two days, closely guarded by a lieutenant and a squad of a dozen armed guards.

When U.S. aircraft attacked the two trucks, the Chinese lieutenant ordered that the vehicles stop and find protective cover.

We had crossed two forks of a river during the night and found ourselves just outside of Chonchun, and were brought to a group of huts to rest. We stayed in these during the day. I was sleeping in an old oxen shed with a Master Sergeant, while the other 17 men were inside a bombed-out house sleeping on the floor.

When artillery rounds began impacting around the huts, the Chinese guards fled the area, leaving the POWs alone. Finding several caves to hide in for the next few days, Maffioli and his fellow Marines then constructed a large sign, which read "RESCUE POW—19" from strips of white wallpaper. The pilot of an Army OY spotter plane saw the message and radioed to three M-4A3 Sherman tanks from the Seventh Army Infantry Division to move up and investigate.

The lieutenant in charge of the tanks leaned down and shouted "You'll never know just how close you guys came to getting it. I had my guys ready to open up on you with our 50-caliber machine guns. I got a message that there were 19 prisoners of war wanting to be rescued, and I was looking through my binoculars when I saw 19 Chinese soldiers come running out of that house. I thought you were Red Chinese until you threw away those hats, and we saw your Caucasian features."

Those Army tankers took us in to Chunchon, and the Army flew in 19 OY spotter planes—one for each of us—and they flew us back to our Corps headquarters. Major General O. P. Smith, commanding general of the First Marine Division, greeted us and congratulated us on our escape. We were taken aboard the Navy hospital ship, USS Haven, for a one-week stay before being flown to the U.S. Naval hospital at Yokosuka, Japan.

Maffioli remained hospitalized for a month to correct the damage done by prolonged malnutrition.

I knew that I owed my life to my fellow Marines who had helped carry me during my last few days as a prisoner of war. If it were not for them, I would not have made it to those Army tanks that came to our rescue. I had been passing nothing but blood through my bowels for more than a week, and I was

in such poor physical shape I doubt I could have lasted more than a day or two. I had lost more than 60 pounds since my capture.

Len Maffioli returned to active duty after five more months of hospitalization and convalescence. In 1967 he requested and received a transfer to duty in Vietnam, where he served for 13 months as the operations chief of the First Tank Battalion, participating in four major campaigns, including the 1968 Tet Offensive. In 1975 he was transferred to the Marine Corps Recruit Depot, San Diego, where he served as the depot's inspection chief until his retirement in 1979. With more than 33 years of military service, he was the last Korean ex-POW and one of the few remaining veterans of World War II on active duty in the Marine Corps.

Source

Norton, Maj. Bruce H. *Grown Gray in War.* New York: Random House, 1997.

Maker, Raymond Whitney (b. 1892) *Private first class, United States Army.*

Born on November 15, 1892, in Weston, Massachusetts, he was the son of Winfield Scott Maker and Rosalba Louise Peck. His sister, Eva (Maker) Sullivan, became a registered nurse, and his brother, Clifford, served as a private with the Engineering Detachment, Boston District Ordance Office, during World War I. Their father owned a hotel, restaurant, and livery stable and enjoyed racing sulky horses.

Not content with life on the farm, young Raymond enlisted in the United States Army and served with distinction during World War I, assigned as a wireman and forward observer to Company C, 101st Field Signal Battalion, from June 1, 1917, to April 29, 1919.

His battalion was organized as the Second Brigade of Massachusetts Volunteer Militia in July 1879. In June 1905, it became the Signal Corps and so continued until May 10, 1916, it was organized as the First Signal Battalion. In May 1917, its designation was changed to the First Battalion Massachusetts Signal Corps, on May 29, 1917, it became the First Field Signal Battalion. On its induction into the service on July 25, 1915, its designation was again changed; it became the 101st Field Signal Battalion, 26th Division.

The battalion sailed under the command of Maj. Harry G. Chase on September 20 for foreign service and arrived at St. Nazaire, France, on October 6.

This battalion was highly trained and saw service on the Mexican border from June to November 1916. On its arrival in France it was immediately called upon to fur-

Raymond Whitney Maker

participated in bloody offensive action at Aisne-Marne, St. Mihiel, and Meuse-Argonne. In one engagement he and a fellow soldier were pinned down in a bomb crater by enemy machine gun fire for more than 24 hours. As a German squad advanced on their position, Maker killed three of them with his Colt .45 automatic.

At the Battle of Verdun, he was wounded twice, gassed, and left for dead. Hospitalized for nearly a month, he survived his ordeal and returned to the United States in 1919. The New England Telephone and Telegraph Company employed him as an equipment installation expert for the next 44 years. He married Gladys G. Bowman on August 2, 1919, and they had four children, Rosalba H., Raymond W., Donald W., and Marjorie G. Maker.

In 1959, Raymond W. Maker became a state veteran celebrity when, learning that Mrs. Charles A. Post, president of the Alliance Française, and Prof. Albert J. Salvan, of Brown University, were going to Verdun to represent the United States as part of a French celebration. Maker volunteered to return to the mayor of Verdun a large iron key that served to lock the famous walled city at night that he had taken as a souvenir.

For his historic gesture, Maker was presented with a certificate of grateful appreciation from François Schleiter, the senator-mayor of Verdun.

Source

Rosalba H. Maker Norton (daughter of Raymond Whitney
    Maker), letter to author, September 2001.

nish all sorts of details, both of officers and of men. In November 1917, it furnished two officers to act as battalion signal officers with the First Division, when units of this division went into the line for the first time.

During the battalion's service in France it had six commanding officers. Major Allbright, who was succeeded by Major Wamsley, who was followed by Major Evans, succeeded by Major Chase; the battalion was next commanded by Major La Crosse and finally Major Crafts, who took it home. The constant change in commanding officers, whatever the reasons may have been, had a depressing effect on the morale of the battalion.

The combat service of this particular battalion was that credited to the units of the 26th Infantry Division. After the Armistice the battalion continued its training and did salvage work. On April 6, 1919, the battalion sailed from Brest, arrived in Boston April 18, and was demobilized on April 29, 1919.

Private First Class Maker first saw combat with Company C, in the Champagne-Marne Defensive Sector, and

Manning, Sidney E. (b. 1892) *Corporal, United States Army, Company G, 167th Infantry, 42d Division, so distinguished himself in combat in France, during World War I, that he was awarded the Medal of Honor for his heroic actions.*

Born: July 17, 1892, Butler County, Ala.; **Entered service at:** Flomation, Ala.; **Place and date:** Near Breuvannes, France, July 28, 1918. **G.O. No.:** 44 W.D. 1919.

Citation: "When his platoon commander and platoon sergeant had both become casualties soon after the beginning of an assault on a strongly fortified heights overlooking the Ourcq River, Corporal Manning took command of his platoon, which was near the center of the attacking line. Though himself severely wounded, he led forward the 35 men remaining in the platoon, and finally succeeded in gaining a foothold on the enemy's position, during which time he had received more wounds and all but 7 of his men had fallen. Directing the consolidation of the position, he held off a large body of the enemy only 50 yards away by fire from his automatic rifle. He declined to take cover until his line had been entirely consolidated with the line of the platoon on the front, when he dragged himself to shelter, suffering from 9 wounds in all parts of the body."

Source
Medal of Honor Citation.

Marion, Francis ("The Swamp Fox") (1732–1795) *A partisan leader in the American Revolution, given the sobriquet by Banastre Tarleton, the British commander of Loyalists in the Carolinas, who was one of his chief adversaries.*

Francis Marion was born in about 1732 in St. John's Parish, Berkeley County, South Carolina, of Huguenot parents who farmed along the Santee River. As a young man of 16, he gave up his ambition of becoming a sailor after surviving a shipwreck. In 1761 he distinguished himself as a lieutenant of militia in an expedition against the Cherokee.

Marion rose to a position of prominence in his community. In 1775 he was a delegate to the South Carolina Provincial Congress and was named a captain in the Second South Carolina Regiment. Promoted to major in February 1776, he participated in the defense of Charleston on June 28. Later in 1776 he was promoted to lieutenant colonel and assumed command of the regiment. In October 1779 he led his command in an unsuccessful assault against Savannah.

A broken ankle caused Marion to be sent away from Charleston and saved him from capture when it fell to the British on May 12, 1780. With all organized resistance in South Carolina at an end, Marion began his career as a guerrilla leader. As a partisan he participated in skirmishes and battles at Great Savannah, Blue Savannah, Black Mingo, Tearcoat Swamp, Georgetown, and Halfway Swamp. Marion was able to use a relatively small striking force to its greatest potential, his primary weapons the elements of speed and surprise. Slashing at troop positions and supply convoys, intercepting communications, and cutting off sources of intelligence, his partisans continually harried British and Tory forces, forcing the British to commit critical resources to fending off and pursuing them.

In late 1780 Marion was appointed brigadier general of the South Carolina militia. In cooperation with troops under the command of Major Henry Lee, he raided Georgetown and took Fort Watson and Fort Motte. He went on to support attacks on Augusta and Ninety-Six. Joining the southern army of Major General Nathanael Greene, Marion's militia fought as regulars in Greene's army at the Battle of Eutaw Springs. Marion was commended by Greene for his conduct during the battle.

Elected to the state senate before the Revolution ended, Marion went to Jacksonboro for the general assembly of 1781. His brigade was given the task of protecting that body, but the British forces routed his command. Though he rallied some of his men, he suffered another defeat at Wambaw Bridge. On August 27 he successfully ambushed the enemy at Fair Lawn.

After the war Francis Marion was appointed commandant of Fort Johnson. He was reelected to the state senate in 1782 and 1784 and sat in the state constitutional convention in 1790. In 1786 he married Mary Esther Videau, a wealthy cousin. Marion died in Pond Bluff South Carolina, on February 27, 1795.

Source and Additional Reading
Adelhaft, Jerome J. *The Disorders of War: The Revolution in South Carolina.* Orono, Me.: University of Maine at Orono Press, 1981.
Gerson, Noel Bertram. *The Swamp Fox, Francis Marion.* New York: Doubleday, 1967.
Rankin, Hugh F. *Francis Marion: The Swamp Fox.* New York: Crowell, 1973.
Simms, William Gilmore. *The Life of Francis Marion.* Freeport, N.Y.: Books for Libraries, 1844.

Marm, Walter Joseph, Jr. (b. 1941) *First lieutenant (then second lieutenant), United States Army, Company A, First Battalion, Seventh Cavalry, First Cavalry Division (Airmobile), so distinguished himself in combat, during the Vietnam War, that he was awarded the Medal of Honor for his heroic actions.*

Born: November 20, 1941, Washington, Pa.; **Entered service at:** Pittsburgh, Penn.; **Place and date:** Vicinity of IA Drang Valley, Republic of Vietnam, November 14, 1965. **G.O. No.:** 7, February 15, 1967.

Citation: "For conspicuous gallantry and intrepidity at the risk of life above and beyond the call of duty. As a platoon leader in the 1st Cavalry Division (Airmobile), 1st Lt. Marm demonstrated indomitable courage during a combat operation. His company was moving through the valley to relieve a friendly unit surrounded by an enemy force of estimated regimental size. 1st Lt. Marm led his platoon through withering fire until they were finally forced to take cover. Realizing that his platoon could not hold very long, and seeing four enemy soldiers moving into his position, he moved quickly under heavy fire and annihilated all 4. Then, seeing that his platoon was receiving intense fire from a concealed machine gun, he deliberately exposed himself to draw its fire. Thus locating its position, he attempted to destroy it with an antitank weapon. Although he inflicted casualties, the weapon did not silence the enemy fire. Quickly, disregarding the intense fire directed on him and his platoon, he charged 30 meters across open ground, and hurled grenades into the enemy position, killing some of the 8 insurgents manning it. Although severely wounded, when his grenades were expended, armed with only a rifle, he continued the momentum of his assault on the position and killed the remainder of the enemy. 1st Lt. Marm's selfless actions reduced the fire on his platoon, broke the enemy assault, and rallied his unit to continue toward the accomplishment of this mission. 1st Lt. Marm's gallantry on the battlefield and his extraordinary intrepidity at the risk of his life are in the highest traditions of the U.S. Army and reflect great credit upon himself and the Armed Forces of his country."

Source
Medal of Honor Citation.

Marquez, Eleuterio Joe *Pharmacist's mate third Class, United States Navy Reserve, so distinguished himself in combat during World War II that he was awarded the Navy Cross for his heroic actions.*

Citation: "For extraordinary heroism as a Hospital Corpsman with an Assault Company attached to FIFTH Marines, FIRST Marine Division, in action against enemy Japanese forces on Peleliu, Palau Islands, on October 13, 1944. Although severely wounded in both legs during an action in which his company was subjected to intense hostile fire, MARQUEZ courageously dragged himself over extremely rough and difficult terrain to aid seven of his wounded comrades, and, although unable to walk, treated each of the casualties in turn, remaining with them and refusing treatment for himself until they were evacuated. His valiant devotion to duty and grave concern for the welfare of others were in keeping with the highest traditions of the United States Naval Service."

Source
Navy Cross Citation.

Martin, Cecil H. (b. 1940) *Machinist Mate, First Class, (MN1) United States Navy, so distinguished himself in naval surface combat that he was awarded the Navy Cross for his heroic actions in the Republic of Vietnam.*

Born on November 6, 1940, at Yale, Illinois, Martin entered service July 23, 1958, in Indianapolis. He retired in 1979 holding the rank of lieutenant. Lieutenant Martin's awards include the Bronze Star with combat V, Purple Heart, Navy Commendation Medal, Combat Action Ribbon, Presidential Unit Citation, Navy Unit Commendation with one Gold Star, United States Navy Good Conduct Medal with three Bronze Stars, National Defense Medal, Vietnam Service Medal with four Bronze Stars, RVN (Republic of Vietnam) Gallantry Cross with Bronze Star, RVN Civil Actions Honor Medal Unit Citation, RVN Gallantry Cross Unit Citation, and RVN Campaign Medal.

Citation: "For extraordinary heroism on the night of 21 November 1968 while serving with River Division 531 during riverine assault operations against enemy aggressor forces in the Mekong Delta region of the Republic of Vietnam. As Senior Boat Captain of a two-boat patrol, MN1 Martin was transiting from Rach Soi to Rach Gia, in conjunction with a concentrated patrol program adopted for the SEALORDS interdiction campaign in the lower Delta, when his patrol came under heavy enemy attack on all sides. During the initial hail of fire, his cover boat received two direct rocket hits, wounding all personnel aboard and causing the craft to veer out of control and run aground directly in front of the enemy firing positions. MN1 Martin ordered his coxswain to reverse course and reenter the ambush area to rescue the cover boat's crewmembers. As his unit approached the stricken craft, MN1 Martin directed effective counterfire and, placing his boat between the beleaguered craft and the blazing enemy batteries, took command of the precarious rescue effort. While affording exemplary leadership and inspiration to the members of his surprised and battered patrol element, he directed the major fire-suppression efforts of his gunners, personally manning and firing a machine gun at crucial intervals. Additionally, MN1 Martin rendered first aid to casualties, extinguished a fire in the beached craft, advised his commanding officer in the Naval Operations Center of the seriousness of the situation, and coordinated the transfer of wounded personnel to his unit. Through his courageous and determined fighting spirit, he succeeded in safely extracting his men, undoubtedly saving numerous lives. His great personal valor in the face of heavy and sustained enemy fire was in keeping with the highest traditions of the United States Naval Service."

Source
Information supplied by Lt. Cecil H. Martin, United States Navy (Retired).

Martini, Gary W. (1948–1967) *Private first class, United States Marine Corps, Company F, Second Battalion, First Marines, First Marine Division, so distinguished himself in combat, in the Republic of Vietnam, that he was awarded (posthumously) the Medal of Honor for his heroic actions.*

Born: September 21, 1948, Lexington, Va.; **Entered service at:** Portland, Oreg.; **Place and date:** Binh Son, Republic of Vietnam, April 21, 1967.

Citation: "For conspicuous gallantry and intrepidity at the risk of his life above and beyond the call of duty. On 21 April 1967, during Operation UNION elements of Company F, conducting offensive operations at Binh Son, encountered a firmly entrenched enemy force and immediately deployed to engage them. The Marines in Pfc. Martini's platoon assaulted across an open rice paddy to within 20 meters of the enemy trench line where they were suddenly struck by hand grenades, intense small arms, automatic weapons, and mortar fire. The enemy onslaught killed 14 and wounded 18 Marines, pinning the remainder of the platoon down behind a low paddy dike. In the face of imminent danger, Pfc. Martini immediately crawled over the dike to a forward open area within 15 meters of the enemy position where, continuously exposed to the hostile fire, he hurled hand grenades, killing several of the enemy. Crawling back through the intense fire, he rejoined his platoon, which had moved to the relative safety of a trench line. From this position he observed several of his wounded comrades lying helpless in the fire-swept paddy. Although he knew that 1 man had been killed attempting to assist the wounded, Pfc. Martini raced through the open area and dragged a comrade back to a friendly position. In spite of a serious wound received during this first daring rescue, he again braved the unrelenting fury of the enemy fire to aid another companion lying wounded only 20 meters in front of the enemy trench line. As he reached the fallen Marine, he received a mortal wound, but disregarding his own condition, he began to drag the Marine toward his platoon's position. Observing men from his unit attempting to leave the security of their position to aid him, concerned only for their safety, he called to them to remain under cover, and through a final supreme effort, moved his injured comrade to where he could be pulled to safety, before he fell, succumbing to his wounds. Stouthearted and indomitable, Pfc. Martini unhesitatingly yielded his life to save 2 of his comrades and insure the safety of the remainder of his platoon. His outstanding courage, valiant fighting spirit and selfless devotion to duty reflected the highest credit upon himself, the Marine Corps, and the U.S. Naval Service. He gallantly gave his life for his country."

Source
Medal of Honor Citation.

Matthews, Daniel P. (b. 1931) *Sergeant, United States Marine Corps, Company F, Second Battalion, Seventh Marines, First Marine Division (Reinforced), so distinguished himself in combat, during the Korean War, that he was awarded the Medal of Honor for his heroic actions.*

Born: 1931, Van Nuys, Calif.; **Entered service at:** Van Nuys, Calif.; **Place and date:** Vegas Hill, Korea, March 28, 1953. **Award presented:** March 29, 1954.

Citation: "For conspicuous gallantry and intrepidity at the risk of his life above and beyond the call of duty while serving as a Squad Leader of Company F, Second Battalion, Seventh Marines, First Marine Division (Reinforced), in action against enemy aggressor forces in Korea on 28 March 1953. Participating in a counterattack against a firmly entrenched and well-concealed hostile force which had repelled six previous assaults on a vital enemy-held outpost far forward of the main line of resistance, Sergeant Matthews fearlessly advanced in the attack until his squad was pinned down by a murderous sweep of fire from an enemy machine gun located on the peak of the outpost. Observing that the deadly fire prevented a corpsman from removing a wounded man lying in an open area fully exposed to the brunt of the devastating gunfire, he worked his way to the base of the hostile machine-gun emplacement, leaped onto the rock fortification surrounding the gun and, taking the enemy by complete surprise, single-handedly charged the hostile emplacement with his rifle. Although severely wounded when the enemy brought a withering hail of fire to bear upon him, he gallantly continued his valiant one man assault and, firing his rifle with deadly effectiveness, succeeded in killing two of the enemy, routing a third and completely silencing the enemy weapon, thereby enabling his comrades to evacuate the stricken Marine to a safe position. Succumbing to his wounds before aid could reach him, Sergeant Matthews, by his indomitable fighting sprit, courageous initiative and resolute determination in the face of almost certain death, served to inspire all who observed him and was directly instrumental in saving the life of his wounded comrade. His great personal valor reflects the highest credit upon himself and enhances the finest traditions of the United States Naval Service. He gallantly gave his life for his country."

Source
Medal of Honor Citation.

Maxam, Larry Leonard (1948–1968) *Corporal, United States Marine Corps, Company D, First Battalion, Fourth Marines, Third Marine Division (Reinforced), FMF, so distinguished himself in combat, during the Vietnam War, that he was awarded (posthumously) the Medal of Honor for his heroic actions.*

Born: January 9, 1948, Glendale, Calif.; **Entered service at:** Los Angeles, Calif.; **Place and date:** Cam Lo District, Quang Tri Province, Republic of Vietnam, February 2, 1968.

Citation: "For conspicuous gallantry and intrepidity at the risk of his life above and beyond the call of duty while serving as a fire team leader with Company D. The Cam

Lo District Headquarters came under extremely heavy rocket, artillery, mortar, and recoilless rifle fire from a numerically superior enemy force, destroying a portion of the defensive perimeter. Cpl. Maxam, observing the enemy massing for an assault into the compound across the remaining defensive wire, instructed his assistant fire team leader to take charge of the fire team, and unhesitatingly proceeded to the weakened section of the perimeter. Completely exposed to the concentrated enemy fire, he sustained multiple fragmentation wounds from exploding grenades as he ran to an abandoned machine gun position. Reaching the emplacement, he grasped the machine gun and commenced to deliver effective fire on the advancing enemy. As the enemy directed maximum firepower against the determined Marine, Cpl. Maxam's position received a direct hit from a rocket-propelled grenade, knocking him backwards and inflicting severe fragmentation wounds to his face and right eye. Although momentarily stunned and in intense pain, Cpl. Maxam courageously resumed his firing position and subsequently was struck again by small-arms fire. With resolute determination, he gallantly continued to deliver intense machine gun fire, causing the enemy to retreat through the defensive wire to positions of cover. In a desperate attempt to silence his weapon, the North Vietnamese threw hand grenades and directed recoilless rifle fire against him inflicting 2 additional wounds. Too weak to reload his machine gun, Cpl. Maxam fell to a prone position and valiantly continued to deliver effective fire with his rifle. After 1½ hours, during which he was hit repeatedly by fragments from exploding grenades and concentrated small-arms fire, he succumbed to his wounds, having successfully defended nearly half of the perimeter single-handedly. Cpl. Maxam's aggressive fighting spirit, inspiring valor and selfless devotion to duty reflected great credit upon himself and the Marine Corps and upheld the highest traditions of the U.S. Naval Service. He gallantly gave his life for his country."

Source
Medal of Honor Citation.

Merrill, Frank Dow (1903–1955) *American general officer, commander of Merrill's Marauders in Burma during World War II.*

Merrill was born in Hopkinton, Massachusetts, on December 4, 1903, and graduated from West Point in 1929.

Stationed in Burma at the time of the Pearl Harbor attack in December 1941, he was assigned to the staff of Lt. Gen. Joseph W. Stilwell, U.S. commander of the China-Burma-India Theater. In 1942 he became Stilwell's operations officer. When Stilwell took personal command of a military thrust to open a land route from India, through Burma, to China, Merrill was named commander of a regiment of crack U.S. combat troops that later came to be known as Merrill's Marauders. After a difficult march over mountainous terrain in tropical heat, Merrill's troops captured the key airfield of Myitkyina in northern Burma in May 1944. Merrill was evacuated as a result of a heart attack, and the Marauders suffered heavy losses and ultimately crumbled as an effective fighting force.

He was promoted to major general in 1944 and retired from the army in 1948. He died in Fernandina Beach, Florida, on December 11, 1955.

Source
Ogburn, Charlton. *The Marauders*. New York: Harper, 1959.
Romanus, Charles F., and Riley Sunderland. *Time Runs Out in CBI*. Washington, D.C.: Office of the Chief of Military History, Department of the Army, 1956.

Michael, Edward S. (b. 1918) *First lieutenant, United States Army Air Corps, 364th Bomber Squadron, 305th Bomber Group, so distinguished himself in aerial combat, during World War II, that he was awarded the Medal of Honor for his heroic actions.*

Born: May 2, 1918, Chicago, Ill.; **Entered service at:** Chicago, Ill.; **Place and date:** Over Germany, April 11, 1944. **G.O. No.:** 5, January 15, 1945.

Citation: "For conspicuous gallantry and intrepidity above and beyond the call of duty while serving as pilot of a B17 aircraft on a heavy-bombardment mission to Germany, 11 April 1944. The group in which 1st Lt. Michael was flying was attacked by a swarm of fighters. His plane was singled out and the fighters pressed their attacks home recklessly, completely disregarding the Allied fighter escort and their own intense flak. His plane was riddled from nose to tail with exploding cannon shells and knocked out of formation, with a large number of fighters following it down, blasting it with cannon fire as it descended. A cannon shell exploded in the cockpit, wounded the copilot, wrecked the instruments, and blew out the side window. 1st Lt. Michael was seriously and painfully wounded in the right thigh. Hydraulic fluid filmed over the windshield making visibility impossible, and smoke filled the cockpit. The controls failed to respond and 3,000 feet were lost before he succeeded in leveling off. The radio operator informed him that the whole bomb bay was in flames as a result of the explosion of 3 cannon shells, which had ignited the incendiaries. With a full load of incendiaries in the bomb bay and a considerable gas load in the tanks, the danger of fire enveloping the plane and the tanks exploding seemed imminent. When the emergency release lever failed to function, 1st Lt. Michael at once gave the order to bail out and 7 of the crew left the plane. Seeing the bombardier firing the navigator's gun at the enemy planes, 1st Lt. Michael ordered him to bail out, as the plane was liable to explode any minute. When the bombardier looked for his parachute he found that it had been riddled with 20 mm fragments and was useless. 1st Lt. Michael, seeing the ruined parachute, realized that if the plane was abandoned the bombardier would perish and decided that the only chance would be a crash landing. Completely disregarding his own painful and profusely bleeding wounds, but thinking only of the safety of the remaining crewmembers, he gallantly evaded the enemy, using violent evasive action despite the battered condition of his plane. After the plane had been under sustained enemy attack for fully 45 minutes, 1st Lt. Michael finally lost the persistent fighters in a cloudbank. Upon emerging, an accurate barrage of flak caused him to come down to treetop level where flak towers poured a continuous rain of fire on the plane. He continued into France, realizing that at any moment a crash landing might have to be attempted, but trying to get as far as possible to increase the escape possibilities if a safe landing could be achieved. 1st Lt. Michael flew the plane until he became exhausted from the loss of blood, which had formed on the floor in pools, and he lost consciousness. The copilot succeeded in reaching England and sighted an RAF field near the coast. 1st Lt. Michael finally regained consciousness and insisted upon taking over the controls to land the plane. The undercarriage was useless; the bomb bay doors were jammed open; the hydraulic system and altimeter were shot out. In addition, there was no airspeed indicator, the ball turret was jammed with the guns pointing downward, and the flaps would not respond. Despite these apparently insurmountable obstacles, he landed the plane without mishap."

Source
Medal of Honor Citation.

Miles, L. Wardlaw (b. 1918) *Captain, United States Army, 308th Infantry, 77th Division, distinguished himself in combat and was awarded the Medal of Honor for his actions in September 1918.*

Born: March 23, 1873, Baltimore, Md.; **Entered service at:** Princeton, N.J.; **Place and date:** Near Revillion, France, September 14, 1918. **G.O. No.:** 44, W.D. 1919.

Citation: "Volunteered to lead his company in a hazardous attack on a commanding trench position near Aisne Canal, which other troops had previously attempted to take without success. His company immediately met with intense machine-gun fire, against which it had no artillery assistance, but Captain Miles preceded the first wave and assisted in cutting a passage through the enemy's wire

entanglements. In so doing he was wounded 5 times by machine-gun bullets, both legs and 1 arm being fractured, whereupon he ordered himself placed on a stretcher and had himself carried forward to the enemy trench in order that he might encourage and direct his company, which by this time had suffered numerous casualties. Under the inspiration of this officer's indomitable spirit his men held the hostile position and consolidated the front line after an action lasting 2 hours, at the conclusion of which Captain Miles was carried to the aid station against his will."

Source
Medal of Honor Citation.

Miller, Andrew (d. 1944) *Staff sergeant, United States Army, Company G, 377th Infantry, 95th Infantry Division, so distinguished himself in combat, during World War II, that he was awarded (posthumously) the Medal of Honor for his heroic actions.*

Born: Manitowoc, Wis., **Entered service at:** Two Rivers, Wis.; **Place and date:** From Woippy, France, through Metz to Kerprich Hemmersdorf, Germany, November 16–29, 1944. **G.O. No.:** 74, September 1, 1945.

Citation: "For performing a series of heroic deeds from 16–29 November 1944, during his company's relentless drive from Woippy, France, through Metz to Kerprich Hemmersdorf, Germany. As he led a rifle squad on 16 November at Woippy, a crossfire from enemy machineguns pinned down his unit. Ordering his men to remain under cover, he went forward alone, entered a building housing 1 of the guns and forced 5 Germans to surrender at bayonet point. He then took the second gun single-handedly by hurling grenades into the enemy position, killing 2, wounding 3 more, and taking 2 additional prisoners. At the outskirts of Metz the next day, when his platoon, confused by heavy explosions and the withdrawal of friendly tanks, retired, he fearlessly remained behind armed with an automatic rifle and exchanged bursts with a German machinegun until he silenced the enemy weapon. His quick action in covering his comrades gave the platoon time to regroup and carry on the fight. On 19 November S/Sgt. Miller led an attack on large enemy barracks. Covered by his squad, he crawled to a barracks window, climbed in and captured 6 riflemen occupying the room. His men, and then the entire company, followed through the window, scoured the building, and took 75 prisoners. S/Sgt. Miller volunteered, with 3 comrades, to capture Gestapo officers who were preventing the surrender of German troops in another building. He ran a gauntlet of machinegun fire and was lifted through a window. Inside, he found himself covered by a machine pistol, but he persuaded the 4 Gestapo agents confronting him to surrender. Early the next morning, when strong hostile forces punished his company with heavy fire, S/Sgt. Miller assumed the task of destroying a well-placed machinegun. He was knocked down by a rifle grenade as he climbed an open stairway in a house, but pressed on with a bazooka to find an advantageous spot from which to launch his rocket. He discovered that he could fire only from the roof, a position where he would draw tremendous enemy fire. Facing the risk, he moved into the open, coolly took aim and scored a direct hit on the hostile emplacement, wreaking such havoc that the enemy troops became completely demoralized and began surrendering by the score. The following day, in Metz, he captured 12 more prisoners and silenced an enemy machinegun after volunteering for a hazardous mission in advance of his company's position. On 29 November, as Company G climbed a hill overlooking Kerprich Hemmersdorf, enemy fire pinned the unit to the ground. S/Sgt. Miller, on his own initiative, pressed ahead with his squad past the company's leading element to meet the surprise resistance. His men stood up and advanced deliberately, firing as they went. Inspired by S/Sgt. Miller's leadership, the platoon followed, and then another platoon arose and grimly closed with the Germans. The enemy action was smothered, but at the cost of S/Sgt. Miller's life. His tenacious devotion to the attack, his gallant choice to expose himself to enemy action rather than endanger his men, his limitless bravery, assured the success of Company G."

Source
Medal of Honor Citation.

Miller, Doris, (1919–1943) *Petty officer third class, United States Navy.*

Doris ("Dorie") Miller was born in Waco, Texas, on October 12, 1919. He enlisted in the navy in September 1939 as a mess attendant third class. On December 7, 1941, while serving aboard USS *West Virginia* (BB-48), he distinguished himself by courageous conduct and devotion to duty during the Japanese attack on Pearl Harbor. He was awarded the Navy Cross for his actions on this occasion.

Doris Miller served aboard USS *Indianapolis* (CA-35) from December 1941 to May 1943. He was then assigned to the escort carrier *Liscome Bay* (CVE-56). Cook Third Class Miller was lost with that ship when a Japanese submarine torpedoed her on November 24, 1943, during the invasion of the Gilbert Islands.

The USS *Miller* (DE-1091) was named in honor of Cook Third Class Doris Miller.

Citation: "For distinguished devotion to duty, extraordinary courage and disregard for his own personal safety during the attack on the Fleet in Pearl Harbor, Territory of Hawaii, by Japanese forces on December 7, 1941.

While at the side of his Captain on the bridge, Miller, despite enemy strafing and bombing and in the face of a serious fire, assisted in moving his Captain, who had been mortally wounded, to a place of greater safety, and later manned and operated a machine gun directed at enemy Japanese attacking aircraft until ordered to leave the bridge."

Source
Naval Historical Center.
Navy Cross Citation.

Millett, Lewis L. (b. 1920) *Captain, United States Army, Company E, 27th Infantry Regiment, so distinguished himself in combat, during the Korean War, that he was awarded the Medal of Honor for his heroic actions.*

Born: 1920, Mechanic Falls, Maine; **Entered service at:** Mechanic Falls, Maine; **Place and date:** Vicinity of Soam-Ni, Korea, February 7, 1951. **G.O. No.:** 69, August 2, 1951.

Citation: "Captain Lewis L Millett, Infantry, United States Army, a member of Company E, 27th Infantry Regiment, distinguished himself by conspicuous gallantry and intrepidity above and beyond the call of duty in action in the vicinity of Soam-Ni, Korea on 7 February 1951. While personally leading his company in an attack against a

Lewis L. Millett

strongly held position he noted that the 1st Platoon was pinned down by small arms, automatic, and antitank fire. Captain Millett ordered the 3d Platoon forward, placed himself at the head of the two platoons, and, with fixed bayonet, led the assault up the fire-swept hill. In the fierce charge Captain Millett bayoneted two enemy soldiers and boldly continued on, throwing grenades, clubbing and bayoneting the enemy, while urging his men forward by shouting encouragement. Despite vicious opposing fire, the whirlwind hand-to-hand assault carried to the crest of the hill. His dauntless leadership and personal courage so inspired his men that they stormed into the hostile position and used their bayonets with such lethal effect that the enemy fled in wild disorder. During this fierce onslaught Captain Millett was wounded by grenade fragments but refused evacuation until the objective was taken and firmly secured. The superb leadership, conspicuous courage, and consummate devotion to duty demonstrated by Captain Millett were directly responsible for the successful accomplishment of a hazardous mission and reflect the highest credit on himself and the heroic traditions of the military service."

Source
Medal of Honor Citation.

Hiroshi H. Miyamura

Miyamura, Hiroshi H. *Corporal, United States Army, Company H, Seventh Infantry Regiment, Third Infantry Division, so distinguished himself in combat, during the Korean War, that he was awarded the Medal of Honor for his heroic actions.*

Born: Gallup, N. Mex.; **Entered service at:** Gallup, N. Mex.; **Place and date:** Near Taejon-ni, Korea, April 24 and 25, 1951. **G.O. No.:** 85, November 4, 1953.

Citation: "Cpl. Miyamura, a member of Company H, distinguished himself by conspicuous gallantry and intrepidity above and beyond the call of duty in action against the enemy. On the night of 24 April, Company H was occupying a defensive position when the enemy fanatically attacked threatening to overrun the position. Cpl. Miyamura, a machine gun squad leader, aware of the imminent danger to his men unhesitatingly jumped from his shelter wielding his bayonet in close hand-to-hand combat killing approximately 10 of the enemy. Returning to his position, he administered first aid to the wounded and directed their evacuation. As another savage assault hit the line, he manned his machine gun and delivered withering fire until his ammunition was expended. He ordered the squad to withdraw while he stayed behind to render the gun inoperative. He then bayoneted his way through infiltrated enemy soldiers to a second gun emplacement and assisted in its operation. When the intensity of the attack necessitated the withdrawal of the company Cpl. Miyamura ordered his men to fall back while he remained to cover their movement. He killed more than 50 of the enemy before his ammunition was depleted and he was severely wounded. He maintained his magnificent stand despite his painful wounds, continuing to repel the attack until his position was overrun. When last seen he was fighting ferociously against an overwhelming number of enemy soldiers. Cpl. Miyamura's indomitable heroism and consummate devotion to duty reflect the utmost glory on himself and uphold the illustrious traditions on the military service."

Source
Medal of Honor Citation.

Mize, Ola L. (b. 1931) *Master sergeant (then Sergeant), United States Army, Company K, 15th Infantry Regiment, Third Infantry Division, so distinguished himself in combat, during the Korean War, that he was awarded the Medal of Honor for his heroic actions.*

Born: August 28, 1931, Marshall County, Ala.; **Entered service at:** Gadsden, Ala.; **Place and date:** Near

Surang-ni, Korea, June 10–11, 1953 **G.O. No.:** 70, September 24, 1954.

Citation: "M/Sgt. Mize, a member of Company K, distinguished himself by conspicuous gallantry and outstanding courage above and beyond the call of duty in action against the enemy. Company K was committed to the defense of "Outpost Harry," a strategically valuable position, when the enemy launched a heavy attack. Learning that a comrade on a friendly listening post had been wounded he moved through the intense barrage, accompanied by a medical aid man, and rescued the wounded soldier. On returning to the main position he established an effective defense system and inflicted heavy casualties against attacks from determined enemy assault forces which had penetrated into trenches within the outpost area. During his fearless actions he was blown down by artillery and grenade blasts 3 times but each time he dauntlessly returned to his position, tenaciously fighting and successfully repelling hostile attacks. When enemy onslaughts ceased he took his few men and moved from bunker to bunker, firing through apertures and throwing grenades at the foe, neutralizing their positions. When an enemy soldier stepped out behind a comrade, prepared to fire, M/Sgt. Mize killed him, saving the life of his fellow soldier. After rejoining the platoon, moving from man to man, distributing ammunition, and shouting words of encouragement he observed a friendly machine gun position overrun. He immediately fought his way to the position, killing 10 of the enemy and dispersing the remainder. Fighting back to the command post, and finding several friendly wounded there, he took a position to protect them. Later, securing a radio, he directed friendly artillery fire upon the attacking enemy's routes of approach. At dawn he helped regroup for a counterattack which successfully drove the enemy from the outpost. M/Sgt. Mize's valorous conduct and unflinching courage reflect lasting glory upon himself and uphold the noble traditions of the military service."

Source
Medal of Honor Citation.

Ola L. Mize

Modrzejewski, Robert J. (b. 1934) *Major (then captain), United States Marine Corps, Company K, Third Battalion, Fourth Marines, Third Marine Division, FMF, so distinguished himself in combat during the Vietnam War that he was awarded the Medal of Honor for his heroic actions.*

Born: July 3, 1934, Milwaukee, Wis.; **Entered service at:** Milwaukee, Wis.; **Place and date:** Republic of Vietnam, July 15–18, 1966.

Citation: "For conspicuous gallantry and intrepidity at the risk of his life above and beyond the call of duty. On 15 July, during Operation HASTINGS, Company K was landed in an enemy-infested jungle area to establish a blocking position at a major enemy trail network. Shortly after landing, the company encountered a reinforced enemy platoon in a well-organized, defensive position. Maj. Modrzejewski led his men in the successful seizure of the enemy redoubt, which contained large quantities of ammunition and supplies. That evening, a numerically superior enemy force counterattacked in an effort to retake the vital supply area, thus setting the pattern of activity for the next 2 $\frac{1}{2}$ days. In the first series of attacks, the enemy assaulted repeatedly in overwhelming numbers but each time was repulsed by the gallant Marines. The second night, the enemy struck in battalion strength, and Maj. Modrzejewski was wounded in this intensive action, which was fought at close quarters. Although exposed to enemy fire, and despite his painful wounds, he crawled 200 meters to provide critically needed ammunition to an exposed element of his command and was constantly present wherever the fighting was heaviest; despite numerous casualties, a

Robert J. Modrzejewski

dwindling supply of ammunition and the knowledge that they were surrounded, he skillfully directed artillery fire to within a few meter of his position and courageously inspired the efforts of his company in repelling the aggressive enemy attack. On 18 July, Company K was attacked by a regimental-size enemy force. Although his unit was vastly outnumbered and weakened by the previous fighting, Maj. Modrzejewski reorganized his men and calmly moved among them to encourage and direct their efforts to heroic limits as they fought to overcome the vicious enemy onslaught. Again he called in air and artillery strikes at close range with devastating effect on the enemy, which together with the bold and determined fighting of the men of Company K, repulsed the fanatical attack of the larger North Vietnamese force. His unparalleled personal heroism and indomitable leadership inspired his men to a significant victory over the enemy force and reflected great credit upon himself, the Marine Corps, and the U.S. Naval Service."

Source and Additional Reading

Editors of Boston Publishing, Company. *Above and Beyond.* Boston: Boston Publishing, 1985.
Medal of Honor Citation.

Montgomery, Jack C. *First lieutenant, United States Army, 45th Infantry Division, so distinguished himself in combat, during World War II, that he was awarded the Medal of Honor for his heroic actions.*

Born: Long, Okla.; **Entered service at:** Sallisaw, Okla.; **Place and date:** Near Padiglione, Italy, February 22, 1944. G.O. No.: January 15, 1945.

Citation: "For conspicuous gallantry and intrepidity at risk of life above and beyond the call of duty on 22 February 1944, near Padiglione, Italy. Two hours before daybreak a strong force of enemy infantry established themselves in 3 echelons at 50 yards, 100 yards, and 300 yards, respectively, in front of the rifle platoons commanded by 1st Lt. Montgomery. The closest position, consisting of 4 machineguns and 1 mortar, threatened the immediate security of the platoon position. Seizing an Ml rifle and several hand grenades, 1st Lt. Montgomery crawled up a ditch to within hand grenade range of the enemy. Then climbing boldly onto a little mound, he fired his rifle and threw his grenades so accurately that he killed 8 of the enemy and captured the remaining 4. Returning to his platoon, he called for artillery fire on a house, in and around which he suspected that the majority of the enemy had entrenched themselves. Arming himself with a carbine, he proceeded along the shallow ditch, as withering fire from the riflemen and machinegunners in the second position was concentrated on him. He attacked this position with such fury that 7 of the enemy surrendered to him, and both machineguns were silenced. Three German dead were found in the vicinity later that morning. 1st Lt. Montgomery continued boldly toward the house, 300 yards from his platoon position. It was now daylight, and the enemy observation was excellent across the flat open terrain which led to 1st Lt. Montgomery's objective. When the artillery barrage had lifted, 1st Lt. Montgomery ran fearlessly toward the strongly defended position. As the enemy started streaming out of the house, 1st Lt. Montgomery, unafraid of treacherous snipers, exposed himself daringly to assemble the surrendering enemy and send them to the rear. His fearless, aggressive, and intrepid actions that morning accounted for a total of 11 enemy dead, 32 prisoners, and an unknown number of wounded. That night, while aiding an adjacent unit to repulse a counterattack, he was struck by mortar fragments and seriously wounded. The selflessness and courage exhibited by 1st Lt. Montgomery in alone attacking 3 strong enemy positions inspired his men to a degree beyond estimation."

Source

Medal of Honor Citation.

Moon, Harold Jr. *Private, United States Army, Company G, 34th Infantry, 24th Infantry Division, so distinguished himself in combat, during World War II, that he was awarded (posthumously) the Medal of Honor for his heroic actions.*

Born: Albuquerque, N. Mex.; **Entered service at:** Gardena, Calif.; **Place and date:** Pawig, Leyte, Philippine Islands, October 21, 1944. **G.O. No.:** 104, November 15, 1945.

Citation: "He fought with conspicuous gallantry and intrepidity when powerful Japanese counterblows were being struck in a desperate effort to annihilate a newly won beachhead. In a forward position, armed with a submachinegun, he met the brunt of a strong, well-supported night attack, which quickly enveloped his platoon's flanks. Many men in nearby positions were killed or injured, and Pvt. Moon was wounded, as his foxhole became the immediate object of a concentration of mortar and machinegun fire. Nevertheless, he maintained his stand, poured deadly fire into the enemy, daringly exposed himself to hostile fire time after time to exhort and inspire what American troops were left in the immediate area. A Japanese officer, covered by machine-gun fire and hidden by an embankment, attempted to knock out his position with grenades, but Pvt. Moon, after protracted and skillful maneuvering, killed him. When the enemy advanced a light machinegun to within 20 yards of the shattered perimeter and fired with telling effects on the remnants of the platoon, he stood up to locate the gun and remained exposed while calling back range corrections to friendly mortars which knocked out the weapon. A little later he killed 2 Japanese as they charged an aid man. By dawn his position, the focal point of the attack for more than 4 hours, was virtually surrounded. In a fanatical effort to reduce it and kill its defender, an entire platoon charged with fixed bayonets. Firing from a sitting position, Pvt. Moon calmly emptied his magazine into the advancing horde, killing 18 and repulsing the attack. In a final display of bravery, he stood up to throw a grenade at a machine-gun, which had opened fire on the right flank. He was hit and instantly killed, falling in the position from which he had not been driven by the fiercest enemy action. Nearly 200 dead Japanese were found within 100 yards of his foxhole. The continued tenacity, combat sagacity, and magnificent heroism with which Pvt. Moon fought on against overwhelming odds contributed in a large measure to breaking up a powerful enemy threat and did much to insure our initial successes during a most important operation."

Source
Medal of Honor Citation.

Morgan, John C. (b. 1914) *(Air mission) second lieutenant, United States Army Air Corps, 326th Bomber Squadron, 92d Bomber Group, so distinguished himself in aerial combat, during World War II, that he was awarded the Medal of Honor for his heroic actions.*

Born: August 24, 1914, Vernon, Tex.; **Entered service at:** London, England; **Place and date:** Over Europe, July 28, 1943. **G.O. No.:** 85, December 17, 1943.

Citation: "For conspicuous gallantry and intrepidity above and beyond the call of duty, while participating in a bombing mission over enemy-occupied continental Europe, 28 July 1943. Prior to reaching the German coast on the way to the target, the B17 airplane in which 2d Lt. Morgan was serving as copilot was attacked by a large force of enemy fighters, during which the oxygen system to the tail, waist, and radio gun positions was knocked out. A frontal attack placed a cannon shell through the windshield, totally shattering it, and the pilot's skull was split open by a .303 caliber shell, leaving him in a crazed condition. The pilot fell over the steering wheel, tightly clamping his arms around it. 2d Lt. Morgan at once grasped the controls from his side and, by sheer strength, pulled the airplane back into formation despite the frantic struggles of the semi-conscious pilot. The interphone had been destroyed, rendering it impossible to call for help. At this time the top turret gunner fell to the floor and down through the hatch with his arm shot off at the shoulder and a gaping wound in his side. The waist, tail, and radio gunners had lost consciousness from lack of oxygen and, hearing no fire from their guns, the copilot believed they had bailed out. The wounded pilot still offered desperate resistance in his crazed attempts to fly the airplane. There remained the prospect of flying to and over the target and back to a friendly base wholly unassisted. In the face of this desperate situation, 2d Lt. Officer Morgan made his decision to continue the flight and protect any members of the crew who might still be in the ship and for 2 hours he flew in formation with one hand at the controls and the other holding off the struggling pilot before the navigator entered the steering compartment and relieved the situation. The miraculous and heroic performance of 2d Lt. Morgan on this occasion resulted in the successful completion of a vital bombing mission and the safe return of his airplane and crew."

Source
Medal of Honor Citation.

Morris, Charles B. (b. 1931) *Staff sergeant (then sergeant), United States Army, Company A, Second Battalion (Airborne), 503d Infantry, 173d Airborne Brigade*

(Separate) so distinguished himself in combat, during the Vietnam War, that he was awarded the Medal of Honor for his heroic actions.

Born: December 29, 1931, Carroll County, Va.; **Entered service at:** Roanoke, Va.; **Place and date:** Republic of Vietnam, June 29, 1966. **C.O. No.:** 51, December 14, 1967.

Citation: "For conspicuous gallantry and intrepidity at the risk of his life above and beyond the call of duty. Seeing indications of the enemy's presence in the area, S/Sgt. Morris deployed his squad and continued forward alone to make a reconnaissance. He unknowingly crawled within 20 meters of an enemy machinegun, whereupon the gunner fired, wounding him in the chest. S/Sgt. Morris instantly returned the fire and killed the gunner. Continuing to crawl within a few feet of the gun, he hurled a grenade and killed the remainder of the enemy crew. Although in pain and bleeding profusely, S/Sgt. Morris continued his reconnaissance. Returning to the platoon area, he reported the results of his reconnaissance to the platoon leader. As he spoke, the platoon came under heavy fire. Refusing medical attention for himself, he deployed his men in better firing positions confronting the entrenched enemy to his front. Then for 8 hours the platoon engaged the numerically superior enemy force. Withdrawal was impossible without abandoning many wounded and dead. Finding the platoon medic dead, S/Sgt. Morris administered first aid to himself and was returning to treat the wounded members of his squad with the medic's first aid kit when he was again wounded. Knocked down and stunned, he regained consciousness and continued to treat the wounded, reposition his men, and inspire and encourage their efforts. Wounded again when an enemy grenade shattered his left hand, nonetheless he personally took up the fight and armed and threw several grenades, which killed a number of enemy soldiers. Seeing that an enemy machinegun had maneuvered behind his platoon and was delivering the fire upon his men, S/Sgt. Morris and another man crawled toward the gun to knock it out. His comrade was killed and S/Sgt. Morris sustained another wound, but, firing his rifle with 1 hand, he silenced the enemy machinegun. Returning to the platoon, he courageously exposed himself to the devastating enemy fire to drag the wounded to a protected area, and with utter disregard for his personal safety and the pain he suffered, he continued to lead and direct the efforts of his men until relief arrived. Upon termination of the battle, important documents were found among the enemy dead revealing a planned ambush of a Republic of Vietnam battalion. Use of this information prevented the ambush and saved many lives. S/Sgt. Morris's gallantry was instrumental in the successful defeat of the enemy, saved many lives, and was in the highest traditions of the U.S. Army."

Source
Medal of Honor Citation.

Mosby, John Singleton (1833–1916) *Confederate partisan ranger.*

It has been claimed by some that the activities of partisan ranger bands in northern and western Virginia, especially those of John S. Mosby, may have prevented a Union victory in the summer or fall of 1864. A Virginian with a penchant for violence, Mosby had been practicing law at the outbreak of the war.

His assignments included the following: private, First Virginia Cavalry (1861); first lieutenant, First Virginia Cavalry (February 1862); captain, Provisional Army of the Confederate State, (PACS) (March 15, 1863); major, PACS (March 26, 1863); major, 43rd Virginia Cavalry Battalion (June 10, 1863); lieutenant colonel, 43rd Virginia Cavalry Battalion (January 21, 1864); and colonel, Mosby's (Va.) Cavalry Regiment (December 7, 1864).

Originally an enlisted man and officer in the First Virginia Cavalry, he came into conflict with that unit's colonel, "Grumble Jones," and joined J. E. B. Stuart's staff as a scout. During the Peninsula Campaign he paved the way for Stuart's famous ride around McClellan. After a brief period of captivity in July 1862 he rejoined Stuart and was rewarded with the authority to raise a band of partisans for service in the Loudoun Valley in northern Virginia. Originally a battalion, his command was raised to a regiment in the last months of the war.

In the meantime he managed to wreak havoc among the Union supply lines, forcing field commanders to detach large numbers of troops to guard their communications. His forays took him within the lines guarding Washington, as Mosby himself often did the advance scouting in disguise. Early in 1863, with 29 men, he rode into Fairfax Court House and roused Union Gen. Edwin H. Stoughton from bed with a slap on the rear end. After the capture of Generals Crook and Kelley by McNeil's partisans, Mosby complimented them, stating that he would have to ride into Washington and take Abraham Lincoln to top their success. On another occasion he almost captured the train on which Grant was traveling.

The disruption of supply lines and the constant disappearance of couriers frustrated army, and lesser-group, commanders to such a degree that some took to the summary execution of guerrillas (partisan rangers). George Custer executed six of Mosby's men in 1864, and the partisan chief retaliated with seven of Custer's. A note attached to one of the bodies stated that Mosby would treat all further captives as prisoners of war unless Custer committed some new act of cruelty. The killings stopped.

With the surrender of Lee, Mosby simply disbanded his command on April 20, 1865, rather than formally surrender. Although the partisans were certainly a nuisance to federal commanders, it is an open question as to how effective they were in prolonging the conflict. Many southerners were very critical of the partisans, [only some Southerners accepting Mosby's command.]

Not pardoned until 1866, Mosby practiced law and befriended Grant. For supporting Grant, a Republican, in the 1868 and 1872 elections, he earned the enmity of many southerners. He received an appointment as U.S. consul in Hong Kong and other government posts.

Source

Jones, Virgil Carrington. *Ranger Mosby.* Chapel Hill, N.C.: Chapel Hill Press, 1944.

Moskala, Edward J. (1921–1946) *Private first class, United States Army, Company C, 383d Infantry, 96th Infantry Division, so distinguished himself in combat, during World War II, that he was awarded (posthumously) the Medal of Honor for his heroic actions.*

Born: November 6, 1921, Chicago, Ill.; **Entered service at:** Chicago, Ill.; **Place and date:** Kakazu Ridge, Okinawa, Ryukyu Islands, April 9, 1945. **G.O. No.:** 21, February 26, 1946.

Citation: "He was the leading element when grenade explosions and concentrated machinegun and mortar fire halted the unit's attack on Kakazu Ridge, Okinawa, Ryukyu Islands. With utter disregard for his personal safety, he charged 40 yards through withering, grazing fire and wiped out 2 machinegun nests with well-aimed grenades and deadly accurate fire from his automatic rifle. When strong counterattacks and fierce enemy resistance from other positions forced his company to withdraw, he voluntarily remained behind with 8 others to cover the maneuver. Fighting from a critically dangerous position for 3 hours, he killed more than 25 Japanese before following his surviving companions through screening smoke down the face of the ridge to a gorge where it was discovered that one of the group had been left behind, wounded. Unhesitatingly, Pvt. Moskala climbed the bullet-swept slope to assist in the rescue, and, returning to lower ground, volunteered to protect other wounded while the bulk of the troops quickly took up more favorable positions. He had saved another casualty and killed 4 enemy infiltrators when he was struck and mortally wounded himself while aiding still another disabled soldier. With gallant initiative, unfaltering courage, and heroic determination to destroy the enemy, Pvt. Moskala gave his life in his complete devotion to his company's mission and his comrades' well-being. His intrepid conduct provided a lasting inspiration for those with whom he served."

Source
Medal of Honor Citation.

Moultrie, William (1730–1805) *American general officer.*

Born in Charleston, South Carolina, on November 23, 1730, Moultrie fought as a captain against the Cherokee in 1761 and at the outbreak of the American Revolution was appointed a colonel in the Second Colonial Regiment. His choice of palmetto logs in the construction of a fort to defend Charleston was vindicated when the fort withstood an attack by the British fleet. Later promoted to brigadier general, Moultrie defeated the British at Beaufort, South Carolina He helped thwart another attack on Charleston, but in 1780 he and his garrison were captured when the city fell, and Moultrie was imprisoned for two years.

After the war, Moultrie served as a South Carolina legislator, as lieutenant governor, and as governor from 1785 to 1787 and from 1792 to 1794. He died in Charleston on September 27, 1805.

Source

Moultrie, William. *Memoirs of the American Revolution.* 2 vols. 1802. Reprint, New York: Longworth, 1968.

Munro, Douglas Albert (1919–1942) *Signalman first class, United States Coast Guard, so distinguished himself in combat, during World War II, that he was awarded (posthumously) the Medal of Honor for his heroic actions.*

Born: October 11, 1919, Vancouver, B.C.; **Entered service at:** Washington.

Citation: "For extraordinary heroism and conspicuous gallantry in action above and beyond the call of duty as Petty Officer in Charge of a group of 24 Higgins boats, engaged in the evacuation of a battalion of Marines trapped by enemy Japanese forces at Point Cruz Guadalcanal, on 27 September 1942. After making preliminary plans for the evacuation of nearly 500 beleaguered Marines, Munro, under constant strafing by enemy machine-guns on the island, and at great risk of his life, daringly led 5 of his small craft toward the shore. As he closed the beach he signaled the others to land, and then in order to draw the enemy's fire and protect the heavily loaded boats, he valiantly placed his craft with its 2 small guns as a shield between the beachhead and the Japanese. When the perilous task of evacuation was nearly completed, Munro was instantly killed by enemy fire, but his crew, 2 of whom were wounded, carried on until the last boat had loaded and cleared the beach. By his outstanding leadership, expert planning, and dauntless devotion to duty, he and his courageous comrades undoubtedly saved the lives of many who otherwise would have perished. He gallantly gave his life for his country."

Source
Medal of Honor Citation.
Editors of Boston Publishing Company. *Above and Beyond.* Boston: Boston Publishing, 1985.

Murphy, Audie Leon (1924–1971) *Second lieutenant, commanding officer, Company B, 15th Infantry, Third Infantry Division, so distinguished in combat, during World War II, that he was awarded the Medal of Honor for his heroic actions.*

Born: Hunt County, near Kingston, Tex.; **Entered service at:** Dallas, Tex.; **Place and date:** Holtzwihr, France, January 26, 1945. **G.O. No.:** 65, August 9, 1945.

Citation: "2d Lt. Murphy commanded Company B, which was attacked by 6 tanks and waves of infantry. 2d Lt. Murphy ordered his men to withdraw to prepared positions in a woods, while he remained forward at his command post and continued to give fire directions to the artillery by telephone. Behind him, to his right, 1 of our tank destroyers received a direct hit and began to burn. Its crew withdrew to the woods. 2d Lt. Murphy continued to direct artillery fire, which killed large numbers of the advancing enemy infantry. With the enemy tanks abreast of his position, 2d Lt. Murphy climbed on the burning tank destroyer, which was in danger of blowing up at any moment, and employed its .50 caliber machinegun against the enemy. He was alone and exposed to German fire from 3 sides, but his deadly fire killed dozens of Germans and caused their infantry attack to waver. The enemy tanks, losing infantry support, began to fall back. For an hour the Germans tried every available weapon to eliminate 2d Lt. Murphy, but he continued to hold his position and wiped out a squad, which was trying to creep up unnoticed on his right flank. Germans reached as close as 10 yards, only to be mowed down by his fire. He received a leg wound, but ignored it and continued the single-handed fight until his ammunition was exhausted. He then made his way to his company, refused medical attention, and organized the company in a counterattack which forced the Germans to withdraw. His directing of artillery fire wiped out many of the enemy; he killed or wounded about 50. 2d Lt. Murphy's indomitable courage and his refusal to give an inch of ground saved his company from possible encirclement and destruction, and enabled it to hold the woods which had been the enemy's objective."

By the end of the war, Audie Murphy had more combat decorations than any other soldier in the United States Army and was considered the World War II equivalent of Alvin C. York. He was offered admission to West Point

after the war, which would lead to a career in the regular army, but he opted for a transfer into the National Guard (in which he eventually attained the rank of major) and pursuit of an acting career in Hollywood after being introduced to the actor James Cagney. His real-life heroism combined with his boyish all-American looks made him a natural matinee idol and star of Westerns, although the film critics were often unkind. Two roles that did receive generally positive reviews were, not surprisingly, that of Henry Fleming, the young infantryman in the adaptation of Stephen Crane's classic Civil War novel *The Red Badge of Courage* (1951) and his self-portrait in the film version of his autobiography.

To Hell and Back follows Murphy's life from late childhood, when, a member of a poor Texas farm family, he dropped out of high school to enlist at the start of the war and then had to overcome several obstacles, particularly his diminutive stature, to be assigned to the infantry. He quickly rose through the enlisted ranks through intense fighting in Italy and France and eventually received a battlefield commission and found himself on top of the burning tank at Holtzwihr. One might assume that in portraying himself on film, Murphy went on the ultimate ego trip with what today would be described as Rambo-like heroics, but in comparing the film with the official combat reports, it is clear that Murphy was actually being extremely modest and self-deprecating.

Other members of Company B, 15th Infantry, did find that Hollywood had "cleaned up" the battlefields far too much. One pointed out that whereas the standoff at Holtzwihr took place in freezing rain and a mire of mud and melting snow, Hollywood made it look like "a sunny day in the park." Another technical inaccuracy, although quite minor by Hollywood standards, is that Murphy did his onscreen standoff on top of a burning M-4 Sherman medium tank, whereas in real life it was an M-36 Hellcat tank destroyer; the two vehicles are similar enough, with the same chassis (the tank destroyer has lighter armor but a larger, more powerful gun), that the average untrained civilian would be unable to tell the difference.

Murphy died in a plane crash in 1971 on a business venture. In his last film role earlier that year, he played Jesse James in *A Time for Dying.*

Source
Graham, Don. *No Name on the Bullet: A Biography of Audie Murphy.* New York: Viking, 1989.
Simpson, Col. Harold B. *Audie Murphy: American Soldier.* Hillsboro, Tex.: Hillsboro Junior College Press, 1982.

Murphy, Raymond G. (b. 1930) *Second lieutenant, United States Marine Corps Reserve, Company A, First Battalion, Fifth Marines, First Marine Division (Reinforced),* *so distinguished himself in combat, during the Korean War, that he was awarded the Medal of Honor for his heroic actions.*

Born: January 14, 1930, Pueblo, Colo.; **Entered service at:** Pueblo, Colo.; **Place and date:** Korea, February 3, 1953.

Citation: "For conspicuous gallantry and intrepidity at the risk of his life above and beyond the call of duty as a platoon commander of Company A, in action against enemy aggressor forces. Although painfully wounded by fragments from an enemy mortar shell while leading his evacuation platoon in support of assault units attacking a cleverly concealed and well-entrenched hostile force occupying commanding ground, 2d Lt. Murphy steadfastly refused medical aid and continued to lead his men up a hill through a withering barrage of hostile mortar and small-arms fire, skillfully maneuvering his force from one position to the next and shouting words of encouragement. Undeterred by the increasing intense enemy fire, he immediately located casualties as they fell and made several trips up and down the fire-swept hill to direct evacuation teams to the wounded, personally carrying many of the stricken Marines to safety. When reinforcements were needed by the assaulting elements, 2d Lt. Murphy employed part of his unit as support and, during the ensuing battle, personally killed 2 of the enemy with his pistol. With all the wounded evacuated and the assaulting units beginning to disengage, he remained behind with a carbine to cover the movement of friendly forces off the hill and, though suffering intense pain from his previous wounds, seized an automatic rifle to provide more firepower when the enemy reappeared in the trenches. After reaching the base of the hill, he organized a search party and again ascended the slope for a final check on missing Marines, locating and carrying the bodies of a machine gun crew back down the hill. Wounded a second time while conducting the entire force to the line of departure through a continuing barrage of enemy small arms, artillery, and mortar fire, he again refused medical assistance until assured that every one of his men, including all casualties, had preceded him to the main lines. His resolute and inspiring leadership, exceptional fortitude, and great personal valor reflect the highest credit upon 2d Lt. Murphy and enhance the finest traditions of the U.S. Naval Service."

Source
Medal of Honor Citation.

Murray, Charles P., Jr. *First lieutenant, United States Army, Company C, 30th Infantry, Third Infantry Division, so distinguished himself in combat, during World War II, that he was awarded the Medal of Honor for his heroic actions.*

Born: Baltimore, Md.; **Entered service at:** Wilmington, N.C.; **Place and date:** Near Kaysersberg, France, December 16, 1944. **G.O. No.:** 63, August 1, 1945.

Citation: "For commanding Company C, 30th Infantry, displaying supreme courage and heroic initiative near Kaysersberg, France, on 16 December 1944, while leading a reinforced platoon into enemy territory. Descending into a valley beneath hilltop positions held by our troops, he observed a force of 200 Germans pouring deadly mortar, bazooka, machinegun, and small arms fire into an American battalion occupying the crest of the ridge. The enemy's position in a sunken road, though hidden from the ridge, was open to a flank attack by 1st Lt. Murray's patrol but he hesitated to commit so small a force to battle with the superior and strongly disposed enemy. Crawling out ahead of his troops to a vantagepoint, he called by radio for artillery fire. His shells bracketed the German force, but when he was about to correct the range his radio went dead. He returned to his patrol, secured grenades and a rifle to launch them and went back to his self-appointed

Charles P. Murray Jr.

outpost. His first shots disclosed his position; the enemy directed heavy fire against him as he methodically fired his missiles into the narrow defile. Again he returned to his patrol. With an automatic rifle and ammunition, he once more moved to his exposed position. Burst after burst he fired into the enemy, killing 20, wounding many others, and completely disorganizing its ranks, which began to withdraw. He prevented the removal of 3 German mortars by knocking out a truck. By that time a mortar had been brought to his support. 1st Lt. Murray directed fire of this weapon, causing further casualties and confusion in the German ranks. Calling on his patrol to follow, he then moved out toward his original objective, possession of a bridge and construction of a roadblock. He cap-

tured 10 Germans in foxholes. An eleventh, while pretending to surrender, threw a grenade which knocked him to the ground, inflicting 8 wounds. Though suffering and bleeding profusely, he refused to return to the rear until he had chosen the spot for the block and had seen his men correctly deployed. By his single-handed attack on an overwhelming force and by his intrepid and heroic fighting, 1st Lt. Murray stopped a counterattack, established an advance position against formidable odds, and provided an inspiring example for the men of his command."

Source
Medal of Honor Citation.

N

Neppel, Ralph G. *Sergeant, United States Army, Company M, 329th Infantry, 83d Infantry Division, so distinguished himself in combat, during World War II, that he was awarded the Medal of Honor for his heroic actions.*

Born: Willey, Iowa; **Entered service at:** Glidden, Iowa; **Place and date:** Birgel, Germany, December 14, 1944. **G.O. No.:** 77, September 10, 1945.

Citation: "He was leader of a machinegun squad defending an approach to the villate of Birgel, Germany, on 14 December 1944, when an enemy tank, supported by 20 infantrymen, counterattacked. He held his fire until the Germans were within 100 yards and then raked the foot soldiers beside the tank killing several of them. The enemy armor continued to press forward and, at the pointblank range of 30 yards, fired a high-velocity shell into the American emplacement, wounding the entire squad. Sgt. Neppel, blown 10 yards from his gun, had 1 leg severed below the knee and suffered other wounds. Despite his injuries and the danger from the onrushing tank and infantry, he dragged himself back to his position on his elbows, remounted his gun and killed the remaining enemy riflemen. Stripped of its infantry protection, the tank was forced to withdraw. By his superb courage and indomitable fighting spirit, Sgt. Neppel inflicted heavy casualties on the enemy and broke a determined counterattack."

Source
Medal of Honor Citation.

Newlin, Melvin Earl (1948–1967) *Private first class, United States Marine Corps, Second Battalion, Fifth Marines, First Marine Division (Reinforced), FMF, so distinguished himself in combat, during the Vietnam War that he was awarded (posthumously) the Medal of Honor for his heroic actions.*

Born: September 27, 1948, Wellsville, Ohio; **Entered service at:** Cleveland, Ohio; **Place and date:** Quang Nam Province, Republic of Vietnam, July 4, 1967.

Citation: "For conspicuous gallantry and intrepidity at the risk of his life above and beyond the call of duty while serving as a machine gunner attached to the 1st Platoon, Company F, 2d Battalion, on 3 and 4 July 1967. Pfc. Newlin, with 4 other Marines, was manning a key position on the perimeter of the Nong Son outpost when the enemy launched a savage and well coordinated mortar and infantry assault, seriously wounding him and killing his 4 comrades. Propping himself against his machinegun, he poured a deadly accurate stream of fire into the charging ranks of the Viet Cong. Though repeatedly hit by small-arms fire, he twice repelled enemy attempts to overrun his position. During the third attempt, a grenade explosion wounded him again and knocked him to the ground unconscious. The Viet Cong guerrillas, believing him dead, bypassed him and continued their assault on the main force. Meanwhile, Pfc. Newlin regained consciousness, crawled back to his weapon, and brought it to bear on the rear of the enemy, causing havoc and confusion among them. Spotting the enemy attempting to bring a captured 106 recoilless weapon to bear on other Marine positions, he shifted his fire, inflicting heavy casualties on the enemy and preventing them from firing the captured weapon. He then shifted his fire back to the primary enemy force, causing the enemy to stop their assault on the Marine bunkers and to once again attack his machinegun position. Valiantly fighting off 2 more enemy assaults, he firmly held his ground until mortally wounded. Pfc. Newlin had single-handedly broken up and disorganized the entire enemy assault force, causing them to lose momentum and delaying them long enough for his fellow

Marines to organize a defense and beat off their secondary attack. His indomitable courage, fortitude, and unwavering devotion to duty in the face of almost certain death reflect great credit upon himself and the Marine Corps and upheld the highest traditions of the U.S. Naval Service."

Source
Medal of Honor Citation.

Nimitz, Chester William (1885–1966) *Fleet Admiral, United States Navy, one of nine "five star" officers.*

Chester William Nimitz was born on February 24, 1885, in a hotel built by his grandfather, Charles Nimitz, a retired sea captain, near the town of Fredericksburg, Texas. As a young man, Nimitz had his sights on an army career and while a student at Tivy High School, in Kerrville, Texas, he tried for an appointment to West Point. With none available, he was appointed to the United States Naval Academy from the 12th Congressional District of Texas in 1901 and graduated with distinction in January 1905, seventh in a class of 114.

He joined the battleship USS *Ohio* at San Francisco and cruised on her to the Far East. In September 1906, he was transferred to the USS *Baltimore,* and on January 31, 1907, after two years at sea (then required by law), he was commissioned ensign. Remaining on Asiatic Station in 1907, he successively served aboard the gunboats USS *Panay,* USS *Decatur,* and USS *Denver* (Nimitz was court-martialed for grounding her, an obstacle in his career that he overcame).

Nimitz returned to the United States aboard the USS *Ranger* and in January 1909 began instruction in the First Submarine Flotilla. In May of that year he was given command of the flotilla, with additional duty in command of *Plunger,* later renamed *A-1.* He commanded *Snapper* when that submarine was commissioned on February 2, 1910 and on November 18, 1910, assumed command of the *Narwhal.* In the latter command he had additional duty from October 10, 1911, as commander, Third Submarine Division, Atlantic Torpedo Fleet. In November 1911, he was ordered to the Boston Navy Yard, to assist in fitting out *Skipjack* and assume command of that submarine, renamed *E-1* at commissioning on February 14, 1912. On March 20, 1912, he rescued W. J. Walsh, fireman, second class, from drowning. A strong tide was running and Walsh, who could not swim, was being rapidly swept away from his ship. Lieutenant Nimitz dove into the water and kept Walsh afloat until a small boat picked up both men. Nimitz was awarded the Silver Lifesaving Medal by the Treasury Department for his heroic actions.

After commanding the Atlantic Submarine Flotilla, from May 1912 to March 1913, Nimitz supervised the building of diesel engines for the tanker *Maumee,* under construction at the New London Ship and Engine Building Company, at Groton, Connecticut.

In the summer of 1913 he studied engines at the diesel engine plants in Nuremberg, Germany, and Ghent, Belgium. Returning to the New York Navy Yard, he became *Maumee*'s executive officer and engineer on her commissioning, October 23, 1916. On August 10, 1917, Nimitz became aide to commander, Submarine Force, United States Atlantic Fleet. On February 6, 1918, he was appointed as chief of staff and was awarded a Letter of Commendation by the secretary of the navy for his meritorious service as chief of staff to the commander of the Atlantic Submarine Force. On September 16, 1918, he reported to the Office of the Chief of Naval Operations and on October 25 was given additional duties as senior member, Board of Submarine Design.

From May 1919 to June 1920, he served as executive officer of the USS *South Carolina.* He then commanded USS *Chicago* with additional duty in command of Submarine Division 14, based at Pearl Harbor. Returning to the United States in the summer of 1922, he studied at the Naval War College, Newport, Rhode Island, in June 1923, he became aide and assistant chief of staff to the commander, Battle Fleet, and later to the commander in chief, United States Fleet. In August 1926, he went to the University of California to help establish one of the navy's first Naval Reserve Officers Training Corps Units.

In June 1929, he took command of Submarine Division 20. In June 1931 he assumed command of USS *Rigel* at San Diego. In October 1933, he took command of the USS *Augusta* and cruised to the Far East, where in December of that year *Augusta* became the flagship of the Asiatic Fleet. In April 1935, he returned home and for three years served as assistant chief of the Bureau of Navigation, before becoming commander, Cruiser Division Two, Battle Force. In September 1938, he took command of Battleship Division One, Battle Force.

On June 15, 1939, Nimitz was appointed chief of the Bureau of Navigation, and on October 17, 1941, he was selected as commander in chief, United States Pacific Fleet, with the rank of admiral, effective December 31. Assuming command at the most critical period of the war in the Pacific, Admiral Nimitz, despite the losses at Pearl Harbor and the tragic shortage of ships, planes, and supplies, successfully organized his forces to halt the Japanese advance. As rapidly as ships, men, and material became available, he shifted to the offensive and, by his brilliant leadership and outstanding tactical skills, defeated the enemy in the Coral Sea, off Midway, and in the Solomon Islands.

On October 7, 1943, Nimitz was designated commander in chief, Pacific Fleet and Pacific Ocean Area. By act of Congress, approved December 14, 1944, the grade of Fleet Admiral of the United States Navy—the highest grade in the navy—was established, and the next day President Roosevelt nominated Admiral Nimitz to that rank. He took the oath of office on December 19, 1944.

In the final phases of World War II, Nimitz attacked the Marianas, invading Saipan, inflicting a decisive defeat on the Japanese Fleet in the Battle of the Philippine Sea, and capturing Guam and Tinian. His Fleet Forces isolated enemy-held bastions of the Central and Eastern Carolines and secured in quick succession Peleliu, Angaur, and Ulithi. In the Philippines, his ships turned back powerful task forces of the Japanese Fleet, a historic victory in the multiphased Battle for Leyte Gulf, in October 1944.

Fleet Admiral Nimitz's successful amphibious assaults on Iwo Jima and the island of Okinawa culminated the long-range strategy.

On September 2, 1945, Admiral Nimitz was the United States signatory to the surrender terms aboard the battleship USS *Missouri,* in Tokyo Bay.

On October 5, 1945, officially designated "Nimitz Day" in Washington, D.C., Admiral Nimitz was personally presented a Gold Star in lieu of the third Distinguished Service Medal by the president of the United States, "For exceptionally meritorious service as Commander in Chief, U.S. Pacific Fleet and Pacific Ocean Areas, from June 1944 to August 1945."

On November 26, 1945, his nomination as chief of naval operations was confirmed by the Senate and on December 15, 1945, he relieved Fleet Admiral Ernest J. King. With characteristic efficiency he tackled the difficult task of reducing the most powerful navy in history to a fraction of its wartime peak while establishing and overseeing programs for the maintenance of active and reserve fleets with the potential strength and readiness required to support national defense policies.

On December 15, 1947, he was detached as chief of naval operations and reported in as special assistant to the secretary of the navy in the Western Sea Frontier. In March 1949, he was nominated as plebiscite administrator for Kashmir under the United Nations (UN). When that did not materialize he asked to be relieved and accepted an assignment as a roving goodwill ambassador of the United Nations, to explain to the public the major issues confronting the UN. In 1951, President Truman appointed him chairman of the nine-man Commission on International Security and Industrial Rights.

Thereafter, he took an active interest in San Francisco community affairs, in addition to continuing actively to participate in affairs of concern to the navy and the country. He was an honorary vice president and later honorary president of the Naval Historical Foundation. He served for eight years as a regent of the University of California and did much to restore goodwill with Japan by raising funds to restore the battleship *Mikasa,* Admiral Togo's flagship at Tsushima in 1905.

Fleet Adm. Chester W. Nimitz died at home on Yerba Buena Island in San Francisco on the evening of February 29, 1966.

Admiral Nimitz is remembered as a heroic naval officer of open mind and wide experience, who was able to achieve his goals without antagonizing his colleagues. He provided the strategic direction for, and much of the impetus behind, the victorious advance across the Central Pacific.

Source and Additional Reading

Dupuy, Trevor N., Curt Johnson, and David L. Bongard. *The Harper Encyclopedia of Military Biography.* New York: HarperCollins, 1992.

Morison, Samuel Eliot. *History of the United States Naval Operations in World War II.* 15 Vols. Boston: Little, Brown, 1947–1962.

Nimitz, Chester W., and E. B. Potter. *Sea Power, a Naval History.* 2 vols. Annapolis, Md.: Naval Institute Press, 1960.

Potter, E. B. *Nimitz.* Annapolis, Md.: Naval Institute Press, 1976.

Norris, Gleason *Gunnery sergeant, United States Marine Corps.*

Marine Administrative Message 533/00 introduced the name of Gunnery Sergeant Gleason Norris to many Marines for the first time. This message provided a brief glimpse of what GySgt Norris did for his country, but that is only part of his story.

His Silver Star medal citation is a vivid rendering of the time that changed his life forever. These harrowing moments, however, capture only a snapshot in time.

Because award citations are brief by nature, they often beg other questions. What was this person like? Where did he come from? What became of him following this action? This is GySgt Norris' story.

The previous company gunnery sergeant for Company M, 3rd Battalion, 26th Marine Regiment was killed in action in early July 1967. Gunny Norris joined the unit as his replacement later that month.

Although the gunny had been with "Mike" Company only a short time, the word was out that you did not mess with him. His calm demeanor belied a no-nonsense presence.

While in garrison, the gunny was responsible for taking care of the sundry needs of the platoons as well as organizing "rear security." For this, he would set up an observation post on the road to their rear area. He also coordinated entertainment for the Marines, including an impromptu singing group known as the Songbirds.

Vietnam was, however, a long way from home. Home for Gunny Norris was the Tohono O'odham Indian reservation.

There are four distinct parts to the Tohono O'odham (pronounced Toe-Ho-No Ah-tomb) nation, with the largest portion located west of Tucson, Arizona.

Situated in the Sonoran Desert and spanning the frontier with Mexico, the Tohono O'odham reservation is the second largest in the country after the Navajo reservation. It is home to 17,340 people. Of this total, 6,570 reside in the capital of Sells.

Gunny Norris came from this background, received his general equivalency diploma in the Marine Corps and contributed 20 years of his life—including combat in both Korea and Vietnam. While the gunny left active ranks more than 30 years ago, his actions were never forgotten.

Following the action that would later earn for him the Silver Star, he returned to Camp Pendleton, California, and served out his 20 years. He was never able to hold an 0369, infantry unit leader billet again because of the severity of his wounds, retiring in 1970 with a 90% disability.

Lieutenant Colonel Andy De Bona—the Mike Company Commander and himself a recipient of the Navy Cross—last saw Gunny Norris on the day he was evacuated for his injuries. De Bona went to Sells to honor a fellow Marine and to close an unfinished chapter in his life.

This chapter, marked by the vagaries of missed opportunities, circumstances and the stubborn reality of law, contained a void: recognition for Gunny Norris' heroic actions on 10 September 1967.

On September 15, 2000, 33 years later, their paths crossed again, this time in the gymnasium at Baboquivari-Indian Oasis Middle School. Almost 1,500 people were present to celebrate one of their own and witness the end of a long journey.

They were also there to hear the reading of the Silver Star citation:

> For conspicuous gallantry and intrepidity in action, while serving as Company Gunnery Sergeant, Company M, Third Battalion (Reinforced), in connection with operations against the enemy in the Republic of Vietnam. On 10 September 1967, in the vicinity of Con Thien, Company M was assaulted by elements of an estimated North Vietnamese Army Regiment. During the enemy assault, a mortar round landed dangerously close to Gunnery Sergeant Norris, painfully wounding him. As the enemy human wave attack spilled around the flank of the platoon in front of Gunnery Sergeant Norris, he courageously moved among the elements of the Company Command Group repositioning Marines and directed their fire on the enemy forces. While

fearlessly exposing himself to a heavy volume of direct enemy fire, he was again painfully wounded by an enemy explosive device, and blown literally off his feet. This did not deter his valiant fighting spirit. With full knowledge of the risks involved, he continued to move up and down the line of Marines, shouting words of encouragement and firing his weapon while in full view of the enemy until wounded yet a third time. After being assisted to a med-evac zone, he took charge of the wounded and calmly integrated those Marines still able to fire a weapon into a defensive perimeter. Only after the threat of enemy ground attack had subsided did he permit medical personnel to attend to his numerous wounds. By his courage, bold initiative, and unwavering devotion to duty in the face of great personal danger, Gunnery Sergeant Norris reflected great credit upon himself and upheld the highest traditions of the Marine Corps and the United States Naval Service.

Source

Coleman, Capt. D. H., USMC. "American Indian Receives Silver Star." *Leatherneck: Magazine of the Marines.* May 2001, p.52.

Norton, John J. *Captain, United States Marine Corps, so distinguished himself while serving as commanding officer, Company E, Second Battalion, Fifth Marines, that he was awarded the Navy Cross for his heroic actions on April 21, 1968.*

Citation: "For extraordinary heroism while serving as Commanding Officer of Company E, Second Battalion, Fifth Marines, First Marine Division (Reinforced), in connection with operations against the enemy in the Republic of Vietnam. On the night of 21 April 1968, during Operation BAXTER GARDEN, the battalion commander was conducting a command and staff conference to review the day's actions and to make plans for the resumption of the attack the following morning. The meeting was held in the semidarkness of a small open area serving as the temporary battalion command post. As the meeting concluded, a trip wire attached to a hand grenade buried in the ground was accidentally pulled, activating the grenade. Instantly realizing the peril to the closely assembled group in the confined area, Captain Norton, completely ignoring the danger to his own life, unhesitatingly clutched the grenade to his chest, fell to the ground, and rolled on top of the grenade to shield other members of the command group from the expected blast. Lying motionless on the grenade, he calmly warned everyone to clear the area. When the device failed to detonate and engineers summoned to examine the grenade could not determine the exact condition of the firing device because of the position of Captain Norton's body on the grenade, he cleared the area of all personnel and courageously rolled away from the grenade. When the grenade failed to detonate, it was determined to have a faulty mechanism and was subsequently destroyed in place. By his courage, bold initiative, and selfless devotion to duty at the risk of his own life, Captain Norton upheld the highest traditions of the Marine Corps and the United States Naval Service."

Source and Additional Reading

Navy Cross Citation.

Stevens, Paul D., ed. *The Navy Cross: Vietnam: Citations of Awards to Men of the United States Marine Corps, 1964–1973*. Forest Ranch, Calif.: Sharp & Dunnigan, 1987.

Michael J. Novosel

Novosel, Michael J. *Chief warrant officer, United States Army, 82d Medical Detachment, 45th Medical Company, 68th Medical Group, so distinguished himself in aerial combat, during the Vietnam War, that he was awarded the Medal of Honor for his heroic actions.*

Born: September 3, 1922, Etna, Pa.; **Entered service at:** Kenner, La.; **Place and date:** Kien Tuong Province, Republic of Vietnam, October 2, 1969.

Citation: "For conspicuous gallantry and intrepidity in action at the risk of his life above and beyond the call of duty. CWO Novosel, 82d Medical Detachment, distinguished himself while serving as commander of a medical evacuation helicopter. He unhesitatingly maneuvered his helicopter into a heavily fortified and defended enemy training area where a group of wounded Vietnamese soldiers were pinned down by a large enemy force. Flying without gunship or other cover and exposed to intense machinegun fire, CWO Novosel was able to locate and rescue a wounded soldier. Since all communications with the beleaguered troops had been lost, he repeatedly circled the battle area, flying at low level under continuous heavy fire, to attract the attention of the scattered friendly troops. This display of courage visibly raised their morale, as they recognized this as a signal to assemble for evacuation. On 6 occasions he and his crew were forced out of the battle area by the intense enemy fire, only to circle and return from another direction to land and extract additional troops. Near the end of the mission, a wounded soldier was spotted close to an enemy bunker. Fully realizing that he would attract a hail of enemy fire, CWO Novosel nevertheless attempted the extraction by hovering the helicopter backward. As the man was pulled on board, enemy automatic weapons opened fire at close range, damaged the aircraft and wounded CWO Novosel. He momentarily lost control of the aircraft, but quickly recovered and departed under the withering enemy fire. In all, 15 extremely hazardous extractions were performed in order to remove wounded personnel. As a direct result of his selfless conduct, the lives of 29 soldiers were saved. The extraordinary heroism displayed by CWO Novosel was an inspiration to his comrades in arms and reflect great credit on him, his unit, and the U.S. Army."

Source

Medal of Honor Citation.

★ ★ ★ ★

O'Brien, George H., Jr. (b. 1926) *Second lieutenant, United States Marine Corps Reserve, Company H, Third Battalion, Seventh Marines, First Marine Division (Reinforced), so distinguished himself in combat during the Korean War that he was awarded the Medal of Honor for his heroic actions.*

Born: September 10, 1926, Fort Worth, Tex.; **Entered service at:** Big Spring, Tex.; **Place and date:** Korea, October 27, 1952.

Citation: "For conspicuous gallantry and intrepidity at the risk of his life above and beyond the call of duty as a rifle platoon commander of Company H, in action against enemy aggressor forces. With his platoon subjected to an intense mortar and artillery bombardment while preparing to assault a vitally important hill position on the main line of resistance, which had been overrun by a numerically superior enemy force on the preceding night, 2d Lt. O'Brien leaped from his trench when the attack signal was given and, shouting for his men to follow, raced across an exposed saddle and up the enemy-held hill through a virtual hail of deadly small-arms, artillery, and mortar fire. Although shot through the arm and thrown to the ground by hostile automatic-weapons fire as he neared the well-entrenched enemy position, he bravely regained his feet, waved his men onward, and continued to spearhead the assault, pausing only long enough to go to the aid of a wounded Marine. Encountering the enemy at close range, he proceeded to hurl handgrenades into the bunkers and, utilizing his carbine to best advantage in savage hand-to-hand combat, succeeded in killing at least 3 of the enemy. Struck down by the concussion of grenades on 3 occasions during the subsequent action, he steadfastly refused to be evacuated for medical treatment and continued to lead his platoon in the assault for a period of nearly 4 hours, repeatedly encouraging his men and maintaining superb

direction of the unit. With the attack halted he set up a defense with his remaining forces to prepare for a counterattack, personally checking each position, attending to the wounded and expediting their evacuation. When a relief of the position was effected by another unit, he remained to cover the withdrawal and to assure that no wounded were left behind. By his exceptionally daring and forceful leadership in the face of overwhelming odds, 2d Lt. O'Brien served as a constant source of inspiration to all who observed him and was greatly instrumental in the recapture of a strategic position on the main line of resistance. His indomitable determination and valiant fighting spirit reflect the highest credit upon himself and enhance the finest traditions of the U.S. Naval Service."

Source
Medal of Honor Citation.

O'Callahan, Joseph Timothy (b. 1904)
Commander (Chaplain Corps), United States Naval Reserve, U.S.S. Franklin, *so distinguished himself in combat, during World War II, that he was awarded the Medal of Honor for his heroic actions.*

Born: May 14, 1904, Boston, Mass.; **Entered service at:** Massachusetts; **Place and date:** Near Kobe, Japan, March 19, 1945.

Citation: "For conspicuous gallantry and intrepidity at the risk of his life above and beyond the call of duty while serving as chaplain on board the U.S.S. *Franklin* when that vessel was fiercely attacked by enemy Japanese aircraft during offensive operations near Kobe, Japan, on 19 March 1945. A valiant and forceful leader, calmly braving the perilous barriers of flame and twisted metal to aid his men and his ship, Lt. Comdr. O'Callahan groped his way through smoke-filled corridors to the open flight deck and into the midst of violently exploding bombs, shells, rockets, and other armament. With the ship rocked by incessant explosions, with debris and fragments raining down and fires raging in ever-increasing fury, he ministered to the wounded and dying, comforting and encouraging men of all faiths; he organized and led fire-fighting crews into the blazing inferno on the flight deck; he directed the jettisoning of live ammunition and the flooding of the magazine; he manned a hose to cool hot, armed bombs rolling dangerously on the listing deck, continuing his efforts, despite searing, suffocating smoke which forced men to fall back gasping and imperiled others who replaced them. Serving with courage, fortitude, and deep spiritual strength, Lt. Comdr. O'Callahan inspired the gallant officers and men of the U.S.S. *Franklin* to fight heroically and with profound faith in the face of almost certain death and to return their stricken ship to port."

Source
Medal of Honor Citation.

O'Hare, Edward Henry (b. 1914) *Lieutenant, United States Navy, so distinguished himself in combat, during World War II, that he was awarded the Medal of Honor for his heroic actions.*

Born: March 13, 1914, St. Louis, Mo.; **Entered service at:** St. Louis, Mo. **Other United States Navy awards:** Navy Cross, Distinguished Flying Cross with one Gold Star.

Citation: "For conspicuous gallantry and intrepidity in aerial combat, at grave risk of his life above and beyond the call of duty, as section leader and pilot of Fighting Squadron 3 on 20 February 1942. Having lost the assistance of his teammates, Lt. O'Hare interposed his plane between his ship and an advancing enemy formation of 9 attacking twin-engine heavy bombers. Without hesitation, alone and unaided, he repeatedly attacked this enemy formation, at close range in the face of intense combined machinegun and cannon fire. Despite this concentrated opposition, Lt. O'Hare, by his gallant and courageous action, his extremely skillful marksmanship in making the most of every shot of his limited amount of ammunition, shot down 5 enemy bombers and severely damaged a sixth before they reached the bomb release point. As a result of his gallant action—one of the most daring, if not the most daring, single action in the history of combat aviation—he undoubtedly saved his carrier from serious damage."

Source
Medal of Honor Citation.

O'Kane, Richard Hetherington (b. 1911)
Commander, United States Navy, commanding U.S.S. Tang, so distinguished himself in subsurface naval warfare, during World War II, that he was awarded the Medal of Honor for his heroic actions.

Born: February 2, 1911, Dover, N.H.; **Entered service at:** New Hampshire; **Place and date:** Vicinity Philippine Islands, October 23 and 24, 1944.

Citation: "For conspicuous gallantry and intrepidity at the risk of his life above and beyond the call of duty as commanding officer of the U.S.S. *Tang* operating against 2 enemy Japanese convoys on 23 and 24 October 1944, during her fifth and last war patrol. Boldly maneuvering on the surface into the midst of a heavily escorted convoy, Comdr. O'Kane stood in the fusillade of bullets and shells from all directions to launch smashing hits on 3 tankers, coolly swung his ship to fire at a freighter and, in a split-second decision, shot out of the path of an onrushing transport, missing it by inches. Boxed in by blazing tankers, a freighter, transport, and several destroyers, he blasted 2 of the targets with his remaining torpedoes and, with pyrotechnics bursting on all sides, cleared the area. Twenty-four hours later, he again made contact with a

Richard Hetherington O'Kane

heavily escorted convoy steaming to support the Leyte campaign with reinforcements and supplies and with crated planes piled high on each unit. In defiance of the enemy's relentless fire, he closed the concentration of ships and in quick succession sent 2 torpedoes each into the first and second transports and an adjacent tanker, finding his mark with each torpedo in a series of violent explosions at less than 1,000-yard range. With ships bearing down from all sides, he charged the enemy at high speed, exploding the tanker in a burst of flame, smashing the transport dead in the water, and blasting the destroyer with a mighty roar which rocked the *Tang* from stem to stern. Expending his last 2 torpedoes into the remnants of a once powerful convoy before his own ship went down, Comdr. O'Kane, aided by his gallant command, achieved an illustrious record of heroism in combat, enhancing the finest traditions of the U.S. Naval Service."

Source
Medal of Honor Citation.

O'Malley, Robert E. (b. 1943) *Sergeant (then Corporal), United States Marine Corps, Company One, Third Battalion, Third Marine Regiment, Third Marine Division (Reinforced), so distinguished himself in combat, during the Vietnam War, that he was awarded the Medal of Honor for his heroic action.*

Born: June 3, 1943, New York, N.Y.; **Entered service at:** New York, N.Y. **Place and date:** Near An Cu'ong 2, South Vietnam, 18 August 1965.

Citation: "For conspicuous gallantry and intrepidity in action against the communist (Viet Cong) forces at the risk of his life above and beyond the call of duty. While leading his squad in the assault against a strongly entrenched enemy force, his unit came under intense small-arms fire. With complete disregard for his personal safety, Sgt. O'Malley raced across an open rice paddy to a trench line where the enemy forces were located. Jumping into the trench, he attacked the Viet Cong with his rifle and grenades, and singly killed 8 of the enemy. He then led his squad to the assistance of an adjacent Marine unit that was suffering heavy casualties. Continuing to press forward, he reloaded his weapon and fired with telling effect into the enemy emplacement. He personally assisted in the evacuation of several wounded Marines, and again regrouping the remnants of his squad, he returned to the point of the heaviest fighting. Ordered to an evacuation point by an officer, Sgt. O'Malley gathered his besieged and badly wounded squad, and boldly led them under fire to a helicopter for withdrawal. Although 3 times wounded in this encounter, and facing imminent death from a fanatic and determined enemy, he steadfastly refused evac-

Robert E. O'Malley

uation and continued to cover his squad's boarding of the helicopters while, from an exposed position, he delivered fire against the enemy until his wounded men were evacuated. Only then, with his last mission accomplished, did he permit himself to be removed from the battlefield. By his valor, leadership, and courageous efforts in behalf of his comrades, he served as an inspiration to all who observed him, and reflected the highest credit upon the Marine Corps and the U.S. Naval Service."

Source
Medal of Honor Citation.

Ortiz, Peter Julien (d. 1988) *Major, United States Marine Corps, served with distinction in the Office of Strategic Services during World War II.*

When CBS NEWS covered the Winter Olympic Games in February 1992, viewers watching cross-country skiers in the French Alps were treated to a surprising story of how United States Marines won medals of a very different sort in those same mountains 48 years earlier. CBS's Charles Kuralt, standing by a jagged stone column as Olympic contestants skied past without a glance, translated the French inscription at its base: "In memory of American Sergeant Charles Perry, fallen on the field of honor in the act of parachuting."

Marine Corps exploits in the Pacific during World War II are legend. But until Kuralt related the story of UNION II, few Americans knew that Marines also fought and died in Europe. UNION II was the Office of Strategic Services (OSS) code name for a mission of the most dangerous kind: dropping a heavily armed elite team into the midst of the German army to train and lead French Resistance units.

There were six Marines on the mission: Maj. Peter Julien Ortiz, Gunnery Sergeant Robert La Salle, and Sergeants John Bodnar, Fred Brunner, Jack Risler, and Perry. Rounding out the team were Army Air Corps Cap. John Coolidge and Joseph Arcelin, a Free French officer carrying papers that identified him as Sergeant George Andrews, United States Marine Corps Reserve (USMCR). Although Arcelin could not speak French, it was thought palming him off as a Marine might be useful. The false papers later saved his life.

On August 1, 1944, Flying Fortresses from Knettershall Airfield in England swooped in over Les Sevoies, the French Alps, and dropped the eight men and 864 containers of weapons, ammunition, and other supplies for the Maquis, who were eager to fight but lacked the means. The B-17s swept across a drop zone so low that Risler remembers being able to see cowbells on the startled cows in the fields beneath him.

The men's parachutes were yanked open by cables attached to their plane. They did not wear backup parachutes; at that height there would have been no time to use them. Sergeant Perry fell to his death when his cable broke apart from the bomber. He was buried in the Catholic cemetery on the Col de Saisies in a grave hastily dug by the French, who decorated it with flowers and a wooden cross. The stone monument marking the spot where he fell was erected after the war.

The drop was Ortiz's second visit to the Haute Sevoie: He had parachuted onto Vecors plateau in early January, five months before D-Day, with an English agent named Thackwaite and a French radio operator who used the code name Monnier. These three composed the first UNION mission. He was then Captain Ortiz and used his command of German to acquire a Gestapo pass and steal German vehicles whenever he or his companions required transportation. While he was at it, he drove four downed Royal Air Force (RAF) flyers to the Spanish border and freedom.

The United States Marine Corps has produced any number of gutsy, sometimes unconventional fighting men,

but Peter Ortiz was something special. For one thing, he wasn't entirely a product of the corps. Born in New York of French parentage, he had been schooled in the United States and France, then enlisted in the Foreign Legion when he was 18. He distinguished himself in several clashes with the Berbers in North Africa, and the legion promoted him to acting lieutenant when he was 19.

At the end of his five-year hitch, Ortiz returned to his family in California. But when Hitler invaded Poland in 1939, and France went to war, he announced his intention to rejoin his old Foreign Legion outfit. No American ships were carrying passengers to France, so Ortiz had to sail from Canada. A U-boat almost ended his career when it torpedoed the vessel off the French coast. Ortiz declared that the sinking removed any doubts from his mind: "I now was mad enough to know I wanted to fight the Nazis."

Joining the 11th Regiment of the legion as a sergeant in October 1939, he had risen to first lieutenant by the time the regiment was overrun by numerically superior German forces two years later. Ortiz always took pride in the fact that the regiment had never surrendered and had fought on until it was engulfed. Severely wounded, Ortiz was patched up by German surgeons and, as soon as he felt well enough, began the escape attempts that caused him to be branded a dangerous prisoner. In October 1941, he made good his escape to Portugal.

Ortiz reached New York four days after the United States entered the war and tried to enlist, but wounds and prison fare had left him a wreck. He returned to La Jolla, California, and worked on building himself up until in June 1942 he had recovered sufficiently to pass the Marine Corps physical. Ortiz later remarked of time in boot camp at Parris Island, "It wasn't as hard as the Legion training."

The corps realized that here was a prize, and Ortiz was given parachute training and a reserve commission. Back in North Africa, this time in American uniform, he had a knowledge of Arabic that enabled him to hone what became his specialty: valuable, sometimes murderous one-man reconnaissance patrols in the enemy's camp. His greatest danger on these expeditions was not from the Germans but from the American army. First they nearly shot him; then, after taking him prisoner, they refused to believe that this "dirty Arab" was actually a United States Marine. It took some persuasion to get an army officer to check with headquarters, who confirmed his identity.

The mission in southern France followed. Ortiz and his Free French and British colleagues wore their military uniforms after landing to impress the Resistance that they represented an Allied military presence. OSS code named UNION, his unit's task was to assess the military potential and needs of the *Maquis* to disrupt German communications and mobility in the mountain region once the Allies invaded Fortress Europe and began moving inland. And what better way to access the *Maquis*'s fighting ability than by blowing up some bridges and carrying out a few raids and ambushes?

Ortiz often concealed his Marine captain's uniform under a voluminous artist's cape so he could roam village streets, drop in on local bistros, and eavesdrop on conversations, both French and German. By now UNION and Ortiz in particular were objects of massive German search efforts, whose repeated failures incensed the local command.

In one café, Ortiz listened as some Germans at a nearby table mentioned his name and discussed in detail what they would do if they ever had the "filthy American swine" in their presence. Ortiz had heard enough. He introduced himself as the villain they sought and opened his cape to reveal his Marine Corps uniform—and a .45 Colt in each hand. He killed the soldiers and left. Before a RAF plane pulled the team out in late May, UNION and Ortiz had made life in the Haute Savoie ever more precarious for its German garrison.

And now Ortiz, promoted to major, was back with a team of American Marines, ready to stir the pot some more. The 173-ton supply drop that arrived with them had alerted the Gestapo to the team's presence, and the Marines were forced to move fast to stay ahead of their pursuers.

The men of UNION II spent their first week training the local battalion of resistance fighters in the use and maintenance of their new weapons and mapping out places to strike. Then they sent out patrols to contact other resistance groups believed to be in the woods around the nearby city of Beaufort.

"On 14 August we proceeded to Beaufort where we made contact with other Forces *Francaises de l'Interieur* companies and from there went on to Montgirod where we were told there were heavy concentrations of Germans," Sergeant Brunner reported. "We were able to enter the town but had no sooner done so than we were heavily shelled by the German batteries located in the hills around the city. We were forced to retire and hid out in the mountains near Montgirod with the (maquis) Bulle Battalion. The Germans quickly surrounded the area."

The farmers of Montgirod had fed the Americans during their brief stay, and the Germans had strict rules about that. Entering the village the following day, the Gestapo found two wounded *Maquis* and executed them on the spot. Next they torched the village, burning every building to the ground. The Germans then took hostages and announced that they would be shot if the villagers sheltered Americans again.

Meanwhile, German troops kept the Marines under heavy fire, finally trapping them in neighboring woods. During the night, however, the team managed to elude the surrounding German lines and escape without a scratch. They crossed a highway bridge over the Isere River, passed through the village of Centron, and took up a position on the slope of the valley. Slipping from concealment, Ortiz went to reconnoiter another village, this one called Longefoy

"I contacted the mayor and requested food," he later wrote in his intelligence report. "He was understandably nervous at first, but as his confidence returned he and others became very hospitable. Food and drink were brought to us at our hideout."

After dark the Americans entered Longefoy and were loddged for the night. Refreshed, they moved on with the dawn. The mayor and inhabitants of the village had taken a very great risk. The Germans missed UNION II at Longefoy but caught up with the unit later that day.

Moving in single file at 50-yard intervals, with full field packs, the little group recrossed the Isere into Centron. They had just passed through the village and were coming up into the highway when a German motorized convoy came around a bend in the road and spotted the uniformed Americans. Soldiers poured out of the trucks and opened fire, while machine guns from the turrets of the armored cars joined in.

Sergeant Brunner and Army Captain Coolidge, in the rear of the column, managed to dive into the river and swim to safety, although Coolidge was wounded. Ortiz, Bodnar, Risler, and "Andrews" retreated into Centron and returned the fire. Risler took shelter in a ditch. It was so shallow his pack protruded and was a target; he undid his pack and slid out of it.

For the next couple of hours four men, fighting from house to house, held off an entire German battalion. If they could hold out until dusk, there was always a chance they might repeat their feat of two days ago and slip through the German net. But Ortiz remembered the hostages of Montgirod and feared similar reprisals against the residents of Centron. He decided to give himself up if he could exact a German promise to spare the villagers.

But first he told Bodnar and Risler to try to escape if they wished. Both made essentially the same reply: "Sir, we're Marines and we're sticking together." Bodnar added: "What you think is right goes for me, too."

Ortiz borrowed a sheet from one of the women, fastened it to a pole, and stepped out into German fire. Bullets chewed up the ground around him as he walked forward, waving his white flag and shouting in German, French, and English his willingness to surrender. Finally, the shooting stopped and he was able to parley with the battalion commander. Ortiz's terms were accepted: The village would be spared if he and his men gave themselves up.

But a hitch cropped up when only three other uniformed men came forward. The German officer was furious; he was convinced he had engaged a much larger enemy force. Finally he was calmed and even accepted the premise that the French-speaking "Sergeant Andrews" was an American of French descent. Had Arcelin's true identity been discovered, the Free French officer would have been shot.

Ortiz had been a difficult prisoner once before and this time was no different. Marine Lt. Colonel Robert E. Mattingly, who chronicled Ortiz's career for *Studies in Intelligence* in 1982, lists at least five attempted escapes by Ortiz before he finally succeeded. As Ortiz was driven away from Centron in a staff car, he tried to set the upholstery on fire with his cigarette lighter, reasoning that he might escape amid the smoke and confusion. That did not work.

Later, when the prisoners were taken to Bessoleno in Italy, his captors found 65,000 francs, a man, and a compass he had hidden on his person. He lost those, but when left alone for a few minutes in a locked office he swiftly searched it and filched more maps.

Another time, in a bus filled with Prisoners of War (POWs) being driven to a transit camp, Ortiz tried to rally the prisoners to rush the guards and take over the bus, but they refused. He never gave up, however, He tried to escape from a prison-bound railway train and had nearly twisted open his boxcar's barbed wire barrier when a guard discovered it.

Imprisoned at last in Marlag-Milag Nord in Westertimke, 17 miles from Bremen, Ortiz was told by the senior Allied POW that there were to be no efforts to escape. This attitude did not suit Oritz, who declared himself the senior American POW and made his own rule: Escape. He laboriously cut through a series of fences, only to be caught and taken back. These attempts invariably led to beatings, but nothing deterred him.

When 2d Lt. Walter L. Taylor, another Marine, who had been attached to the OSS and captured near Grasse, arrived at the camp, Ortiz recruited him in his escape plans. The two were industriously secreting food, maps, and clothes for their next attempt when the prisoners were formed into a column and forced to march north as the Germans retreated before the Allied advance. When RAF fighters strafed the column, however, Ortiz and Taylor, along with two others, fled into the woods and kept going.

For 10 days they remained in hiding, waiting for Allied soldiers to appear. When none did, the sick and starving quartet made their way back to Marlag. There they found other POWs who had hidden during the hasty evacuation, among them Bodnar, Risler, and Arcelin. The camp was liberated by British troops on April 29, 1945, after two days of fierce resistance by Waffen SS troops during which Arcelin was wounded.

As the POWs were being sent to the rear, the four Marines, Ortiz, Bodnar, Risler, and Taylor, went as a group to the British commander and tried to join his outfit.

"We Marines wanted to join this unit in order to bag a few more Germans" was the way Ortiz explained it. The request was denied; their war was over. And 10 days later, so was the war in Europe.

Ortiz came out of the conflict with a Navy Cross with a Gold Star in lieu of a second award, the Legion of Merit, and two Purple Hearts.

France made him a chevalier of the Legion d'Honneur and gave him the croix de guerre with palm, as well as the Ouissam Alouite and the Medaille Colonaile; Britain made him an officer of the Most Excellent Order of the British Empire.

After the war two movies used Ortiz's adventures in their plots: *13 Rue Madeleine,* with James Cagney, and *Operation Top Secret,* starring Cornel Wilde. Hollywood even used Colonel Ortiz as a technical adviser. He died in 1988.

Centron, today, is a thriving village, presided over by a white-haired mayor, Fernand Bal. As a child, he watched as three United States Marines and a Frenchman held off a German mechanized column there; it was his aunt who supplied the bedsheet Ortiz used as a truce flag.

"They surrendered to the Germans to save the village," Bal told Kuralt on the CBS newscast. "Otherwise, the village certainly would have been burned like Montgirod, with many victims—a lot of dead."

And he added, "On the one hand, the townspeople were happy Ortiz surrendered to save the village. On the other hand, they were very sad to see this wonderful officer give himself up."

But the hero of the Haute Savoie is not forgotten. On the wall of the office of Centron's mayor hangs a plaque inscribed, "In memory of the passage of Commander Ortiz and his Valiant Companions, 16th of August, 1944."

Source

O'Neill, William J. "The Derring-Do of Peter Ortiz." *Marine Corps League Magazine* vol. 48, no. 3 (Autumn 1992): 22–26.

Osceola (Billy Powell) (1804–1838) *Seminole leader.*

Born in a Creek village in Alabama (1804), Osceola had a father who was an Englishman and a mother who was a Creek. He moved with his mother to an Upper Creek village in Florida in 1812. At the age of 14 he and his mother were captured by United States troops during the First Seminole War (1817–18). Released from captivity that same year, he settled in a Seminole village near Tampa Bay. With two wives Osceola moved to an island reservation established in the Moultrie Creek Treaty of 1823. He then became a minor chief and was among a group of Seminole chiefs who resisted the Removal Bill of 1830 and the Treaty of Paynes Landing, which was used to impose the removal of Seminoles for specific areas of Florida. He was arrested on the orders of United States Indian Agent Wiley Thompson for his refusal to sign a removal agreement in 1835. After spending five days in jail Osceola signed an agreement and was released. He then renounced the paper and entered into a pact with other Seminole chiefs to resist relocation. In the Wahoo Swamp of the Withlacoochie River, Osceola's war party ambushed 150 U.S. regular troops under the command of Major Francis Dade, killing all but three men (December 28, 1835). This began the Second Seminole War. An 800-man force commanded by Gen. Duncan Lamon Clinch then pursued Osceola. Wounded in a later engagement, Osceola fled with a small group of followers into the swamp, where he continued to use hit-and-run tactics against government troops. After heavy losses, the Seminole chiefs Micanopy, Jumper, and Alligator concluded an armistice in January 1837. Osceola turned himself in to authorities at Fort Mellon, near Lake Monroe, in May 1837. He then fled back into the safety of the swamps after U.S. troops allowed slavers to enter Florida and seize blacks and Seminoles.

Brigadier General Joseph Hernandez finally captured Osceola during negotiations, on orders from Gen. Thomas S. Jessup. He was imprisoned at Fort Marion, near St. Augustine, and then moved to Fort Moultrie, South Carolina, where he died of malaria, on January 30, 1838.

Source and Additional Reading

Dupuy, Trevor N., Curt Johnson, and David L. Bongard. *The Harper Encyclopedia of Military Biography.* New York: HarperCollins, 1992.

Mahor, John K. *History of the Second Seminole War.* Gainesville: University of Florida Press, 1967.

McReynolds, Edwin C. *The Seminoles.* Norman: University of Oklahoma Press, 1957.

Ouellet, David George Seman (1944–1967) *SN, United States Navy, so distinguished himself in combat, during the Vietnam War, that he was awarded the Medal of Honor for his heroic actions.*

Born: June 13, 1944, Newton, Mass.; **Entered service at:** Boston, Mass.; **Place and date:** Mekong River, Republic of Vietnam, March 6, 1967.

David George Ouellet was born to Chester J. and Elizabeth E. Ouellet. He graduated from Hardy School, Wellesley, Massachusetts, in 1958; attended Wellesley Junior High School; and subsequently was employed by the Alfred Fisher Trucking Company in Wellesley. On July 28, 1964, he enlisted in the United States Navy and had recruit training at the Naval Training Center, Great Lakes, Illinois. Completing his training in October 1964, he joined Assault Craft Division 12 and while attached to that division served for five months in 1965 in the Vietnam era. Between June and August 1966 he had river patrol boat training at the Naval Schools Command, Vallejo, California, after which he had training at the Naval Amphibious Base, Coronado, California. On September 21, 1966, he reported for duty with River Squadron Five and was attached to River Section 532, My Tho.

Citation: "For conspicuous gallantry and intrepidity at the risk of his life above and beyond the call of duty. As the forward machine gunner on River Patrol Boat (PBR) 124, which was on patrol during the early evening hours, SN Ouellet observed suspicious activity near the river bank, alerted his boat captain, and recommended movement of the boat to the area to investigate. While the PBR was making a high-speed run along the riverbank, Seaman Ouellet spotted an incoming enemy grenade falling toward the boat. He immediately left the protected position of his gun mount and ran for the full length of the speeding boat, shouting to his fellow crewmembers to take cover. Observing the boat captain standing unprotected on the boat, SN Ouellet bounded on to the engine compartment cover, and pushed the boat captain down to safety. In the split second that followed the grenade's landing, and in the face of certain death, SN Ouellet fearlessly placed himself between the deadly missile and his shipmates, courageously absorbing most of the blast fragments with his body in order to protect his shipmates from injury and death. His extraordinary heroism and his selfless and courageous actions on behalf of his comrades at the expense of his life were in the finest traditions of the U.S. Naval Service."

In recognition of his bravery, the United States Navy posthumously awarded Ouellet the Medal of Honor and the Purple Heart (for wounds received in enemy action) and later named a frigate (FF 1077) after him.

Source
Medal of Honor Citation.

P

Paige, Mitchell *Platoon sergeant, United States Marine Corps, so distinguished himself in combat, during World War II, that he was awarded the Medal of Honor for his heroic actions.*

"That night, twenty-four-year-old Platoon Sgt. Mitchell Paige from Charlerio, Pennsylvania, won a battlefield commission and became the second enlisted Marine to receive the Medal of Honor in World War II. Paige commanded a machine-gun section in a saddle between E and F Companies (2d Battalion, 7th Marines). In the darkness and pelting rain, the Japanese stormed the Marines' position; and they battled hand-to-hand until Paige's men were killed or wounded. Alone, the sergeant fought the gun, killed the oncoming soldiers; and when the gun was destroyed, he moved to his right and brought back another gun and a few riflemen. They opened fire. As dawn came, Paige saw Japanese crawling to an unattended gun; he raced them to it, while the enemy concentrated their fire on him. He won. Three Marines started to bring him belts of ammunition; each in turn was hit. Paige would fire a burst and then move; grenades would hit where he had been. He would fire again. He threw two ammo belts around his shoulders, picked up the hot machine gun and led the riflemen he had collected down the ridge, their bayonets fixed, whooping like Indians. The enemy melted away. And then all was quiet. The battle was over. Paige's arms were blistered from fingertips to elbows. There were more than 100 Japanese bodies in front of his sector. That was the end of the enemy's strongest effort to recapture Henderson Field. Bulldozers shoved 2,000 Japanese corpses into mass graves (Moskin)."

Citation: "For extraordinary heroism and conspicuous gallantry in action above and beyond the call of duty while serving with a company of Marines in combat against enemy Japanese forces in the Solomon Islands on 26 October 1942. When the enemy broke through the line directly in front of his position, P/Sgt. Paige, commanding a machinegun section with fearless determination, continued to direct the fire of his gunners until all his men were either killed or wounded. Alone, against the deadly hail of Japanese shells, he fought with his gun and when it was destroyed, took over another, moving from gun to gun, never ceasing his withering fire against the advancing hordes until reinforcements finally arrived. Then, forming a new line, he dauntlessly and aggressively led a bayonet charge, driving the enemy back and preventing a breakthrough in our lines. His great personal valor and unyielding devotion to duty were in keeping with the highest traditions of the U.S. Naval Service."

Source and Additional Reading
Medal of Honor Citation.
Blakeney, Jane. *Heroes: U.S. Marine Corps 1861–1955.* Washington, D.C.: Guthrie Lithographic, 1956.
Moskin, J. Robert. *The U.S. Marine Corps Story.* New York: McGraw-Hill, 1987.

Patton, George Smith, Jr. (1885–1945) *General, United States Army, tank commander whose bold armored advance across France and Germany in 1944 and 1945 made a significant contribution to Allied victory in World War II.*

George Patton was born in San Gabriel, California, on November 11, 1885, into a family with a long tradition of military service. He attended the Virginia Military Institute and graduated from the United States Military Academy in 1909, when he was commissioned a second lieutenant in the 15th Cavalry. He graduated from the Mounted Service School, Fort Riley, Kansas, in 1913 and a year later from the Advanced Course at the Cavalry School, Fort Riley. In 1916 he went as acting aide to Gen. John J. Pershing in the Mexican expedition, and in 1917 Pershing took him to France as commander of his headquarters troops.

In November 1917, Patton was one of the first men detailed to the newly established Tank Corps of the United States Army and was assigned the task of organizing and training the First Tank Brigade near Langres, France. He led this unit in the St. Mihiel drive in mid-September 1918 and was wounded later in the month at the opening of the Meuse-Argonne offensive. He was awarded the Distinguished Service Cross and the Distinguished Service Medal and promoted temporarily to the rank of colonel.

Between the two world wars Patton graduated from the Command and General Staff School in 1924 and from the Army War College in 1932. His assignments during this period included two tours in Hawaii; a tour in the office of the chief of cavalry, War Department; and three tours with the Third Cavalry at Fort Myer, Virginia.

In July 1940, Patton was appointed to the command of a brigade of the Second Armored Division at Fort Benning, Georgia. Less than a year later he was given command of the division and promoted temporarily to the rank of major general. Early in 1942 he became commander of the First Armored Corps, which he trained at the Desert Training Center, near Indio, California. Patton played a leading role in the Allied invasion of North Africa in November 1942, commanding the ground elements of the western task forces that entered Casablanca and soon occupied French Morocco. When in March 1943 the United States Second Corps in Tunisia was reorganized after an earlier rebuff at Kasserine Pass by General Erwin Rommel's forces, Patton became its commander. Within a month he was promoted temporarily to the rank of lieutenant general and put in charge of American preparations for the invasion of Sicily. On July 10 he commanded the United States Seventh Army in its assault on that island. In conjunction with the British Eighth Army, he cleared Sicily of the enemy in 38 days. His victory was marred by an incident in which he struck an army hospital patient being treated for shell shock, an action for which he later made a public apology.

In March 1944, Patton assumed command of the Third Army in Britain and began to plan future operations in northwestern Europe. Shortly before the invasion Gen. Dwight D. Eisenhower reprimanded him for indiscreet political statements. On August 1 his army became operational in France, and he began the exploitation of the breakthrough near Avranches made by the First Army a few days before. He thrust one corps westward into Brittany toward Brest, while his other three corps pushed southward toward the Loire and then swung eastward in a series of broad sweeps toward the Seine. In one of the most spectacular actions of the campaign in northern France, he drove toward Paris, bypassed it, and reached the area near Metz and Nancy before being stopped by dwindling supplies and stiffening enemy resistance.

While Patton was preparing an attack eastward into the Saar area, in conjunction with the Seventh Army, the Germans launched their Ardennes counteroffensive of December 16. In an action characterized by Gen. Omar N. Bradley as "one of the most astonishing feats of generalship of our campaign in the west," Patton turned his forces quickly northward against the southern flank of the bulge and helped contain the enemy.

By the end of January 1945, the Third Army was ready to drive against the Siegfried Line between Saarlautern (now Saarlouis) north to St. Vith. Patton's four corps had pierced these defenses by the end of February and by mid-March had pushed forward through the Eifel to gain control of the Moselle from the Saar River to Coblenz and of the Rhine from Andernach to Coblenz. In the following week his forces raced through the Palatinate region to the Rhine south of Coblenz. On the evening of March 22–23, units crossed the river near Oppenheim; Frankfurt am Main fell three days later. By the third week in April his forces had driven across southern Germany to the Czechoslovak border, and some of his units were in Austria before the month's end. During the first week in May, Third Army columns pushed into Czechoslovakia, and Plze (Pilsen) was freed just before the armistice.

Patton was promoted to temporary four-star rank in mid-April. Shortly after the end of the war he began his duties as military governor of Bavaria. His outspoken criticisms of denazification policies led to an outcry in the United States, followed in October 1945 by his relief as Third Army commander and assignment to the 15th Army, then a small headquarters engaged in studying military operations in northwestern Europe. Near the end of the year Patton was seriously injured in an automobile accident near Mannheim. He died in a nearby hospital in Heidelberg on December 21, 1945.

Profane, impetuous, and flamboyant, Patton was easily the most colorful of the United States Army's commanders in the west, and its leading genius in tank warfare. Behind his showmanship and audacity lay the imaginative planning and shrewd judgment that made him one of the great combat commanders of World War II.

Sources and Additional Reading

Blumenson, Martin, ed. *The Patton Papers*. 2 Vols. Boston: Houghton Mifflin, 1974.

Blumenson, Martin. *Patton: The Man behind the Legend.* New York: Morrow, 1985.

Farago, Ladislas. *The Last Days of Patton.* New York: McGraw-Hill, 1981.

Patton, George S. Jr. *War as I Knew It.* Boston: Houghton Mifflin, 1947.

Pogue, Forrest C. *U.S. Army in World War II: European Theater of Operations: The Supreme Command Bibliography.* Washington, D.C.: Dept. of the Army; 1954.

Pelham, John (1838–1863) *Major, Confederate States Army.*

Although "The Gallant Pelham" served the entire war with the artillery, he was destined to fall while moonlighting in a cavalry charge. A native of Alabama, he withdrew from West Point on the outbreak of hostilities and joined the Confederate army. His assignments included the following: lieutenant, Wise (Virginia) Artillery (early 1861); captain, Stuart Horse Artillery (March 23, 1862); major, Artillery (August 9, 1862); lieutenant colonel, Artillery (April 4, 1863, to rank from March 2); and commander, Horse Artillery Battalion, Cavalry Division, Army of Northern Virginia (August 1862–March 17, 1863).

After fighting at First Bull Run, he became the captain of the first horse artillery battery that served with J. E. B. Stuart, becoming close friends with the general. Commanding his unit, he saw action at Yorktown and during the Seven Days. Promoted, he commanded all of Stuart's horse batteries at Second Bull Run and Antietam. At Fredericksburg he held up the advance of a Union division against the Confederate right with only two guns. With only one gun left, he continued to shift positions despite the fact that 24 enemy guns were now concentrating their fire on him. Disobeying repeated orders to withdraw, he only did so on running out of ammunition. General Lee, who had observed the action, said, "It is glorious to see such courage in one so young!"

Known as the "Boy Major," Pelham heard of an impending action at Kelly's Ford on March 17, 1863. Away from his battalion at the time, he joined the fray with the cavalry. He fell victim to a shell fragment while directing a column past a fence. Thought to be dead, he was thrown over a horse and led from the field. Quite a while later he was lowered to the ground and found to be still alive. He died shortly thereafter. Some believed that prompt attention might have saved his life.

Source
Hassler, William Woods. *Colonel John Pelham, Lee's Boy Artillerist.* Richmond, Va.: Garrett and Massie, 1957.

Perez, Manuel, Jr. (1923–1945) *Private first class, United States Army, Company A, 511th Parachute Infantry, 11th Airborne Division, so distinguished himself in combat, during World War II, that he was awarded (posthumously) the Medal of Honor for his heroic actions.*

Born: March 3, 1923, Oklahoma City, Okla.; **Entered service at:** Chicago, Ill.; **Place and date:** Fort William McKinley, Luzon, Philippine Islands, February 13, 1945. **G.O. No.:** 124, December 27, 1945.

Citation: "He was lead scout for Company A, which had destroyed 11 of 12 pillboxes in a strongly fortified sector defending the approach to enemy-held Fort William McKinley on Luzon, Philippine Islands. In the reduction of these pillboxes, he killed 5 Japanese in the open and blasted others in pillboxes with grenades. Realizing the urgent need for taking the last emplacement, which contained 2 twin-mount .50-caliber dual-purpose machine guns, he took a circuitous route to within 20 yards of the position, killing 4 of the enemy in his advance. He threw a grenade into the pillbox, and, as the crew started withdrawing through a tunnel just to the rear of the emplacement, shot and killed 4 before exhausting his clip. He had reloaded and killed 4 more when an escaping Japanese threw his rifle with fixed bayonet at him. In warding off this thrust, his own rifle was knocked to the ground. Seizing the Jap rifle, he continued firing, killing 2 more of the enemy. He rushed the remaining Japanese, killed 3 of them with the butt of the rifle and entered the pillbox, where he bayoneted the 1 surviving hostile soldier. Singlehandedly, he killed 18 of the enemy in neutralizing the position that had held up the advance of his entire company. Through his courageous determination and heroic disregard of grave danger, Pfc. Perez made possible the successful advance of his unit toward a valuable objective and provided a lasting inspiration for his comrades."

Source
Medal of Honor Citation.

Perry, Oliver Hazard *Admiral, United States Navy, War of 1812.*

Born in South Kingston, Rhode Island, Perry became a lieutenant (1807) and commanded coastal gunboats (1807–09) and the USS *Revenge* on the south Atlantic coast (1809–11). Promoted to master commandant (1812), he went to Presque Isle (now Erie), Pennsylvania, to build an American fleet for use on Lake Erie during the War of 1812. Leading the fleet against the British fleet in September 1813, he won the battle (although he had to transfer his flag from the USS *Lawrence* to the USS *Niagara*) and sent a famous message to Gen. William Henry

Harrison, "We have met the enemy and they are ours." He transported Harrison's army across Lake Erie and led a cavalry charge at the Battle of the Thames. After the war he commanded a squadron sent to Venezuela (1819), where he died of yellow fever. His remains were taken to Newport, Rhode Island, in 1826.

Source
United States Naval Historical Center.

Pershing, John Joseph ("Black Jack") (1860–1948)
Commander of the American Expeditionary Forces (AEF) in World War I.

After his graduation from the United States Military Academy in 1886 Pershing served in the cavalry in the West. He received a law degree from the University of Nebraska and joined (1896) the staff at army headquarters in Washington, D.C. He returned to West Point in 1897 as a member of the tactical staff. During the Spanish-American War, Pershing distinguished himself at Kettle and San Juan Hills; he later served as head of the War Department's new Division of Customs and Insular Affairs. He went in 1899 to the Philippines, where he led a series of important expeditions among the hostile Moros.

In 1905 he became military attaché in Tokyo and then went to Manchuria as an observer of the Russo-Japanese War. In 1906, President Theodore Roosevelt elevated Pershing in rank from captain to brigadier general. Pershing took command of Fort McKinley near Manila and then became (1909) governor of Moro province in the southern Philippines, thoroughly defeating the Moros by 1913.

Given command of the Eighth Brigade in 1914, he led (1916–17) the difficult punitive expedition against Pancho Villa in Mexico. Experience and seniority gave him command of the AEF in 1917. Pershing's tasks in France during World War I were more managerial than warlike: he had to organize, train, and supply an inexperienced force that eventually numbered more than 2 million. Constantly rebuffing British and French efforts to siphon off his men into their depleted ranks, Pershing found himself waging two wars, against the Germans and against the Allies. AEF successes in the war were largely credited to Pershing, and he emerged from it the most celebrated American hero.

Congress created for him a new rank, general of the armies. His memoir, *My Experiences in the World War,* won him the 1932 Pulitzer Prize in history.

Source and Additional Reading

Braddy, Haldeen. *Pershing's Mission in Mexico.* Reprint, El Paso, Tex.: Western Press, 1966.
Cooke, James. *Pershing and His Generals: Command and Staff in the AEF.* Westport, Conn.: Praeger, 1997.
Goldhurst, Richard. *Pipe Clay and Drill: John J. Pershing: The Classic American Soldier.* New York, Reader's Digest Press, 1977.
Mason, Herbert Malloy, Jr. *The Great Pursuit: Pershing's Expedition to Destroy Pancho Villa.* New York: Random House, 1970.
Palmer, Frederick. *John J. Pershing, General of the Armies: A Biography.* 1948. Reprint Temeculo, Calif.: Reprint Services Corp., 1993.
Smith, Gene. *Until the Last Trumpet Sounds: The Life of General of the Armies John J. Pershing.* New York: Wiley, 1999.
Vandiver, Frank E. *Black Jack. The Life and Times of John J. Pershing* 2 Vols. College Station, Tex.: Texas A&M University Press, 1977.

Peters, George J. *Private, United States Army, Company G, 507th Parachute Infantry, 17th Airborne Division, so distinguished himself in combat, during World War II, that he was awarded (posthumously) the Medal of Honor for his heroic actions.*

Born: Cranston, R.I.; **Entered service at:** Cranston, R.I.; **Place and date:** Near Fluren, Germany, March 24, 1945. **G.O. No.:** 16, February 8, 1946.

Citation: "Pvt. Peters, a platoon radio operator with Company G, made a descent into Germany near Fluren, east of the Rhine. With 10 others, he landed in a field about 75 yards from a German machinegun supported by riflemen, and was immediately pinned down by heavy, direct fire. The position of the small unit seemed hopeless with men struggling to free themselves of their parachutes in a hail of bullets that cut them off from their nearby equipment bundles, when Pvt. Peters stood up without orders and began a l-man charge against the hostile emplacement armed only with a rifle and grenades. His single-handed assault immediately drew the enemy fire away from his comrades. He had run halfway to his objective, pitting rifle fire against that of the machinegun, when he was struck and knocked to the ground by a burst. Heroically, he regained his feet and struggled onward. Once more he was torn by bullets, and this time he was unable to rise. With gallant devotion to his self-imposed mission, he crawled directly into the fire that had mortally wounded him until close enough to hurl grenades which knocked out the machinegun, killed 2 of its operators, and drove protecting riflemen from their positions into the safety of a woods. By his intrepidity and supreme sacrifice, Pvt. Peters saved the lives of many of his fellow soldiers and made it possible for them to reach their equipment, organize, and seize their first objective."

Source
Medal of Honor Citation.

Pettigrew, James Johnston (1828–1863) *General officer, Confederate States Army.*

Lacking combat experience, J. Johnston Pettigrew was loath to accept a brigadier generalship and actually sent the commission back to the Confederate War Department. The North Carolinian had taught at the Washington Naval Observatory and studied law in the United States and Germany. Practicing in Charleston, he was involved in the militia and became an officer.

His military assignments included the following: colonel, First South Carolina Rifles (November 1860); private, Hampton (South Carolina) Legion (1861); colonel, 12th North Carolina Volunteers (July 11, 1861); colonel, 22nd North Carolina (designation change on November 14, 1861); brigadier general, Confederate States Army (CSA) (February 26, 1862); commander, French's (old) brigade, Aquia District, Department of Northern Virginia (March 12–mid-April 1862); commander of brigade, Whiting's–G. W. Smith's division, Department of Northern Virginia (April–May 31, 1862); commander, Martin's (old) brigade, Department of North Carolina (September 1862–February and April 1–May, 1863); commander of brigade, Hill's command, Department of Virginia and North Carolina (February–April 1, 1863); commander of brigade, Heth's division, Third Corps, Army of Northern Virginia (May 30–July 1 and July 14, 1863); and commander of division (July 1–mid-July 1863).

After commanding his rifles at Fort Sumter, he went to Virginia as a private but was appointed to the colonelcy of the North Carolina regiment before First Bull Run. He served that winter in the Fredericksburg area and the next spring moved to the Peninsula. After the Yorktown siege he was wounded and captured at Seven Pines. Exchanged in late August 1862, he commanded a brigade in southern Virginia and North Carolina until May 1863, when it was ordered to Lee's army. At Gettysburg he succeeded the wounded Herb in charge of the division and led it in Pickett's Charge two days later. During the retreat he was mortally wounded on July 14 at Falling Waters while commanding his brigade. Carried back to Virginia, he died three days later.

Source
Freeman, Douglas S. *Lee's Lieutenants*. 3 Vols. 1942–44.

Pickett, George Edward (1825–1875) *General officer, Confederate States Army. Born in Richmond, Virginia, on January 28, 1825, Pickett graduated last in a class of 59 from West Point in 1846. Among his several classmates who became generals were George B. McClellan and Thomas J. Jackson. In the war with Mexico Pickett was brevetted lieutenant and captain for his service in the Siege of Vera Cruz and during the subsequent advance on Mexico City. He served in Texas, Virginia, and Washington Territory until 1861, when he resigned his commission to enter the Confederate army.*

First a colonel, then a brigadier general (as of January 14, 1862), he served under Major General James Longstreet during the Seven Days Campaign and was wounded at Gaines' Mill. As a major general (October 10, 1862) commanding a division, he was at Fredericksburg.

His name in Civil War history was secured in a losing cause, the charge against the federal center on the third day at Gettysburg. After bloody but inconclusive movements July 1–2, Lee ordered the massive assault, which followed an intensive but basically ineffectual cannonade. Under Pickett's immediate command were the brigades of Brig. Gens. James L. Kemper, Richard B. Garnett, and Lewis A. Armistead. According to reports, Pickett was in excellent spirits and expected to carry the Union defenses. At midafternoon the forward movement began with the troops dressed as if on parade as they marched into the federal guns. Pickett, as division commander, attempted to coordinate the ill-fated movement and, contrary to the view of some critics, acquitted himself bravely and well. But the task was impossible, and he ordered his men to withdraw when clearly they could not break the Union center.

Notwithstanding the bravery of his troops and his own efforts on the field, Pickett's military reputation was afterward in decline. He fought in battles at New Berne, Petersburg, and Five Forks. General R. E. Lee relieved him of his command after Sayler's Creek, only days before the final surrender at Appomattox. After the war Pickett worked as an insurance salesman in Richmond; he died in Norfolk on July 30, 1875.

Source
Longarce, Edward G. *Leader of the Charge.* Shippensburg, PA, 1998.

Pitcher, Molly (Mary Hays McCauly) (1753–1832) *Revolutionary War heroine of the Battle of Monmouth Court House.*

During the American Revolution, Mary's McCauly's husband, who was a member of the First Pennsylvania Artillery, fought at the Battle of Monmouth Court House on June 28, 1778. Mary (Molly), who had accompanied him onto the battlefield, carried water in a pitcher to her husband and others, earning the nickname "Molly Pitcher." With the temperature close to 100 degrees, she carried water to her husband's battery. When her husband collapsed, wounded or overcome by the heat, she took his place in the gun crew and continued firing his cannon.

Joseph Plumb Martin of Connecticut saw her in action. In his war memoir he wrote:

> While in the act of reaching for a cartridge, a cannon shot from the enemy passed directly between her legs without doing any other damage than carrying away all the lower part of her petticoat. Looking at it with apparent unconcern she observed that it was lucky it did not pass a little higher, for in that case it might have carried away something else.

According to one version of the story, Mary was presented to General George Washington after the battle, and he praised her courage. For decades American artillerymen offered a toast to Mary: "Drunk in a beverage richer and stronger than was poured that day from Molly Pitcher's pitcher."

For many years it was believed she was born Mary Ludwig and that she had married John Casper Hayes in Carlisle, Pennsylvania. Her identification with Mary Ludwig was later challenged in favor of another Mary, who married William Hays.

Pitcher was named for the thousands of water pitchers she carried to the troops during the battle. After her husband's death in 1789, she married George MacCauly. In 1822 the Pennsylvania legislature passed an act "for the relief of Molly McCauly, for her services during the revolutionary war." She was awarded $40, and the same amount was to be paid to her annually during her lifetime. She died in Carlisle on January 22, 1832, and is buried beside the Molly Pitcher monument in Carlisle, Pennsylvania.

Sources and Additional Reading

Fleming, Thomas. *Liberty! The American Revolution*. New York: Viking Penguin, 1997.

McKenney, Janice E. *"Women in Combat: Comment," Armed Forces in Society* 8, no. 4 (Summer 1982): 686–692.

Pollock, Edwin ("Cootie") (1899–1989) *General, United States Marine Corps.*

Born in 1899, Edwin "Cootie" Pollock began his military career attending Staunton Military Academy, before entering the Citadel in 1917. Having served all four of his cadet years on the old Citadel grounds, in Charleston, next to Francis Marion Square, he graduated in 1921. He earned the college's Star of the West Medal, signifying that he was the "best-drilled" cadet on campus.

While he was attending the Citadel, the school offered no internal Navy/Marine Corps Commissioning program, prompting Pollock to pursue a commission through a Marine Corps Platoon Leader's Course (PLC) type of commissioning program. As a young Marine officer, Pollock served a variety of tours, including combat in Nicaragua under the future Raider commander Merritt "Red Mike" Edson. However, it was not until World War II that Pollock would achieve his greatest feats of combat leadership.

As commanding officer, Second Battalion, First Marine Regiment, under Lt. Gen. Alexander A. Vandergrift during Operation WATCHTOWER, Pollock with his Marines would find himself in fierce combat against the Japanese. Pollock and his fellow officers shared every hardship with their Marines in the steamy jungles of Guadalcanal, and he found himself in close combat on more than one occasion. At one point, a Japanese soldier, pistol drawn, leaped at Pollock. The soldier fired directly at Pollock at point blank range, but his weapon failed to discharge. Evidently discouraged, the enemy soldier turned the weapon back on himself and fired—this time, successfully.

Lieutenant Colonel Pollock's greatest moment occurred on August 20, 1942, during the defense of Henderson Field on Guadalcanal. Having engaged and killed 900 Japanese infantrymen, under the command of Colonel Kiyano Ichiki, at Alligator Creek on the Tenaru River, Pollock and his depleted force of Marines displayed tremendous courage and tenacity under fire. The Japanese threatened to breach his lines on several occasions and at one point crossed the Tenaru River and set up a machine gun position in an abandoned Marine Amtrak. Pollock supervised the battle from just a few yards behind his firing line, always remaining calm and inspiring his men. During several days of constant battle, including several nighttime engagements, Pollock's Marines repulsed every Japanese assault, wiping out Colonel Ichiki's crack shock troops. After the conclusion of the Guadalcanal Campaign, Pollock was awarded the Navy Cross for his heroism, as well as the Legion of Merit and the Bronze Star, both with the Combat V devices.

General Pollock's distinguished military career continued, and during the postwar period he proved to be an ardent supporter of a revolutionary new doctrine involving the primary use of helicopters, known as the vertical envelopment. As a brigadier general, he commanded the First Marine Division in Korea from 1952 to 1953, for which he received the Korean Order of Military Merit of Taiguk. After the war, he served as commanding general of Marine Corps Recruit Depot, Parris Island, and Marine Corps Base, Quantico, Virginia. He is the only Marine to have commanded both Fleet Marine Forces, Atlantic and Pacific.

After his promotion to general and subsequent retirement in 1959, General Pollock returned to the Citadel and served the school that he credited with having given him his leadership skills. He served as chairman of the Board of Visitors from 1965 to 1968 and was granted the title of chairman emeritus until his death in 1989.

Today, General Pollock's portrait hangs in a place of honor with those of his classmates in the Daniel Library.

Source and Additional Reading

Frank, Richard B. *Guadalcanal*. New York: Random House, 1990.

Marine Corps Historical Center.

Whittle, Frank. "The Citadel Marine." Unpublished work, 1980.

Pope, John (1822–1892) *Union General officer.*

The only army commander operating against the Army of Northern Virginia to earn the personal animosity of Robert E. Lee was John Pope. The Kentucky native had spent his entire career in the military service. Receiving an appointment to West Point from Illinois, he was graduated in 1842 and was posted to the Topographical Engineers. Performing creditably, he was considered a top soldier. The Mexican War earned him two brevets and he continued to rise regularly in rank.

His Civil War–era assignments, which were somewhat less happy, included the following: captain, Topographical Engineers (from July 1, 1856); brigadier general, United States Volunteers (USV) (June 14, 1861, to rank from May 17); commander, District of North Missouri, Western Department (July 29–October 1861); commander, Second Division, Army of Southwest Missouri, Western Department (October–November 9, 1861); commander, Second Division, Army of Southwest Missouri, Department of the Missouri (November 9–December 1861); commander, District of Central Missouri, Department of the Missouri (December 1861–February 18, 1862); commander, Army of the Mississippi (February 23–June 26, 1862); major general, USV (March 21, 1862); commander, Army of Virginia (June 26–September 2 1862); brigadier general, USA (July 14, 1862); and commander, Department of the Northwest (September 16–November 28, 1862, and February 13, 1863–February 13, 1865).

Having served in the escort of Lincoln to the Washington inaugural ceremonies, Pope was named to be a brigadier of volunteers and performed organizational duties in Illinois before serving under Fremont in the Western Department. His capabilities having been displayed in Missouri, he was eventually given charge of the operations along the Mississippi River.

In early 1862 he scored major successes at New Madrid and Island 10 and the advance on Memphis. He then led one of the three field armies serving under Henry W. Halleck in a painfully slow advance on Corinth, Mississippi. In the meantime he had been awarded a second star in the volunteer service and was marked for advancement. With the scattered forces in northern Virginia unable to contain Stonewall Jackson's small mobile command in the Shenandoah Valley and thus unable to advance on Richmond from the north, Pope was called east. Three departments were merged into his newly formed Army of Virginia. His former commander, Fremont, refused to be one of his corps commanders and was relieved of duty. Pope was then advanced to a brigadier generalship in the regular establishment. Not taking command of his scattered forces in the field until late July, he lost the faith of his men when he made an address praising the western armies and disparaging the efforts of the eastern forces up to that time. In bombastic fashion he declared his headquarters would be in the saddle. This led to a quip that he did not know his "headquarters from his hindquarters."

His proposals on how to deal with the secessionist population raised the ire of his opponents, especially Lee. Part of Pope's command was defeated at Cedar Mountain. Later that month his command and parts of McClellan's Army of the Potomac fought at Second Bull Run. Pope had no idea of the true situation on the field and was routed.

Blaming the defeat on his subordinates, he came into conflict with those officers who were McClellan partisans. He charged Fitz-John Porter with disobedience of orders in failing to launch an attack that was in fact impossible. Nonetheless Porter was cashiered, but Pope also lost his command on September 21, 1862, and the Army of Virginia was merged into the Army of the Potomac 10 days later.

Although there was recognition of a lack of support from McClellan and his officers, Lincoln believed he had little choice but to give the consolidated command to McClellan in the face of the Confederate invasion of Maryland. Pope then spent most of the balance of the war commanding the Department of the Northwest and dealing with the Sioux uprising. He performed his job ably and in 1865 was brevetted a regular army major general for Island 10.

Mustered out of the volunteers on September 1, 1866, he held departmental commands in the regular army, mostly in the West, until his 1886 retirement. Four years later he was named a full major general.

Source

Ellis, Richard N. *General Pope and U.S. Indian Policy*. Albuquerque: University of New Mexico Press, 1970.

Ropes, John C. *The Army under Pope and Ellis*. New York: Charles Scribner's Sons, 1881.

Puller, Lewis B. ("Chesty") (1898–1971) *Lieutenant general, United States Marine Corps.*

"Chesty" Puller, colorful veteran of the Korean fighting, four World War II campaigns, and expeditionary service in China, Nicaragua, and Haiti, was one of the most decorated Marines in the corps, and the only Leatherneck ever awarded the Navy Cross five times for heroism and gallantry in action.

The general's last active duty station was Camp Lejeune, North Carolina, where he was commanding the Second Marine Division when he became seriously ill in August 1954. After that he served as deputy camp commander until his illness forced him to retire from his beloved Marine Corps.

Born in the tidewater village of West Point, Virginia, where his father had a wholesale grocery business, Puller was reared on tales of Confederate glory. His grandfather, Major John Puller, a heroic cavalryman, was killed in 1863. Determined to pursue a military career, Puller completed one year at the Virginia Military Institute (VMI) before enlisting in the Marine Corps in August 1918. VMI may have given him the exaggerated military bearing for which he was nicknamed, but it was during more than four years as a Marine noncommissioned officer (NCO) and concurrent time as a lieutenant of the Gendarmerie d'Haiti (1919–23) that Puller developed his distinctive leadership style; perfectionism; mission overachievement; and fearless, inspirational conduct under fire.

A Marine officer and enlisted man for 37 years, General Puller served at sea or overseas for all but 10 of those years, including a hitch as commander of the "Horse Marines" in China. Excluding medals from foreign governments, he was awarded a total of 14 personal decorations in combat, plus a long list of campaign medals, unit citation ribbons, and other awards.

Varied assignments followed his commissioning in 1924, including two tours in Nicaragua, in each of which he was awarded the Navy Cross. His third and fourth Navy Crosses were awarded during World War II for heroic action at the Battle of Guadalcanal and at Cape Gloucester on New Britain Island; and his fifth Navy Cross for service in Korea, where Puller commanded the First Marine Regiment in the assault landing at Inchon, the seizure of Seoul, and the fighting at the Chosin Reservoir. His last Navy Cross Citation states in part as follows:

> Fighting continuously in sub-zero weather against a vastly outnumbering hostile force, (then) Colonel Puller drove off repeated and fanatical enemy attacks upon his Regimental defense sector and supply points. Although the area was frequently covered by grazing machine gun fire and intense artillery and mortar fire, he coolly moved among his troops to insure their correct tactical employment, reinforced the lines as the situation demanded and successfully defended his perimeter, keeping open the main supply routes for the movement of the Division. During the attack from Koto-ri to Hungman, he expertly utilized his Regiment as the Division rear guard, repelling two fierce enemy assaults, which severely threatened the security of the unit,

and personally supervised the care and prompt evacuation of all casualties. By his unflagging determination, he served to inspire his men to heroic efforts in defense of their positions and assured the safety of much valuable equipment, which would otherwise have been lost to the enemy. His skilled leadership, superb courage and valiant devotion to duty in the face of overwhelming odds reflect the highest credit upon Colonel Puller and the United States Naval Service.

Serving in Korea from September 1950 to April 1951, the general was awarded the Army Silver Star Medal during the Inchon landing, his second Legion of Merit with Combat V in the Inchon-Seoul fighting and the early phases of the Chosin Reservoir Campaign, and three Air Medals for reconnaissance flights over enemy territory.

General Puller had served with the First Marine Division in the World War II campaigns on Guadalcanal, Eastern New Guinea, Camp Gloucester, and Peleliu, earning his third Navy Cross and the Bronze Star and Purple Heart Medals at Guadalcanal; his fourth Navy Cross at Cape Gloucester; and his first Legion of Merit with Combat V at Peleliu. He won his first Navy Cross in November 1930 and his second in September and October 1932, while fighting bandits in Nicaragua.

In January 1933, General Puller left Nicaragua for the West Coast of the United States. A month later he sailed from San Francisco to join the Marine Detachment of the American Legion at Peiping, China. There, in addition to other duties, he commanded the famed Horse Marines. Without returning to the United States, he began a tour of sea duty in September 1934, as commanding officer of the Marine Detachment aboard the USS *Augusta* of the Asiatic Fleet. In June 1936, he returned to the United States to become an instructor at the Basic School at Philadelphia. He left there in May 1939 to serve another year as commander of the *Augusta's* Marine Detachment and from that ship joined the Fourth Marines at Shanghai, China, in May 1940.

After serving as a battalion executive officer with the Fourth Marines, Puller sailed for the United States in August 1941, just four months before the attack on Pearl Harbor. In September, he took command of the First Battalion, Seventh Marines, First Marine Division, at Camp Lejeune. That regiment was detached from the First Marine Division in March 1942 and the following month, as part of the Third Marine Brigade, sailed for the Pacific Theater. The Seventh Marines rejoined the First Marine Division in September 1942, and General Puller, still commanding its First Battalion, went on to earn his third Navy Cross at Guadalcanal.

The action that earned that medal occurred on the night of October 24–25, 1942. For a desperate three hours his battalion, stretched over a mile-long front, was the only defense between vital Henderson Airfield and a regiment of seasoned Japanese troops. In pouring tropical rain, the Japanese smashed repeatedly at his thin line, as General Puller moved up and down its length to encourage his Marines and direct the defense. After reinforcements arrived, he commanded the augmented force until late the next afternoon. The defending Marines suffered fewer than 70 casualties in the engagement, whereas 1,400 of the enemy were killed and the Marines recovered 17 truckloads of Japanese equipment.

After Guadalcanal the general became executive officer of the Seventh Marines. He was fighting in that capacity when he was awarded his fourth Navy Cross at Cape Gloucester in January 1944. When the commanders of two battalions were wounded, he took over their units and moved through heavy machine gun and mortar fire to reorganize them for attack, then led them in taking a strongly fortified enemy position.

In February 1944, Puller took command of the First Marines at Cape Gloucester. After leading that regiment for the remainder of the campaign, he sailed with it for the Russell Islands in April 1944 and went on from there to command it at Peleliu in September and October 1944. He returned to the United States in November, was named executive officer of the Infantry Training Regiment at Camp Lejeune in January 1945, and took command of that regiment the next month.

In August 1946, General Puller became director of the Eighth Marine Corps Reserve District, with headquarters at New Orleans, Louisiana. After that assignment he commanded the Marine Barracks at Pearl Harbor until August 1950, when he arrived at Camp Pendleton, California, to reestablish and take command of the First Marines, the same regiment he had led at Cape Gloucester and on Peleliu.

Landing with the Fourth Marines at Inchon, Korea, in September 1950, he continued to head that regiment until January 1951, when he was promoted to brigadier general and named assistant commander of the First Marine Division. That May he returned to Camp Pendleton to command the newly activated Third Marine Brigade, which was redesignated the Third Marine Division in January 1952. After that, he was the assistant division commander until he took over the Troop Training Unit, Pacific, at Coronado, California, that June. He was promoted to major general in September 1953 and in July 1954 assumed command of the Second Marine Division, at Camp Lejeune. Despite his illness he retained that command until February 1955, when he was appointed deputy camp commander. He served in that capacity until August, when he entered the United States Naval Hospital at Camp Lejeune prior to retirement.

During the 1950s, the outspoken "Chesty" Puller gained attention as a champion of tough, realistic train-

Lewis B. "Chesty" Puller

ing; a defender of the basic soundness of American youth; and a critic of higher leadership. His legend continued to grow: photographs of his bulldog visage were displayed in homes and service clubs across the country as a symbol of invincible heroism and fidelity to traditional military standards.

Lieutenant General Puller was the recipient of five Navy Crosses; the Army Distinguished Service Cross; the Army Silver Star; the Legion of Merit with combat V and Gold Star in lieu of a second award; the Bronze Star Medal; the Air Medal with Gold Stars in lieu of second and third awards; and the Purple Heart Medal. His other medals and decorations include the Presidential Unit Citation Ribbon with four Bronze Stars; the Marine Corps Good Conduct Medal with one Bronze Star; the World War I Victory Medal with West Indies clasp; the Haitian Campaign Medal; the Second Nicaraguan Campaign Medal; the Marine Corps Expeditionary Medal with one Bronze Star; the China Service Medal; the American Defense Service Medal with base clasp; the American Area Campaign Medal; the Asiatic-Pacific Area Campaign Medal with four Bronze Stars; the World War II Victory Medal; the National Defense Service Medal; the Korean Service Medal with one Silver Star in lieu of five Bronze Stars; the United Nations Service Medal;

the Haitian Medaille Militarie; the Nicaraguan Presidential Medal of Merit with Diploma; the Nicaraguan Cross of Valor with Diploma; the Republic of Korea's Ulchi Medal with Gold Star; and the Korean Presidential Unit Citation with Oak Leaf Cluster.

Promoted to his final rank and placed on the temporary disability list on November 1, 1955, he died on October 11, 1971, in Hampton, Virginia, after a long illness.

Source and Additional Reading

Chambers, John Whiteclay III. *The Oxford Companion to American Military History.* New York: Oxford University Press, 1999.

Davis, Burk. *Marine! The Life of Lt. Gen. Lewis B. (Chesty) Puller, USMC.* New York: Bantam, 1962.

Marine Corps Historical Center.

Pyle, Ernie (1900–1945) *American journalist of World War II.*

A native of Dana, Indiana, Pyle worked on a local newspaper before joining the *Washington* [DC] *Daily News* in 1923, initially covering aviation and later serving as managing editor. In 1935, Pyle began a syndicated column for the Scripps-Howard organization, describing his experiences motoring around the United States. Over the next four years, his stories focused on the lives of average citizens.

In 1940, Pyle received his first wartime assignment from Scripps-Howard, covering the Blitz in England. Two years later, he started reporting on the North Africa Campaign and followed United States combat troops to Sicily, Italy, and France. Widely respected by both the public and the average G.I., Pyle succeeded in conveying a sense of the hardship, fear, and endurance of the individual soldier, with a special focus on the combat infantryman. At the height of his fame, over 400 newspapers carried his columns. In 1944, he won the Pulitzer Prize, and *Time* magazine featured him on its cover.

In 1945, Pyle, at the behest of the navy, shifted to covering the Pacific Theater. In one of his articles he submitted the following insight:

> *Marine Philosophy:* Marines have a cynical approach to war, they believe in three things: liberty, payday and that when two Marines are together in a fight, one is being wasted. Being in a minority group militarily, they are proud and sensitive in their dealings with other military organizations. A Marine's concept of a perfect battle is to have other Marines on the right and the left flanks, Marine aircraft overhead and Marine artillery and naval gunfire backing them up.

Ernie Pyle was killed by enemy fire on the tiny island of Ie Shima, near Okinawa, serving with his beloved Marines, on April 18, 1945.

Source and Additional Reading

Chambers, John Whiteclay III. *The Oxford Companion to American Military History.* New York: Oxford University Press, 1999.

Tobin, James. *Ernie Pyle's War: America's Eyewitness to World War II.* New York: Free Press, 1997.

Voss, Frederick S. *Reporting the War: The Journalistic Coverage of World War II.* Washington, D.C.: Smithsonian Institution Press, 1994.

R

✶ ✶ ✶ ✶

Ramage, Lawson Paterson (b. 1920) *Commander, United States Navy, commander of the USS* Parche *in subsurface combat, so distinguished himself in combat, during World War II, that he was awarded the Medal of Honor for his heroic actions.*

Born: January 19, 1920, Monroe Bridge, Mass.; **Entered service at:** Vermont; **Place and date:** Pacific, July 31, 1944.

Citation: "For conspicuous gallantry and intrepidity at the risk of his life above and beyond the call of duty as commanding officer of the U.S.S. *Parche* in a predawn attack on a Japanese convoy, 31 July 1944. Boldly penetrating the screen of a heavily escorted convoy, Comdr. Ramage launched a perilous surface attack by delivering a crippling stern shot into a freighter and quickly following up with a series of bow and stern torpedoes to sink the leading tanker and damage the second one. Exposed by the light of bursting flares and bravely defiant of terrific shellfire passing close overhead, he struck again, sinking a transport by two forward reloads. In the mounting fury of fire from the damaged and sinking tanker, he calmly ordered his men below, remaining on the bridge to fight it out with an enemy now disorganized and confused. Swift to act as a fast transport closed in to ram, Comdr. Ramage daringly swung the stern of the speeding *Parche* as she crossed the bow of the onrushing ship, clearing by less than 50 feet but placing his submarine in a deadly crossfire from escorts on all sides and with the transport dead ahead. Undaunted, he sent 3 smashing "down the throat" bow shots to stop the target, then scored a killing hit as a climax to 46 minutes of violent action with the *Parche* and her valiant fighting company retiring victorious and unscathed."

Source
Medal of Honor Citation.

Rascon, Alfred V. (b. 1945) *Specialist fourth class, U.S Army, Reconnaissance Platoon, Headquarters Company, First Battalion (Airborne), 503rd Infantry, 173d Airborne Brigade (Separate), so distinguished himself in combat, in*

Alfred V. Rascon

the Republic of Vietnam, on March 16, 1966, that he was awarded the Medal of Honor for his heroic actions.

Born: 1945, Chihuahua, Mexico.

Citation: "Specialist Four Alfred Rascon distinguished himself by a series of extraordinarily courageous acts on 16 March 1966, while assigned as a medic to the Reconnaissance Platoon, Headquarters Company, 1st Battalion (Airborne), 503rd Infantry, 173d Airborne Brigade (Separate). While moving to reinforce its sister battalion under intense enemy attack, the Reconnaissance Platoon came under heavy fire from a numerically superior enemy force. The intense enemy fire from crew-served weapons and grenades severely wounded several point squad soldiers. Specialist Rascon, ignoring directions to stay behind shelter until covering fire could be provided, made his way forward. He repeatedly tried to reach the severely wounded point machingunner lying on an open enemy trail, but was driven back each time by the withering fire. Disregarding his personal safety, he jumped to his feet, ignoring flying bullets and exploding grenades to reach his comrade. To protect him from further wounds, he intentionally placed his body between the soldier and enemy machine guns, sustaining numerous shrapnel injuries and a serious wound to the hip. Disregarding his serious wounds he dragged the larger soldier from the fire-raked trail. Hearing the second machine-gunner yell that he was running out of ammunition, Specialist Rascon, under heavy enemy fire crawled back to the wounded machine-gunner stripping him of his bandoliers of ammunition, giving them to the machine-gunner who continued his suppressive fire. Specialist Rascon fearing the abandoned machine gun, its ammunition and spare barrel could fall into enemy hands made his way to retrieve them. On the way, he was wounded in the face and torso by grenade fragments, but disregarded these wounds to recover the abandoned machine gun, ammunition and spare barrel items, enabling another soldier to provide added suppressive fire to the pinned-down squad. In searching for the wounded, he saw the point grenadier being wounded by small arms fire and grenades being thrown at him. Disregarding his own life and his numerous wounds, Specialist Rascon reached and covered him with his body absorbing the blasts from the exploding grenades, and saving the soldier's life, but sustaining additional wounds to his body. While making his way to the wounded point squad leader, grenades were hurled at the sergeant. Again, in complete disregard for his own life, he reached and covered the sergeant with his body, absorbing the full force of the grenade explosions. Once more Specialist Rascon was critically wounded by shrapnel, but disregarded his own wounds to continue to search and aid the wounded. Severely wounded, he remained on the battlefield, inspiring his fellow soldiers to continue the battle. After the enemy broke contact, he disregarded aid for himself, instead treating the wounded and directing their evacuation. Only after being placed on the evacuation helicopter did he allow aid to be given to him. Specialist Rascon's extraordinary valor in the face of deadly enemy fire, his heroism in rescuing the wounded, and his gallantry by repeatedly risking his own life for his fellow soldiers are in keeping with the highest traditions of military service and reflect great credit upon himself, his unit, and the United States Army."

Source
Medal of Honor Citation.

Red Cloud (Makhpiya Luta) 1822–1909 *Head chief of the Oglala Lakota, a Sioux group, for years frustrated efforts of the U.S. government to open up the West.*

From 1859 on Red Cloud and his band, living near Fort Laramie, Wyoming attacked white immigrants encroaching on Indian Territory along the North Platte River. By 1865 he was effectively discouraging white intrusion by way of the Bozeman Trail. Red Cloud led the 1866 massacre of 80 troops from Fort Kearney, one of the posts built

Red Cloud

to protect the trail, an event that led to the abandonment of the trail by the whites in 1868. A peace treaty of that year, which Red Cloud signed, seems to have been a turning point for the war chief. After visiting Washington, D.C., where the numbers and power of white people perhaps impressed him, he agreed to settle down as a reservation chief. According to some of his contemporaries, such as Sitting Bull and Crazy Horse, he sold out to the whites, permitting corrupt and deplorable conditions on Sioux reservations. He lost his status as head chief in 1881. After the Wounded Knee massacre (1890) he lived quietly on Pine Ridge Reservation.

Sources and Additional Reading

Hyde, George E. *Red Cloud's Folk.* 1957; Reprint, Norman: University of Oklahoma Press, 1976.

Larson, Robert W. *Red Cloud: Warrior-Statesman of the Lakota Sioux.* Norman: University of Oklahoma Press, 1997.

Olson, James C. *Red Cloud and the Sioux Problem.* Lincoln: University of Nebraska Press, 1965.

Reese, John N., Jr. *Private first class, United States Army, Company B, 148th Infantry, 37th Infantry Division.*

Born: Muskogee, Okla.; **Entered service at:** Pryor, Okla.; **Place and date:** Paco Railroad Station, Manila, Philippine Islands, February 9, 1945. **G.O. No.:** 89, October 19, 1945.

Citation: "He was engaged in the attack on the Paco Railroad Station, which was strongly defended by 300 determined enemy soldiers with machine-guns and rifles, supported by several pillboxes, three 20 mm. guns, one 37-mm. gun and heavy mortars. While making a frontal assault across an open field, his platoon was halted 100 yards from the station by intense enemy fire. On his own initiative he left the platoon, accompanied by a comrade, and continued forward to a house 60 yards from the objective. Although under constant enemy observation, the 2 men remained in this position for an hour, firing at targets of opportunity, killing more than 35 Japanese and wounding many more. Moving closer to the station and discovering a group of Japanese replacements attempting to reach pillboxes, they opened heavy fire, killed more than 40 and stopped all subsequent attempts to man the emplacements. Enemy fire became more intense as they advanced to within 20 yards of the station. From that point Pfc. Reese provided effective covering fire and courageously drew enemy fire to himself while his companion killed 7 Japanese and destroyed a 20-mm. gun and heavy machinegun with hand grenades. With their ammunition running low, the 2 men started to return to the American lines, alternately providing covering fire for each other as they withdrew. During this movement, Pfc. Reese was killed by enemy fire as he reloaded his rifle. The intrepid team, in 2 ¹/₂ hours of fierce fighting, killed more than 82 Japanese, completely disorganized their defense and paved the way for subsequent complete defeat of the enemy at this strong point. By his gallant determination in the face of tremendous odds, aggressive fighting spirit, and extreme heroism at the cost of his life, Pfc. Reese materially aided the advance of our troops in Manila and provided a lasting inspiration to all those with whom he served."

Source
Medal of Honor Citation.

Revere, Paul (1735–1818) *American patriot.*

Paul Revere was born in Boston, Massachusetts, on January 1, 1735. He became a legendary hero at the start of the American Revolution, when he rode from Charlestown to Lexington, Massachusetts, on the night of April 18, 1775, to warn the countryside of approaching British troops.

An official courier for the Massachusetts Committee of Correspondence, Revere arrived in Lexington shortly before another rider, William Dawes, and warned John Hancock and Samuel Adams to escape. Revere then started for Concord accompanied by Dawes and Samuel Prescott but was halted by a British patrol. Only Prescott reached Concord. Revere's exploit was celebrated in Henry Wadsworth Longfellow's famous (but generally inaccurate) poem "Paul Revere's Ride" (1863).

In his portrait painted by John Singleton Copley around 1765, Paul Revere holds an unfinished silver teapot. The energetic, colorful Revere organized a network of more than 60 fellow artisans that formed the secret heart of Boston's revolutionary movement.

His father, Apollos Rivoire (or De Rivoire), was a Huguenot who had immigrated to Boston while still a boy as a refugee from religious persecution in France. Apprenticed to the silversmith John Coney, Rivoire had married Deborah Hitchbourn (Hitchborn) and gradually anglicized his name to *Paul Revere.* As an independent silversmith, the elder Revere had become a man of substance by the time his son Paul was born in 1735.

Young Paul learned the trade of silversmith in his father's shop and probably attended the North Writing (or Grammar) School while serving his apprenticeship. In 1756 he enlisted for the unsuccessful expedition against the French post at Crown Point, serving as second lieutenant. A few months after his return, in the summer of 1757, he married Sarah ("Sary") Orne, with whom he would have eight children.

Revere is remembered as much as a craftsman as he is as a patriot. His anti-British engravings of episodes such as the Boston Massacre were effective propaganda. He cast musket balls and cannon during the war and designed and printed the first Continental currency. After the war he became one of New England's leading silversmiths and a pioneer in the production of copper plating in America.

When tension developed between the colonies and the mother country after the end of the Seven Years' War (1756–63), Paul Revere emerged as one of the leaders of the group of artisans who identified themselves with the critics of the policies of England. As a Mason he was already associated with James Otis, Joseph Warren, and other libertarians. He now became a member of various Whig groups, organized and unorganized, such as the Sons of Liberty, the North End Caucus, and the Long Room Club. He was probably a witness of, although not certainly a participant in, the Stamp Act riots and the looting of Governor Thomas Hutchinson's house.

Meanwhile, although his fame as a silversmith steadily mounted, business fell off for several years, and Revere turned to other trades to supplement his income. He did copper engraving, although his skill as a draftsman was woefully inadequate; drew political cartoons for the Whig polemicists; published music; and even went in for dentistry, a craft that he soon dropped. He was not only one of the most versatile and outstanding artisans of Boston; he was also an active political leader.

He observed the arrival of the customs commissioners and the British troops in Boston in 1768 and published a series of engravings that commemorated the latter event. When the so-called Boston Massacre took place in 1770, he published a famous drawing of the scene that doubtless aroused as much resentment against the British troops as the event itself.

In the years between 1770 and 1773, Revere became an express (mounted messenger) for the Whig patriots of Boston. At the time of the arrival of the tea ships in the autumn of 1773, he rode out to warn the Committees of Correspondence of the other ports along the coast not to permit the ships to land their cargoes. A little later, after he himself had been one of the "Indians" in the Boston Tea Party, he rode to Pennsylvania for the Boston committee to carry the news of the party to the committees of New York and Philadelphia.

It was in the spring of 1775 that Revere made the famous ride described by Henry Wadsworth Longfellow that placed him among the immortals of the American national tradition. General Thomas Gage, the British military governor of Massachusetts, had decided to arrest John Hancock and Samuel Adams, who were at Lexington, and to confiscate the military supplies stored by the Whigs at Concord. On Sunday, April 16, four days before the projected Gage expedition, Revere rode out to Lexington to warn Hancock and Adams and sent word to the Whigs at Concord to hide the stores. At this time he arranged to signal the patriots by showing two lanterns in Boston's North Church steeple if the British moved by sea or one if by land.

On the night of Tuesday, April 18, Revere and William Dawes rode out, Dawes by way of Boston Neck and Revere by way of Charlestown, to alert the countryside that the British troops would move the next morning. Revere arrived in Lexington about half an hour before Dawes, and Hancock and Adams fled to Woburn. Revere, Dawes, and Dr. Samuel Prescott started for Concord, but Dawes and Revere were stopped by a British patrol; Prescott got through. Revere was released by the British and returned to Lexington to help in saving John Hancock's trunk and papers.

During the first years of the war, Revere served as a messenger for the Committee of Safety, with headquarters at Cambridge. He was then commissioned by the Provincial Congress to manufacture gunpowder. He also designed and printed the first issue of Continental money and made the first official seal for the colonies and the state seal of Massachusetts. After the reoccupation of Boston in 1776, he again took up his old trade. He reached the rank of lieutenant colonel and was placed in command of Castle William (Castle Island) in Boston Harbor. Meanwhile he had begun to cast cannon for the American army.

"Sary" Revere died on May 3, 1773, and Revere married Rachel Walker on October 10. They had eight children. After the war he went into merchandising and, later, bell casting, but silversmithing, with the assistance of his son, continued to be his most dependable and rewarding business. Presently, at the age of 65, he learned how to roll sheet copper and furnished the new sheeting for the dome of the Massachusetts State House and other public buildings, as well as for the hulls of ships in the young American navy, including the *Constitution* for which he had earlier furnished bolts, spikes, braces, and other fittings. Paul Revere's outstanding characteristic was the versatility of his craftsmanship; his reputation as an artist in the working of silver is hardly less great or enduring than his fame as a patriot. For him, that famous ride to Lexington was hardly more than an exciting incident that was, in fact, shared by William Dawes. Because of its dramatic nature, however, it is the ride for which he is most popularly remembered by succeeding generations.

Sources and Additional Reading

Bigelow, Francis H. *Historic Silver of the Colonies and Its Makers.* New York: Macmillan, 1917.

Brigham, Clarence. *Paul Revere's Engraving.* Worcester, Mass.: American Antiquarian Society, 1954.

Buhler, Kathryn C. *Paul Revere, Goldsmith: 1735–1818.* Boston: Museum of Fine Arts, 1956.

Forbes, Esther. *Paul Revere and the World He Lived In.* 1942. Reprint, New York: Houghton Mifflin, 1962.

Goss, Elbridge. *The Life of Colonel Paul Revere.* 1891. Reprint, New York: Irvington, 1972.

Stevenson, Augusta. *Paul Revere: Boston Patriot.* Indianapolis, Ind.: Bobbs Merrill, 1946.

Richards, Thomas A. *Corporal, United States Marine Corps, so distinguished himself in combat, in June 1969, that he was awarded the Navy Cross for his heroic actions.*

Citation: "For extraordinary heroism on 5 and 6 June 1969, as a Fire Team Leader with Company H, Second Battalion, Ninth Marines, Third Marine Division, during operations against an armed enemy in the Republic of Vietnam. When his platoon initiated contact with a company-sized hostile force occupying well-camouflaged positions of a cliff overlooking a trail, and were subjected to a heavy volume of fire, Corporal Richards, during the initial attack, skillfully regrouped his platoon and led his men in a counterattack, enabling them to establish a defensive perimeter. Throughout the night, he assisted in countering enemy attacks and in moving casualties to areas of relative safety. Although wounded by fragments of an enemy grenade, he steadfastly refused to be evacuated in order to remain with his men and continue the fight. Observing that a machinegun in his area was dangerously short of ammunition, he made several trips across the fire-swept zone to obtain and replenish ammunition for the weapon. When the machine gunner and assistant gunner sustained wounds, Corporal Richards unhesitatingly dashed to the gun position, and although exposed to the brunt of the enemy attack, concentrated a heavy volume of fire on the hostile troops, causing the attack to falter long enough for the Marines to repulse it. His gallant actions resulted in the death of eight enemy soldiers and prevented the Marine perimeter from being penetrated. Through his superb leadership, courage, initiative and inspiring dedication, he contributed significantly to the defeat of the enemy and upheld the highest traditions of the Marine Corps and of the United States Naval Service."

Source
Navy Cross Citation.

Rickenbacker, Edward V. (1890–1973) *First lieutenant, United States Army Air Corps, 94th Aero squadron, Air Service, American ace during World War I, so distinguished himself in combat that he was awarded the Medal of Honor for his heroic actions.*

Born: October 8, 1890, Columbus, Ohio; **Entered service at:** Columbus, Ohio; **Place and date:** Near Billy, France, September 25, 1918. **G.O. No.:** 2, W.D., 1931.

Born on October 8, 1890, in Columbus, Ohio, Rickenbacker developed an early interest in internal-combustion engines and automobiles, and, by the time the United States entered World War I, he was one of the country's top three racing drivers. He entered the army in 1917 as a driver attached to Gen. John J. Pershing's staff and drove a car for Colonel William ("Billy") Mitchell, the noted advocate of tactical air power.

With Mitchell's help, he became a fighter pilot and was assigned to the 94th Aero Pursuit Squadron. He accumulated 26 air victories and numerous decorations, including the Medal of Honor. His war exploits are published in his 1919 book, *Fighting the Flying Circus.*

Rickenbacker returned to work in the automobile industry after the war, first with his own company and later with the Cadillac Motor Car Company. He joined American Airways in 1932; he moved to North American Aviation, Inc., in 1933, then to Eastern Air Lines in 1935. Rickenbacker became president, general manager, and director of Eastern three years later. After leading the company ably for many years, he resigned as president in 1959 and as director and chairman of the board in 1963. He died on July 23, 1973, in Zürich.

Citation: "For conspicuous gallantry and intrepidity above and beyond the call of duty in action against the enemy near Billy, France, 25 September 1918. While on a voluntary patrol over the lines, 1st Lt. Rickenbacker attacked 7 enemy planes (5 type Fokker, protecting two Halberstadts). Disregarding the odds against him, he dived on them and shot down one of the Fokkers out of control. He then attacked one of the Halberstadts and sent it down also."

Source
Medal of Honor Citation.

Ridgway, Matthew Bunker (1895–1993) *General officer, United States Army, in World War II planned and executed the first major airborne assault in U.S. military history with the attack on Sicily, July 1943.*

Born on March 3, 1895, at Fort Monroe, Virginia, Ridgway was a 1917 graduate of the United States Military Academy at West Point, New York, and served in various staff positions before World War II. In 1942 he took command of the 82nd Infantry Division and oversaw its conversion to the 82nd Airborne Division, which he then commanded in the Sicily Campaign. Ridgway parachuted with his troops into Normandy in June 1944 during the Normandy Invasion, and he subsequently led the 18th Airborne Corps in action in the Netherlands, Belgium, and Germany.

Assuming command of the United States Eighth Army in Korea during the Chinese Communist offensive in late 1950, Ridgway rallied the United Nations forces and initiated a counteroffensive that drove the Chinese out of South Korea. Promoted in 1951 to the rank of general, he succeeded General Douglas MacArthur as Allied commander in the Far East and continued the successful defense of South Korea. He subsequently oversaw the end of the United States occupation of Japan in 1952.

In 1952 Ridgway succeeded Gen. Dwight D. Eisenhower as supreme commander of the Allied forces in Europe, and the following year he was appointed chief of staff of the United States Army. He retired in 1955 as a general. Ridgway's war memoirs, entitled *Soldier*, were published in 1956.

Source and Additional Reading

Edwards, Paul M. *General Mathew B. Ridgway: An Annotated Bibliography*. Westort, Conn.: Greenwood Press, 1993.

Ridgway, Matthew B. *Soldier: The Memoirs of Matthew B. Ridgway*. New York: Harper, 1956.

Soffer, Jonathan M., *Matthew B. Ridgway*. Westport, Conn.: Greenwood Press, 1988.

Roosevelt, George W. *First sergeant, Company K, 26th Pennsylvania Infantry, father of President "Teddy" Roosevelt, so distinguished himself in combat, during the American Civil War, that he was awarded the Medal of Honor for his heroic actions.*

Born: Chester, Pa.; **Entered service at:** Chester, Pa.; **Place and date:** At Bull Run, Va., August 30, 1862, at Gettysburg, Pa., July 2, 1863. **Date of issue:** July 2, 1887.

Citation: "At Bull Run, Va., recaptured the colors, which had been seized by the enemy. At Gettysburg captured a Confederate color bearer and color, in which effort he was severely wounded."

Source
Medal of Honor Citation.

Roosevelt, Theodore, Jr. (1887–1944) *Brigadier general, assistant division commander, Fourth Infantry Division, First Army, so distinguished himself in combat, during World War II, that he was awarded the Medal of Honor for his heroic actions.*

Born: 1887, Oyster Bay, N.Y.; **Entered service at:** Oyster Bay, N.Y.; **Place and date of action:** Utah Beach, Normandy, France, June 6 1944. **G.O. No.:** 77, September 28, 1944.

Citation: "For gallantry and intrepidity at the risk of his life above and beyond the call of duty on 6 June 1944, in France. After 2 verbal requests to accompany the leading assault elements in the Normandy invasion had been denied, Brig. Gen. Roosevelt's written request for this mission was approved and he landed with the first wave of the forces assaulting the enemy-held beaches. He repeatedly led groups from the beach, over the seawall and established them inland. His valor, courage, and presence in the very front of the attack and his complete unconcern at

being under heavy fire inspired the troops to heights of enthusiasm and self-sacrifice. Although the enemy had the beach under constant direct fire, Brig. Gen. Roosevelt moved from one locality to another, rallying men around him, directed and personally led them against the enemy. Under his seasoned, precise, calm, and unfaltering leadership, assault troops reduced beach strong points and rapidly moved inland with minimum casualties. He thus contributed substantially to the successful establishment of the beachhead in France."

Theodore Roosevelt Jr. was the first Allied general officer to wade ashore on the Normandy beachhead (not counting those who landed in the airborne assault farther inland) and the only general in the first amphibious wave. Because of a navigational error by the landing craft crews, the first wave of the Fourth Infantry Division landed on the wrong inlet on Utah Beach, which, fortunately for them, was less heavily defended than their original objective. Quickly assessing the situation and seizing the initiative and advantage, Roosevelt rerouted the remainder of the division into the new sector ("We'll start the war from here!" was his famous line, later echoed by the actor Henry Fonda onscreen), overwhelmed the defenses, and rapidly drove inland. The Fourth Infantry Division then proceeded to outflank the Germans on their initial objective, clear the entire beachhead, and link up with the airborne assault forces with fewer casualties than the divisions on the other four beachheads. Armed only with a pistol and walking with a cane because of arthritis, he led several assaults along the beachhead in what then–Lt. Gen. Omar N. Bradley, commander of the United States First Army and of the overall amphibious operation, would later describe as the single bravest act he witnessed in the entire war.

Bravery in battle was, of course, nothing new to the Roosevelts of Oyster Bay. Roosevelt and his three brothers had all been bloodied in combat in the First World War. The youngest brother, Quentin, was killed in action as a fighter pilot with the 95th "Kicking Mule" Squadron (sister unit to Eddie Rickenbacker's famed 94th "Hat in the Ring" Squadron) in July 1918. Their father had himself sought to be reactivated in the army for combat in that war (at the age of 58, eight years after retiring from the presidency of the United States!). Elsewhere on the Normandy beaches that June morning in 1944 was Theodore Roosevelt Jr.'s own son, Quentin Roosevelt II, whom he had named, of course, for his fallen brother and who was returning to combat after being severely wounded in the North African Campaign; Theodore Jr. and Quentin II are the only father-and-son pair known to have landed in Normandy on D-Day.

The two Theodore Roosevelts were also the second father-and-son pair to become Medal of Honor recipients after Arthur and Douglas MacArthur, although not until after both men had been dead and buried for decades. By all objective criteria, the elder Roosevelt's valor and gallantry, in leading the legendary charge of his First United States Volunteer Cavalry "Rough Riders" Regiment up Kettle and San Juan Hills in Cuba on July 1, 1898, during the Spanish-American War, should have earned him the medal. A nomination was duly submitted by his chain of command. While it was en route, however, he made the fatal mistake of criticizing the War Department in a letter to the press, after the U.S. troops' departure from Cuba was delayed and the Rough Riders had been forced to bivouac in a mosquito-infested swamp, losing more men to malaria than they had in combat. The secretary of war quickly squashed the award in retaliation, and 46 years would elapse before the name of Theodore Roosevelt would be seen on a Medal of Honor citation, and over a century would elapse before, in January 2001 after years of review by Congress and the Department of the Army, the elder Theodore Roosevelt received his Medal of Honor for the Battle of San Juan Hill, 82 years posthumously. As it was, the elder Theodore Roosevelt would become more responsible than any other individual for inflating the value of the Medal of Honor and making it the ultimate decoration it has become; on ascending to the presidency in 1901, he took measures to ensure that only those actions that surpassed his own in Cuba would be worthy of the medal, and his charge up San Juan Hill (Kettle Hill) became the yardstick for future Medals of Honor.

In the film, there is a scene where, before the assault, Roosevelt gets into a discussion with Maj. Gen. Raymond O. Barton (played by Edmond O'Brien), the division commander, about his need to live up to his father's name and heroism. Whether or not such a conversation actually took place as depicted, it is interesting to note that in the book by Cornelius Ryan on which the screenplay was based, there is absolutely no mention of, or even any allusion to, the elder Theodore Roosevelt. In fact, Ryan's book, *The Longest Day* (Simon & Schuster, 1959) the basis for the film, refers only to "Brigadier General Theodore Roosevelt"; *Jr.* is omitted.

Conversely, there is no depiction or mention of Quentin Roosevelt II in the film *The Longest Day,* but he is mentioned briefly in the book. With the broad scope of the film, Henry Fonda's portrayal of Roosevelt was only one in literally a cast of thousands, and with the frequent scene shifting of the film, the depiction of his heroism unfortunately becomes somewhat disjointed and diluted. This becomes more evident when contrasted with the depiction of the Medal of Honor–earning acts of Joshua Lawrence Chamberlain in *Gettysburg,* because the two films and the respective battles depicted in them are quite comparable in scope.

Roosevelt was actually the second of two Medal of Honor recipients who were sons of former presidents of the United States: Lt. Col. Webb C. Hayes, the son of Rutherford B. Hayes, received his medal for action during the Philippine Insurrection in 1899. (Any person who suggests the involvement of political favoritism in these awards should be aware that both fathers were deceased, and had been out of office for decades, at the time of their sons' actions. We are also reminded that although the incumbent president at the time of Roosevelt's action was his cousin, Franklin, the "Hyde Park branch" of the family, of which Franklin was the patriarch, were of the opposing political party to, and in the midst of a family feud with, the "Oyster Bay branch."

Theodore Roosevelt Jr. died of a heart attack on the battlefield in Normandy five weeks after D-Day, just before word arrived at his headquarters that he had been promoted to major general and reassigned to command of another division. Setting aside the family feud as he presented Roosevelt's widow the Medal of Honor, Franklin D. Roosevelt said simply, "His father would have been proudest."

Sources

Hagedorn, Herman. *The Boy's Life of Theodore Roosevelt*. New York: Harper, 1918.
Miller, Nathan. *Theodore Roosevelt: A Life*. New York: William Morrow, 1992.
Pringle, Henry F. *Theodore Roosevelt: A Biography*. New York: Harcourt Brace, 1931.
Roosevelt, Theodore. *The Rough Riders*. New York: Charles Scriber's Sons, 1898.
Ryan, Cornelius. *The Longest Day*. New York: Simon & Schuster, 1959.

Rosecrans, William Starke (1819–1898) *Union general officer.*

William S. Rosecrans was born September 6, 1819, at Delaware City, Ohio, the son of Crandell Rosecrans and Jane Hopkins and the great-grandson of Stephen Hopkins, colonial governor of Rhode Island and a signer of the Declaration of Independence. Hopkins also coauthored with John Adams, the draft of the Articles of Confederation.

Rosecrans was a graduate of the class of 1842 at West Point (Fifth in the class of 56). Among his classmates were James Longstreet, Richard H. Anderson, Abner Doubleday, John Newton, George Sykes, Seth Williams, Lafayette McClaws, Alexander P. Stewart, John Pope, D. H. Hill, and Earl Van Dorn. He was the roommate of James Longstreet and A. P. Stewart.

Rosecrans was assigned engineering duty on graduation but resigned from the army in 1854 and became an architect and a civil engineer. His rise in business was astounding. He took over direction of mining in western Virginia (West Virginia today), where his geological surveys pointed with remarkable accuracy to profitable new veins of coal. He became president of a navigation company formed to transport coal. He was also an inventor. Numbered among his inventions were odorless oil, a round lamp wick, a short practical lamp chimney, and a new and economical method of manufacturing soap. While he was in the laboratory a safety lamp exploded and burned him severely.

He was bedridden for 18 months recovering from the burns. Just as he was completing his recovery from burns, the Civil War broke out. His first duties in the war were for the state of Ohio when he became the drillmaster for the Marion Rifles. Afterward he became the engineering officer who laid the plan for Camp Dennison, Ohio, and eventually became the commanding officer of the 23rd Ohio Volunteer Infantry, among whose members were the future presidents Rutherford B. Hayes and William McKinley and Stanley Matthews, a future associate justice of the Supreme Court.

Rosecrans was soon appointed a brigadier general in the regular army, in which he was a successful commander at Rich Mountain, Virginia. After Rich Mountain, George McClellan received much credit for the success there and was promoted to commanding general of the Army of the Potomac and eventually general in chief of the Union Armies. Yet it was Rosecrans who developed and carried out the plans that gained the victory at Rich Mountain. McClellan did not give him any credit in the official reports. Thus Rosecrans refused to go east with McClellan and requested a transfer to the west.

In the west, Rosecrans was placed in charge of the left wing of the Army of the Mississippi at Iuka and Corinth. At both he performed ably. After Corinth animosities between Grant and Rosecrans arose. Grant blamed Rosecrans for not pursuing the Confederate army after Corinth, and Rosecrans placed blame on Grant for not sending reinforcements during and immediately after the battle.

After Corinth, Rosecrans was given command of the 14th Corps and promotion to major general. The promotion was backdated to March 1862 so that Rosecrans would outrank Major General Thomas. As commanding general of the 14th Corps Rosecrans secured a victory at Stones River (Murfreesboro) and immediately began the reorganization of the corps into the Army of the Cumberland. He then embarked on the Tullahoma Campaign and ousted the Confederates from Chattanooga with fewer than 500 casualties in the whole army.

Rosecrans was loved by the men of his army but was harsh on his officers. A severe problem for Rosecrans was that once a battle began he became very excitable and began stuttering becoming very difficult to understand. Another shortcoming was his micromanagement of the movements of units instead of delegation of that responsibility through the chain of command.

These problems were never more apparent than at Chickamauga. Rosecrans issued an order to General Wood "to close in and support his left." This order created a hole in the Union line, which coincided with Longstreet's attack and led to the Confederate victory. Because of the defeat, Rosecrans was relieved of command of the Army of the Cumberland and would eventually be given command of the Department of Missouri until war's end.

Rosecrans resigned from the army in 1867 to resume his career in business. He eventually would minister to Mexico, serve in Congress representing California, and be appointed registrar of the Treasury. William S. Rosecrans died March 11, 1898, at Redondo, California, and is buried at Arlington National Cemetery.

Source

Dupuy, Trevor N., Curt Johnson, and David L. Bongard. *The Harper Encyclopedia of Military Biography*. New York: HarperCollins, 1992.

★ ★ ★ ★

Safford, Mary Jane (1831–1891) *American Civil War nurse, known as the "Angel of Cairo"*

Mary Safford was born in Hyde Park, Vermont, and lived in Crete, Illinois, from age three. In 1849, after her parents' death, family members secured her education at an academy in Bakersfield, Vermont, she then traveled in Canada to learn French and acted as governess to a German-speaking family to acquire skill in German. Unmarried, she took up residence with her elder brother, Alfred Safford, a Joliet, Illinois, businessman, then moved with him to Shawneetown, and in 1858 to Cairo, Illinois. Safford's exact birth date is unknown, but she is thought to have been 29 at the outbreak of the Civil War.

On the arrival of the nurse Mary Ann "Mother" Bickerdyke in Cairo in summer 1861, Safford volunteered to work with her as a nursing aide; she showed talent and was pressed into full-time nursing. With Bickerdyke, she cared for troops succumbing to camp diseases and the large numbers of wounded from the Battles of Belmont and Fort Donelson. Though based at the large field hospital in Cairo, she often left the facilities to care for the sick in surrounding camps and is remembered for walking the Belmont battlefield under her own flag of truce searching out the wounded. After the Battle of Fort Donelson, Bickerdyke recalled that Safford worked 10 days in the Cairo hospital with little sleep, neared collapse, then accepted nursing duties aboard the transport ship *City of Memphis.* These exertions forced her to retire to her brother's home in poor health.

Safford returned to nursing for the Battle of Shiloh, working aboard the *Hazel Dell* and with Bickerdyke in Savannah, Tennessee, field hospitals. An attractive, polished, compassionate woman, she impressed her patients aboard the *Hazel Dell* and won the sobriquet "Angel of Cairo." However, overworked and weak, she suffered a breakdown after caring for the Shiloh wounded, was con-

fined to bed for several months, then, at her brother's urging, accompanied the family of the former Illinois governor Joel Matteson on a lengthy European tour to recuperate. She did not return to the United States until autumn 1866.

Interested in resuming medical work, Safford entered the New York Medical College for Women in 1867; graduated in 1869; studied surgery at the General Hospital of Vienna, Austria, through 1871; continued studies at the University of Breslau, Germany, for several months, where she performed the first ovariotomy ever done by a woman; returned to the United States late in 1872; and in 1873 opened a private practice in Chicago. In 1872 she married James Blake. When the marriage proved unworkable, Safford joined the Boston University School of Medicine faculty, divorced Blake in 1880, then retired from the school in poor health in 1886. She took up residence in Tarpon Springs, Florida, where she died in 1891.

Source

Faust, Patricia L., ed. *Historical Times Illustrated Encyclopedia of the Civil War.* New York: Harper & Row, 1986.

Schwartzkopf, H. Norman (b. 1934) *United States Army, General, commander of the United States–led coalition of land, sea, and air forces that won decisive victory in the Persian Gulf War in 1991.*

Schwartzkopf was born in Trenton, New Jersey, on August 22, 1934. His father, Herbert Norman Schwarzkopf, was a West Point graduate. The senior Schwarzkopf gave his name to his son but, disliking the name *Herbert,* gave him only the letter *H.* The senior Schwarzkopf became superintendent of the New Jersey State Police and was the chief investigator in the kidnaping case of Charles Lindbergh's son. He later (1942–48) worked in Iran, where he helped establish the shah's police force. At the age of 12, young Norman lived in Tehran with his father.

At West Point, a young Schwarzkopf gained a reputation among his lower-class subordinates for handing out unnecessarily humiliating beratings over minor infractions. At the same time, out of uniform, he proved to be a kind, tireless mentor to younger cadets whom he coached in wrestling. He graduated from the academy in 1956, earning both a bachelor's degree in science in mechanical engineering and a commission in the army as a second lieutenant in the infantry.

His first assignment was platoon leader in the Second Airborne Battle Group at Fort Benning, Georgia. There he received advanced infantry and airborne training, followed by an assignment with the 101st Airborne in Kentuck, and the 6th Infantry Division in Germany, where he stayed until 1961.

In 1964, H. Norman received a master's degree from the University of Southern California, with a specialization in guided missile engineering. He married Brenda Holsinger on July 6, 1968.

He served two tours in the Vietnam War, first as an adviser to the South Vietnamese Airborne Division and then as commander of the First Battalion, Sixth Infantry, 23rd American Infantry Division. He was awarded the Silver Star Medal on three occasions during the war.

One incident, in May 1970, cemented his reputation as an officer who risked his personal safety for his men. At the time, several of Schwartzkopf's men had crossed into an unmarked minefield. Schwartzkopf arrived on scene and urged his men to retrace their steps slowly in the hope of extracting them without their encountering any of the deadly mines. One of his young troops triggered a land mine, severely injuring himself and Schwartzkopf. Schwartzkopf crawled out to the man and began to assist in splinting his broken leg. The first-aid team needed a tree branch to act as a splint, and as one soldier moved to reach a small tree, he detonated another land mine, resulting in his death and the wounding of two more U.S. soldiers. Colonel Schwartzkopf eventually led the surviving men to safety, and for this action he was awarded both the Silver Star and the Purple Heart. He returned to the United States in 1971.

Schwarzkopf had served as the military assistant (liaison officer) to the assistant secretary of the army in Washington, D.C. (1973–74); deputy commander of the 172d Infantry Brigade, Fort Richardson, Alaska (1974–76); commander of the First Brigade, Ninth Infantry Division, Fort Lewis, Washington (1976–78); and deputy director for plans of the United States Pacific Command, Camp Smith, Hawaii (1978–80). He was assistant division commander, Eighth Infantry Division, United States Army Europe (1980–82); deputy director of military personnel management and deputy chief of staff personnel

(1982–83), then commanding general of the 24th Infantry Division and Fort Stewart, Georgia (1983–85).

Schwarzkopf was the deputy commander of United State forces in the Grenada operation in 1983. He later served with the Department of the Army (1985–86); as commanding general of First Corps at Fort Lewis, Washington (1986–87); and in another tour with the Department of the Army (1987–88). In 1988, he became commander in chief of the United States Central Command, then headquartered at MacDill Air Force Base, Florida. The Central Command was involved with U.S. military concerns in nations in the Middle East, Africa, and the Persian Gulf. During 1988, Schwarzkopf received his fourth star as general. As commander in chief of the United States–led coalition forces sent to Saudi Arabia in Operation Desert Shield, after the Iraqi invasion of Kuwait in August 1990, General Schwarzkopf coordinated the armed forces of the many nations opposed to the expansionism of the Iraqi ruler, Saddam Hussein. He played a key role in the rapid and decisive defeat of Iraqi forces in early 1991 in Operation Desert Storm.

In addition to three Silver Star Medals, General Schwarzkopf was awarded the Distinguished Service Medal with Oak Leaf Cluster, the Distinguished Flying Cross, the Legion of Merit, the Bronze Star with three Oak Leaf Clusters, the Purple Heart with Oak Leaf Cluster, the Combat Infantryman Badge, the Master Parachutist Badge, and other unit decorations.

Source and Additional Reading

Anderson, Jack, and Van Atta, Dale. *Stormin' Norman.* New York: Kensington, 1991.

Schwarzkopf, H. Norman. *It Doesn't Take a Hero.* New York: Bantam, 1992.

Sedgwick, John (1813–1864) *Union general officer*

Born in Cornwall Hollow, Connecticut, on September 13, 1813, Sedgwick attended Sharon Academy briefly and taught school for two winters before entering West Point, where he graduated 24th in the class of 1837. Affectionately called "Uncle John" Sedgwick by his troops, he became the third and last corps commander in the Army of the Potomac killed in action.

This Connecticut-born West Pointer had an unusually active prewar career. Originally posted to the artillery, he fought in the Seminole War, was involved in the Trail of Tears, episode, and earned two brevets in the Mexican War. On the expansion of the regular establishment in 1855 he transferred to the mounted arm. In this branch he served in "Bleeding Kansas," on the Mormon Expedition, and in further fighting, with Native Americans. During the secession crisis he was twice in a matter of weeks promoted to replace Robert E. Lee, once when that officer was himself promoted and once when Lee resigned.

Sedgwick's Civil War assignments included the following: major, First Cavalry (from March 3, 1855); lieutenant colonel, Second Cavalry (March 16, 1861); colonel, First Cavalry (April 25, 1861); colonel, Fourth Cavalry (change of designation August 3, 1861); brigadier general United States Volunteers (USV) (August 31, 1861); commander, Second Brigade, Heintzelman's division, Army of the Potomac (October 31, 1861–February 9, 1862); commander, Stone's (old) division, Army of the Potomac (February 9–March 13, 1862); commander, Second Division, Second Corps, Army of the Potomac (March 13–September 17, 1862); major general, USV (July 4, 1862); commander, Second Corps, Army of the Potomac (December 26, 1862–January 26, 1863); commander, Ninth Corps, Army of the Potomac (January 16–February 5, 1863); and commander, Sixth Corps, Army of the Potomac (February 4, 1863–April 6, 1864, and April 13–May 9, 1865).

Initially in charge of a brigade in the fall of 1861, Sedgwick took over a division when Gen. Charles P. Scone was placed under arrest. This division he led to the Peninsula, where he fought at Yorktown and Seven Pines. During the Seven Days he was wounded at Frayser's Farm. On the nation's birthday he received the second star of a major general and continued in division command until Antietam, when his division marched into a trap, being struck on three sides. Sedgwick himself suffered three wounds and was out of action until after Fredericksburg, when he returned to lead first the Second Corps, then the Ninth, and finally the Sixth. In the Chancellorsville Campaign he commanded Hooker's force at Fredericksburg. He broke through Marye's Heights in an effort to relieve the pressure on his chief but was stopped at Salem Church and forced to withdraw north of the river. At Gettysburg his corps was in reserve, but he scored a signal success at Rappahannock Bridge that fall.

One of the top corps commanders with the army, he retained command when the five corps were reduced to three. He led his men into the tangled fighting of the Wilderness and then on to Spotsylvania. While placing his corps artillery he was shot by a Confederate sharpshooter in the head. Ironically he had just declared that they could not fire accurately at that distance. He died almost immediately. Sedgwick was buried where he was born, in Cornwall Hollow, Connecticut.

Source

Winslow, Richard Elliott. *General John Sedgwick: The Story of a Union Corps Commander.* Novato, Calif.: Presidio Press, 1982.

Sexton, Charles T. *Corporal, United States Marine Corps, so distinguished himself in combat, during the* *Vietnam War, that he was awarded the Navy Cross for his heroic actions in February 1970.*

Citation: "For extraordinary heroism while serving as a Radio Operator with the Third Force Reconnaissance Company, Third Marine Amphibious Force, in connection with combat operations against the enemy in the Republic of Vietnam. Corporal Sexton was a member of a six-man reconnaissance team which was patrolling deep in the A Shau valley when it came under a heavy volume of small-arms and automatic weapons fire from approximately fifty enemy soldiers occupying well-concealed emplacements in the dense elephant grass. During the initial moments of the attack; three Marines were mortally wounded and two were seriously wounded. After a rapid assessment of the precarious situation, Corporal Sexton directed the fire of his two wounded companions and moved about the fire-swept area to collect hand grenades and ammunition from his fallen comrades. Utilizing his radio, he then reported the situation to his commanding officer and requested assistance. For the next several hours, while the enemy attempted to encircle and overrun his position, Corporal Sexton repeatedly adjusted helicopter and fixed-wing air strikes on the hostile unit, hurled hand grenades, shouted encouragement to his wounded companions, and simultaneously furnished a running commentary to his company commander until a reaction force arrived to lend support. His heroic and determined actions were an inspiration to all who observed him and undoubtedly saved his fellow Marines from further serious injury or even death. By his courage, superb leadership, and valiant devotion to duty in the face of grave personal danger, Corporal Sexton upheld the highest traditions of the Marine Corps and the United States Naval Service."

Source

Navy Cross Citation.

Norton, Maj. Bruce H. New York *Force Recon Diary, 1969.* New York: Ballantine, 1990.

Shaw, Robert Gould (1837–1863) *Colonel, Union army: "He Laid Down His Life for a Race."*

Robert Gould Shaw is best remembered as the brave colonel who led the 54th Massachusetts in their fearless charge at Fort Wagner. But what makes him an extraordinary individual lies beyond this noble deed. In what would be a few months with the regiment, Shaw's remarkable personal growth found him transformed from "an ordinary mortal" to a compassionate and selfless leader who "laid down his life" for his men and "for a race." This is what makes him a true hero.

A Prosperous and Humanitarian Upbringing   Robert Gould Shaw was born on October 10, 1837, in Boston, Massachusetts, the second child and only son of Francis George and Sarah Blake (Sturgis) Shaw. As the grandchild of successful merchants who had amassed millions of dollars as merchants, Robert enjoyed a comfortable upbringing with his four sisters. From the early years of his sheltered childhood, he demonstrated a fondness for family, companionship, and social events. When Robert was four, his father, a merchant and part-time lawyer, retired at age 32 to pursue a literary career and philanthropic interests and to spend more time with his family. Francis relocated the family to the country near Brook Farm, an experimental commune inhabited by intellectuals such as Ralph Waldo Emerson, Nathaniel Hawthorne, and Margaret Fuller. Living in this area until he was nine, Robert was introduced to these freethinkers' beliefs as well as the open-minded ideals of the local Unitarian church members. He began to develop an understanding of abolitionism, a cause supported by his parents, who were prominent and well-respected humanitarians, social reformers, and antislavery activists in their community. However, at this young age Robert did not yet fully embrace his parents' philosophies on life.

After the decline of Brook Farm, the Shaws lived at residences on the East Coast and in Europe. Robert briefly attended a preparatory school in New York, with lessons in languages and violin. At a boarding school in Switzerland, he studied math, various languages, and violin and piano. His life was miserable at these institutions, because he missed his family and disliked authority and discipline. Seeking diversion in Europe, Robert frequented the theater, opera, concerts, and parties.

He widely toured the Continent with friends, much to his parents' displeasure. Away from home, he began to ponder his own identity and questioned his parents' principles. But through his wayward adolescent years, he still felt close to his mother and siblings.

In 1856, Robert passed the entrance exam to Harvard but did not excel in academics, preferring to spend more time on extracurricular activities such as sports and a musical group in which he played violin. Initially insecure about his diminutive stature at five feet, five inches, he gained more confidence when he was elected president of many clubs in which he participated. Yet he remained uncertain about his career goals and therefore was not disappointed when he left the university in spring 1859, after the Panic of 1857 cut the family fortune in half. At first Robert was enthusiastic about working for Henry P. Sturgis and Co., his uncle's mercantile office in New York City. But half a year later, he became bored with the daily monotony of inventory.

A New Family and a New Life   In 1860, after Abraham Lincoln became president and the southern states seceded from the Union, Robert enlisted with the Seventh New York National Guard. This exclusive military regiment comprised sons from New York society who were intent on proving their worthiness and patriotism. The Seventh sprang to the call immediately after the firing on Fort Sumter on April 12, 1861. In their naïve optimism, the young men believed that the conflict would be brief and so agreed to volunteer their services for only 30 days. After the unit disbanded, Robert decided to remain in the military. On May 10, 1861, he obtained an officer's commission as a second lieutenant with the Second Massachusetts, a newly formed infantry, and for the next 20 months these men were comrades and family to him. Life with the Second Massachusetts gradually changed Shaw's outlook on the war and his own existence. Though as an officer he was able to attend elegant parties and eat and sleep well, for the first time he was among men of other social classes, whom he had to depend on for his survival. Shaw quickly adapted to his new environments at each camp and, being fond of traveling, took in the vistas of Virginia and Maryland with great pleasure while on the march. Through the daily routine of drilling and soldiering he began to appreciate discipline, having witnessed the success of regiments that maintained strict order. Given a goal in the army, he now began to feel more alive and purposeful. But he also yearned for action on the battlefield to prove his manhood. Shaw's wish would soon be fulfilled. During the Shenandoah Valley Campaign, the Second was ordered to cover the retreat from Strasburg, Virginia, in the battle at Front Royal on May 23, 1862.

In this engagement Shaw received a minor wound and was recognized by his men for exhibiting courage and cool composure during the fray. But the Second would not experience their real baptism of fire until the Northern Virginia Campaign at the Cedar Mountain wheatfield, August 9, 1862. The regiment suffered terrible losses and would be tested again on September 17 at the Battle of Antietam, considered the bloodiest single day in the war. Shaw, now a captain in the unit, received a minor wound but felt the excitement of the battle as never before. However, after enduring the horrors of this event, he wished more than ever that the war would end.

The autumn and winter of 1862 found Shaw and the Second Massachusetts inactive, as they were not ordered to participate in the Battle of Fredericksburg in December. During this lull, Shaw briefly entertained thoughts about joining the cavalry, then—ever vacillating between ideas—decided to continue the fight with the Second, determined to remain in service until the end of the war. Missing home and family, he also thought about Annie Haggerty, a young woman from a prosperous family in Lenox, Massachusetts, who had won his heart prior to the war. In late November he proposed to her in a letter and they planned a wedding early next year.

A Regiment of Black Soldiers   After the federal victory in the Battle of Antietam, President Lincoln had declared a preliminary Emancipation Proclamation, warning the Confederacy that if they did not return to the Union their slaves would be freed. The proclamation, which was officially issued on January 1, 1863, liberated more than 3 million slaves in the southern states, changing the dynamics of the war. With the war soon to be entering its third year and the ranks depleted by battlefield casualties and desertions, the Union army was in great need of new recruits. By the end of January 1863, Lincoln authorized Secretary of War Edwin M. Stanton to allow black men to enlist in volunteer regiments. Though the idea of arming black men was controversial and unpopular among many white soldiers and citizens, this move found great favor among the abolitionists, with whom the topic already had been discussed. Early the next month, the proabolitionist Governor John A. Andrew of Massachusetts executed his plan to form a black volunteer regiment. This unit, the 54th Massachusetts, would be the first of its kind in the northern states. Governor Andrew approached Shaw to lead the new regiment as its colonel, because of his family's powerful and respectable status in society and their antislavery principles. At first Robert was reluctant to leave the Second Massachusetts, unsure about assuming this great responsibility and his ability to live up to everyone's expectations. He initially turned down the governor's offer then reconsidered, feeling that his mother would be greatly disappointed in him if he refused. Accepting the colonelcy, on February 15 he arrived in Boston to assist with the formation of the regiment.

The most ardent speaker urging black men to enlist in the 54th was Frederick Douglass, a great orator, writer, and social reformer, who, born a slave and having escaped to freedom, would help to emancipate thousands of slaves during his lifetime. Borrowing a line from the English Romantic poet Lord George Gordon Byron, Douglass proclaimed to black men: "Who would be free themselves must strike the blow . . . I urge you to fly to arms and smite to death the power that would bury the Government and your liberty in the same hopeless grave. This is your golden opportunity." To encourage the men and show his support, Douglass sent his sons Lewis and Charles to be enlisted.

From February through March, Shaw organized and drilled the recruits at Camp Meigs near Boston. As a commanding officer he was a strict disciplinarian, largely because of his concern that the failure of this experimental regiment would generate ridicule and shame for all, damaging future chances for more regiments of its kind. The men were issued uniforms and housed in wooden barracks. Shaw ensured that they were properly nourished and furnished with necessary supplies. However, despite his provision for the comfort of his men, he initially harbored some prejudices about their mannerisms. Shaw supported the Emancipation Proclamation and wished for the abolition of slavery, but in his early days as their officer he did not see his men as individuals. Twenty-five years old and lacking in wisdom and experience, he had yet to learn about members of a race other than his own. By the end of March, Shaw was enlightened on the intelligence of the many educated men in his unit. He also admired their resolve and relative ease in adjusting to military life. As Shaw gradually began to treat his men with more respect, they respected him more in return.

The Greatest Sacrifice   On May 2, Robert and Annie were married in New York City, and not long afterward he was ordered to return to camp. Major General David Hunter, commander of the Department of the South, had requested the 54th's presence at his headquarters on the island of Hilton Head, South Carolina. Impressed with the unit, Hunter dispatched the 54th to serve alongside the Second South Carolina, a contraband regiment under the command of Colonel James Montgomery, an abolitionist from Kansas.

Early in June, the 54th reported to Colonel Montgomery on St. Simons Island, off the coast of Georgia. With Montgomery's troops they embarked on an "expedition" to Darien. Carrying out orders from General Hunter, Montgomery had his men pillage then burn the town with the assistance of one of Shaw's companies. Appalled by this barbarism, Shaw protested but had to yield to higher authority. The incident plagued him until the end of his days. The negative publicity that resulted from the raid made Shaw twice as determined to prove the validity and capability of the 54th as a competent, honorable regiment. After the destruction of Darien, General Hunter was relieved of his command and replaced by Gen. Quincy A. Gillmore. The 54th remained with the Second South Carolina for a while, and Shaw came to appreciate Montgomery as a well-spoken, religious man devoted to his cause, though he also found him repulsive for his fanaticism. Colonel Shaw invested much time and energy looking after his men and becoming better acquainted with them. He wrote to Governor Andrew arguing against the pay cut Stanton had imposed on black regiments on June 4, 1863. Shaw insisted that his men should be mustered out of the army if they could not be paid equally to white soldiers at 13 dollars a month. On a social level, he attended one of the men's praise meetings and took a genuine, unbiased interest in the song and dance of the performers. At the beginning of July, a plan to attack Charleston was launched. Capturing the affluent harbor town would be a major victory for the Union, because of the town's importance to the Confederacy and its strategic location at the juncture of the Ashley and Cooper Rivers. Should this campaign succeed, the federals would also regain possession of Fort Sumter. On discovering that the 54th was not to be included in the campaign, Shaw wrote to his brigade commander, Gen. George C. Strong, expressing his disappointment. He had high hopes for his regiment and wanted them to engage in battle alongside white troops so they could prove their worth as soldiers and be proud.

The men would finally be put to the test on July 16, eight days after being ordered to James Island. The rebels made an attack on the federal army and Shaw's men staunchly resisted the blow and prevailed. They had, as Shaw wished, fought hard and fought well with white soldiers against white Confederates. But there would be no rest for the weary. That night, the 54th received orders to march through the treacherous mud flats. Bound for General Strong's headquarters on Morris Island, just within reach of Charleston, the regiment had to traverse one small island after another to arrive at their destination. The following day, tired and hungry, the men lingered for hours in the scorching heat awaiting a steamer to Folly's Island. Just before midnight they were on board, and on July 18 Shaw reported to Strong's headquarters. The colonel was presented a great challenge and opportunity: Would he have his men lead the charge to attack the indomitable Fort Wagner? Only a few days ago other troops had attempted to take the fort and failed. However, if the 54th could, a significant victory would be celebrated by all in the Union. To this request, Shaw answered a firm yes. He would place his duty and loyalty to country, family, and regiment above his own personal desires, for deep within he held a secret fear that this would be his last engagement.

That evening, the brave colonel led his men in the charge along the beach to the fort, as shells and shot rained down relentlessly on the gallant 54th. Though their lines were mowed down and bodies strewn across the sand, he rallied the surviving men onward to scale the walls of Fort Wagner. As Shaw reached the top of the parapet, he was struck by a bullet and killed. The following day, his body was buried in the sand along with those of his men. The mission to take the fort did not succeed, but the efforts they made and the significance of what was achieved in that fateful event would not be forgotten.

Storming Fort Wagner, a famous chromolithograph by Louis Kurz and Alexander Allison printed in 1890, depicts Col. Robert Gould Shaw and the men of the 54th Massachusetts. The Shaw Memorial, a bronze relief honoring the colonel and the 54th Massachusetts, would be completed in 1897 and stands in Boston today. The artist, Augustus Saint-Gaudens, worked on this masterpiece for 14 years, from in 1883. The original plaster cast is housed in the Saint-Gaudens National Historic Site in Cornish, New Hampshire, a copy of the plaster cast is located in the National Gallery of Art in Washington, D.C. *The Raid on Darien, Georgia* includes a letter by Shaw to his wife, Annie, about the "expedition" to Darien and includes a

photograph of Shaw and of St. Simons Island, where his letter was written. In the Battle of Olustee (Ocean Pond), February 20, 1864, the 54th fought alongside two other black regiments: the 8th U.S. Colored Troops and the 35th U.S. Colored Troops. This was the largest Civil War battle in the state of Florida, and a terrible defeat for the Union army.

Source and Additional Reading

Burchard, Peter. *One Gallant Rush: Robert Gould Shaw and His Brave Black Regiment.* New York: St. Martin's Press, 1965.

Catton, Bruce. *The American Heritage Picture History of the Civil War.* New York: American Heritage, 1988.

Davis, Kenneth C. *Don't Know Much about the Civil War: Everything You Need to Know about America's Greatest Conflict but Never Learned.* New York: William Morrow, 1996.

Duncan, Russell. *Blue-Eyed Child of Fortune: The Civil War Letters of Colonel Robert Gould Shaw.* Athens: University of Georgia Press, 1992.

Redkey, Edwin S. *A Grand Army of Black Men: Letters from African-American Soldiers in the Union Army, 1861–1865.* New York: Cambridge University Press, 1992.

Sheridan, Philip Henry (1831–1888) *Union general officer.*

While on his meteoric rise in the Union army, Philip H. Sheridan earned the enmity of many Virginians for laying waste to the Shenandoah Valley. His date and place of birth are uncertain, but he claimed to have been born in New York in 1831. Although he was destined to emerge from the Civil War with the third greatest reputation among the victors, his military career had not begun auspiciously. It took him five years to graduate from West Point (1853) because of an altercation with a fellow cadet and future Union general, William R. Terrill.

Posted to the infantry, he was still a second lieutenant at the outbreak of the Civil War. His assignments included the following: second lieutenant, Fourth Infantry (From November 22, 1854); first lieutenant, Fourth Infantry (March 1, 1861); captain, 13th Infantry (May 14, 1861); chief quartermaster and chief commissary of subsistence, Army of Southwest Missouri, Department of the Missouri (ca. December 25, 1861–early 1862); colonel, Second Michigan Cavalry (May 25, 1862); commander, Second Brigade, Cavalry Division, Army of the Mississippi (June 1–September 4, 1862); brigadier general, United States Volunteers (USV) (July 1, 1862); commander, 11th Division, Army of the Ohio (September 1–September 29, 1862); commander, 11th Division, Third Corps, Army of the Ohio (September 29–November 5, 1862); commander, Third

Division, Right Wing, 14th Corps, Army of the Cumberland (November 5, 1862–January 9, 1863); major general, USV (December 31, 1862); commander, Third Division, 20th Corps, Army of the Cumberland (January 9–October 9, 1863); commander, Second Division, Fourth Corps, Army of the Cumberland (October 10, 1863–February 17, 1864, and February 27–April 1864); commander, Cavalry Corps, Army of the Potomac (April 4–August 2, 1864); commander, Army of the Shenandoah (August 6–October 16, 1864, and October 19, 1864–February 28, 1865); also commander, Middle Military Division (August 6, 1864–February 27, 1865); brigadier general, USA (September 20, 1864); major general, USA (November 8, 1864); and commander, Sheridan's cavalry command (March–April 1865).

After serving in a staff position during the early part of the war he was recommended for the command of a cavalry regiment by Gordon Granger. Within days of taking command he was in charge of the brigade with which he earned his first star, at Booneville in northern Mississippi. In the late summer of 1862 he was given a division in Kentucky and middle Tennessee. He fought well at Perryville and Murfreesboro and was given a second star in the volunteers to date from the latter. At Chickamauga his division, along with almost two-thirds of the army, was swept from the field. However, at Chattanooga he regained his somewhat tarnished reputation when his division broke through the rebel lines atop Missionary Ridge. There was some question of who, if anyone, had ordered the troops all the way up to the crest. His division made a limited pursuit. When Grant went to the East, he placed Sheridan in command of the Army of the Potomac's mounted arm. Against J. E. B. Stuart's depleted horsemen Sheridan met with mixed success in the Overland Campaign but did manage to wound the Confederate cavalryman mortally at Yellow Tavern. His purposes were thwarted at Haws' Shop and Trevilian Station. His temperament put him in conflict with Generals Meade, Warren, Duffie, and Stevenson.

After General Early's threat to Washington, Grant tapped Sheridan to command a new military division, which comprised three departments, and charged him with clearing out the Shenandoah Valley. Despite being plagued by irregulars along his supply lines, he managed to best Early at Third Winchester, Fisher's Hill, and Cedar Creek. At the outbreak of the latter battle he was returning from a meeting with Grant and rode at a gallop from Winchester to the scene of the early morning reverse. Re-forming his men, he drove the enemy—who had lost all sense of order while plundering the camps—from the field, taking many prisoners. For this campaign he was named brigadier and major general in the regular army, vacating his volunteer commission, and received the thanks of Congress. He also burned his way through the valley, preventing future Confederate use of its grain and other stores.

The next March he destroyed Early's remaining forces at Waynesboro and then went on a raid, threatening Lynchburg. Rejoining Grant, he smashed through the Confederate lines at Five Forks, necessitating the evacuation of both Petersburg and Richmond. During the action he unfairly removed Warren for slowness. It was Sheridan's cavalry command, backed by infantry, that finally blocked Lee's escape at Appomattox. His role in the final campaign even eclipsed that of the army commander Meade.

After a postwar show of force against Maximilian in Mexico, he headed the Reconstruction government of Texas and Louisiana. His severity forced his removal within half a year. Remaining in the regular army, he died as a full general in 1888, having been the commander in chief since 1884. In the meantime he had commanded the Division of the Missouri, observed the Franco-Prussian War, and worked for the creation and preservation of Yellowstone National Park. By the use of troops to protect the park he may have been trying to salve his conscience for the destruction in the Shenandoah.

Source and Additional Reading

O'Connor, Richard. *Sheridan the Inevitable.* Indianapolis, Ind.: Bobbs Merrill, 1953.

Sheridan, Philip H. *Personal Memoirs of P. H. Sheridan, General United States Army.* New York: Charles L. Webster, 1888.

Sherman, William Tecumseh (1820–1891) *Union general officer.*

He never commanded in a major Union victory and his military career had repeated ups and downs, but William T. Sherman is the second best known of northern civil war commanders. His father had died when he was nine years old, and Sherman was raised by Senator Thomas Ewing and eventually married into his family. Through the influence of his patron, he obtained an appointment to West Point. Only five cadets of the class of 1840 graduated ahead of him, and he was appointed to the artillery. He received a brevet for his services in California during the Mexican War but resigned in 1853 as a captain and commissary officer.

The years until the Civil War were not filled with success. Living in California and Kansas, he failed in banking and law. In 1859 he seemed to have found his niche as the superintendent of a military academy, which is now Louisiana State University. However, he resigned this post on the secession of the state and went to St. Louis as head of a streetcar company and then volunteered for the Union army.

His assignments included the following: colonel, 13th Infantry (May 14, 1861); commander, Third

Brigade, First Division, Army of Northeastern Virginia (June–August 17, 1861); brigadier general, USV (August 7, 1861, to rank from May 17); commander of brigade, Division of the Potomac (August 17–28, 1861); second in command, Department of the Cumberland (August 28–October 8, 1861); commander of department (October 8–November 9, 1861); commander, District of Cairo, Department of the Missouri (February 14–March 1, 1862); commander, Fifth Division, Army of the Tennessee (March 1–July 21, 1862); major general, USV (May 1, 1862); commander, Fifth Division, District of Memphis, Army of the Tennessee (July 21–September 24, 1862); commander, First Division, District of Memphis, Army of the Tennessee (September 24–October 26, 1862); also commander, of district (July 21–October 26, 1862); commander, District of Memphis, 13th Corps, Army of the Tennessee (October 24–November 25, 1862); commander, Yazoo Expedition, Army of the Tennessee (December 18, 1862–January 4, 1863); commander, Second Corps, Army of the Mississippi (January 4–12, 1863); commander, 15th Corps, Army of the Tennessee (January 12–October 29, 1863); brigadier general, USA (July 4, 1863); commander, Army and Department of the Tennessee (October 24, 1863–March 26, 1864); commander, Military Division of the Mississippi (March 18, 1864–June 27, 1865); major general, USA (August 12, 1864); lieutenant general, USA (July 25, 1866); general, USA (March 4, 1869); and commander in chief, USA (March 8, 1869–November 1, 1883).

Appointed to the colonelcy of one of the regular army's newly authorized infantry regiments, he led the brigade of volunteers of the First Division that crossed Bull Run to aid the Second and Third Divisions after the attack on the enemy left had begun. Despite being caught up in the route—he already had a low opinion of volunteers—he was named a brigadier general the next month. Briefly commanding a brigade around Washington, D.C., he was then sent to Kentucky as deputy to Robert Anderson. He soon succeeded the hero of Fort Sumter in command of the department but got into trouble over his overestimates of the enemy strength. The newspapers actually reported him as being insane. Removed from command, he was given another chance by his friend Henry W. Halleck in Missouri. But again, while inspecting troops in the central part of the state, he allowed his overactive imagination to run away with him. During the campaign against Forts Henry and Donelson he was stationed at Paducah, Kentucky, and charged with forwarding reinforcements to Grant. Forming a good working relationship with the future commander in chief, Sherman offered to waive his seniority rights and take a command under him.

Commanding a division, he was largely responsible for the poor state of preparedness at Shiloh but redeemed himself during the defensive fighting of the first day and

was wounded. The next day his command played only a minor role. Praised by Grant, he was soon made a major general of volunteers. He was instrumental in persuading Grant to remain in the army during his difficulties with Halleck during the advance on Corinth, Mississippi.

During the early operations against Vicksburg he ordered a doomed assault at Chickasaw Bluffs and a few days later was superseded by John A. McClernand, who accepted Sherman's proposal to attack Arkansas Post. Grant initially criticized this movement as unnecessary but declared it an important achievement when it succeeded and he learned that Sherman had suggested it. Sherman's corps did little fighting in the advance on Vicksburg in May until the disastrous assaults were made.

After the fall of the river city he was named a brigadier general in the regular army and led an expedition against Jackson. That fall he went to the relief of Chattanooga, where he failed to achieve his objectives in the assault against Tunnel Hill at the end of Missionary Ridge. Nonetheless, he was highly praised by Grant, who then sent him to relieve the pressure on Gen. Ambrose E. Burnside at Knoxville. Back in Mississippi, he led the Meridian Expedition and then succeeded Grant in overall command in the West, Facing Joseph E. Johnston's army, he forced it all the way back to Atlanta, where the Confederate was replaced by John B. Hood, who launched three disastrous attacks against the Union troops near the city. Eventually taking possession of Atlanta, Sherman ordered the population evacuated and the military value of the city destroyed. Sending George H. Thomas back to Middle Tennessee to deal with Hood, he embarked on his March to the Sea. Taking Savannah, he announced the city as a Christmas gift to the president and the country. Marching north to aid Grant in the final drive against Richmond, he drove through the Carolinas and accepted Johnston's surrender at Durham Station. His terms were considered too liberal and touching on political matters and were disapproved by Secretary of War Stanton. This led to a long-running feud between the two. Terms were finally arranged on the basis of the Appomattox surrender.

During the last two campaigns Sherman had earned a reputation for destruction and for the lack of discipline of his troops—his marauding stragglers were known as "Sherman's bummers." Especially resented by southerners was the burning of Columbia, South Carolina. But there are indications that the fires had spread from cotton set ablaze by the retreating Confederates under Wade Hampton.

On August 12, 1864, Sherman had been promoted to major general in the regular army and vacated his volunteer commission. Also, he was the only man twice to receive the thanks of Congress during the Civil War—first for Chattanooga and second for Atlanta and Savannah. After the war he remained in the service and was promoted to full general, replacing Grant as commander in chief. One of his most important contributions after the war was the establishment of the Command School at Ft. Leavenworth. He retired from the army on February 8, 1884.

He was noted for this absolute refusal to be drawn into politics. In 1886 he made his home in New York City, where he died on February 14, 1891. He is buried in Calvary Cemetery, St. Louis.

Source and Additional Reading

Hart, B. H. Liddell. *Sherman: Soldier, Realist, American.* Dodd, Mead, New York, 1929.

Lewis, Lloyd. *Sherman: Fighting Prophet.* New York, Harcourt Brace, 1932.

Shields, Marvin G. (1939–1965) *Construction mechanic third class, United States Navy, Seabee Team 1104, so distinguished himself in combat, during the Vietnam War, that he was awarded (posthumously) the Medal of Honor.*

Born: December 30, 1939, Port Townsend, Wash.; **Entered service at:** Seattle, Wash.; **Place and date:** Dong Xoai, Republic of Vietnam, June 10, 1965.

Citation: "For conspicuous gallantry and intrepidity at the risk of his life above and beyond the call of duty. Although wounded when the compound of Detachment A342, 5th Special Forces Group (Airborne), 1st Special Forces, came under intense fire from an estimated reinforced Viet Cong regiment employing machineguns, heavy weapons and small arms, Shields continued to resupply his fellow Americans who needed ammunition and to return the enemy fire for a period of approximately 3 hours, at which time the Viet Cong launched a massive attack at close range with flame-throwers, hand grenades and small-arms fire. Wounded a second time during this attack, Shields nevertheless assisted in carrying a more critically wounded man to safety, and then resumed firing at the enemy for 4 more hours. When the commander asked for a volunteer to accompany him in an attempt to knock out an enemy machinegun emplacement which was endangering the lives of all personnel in the compound because of the accuracy of its fire, Shields unhesitatingly volunteered for this extremely hazardous mission. Proceeding toward their objective with a 3.5-inch rocket launcher, they succeeded in destroying the enemy machinegun emplacement, thus undoubtedly saving the lives of many of their fellow servicemen in the compound. Shields was mortally wounded by hostile fire while returning to his defensive position. His heroic initiative and great personal valor in the face of intense enemy fire sustain and enhance the finest traditions of the U.S. Naval Service."

Source and Additional Reading

Medal of Honor Citation.

Stanton, Shelby L. *Special Forces at War: An Illustrated History, Southeast Asia, 1957–1975.* Charlottesville, Va.: Howell Press, 1990.

Shofner, Austin C. "Shifty" (1916–1999) *Brigadier general, United States Marine Corps.*

Although BGen. Austin C. Shofner, United States Marine Corps (Retired), died at his Shelbyville, Tennessee, home in November 1999, his accomplishments as a war hero, athletic coach, and businessman live on.

He was born on March 3, 1916, in Chattanooga to Austin W. and Rachel Conner Shofner, with a very definite military background on both sides of his family.

His great great-grandfather, Martin Shofner, had fought as an infantryman in the Battle of Kong Mountain during the Revolutionary War and for that service had received a land grant of a large area of property that would later become a part of Bedford County, Tennessee.

Shofner's grandfather, Monroe Shofner, was a cavalryman for the Confederate State of America during the Civil War, who served under Gen. Nathan Bedford Forrest.

On the maternal side, his great-uncle, Lewis Shepherd, also fought for the Confederate States of America. He was captured in March 1864, near Graysville, Georgia, and was first imprisoned near Chattanooga and later moved to Camp Morton in Indiana. He escaped from Camp Morton in November 1864 but was recaptured two days later. So there was also a history of escape in Shofner's background. Shepherd later became a lawyer, served many years as a judge, and twice served in the Tennessee House of Representatives.

Shofner's family moved to Bedford County when he was three years old and lived on a farm on the Shofner Land Grant. He said spending his early years on that farm along Thompson Creek and Duck River taught him many things, such as hard work as a means to achieve goals, the value of a high-quality education, and even at an early age ways to turn a buck by hunting and trapping.

His involvement in sports began when his father became principal of the high school in Tullahoma. He played tackle on the football team and was an outfielder on the baseball team and played his senior seasons at Shelbyville. After graduating from Shelbyville, he attended the University of Tennessee, where he was a member of the football and wrestling teams.

He played football under Major, later General Bob Neyland, a graduate of West Point, whose coaching career at Tennessee was interrupted twice by returning to military service.

Those four years under Coach Neyland were partially responsible for my choosing a military career.

The first time I ever heard, "When the going gets tough, the tough get going," was from Coach Neyland. He also taught us "Play for the breaks and when they come your way . . . score."

Shofner credited the teachings and concepts of Coach Neyland with helping him survive his early battles, stints in prisoner-of-war (POW) camps, and ultimate escape to fight again in World War II.

As a member of the wrestling team, he once pinned his opponent in the 165-pound class and then learned that Tennessee's wrestler in the 175-pound class had failed to make weight and would have to forfeit. Shofner talked the coach into letting him wrestle in the 175-pound class and pinned his opponent in about three minutes.

Into the Military He had signed up for Army Reserve Officers Training Corps (ROTC) at Tennessee and shortly before graduation, in 1937, learned there was only one opening for the Marine Corps for all the graduates in the ROTC program. Shofner applied for that spot and was accepted. He reported for duty July 1, 1937, at Marine Corps Basic Officers School at Philadelphia Naval Yard. The school lasted 10 months and covered all phases of military training. He qualified as expert in every weapon in use by the Marine Corps at that time.

A member of that class was Gregory "Pappy" Boyington, the legendary fighter pilot who left the Marines to fight with the Flying Tigers in China before the United States entered World War II and later returned to the Marine Corps as leader of the famous Black Sheep Squadron (and a recipient of the Medal of Honor).

After completion of Basic Officers School, Shofner's first duty assignment was aboard the battleship USS *Oklahoma*, where he was second battery gunnery officer. While aboard he qualified as a deep-sea diver.

In the spring of 1939, he was transferred to San Diego Marine Base and was platoon commander of Company E, Second Battalion, Sixth Marine Regiment. While assigned there, he became player-coach on one of the outstanding Marine Corps football teams of all time during the 1939 and 1940 seasons.

Shofner, by now a first lieutenant, was transferred from San Diego to the Fourth Marine Regiment, then located in the International Settlement, in Shanghai, China, in June 1941. He was assigned to a variety of duties, including battalion athletic officer, and coached a six-man football team to the regimental championships.

The Fourth Marine Regiment actually served as guards of the International Settlement, providing security for the countries established there, including the United States, Great Britain, France, Italy, Germany, and Japan. War was raging in China and Japanese forces were in total control of the area around the settlement.

"Our primary job was to keep the Japanese forces out of the International Settlement although they controlled the rest of Shanghai. We suddenly became aware of the growing tensions between the United States and Japan. It was generally accepted that we would be fighting the Japanese. It was only a matter of where and when," Shofner explained.

The Fourth Marine Regiment departed Shanghai on November 27, 1941. Rumor had it we [the regiment] were bound for the Philippine Islands. Two days out of Shanghai, possibly somewhere north of Formosa, six Japanese destroyers approached one of the ships. The Marines on the deck of the liner *President Madison* set up machine guns, but nothing happened. The Japanese destroyers stopped their aggressive actions and steamed away in another direction.

At dawn on the morning of December 1, the Marines arrived in the Philippines, docking at Subic Bay, only a few days before the Japanese attack on Pearl Harbor.

Before leaving Shanghai, Shofner had started keeping a diary; he continued to do so during the early days of the war, his time in prison camps, his escape, and time spent fighting with guerrilla forces until he was evacuated by submarine to Australia in December 1943.

"This was extremely risky, especially during the time I was in the Japanese prison camps. I saw men beaten or killed for less than keeping a dairy of daily events. I was able to keep it hidden. One Jap guard found the diary but the obviously couldn't read English He just glanced at it and threw it aside," said Shofner.

Some excerpts from the diary told of early fighting.

Dec. 12, 1941—Japanese Zero fighters picked off 7 PBYs, the big Catalina Flying Boats, at anchorage in Subic Bay. Our regiment fired .30-caliber machine guns at the low-flying fighters with no apparent damage. Went out in afternoon and tried to salvage the .50-caliber machine guns off the sunken PBYs.

Japanese landings were taking place all around the Subic Bay area in the vicinity of the town of Olonagapo, where Shofner and his men were constantly being bombed and strafed by the Japanese, who had quickly taken complete control of the air.

Dec. 25th, 1941—I left Olongapo at 3 p.m. and arrived at Mariveles on Manila Bay about 8 p.m. One of my friends, Captain Noel Castle, got me a turkey sandwich—my Christmas dinner. I went down to the beach and watched a freighter burn. Found a bunk in officers quarters at Mariveles. Air alarm went off about midnight. Everyone ran outside, according to plan, into open spaces. I looked out—Manila was being burned—then went back to sleep as I was very tired.

Shofner's unit was moved to Corregidor, a small volcanic island guarding the entrance to Manila Bay, on December 27. The Japanese bombed and shelled Corregidor almost constantly, but the American and Filipino forces continued to hold out, upsetting the Japanese timetable and their plans to attack Australia and other areas.

Soon the lack of food, disease, and lack of medicines, ammunition, and modern weapons made the situation terrible. Shofner was wounded; he received the Silver Star for his actions during those desperate days.

"At times the Japanese artillery shells were falling on us so fast it practically sounded like a machine gun firing," he once remarked.

Prison Camp   General Douglas MacArthur, who had been evacuated to Australia earlier, ordered American forces on Corregidor to surrender on May 6, 1942. Japanese forces arrived the next morning and immediately started kicking, slapping, and taking anything of value from their prisoners. Resistance meant instant death. Shofner told of seeing Japanese soldiers with three or four wristwatches on their arms and one with watches from his wrist to his elbow. An American's finger was chopped off when he could not remove his ring quickly enough.

The Americans were taken to the Bilibid Prison in Manila and then moved in hot, tightly jammed cattle cars to Cabanatuan, known to many as the Camp of Death. Many of those held at Cabanatuan were survivors of the Death March and of Corregidor.

They received practically no food, only small amounts of worm-infested rice. Shofner said he ate the rice, worms and all, since the worms wre the only source of protein. There was no medicine for the sick or the wounded. Americans were forced to dig ditches each morning to bury those who died during the night, usually as many as 30–50 men.

On the morning of October 26, 1942, Shofner was one of 1,000 prisoners ordered aboard the *Erie Maru*, a rusty Japanese freighter, to be moved to Davao Penal Colony on the island of Mindanao. They arrived in the rain on November 7 and were forced to march to the penal colony.

Escape   Shofner, nine other Americans, and two Filipino guides escaped from Davao Penal Colony on Sunday morning, April 4, 1943. They pretended to be going out on work details and fled into the jungle, chopping their way through the thick growth with bolos.

As night fell, they found themselves in a deep swamp. The jungle and swamp, marked as *unexplored* on available maps, were occupied by wild tribes. The cold, wet escapees climbed atop a log and ate a cold meal. Soon they heard drums beating in the distance.

Shofner softly chanted, "Heads are available, heads are available," in time to the drumbeats.

"The others quickly told me to knock it off, but it broke the spell and we stopped feeling sorry for ourselves and talked over our situation. At least we were free," Shofner once remarked while describing their first day of freedom.

They made contact with Filipino guerrillas three days later.

After making their way along mountains and through dense jungles to the northern area of Mindanao, they joined the guerrillas and fought with them until evacuated by submarine to Australia.

Shofner was promoted from captain to major while with the guerrillas and served as deputy chief of staff and operations officer of a guerrilla division. They had little ammunition and no modern weapons but their hit-and-run tactics held the Japanese invaders to only a few coastal towns.

On Monday, November 15, 1943, Shofner and two other Marines in his escape party were evacuated by submarine.

"As we pulled away from the dock, our guerrilla band was playing 'God Bless America.' I don't mind saying that there were tears in my eyes," said Shofner.

After a brief stay in Australia, during which he was interviewed by General MacArthur and presented the Legion of Merit, Shofner returned to the United States in December 1943. During his flight to Washington he had a brief layover in Knoxville and noticed a woman he had dated during his days at the University of Tennessee working at the ticket counter of a civilian airline. She was Kathleen King, a beautiful brunette, the former Miss Tennessee. He was still dressed in ragged clothing he had worn during his time with the guerrillas and had lost much weight since she had seen him.

"She was busy. I got in the line and made my way to the counter. She said, 'May I help you?' I just smiled and said, 'Hi!' As she looked up and saw me, her mouth flew open and she started to scream. She'd heard I was dead. She thought she was seeing a ghost."

Shofner returned to Shelbyville on Christmas Eve 1943 for a brief stay before returning to duty, at his request, in the South Pacific.

He was a battalion commander in the invasion of Peleliu in 1944 and was wounded late in the first day ashore. After being treated for his wounds, he was taken to a hospital ship and treated for his wounds. Wanting to return to the battle and without seeking permission, he caught a landing craft and headed back to the island.

Ironically, he was placed in charge of Japanese who had been taken prisoner, who complained to an interpreter they were not receiving enough food and Shofner was not treating them well. Shofner had the interpreter inform them that he had been a prisoner of the Japanese and would be very happy to treat them just as he had been treated. They quickly dropped their complaints.

Shofner was later assigned to temporary duty with an army unit during MacArthur's return to the Philippines. He and an interpreter went behind Japanese lines to talk with Filipino guerrillas about a planned move to free prisoners being held at Cabanatuan. Although Shofner was not allowed to take part in the actual raid, army rangers and scouts hit Cabanatuan, the Camp of Death, and freed over 500 prisoners after wiping out the Japanese garrison.

He later was in the thick of the battle for Okinawa and troops under his command captured some Japanese strongholds after a long, bloody battle.

Shofner was on Okinawa, where he and his men were preparing to invade Japan, when America dropped the atomic bombs and Japan surrendered a few days later.

"I've heard a lot of people criticize America for dropping the atomic bomb, but none of them were being asked to invade Japan, where American losses were going to be extremely heavy," he once remarked.

Postwar Life   After retiring from the Marine Corps as a brigadier general in 1959, he returned to Bedford County, Tennessee, and became a founder of an insurance company and finance company, in addition to other business interests.

He married the late Kathleen King in 1947. They had five sons, four of whom are still living.

Wes Shofner, a graduate of Harvard and Vanderbilt Law School, is a partner in one of Nashville's largest law firms.

Martin Shofner, an architect, earned degrees at Harvard and Yale.

Dr. Stewart Shofner, an ophthalmologist, attended Harvard Medical School at the University of Virginia and had additional studies at Yale and Louisiana State University.

Michael Shofner is a graduate of Southwestern University. He oversees several finance companies in Shelbyville and Tullahoma, Tennessee.

Source
Melson, B. *Shelbyville* [Tenn.] *Times-Gazette*, November 17, 1999. pp. 1, 5, 6.

Shughart, Randall D. (d. 1993) *Sergeant first class, United States Army, so distinguished himself in combat in Somalia, in 1993, that he was awarded (posthumously) the Medal of Honor for his heroic actions.*

Born: Newville, Penn.; **Place and date:** October 3, 1993, Mogadishu, Somalia.

Citation: "Sergeant First Class Shughart, United States Army, distinguished himself by actions above and beyond the call of duty on 3 October 1993, while serving as a Sniper Team Member, United States Army Special Operations Command with Task Force Ranger in Mogadishu, Somalia. Sergeant First Class Shughart provided precision sniper fires from the lead helicopter during an assault on a building and at two helicopter crash sites, while subjected to intense automatic weapons and rocket propelled grenade fires. While providing critical suppressive fires at the second crash site, Sergeant First Class Shughart and his team leader learned that ground forces were not immediately available to secure the site. Sergeant First Class Shughart and his team leader unhesitatingly volunteered to be inserted to protect the four critically wounded personnel, despite being well aware of the growing number of enemy personnel closing in on the site. After their third request to be inserted, Sergeant First Class Shughart and his team leader received permission to perform this volunteer mission. When debris and enemy ground fires at the site caused them to abort the first attempt, Sergeant First Class Shughart and his team leader were inserted one hundred meters south of the crash site. Equipped with only his sniper rifle and a pistol, Sergeant First Class Shughart and his team leader, while under intense small arms fire from the enemy, fought their way through a dense maze of shanties and shacks to reach the critically injured crewmembers. Sergeant First Class Shughart pulled the pilot and the other crewmembers from the aircraft, establishing a perimeter, which placed him and his fellow sniper in the most vulnerable position. Sergeant First Class Shughart used his long-range rifle and side arm to kill an undetermined number of attackers while traveling the perimeter, protecting the downed crew. Sergeant First Class Shughart continued his protective fire until he depleted his ammunition and was fatally wounded. His actions saved the pilot's life. Sergeant First Class Shughart's extraordinary heroism and devotion to duty were in keeping with the highest standards of military service and reflect great credit upon him, his unit and the United States Army."

Source
Medal of Honor Citation.

Sickles, Daniel Edgar (1819–1914) *Union general officer, so distinguished himself in combat, during the American Civil War, that he was awarded the Medal of Honor for his heroic actions.*

In his pre– and post–Civil War careers, as well as during the conflict, Daniel E. Sickles proved to be one of the most controversial of Union corps commanders. Before the war, the New York City native had already become the first man acquitted of a murder charge on the grounds of temporary insanity.

Sickles, a congressman, shot down Philip Barton Key, the son of the composer of "The Star Spangled Banner," in Lafayette Park, across the street from both Sickles's home and the White House. Key had been having an affair with Sickles's wife, whom Sickles had married while serving as secretary of the U.S. legation in London. The defense attorney Edwin M. Stanton gained the innovative verdict. Sickles then publicly forgave his wife, outraging the public, who had applauded his role in the shooting, and apparently ending his political career. Just then the Civil War broke out and he saw his chance to get a new start by offering his services.

Sickles's assignments included the following: colonel, 70th New York (June 20, 1861); brigadier general, United States Volunteers (USV) (September 3, 1861); commander, second ("Excelsior") Brigade, Hooker's division, Army of the Potomac (October 3, 1861–March 13, 1862); commander, Second ("Excelsior") Brigade, Second Division, Third Corps, Army of the Potomac (May 24–July 16, 1862); commander of division (September 5, 1862–January 12, 1863); major general, USV (November 29, 1862); and commander of corps (February 5–May 29, and June 3–July 2, 1863).

When authorized to raise a regiment he proceeded to recruit enough men for a brigade and was soon rewarded with a brigadier's star. Frequently absent from his command seeking advancement in Washington, he nonetheless commanded his brigade at Seven Pines and during the Seven Days. In charge of the division, he fought at Fredericksburg and received the regular army brevet of brigadier general in 1867. His prewar reputation as a womanizer and heavy drinker was revived during his career as a brigade and division commander, and his brigade was considered a rowdy bunch. But his heyday occurred when Joseph Hooker took command of the army, many officers complained that Hooker, Sickles, and Daniel Butterfield had converted the army headquarters into a combination of bar and brothel.

Sickles's own headquarters were considered to be even worse. After fighting at Chancellorsville, Sickles retained charge of the Third Corps even after Hooker's removal. Then on the second day of Gettysburg he did not like the sector assigned to his men along Cemetery Ridge. It was too long and low for his liking, and he unilaterally decided to advance to the Peach Orchard. If he had survived the battle unscathed, he probably would have been court-martialed. But some claim that his advanced position absorbed the shock of Longstreet's assault before it could reach the ridge; according to that interpretation, if the assault had hit the ridge in full strength, it would have broken the Union line. This conclusion is, however, highly debatable since his move-

ment put the left flank of the second Corps in the air as well as both of his own. Always courageous on the field of battle, he was struck in the leg by a shell as his command was beginning its withdrawal. The leg was amputated within half an hour. In 1867 he was brevetted regular army major general for his role in the battle and three decades later was awarded the Medal of Honor. He donated his leg to an army medical museum and in later years is said to have visited it.

During his recovery he engaged in a feud with Meade over his generalship and who had won the battle. As a result he was denied further field command and was assigned a series of special missions by the War Department. Made colonel, 42nd Infantry, in the 1866 regular army reorganization, he was mustered out of the volunteer service as a major general (from late 1862) on January 1, 1868.

The next year, he was retired with the advanced rank of major general in the regular establishment. Appointed U.S. minister to Spain by Grant, he furthered his reputation as a ladies' man. In the 1890s he served a term in Congress. For 26 years—until forced out in a financial scandal—he chaired the New York State Monuments Commission.

Source and Additional Reading

Pinchon, Edgcumb. *Dan Sickles: Hero of Gettysburg*. New York: Doubleday, Doran, 1945.

Swanberg, W. A. *Sickles the Incredible*. New York: Charles Scribner's Sons, 1985.

Sijan, Lance Peter *Lieutenant, United States Air Force, Vietnam War Prisoner of War, so distinguished himself in combat that he was (posthumously) awarded the Medal of Honor for his heroic actions.*

Born: April 13, 1942, Milwaukee, Wis.; **Entered service at:** Milwaukee, Wis.; **Place and date:** North Vietnam, November 9, 1967.

Home City of Record: Milwaukee, Wis.; Date of loss: November 9, 1967. Country of loss: Laos. Loss coordinates: 171500N 1060800E. Status (in 1973): Killed in captivity. Acft/vehicle/ground: F4C. Other personnel in incident: John W. Armstrong (missing).

First Lieutenant Lance P. Sijan was the pilot and Lt. Col. John W. Armstrong the bombardier/navigator of an F4C Phantom fighter/bomber sent on a mission over Laos on November 9, 1967. Sijan and Armstrong were flying low over the Ho Chi Minh Trail when, at approximately 9 P.M., the aircraft was hit by a surface-to-air missile (SAM) and crashed. The two went down near the famed Mu Gia Pass, a pass in the mountainous border region of Laos and Vietnam. It was not until nearly six years later that what happened to Sijan and Armstrong was learned. They were classified missing in action (MIA).

Sijan evaded capture for nearly six weeks. During that time, he was seriously injured and suffering from shock and extreme weight loss due to lack of food. The extremely rugged terrain was sometimes almost impassable, but Sijan continued to try to reach friendly forces. After being captured by North Vietnamese forces, Sijan was taken to a holding point for subsequent transfer to a prisoner of war (POW) camp. In his emaciated and crippled condition, he overpowered one of his guards and crawled into the jungle, only to be recaptured after several hours. He was then transferred to another prison camp, where he was kept in solitary confinement and interrogated at length. During the interrogation he was severely tortured yet did not reveal information to his captors. Sijan lapsed into delirium and was placed in the care of another American POW. During intermittent periods of consciousness, he never complained of his physical condition and kept talking about escaping. He was barely alive yet continued to fight.

During the period he was cared for, he also told the story of his shootdown and evasion to other Americans. After their release, his incredible story was told in *Into the Mouth of the Cat,* a book written by Malcolm McConnell from stories brought back by returning American POWs.

Sijan related to fellow POWs that the aircraft had climbed to approximately 10,000 feet after being struck. Sijan bailed out but was unable to see what happened to LTC Armstrong because of the darkness. In 1977, a Pathet Lao defector, who claimed to have been a prison camp guard, stated he had been guarding several Americans. According to his report, one was named "Armstrong." There are only two Armstrongs listed as MIA. There is little question that the other Armstong died at the time of his crash. The Defense Intelligence Agency gives this report no credence.

Sijan was finally removed from the care of other POWs and they were told he was being taken to a hospital. They never saw him again. His remains were returned on March 13, 1974. In the early 1980s, Lt. Col. James "Bo" Gritz conducted a number of missions into Laos attempting to obtain positive proof of live POWs there or, better, to secure the release of at least one POW. Although Gritz failed to free any POWs, he returned with a wealth of information on Americans. One thing Gritz recovered was a United States Air Force Academy ring, dated class of 1965, inscribed "Lance Peter Sijan." The ring was returned to Sijan's family in Wisconsin.

The North Vietnamese captured Lance Sijan. It is theorized that since the Pathet Lao also operated throughout Laos, it is possible that Armstrong, if he was captured, was captured by the Pathet Lao. Although the Pathet Lao stated publicly they held "tens of tens" of American POWs, the United States never negotiated their release because it did not officially recognize the Pathet Lao as a governmental entity. Consequently, nearly 600 Americans lost in Laos disappeared. Not one American held by the Lao was ever released.

Lance P. Sijan graduated from the United States Air Force Academy in 1965. He was promoted to the rank of captain during his captivity and was awarded the Medal of Honor for his extraordinary heroism during his evasion and captivity. Sijan became legendary in his escape attempts and endurance, even among his Vietnamese captors.

Citation: "While on a flight over North Vietnam, Capt. Sijan ejected from his disabled aircraft and successfully evaded capture for more than 6 weeks. During this time, he was seriously injured and suffered from shock and extreme weight loss due to lack of food. After being captured by North Vietnamese soldiers, Capt. Sijan was taken to a holding point for subsequent transfer to a prisoner of war camp. In his emaciated and crippled condition, he overpowered 1 of his guards and crawled into the jungle, only to be recaptured after several hours. He was then transferred to another prison camp where he was kept in solitary confinement and interrogated at length. During interrogation, he was severely tortured, however, he did not divulge any information to his captors. Capt. Sijan lapsed into delirium and was placed in the care of another prisoner. During his intermittent periods of consciousness until his death, he never complained of his physical condition and, on several occasions, spoke of future escape attempts. Capt. Sijan's extraordinary heroism and intrepidity above and beyond the call of duty at the cost of his life are in keeping with the highest traditions of the U.S. Air Force and reflect great credit upon himself and the U.S. Armed Forces."

Source and Additional Reading

Medal of Honor Citation.

McConnell, Malcom. *Into the Mouth of the Cat: The Story of Lance Sijan, Hero of Vietnam.* Bridgewater, N.J.: 1997.

U.S. Air Force Military Museum Website: www.wbafb.afmil/museum/history/vietnam/sijan/htm

Sitting Bull (Tatanka Iyotake) (1831–1890) *Great Sioux leader of the Hunkpapa Lakota group who helped defeat General George Custer at the Battle of the Little Bighorn.*

Born on Grand River, South Dakota, Sitting Bull fought hostile tribes and white intruders on Sioux lands from his early adulthood. He excelled in the virtues most admired by the Sioux: bravery, fortitude, generosity, and wisdom.

With Chiefs Crazy Horse and Gall, he stood fast against surrendering land or mining rights in the Black

Hills after gold was discovered there in the mid-1870s. The three chiefs successfully attacked Custer at the Little Bighorn (1876), after which Sitting Bull and other Sioux fled to Canada. Returning in 1881, he was imprisoned for two years before returning to Standing Rock Reservation. Some observers have said that the reason Sitting Bull was allowed to travel with Buffalo Bill and his Wild West Show, organized in 1883, was to keep him away from the reservation.

In 1890, shortly before the massacre of the Sioux at Wounded Knee, Sitting Bull permitted Grand River people to join the antiwhite ghost dance cult and was therefore arrested. In the fracas that followed, Native American police killed him. His remains are buried near Mobridge, South Dakota. He is still revered at Standing Rock Reservation.

Sources and Additional Reading

Manzione, Joseph. *I Am Looking to the North for My Life.* Salt Lake City: University of Utah Press, 1990.

Utley, Robert M. *The Lance and the Shield.* New York: Holt, 1993.

Vestal, Stanley. *Sitting Bull, Champion of the Sioux: A Biography,* rev. ed. 1957. Reprint, Norman: University of Oklahoma Press, 1980.

Smith, Chester B. *SM1, United States Navy.*

Born in Celina, Ohio, Chester B. Smith enlisted in 1954 and progressed through the enlisted ranks to warrant officer and then to commissioned officer status in 1971. During his career he spent 22 years at sea, including two tours in command. He retired from the United States Navy in September 1993 with the rank of captain after 39 years of active naval service and currently (February 2002) serves as the chief of Veterans Services for the city of Jacksonville, Florida.

Citation: "For extraordinary heroism in action against communist insurgent forces in the Republic of Vietnam, while serving with River Section 531 on 11 December 1966. As Patrol Officer on a PBR combat patrol on the Mekong River, SM1 (Signalman First Class) Smith pursued a sampan, with three Viet Cong aboard, into a narrow canal where the sampan's occupants, aided by eight other Viet Cong along the canal banks, opened fire on the patrol boat. SM1 Smith promptly directed his crew in returning suppressive fire, which accounted for eight Viet Cong killed. Bringing in his cover boat from the main river, SM1 Smith reentered the canal where he came upon a company-size Viet Cong force preparing to board forty sampans. The enemy opened fire on the patrol boats, but were completely repulsed and demoralized by SM1 Smith's sudden attack, causing them to retreat in confu-

sion. At least two of the enemy were confirmed as killed. While returning the heavy fire the Viet Cong were directing at him, SM1 Smith systematically destroyed their water transport and equipment. After extracting his patrol to rearm, he reentered the canal for a third time and personally directed his machine gunners in silencing six enemy weapon positions. SM1 Smith then vectored a USN helicopter in a rocket run on a cleverly camouflaged bunker. A large secondary explosion resulted, completely destroying an enemy ammunition cache. When the overall four-hour engagement had ended, SM1 Smith's PBR's had accounted for fifteen enemy confirmed killed, twenty-eight enemy sampans sunk, twelve damaged, three captured, and an enemy ammunition cache destroyed. His aggressive actions, outstanding initiative, extraordinary courage, and gallant leadership were in keeping with the highest traditions of the United States Naval Service."

Captain Smith's awards include the Navy Cross, Silver Star, Legion of Merit, Purple Heart, Navy Commendation, Navy Achievement with two Stars, National Defense Service Medal, Good Conduct Medal with five stars, Vietnam Service Medal, Vietnamese Cross of Gallantry with Palm, Vietnam Campaign Medal, as well as numerous ribbons.

Source

Information supplied by Capt. Chester B. Smith, USN (Retired).

Smith, Edmund Kirby (1824–1893) *General officer, Confederate States Army.*

After the fall of Vicksburg and Port Hudson and the closing of the Mississippi, the Confederate Gen. E. Kirby Smith was confronted with the command of a virtually independent area of the Confederacy and all of its inherent administrative problems. The Floridian West Pointer (1845) nicknamed "Seminole" at the academy had been posted to the infantry on his graduation and won two brevets in the Mexican War. In 1855 he transferred to the cavalry and served until his resignation as major in the Second Cavalry on April 6, 1861. In the meantime he had taught mathematics at his alma mater and been wounded in 1859 fighting Native Americans in the Nescutunga Valley of Texas. When Texas seceded, Smith refused to surrender his command to the state forces under Ben McCulloch.

Joining the Confederacy, he had the following assignments: lieutenant colonel, Cavalry (spring 1861); chief of staff, Army of the Shenandoah (spring–summer 1861); brigadier general, Confederate States Army (CSA) (June 17, 1861); commander, Fourth Brigade, Army of the Shenandoah (ca. June–July 20, 1861); commander, Fourth Brigade, Second Corps, Army of the Potomac

(July 20–21, 1861); major general, CSA (October 11, 1861); commander, Fourth Division, Potomac District, Department of Northern Virginia (October 22, 1861–February 21, 1862); commander, Department of East Tennessee (March 8–August 25, ca. October 31–December 1862, and December 23, 1862–January 1863); commander, Army of Kentucky, Department Two (August 25–November 20, 1862); lieutenant general, CSA (October 9, 1862); also commander of corps, Army of Tennessee (November 20–December 1862); commander, Southwestern Army (January 14–March 7, 1863); commander, Trans-Mississippi Department (March 7, 1863–April 19, 1865, and April 22–May 26, 1865); and general, Provisional Army of the Confederate States (PACS) (February 19, 1864).

After serving as Joseph E. Johnston's staff head in the Shenandoah Valley he was promoted to brigadier general and given command of a brigade that he led at First Bull Run. Wounded severely in that action, he returned to duty as a major general and division commander in northern Virginia. Early in 1862 he was dispatched to command in East Tennessee. Cooperating with Braxton Bragg in the invasion of Kentucky, he scored a victory at Richmond and was soon named to the newly created grade of lieutenant general.

Early in 1863 he was transferred to the Trans-Mississippi West, where he remained for the balance of the war. With the fall of the Mississippi River to the Union forces he was virtually cut off from Richmond. He was forced to deal alone with such matters as impressment of supplies, destruction of cotton to prevent capture, and blockade running through Mexico, in addition to his normal military duties. He also, in an irregular fashion, promoted officers to general's rank, sometimes making his actions subject to the president's approval and sometimes not. Davis approved some and never acted on others. Smith could be forgiven for exceeding his authority in such matters because of the situation of his command as an almost separate country.

In the spring of 1864 he soundly defeated Nathaniel P. Banks's Red River Campaign and then dispatched reinforcements northward to defeat Steele's cooperating column in Arkansas. With the pressure relieved, Smith attempted to send reinforcements east of the Mississippi, but as did his earlier attempts to relieve Vicksburg, it proved impracticable because of Union naval control of the river. Instead he dispatched Sterling Price, with all available cavalry, on an unsuccessful invasion of Missouri. Thereafter the war west of the river was principally one of small raids and guerrilla activity. By now a full general, he surrendered his department—the only significant Confederate army left—on May 26, 1865.

After the war he was active in the telegraph business and in education. At the time of his death he was the last of the full Confederate generals.

Source

Kierby, Robert L. *Kirby Smith's Confederacy: The Trans-Mississippi South, 1863–1865.* New York: Columbia University Press, 1972.

Noll, Arthur Howard. *General Kirby Smith.* Sewanee, Tenn.: University Press at the University of the South, 1907.

Parks, Joseph Howard. *General Edmund Kirby-Smith. C.S.A.* Baton Rouge: Louisiana State University Press, 1954.

Smith, Holland McTyeire ("Howlin' Mad")
(1882–1967) *Marine general officer.*

Born in Seale, Alabama, on April 20, 1882, Smith graduated from Alabama Polytechnic Institute in 1901. After two years of law practice, he took a commission as a second lieutenant of Marines in March 1905. He served in the Philippines from 1906 to 1908, in Panama in 1909–1910, and again in the Philippines from 1912 to 1914, before duty in the Dominican Republic in 1916–1917. During this time he was promoted to captain and earned his nickname, "Howlin' Mad."

Smith went to France with the Fifth Marine Regiment in June 1917 and then became adjutant of the Fourth Marine Brigade. He was assigned to First Corps Staff in July 1918 and saw combat action in the Aisne-Marne from July 25 to August 2; in Saint-Mihiel, September 12–17; and at the Meuse-Argonne, October 4–November 11, offensives, serving on Third Army's staff by the war's end.

After occupation duty, he graduated from the Naval War College in 1921 and served in the navy's War Plans Office from 1921 to 1923. Smith served as the chief of staff of the Marine Brigade in Haiti in 1924–1925 and of the First Marine Brigade in 1925–1926. He served next at the Philadelphia Navy Yard, from 1927 to 1931, then on the staff of the battle force commander, from 1931 to 1933. Promoted to colonel in 1933, he was assigned to a series of staff assignments before being promoted to brigadier general in 1938. He served as the director of operations and training before being named assistant to Marine Corps Commandant General Thomas Holcomb in April 1939.

General Smith helped develop new techniques and equipment for amphibious warfare; commanded the First Marine Brigade, which became the First Marine Division, in May 1941; and was promoted to major general in February 1941. He was assigned to Amphibious Force, Atlantic Fleet, and worked with Adm. Richmond K. Turner to create a combat-ready force. He transferred west to organize the Pacific Fleet Amphibious Force in September 1942 and then planned and directed the invasion of Tarawa, November 20–23, 1943.

As the commander of the Fifth Amphibious Corps, he personally led Marines ashore there; he planned and directed the successful assaults on Kawajalein, January

31–February 5, 1944, and on Eniwetok, February 18–23. Promoted to lieutenant general, he then planned and led the invasions of Saipan (June 15–July 12), Guam (July 21–August 10), and Tinian (July 24–August 1) in the Marianas Islands.

General Smith sparked a major controversy when he relieved Maj. Gen. Ralph C. Smith, United States Army, of command of the 27th Infantry Division during the Battle for Saipan, on June 24, 1944. This incident revealed the difference between the aggressive Marine Corps operational style and the army's more moderate approach to combat.

Given command of Fleet Marine Force, Pacific, in July 1944, General Smith went on to plan and direct the invasions of Iwo Jima (February 19–March 24, 1945) and Okinawa (April 1–June 21).

On his return to the United States, he was named commander of the infantry training center at Camp Pendleton, California, in July 1945. General Smith retired from active duty and was promoted to general in August 1946. A published record of his heroic wartime experiences, *Coral and Brass,* was published in 1949. The general died in San Diego, California, on January 12, 1967.

General "Howlin' Mad" Smith was one of the fathers of modern amphibious warfare and was, with General Douglas MacArthur, one of its foremost practitioners; he was a vigorous and demanding commander, irascible and quarrelsome, and one of America's more colorful field commanders in World War II.

Source and Additional Reading

Dupuy, Trevor N., Curt Johnson, and David L. Bongard. *Harper Encyclopedia of Military Biography.* New York: HarperCollins, 1992.

Morison, Samuel Eliot. *History of the United States Naval Operations in World War II.* 15 Vols. Boston: Little, Brown, 1947–62.

Smith, Holland M., and Finch, Percy. *Coral and Brass.* New York: Charles Scribner's Sons, 1949.

Smith, Nathan R. (b. 1920) *Colonel, United States Marine Corps.*

Nathan R. Smith was born on March 12, 1920, in White Haven, Pennsylvania, where he graduated from high school in 1937. He joined the Civilian Conservation Corps but left in 1938 to enlist in the Marine Corps.

After recruit training at Parris Island, he served at the Naval Gun Factory in Washington, D.C.; when the First Marine Division was formed at Guantanamo Bay, Cuba, in 1941, he served with the First and Seventh Marine Regiments as they formed for war.

When the division returned to the United States he rejoined First Battalion, Fifth Marines, then located at Quantico, Virginia. Colonel Smith subsequently transferred to the Fifth Amphibious Corps Headquarters, where, while acting first sergeant of Headquarters Company, he received a field appointment to second lieutenant.

Colonel Smith's combat history and participation in expeditions and campaigns include Corps Troops, Fifth Amphibious Corps, Saipan and Tinian, 1944; Corps Troops, Iwo Jima, 1945; and Occupation of Sasebo, Japan, 1945.

He served as company commander, Company A, First Battalion, Seventh Marines, in Korea Winter and Spring Operation in 1951. Colonel Smith also participated in the evacuation operations in South Vietnam and Tachen Islands, 1954–55. He served as G-2, Landing Force, during the Lebanon Operation in 1958.

His other command and staff assignments included tours with the Second and Third Marine Divisions. He served as a tactics instructor at the Basic School, Quantico, Virginia, from 1951 to 1954. He also served as director, Troop Training School, LFTC, Coronado, California, 1966–67, and transferred to Washington, D.C., to serve with OPNAV in Research and Development of Landing Forces and Riverine Warfare. Colonel Smith retired from active duty in August 1968.

After his retirement, Colonel Smith attended San Diego State College to do undergraduate and graduate work. He received a master's degree in public administration in 1972 and was employed by San Diego County until 1984. He currently serves as a volunteer at the MCRD, San Diego, Command Museum. Colonel Smith and his wife, Janet, reside in Coronado, California.

Source

U.S. Marines: Mustangs of the Corps. Dallas: Taylor, 1991.

Spruance, Raymond Ames (1886–1969) *Admiral, United States Navy, during World War II.*

Raymond A. Spruance was born in Baltimore, Maryland, on January 3, 1886. An instructor at the United States Naval War College before the war, Spruance was a rear admiral when hostilities with Japan broke out in 1941. He joined the United States Pacific Fleet under Adm. Chester W. Nimitz and distinguished himself in the Battle of Midway (1942). As commander of the Central Pacific Area, he directed naval forces in the successful assaults on the Japanese-held Gilbert Islands in 1943, on the Marshall Islands and Saipan in 1944, and on Iwo Jima and Okinawa in 1945. Made a full admiral in 1944, Spruance succeeded Nimitz as commander of the Pacific Fleet (November 1945–February 1946). He later served as president of the Naval War College (1946–48) and as U.S. ambassador to the Philippines (1952–55). He died December 13, 1969.

Source and Additional Reading

Buell, Thomas B. *The Quiet Warrior: A Biography of Admiral Raymond A. Spruance.* Annapolis, Md.: Naval Institute Press, 1987.

Fuchida, Mitsuo, and Okumiya, Masatake. *Midway: The Battle That Doomed Japan.* Annapolis, Md.: Naval Institute Press, 1955.

Stilwell, Joseph ("Vinegar Joe") (1883–1946)

General, United States Army, in World War II commander of U.S. forces in the China-Burma-India Theater during World War II.

He was born in Palatka, Florida, on March 19, 1883. After graduating from West Point in 1904 he served in the Philippines and was an instructor at the Military Academy. During World War I he was a staff officer in France and was awarded the Distinguished Service Medal.

After the war Stilwell learned Chinese. He was posted in China from 1926 to 1929 and was military attaché in Peking from 1932 to 1939. In 1942, during World War II, he returned to China as chief of staff to General Chiang Kai-shek and commander of U.S. forces in the China-Burma-India Theater. After his troops were defeated by the Japanese, he led a 140-mile (225-kilometer) retreat through dense jungles to India. In 1943 he was made deputy commander of the Anglo-American Southeast Asia Command, and the next year he led a successful offensive in Burma. He was promoted to full general in August 1944 but was recalled to Washington in October because of his differences with Chiang.

Stilwell was appointed commander of United States Army ground forces in January 1945. In June he was named commander of the 10th Army in Okinawa; when Japan was defeated, he received the surrender of over 100,000 Japanese troops in the Ryukyu Islands. After the war he was commander of the Sixth Army. He died in San Francisco on October 12, 1946.

During the war Stilwell became known as "Vinegar Joe" because of his strongly stated opinions. Parts of his wartime diaries and notebook, not intended for print, were published in 1948 as the controversial *Stilwell Papers.*

Source and Additional Reading

Larrabee, Eric. *Commander in Chief: Franklin D. Roosevelt, His Lieutenants, and Their War.* New York: Harper & Row, 1987.

Tuchman, Barbara. *Stilwell and the American Experience in China, 1911–1945.* New York: Macmillan, 1970.

Stockdale, James Bond (b. 1923) *Vice Admiral, United States Navy.*

Born: December 23, 1923, Abingdon, Ill. **Entered service at:** Abingdon, Ill. **Place and Date:** Hoa Lo Prison, Hanoi, Vietnam, September 4, 1969. **Rank and organization:** Rear Admiral (then Captain), U.S. Navy.

James B. Stockdale was born on December 23, 1923, in Abingdon, Illinois. As a high school student and at Knox and Monmouth Colleges, he was accomplished in scholarship, music, and athletics. In 1943 he entered the U.S. Naval Academy and graduated in 1946. After a three-year tour on destroyers he began flight training. After squadron and test pilot tours, he spent two years at Standford University, where he earned a master's degree in international relations. After commanding VF 51 (fighter squadron) in Southeast Asia, 1965, he assumed command of Carrier Wing 16 aboard the USS *Oriskany.*

By midsummer 1964, events were taking place in the Gulf of Tonkin that would lead to the first clash between U.S. and North Vietnamese forces. In late July, the destroyer USS *Maddox* cruised unencumbered along a predesignated route off the North Vietnamese coast. In the early morning hours of August 2, however, intelligence sources learned of a possible attack against the destroyer. The attack by three North Vietnamese P-4 torpedo boats (PT boats) materialized just after 4:00 P.M. on August 2. The *Maddox* fired three warning volleys and then opened fire. Four F-8 Crusaders, led by Commander James B. Stockdale from the aircraft carrier USS *Ticonderoga,* also took part in the skirmish. The result of the 20-minute confrontation saw one gunboat sunk and another crippled. The *Maddox,* ordered out of the gulf after the incident, was hit by one 14.5 mm shell.

A day later the *Maddox,* accompanied by the destroyers USS *C. Turner Joy,* received instructions to reenter the gulf and resume patrol. The aircraft carrier USS *Constellation,* on a Hong Kong port visit, was ordered to join the *Ticonderoga,* which was stationed at the mouth of the Gulf of Tonkin in the South China Sea. The two destroyers cruised without incident on August 3 and, in the daylight hours of August 4, moved to the middle of the gulf. Parallel to the movements of the *C. Turner Joy* and *Maddox,* South Vietnamese gunboats launched attacks on several North Vietnamese radar installations. The North Vietnamese believed the U.S. destroyers were connected with these strikes.

At 8:41 P.M. on August 4, both destroyers reportedly picked up fast-approaching contacts on their radars. Navy documents show the ships changed course to avoid the unknown vessels, but the contacts continued intermittently. At 10:39 P.M., when the *Maddox* and *C. Turner Joy* radars indicated one enemy vessel had closed to within 7,000 yards, the *C. Turner Joy* was ordered to open fire, and the *Maddox* soon followed. For the next several hours, the destroyers, covered by the *Ticonderoga's* and the *Constellation's* aircraft, reportedly evaded torpedoes and fired on their attackers.

Historians have and will continue to debate whether the destroyers actually were attacked. Most of the pilots flying that night spotted nothing. Stockdale stated that a gunboat attack did not occur. The skipper of the *Ticonderoga's* Attack Squadron 56, Commander Wesley L. McDonald, said he "didn't see anything that night except the *Maddox* and the *C. Turner Joy.*"

President Lyndon B. Johnson reacted at once to the supposed attacks on the *Maddox,* ordering retaliatory strikes on strategic points in North Vietnam. Even as the president spoke to the nation, aircraft from the *Constellation* and *Ticonderoga* were airborne and heading for four major PT-boat bases along the North Vietnamese coast. The area of cover ranged from a small base at Quang Khe 50 miles north of the demarcation line between North and South Vietnam to the large base at Hon Gai.

On August 5, 1964, Stockdale led a flight of 16 aircraft from the *Ticonderoga* on the Vinh petroleum storage complex at 1:30 P.M. in response to the presidential directive to destroy gunboats and supporting facilities in North Vietnam, which the president indicated were used in the attack on the *Maddox.* The results saw 90 percent of the storage facility at Vinh go up in flames.

Meanwhile, from the *Constellation,* nearby Ben Thuy Naval Base, Quang Khe, Hon Me Island, and Hon Gai's inner harbor aircraft made other coordinated attacks. Skyraiders and F-8's bombed and rocketed four areas, destroying or damaging an estimated 25 PT-boats, more than half of the North Vietnamese force.

Air wing command was usually placed under an individual who had completed a tour as a squadron commander of an attack or fighter unit. The CAG was (commander air group) was typically a better-than-average pilot with a solid record of performance and more than likely a pretty fair politician. By another definition, he had survived in a profession unforgiving of error.

On his second Vietnam tour, Commander James B. Stockdale was the commander of Air Wing 16 onboard the USS *Oriskany.* He had led the successful strike off the Ticonderoga against the petroleum storage facility at Vinh on August 4, 1964. On one mission, he had the canopy blown off his aircraft and had to ditch in the Gulf of Tonkin, where he was rescued. Then on September 9, 1965, flying an A4E Skyhawk, he led another strike mission over North Vietnam.

A major strike had been scheduled against the Thanh Hoa (Dragon Jaw) Bridge, and the weather was so critical there was a question whether or not to launch. Finally the decision was made to launch. Halfway through, weather reconnaissance aircraft reported the weather in the target area was zero, and Stockdale had no choice but to send the aircraft on to secondary targets. Stockdale and his wing-man, Commander Wynn Foster, circled the Gulf of Tonkin while another strike element departed to look for a SAM (surface-to-air missile) site as their secondary target. Had anything been found, Wynn and Stockdale were to join them.

After fifteen minutes or so, the other group came up empty. The group made the decision to hit a secondary target, a railroad facility near the city of Thanh Hoa.

Commander Stockdale's aircraft was hit by flak, and he ejected, landing in a village. His wingman saw Stockdale's parachute go down, but he could not see what was happening to Stockdale on the ground. On a low pass, Foster saw that the villagers were brutally beating Stockdale. There was nothing he could do. The village was an unauthorized target. Throughout the rest of the war, Foster carried the guilt of being unable to do something to help Commander Stockdale.

James Stockdale was captured by the North Vietnamese and taken to Hanoi, where he spent the next seven and one-half years as a prisoner of war. He had briefed his pilots during the period he was CAG on the *Oriskany* that the Code of Conduct would apply to anyone captured. There had been some dispute about the validity of the Code in an undeclared war, such as that in Vietnam.

American POWs who had flown with Stockdale had no doubt as to what was expected of them as prisoners. The knowledge, however, was a two-edged sword. On the one hand, the captives were glad to understand the guidelines. On the other, when they "broke" (which inevitably they did), immense guilt and shame ensued. Eventually, as they communicated with one another, everyone understood that they had only to do their best.

It was not possible to resist utterly and survive. A few prisoners cooperated with the enemy "above and beyond" what was considered appropriate and received special treatment from their guards in return. Fellow POWs who were doing their best to adhere to the Code of Conduct despised these men. Upon his return, Jim Stockdale accused two POWs of mutiny. Official charges were never brought against these men or any other similarly accused POWs.

During his captivity, Stockdale was considered to be a troublemaker by the North Vietnamese. As a senior officer, Stockdale developed a policy of behavior for the POWs called Back Us. The policy provided guidance on such behavior as propaganda broadcasts, bowing to guards, and unity, thwarting the "obedience" the North Vietnamese tried to extract from the American POWs. The POWs where shuffled from one camp to another, many times based on "unsatisfactory" behavior; many were held in long periods of solitary confinement; many were tortured during brutal "interrogation" sessions.

In early 1969, one of the POWs became seriously ill and was in great pain at a camp known as Alcatraz, located some 10 blocks from the infamous Hoa Lo (Hanoi Hilton) prison. The man was receiving no medical care, and fellow prisoners put the pressure on. What ensued might be called a prison riot. The effort did bring a doctor to the ill POW's cell, although the doctor did nothing to ease his pain. The next morning, Stockdale organized a 48-hour fast to demand medical attention for the ailing officer. The next evening each prisoner was interrogated and, on the morning of January 27, Stockdale was taken away to another prison center.

Finally, on February 12, 1973, James Stockdale and his fellow POWs were released from their prisoner-of-war camps and sent home. In all, 591 Americans were released.

Since the war ended, nearly 10,000 reports relating to Americans missing, prisoner, or unaccounted for in Southeast Asia have been received by the U.S. government. Many authorities who have examined this largely classified source of information are still convinced that hundreds of Americans are still held as captives today. These reports are the source of serious distress to many returned American POWs. They had a code that no one honorably return unless all of the prisoners returned.

James B. Stockdale's personal statement:

Ten years ago, (1963), I toured the Old Yuma Territorial Prison with my two eldest sons, ages 12 and 8. Their boyish reactions to the filthy cells used for solitary confinement were predictable. A blend of wonderment and horror crossed their faces as they peered in at leg irons in the tiny, windowless concrete boxes. I assured the boys that the day's of old Western desperadoes, as well as jails like these were gone forever.

Little did I know that within a few years I would find myself in an old French-built isolated cellblock in Hanoi. This jail we called Alcatraz. I was one of eleven Americans living in tiny windowless boxes (complete with leg irons) finding out first hand the capabilities of the human spirit in such a situation. Pedantic arguments of international politics were wasted on us. We had a war to fight and were committed to fighting it from lonely concrete boxes. Our very fiber and sinew were the only weapons at our disposal. Each man's values from his own private sources provided the strength enabling him to maintain his sense of purpose and dedication. They placed unity above self. Self-indulgence was a luxury that could not be afforded.

Each member of our "Alcatraz gang" fought his war well from a filthy cell. All but one of us, Ron Storz, came home alive. Ron was a tiger to the end. For us he will always remain a symbol of courage, fidelity and dedication.

In December 1996, James B. Stockdale retired from the United States Navy as a Vice Admiral. He and his wife, Sybil, reside in California.

Citation: For conspicuous gallantry and intrepidity at the risk of his life above and beyond the call of duty while senior naval officer in the Prisoner of War camps North Vietnam. Recognized by his captors as the leader of the Prisoners of War resistance to interrogation and in their refusal to participate in propaganda exploitation, Rear Admiral Stockdale was singled out for interrogation and attendant torture after he was detected in a covert communications attempt. Sensing the start of another purge, and aware that his earlier efforts at self-disfigurement to dissuade his captors from exploiting him for propaganda purposes had resulted in cruel and agonizing punishment, Rear Admiral Stockdale resolved to make himself a symbol of resistance regardless of personal sacrifice.

He deliberately inflicted a near-mortal wound to his person in order to convince his captors of his willingness to give up his life rather than capitulate. He was subsequently discovered and revived by the North Vietnamese who, convinced of his indomitable spirit, abated in their employment of excessive harassment and torture toward all of the Prisoners of War. By his heroic actions, at great peril to himself, he earned the everlasting gratitude of his fellow prisoners and of his country. Rear Admiral Stockdale's valiant leadership and extraordinary courage in a hostile environment sustain and enhance the finest traditions of the U. S. Naval Service."

Sources

Medal of Honor Citation

Stockdale, James B. *Courage Under Fire: Testing Epictetus's doctrine in a laboratory of human behavior.* Stanford, Calif.: Stanford University Press, Hoover Institution, 1993.

Stockdale, James B. and Sybil Stockdale. *In Love and War: The Story of a Family's Ordeal and Sacrifice during the Vietnam Years.* New York: Harper & Row, 1984.

Wyatt, Frederick, and Barbara Wyatt. *We Came Home.* Toluca Lake, Calif.: P.O.W. Publications, 1977.

Street, George Levick, III (b. 1913) *Commander, United States Navy, commanding the USS* Tirante, *so distinguished himself in subsurface combat, during World War II, that he was awarded the Medal of Honor for his heroic actions.*

Born: July 27, 1913, Richmond, Va.; **Entered service at:** Virginia; **Place and date:** Harbor of Quelpart Island, off the coast of Korea, April 14, 1945. **Other United States Navy awards:** Navy Cross, Silver Star with one Gold Star.

Citation: "For conspicuous gallantry and intrepidity at the risk of his life above and beyond the call of duty as commanding officer of the USS *Tirante* during the first war patrol of that vessel against enemy Japanese surface forces in the harbor of Quelpart Island, off the coast of Korea, on 14 April 1945. With the crew at surface battle stations, Comdr. (then Lt. Comdr.) Street approached the hostile anchorage from the south within 1,200 yards of the coast to complete a reconnoitering circuit of the island. Leaving the 10-fathom curve far behind he penetrated the mined and shoal-obstructed waters of the restricted harbor despite numerous patrolling vessels and in defiance of 5 shore-based radar stations and menacing aircraft. Prepared to fight it out on the surface if attacked, Comdr. Street went into action, sending 2 torpedoes with deadly accuracy into a large Japanese ammunition ship and exploding the target in a mountainous and blinding glare of white flames. With the *Tirante* instantly spotted by the enemy as she stood out plainly in the flare of light, he ordered the torpedo data computer set up while retiring and fired his last 2 torpedoes to disintegrate in quick succession the leading frigate and a similar flanking vessel. Clearing the gutted harbor at emergency full speed ahead, he slipped undetected along the shoreline, diving deep as a pursuing patrol dropped a pattern of depth charges at the point of submergence. His illustrious record of combat achievement during the first war patrol of the *Tirante* characterizes Comdr. Street as a daring and skilled leader and reflects the highest credit upon himself, his valiant command, and the U.S. Naval Service."

Source
Medal of Honor Citation.

Stuart, James Ewell Brown (J. E. B. Stuart)
(1833–1864) *General officer, Confederate States Army.*

Known as "Jeb," Stuart was probably the most famous cavalryman of the Civil War. A Virginia-born West Pointer (1854), Stuart was already a veteran of Native American fighting on the plains and of Bleeding Kansas when, as a first lieutenant in the First Cavalry, he carried orders for Robert E. Lee to proceed to Harper's Ferry to crush John Brown's raid. Stuart, volunteering as aide-de-camp, went along and read the ultimatum to Brown before the assault in which he distinguished himself. Promoted to captain on April 22, 1861, Stuart resigned on May 14, 1861, having arrived May 6 in Richmond and been made a lieutenant colonel of Virginia Infantry.

His later appointments included the following: captain of Cavalry, Confederate States Army (CSA) (May 24, 1861); colonel, First Virginia Cavalry (July 16, 1861); brigadier general, CSA (September 24, 1861); and major general, CSA (July 25, 1862). His commands in the Army of Northern Virginia included the following: Cavalry Brigade (October 22, 1861–July 28, 1862); Cavalry Division (July 28, 1862–September 9, 1863); temporarily Jack-

son's Second Corps (May 3–6, 1863); and Cavalry Corps (September 9, 1863–May 11, 1864).

After early service in the Shenandoah Valley, Stuart led his regiment in the Battle of First Bull Run and participated in the pursuit of the routed federals. He then directed the army's outposts until given command of the cavalry brigade. Besides leading the cavalry in the Army of Northern Virginia's fights at the Seven Days, Second Bull Run, Antietam, Fredericksburg, Chancellorsville, Gettysburg, and the Wilderness, Stuart was a raider. Twice he led his command around McClellan's army, once in the Peninsula Campaign and once after the Battle of Antietam. Although his exploits were militarily important, they provided a boost to the southern morale. During the Second Bull Run Campaign, he lost his famed plumed hat and cloak to pursuing federals. In a later Confederate raid, Stuart managed to overrun Union army commander Pope's headquarters and capture his full uniform and orders, thus providing Robert E. Lee with much valuable intelligence. At the end of 1862, Stuart led a raid north of the Rappahannock River, inflicting some 230 casualties while losing only 27 of his own men.

At Chancellorsville he took over command of his friend Stonewall Jackson's corps after that officer had been mortally wounded by his own men. Returning to the cavalry shortly after, he commanded the southern horsemen in the largest cavalry engagement ever fought on the American continent, Brandy Station, on June 9, 1863. Although the battle was a draw, the Confederates did hold the field. However, the fight represented the rise of the Union cavalry and foreshadowed the decline of the formerly invincible southern mounted arm. During the Gettysburg Campaign, Stuart, acting under ambiguous orders, again circled the Union army but in the process deprived Lee of his eyes and ears while in enemy territory. Arriving late on the second day of the battle, Stuart failed the next day to get into the enemy's rear flank, defeated by Generals Gregg and Custer.

During Grant's drive on Richmond in the spring of 1864, Stuard halted Sheridan's cavalry at Yellow Tavern on the outskirts of Richmond on May 11. In the fight he was mortally wounded and died the next day in the rebel capital. He is buried in Hollywood Cemetery there. Like his intimate friend, Stonewall Jackson, General Stuart soon became a legendary figure, ranking as one of the great cavalry commanders of America. His death marked the beginning of the decline of the superiority that the Confederate horse had enjoyed over that of the Union. Stuart was a son-in-law of Brig. Gen. Philip St. George Cooke of the federal service; his wife's brother was Brig. Gen. John Rogers Cooke of the Confederacy.

Source
Davis, Burke. *Jeb Stuart: The Last Cavalier.* New York: Charles Scribner's Sons, 1992.

Sullivan Brothers

The five Sullivan brothers (Albert, Francis, George, Joseph, and Madison) served together as shipmates aboard the cruiser USS *Juneau* after requesting special permission from the secretary of the navy. The *Juneau* was sunk on November 13, 1942, off the island of Guadalcanal by Japanese submarine *I-26*. Of the crew of more than 600 sailors, only 11 survived. The death of the five brothers caused Congress to consider enacting a law prohibiting members of a family from serving in a combat zone at the same time, but such a law has never been passed.

Even after hearing rumors of the death of her five sons, Mrs. Sullivan continued to support the war effort, as evidenced by a letter she wrote to the Bureau of Naval Personnel. Franklin D. Roosevelt sent a personal letter to Mrs. Sullivan expressing his and the nation's sorrow. For wartime America, the Sullivan brothers became the ultimate symbol of heroic sacrifice. The guided missile destroyer USS *The Sullivans*, DDG-68 was commissioned in honor of the brothers.

Source
Naval Historical Center.

Tecumseh (1768–1813) *Shawnee chief who sought to organize a confederacy of midwestern Native American tribes against the encroaching whites.*

A Shawnee, Tecumseh was born near the Mad River in Ohio. He fought the Americans as a young man but achieved general fame only after 1805. In that year his brother Tenskwatawa, known as "The Prophet," began to preach a Native American religious revival at Greenville, Ohio. Tecumseh made use of this movement in an attempt to create a Native American political alliance.

In 1808 the brothers moved their village to the Tippecanoe River in Indiana. From there Tecumseh traveled widely, urging resistance to the Americans. He argued that because the land belonged to the Native Americans in common, no one tribe could legally make cessions to the U.S. government. From 1808 the brothers received advice and supplies from the British in Upper Canada. Hopes for an effective confederacy were soon dashed, however. While Tecumseh was traveling to recruit southern tribes, Native American forces led by the Prophet clashed with troops commanded by Gen. William Henry Harrison at the Battle of Tippecanoe on November 7, 1811, and the forces of the confederacy were dispersed.

In the War of 1812, Tecumseh was commissioned a brigadier general, fought for the British on the Detroit frontier, and recruited Native American tribes for the British cause. He was killed at the Battle of the Thames in Upper Canada on October 5, 1813.

Sources and Additional Reading

Edmunds, R. David. *Tecumseh and the Quest for Indian Leadership.* Boston: Little, Brown, 1984.
Sugden, John. *Tecumseh, A Life.* New York: Henry Holt, 1998.

Thomas, George Henry (1816–1870) *Major general, Union army.*

Unlike his fellow Virginian, Robert E. Lee, George Thomas remained loyal to the Union. During Nat Turner's bloody slave revolt, Thomas had led his family to safety; subsequently he attended West Point (1840). A veteran of the Seminole and Mexican Wars and an artillery and cavalry instructor at the Academy, he was a major in the Second, soon to be the Fifth Cavalry at the time of the secession crisis. His war assignments included the following: lieutenant colonel, Second Cavalry (April 25, 1861); colonel, Second Cavalry (May 3, 1861); commander, First Brigade, First Division, Department of Pennsylvania (June–July 25, 1861), Department of the Shenandoah (July 25–August 17, 1861), Banks's division, Army of the Potomac (August 17–28, 1861); brigadier general, United States Volunteers (USV) (August 3, 1861); commander, Camp Dick Robinson, Ken., Department of the Ohio (October–December 2, 1861); commander, First Division, Army of the Ohio (December 2, 1861–April 30, 1862, and June 10–September 29, 1862); major general, USV (April 25, 1862); commander, Army of the Tennessee (April 30–June 10, 1862); second in command, Army of the Ohio (September 29–October 24, 1862); commander of Center, 14th Corps, Army of the Cumberland (November 5, 1862–January 9, 1863); commander of corps (January 9–October 28, 1863); brigadier general, USA (October 27, 1863); commander of army (October 28, 1863–September 26, 1864); commander, Department of the Cumberland (October 28, 1863–June 27, 1865); and major general, USA (December 15, 1864).

After brief service in the East, Thomas was sent to Kentucky and commanded at Mill Springs. After arriving too late for the fighting at Shiloh, he commanded the Army of the Tennessee, replacing Grant, who was shelved by being made second in command to Halleck. After participating in the slow drive on Corinth, Thomas returned to Kentucky and fought at Perryville and later at Stones River and in the Tullahoma Campaign. At Chickamauga, after most of the army had fled the field, Thomas stubbornly held out on the second day at Snodgrass Hill, earning the nickname "The Rock of Chickamauga."

After the defeat the army was besieged at Chattanooga and Grant was promoted to overall command in the West and sent with reinforcements. He was given duplicate orders, one leaving General Rosecrans in command of the Army of the Cumberland and the other giving Thomas the post. Grant chose the latter, although he resented Thomas for his replacement after Shiloh. Thomas's men broke through the Confederate lines at Missionary Ridge and later took part in the capture of Atlanta.

With General Hood's Army of Tennessee threatening Tennessee in Sherman's rear, Thomas was detached with two corps to deal with him. This was effectively the end of the Army of the Cumberland. After being briefly besieged at Nashville, Thomas, who was about to be removed for being too slow, attacked and routed the rebels. For this, one of the most decisive battles of the war, Thomas became one of 13 officers to receive the Thanks of Congress. Hood's command was no longer a real threat to anyone. With most of his forces sent to other theaters of operations, Thomas remained in command in Tennessee until 1867, when he was assigned to command on the Pacific coast until his death in 1870.

Source
McKinney, Francis F. *Education in Violence: The Life of George H. Thomas and the History of the Army of the Cumberland.* Chicago: American House, 1966.

Thomas, William H. *Private first class, United States Army, 149th Infantry, 38th Infantry Division, so distinguished himself in combat, during World War II, that was awarded (posthumously) the Medal of Honor for his heroic actions.*

Born: Wynne, Ark.; **Entered service at:** Ypsilanti, Mich.; **Place and date:** Zambales Mountains, Luzon, Philippine Islands, April 22, 1945. **G.O. No.:** 81, September 24, 1945.

Citation: "He was a member of the leading squad of Company B, which was attacking along a narrow, wooded ridge. The enemy strongly entrenched in camouflaged emplacements on the hill beyond directed heavy fire and hurled explosive charges on the attacking riflemen. Pfc. Thomas, an automatic rifleman, was struck by 1 of these charges, which blew off both his legs below the knees. He refused medical aid and evacuation, and continued to fire at the enemy until his weapon was put out of action by an enemy bullet. Still refusing aid, he threw his last 2 grenades. He destroyed 3 of the enemy after suffering the wounds from which he died later that day. The effective fire of Pfc. Thomas prevented the repulse of his platoon and assured the capture of the hostile position. His magnificent courage and heroic devotion to duty provided a lasting inspiration for his comrades."

Source
Medal of Honor Citation.

Thompson, Robert H. *Colonel (then major), United States Marine Corps, so distinguished himself as the commanding officer of First Battalion, Fifth Marines, during combat operations in Hue City, during the Vietnam War, that he was awarded the Navy Cross.*

Citation: "For extraordinary heroism while serving as the Commanding Officer, First Battalion, Fifth Marines, First Marine Division (Reinforced), in the Republic of Vietnam, from 12 February to 3 March 1968, while participating in Operation HUE CITY, Lieutenant Colonel (then Major) Thompson aggressively led his battalion in intense fighting against well-entrenched North Vietnamese forces within the Citadel. On 13 February, he deployed elements of his unit across the Perfume River to reduce enemy resistance in the southeast corner of the walled city. Almost immediately, small arms, automatic weapons, and rocket fire from a large North Vietnamese force slowed his advance. Ignoring the intense enemy fire, he moved to an exposed vantage point where he rapidly assessed the situation and unhesitatingly moved across the fire-swept front of his battalion, directing the efforts of the company commanders and shouting words of encouragement to individual Marines, inspiring them to resume the momentum of the attack. Ordered to commence an attack northwest of the city on 28 February, Colonel Thompson fearlessly moved his command group with the attacking companies, repeatedly moving to the areas of heaviest contact in order to personally assist his unit commanders and influence the course of the engagement. When an attached company engaged a well-entrenched North Vietnamese force on 1 March, Colonel Thompson accompanied a reinforcing unit dispatched to establish a blocking position to prevent the enemy's escape. Located with the lead elements, he personally coordinated supporting arms fire with the movements of the advancing Marines as they overwhelmed the enemy and accomplished their mission. By his intrepid fighting spirit, inspiring leadership, and selfless devotion to duty at great personal risk, Colonel Thompson upheld the highest traditions of the Marine Corps and the United States Naval Service."

Source and Additional Reading

Navy Cross Citation.

Nolan, Keith W. *Battle for Hue: Tet. 1968.* Novato, Calif.: Presidio Press, 1983.

Tominac, John J. *First lieutenant, United States Army, Company One, 15th Infantry, Third Infantry Division, so distinguished himself in combat, during World War II, that he was awarded the Medal of Honor for his heroic actions.*

Born: Conemaugh, Penn.; **Entered service at:** Conemaugh, Penn.; **Place and date:** Saulx de Vesoul, France, September 12, 1944. **G.O. No.:** 20, March 29, 1945.

Citation: "For conspicuous gallantry and intrepidity at risk of life above and beyond the call of duty on 12 September 1944, in an attack on Saulx de Vesoul, France 1st Lt. Tominac charged alone over 50 yards of exposed terrain onto an enemy roadblock to dispatch a 3-man crew of German machine gunners with a single burst from his Thompson machinegun. After smashing the enemy outpost, he led 1 of his squads in the annihilation of a second hostile group defended by mortar, machinegun, automatic pistol, rifle and grenade fire, killing about 30 of the enemy. Reaching the suburbs of the town, he advanced 50 yards ahead of his men to reconnoiter a third enemy position, which commanded the road with a 77-mm. SP gun supported by infantry elements. The SP gun opened fire on his supporting tank, setting it afire with a direct hit. A fragment from the same shell painfully wounded 1st Lt. Tominac in the shoulder, knocking him to the ground. As the crew abandoned the M-4 tank, which was rolling down hill toward the enemy, 1st Lt. Tominac picked himself up and jumped onto the hull of the burning vehicle. Despite withering enemy machinegun, mortar, pistol, and sniper fire, which was ricocheting off the hull and turret of the M-4, 1st Lt. Tominac climbed to the turret and gripped the 50-caliber antiaircraft machinegun. Plainly silhouetted against the sky, painfully wounded, and with the tank burning beneath his feet, he directed bursts of machinegun fire on the roadblock, the SP gun, and the supporting German infantrymen, and forced the enemy to withdraw from his prepared position. Jumping off the tank before it exploded, 1st Lt. Tominac refused evacuation despite his painful wound. Calling upon a sergeant to extract the shell fragments from his shoulder with a pocketknife, he continued to direct the assault, led his squad in a hand grenade attack against a fortified position occupied by 32 of the enemy armed with machineguns, machine pistols, and rifles, and compelled them to surrender. His outstanding heroism and exemplary leadership resulted in the destruction of 4 successive enemy defensive positions, surrender of a vital sector of the city Saulx de Vesoul, and the death or capture of at least 60 of the enemy."

Source

Medal of Honor Citation.

Tompkins, Sally Louisa (1833–1916) *The only woman to hold a commission in the Confederate States Army.*

Born in Poplar Grove, Mathews City, Virginia, on November 9, 1833, Sally and her family moved to Richmond, where they lived at the outbreak of Civil War, after her father's death. When the government asked the public to help care for the wounded of First Bull Run, Sally responded by opening a private hospital in a house donated for that purpose by Judge John Robertson. Robertson Hospital, subsidized by Tompkins's substantial inheritance, treated 1,333 Confederate soldiers from its opening until the last patients were discharged June 13, 1865.

Because the hospital returned more of its patients to the ranks than any other medical-care facility, officers tried to place their most seriously wounded men in Tompkins's care. She used her high rate of success to convince President Jefferson Davis to allow her hospital to stay open even as his orders shut down other private hospitals in the city. To circumvent the regulation calling for all hospitals to be run by military personnel, on September 9, 1861, Davis appointed Tompkins captain of cavalry, unassigned, making her the only woman to hold a commission in the Confederate States Army. Her military rank allowed her to draw government rations and a salary to help defray some of her operating costs. Only 73 deaths were recorded at Robertson Hospital during its 45-month existence. Tompkins remained a beloved celebrity in postwar Richmond, active in the Episcopal church and a popular guest at veterans' reunions and Daughters of the Confederacy meetings. The war, her continued charity work, and her generous hospitality to veterans eventually exhausted her fortune. In 1905 "Captain Sally" moved into the Confederate Women's Home in Richmond as a lifetime guest; she died there July 26, 1916, in her 83d year. An honorary member of the R. E. Lee Camp of the Confederate Veterans, she was honored with a full military funeral. Four chapters of the United Daughters of the Confederacy are named in Sally Tompkins's honor.

Source

Boatner, Mark M. *The Civil War Dictionary.* New York: Random House, 1991.

Treadwell, Jack L. *Captain, United States Army, Company F, 180th Infantry, 45th Infantry Division, so distinguished himself in combat, during World War II, that he was awarded the Medal of Honor for his heroic actions.*

Born: Ashland, Ala.; **Entered service at:** Snyder, Okla.; **Place and date:** Near Nieder-Wurzbach, Germany, March 18, 1945. **G.O. No.:** 79, September 14, 1945.

Citation: "Capt. Treadwell (then 1st Lt.), commanding officer of Company F, near Nieder-Wurzbach, Germany, in the Siegfried line, single-handedly captured 6 pillboxes and 18 prisoners. Murderous enemy automatic and rifle fire with intermittent artillery bombardments had pinned down his company for hours at the base of a hill defended by concrete fortifications and interlocking trenches. Eight men sent to attack a single point had all become casualties on the bare slope when Capt. Treadwell, armed with a submachinegun and handgrenades, went forward alone to clear the way for his stalled company. Over the terrain devoid of cover and swept by bullets, he fearlessly advanced, firing at the aperture of the nearest pillbox and, when within range, hurling grenades at it. He reached the pillbox, thrust the muzzle of his gun through the port, and drove 4 Germans out with their hands in the air. A fifth was found dead inside. Waving these prisoners back to the American line, he continued under terrible, concentrated fire to the next pillbox and took it in the same manner. In this fort he captured the commander of the hill defenses, whom he sent to the rear with the other prisoners. Never slackening his attack, he then ran across the crest of the hill to a third pillbox, traversing this distance in full view of hostile machine gunners and snipers. He was again successful in taking the enemy position. The Germans quickly fell prey to his further rushes on 3 more pillboxes in the confusion and havoc caused by his whirlwind assaults and capture of their commander. Inspired by the electrifying performance of their leader, the men of Company F stormed after him and overwhelmed resistance on the entire hill, driving a wedge into the Siegfried line and making it possible for their battalion to take its objective. By his courageous willingness to face nearly impossible odds and by his overwhelming one-man offensive, Capt. Treadwell reduced a heavily fortified, seemingly impregnable enemy sector."

Source
Medal of Honor Citation.

Turner, Day G. (d. 1945) *Sergeant, United States Army, Company B, 319th Infantry, 80th Infantry Division, so distinguished himself in combat, during World War II, that he was awarded (posthumously) the Medal of Honor.*

Born: Berwick, Pa.; **Entered service at:** Nescopek, Pa.; **Place and date:** At Dahl, Luxembourg, January 8, 1945. G.O. No.: 49, June 28, 1945.

Citation: "He commanded a 9-man squad with the mission of holding a critical flank position. When overwhelming numbers of the enemy attacked under cover of withering artillery, mortar, and rocket fire, he withdrew his squad into a nearby house, determined to defend it to the last man. The enemy attacked again and again and was repulsed with heavy losses. Supported by direct tank fire, they finally gained entrance, but the intrepid sergeant refused to surrender although 5 of his men were wounded and 1 was killed. He boldly flung a can of flaming oil at the first wave of attackers, dispersing them, and fought doggedly from room to room, closing with the enemy in fierce hand-to-hand encounters. He hurled hand-grenade for hand-grenade, bayoneted 2 fanatical Germans who rushed a doorway he was defending and fought on with the enemy's weapons when his own ammunition was expended. The savage fight raged for 4 hours, and finally, when only 3 men of the defending squad were left unwounded, the enemy surrendered. Twenty-five prisoners were taken, 11 enemy dead and a great number of wounded were counted. Sgt. Turner's valiant stand will live on as a constant inspiration to his comrades. His heroic, inspiring leadership, his determination and courageous devotion to duty exemplify the highest tradition of the military service."

Source
Medal of Honor Citation.

Twining, Merrill B. (1902–1996) *General officer, United States Marine Corps, whose vision, skill, and determination helped to shape the Marine Corps after World War II.*

Died May 11, 1996, in Fallbrook, California. He had retired from active duty with the Marine Corps on October 31, 1959. He was advanced to the rank of general on his retirement as a result of his special commendation in combat.

Twining was born on November 28, 1902, at Monroe, Wisconsin, and was commissioned a Marine second lieutenant on graduation from the United States Naval Academy in June 1923. During the next two years, the lieutenant completed the Marine Officers Basic School; served at Quantico, Virginia; participated in Caribbean maneuvers with the 10th Marines; and was stationed at the Marine Barracks, Pensacola, Florida.

Lieutenant Twining was ordered to the Marine Barracks at Pearl Harbor in November 1925, and after six months in Hawaii, he sailed for duty in China, via the Philippine Islands. In China he served with the 4th and 12th Marine Regiments at Shanghai, Taku, Hsin Ho, Tientsin, and Peking. He returned to the United States in August 1928 and in December was promoted to first lieutenant while serving as commander of the Marine Barracks at the Pacific Coast Torpedo Station, Keyport,

Washington. He then served briefly as editor and publisher of *Leatherneck Magazine* in Washington, D.C.

In September 1929, Lieutenant Twining was assigned to the Office of the Judge Advocate General of the Navy. While stationed there, he obtained his bachelor of laws degree from George Washington University in 1932. He reported again to the Marine Barracks at Pearl Harbor in November 1932 and remained there until January 1935. In March 1935, while attached to the Marine Barracks at the Naval Air Station, Sunnyvale, California, he earned the Distinguished Pistol Shot's Gold Badge in the Western Rifle and Pistol Matches at San Diego, California. He was promoted to the rank of captain in May 1935.

From July 1935 to August 1936, Captain Twining was a student in the Army Infantry School, Fort Benning, Georgia. During the next year he served at Philadelphia as an instructor in the Marine Officers' Basic School. In Quantico in June 1937, he served as a company commander with the Fifth Marines; two years later he became an instructor in the Marine Corps Schools. He also participated in Caribbean maneuvers in 1938 and 1939. He was promoted to major in July 1939.

In November 1941, Major Twining joined the First Marine Division at Camp Lejeune, North Carolina. He was promoted to lieutenant colonel in January 1942 and moved with the division to the Pacific area in May 1942. He earned his first Legion of Merit with Combat V for his meritorious service June 25–December 10, 1942, as the division's assistant operations officer, and later assistant chief of staff, G-3 (operations and training officer). In that capacity he prepared and executed the plans for the Guadalcanal Campaign.

During the planning phase, Lieutenant Colonel Twining and Maj. William B. McKean were flown over the then-Japanese-held island on July 17, 1942, the first sighting of Guadalcanal by U.S. Marines during World War II. After the Guadalcanal Campaign, he served as assistant chief of staff, G-3, of the First Marine Amphibious Corps, then commanded by Gen. Alexander A. Vandergrift.

After returning to the United States in November 1943, Lieutenant Colonel Twining remained until 1947 at the Marine Corps Schools, Quantico. While there, he served successfully as chief of operations and training, executive officer, and member of the schools' administrative staff. He was promoted to colonel in February 1945.

In August 1947, Colonel Twining reported to Pearl Harbor as chief of staff, Fleet Marine Force, Pacific. The following June, he was named fleet Marine officer on staff of the commander in chief, Pacific Fleet. He served in that capacity until July 1949, when he returned to the Marine Corps Schools, as senior resident member of the Marine Corps Board.

In August 1950, he reported to Camp Pendleton and the following month was promoted to brigadier general. He served there as commanding general, Marine Corps Training and Replacement Command, until November 1951, and later as commander of fleet Marine force troops and commanding general, Third Marine Division.

After leaving Camp Pendleton, General Twining joined the First Marine Division in Korea in March 1952. For outstanding service as assistant division commander from March through May 1952, he received a Gold Star in lieu of his second Legion of Merit with Combat V. He returned to the States that June and subsequently served in the Office of the Commandant of the Marine Corps. He was promoted to major general in September 1952. In January 1954, he was named deputy chief of staff at Headquarters Marine Corps.

General Twining returned to Korea in January 1955 as commander of the First Marine Division. In March of that year, he accompanied the division to Camp Pendleton, where he served until August 1956. In September 1956, he was promoted to lieutenant general and assumed duties as commandant, Marine Corps Schools, Quantico, 25th Marine Corps officer to head the schools. He served in that capacity until his retirement October 31, 1959.

In 1996, at the age of 94, General Twining authored his memoirs, *No Bended Knee: The Battle for Guadalcanal.* The title is from a statement made by Marine Gen. Alexander A. Vandergrift, commandant of the Marine Corps in 1946, in his testimony before the Senate Naval Affairs Committee:

> The bended knee is not a tradition of our Corps. If the Marine as a fighting man has not made a case for himself after 170 years of service, he must go. But I think that you will agree with me that he has earned the right to depart with dignity and honor, not by subjugation to the status of uselessness and servility planned for him by the War Department.

In addition to the Legion of Merit with Combat V and Gold Star in lieu of a second award, the general's medals and decorations include the Letter of Commendation with Commendation Ribbon, the Presidential Unit Citation, the Expeditionary Medal, the Yangtze Service Medal, the American Defense Medal, the Asiatic-Pacific Campaign Medal with two Bronze Stars, the American Campaign Medal, the World War II Victory Medal, the National Defense Medal, the Korean Service Medal with two Bronze Stars, the United Nations Service Medal, the Korean Presidential Unit Citation, and the Order of Orange Nassau with Swords (awarded by Queen Wilhelmina of the Netherlands).

Several members of General Twining's family also had distinguished careers in the military. President Dwight D.

Eisenhower named his brother, Gen. Nathan F. Twining, former United States Air Force chief of staff, to serve as chairman of the Joint Chiefs of Staff. Another brother, Robert Twining, was a retired navy captain. His grandfather, Nathan C. Twining, was a Civil War army captain; his uncle, Nathan C., was a rear admiral.

Source

Marine Corps Historical Center.

Twining, Merrill B. *No Bended Knee*. Novato, Calif.: Presidio Press, 1996.

U

Urban, Matt (b. 1919) *Lieutenant colonel (then captain), Second Battalion, 60th Infantry Regiment, Ninth Infantry Division, so distinguished himself in combat, during World War II, that he was awarded the Medal of Honor for his heroic actions.*

Born: August 25, 1919, Buffalo, N.Y.; **Entered service at**: Fort Bragg, N.C., July 2, 1941; **Place and date**: Renouf, France, June 14–September 3, 1944.

Citation: "Lieutenant Colonel (then Captain) Matt Urban, l 12-22-2414, United States Army, who distinguished himself by a series of bold, heroic actions, exemplified by singularly outstanding combat leadership, personal bravery, and tenacious devotion to duty, during the period 14 June to 3 September 1944 while assigned to the 2d Battalion, 60th Infantry Regiment, 9th Infantry Division. On 14 June, Captain Urban's company, attacking at Renouf, France, encountered heavy enemy small arms and tank fire. The enemy tanks were unmercifully raking his unit's positions and inflicting heavy casualties. Captain Urban, realizing that his company was in imminent danger of being decimated, armed himself with a bazooka. He worked his way with an ammo carrier through hedgerows, under a continuing barrage of fire, to a point near the tanks. He brazenly exposed himself to the enemy fire and, firing the bazooka, destroyed both tanks. Responding to Captain Urban's action, his company moved forward and routed the enemy. Later that same day, still in the attack near Orglandes, Captain Urban was wounded in the leg by direct fire from a 37 mm tank-gun. He refused evacuation and continued to lead his company until they moved into defensive positions for the night. At 0500 hours the next day, still in the attack near Orglandes, Captain Urban, though badly wounded, directed his company in another attack. One hour later he was again wounded. Suffering from two wounds, one serious, he was evacuated to England. In mid-July, while recovering from his wounds, he learned of his unit's severe losses in the hedgerows of Normandy. Realizing his unit's need for battle-tested leaders, he voluntarily left the hospital and hitchhiked his way back to his unit hear St. Lo, France. Arriving at the 2d Battalion Command Post at 1130 hours, 25 July, he found that his unit had jumped-off at 1100 hours in the first attack of Operation Cobra. Still limping from his leg wound, Captain Urban made his way forward to retake command of his company. He found his company held up by strong enemy opposition. Two supporting tanks had been destroyed and another, intact but with no tank commander or gunner, was not moving. He located a lieutenant in charge of the support tanks and directed a plan of attack to eliminate the enemy strong point. The heavy enemy fire immediately killed the lieutenant and a sergeant when they tried to mount the tank. Captain Urban, though physically hampered by his leg wound and knowing quick action had to be taken, dashed through the scathing fire and mounted the tank. With enemy bullets ricocheting from the tank, Captain Urban ordered the tank forward and, completely exposed to the enemy fire, manned the machine gun and placed devastating fire on the enemy. His action, in the face of enemy fire, galvanized the battalion into action and they attacked and destroyed the enemy position. On 2 August, Captain Urban was wounded in the chest by shell fragments and, disregarding the recommendation of the Battalion Surgeon, again refused evacuation. On 6 August, Captain Urban became the commander of the 2d Battalion. On 15 August, he was again wounded but remained with his unit. On 3 September, the 2d Battalion was given the mission of establishing a crossing-point on the Meuse River near Heer, Belgium. The enemy planned to stop the advance of the Allied Army by concentrating heavy forces at the Meuse. The 2d Battalion, attacking toward the crossing-point, encountered fierce enemy artillery, small arms and mortar fire, which stopped the attack. Captain Urban quickly moved from his command post to the lead position of the battalion. Reorganizing the attacking elements, he personally led a charge toward the enemy's strong point. As the charge moved across the open terrain, Captain Urban was seriously wounded in the neck. Although unable to talk above a whisper from the paralyzing neck wound, and in danger of losing his life, he refused to be evacuated until the enemy was routed and his battalion had secured the crossing-point on the Meuse River.

Captain Urban's personal leadership, limitless bravery, and repeated extraordinary exposure to enemy fire served as an inspiration to his entire battalion. His valorous and intrepid actions reflect the utmost credit on him and uphold the noble traditions of the United States."

Source
Medal of Honor Citation.

Vandergrift, Alexander Archer (1887–1973)

General officer, United States Marine Corps, 18th commandant of the Marine Corps, so distinguished himself in combat, during World War II, that he was awarded the Medal of Honor for his heroic actions.

Born: March 13, 1887, Charlottesville, Va.; **Entered service at**: January 22, 1909; **Place and date**: Solomon Islands, August 7–December 9, 1942.

Vandergrift studied at the University of Virginia and was commissioned in the Marine Corps as a second lieutenant in 1909. After instruction at the Marine Officers School, Port Royal, South Carolina, and a tour of duty at the Marine Barracks, Portsmouth, New Hampshire, he began foreign shore duty in the Caribbean, where he participated in the bombardment, assault, and capture of Coyotope in Nicaragua. He further participated in the engagement and occupation of Vera Cruz, Mexico.

In December 1914, after promotion to first lieutenant, he attended the Advanced Base Course at the Marine Barracks, Philadelphia. On completion of schooling, he sailed for Haiti with the First Marine Brigade and participated in action against hostile Cacos forces at LeTrou and Fort Capois.

In August 1916, he was promoted to captain and became a member of the Haitian Constabulary at Port-au-Prince, where he remained until detached to the United States in December 1918. He returned to Haiti again in 1919, to serve with the Gendarmerie d'Haiti as an inspector of constabulary. He was promoted to major in June 1920.

Vandergrift returned to the United States in April 1923 and was assigned to the Marine Barracks at Quantico, Virginia. He then completed the Field Officers' Course at Marine Corps Schools in May 1926 and was later transferred to the Marine Corps Base, San Diego, California, as the assistant chief of staff.

In February 1927, he sailed for China, where he served as operations and training officer for the Third Marine Brigade with Headquarters at Tientsin. He was ordered to Washington, D.C., in September 1928; there he became assistant chief coordinator, Bureau of the Budget. After duty in Washington, he joined the Marine Barracks, Quantico, where he became assistant chief of staff, G-1 Section, Fleet Marine Force. During this assignment he was promoted to lieutenant colonel in June 1934.

Ordered to China in June 1935, Vandergrift served successively as executive officer and commanding officer of the Marine Detachment at the American Embassy in Peiping. Promoted to colonel in September 1936, Vandergrift reported to Headquarters Marine Corps in June 1937; there he became military secretary to the major general commandant. In March 1940, he was appointed assistant to the major general commandant and the following month was promoted to brigadier general.

General Vandergrift was detached to the First Marine Division in November 1941 shortly before the outbreak of World War II. He was promoted to major general in March 1942 and in May sailed for the South Pacific area as commanding general of the first Marine division to leave the shores of the United States. On August 7, 1942, in the Solomon Islands, he led ashore the First Marine Division, Reinforced, in the first large-scale offensive action against the Japanese. For his heroic and outstanding service as the commanding general of the First Marine Division during the attacks on Guadalcanal, Tulagi, and Gavutu, he was awarded the Navy Cross. For the subsequent occupation and defense from August 7 to December 9, 1942, he was awarded the Medal of Honor.

In July 1943, he assumed command of the First Marine Amphibious Corps; he commanded this organization in the landing at Empress Augusta Bay, Bougainville,

Alexander Archer Vandergrift

Northern Solomon Islands, on November 1, 1943. After establishing the initial beachhead, he relinquished command and returned to Washington, D.C., as commandant-designate.

On January 1, 1944, as a lieutenant general, he was sworn in as the 18th commandant of the Marine Corps. On April 4, 1945, he was appointed general, with a date of rank from March 21, 1945, the first Marine officer on active duty to attain the four-star rank.

For his outstanding service as commandant of the Marine Corps from January 1, 1944, to June 30, 1946, the general was awarded the Distinguished Service Medal. He left active service on December 31, 1947, and was placed on the retired list April 1, 1949.

General Vandergrift held an honorary degree of doctor of military science from Pennsylvania Military College and honorary degrees of doctor of law from Harvard, Colgate, Brown, Columbia, and Maryland Universities and John Marshall College.

General Vandergrift died May 8, 1973, at the National Naval Medical Center, Bethesda, Maryland, after a long illness, at 86 years old.

Citation: "For outstanding and heroic accomplishment above and beyond the call of duty as commanding officer of the 1st Marine Division in operations against

enemy Japanese forces in the Solomon Islands during the period 7 August to 9 December 1942. With the adverse factors of weather, terrain, and disease making his task a difficult and hazardous undertaking, and with his command eventually including sea, land, and air forces of Army, Navy, and Marine Corps, Maj. Gen. Vandegrift achieved marked success in commanding the initial landings of the U.S. forces in the Solomon Islands and in their subsequent occupation. His tenacity, courage, and resourcefulness prevailed against a strong, determined, and experienced enemy, and the gallant fighting spirit of the men under his inspiring leadership enabled them to withstand aerial, land, and sea bombardment, to surmount all obstacles, and leave a disorganized and ravaged enemy. This dangerous but vital mission, accomplished at the constant risk of his life, resulted in securing a valuable base for further operations of our forces against the enemy, and its successful completion reflects great credit upon Maj. Gen. Vandegrift, his command, and the U.S. Naval Service."

Source and Additional Reading
Medal of Honor Citation.
Vandergrift, A. A. *Once a Marine: The Memoirs of General A. A. Vandergrift, USMC.* New York: Norton, 1964.

Van Lew, Elizabeth (1818–1900) *Famous Union spy who raised the first Union flag to wave over Richmond in four years in 1865.*

Born into a prominent Richmond family, Elizabeth Van Lew returned from her schooling in Philadelphia an adamant abolitionist determined to fight slavery in the bastion of the South. "Slave power," she wrote in her diary, "is arrogant, is jealous and intrusive, is cruel, is despotic." Outspoken and rebellious, she appeared to her neighbors to be more than a little eccentric and soon became known as "Crazy Bet."

After Virginia seceded and Fort Sumter fell, she used her reputation for innocuous idiosyncrasy as a shield behind which her shrewd and resourceful mind devised schemes to abet the Union cause from within Richmond. Her first target was the Confederate Libby Prison, which imprisoned Union captives. Pretending to make a merely humanitarian gesture, Van Lew took baskets of food, medicine, and books to the prisoners. What she took out would have shocked the guards she learned to charm and deceive. Not only did Van Lew help some prisoners escape, she also gleaned valuable information from various sources inside the prison. Newly arrived Union prisoners secretly recounted the strength and dispositions of Confederate troops they had seen on their way from the front to Richmond. Of even more use was information carelessly conveyed to the "harmless Crazy Bet" by Confederate guards and by the prison's Confederate commandant, Lt. David H. Todd (Mary Todd Lincoln's half-brother).

She even managed to penetrate the home of President Jefferson Davis by convincing one of her former servants to secure a position in the Davis household staff. At first, Van Lew simply mailed the information she retrieved in letters to federal authorities. As her work continued, her methods grew more sophisticated. She devised a code involving words and letters that prisoners would underline in the books she lent them.

Van Lew also sent her household servants—though she had freed the family's slaves, many of them chose to stay with her—northward carrying baskets of farm produce. Each basket held some eggs, one of which contained encoded messages in place of its natural contents. She sent her information directly to Benjamin Butler as well as to Grant through an elaborate courier system. It was so fast and effective that General Grant often received flowers still fresh from his spy's large garden. Grant would later say of her efforts, "You have sent me the most valuable information received from Richmond during the war."

After the war, President Grant rewarded Van Lew with a job as postmistress of Richmond, which she held from 1869 to 1877. Although revered in the North, she was, needless to say, ostracized by her Richmond neighbors. "No one will walk with us on the street," she wrote, "no one will go with us anywhere; and it grows worse and worse as the years roll on." Failing to be reappointed postmistress under Rutherford B. Hayes, she lived on an annuity from the family of a Union soldier she had helped in Libby Prison. She died in Richmond, probably in 1900.

Source
Boatner, Mark M. *The Civil War Dictionary.* New York: David McKay, 1959.

Van Winkle, Archie (b. 1925) *Staff sergeant, United States Marine Corps Reserve, Company B, First Battalion, Seventh Marines, First Marine Division (Reinforced), so distinguished himself in combat, during the Korean War, that he was awarded the Medal of Honor for his heroic actions.*

Born: March 17, 1925, Juneau, Ala.; **Entered service at:** Arlington, Wash.; **Place and date:** Vicinity of Sudong, Korea, November 2, 1950.

Citation: "For conspicuous gallantry and intrepidity at the risk of his life above and beyond the call of duty while serving as a platoon sergeant in Company B, in action

against enemy aggressor forces. Immediately rallying the men in his area after a fanatical and numerically superior enemy force penetrated the center of the line under cover of darkness and pinned down the platoon with a devastating barrage of deadly automatic weapons and grenade fire, S/Sgt. Van Winkle boldly spearheaded a determined attack through withering fire against hostile frontal positions and, though he and all the others who charged with him were wounded, succeeded in enabling his platoon to gain the fire superiority and the opportunity to reorganize. Realizing that the left flank squad was isolated from the rest of the unit, he rushed through 40 yards of fierce enemy fire to reunite his troops despite an elbow wound, which rendered 1 of his arms totally useless. Severely wounded a second time when a direct hit in the chest from a hostile hand grenade caused serious and painful wounds, he staunchly refused evacuation and continued to shout orders and words of encouragement to his depleted and battered platoon. Finally carried from his position unconscious from shock and from loss of blood, S/Sgt. Van Winkle served to inspire all who observed him to heroic efforts in successfully repulsing the enemy attack. His superb leadership, valiant fighting spirit, and unfaltering devotion to duty in the face of heavy odds reflect the highest credit upon himself and the U.S. Naval Service."

Source
Medal of Honor Citation.

Vargas, Jay, Jr. (b. 1940) *Major (then captain), United States Marine Corps, Company G, Second Battalion, Fourth Marines, Ninth Marine Amphibious Brigade, so distinguished himself in combat, during the Vietnam War, that he was awarded the Medal of Honor for his heroic actions.*

Born: July 29, 1940, Winslow, Ariz.; **Entered service at:** Winslow, Ariz.; **Place and date:** Dai Do, Republic of Vietnam April 30–May 2, 1968.

Citation: "For conspicuous gallantry and intrepidity at the risk of his life above and beyond the call of duty while serving as commanding officer, Company G, in action against enemy forces from 30 April to 2 May 1968. On 1 May 1968, though suffering from wounds he had incurred while relocating his unit under heavy enemy fire the preceding day, Maj. Vargas combined Company G with two other companies and led his men in an attack on the fortified village of Dai Do. Exercising expert leadership, he maneuvered his Marines across 700 meters of open rice paddy while under intense enemy mortar, rocket and artillery fire and obtained a foothold in 2 hedgerows on the enemy perimeter, only to have elements of his company become pinned down by the intense enemy fire.

Jay Vargas Jr.

Leading his reserve platoon to the aid of his beleaguered men, Maj. Vargas inspired his men to renew their relentless advance, while destroying a number of enemy bunkers. Again wounded by grenade fragments, he refused aid as he moved about the hazardous area reorganizing his unit into a strong defense perimeter at the edge of the village. Shortly after the objective was secured the enemy commenced a series of counterattacks and probes, which lasted throughout the night but were unsuccessful, as the gallant defenders of Company G stood firm in their hard-won enclave. Reinforced the following morning, the Marines launched a renewed assault through Dai Do on the village of Dinh To, to which the enemy retaliated with a massive counterattack resulting in hand-to-hand combat. Maj. Vargas remained in the open, encouraging and rendering assistance to his Marines when he was hit for the third time in the 3-day battle. Observing his battalion commander sustain a serious wound, he disregarded his excruciating pain, crossed the fire-swept area and carried his commander to a covered position, then resumed supervising and encouraging his men while simultaneously assisting in organizing the battalion's perimeter defense. His gallant actions uphold the highest traditions of the Marine Corps and the U.S. Naval Service."

Source
Above and Beyond. Boston: Boston Publishing, 1985.
Medal of Honor Citation.

W

Wahlen, George Edward (b. 1929) *Pharmacist's mate second class, United States Navy, Second Battalion, 26th Marines, Fifth Marine Division, so distinguished himself in combat, during World War II, that he was awarded the Medal of Honor for his heroic actions.*

Born: August 8, 1924, Ogden, Utah; **Entered service at:** Utah; **Place and date:** Iwo Jima, Volcano Islands group, March 3, 1945.

Citation: "For conspicuous gallantry and intrepidity at the risk of his life above and beyond the call of duty while serving with the 2d Battalion, 26th Marines, 5th Marine Division, during action against enemy Japanese forces on Iwo Jima in the Volcano group on 3 March 1945. Painfully wounded in the bitter action on 26 February, Wahlen remained on the battlefield, advancing well forward of the front lines to aid a wounded Marine and carrying him back to safety despite a terrific concentration of fire. Tireless in his ministrations, he consistently disregarded all danger to attend his fighting comrades as they fell under the devastating rain of shrapnel and bullets, and rendered prompt assistance to various elements of his combat group as required. When an adjacent platoon suffered heavy casualties, he defied the continuous pounding of heavy mortars and deadly fire of enemy rifles to care for the wounded, working rapidly in an area swept by constant fire and treating 14 casualties before returning to his own platoon. Wounded again on 2 March, he gallantly refused evacuation, moving out with his company the following day in a furious assault across 600 yards of open terrain and repeatedly rendering medical aid while exposed to the blasting fury of powerful Japanese guns. Stouthearted and indomitable, he persevered in his determined efforts as his unit waged fierce battle and, unable to walk after sustaining a third agonizing wound, resolutely crawled 50 yards to administer first aid to still another fallen fighter. By his dauntless fortitude and valor, Wahlen served as a constant inspiration and contributed vitally to the high morale of his company during critical phases of this strategically important engagement. His heroic spirit of self-sacrifice in the face of overwhelming enemy fire upheld the highest traditions of the U.S. Naval Service."

Source
Medal of Honor Citation.

Wainwright, Jonathan Mayhew IV (1883–1953) *General, United States Army so distinguished himself in combat, during World War II, that he was awarded the Medal of Honor for his heroic actions.*

Born: August 23, 1883, Fort Walla Walla, Washington Territory; **Entered service at:** Texas; **Place and date:** Corregidor, May 1942.

Jonathan Wainwright was born the son of a cavalry officer and a descendant in a line of distinguished U.S. naval officers on August 23, 1883, at Fort Walla Walla, Washington Territory. His father, Robert, commanded a squadron in the Battle of Santiago during the Spanish-American War and died in 1901 while serving in the suppression of the Philippine Insurrection. A year later, Jonathan was appointed to the United States Military Academy at West Point.

Wainwright received his commission in 1906 and began his career with the First Cavalry Regiment in Texas, which was sent to the Philippines in 1908 as part of an expedition sent to quell the Moro uprising on the island of Jolo. Wainwright also participated in the St. Mihiel and Meuse-Argonne offensives near the end of World War I. After the Armistice, he served as assistant chief of staff with the Army of Occupation in Koblenz, Germany, and was awarded the Distinguished Service Medal for his work in that capacity. The years between the wars were spent in postgraduate studies and training commands.

He graduated from the Mounted Service School, Fort Riley, Kansas, 1916. Promoted to captain, in 1917 he was on the staff of the first officer training camp at Plattsburg, New York. In February 1918 he was ordered to France. In June he became assistant chief of staff of the 82nd Infantry Division, with which he took part in the St. Mihiel and Meuse-Argonne offensives. Promoted to temporary lieutenant colonel in October he was assigned to occupation duty in Germany with the Third Army until 1920, when, having reverted to captain, he was promoted to major.

After a year as an instructor at the remaned Cavalry School at Fort Riley, he was attached to the General Staff during 1921–23 and assigned to the Third Cavalry, Fort Myer, Virginia, 1923–25. He was promoted to lieutenant colonel in 1929 and graduated from the Command and General Staff School, Fort Leavenworth, Kansas, 1931, and the Army War College, 1934. He was promoted to colonel in 1935 and commanded the Third Cavalry until 1938, when he was advanced to brigadier general in command of the First Cavalry Brigade at Fort Clark, Texas. In September 1940, he was promoted to temporary major general and returned to the Philippines to take command

Jonathan Mayhew Wainwright IV

of the Philippine Division, which began in late December 1941.

Wainwright had little inkling of what the future held. The war in Europe was already raging and he feared "that something might break over here and there he would be stuck in the Philippines missing everything." He was commanding American and Filipino troops in northern Luzon when the Japanese attacked on December 8, 1941. Wainwright commanded from the front, and his skillful series of holding actions helped to make the American stand on Bataan possible.

On February 7, 1942, General MacArthur decorated him with the Distinguished Service Cross for extraordinary heroism. MacArthur was ordered to leave for Australia on March 11, 1942. Wainwright succeeded him as commander of all American and Filipino forces on Bataan and was promoted to lieutenant general.

As the senior field commander of U.S. and Filipino forces, he had tactical responsibility for resisting the Japanese invasion. Pushed back from beachheads in Lingayen Gulf, his Philippine forces withdrew onto the Bataan Peninsula, where they occupied well-prepared defensive positions and commanded the entrance to Manila Bay. In throwing back a major Japanese assault in January, the defenders earned the name "battling bastards of Bataan." When MacArthur was ordered off Bataan in March 1942, Wainwright, promoted to temporary lieutenant general, succeeded to command of United States Army Forces in the Far East, a command immediately afterward redesignated United States Forces in the Philippines. The Japanese attacks resumed in earnest in April.

The Japanese high command issued an ultimatum on March 22, urging the defenders of Bataan to surrender in the name of humanity. Continuous air bombardment was followed by two human wave assaults, which were repulsed, but the defenders were running low on supplies and morale.

Bataan fell on April 9, 1942. President Roosevelt authorized Wainwright to continue the fight or make terms, as he saw fit. Wainwright chose to continue the battle from Corregidor despite the urgings of some that he leave:

> I have been one of the battling bastards of Bataan and I'll play the same role on the rock as long as it is humanly possible. I have been with my men from the start, and if captured I will share their lot. We have been through so much together that my conscience would not let me leave before the final curtain.

Wainwright and 11,000 survivors held on in the tunnels beneath the rock for another month deprived of food, sleep, or hope of relief. On May 5 to Wainwright wrote to MacArthur: "As I write this we are being subjected to terrific air and artillery bombardment and it is unreasonable to expect that we can hold out for long. We have done our best, both here and on Bataan, and although we are beaten we are still unashamed." The Japanese began landing on the island that night, and at noon the next day Wainwright called for terms. General Homma insisted that Wainwright surrender all remaining American and Filipino forces or risk the annihilation of his troops on Corregidor. Wainwright complied. MacArthur countermanded the order but was ignored. MacArthur was livid and later refused to sign General Marshall's recommendation of Wainwright for a Medal of Honor.

Wainwright spent the next three years in Japanese prison camps in the Philippines, China, and Formosa (Taiwan). The man who was known to his friends as Skinny emerged from captivity little more than a skeleton. He was liberated on August 25, 1945, in time to attend the surrender ceremonies aboard USS *Missouri* in Tokyo Bay on September 2, 1945, after which he returned to the Philippines to receive the surrender of the local Japanese commander. A hero's welcome in the United states was accompanied by promotion to general and the awarding of the Medal of Honor. *Memoir, General Wainwright's Story,* was published in 1945. In January 1946 he took command of the Fourth Army, Fort Sam Houston, Texas. He retired from the army in 1947 and died on September 3, 1953.

Citation: "Distinguished himself by intrepid and determined leadership against greatly superior enemy forces. At the repeated risk of life above and beyond the call of duty in his position, he frequented the firing line of his troops where his presence provided the example and incentive that helped make the gallant efforts of these men possible. The final stand on beleaguered Corregidor, for which he was in an important measure personally responsible, commanded the admiration of the Nation's allies. It reflected the high morale of American arms in the face of overwhelming odds. His courage and resolution were a vitally needed inspiration to the then sorely pressed freedom-loving peoples of the world."

Source

Wainwright, Gen. Jonathan M. *General Wainwright's Story.* New York: Doubleday, 1946.

Walker, Dr. Mary E. (b. 1832) *Contract acting assistant surgeon (civilian), United States Army, the sole female recipient of the Medal of Honor.*

Born: November 26, 1832, Oswego County, N.Y.; **Entered service at:** Louisville, Ky.; **Place and date:** Battle of Bull Run, July 21, 1861; Patent Office Hospital, Washington, D.C., October 1861; Chattanooga, Tenn., following Battle of Chickamauga, September 1863; Prisoner of War, April 10, 1864–August 12, 1864, Richmond, Va.; Battle of Atlanta, September 1864.

Citation: "Whereas it appears from official reports that Dr. Mary E. Walker, a graduate of medicine, 'has rendered valuable service to the Government, and her efforts have been earnest and untiring in a variety of ways,' and that she was assigned to duty and served as an assistant surgeon in charge of female prisoners at Louisville, Ky., upon the recommendation of Major-Generals Sherman and Thomas, and faithfully served as contract surgeon in the service of the United States, and has devoted herself with much patriotic zeal to the sick and wounded soldiers, both in the field and hospitals, to the detriment of her own health, and has also endured hardships as a prisoner of war four months in a Southern prison while acting as contract surgeon; and Whereas by reason of her not being a commissioned officer in the military service, a brevet or honorary rank cannot, under existing laws, be conferred upon her; and Whereas in the opinion of the President an honorable recognition of her services and sufferings should be made: It is ordered, That a testimonial thereof shall be hereby made and given to the said Dr. Mary E. Walker, and that the usual medal of honor for meritorious services be given her."

Given under my hand in the city of Washington, D.C., this 11th day of November, AD 1865. Andrew Johnson, President.

The medal was rescinded in 1917 along with 910 others and restored by President Carter June 10, 1977.

Source

Above and Beyond. Editors of Boston Publishing Company. Boston: Boston Publishing, 1985.

Walt, Lewis W. (1913–1989) *General, United States Marine Corps, First assistant Commandant of the Marine Corps to attain the rank of four-star general.*

Lewis William Walt was born February 16, 1913, in Wabaunsee County, Kansas. He graduated from high school in Fort Collins, Colorado, then entered Colorado State University, where he earned a bachelor of science degree in chemistry in 1936. Highlights of his student activities include: honor graduate, president of Student Body and Student Council, captain of the football and wrestling teams, cadet colonel of Reserve Officer Training Corps (ROTC), president of chemistry club, and captain of Scabbard and Blade. He enlisted in the Colorado National Guard at the age of 17. On graduation he was commissioned a second lieutenant in the Army Field Artillery Reserve but resigned that commission to accept an appointment as a Marine second lieutenant, July 6, 1936.

Lieutenant Walt completed Basic School at Philadelphia and in April 1937 was assigned to the Sixth Marine

Regiment in San Diego, California, as a machine gun platoon leader. Embarking for China in August 1937, he took part in the defense of the International Settlement of Shanghai until February 1938, at which time he returned to San Diego. In June 1939, he began his second tour of overseas duty when he was assigned to the Marine Barracks, Guam, Mariana Islands. He was promoted to first lieutenant in October 1939.

Returning to the United States in June 1941, shortly before his country's entry into World War II, Lieutenant Walt was assigned as a company commander in the Officer Candidates Class, Marine Corps Schools, Quantico, Virginia. He was promoted to captain in December 1941.

Early in 1942, Captain Walt volunteered to join the First Marine Raider Battalion, in April 1942 he arrived with the battalion on Somoa. On August 7, 1942, as commander of Company A, First Raider Battalion, he landed his company in the assault on Tulagi Island in the British Solomon Islands. He was awarded the Silver Star Medal for conspicuous gallantry during this landing. After this action, he joined the Fifth Marines on Guadalcanal, where he took part in combat as commanding officer of the Second Battalion, Fifth Marines. He was promoted to major in September 1942.

In October 1942, as battalion commander, Second Battalion, Fifth Marines, First Marine Division, Major Walt was wounded in action but continued in combat. On December 22, 1942, he was spot promoted to lieutenant colonel for his distinguished leadership and gallantry in action during the Guadalcanal Campaign.

In December 1943, after hospitalization and training in Australia, Lieutenant Colonel Walt led the Second Battalion, Fifth Marines, in assaults at Cape Gloucester, New Britain, and shortly thereafter was assigned as regimental executive officer. In the middle of this campaign he was ordered to take over command of the Third Battalion, Fifth Marines, during the intense battle for Aogiri Ridge. During this action, he earned his first Navy Cross, and Gen. Lemuel C. Shepherd Jr., the First Marine Division commander, named Aogiri Ridge *Walt Ridge* in his honor.

Departing Cape Gloucester in late February 1944, Lieutenant Colonel Walt was ordered to the Naval Hospital, Oakland, California, for treatment of wounds and malaria. In June 1944, he returned to the Pacific Theater. That September, he landed at Peleliu as regimental executive officer, Fifth Marines. On D-Day he was again ordered to take over command of the Third Battalion, Fifth Marines, in the midst of the battle for the beachhead, when the commanding officer and the executive officer were both killed. His second Navy Cross was awarded to him for gallantry in this action.

In November 1944, Lieutenant Colonel Walt returned to the United States, and the following month he assumed duty at Marine Corps Schools, Quantico, as chief of the Officer Candidates' School Tactics Section.

Assigned to Camp Pendleton in January 1947, Lieutenant Colonel Walt served as assistant chief of staff, G-3, Third Marine Brigade, and then as G-3, (Operating and Training Officer) First Marine Division. In November 1947, he assumed duty as operations and training officer, First Provisional Marine Brigade, on Guam; he later served as chief of staff of that organization from February to April 1949. Returning to Marine Corps Schools, Quantico, in May 1949, he saw duty as a battalion commander with the Special Training Regiment; in September, he entered the Amphibious Warfare School, Senior Course. On completing the course in June 1950, he remained at Marine Corps Schools to serve as chief of Tactics Section, S-3, and finally executive officer, Basic School. He was promoted to colonel in November 1951.

Ordered to Korea in November 1952, Colonel Walt was in combat with the First Marine Division until August 1953, serving consecutively as commanding officer, Fifth Marines, assistant chief of staff, G-3, and chief of staff of the division. The Legion of Merit and Bronze Star Medal, both with Combat V, were awarded to him for exceptionally meritorious service during this assignment. The Republic of Korea government also awarded Colonel Walt the Ulchi Medal and the Ulchi Medal with Silver Star for this period of combat.

On arrival at Marine Corps Schools, Quantico, in August 1953, Colonel Walt saw duty as director, Advanced Base Problem Section, Marine Corps Educational Center, through May 1954, followed by duty as commanding officer, Officers' Basic School, until August 1956. He also served as a member of the Advanced Research Group, Marine Corps Educational Center, until June 1957.

Transferred to Washington, D.C., Colonel Walt served as assistant director of personnel until August 1959; he then entered the National War College, Washington, D.C., and completed that course in June 1960.

In July 1960, Colonel Walt began a one-year assignment as Marine Corps representative on the Joint Advanced Study Group of the Joint Chiefs of Staff. On completing this assignment, he was promoted to brigadier general and reported for duty at Camp Lejeune as assistant division commander, Second Marine Division.

In September 1962, General Walt returned to Marine Corps Schools, Quantico, he was director of the Marine Corps Landing Force Development Center until May 1965. That same month, he was promoted to major general and in June 1965 assumed command of the Third Marine Amphibious Force and Third Marine Division in Vietnam. He was also chief of Naval Forces, Vietnam, and senior adviser, First Corps and First Corps coordinator, Republic of Vietnam.

Ten months later, President Lyndon B. Johnson nominated General Walt for lieutenant general, and the Senate approved his promotion on March 7, 1966. He continued in Vietnam as commanding general, Third Marine Amphibious Force, and senior adviser, First Corps and First Corps coordinator, Republic of Vietnam. During this period, General Walt was awarded his first Distinguished Service Medal. In addition, the Vietnamese government awarded him the Vietnamese National Order, Third Class; the Vietnamese National Order, Fourth Class; the Cross of Gallantry with Palm; the Chuong My Medal, and the Vietnamese Armed Forces Meritorious Unit Citation of Gallantry Cross with Palm. The government of South Korea also awarded him the senior Ulchi Medal.

On his return to the United States, General Walt served as the deputy chief of staff, director of personnel, at Headquarters Marine Corps, and on January 1, 1968, he was designated assistant commandant of the United States Marine Corps.

In April 1969, the Senate passed, and sent to the White House, a bill to make the assistant commandant of the United States Marine Corps a general (Four Stars), when the active duty strength of the Corps exceeds 200,000 men. On May 5, President Richard M. Nixon signed the bill, and General Walt was promoted to four-star rank on June 2, 1969, thus becoming the first Assistant Commandant of the Marine Corps to attain that rank. He retired from active duty on February 1, 1971.

General Walt, who courageously led Marines in combat during three wars, died March 26, 1989, in Gulfport, Mississippi, after more than 34 years as a Marine officer.

Source
Marine Corps Historical Center.

Washington, George (1732–1799) *Commander in chief of the Continental army during the American Revolution and first president of the United States (1789–1797).*

Born in Westmoreland County, Virginia, on February 22. 1732, George Washington was the eldest son of Augustine Washington and his second wife, Mary Ball Washington, who were prosperous Virginia gentry of English descent.

George spent his early years on the family estate on Pope's Creek along the Potomac River. His early education included the study of such subjects as mathematics, surveying, the classics, and "rules of civility." His father died in 1743, and soon thereafter George went to live with his half-brother, Lawrence, at Mount Vernon, Lawrence's plantation on the Potomac. Lawrence, who became something of a substitute father for his brother, had married into the Fairfax family, prominent and influential Virginians who helped launch George's career. An early ambition to go to sea had been effectively discouraged by George's mother, instead, he turned to surveying, securing (1748)

an appointment to survey Lord Fairfax's lands in the Shenandoah Valley. He helped lay out the Virginia town of Belhaven (now Alexandria) in 1749 and was appointed surveyor for Culpeper County. George accompanied his brother to Barbados in an effort to cure Lawrence of tuberculosis, but Lawrence died in 1752, soon after the brothers returned. George ultimately inherited the Mount Vernon estate.

By 1753 the growing rivalry between the British and French over control of the Ohio Valley, soon to erupt into the French and Indian War (1754–63), created new opportunities for the ambitious young Washington. He first gained public notice when as adjutant of one of Virginia's four military districts, he was dispatched (October 1753) by Governor Robert Dinwiddie on a fruitless mission to warn the French commander at Fort Le Boeuf against further encroachment on territory claimed by Britain. Washington's diary account of the dangers and difficulties of his journey, published at Williamsburg on his return, may have helped win him his ensuing promotion to lieutenant colonel.

Although only 22 years of age and lacking experience, he learned quickly, meeting the problems of recruitment, supply, and desertions with a combination of brashness and native ability that earned him the respect of his superiors.

In April 1754, on his way to establish a post at the Forks of the Ohio (the current site of Pittsburgh), Washington learned that the French had already erected a fort there. Warned that the French were advancing, he quickly threw up fortifications at Great Meadows, Pennsylvania, aptly naming the entrenchment Fort Necessity, and marched to intercept advancing French troops. In the resulting skirmish the French commander, Joseph Coulon de Villiers de Jumonville, was killed and most of his men were captured. Washington pulled his small force back into Fort Necessity, where he was overwhelmed (July 3) by the French in an all-day battle fought in a drenching rain. Surrounded by enemy troops, with his food supply almost exhausted and his dampened ammunition useless, Washington capitulated. Under the terms of the surrender signed that day, he was permitted to march his troops back to Williamsburg.

Discouraged by his defeat and angered by discrimination between British and colonial officers in rank and pay, he resigned his commission near the end of 1754. The next year, however, he volunteered to join British general Edward Braddock's expedition against the French. When Braddock was ambushed by the French and their Native American allies on the Monongahela River, Washington, although seriously ill, tried to rally the Virginia troops. Whatever public criticism attended the debacle, Washington's own military reputation was enhanced, and in 1755, at the age of 23, he was promoted to colonel and appointed commander in chief of the Virginia militia, with responsibility for defending the frontier. In 1758 he took an active part in General John Forbes's successful campaign against Fort Duquesne. In his correspondence during these years, Washington can be seen evolving from a brash, vain, and opinionated young officer, impatient with restraints and given to writing admonitory letters to his superiors, to a mature soldier with a grasp of administration and a firm understanding of how to deal effectively with civil authority.

Assured that the Virginia frontier was safe from French attack, Washington left the army in 1758 and returned to Mount Vernon, directing his attention to restoring his neglected estate. He erected new buildings, refurbished the house, and experimented with new crops. With the support of an ever-growing circle of influential friends, he entered politics, serving (1759–74) in Virginia's House of Burgesses. In January 1759 he married Martha Dandridge Custis, a wealthy and attractive young widow with two small children. It was to be a happy and satisfying marriage.

After 1769, Washington became a leader in Virginia's opposition to Great Britain's colonial policies. At first he hoped for reconciliation with Britain, although some British policies had touched him personally. Discrimination against colonial military officers had rankled deeply, and British land policies and restrictions on western expansion after 1763 had seriously hindered his plans for western land speculation. In addition, he shared the usual planter's dilemma in being continually in debt to his London agents. As a delegate (1774–75) to the First and Second Continental Congress, Washington did not participate actively in the deliberations, but his presence was undoubtedly a stabilizing influence.

In June 1775 he was Congress's unanimous choice as commander in chief of the Continental forces.

Washington took command of the troops surrounding British-occupied Boston on July 3 and devoted the next few months to training the undisciplined 14,000-man army and trying to secure urgently needed powder and other supplies. Early in March 1776, using cannon transported down from Fort Ticonderoga by Henry Know, Washington occupied Dorchester Heights, effectively commanding the city and forcing the British to evacuate on March 17. He then moved to defend New York City against the combined land and sea forces of Sir William Howe. In New York he committed a military blunder by occupying an untenable position in Brooklyn, however, he saved his army by skillfully retreating from Manhattan into Westchester County and through New Jersey into Pennsylvania. In the last months of 1776, desperately short of men and supplies Washington almost despaired. He had lost New York City to the British; enlistment was almost up for a number of the troops, and others were deserting in droves; civilian morale was falling rapidly; and Congress, faced with the possibility of a British attack on Philadelphia, had withdrawn from the city.

Colonial morale was briefly revived by the capture of Trenton, New Jersey, a brilliantly conceived attack in which Washington crossed the Delaware River on Christmas night 1776 and surprised the predominantly Hessian garrison. Advancing to Princeton, New Jersey, he routed the British there on January 3, 1777, but in September and October 1777 he suffered serious reverses in Pennsylvania at Brandywine and Germantown. The major success of that year, the defeat (October 1777) of the British at Saratoga, New York, had belonged not to Washington but to Benedict Arnold and Horatio Gates. The contrast between Washington's record and Gates's brilliant victory was one factor that led to the so-called Conway Cabal, an intrigue by some members of Congress and army officers to replace Washington with a more successful commander, probably Gates. Washington acted quickly, and the plan eventually collapsed as a result of lack of public support as well as Washington's overall superiority to his rivals.

After holding his bedraggled and dispirited army together during the difficult winter at Valley Forge, Washington learned that France had recognized American independence. With the aid of the Prussian baron von Steuben and the French marquis de Lafayette, he concentrated on turning the army into a viable fighting force, and by spring he was ready to take the field again. In June 1778 he attacked the British near Monmouth Courthouse, New Jersey, on their withdrawal from Philadelphia to New York. Although the American general Charles Lee's lack of enterprise ruined Washington's plan to strike a major blow at Sir Henry Clinton's army at Monmouth, the commander in chief's quick action on the field prevented an American defeat.

In 1780 the main theater of the war shifted to the south. Although the campaigns in Virginia and the Carolinas were conducted by other generals, including Nathanael Greene and Daniel Morgan, Washington was still responsible for the overall direction of the war. After the arrival of the French army in 1780 he concentrated on coordinating allied efforts and in 1781 launched, in cooperation with the comte de Rochambeau and the comte d'Estaing, the brilliantly planned and executed Yorktown Campaign against Charles Cornwallis, securing (October 19, 1781) the American victory.

Washington had grown enormously in stature during the war. A man of unquestioned integrity, he began by accepting the advice of more experienced officers such as Gates and Charles Lee but quickly learned to trust his own judgment. He sometimes railed at Congress for its failure to supply troops and for the bungling fiscal measures that frustrated his efforts to secure adequate matériel. Gradually, however, he developed what was perhaps his greatest strength in a society suspicious of the military, his ability to deal effectively with civil authority. Whatever his private opinions, his relations with Congress and with the state governments were exemplary despite the fact that his wartime powers sometimes amounted to dictatorial authority. On the battlefield Washington relied on a policy of trial and error, eventually becoming a master of improvisation. Often accused of being overly cautious, he could be bold when success seemed possible. He learned to use the short-term militia skillfully and to combine green troops with veterans to produce an efficient fighting force.

After the war Washington returned to Mount Vernon, which had declined in his absence. Although he became president of the Society of the Cincinnati, an organization of former Revolutionary War officers, he avoided involvement in Virginia politics. Preferring to concentrate on restoring Mount Vernon, he added a greenhouse, a mill, an icehouse, and new land to the estate. He experimented with crop rotation, bred hunting dogs and horses, investigated the development of Potomac River navigation, undertook various commercial ventures, and traveled (1784) west to examine his land holdings near the Ohio River. His diary notes a steady stream of visitors, native and foreign; Mount Vernon, like its owner, had already become a national institution. In May 1787, Washington headed the Virginia delegation to the Constitutional Convention in Philadelphia and was unanimously elected presiding officer. His presence lent prestige to the proceedings, and although he made few direct contributions, he generally supported the advocates of a strong central government. After the new Constitution was submitted to the states for ratification and became legally operative, he was unanimously elected president (1789).

Taking office (April 30, 1789) in New York City, Washington acted carefully and deliberately, aware of the need to build an executive structure that could accommodate future presidents. Hoping to prevent sectionalism from dividing the new nation, he toured the New England states (1789) and the South (1791). An able administrator, he nevertheless failed to heal the widening breach between factions led by Secretary of State Thomas Jefferson and Secretary of the Treasury Alexander Hamilton. Because he supported many of Hamilton's controversial fiscal policies—such as the assumption of state debts, the Bank of the United States, and the excise tax—Washington became the target of attacks by Jeffersonian Democratic-Republicans. Washington was reelected president in 1792, and the following year the most divisive crisis arising out of the personal and political conflicts within his cabinet occurred over the issue of American neutrality during the war between England and France. Washington, whose policy of neutrality angered the pro-French Jeffersonians, was horrified by the excesses of the French Revolution and enraged by the tactics of Edmond Genêt, the French minister in the United States, which amounted to foreign interference in American politics. Further, with an eye toward developing closer commercial ties with the British, the president agreed with the Hamiltonians on the need for peace with Great Britain. His acceptance of the 1794 Jay's Treaty, which settled outstanding differences between the United States and Britain but Democratic-Republicans viewed as an abject surrender to British demands, revived vituperation against the president, as did his vigorous upholding of the excise law during the Whiskey Rebellion in western Pennsylvania.

By March 1797, when Washington left office, the country's financial system was well established; the Native American threat east of the Mississippi had been largely eliminated; and Jay's Treaty and Pinckney's Treaty (1795) with Spain had enlarged U.S. territory and removed serious diplomatic difficulties. In spite of the animosities and conflicting opinions between Democratic-Republicans and members of the Hamiltonian Federalist Party, the two groups were at least united in acceptance of the new federal government. Washington refused to run for a third term and, after a masterly Farewell Address in which he warned the United States against permanent alliances abroad, he went home to Mount Vernon.

Although Washington reluctantly accepted command of the army in 1798, when war with France seemed imminent, he did not assume an active role. He preferred to spend his last years in happy retirement at Mount Vernon. In mid-December, Washington contracted what was probably quinsy or acute laryngitis; he declined rapidly and died at his estate on December 14, 1799.

Even during his lifetime, George Washington loomed large in the national imagination. Mason L. Weems, author of *A History of the Life and Death Virtues and Exploits of General George Washington*, enhanced his role as a symbol of American virtue after his death. George Washington's own works have been published in various editions, including *The Diaries of George Washington*, edited by Donald Jackson and Dorothy Twohig, and *The Writings of George Washington, 1748–1799*, by John C. Fitzpatrick.

Sources

Fitzpatrick, John C.A.M., ed. *The Diaries of George Washington; 1748–1799. Vol. II, 1771–1785*. Boston: Houghton Mifflin, 1925.

Flexner, James Thomas. *George Washington: The Forge of Experience, 1732–1775*. Boston: Little, Brown, 1965.

Ford, Worthington Chauncey. *George Washington*. New York: Charles Scribner's Sons, 1900.

Judson, Clara Ingram. *George Washington: Leader of the People*. New York: Wilcox & Follett, 1951.

Washington, Irving. *George Washington; A Biography*. New York: Putnam, 1855.

Watkins, Travis E. (d. 1950) *Master sergeant, United States Army, Company H, Ninth Infantry Regiment, Second Infantry Division, so distinguished himself in combat, during the Korean War, that he was awarded (posthumously) the Medal of Honor for his heroic actions.*

Born: Waldo, Ark.; **Entered service at:** Texas; **Place and date:** Near Yongsan, Korea, August 31–September 3, 1950. **G.O. No.:** 9, February 16, 1951.

Citation: "M/Sgt. Watkins distinguished himself by conspicuous gallantry and intrepidity above and beyond the call of duty in action against the enemy. When an overwhelming enemy force broke through and isolated 30 men of his unit, he took command, established a perimeter defense and directed action that repelled continuous, fanatical enemy assaults. With his group completely surrounded and cut off, he moved from foxhole to foxhole exposing himself to enemy fire, giving instructions and offering encouragement to his men. Later when the need for ammunition and grenades became critical he shot 2 enemy soldiers 50 yards outside the perimeter and went out alone for their ammunition and weapons. As he picked up their weapons he was attacked by 3 others and wounded. Returning their fire he killed all 3 and gathering up the weapons of the 5 enemy dead returned to his amazed comrades. During a later assault, 6 enemy soldiers gained a defiladed spot and began to throw grenades into the perimeter making it untenable. Realizing the desperate situation and disregarding his wound he rose from his foxhole to engage them with rifle fire. Although immediately hit by a burst from an enemy machine gun he continued to fire until he had killed the grenade throwers. With this threat eliminated he collapsed and despite being paralyzed from the waist down, encouraged his men to hold on. He refused all food, saving it for his comrades, and when it became apparent that help would not arrive in time to hold the position ordered his men to escape to friendly lines. Refusing evacuation, as his hopeless condition would burden his comrades, he remained in his position and cheerfully wished them luck. Through his aggressive leadership and intrepid actions, this small force destroyed nearly 500 of the enemy before abandoning their position. M/Sgt. Watkins' sustained personal bravery and noble self-sacrifice reflect the highest glory upon himself and is in keeping with the esteemed traditions of the U.S. Army."

Source
Medal of Honor Citation.

Watson, Wilson Douglas (b. 1921) *Private, United States Marine Corps Reserve, Second Battalion, Ninth Marines, Third Marine Division, so distinguished himself in combat, during World War II, that he was awarded the Medal of Honor for his heroic actions.*

Born: February 18, 1921, Tuscumbia, Ala.; **Entered service at:** Arkansas; **Place and date:** Iwo Jima, Volcano Islands, February 26–27, 1945.

Citation: "For conspicuous gallantry and intrepidity at the risk of his life above and beyond the call of duty as automatic rifleman serving with the 2d Battalion, 9th Marines, 3d Marine Division, during action against enemy Japanese forces on Iwo Jima, Volcano Islands, 26 and 27 February 1945. With his squad abruptly halted by intense fire from enemy fortifications in the high rocky ridges and crags commanding the line of advance, Pvt. Watson boldly rushed 1 pillbox and fired into the embrasure with his weapon, keeping the enemy pinned down single-handedly until he was in a position to hurl in a grenade, and then running to the rear of the emplacement to destroy the retreating Japanese and enable his platoon to take its objective. Again pinned down at the foot of a small hill, he dauntlessly scaled the jagged incline under fierce mortar and machinegun barrages and, with his assistant BAR man, charged the crest of the hill, firing from his hip. Fighting furiously against Japanese troops attacking with grenades and knee mortars from the reverse slope, he stood fearlessly erect in his exposed position to cover the hostile entrenchment's and held the hill under savage fire for 15 minutes, killing 60 Japanese before his ammunition was exhausted and his platoon was able to join him. His courageous initiative and valiant fighting spirit against devastating odds were directly responsible for the continued advance of his platoon, and his inspiring leadership throughout this bitterly fought action reflects the highest credit upon Pvt. Watson and the U.S. Naval Service."

Source
Medal of Honor Citation.

Watters, Charles Joseph (1927–1967) *Chaplain (major) United States Army, Company A, 173d Support Battalion, 173d Airborne Brigade, so distinguished himself in combat, during the Vietnam War, that he was awarded (posthumously) the Medal of Honor for his heroic actions.*

Born: January, 17, 1927, Jersey City, N.J.; **Entered service at:** Fort Dix, N.J.; **Place and date:** Near Dak To Province, Republic of Vietnam, November 19, 1967.

Citation: "For conspicuous gallantry and intrepidity in action at the risk of his life above and beyond the call of duty. Chaplain Watters distinguished himself during an assault in the vicinity of Dak To. Chaplain Watters was moving with one of the companies when it engaged a heavily armed enemy battalion. As the battle raged and the casualties mounted, Chaplain Watters, with complete disregard for his safety, rushed forward to the line of contact. Unarmed and completely exposed, he moved among, as well as in front of the advancing troops, giving aid to the wounded, assisting in their evacuation, giving words of encouragement, and administering the last rites to the dying. When a wounded paratrooper was standing in shock in front of the assaulting forces, Chaplain Watters ran forward, picked the man up on his shoulders and carried him to safety. As the troopers battled to the first enemy entrenchment, Chaplain Watters ran through the intense enemy fire to the front of the entrenchment to aid a fallen comrade. A short time later, the paratroopers pulled back in preparation for a second assault. Chaplain Watters exposed himself to both friendly and enemy fire between the 2 forces in order to recover 2 wounded soldiers. Later, when the battalion was forced to pull back into a perimeter, Chaplain Watters noticed that several wounded soldiers were lying outside the newly formed perimeter. Without hesitation and ignoring attempts to restrain him, Chaplain Watters left the perimeter three times in the face of small arms, automatic weapons, and mortar fire to carry and to assist the injured troopers to safety. Satisfied that all of the wounded were inside the perimeter, he began aiding the medics—applying field bandages to open wounds, obtaining and serving food and water, giving spiritual and mental strength and comfort. During his ministering, he moved out to the perimeter from position to position redistributing food and water, and tending to the needs of his men. Chaplain Watters was giving aid to the wounded when he himself was mortally wounded. Chaplain Watters' unyielding perseverance and selfless devotion to his comrades was in keeping with the highest traditions of the U.S. Army."

Source
Medal of Honor Citation.

Wayne, Anthony ("Mad") (1745–1796) *American Revolutionary War brigadier general.*

Anthony Wayne, born in Chester County, Pennsylvania, near Paoli, Pennsylvania, January 1, 1745, died December 15, 1796. Privately educated in Philadelphia, General Wayne won major recognition in the American Revolution and in warfare against Native American forces.

A dashing, brave soldier, "Mad Anthony" Wayne served in Canada in 1776 and at Brandywine and Germantown in 1777; he encamped at Valley Forge during the winter of 1777–78. At the end of 1778 he was given command of a corps of light infantry. His most successful action was a surprise attack on the British at Stony Point on the Hudson River in July 1779; he continued to see action throughout the war.

In 1776, after the outbreak of the American Revolution, he entered military service as a commander of a Pennsylvania regiment assigned to cover the retreat of American forces from Québec. In 1777, after being promoted to brigadier general, he was posted to Morristown, New Jersey. The Pennsylvania regiments participated in the maneuvering near New Brunswick during June. After a brief stay at Ramapo in July, Wayne's men marched to defend Philadelphia. At the Battle of Brandywine, Wayne's division was at Chadd's Ford. For three hours Wayne fought to repulse Hessian advances over the river as the American left wing deteriorated. In the retreat to Chester, Wayne inspired his men by his bravery.

As the British converged on Philadelphia, Wayne's 1,500 troops attempted to harass the enemy. Assuming that the American presence was undetected, Wayne camped close to the British lines. What became famous as the "Paoli Massacre" ensued. On September 20–21, in a skillful night attack led by Major General Sir Charles Grey, the British bayoneted patriot soldiers. With 300 casualties, Wayne was inevitably subject to criticism. An official inquiry by five ranking officers held that Wayne was not guilty of misconduct but that he had erred in tactics. Enraged, the tempestuous Wayne demanded a full court-martial. On November 1, a board of 13 ranking officers declared that Wayne had acted with honor. Yet Paoli, where British troops, using only their bayonets, had inflicted over 300 casualties, remained a stigma on his record for the rest of his career.

Wayne participated in the Battles of Brandywine and Germantown and in 1778 distinguished himself in the Battle of Monmouth. His greatest achievement was a brilliant victory at Stony Point in 1779. In 1781 he contributed to the British defeat at Yorktown. Wayne retired to civilian life in 1783. After the Revolution, Arthur St. Clair's defeat by the Indians in 1791—the culmination of a series of American defeats in the Old Northwest—caused Wayne to be given (1792) command of the Northwest army.

After spending more than two years training his troops, he led an American army north from the Ohio River and, on August 10, 1794, won a decisive victory at the Battle of Fallen Timbers, on the Maumee River near the site of present-day Toledo, Ohio. Ignoring the protests of the British commander at Fort Miami, Wayne remained for several days, burning the Indian villages and destroying crops before leading the legion back to Cincinnati. The western tribes, their resistance broken, finally agreed, on August 3, 1795, in the Treaty of Greenville, to make peace and cede their lands in Ohio to the United States.

Noted for his bravery and quick temper, Wayne was popularly known as "Mad Anthony." Under provisions of the ensuing Treaty of Greenville (1795), Wayne obtained a large cession from the Native Americans. After the British had agreed in Jay's Treaty to vacate their posts in the Old Northwest, Wayne led the American force that took possession of the forts in 1796.

Source and Additional Reading

Blanco, Richard L. *The American Revolution, 1775–1783.* New York: Garland, 1984.

Pleasants, Henry J. "The Battle of Paoli." *Pennsylvania Magazine of History and Biography,* 72 (1948).

Tucker, Glenn. *Mad Anthony Wayne and the New Nation: The Story of Washington's Front-Line General.* Harrisburg, Pa.: Stackpole Books, 1973.

Wildes, Harry E. *Anthony Wayne: Trouble Shooter of the American Revolution.* New York: Harcourt Brace, 1941.

Webb, James H., Jr. (b. 1946) *Captain, United States Marine Corps, awarded the Navy Cross for his heroic action in combat during the Vietnam War.*

James Webb was born on February 9, 1946, in St. Joseph, Missouri. Both his mother, Vera Lorraine Hodges, and his father, James Henry Webb Sr., were descended principally from the Scotch-Irish settlers who immigrated to the United States from Northern Ireland in the 18th century and became pioneers in the Virginia mountains. Through the 1800s and early 1900s Webb's ancestors moved steadily west and south from Virginia, most often to settlements in North Carolina, Tennessee, Kentucky, Arkansas, and Missouri. In the mid-1900s many members of the family joined the westward migration to California, and the family is now scattered throughout the continental United States.

Both sides of Webb's family have a strong citizen-soldier military tradition that predates the Revolutionary War. Family members have served during the Revolutionary War, the War of 1812, the Mexican War, the Civil War, the Spanish-American War, World War II, the Korean War, the Vietnam War, and the Gulf War. Webb's father was a career Air Force officer who flew B-17s and B-29s during World War II and cargo planes during the Berlin Airlift and was a pioneer in the United States missile program. Colonel Webb, who was the first family member to finish high school and who graduated from the University of Omaha in 1962 after 26 years of night school, put the first Atlas missile into place for the Air Force in the late 1950s and had an unsurpassed success rate as commander of an Atlas, Thor, and Scout Junior missile squadron during the early 1960s.

During the Vietnam War he served at Air Force Systems command on sensitive satellite link programs and as a legislative affairs officer in the Pentagon, leading him to become a vocal critic of Defense Secretary Robert McNamara's leadership methods and causing him eventually to retire from the Air Force, partially in protest of the manner in which the Vietnam War was being micromanaged by the political process.

James Webb grew up on the move, attending more than a dozen different schools across the United States and in England. He graduated from high school in Bellevue, Nebraska. First attending the University of Southern California on an Navy Reserve Officer Training Corps (NROTC) academic scholarship, he left for the Naval Academy after one year. At the Naval Academy he was a four-year member of the Brigade Honor Committee, a varsity boxer, and one of six finalists in the interviewing process for brigade commander during his senior year. Graduating in 1968 he chose a commission in the United States Marine Corps and was one of 18 in his class of 841 to receive the Superintendent's Commendation for outstanding leadership contributions while a midshipman. First in his class of 243 at the Marine Corps Officer's Basic School in Quantico, Virginia, he then served with the Fifth Marine Regiment in Vietnam, where as a rifle platoon and company commander in the infamous An Hoa Basin west of Da Nang he was awarded the Navy Cross, the Silver Star Medal, two Bronze Star Medals, and two Purple Hearts.

He later served as a platoon commander and as an instructor in tactics and weapons at Marine Corps Officer Candidates School, and then as a member of the secretary of the navy's immediate staff, before leaving the Marine Corps in 1972. Webb spent the "Watergate years" as a student at the Georgetown University Law Center, arriving just after the Watergate break-in in 1972 and receiving his J.D. just after the fall of South Vietnam in 1975. While at Georgetown he began a six-year pro bono representation of a Marine who had been convicted of war crimes in Vietnam (he finally cleared the man's name in 1978, three years after his suicide), won the Horan Award for excellence in legal writing, and wrote his first book, *Micronesia and U.S. Pacific Strategy.* He also worked in Asia as a consultant to the governor of Guam, conducting a study of U.S. military land needs in Asia and their impact on Guam's political future.

In government, Webb served in the U.S. Congress as counsel to the House Committee on Veterans Affairs from 1977 to 1981, the first Vietnam War veteran to serve as a full committee counsel in the Congress. During the Reagan administration he was the first assistant secretary of defense for reserve affairs, from 1984 to 1987, and directed considerable research and analysis of the U.S. military's mobilization capabilities and spent much time with the North Atlantic Treaty Organization (NATO) allies. In 1987 he became the first Naval Academy graduate in history to serve in the military and then become secretary of the navy. He resigned from that position in 1988 after refusing to agree to the reduction of the navy's force structure during congressionally mandated budget cuts.

Among Webb's other awards for community service and professional excellence are the Department of Defense Distinguished Public Service Medal, the Medal of Honor Society's Patriot Award, the American Legion National Commander's Public Service Award, the Marine Corps League's Military Order of the Iron Mike Award, the John Russell Leadership Award, and the Robert L. Denig Distinguished Service Award. He was a fall 1992 fellow at Harvard's Institute of Politics.

Citation: "For extraordinary heroism while serving as a Platoon Commander with Company D, First Battalion, Fifth Marines, First Marine Division in connection with combat operations against the enemy in the Republic of Vietnam. On 10 July 1969, while participating in a company-sized search and destroy operation deep in hostile territory, First Lieutenant Webb's platoon discovered a well-camouflaged bunker complex, which appeared to be unoccupied. Deploying his men into defensive positions, First Lieutenant Webb was advancing to the first bunker when three enemy soldiers armed with hand grenades jumped out. Reacting instantly, he grabbed the closest man and, brandishing his .45 caliber pistol at the others, apprehended all three of the soldiers. Accompanied by one of his men, he then approached the second bunker and called for the enemy to surrender. The hostile soldiers failed to answer him and threw a grenade, which detonated dangerously close to him. First Lieutenant Webb detonated a claymore mine in the bunker aperture, accounting for two enemy casualties and disclosing the entrance to a tunnel. Despite the smoke and debris from the explosion and the possibility of enemy soldiers' hiding in the tunnel, he then conducted a thorough search, which yielded several items of equipment and numerous documents containing valuable intelligence data. Continuing the assault, he approached a third bunker and was preparing to fire into it when the enemy threw another grenade. Observing the grenade land dangerously close to his companion, First Lieutenant Webb simultaneously fired his weapon at the enemy, pushed the Marine away from the grenade and shielded him from the explosion with his own body. Although sustaining painful fragmentation wounds from the explosion, he managed to throw a grenade into the aperture and completely destroy the remaining bunker. By his courage, aggressive leadership, and selfless devotion to duty, First Lieutenant Webb upheld the highest traditions of the Marine Corps and of the United States Naval Service."

Source
Navy Cross Citation.
James Webb Enterprises. "James Webb." http://www.jameswebb.com/bio/htm.

Webster, Timothy (1822–1862) *Union spy during the American Civil War. Timothy Webster was recognized as Allan Pinkerton's most famous active agent in the Civil War and was partially responsible for thwarting an assassination attempt on President-Elect Abraham Lincoln. It is impossible to know exactly how events would have transpired at that time without Lincoln at the helm, but it is certainly true that the history of the United States would have been dramatically different if Pinkerton and Webster had failed in their mission and Lincoln had been killed before beginning the presidency.*

Born on March 12, 1822, in Newhaven, Sussex County, England, Webster immigrated to America in August 1830 with his parents and settled in Princeton, New Jersey. After finishing school in 1853 he became a policeman in New York City and performed skillfully. Around 1854 was he was noticed by a friend of Allan Pinkerton's, who recommended him for detective work. After accepting work with Pinkerton, Webster quickly became their best agent. Timothy married Charlotte Sprowles on October 23, 1841, in Princeton, New Jersey, and the couple had four children, two of whom died young. Their son, Timothy Jr., born in 1843, joined the Union army from Onarga, Illinois, on July 30, 1862, and was wounded in the Battle of Brices Crossroads near Ripley, Mississippi, on June 11, 1864, and taken to a Confederate prison in Mobile, Alabama, where his leg was amputated. He subsequently died there on July 4, 1864. His body was transported north to Onarga, Illinois, and buried in the Onarga Cemetery beside his grandfather, Timothy Webster Sr., who died in Onarga in 1860.

At the beginning of the Civil War General George McClellan asked Pinkerton to enter federal service, and he readily agreed. Timothy Webster joined him in this effort, thereby changing from detective to Union spy. Because of the nature of his work, Pinkerton suggested that Webster move his family to a safer place and work out of the Chicago office. Pinkerton suggested Onarga, Illinois, located south of Chicago on the Illinois Central Railroad. Pinkerton was familiar with the area and had said that he would like to have a farm and house there someday, an ambition that was fulfilled. Charlotte and the children moved from New York to Onarga around 1858; Webster commuted easily and his family was safe.

Sent to pose as a southern gentleman in the Baltimore area, Webster managed to become a member of the rebel group "Sons of Liberty" in order to report on their plans and activities. In February 1861 President-Elect Lincoln was to travel from Harrisburg through Baltimore and on to Washington for his inauguration. While Webster was investigating rumors that secessionists were planning to blow up the steamers that ferried trains across the Susquehanna River, he uncovered a plan to assassinate Lincoln as he changed trains in Baltimore. Because Timothy Webster was able to send a warning,

Pinkerton was able to foil the attempt on Lincoln's life. In 1862, Webster was continuing to gather information on the Confederacy in Richmond when he was stricken with inflammatory rheumatism, the result of several previous crossings of the Potomac River in frigid weather, and was too ill to send reports back to Pinkerton. As a result, two men, C. Lewis and C. Scully, were sent to locate him. The men, recognized as being Union spies, were captured by the Confederacy, and eventually revealed secret information incriminating Webster.

Confederate officers had trusted Webster many times with valuable documents and information, and the Confederacy was extremely embarrassed by Webster's betrayal. Whereas Lewis and Scully were eventually released, Webster was arrested, tried, and sentenced to death by hanging. When Pinkerton heard the news of the sentence, he and President Lincoln sent a message to the Confederacy threatening that if Webster were put to death, the Union would reciprocate by hanging a Confederate spy. Previously, Union policy had been to keep spies in jail and eventually exchange them for Union prisoners. The Confederacy ignored the threat, and on April 29, 1862, Timothy Webster climbed the gallows in Richmond, Virginia. The noose was put around his neck and a black hood was fitted over his face. The trap was sprung, but the knot slipped and Webster fell to the ground. After being helped back up the steps and refitted with the noose he said, "I suffer a double death!" The noose held the second time, and Webster died within minutes and was hastily buried in Richmond.

In 1871, at the pleadings of his widow, Charlotte, and in fulfillment of a promise he had made to himself on hearing of Timothy's death, Pinkerton sent George Bangs and Thomas G. Robinson (Timothy's son-in-law) to Richmond to locate his body and take it north for proper burial in "northern soil." With the help of Elizabeth ("Crazy Bet") Van Lew, a southern-born Union sympathizer who operated out of Richmond during the war, they located Timothy's body and transported him to his final resting place in Onarga, Illinois. He was buried beside his father, Timothy Webster Sr., and his son, Timothy Webster Jr. Timothy's widow, Charlotte, went to live with her daughter and son-in-law, Sarah and Thomas Robinson, in Onarga. In September 1874, this family moved to California, where Charlotte received a pension and lived with her daughter until she died on December 1, 1907. She is buried in the Old City Cemetery in Sacramento. Sarah Webster Robinson is buried in the Masonic Cemetery on Riverside Boulevard in Sacramento. Because Sarah's children never married, there are no direct descendants of Timothy Webster.

Source
Courtesy of Patricia Dissmeyer Goff.

Wetzel, Gary George (b. 1947) *Specialist fourth class (then private first class), United States Army, 173d Assault Helicopter Company, so distinguished himself in combat, during the Vietnam War, that he was awarded the Medal of Honor for his heroic actions.*

Born: September 29, 1947, South Milwaukee, Wis.; **Entered service at:** Milwaukee, Wis.; **Place and date:** Near Ap Dong An, Republic of Vietnam, January 8, 1968.

Citation: "Sp4c. Wetzel, 173d Assault Helicopter Company, distinguished himself by conspicuous gallantry and intrepidity at the risk of his life, above and beyond the call of duty. Sp4c. Wetzel was serving as door gunner aboard a helicopter which was part of an insertion force trapped in a landing zone by intense and deadly hostile fire. Sp4c. Wetzel was going to the aid of his aircraft commander when he was blown into a rice paddy and critically wounded by 2 enemy rockets that exploded just inches from his location. Although bleeding profusely due to the loss of his left arm and severe wounds in his right arm, chest, and left leg, Sp4c. Wetzel staggered back to his original position in his gun-well and took the enemy forces under fire. His machinegun was the only weapon placing effective fire on the enemy at that time. Through a resolve that overcame the shock and intolerable pain of his injuries, Sp4c. Wetzel remained at his position until he had eliminated the automatic weapons emplacement that had been inflicting heavy casualties on the American troops and preventing them from moving against this strong enemy force. Refusing to attend his own extensive wounds, he attempted to return to the aid of his aircraft commander but passed out from loss of blood. Regaining consciousness, he persisted in his efforts to drag himself to the aid of his fellow crewman. After an agonizing effort, he came to the side of the crew chief who was attempting to drag the wounded aircraft commander to the safety of a nearby dike. Unswerving in his devotion to his fellow man, Sp4c. Wetzel assisted his crew chief even though he lost consciousness once again during this action. Sp4c. Wetzel displayed extraordinary heroism in his efforts to aid his fellow crewmen. His gallant actions were in keeping with the highest traditions of the U.S. Army and reflect great credit upon himself and the Armed Forces of his country."

Source
Medal of Honor Citation.

Wheeler, Joseph (1836–1906) *One of only a handful of Confederates to be buried in Arlington National Cemetery, his later service as a major general of volunteers, Dragoons-Mounted, in the Spanish-American War. He served as a*

Second lieutenant until 1861. He was commissioned a First lieutenant C.S.A. (Confederate States Army), at first. Later he was named colonel, 19th Alabama, and fought at Shiloh. He was appointed a brigadier general on October 30, 1862. He was promoted to major general on January 20, 1863.

The Georgia-born West Pointer (1859) had resigned his commission as a second lieutenant in the Regiment of Mounted Riflemen—he had briefly been posted to the dragoons in 1859—and, joining the South, had a meteoric rise. The cavalryman's assignments included the following: first lieutenant, Artillery (1861); colonel, 19th Alabama (September 4, 1861); commander Cavalry Brigade, Left Wing, Army of the Mississippi (September 14–November 20, 1862); brigadier general, Confederate States Army (CSA) (October 30, 1862); commander, of cavalry brigade, Polk's corps, Army of Tennessee (November 20–22, 1862); commander, of cavalry brigade, Hardee's corps, Army of Tennessee (November 22–December 1862); commander of cavalry division, Army of Tennessee (December 1862–March 16, 1863); major general, CSA (January 30, 1863); commander of cavalry corps, Army of Tennessee (March 16, 1863–fall 1864); commander, of cavalry corps, Department of South Carolina, Georgia and Florida (fall 1864–March 1865); lieutenant general, CSA (February 28, 1865); and commander of corps, Hampton's cavalry command, Army of Tennessee (March–April 26, 1865). He led an infantry regiment at Shiloh and during the operations around Corinth, Mississippi, but was then assigned in the summer of 1862 to be chief of cavalry for Bragg's Army of the Mississippi. He led a mounted brigade at Perryville and a division at Murfreesboro. Given command of a corps of mounted troopers, he led it in the Tullahoma Campaign and at Chickamauga was in charge of one of the two cavalry corps (the other was under Nathan Bedford Forrest). However, soon after the battle, conflicts between Forrest and Wheeler and Forrest and Bragg led to the reassignment of Forrest. Thus Wheeler was again in charge of all the mounted troops with the Army of Tennessee. He fought thus at Chattanooga and led his men in the Atlanta Campaign. During these last two campaigns he was noted for his raids on the Union supply lines. After the fall of Atlanta, Wheeler's corps was left behind to deal with Sherman while Hood launched his invasion of middle Tennessee. With the small force at hand Wheeler proved unsuccessful in hindering Sherman's March to the Sea.

During the course of the campaign in the Carolinas, Wheeler was placed under the orders of Wade Hampton, who had been transferred from Virginia. Taken prisoner in Georgia in May 1865, Wheeler was held at Fort Delaware until June 8. A longtime congressman from Alabama in the postwar years, he donned the blue as a major general of volunteers in the war with Spain. In 1900 he was retired with the regular army rank of brigadier general. His Confederate career had earned him the sobriquet "Fightin' Joe."

Source

Dyer, John Percy. *From Shiloh to San Juan. The Life of "Fightin' Joe" Wheeler* Rev. ed. Baton Rouge: Louisiana State University, 1989.

Wilkin, Edward G. (d. 1945) *Corporal, United States Army, Company C, 157th Infantry, 45th Infantry Division, so distinguished himself in combat, during World War II, that he was awarded (posthumously) the Medal of Honor for his heroic actions.*

Born: Burlington, Vt.; **Entered service at:** Longmeadow, Mass.; **Place and date:** Siegfried Line in Germany, March 18, 1945. **G.O. No.:** 119, December 17, 1945.

Citation: "He spearheaded his unit's assault of the Siegfried Line in Germany. Heavy fire from enemy riflemen and camouflaged pillboxes had pinned down his comrades when he moved forward on his own initiative to reconnoiter a route of advance. He cleared the way into an area studded with pillboxes, where he repeatedly stood up and walked into vicious enemy fire, storming 1 fortification after another with automatic rifle fire and grenades, killing enemy troops, taking prisoners as the enemy defense became confused, and encouraging his comrades by his heroic example. When halted by heavy barbed wire entanglements, he secured bangalore torpedoes and blasted a path toward still more pillboxes, all the time braving bursting grenades and mortar shells and direct rifle and automatic-weapons fire. He engaged in fierce fire fights, standing in the open while his adversaries fought from the protection of concrete emplacements, and on 1 occasion pursued enemy soldiers across an open field and through interlocking trenches, disregarding the crossfire from 2 pillboxes until he had penetrated the formidable line 200 yards in advance of any American element. That night, although terribly fatigued, he refused to rest and insisted on distributing rations and supplies to his comrades. Hearing that a nearby company was suffering heavy casualties, he secured permission to guide litter bearers and assist them in evacuating the wounded. All that night he remained in the battle area on his mercy missions, and for the following 2 days he continued to remove casualties, venturing into enemy-held territory, scorning cover and braving devastating mortar and artillery bombardments. In 3 days he neutralized and captured 6 pillboxes single-handedly, killed at least 9 Germans, wounded 13, took 13 prisoners, aided in the capture of 14 others, and saved many American lives by his fearless performance as a litter bearer. Through his superb fighting skill, dauntless courage, and gallant, inspiring actions, Cpl. Wilkin contributed in large measure to his company's success in cracking the Siegfried Line. One month later he was killed in action while fighting deep in Germany."

Source
Medal of Honor Citation.

Williams, Charles Q. (b. 1933) *First lieutenant (then second lieutenant, United States Army, Fifth Special Forces Group, so distinguished himself in combat, during the Vietnam War, that he was awarded the Medal of Honor for his heroic actions.*

Born: September 17, 1933, Charleston, S.C.; **Entered service at:** Fort Jackson, S.C.; **Place and date:** Dong Xoai, Republic of Vietnam, June 9–10, 1965. **G.O. No.:** 30, July 5, 1966.

Citation: "1st Lt. Williams distinguished himself by conspicuous gallantry and intrepidity at the risk of his life above and beyond the call of duty while defending the Special Forces Camp against a violent attack by hostile forces that lasted for 14 hours. 1st Lt. Williams was serving as executive officer of a Special Forces Detachment when an estimated Vietcong reinforced regiment struck the camp and threatened to overrun it and the adjacent district headquarters. He awoke personnel, organized them, determined the source of the insurgents' main effort and led the troops to their defensive positions on the south and west walls. Then, after running to the District Headquarters to establish communications, he found that there was no radio operational with which to communicate with his commanding officer in another compound. To reach the other compound, he traveled through darkness but was halted in this effort by a combination of shrapnel in his right leg and the increase of the Vietcong gunfire. Ignoring his wound, he returned to the district headquarters and directed the defense against the first assault. As the insurgents attempted to scale the walls and as some of the Vietnamese defenders began to retreat, he dashed through a barrage of gunfire, succeeded in rallying these defenders, and led them back to their positions. Although wounded in the thigh and left leg during this gallant action, he returned to his position and, upon being told that communications were reestablished and that his commanding officer was seriously wounded, 1st Lt. Williams took charge of actions in both compounds. Then, in an attempt to reach the communications bunker, he sustained wounds in the stomach and right arm from grenade fragments. As the defensive positions on the walls had been held for hours and casualties were mounting, he

ordered the consolidation of the American personnel from both compounds to establish a defense in the district building. After radio contact was made with a friendly air controller, he disregarded his wounds and directed the defense from the district building, using descending flares as reference points to adjust air strikes. By his courage, he inspired his team to hold out against the insurgent force that was closing in on them and throwing grenades into the windows of the building. As daylight arrived and the Vietcong continued to besiege the stronghold, firing a machinegun directly south of the district building, he was determined to eliminate this menace that threatened the lives of his men. Taking a 3.5 rocket launcher and a volunteer to load it, he worked his way across open terrain, reached the berm south of the district headquarters, and took aim at the Vietcong machinegun 150 meters away. Although the sight was faulty, he succeeded in hitting the machinegun. While he and the loader were trying to return to the district headquarters, they were both wounded. With a fourth wound, this time in the right arm and leg, and realizing he was unable to carry his wounded comrade back to the district building, 1st Lt. Williams pulled him to a covered position and then made his way back to the district building where he sought the help of others who went out and evacuated the injured soldier. Although seriously wounded and tired, he continued to direct the air strikes closer to the defensive position. As morning turned to afternoon and the Vietcong pressed their effort with direct recoilless rifle fire into the building, he ordered the evacuation of the seriously wounded to the safety of the communications bunker. When informed that helicopters would attempt to land as the hostile gunfire had abated, he led his team from the building to the artillery position, making certain of the timely evacuation of the wounded from the communications area, and then on to the pickup point. Despite resurgent Vietcong gunfire, he directed the rapid evacuation of all personnel. Throughout the long battle, he was undaunted by the vicious Vietcong assault and inspired the defenders in decimating the determined insurgents. 1st Lt. Williams' extraordinary heroism, was in the highest traditions of the U.S. Army and reflect great credit upon himself and the Armed Forces of his country."

Sources
Medal of Honor Citation.
Stanton, Stanley L. *Special Forces at War: An Illustrated History, Southeast Asia, 1957–1975.* Charlottesville, Va.: Howell Press, 1990.

Williams, Hershel Woodrow (b. 1923) *Corporal, United States Marine Corps Reserve, 21st Marines, Third Marine Division, so distinguished himself in combat, during*

World War II, that he was awarded the Medal of Honor for his heroic actions.

Born: October 2, 1923, Quiet Dell, W.V.; **Entered service at:** West Virginia; **Place and date:** Iwo Jima, Volcano Islands, February 23, 1945.

Citation: "For conspicuous gallantry and intrepidity at the risk of his life above and beyond the call of duty as demolition sergeant serving with the 21st Marines, 3d Marine Division, in action against enemy Japanese forces on Iwo Jima, Volcano Islands, 23 February 1945. Quick to volunteer his services when our tanks were maneuvering vainly to open a lane for the infantry through the network of reinforced concrete pillboxes, buried mines, and black volcanic sands, Cpl. Williams daringly went forward alone to attempt the reduction of devastating machinegun fire from the unyielding positions. Covered only by 4 riflemen, he fought desperately for 4 hours under terrific enemy small-arms fire and repeatedly returned to his own lines to prepare demolition charges and obtain serviced flame-throwers, struggling back, frequently to the rear of hostile emplacements, to wipe out 1 position after another. On 1 occasion, he daringly mounted a pillbox to insert the nozzle of his flame-thrower through the air vent, killing the occupants and silencing the gun; on another he grimly charged enemy riflemen who attempted to stop him with bayonets and destroyed them with a burst of flame from his weapon. His unyielding determination and extraordinary heroism in the face of ruthless enemy resistance were directly instrumental in neutralizing one of the most fanatically defended Japanese strong points encountered by his regiment and aided vitally in enabling his company to reach its objective. Cpl. Williams' aggressive fighting spirit and valiant devotion to duty throughout this fiercely contested action sustain and enhance the highest traditions of the U.S. Naval Service."

Source
Medal of Honor Citation.

Williams, James E. (1930–1999) *Boatswains Mate, First Class (BM 1), United States Navy, so distinguished himself in combat, during the Vietnam War, that he was awarded the Navy Cross for his heroic actions.*

Born June 13, 1930, in Rock Hill, South Carolina, Williams entered the United States Navy at Columbia, South Carolina. His awards include the Navy Cross, Silver Star with Star, Legion of Merit with Combat V, USN/MC Medal with Star, Bronze Star with two Stars and Combat V, Purple Heart with two Stars, Navy Commendation Medal with one Star and Combat V, Combat Action Ribbon, Presidential Unit Citation with one Star, U.S Navy Good Conduct Medal with four Stars, Navy Expeditionary Medal, National Defense Medal with Star, Korean Service Medal with two Stars, Armed Forces Expeditionary Medal, Vietnam Service Medal with two Stars, Korean Presidential Unit Citation, UN Service Medal, RVN Gallantry Cross with Palm and Star, and RVN Campaign Medal.

Citation: "For conspicuous gallantry and intrepidity at the risk of his life above and beyond the call of duty. BM1 Williams was serving as Boat Captain and Patrol Officer aboard River Patrol Boat (PBR) *105* accompanied by another patrol boat when the patrol was suddenly taken under fire by 2 enemy sampans. BM1 Williams immediately ordered the fire returned, killing the crew of 1 enemy boat and causing the other sampan to take refuge in a nearby river inlet. Pursuing the fleeing sampan, the U.S. patrol encountered a heavy volume of small-arms fire from enemy forces, at close range, occupying well-concealed positions along the riverbank. Maneuvering through this fire, the patrol confronted a numerically superior enemy force aboard 2 enemy junks and 8 sampans augmented by heavy automatic weapons fire from ashore. In the savage battle that ensued, BM1 Williams,

James E. Williams

with utter disregard for his safety exposed himself to the withering hail of enemy fire to direct counter-fire and inspire the actions of his patrol. Recognizing the overwhelming strength of the enemy force, BM1 Williams deployed his patrol to await the arrival of armed helicopters. In the course of his movement he discovered an even larger concentration of enemy boats. Not waiting for the arrival of the armed helicopters, he displayed great initiative and boldly led the patrol through the intense enemy fire and damaged or destroyed 50 enemy sampans and 7 junks. This phase of the action completed, and with the arrival of the armed helicopters, BM1 Williams directed the attack on the remaining enemy force. Now virtually dark, and although BM1 Williams was aware that his boats would become even better targets, he ordered the patrol boats' search lights turned on to better illuminate the area and moved the patrol perilously close to shore to press the attack. Despite a waning supply of ammunition the patrol successfully engaged the enemy ashore and completed the rout of the enemy force. Under the leadership of BM1 Williams, who demonstrated unusual professional skill and indomitable courage throughout the 3-hour battle, the patrol accounted for the destruction or loss of 65 enemy boats and inflicted numerous casualties on the enemy personnel. His extraordinary heroism and exemplary fighting spirit in the face of grave risks inspired the efforts of his men to defeat a larger enemy force, and are in keeping with the finest traditions of the U.S. Naval Service."

Second Citation: "For extraordinary heroism on 15 January 1967 while serving with River Section 531 and friendly foreign forces during combat operations against communist insurgent (Viet Cong) forces on the Mekong River in the Republic of Vietnam. As Patrol Officer of a combat PBR patrol BM1 Williams interdicted a major enemy supply movement across the Nam Thon branch of the Mekong River. He directed his units to the suspected crossing area, and was immediately taken under intense hostile fire from fortified positions and from along the riverbanks. After coordinating Vietnamese Artillery Support and USAF air strikes, BM1 Williams courageously led his three PBRs back into the hazardous river to investigate and destroy the enemy sampans and supplies. Blistering fire was again unleashed upon his forces. Frequently exposing himself to enemy fire, he directed his units in silencing several automatic-weapons positions, and directed one PBR to investigate several sampans, which could be seen, while the other PBRs provided cover fire. Almost immediately, the enemy renewed their fire in an effort to force the PBRs away from the sampans. BM1 Williams ordered the destruction of the sampan and the extraction of all his units. During the fierce firefight following the temporary immobilization of one of the units, BM1 Williams was wounded. Despite his painful injuries, he was able to lead his patrol back through the heavy enemy fire. His patrol had successfully interdicted a crossing attempt of three heavy-weapons companies totaling nearly four hundred men, had accounted for sixteen enemy killed in action, twenty wounded, the destruction of nine enemy sampans and junks, seven enemy structures, about 2400 pounds of enemy rice. By his outstanding display of decisive leadership, his unlimited courage in the face of enemy fire, and his utmost devotion to duty, BM1 Williams upheld the highest traditions of the United States Naval Service."

Source
Information supplied by BMC James E. Williams, USN (Retired).

Wilson, Benjamin F. *First lieutenant (then master sergeant), United States Army, Company One, 31st Infantry Regiment, Seventh Infantry Division, so distinguished himself in combat, during the Korean War, that he was awarded the Medal of Honor for his heroic action.*

Born: Vashon, Wash.; **Entered service at:** Vashon, Wash.; **Place and date:** Near Hwach'on-Myon, Korea, June 5, 1951. **G.O. No.:** 69, September 23, 1954.

Citation: "1st Lt. Wilson distinguished himself by conspicuous gallantry and indomitable courage above and beyond the call of duty in action against the enemy. Company I was committed to attack and secure commanding terrain stubbornly defended by a numerically superior hostile force emplaced in well-fortified positions. When the spearheading element was pinned down by withering hostile fire, he dashed forward and, firing his rifle and throwing grenades, neutralized the position denying the advance and killed 4 enemy soldiers manning submachineguns. After the assault platoon moved up, occupied the position, and a base of fire was established, he led a bayonet attack which reduced the objective and killed approximately 27 hostile soldiers. While friendly forces were consolidating the newly won gain, the enemy launched a counterattack and 1st Lt. Wilson, realizing the imminent threat of being overrun, made a determined lone-man charge, killing 7 and wounding 2 of the enemy, and routing the remainder in disorder. After the position was organized, he led an assault carrying to approximately 15 yards of the final objective, when enemy fire halted the advance. He ordered the platoon to withdraw and, although painfully wounded in this action, remained to provide covering fire. During an ensuing counterattack, the commanding officer and 1st Platoon leader became casualties. Unhesitatingly, 1st Lt. Wilson charged the enemy ranks and fought valiantly, killing 3 enemy soldiers with his rifle before it was wrested from his hands, and annihilating 4 others with his entrenching tool. His courageous delaying action enabled his comrades to reorganize and affect an orderly withdrawal. While directing evacuation of the wounded, he suffered a second wound, but elected to remain on the position until assured that all of the men had reached safety. 1st Lt. Wilson's sustained valor and intrepid actions reflect utmost credit upon himself and uphold the honored traditions of the military service."

Source
Medal of Honor Citation.

Wilson, Louis Hugh, Jr. (b. 1920) *General, United States Marine Corps; 26th commandant of the United States Marine Corps, so distinguished himself in combat, during World War II, that he was awarded the Medal of Honor for his heroic actions.*

Born: February 11, 1920, Brandon, Miss.; **Place and date:** Fante Hill, Guam, July 25–26, 1944.

Born in 1920, Wilson earned a B.A. in 1941 from Millsaps College, Jackson, Mississippi, where he participated in football and track. He enlisted in the Marine Corps Reserve in May 1941 and was commissioned a second lieutenant in November of that year. After officers' basic training, he was assigned to the Ninth Marine Regiment at Marine Corps Base, San Diego, California.

General Wilson went overseas with the Ninth Marines in February 1943, making stops at Guadalcanal, Efate, and Bougainville. He was promoted to captain in April 1943.

During the Marines' assault on the island of Guam, on July 25–26, 1944, Wilson commanded Company F, Second Battalion, Ninth Marines and earned the nation's highest military honor for his heroism in combat when he and his company repelled and destroyed a numerically superior enemy force. Because of wounds received in battle, he was evacuated to the U.S. Naval Hospital, San Diego, where he remained until October 16, 1944.

General Wilson returned to duty as commanding officer, Company D, Marine Barracks, Camp Pendleton, California, and in December 1944, he was transferred to Washington, D.C., where he served as a detachment commander at the Marine Barracks. While in Washington he was presented the Medal of Honor by President Harry S. Truman. He was promoted to major in March 1945.

From June 1946 until August 1951, General Wilson had consecutive tours as dean and assistant director, Marine Corps Institute; aide-de-camp, commanding general, Fleet Marine Force, Pacific; and officer in charge, District Headquarters Recruiting Station, New York City.

Promoted to lieutenant colonel in November 1951, while stationed at Quantico, Virginia, he served consecu-

tively as commanding officer of the Basic School's First Training Battalion, commanding officer of Camp Barrett, and executive officer of the Basic School. He completed the Officer's Senior Course in August 1954.

After a brief tour as a senior school instructor, Marine Corps Schools, Quantico, he departed for Korea to serve as assistant G-3, First Marine Division. In August 1955, he returned to the United States with the First Marine Division and was named commanding officer, Second Battalion, Fifth Marines, First Marine Division.

In March 1956, General Wilson was assigned to Headquarters Marine Corps, where he served for two years as head, Operations Section, G-3 (operations and training officer) Division. He returned to duty at Quantico, first as commanding officer of the Test and Training Regiment, later as commanding officer of the Basic School.

In June 1962, after his graduation from the National War College, he was assigned as joint plans coordinator to the deputy chief of staff, Plans and Programs, Headquarters Marine Corps. He transferred to the First Marine Division and deployed with the division in August 1965, stopping at Okinawa before going on to Vietnam. As assistant chief of staff, G-3, First Marine Division, he was awarded the Legion of Merit and the Republic of Vietnam's Cross of Gallantry with Gold Star.

On his return to the United States in August 1966, General Wilson assumed command of the Sixth Marine Corps District, Atlanta, Georgia. He was promoted to brigadier general in November 1966 and was assigned to Headquarters Marine Corps in January 1967 as the legislative assistant to the commandant of the Marine Corps, until July 1968. He then served as chief of staff, Headquarters, Fleet Marine Force, Pacific, until March 1970, earning a second Legion of Merit Medal.

He was advanced to the grade of major general in March 1970 and assumed command of First Marine Amphibious Force, Third Marine Division, on Okinawa. He was awarded a third Legion of Merit for his exemplary service.

In April 1971, he returned to Quantico for duty as deputy for education and director, Education Center, Marine Corps Development and Education Command. He was promoted to lieutenant general in August 1972, and on September 1, 1972, assumed command of the Fleet Marine Force, Pacific. During that tour, General Wilson was presented the Korean Order of National Security Merit GUK-SEON Medal, Second Class, and the Philippine Legion of Honor, Degree of Commander, for his services to those countries.

He was promoted to general officer on July 1, 1975. General Wilson served as the 26th commandant of the Marine Corps from July 1, 1975, until July 1, 1979. For his "exceptionally distinguished service" during his four-year tenure as commandant and his contributions as a member of the Joint Chiefs of Staff, he received the Defense Distinguished Service Medal, First Oak Leaf Cluster, on his retirement on July 1, 1979.

Citation: "For conspicuous gallantry and intrepidity at the risk of his life above and beyond the call of duty as commanding officer of a rifle company attached to the 2d Battalion, 9th Marines, 3d Marine Division, in action against enemy Japanese forces at Fonte Hill, Guam, 25–26 July 1944. Ordered to take that portion of the hill within his zone of action, Capt. Wilson initiated his attack in mid-afternoon, pushed up the rugged, open terrain against terrific machinegun and rifle fire for 300 yards and successfully captured the objective. Promptly assuming command of other disorganized units and motorized equipment in addition to his own company and 1 reinforcing platoon, he organized his night defenses in the face of continuous hostile fire and, although wounded 3 times during this 5-hour period, completed his disposition of men and guns before retiring to the company command post for medical attention. Shortly thereafter, when the enemy launched the first of a series of savage counter-attacks lasting all night, he voluntarily rejoined his besieged units and repeatedly exposed himself to the merciless hail of shrapnel and bullets, dashing 50 yards into the open on 1 occasion to rescue a wounded Marine lying helpless beyond the front lines. Fighting fiercely in hand-to-hand encounters, he led his men in furiously waged battle for approximately 10 hours, tenaciously holding his line and repelling the fanatically renewed counter-thrusts until he succeeded in crushing the last efforts of the hard-pressed Japanese early the following morning. Then organizing a 17-man patrol, he immediately advanced upon a strategic slope essential to the security of his position and, boldly defying intense mortar, machinegun, and rifle fire, which struck down 13 of his men, drove relentlessly forward with the remnants of his patrol to seize the vital ground. By his indomitable leadership, daring combat tactics, and valor in the face of overwhelming odds, Capt. Wilson succeeded in capturing and holding the strategic high ground in his regimental sector, thereby contributing essentially to the success of his regimental mission and to the annihilation of 350 Japanese troops. His inspiring conduct throughout the critical periods of this decisive action sustains and enhances the highest traditions of the U.S. Naval Service."

Source
Marine Corps Historical Center.
Medal of Honor Citation.

Winans, Roswell (b. 1887) *First Sergeant, later Brigadier General, United States Marine Corps, so*

distinguished himself in combat, in the Dominican Republic, that he was awarded the Medal of Honor for his heroic actions.

Born: December 9, 1887, Brookville, Ind.; **Entered service at:** Washington; **Place and date:** Guayacanas, Dominican Republic, July 3, 1916. **G.O. No.:** 244, October 30, 1916.

Citation: "During an engagement at Guayacanas on 3 July 1916, 1st Sgt. Winans participated in action against a considerable force of rebels on the line of march. During a running fight of 1,200 yards, our forces reached the enemy entrenchments and Cpl. Joseph A. Glowin, U.S.M.C., placed the machinegun, of which he had charge, behind a large log across the road and immediately opened fire on the trenches. He was struck once but continued firing his gun, but a moment later he was again struck and had to be dragged out of the position into cover. 1st Sgt. Winans, U.S.M.C., then arrived with a Colt's gun, which he placed in a most exposed position, coolly opened fire on the trenches and when the gun jammed, stood up and repaired it under fire. All the time Glowin and Winans were handling their guns they were exposed to a very heavy fire, which was striking into the logs and around the men, 7 men being wounded, and 1 killed within 20 feet. 1st Sgt. Winans continued firing his gun until the enemy had abandoned the trenches."

Source
Medal of Honor Citation.

Womack, Bryant E. (d. 1952) *Private first class, United States Army, Medical Company, 14th Infantry Regiment, 25th Infantry Division, so distinguished himself in combat, during the Korean War, that he was awarded (posthumously) the Medal of Honor for his heroic actions.*

Born: Mill Springs, N.C.; **Entered service at:** Mill Springs, N.C., **Place and date:** Near Sokso-ri, Korea, March 12, 1952. **G.O. No.:** 5, January 12, 1953.

Citation: "Pfc. Womack distinguished himself by conspicuous gallantry above and beyond the call of duty in action against the enemy. Pfc. Womack was the only medical aid man attached to a night combat patrol when sudden contact with a numerically superior enemy produced numerous casualties. Pfc. Womack went immediately to their aid, although this necessitated exposing himself to a devastating hail of enemy fire, during which he was seriously wounded. Refusing medical aid for himself, he continued moving among his comrades to administer aid. While he was aiding 1 man, he was again struck by enemy mortar fire, this time suffering the loss of his right arm. Although he knew the consequences should immediate aid not be administered, he still refused aid and insisted that all efforts be made for the benefit of others that were wounded. Although unable to perform the task himself, he remained on the scene and directed others in first aid techniques. The last man to withdraw, he walked until he collapsed from loss of blood, and died a few minutes later while being carried by his comrades. The extraordinary heroism, outstanding courage, and unswerving devotion to his duties displayed by Pfc. Womack reflect the utmost distinction upon himself and uphold the esteemed traditions of the U.S. Army."

Source
Medal of Honor Citation.

Woodfill, Samuel *First lieutenant, United States Army, 60th Infantry, Fifth Division, so distinguished himself in combat, during World War I, that he was awarded the Medal of Honor for his heroic actions.*

Born: Jefferson Country, Ind.; **Entered service at:** Bryantsburg, Ind.; **Place and Date:** At Cunel, France, October 12, 1918. **G.O. No.:**16, 1919.

Citation: "While he was leading his company against the enemy, his line came under heavy machinegun fire, which threatened to hold up the advance. Followed by 2 soldiers at 25 yards, this officer went out ahead of his first line toward a machinegun nest and worked his way around its flank, leaving the 2 soldiers in front. When he got within 10 yards of the gun it ceased firing, and 4 of the enemy appeared, 3 of whom were shot by 1st Lt. Woodfill. The fourth, an officer, rushed at 1st Lt. Woodfill, who attempted to club the officer with his rifle. After a hand-to-hand struggle, 1st Lt. Woodfill killed the officer with his pistol. His company thereupon continued to advance, until shortly afterwards another machinegun nest was encountered. Calling on his men to follow, 1st Lt. Woodfill rushed ahead of his line in the face of heavy fire from the nest, and when several of the enemy appeared above the nest he shot them, capturing 3 other members of the crew and silencing the gun. A few minutes later this officer for the third time demonstrated conspicuous daring by charging another machinegun position, killing 5 men in one machinegun pit with his rifle. He then drew his revolver and started to jump into the pit, when 2 other gunners only a few yards away turned their gun on him. Failing to kill them with his revolver, he grabbed a pick lying nearby and killed both of them. Inspired by the exceptional courage displayed by this officer, his men pressed on to their objective under severe shell and machinegun fire."

Source
Medal of Honor Citation.

Wright, Raymond R. (b.1945) *Specialist fourth class, United States Army, Company A, Third Battalion, 60th Infantry, Ninth Infantry Division, so distinguished himself in combat, during the Vietnam War, that he was awarded the Medal of Honor for his heroic actions.*

Born: December 5, 1945, Moriah, N.Y.; **Entered Service at:** Moriah, N.Y.; **Place and Date:** Ap Bac Zone Republic of Vietnam, May 2, 1967.

Citation: "For conspicuous gallantry and intrepidity at the risk of his life above and beyond the call of duty. While serving as a rifleman with Company A, Sp4c. Wright distinguished himself during a combat patrol in an area where an enemy ambush had occurred earlier. Sp4c. Wright's unit suddenly came under intense automatic weapons and small arms fire from an enemy bunker system protected by numerous snipers in nearby trees. Despite the heavy enemy fire, Sp4c. Wright and another soldier leaped to the top of a dike to assault the position. Armed with a rifle and several grenades, he and his comrade exposed themselves to intense fire from the bunkers as they charged the nearest one. Sp4c. Wright raced to the bunker, threw in a grenade, killing its occupant. The 2 soldiers then ran through a hail of fire to the second bunker. While his comrade covered him with his machinegun, Sp4c. Wright charged the bunker and succeeded in killing its occupant with a grenade. A third bunker contained an automatic rifleman who had pinned down much of the friendly platoon. While his comrade again covered him with machinegun fire, Sp4c. Wright charged in and killed the enemy rifleman with a grenade. The 2 soldiers worked their way through the remaining bunkers, knocking out 4 of them. Throughout their furious assault, Sp4c. Wright and his comrade had been almost continuously exposed to intense sniper fire from the treeline as the enemy desperately sought to stop their attack. Overcoming stubborn resistance from the bunker system, the men advanced into the treeline forcing the snipers to retreat, giving immediate chase, and driving the enemy away from the friendly unit so that it advanced across the open area without further casualty. When his ammunition was exhausted, Sp4c. Wright returned to his unit to assist in the evacuation of the wounded. This 2-man assault had driven an enemy platoon from a well-prepared position, accounted for numerous enemy casualties, and averted further friendly casualties. Sp4c. Wright's extraordinary heroism, courage, and indomitable fighting spirit saved the lives of many of his comrades and inflicted serious damage on the enemy. His acts were in keeping with the highest traditions of the military service and reflect great credit upon himself and the U.S. Army."

Source
Medal of Honor Citation.

Yabes, Maximo

Yabes, Maximo (1932–1967) *First sergeant, United States Army, Company A, Fourth Battalion, Ninth Infantry, 25th Infantry Division, so distinguished himself in combat, during the Vietnam War, that he was awarded (posthumously) the Medal of Honor, for his heroic actions.*

Born: January 29, 1932, Lodi, Calif.; **Entered service at:** Eugene, Oreg.; **Place and date:** Near Pho Hoa Dong; Republic of Vietnam, February 26, 1967.

Citation: "For conspicuous gallantry and intrepidity at the risk of his life above and beyond the call of duty. 1st Sgt. Yabes distinguished himself with Company A, which was providing security for a land clearing operation. Early in the morning the company suddenly came under intense automatic weapons and mortar fire followed by a battalion sized assault from 3 sides. Penetrating the defensive perimeter the enemy advanced on the company command post bunker. The command post received increasingly heavy fire and was in danger of being overwhelmed. When several enemy grenades landed within the command post, 1st Sgt. Yabes shouted a warning and used his body as a shield to protect others in the bunker. Although painfully wounded by numerous grenade fragments, and despite the vicious enemy fire on the bunker, he remained there to provide covering fire and enable the others in the command group to relocate. When the command group had reached a new position, 1st Sgt. Yabes moved through a withering hail of enemy fire to another bunker 50 meters away. There he secured a grenade launcher from a fallen comrade and fired point blank into the attacking Viet Cong stopping further penetration of the perimeter. Noting 2 wounded men helpless in the fire swept area, he moved them to a safer position where they could be given medical treatment. He resumed his accurate and effective fire killing several enemy soldiers and forcing others to withdraw from the vicinity of the command post. As the battle continued, he observed an enemy machinegun within the perimeter which threatened the whole position. On his own, he dashed across the exposed area, assaulted the machinegun, killed the crew, destroyed the weapon, and fell mortally wounded. 1st Sgt. Yabes' valiant and selfless actions saved the lives of many of his fellow soldiers and inspired his comrades to effectively repel the enemy assault. His indomitable fighting spirit, extraordinary courage and intrepidity at the cost of his life are in the highest military traditions and reflect great credit upon himself and the Armed Forces of his country."

Source
Medal of Honor Citation.

Yeager, Charles E.

Yeager, Charles E. "Chuck" *American test pilot and United States Air Force officer who was the first man to exceed the speed of sound in flight.*

Yeager enlisted in the United States Army in September 1941, shortly after graduating from high school, and was assigned to the Army Air Corps. He was commissioned a reserve flight officer in 1943 and became a pilot in the fighter command of the Eighth Air Force, stationed in England. He flew 64 missions over Europe during World War II, shot down 13 German aircraft, and was himself shot down over France (he escaped capture with the help of the French underground). After the war he became a flight instructor and then a test pilot and secured a commission as a captain in 1947.

Yeager was chosen from several volunteers to test-fly the secret experimental X-1 aircraft, built by the Bell Aircraft Company to test the capabilities of the human pilot and a fixed-wing aircraft against the severe aerodynamic stresses of sonic flight. On October 14, 1947, over Rogers Dry Lake in southern California, he rode the X-1, attached to a B-29 mother ship, to an altitude of 25,000 feet (7,600 meters). The X-1 then rocketed separately to 40,000 feet (12,000 meters), and Yeager became the first man to break the sound barrier, which was approximately 662 miles (1,066 kilometers) per hour at that altitude. The feat was not announced publicly until June 1948. Yeager continued to make test flights, and, on December 12, 1953, he established a world speed record of 1,650 miles (2,660 kilometers) per hour in an X-1A rocket plane.

In 1954 Yeager left his post as assistant chief of test-flight operations at Edwards Air Force Base in California to join the staff of the 12th Air Force in West Germany. After other routine assignments, he returned to Edwards in 1962 as commandant of the Aerospace Research Pilot School with the rank of colonel. In 1968 he took command of the Fourth Tactical Fighter Wing. He retired from the Air Force with the rank of brigadier general in 1975. His autobiography, *Yeager,* was published in 1985.

Sources and Additional Reading

Lundgren, William R. *Across the High Frontier.* New York: Bantam, 1987.

Yeager, Gen. Chuck, and Leo. Janus. *Yeager.* New York: Bantam, 1985.

Yntema, Gordon Douglas (1945–1968) *Sergeant, United States Army, Company D, Fifth Special Forces Group (Airborne), so distinguished himself in combat, during the Vietnam War, that he was awarded (posthumously) the Medal of Honor for his heroic actions.*

Born: June 26, 1945, Bethesda, Md.; **Entered service at:** Detroit, Mich.; **Place and date:** Near Thong Binh, Republic of Vietnam, January 16–18, 1968.

Citation: "For conspicuous gallantry and intrepidity in action at the risk of his life and above and beyond the call of duty. Sgt. Yntema, U.S. Army, distinguished himself while assigned to Detachment A-431, Company D. As part of a larger force of civilian irregulars from Camp Cai Cai, he accompanied 2 platoons to a blocking position east of the village of Thong Binh, where they became heavily engaged in a small-arms fire fight with the Viet Cong. Assuming control of the force when the Vietnamese commander was seriously wounded, he advanced his troops to within 50 meters of the enemy bunkers. After a fierce 30-minute firefight, the enemy forced Sgt. Yntema to withdraw his men to a trench in order to afford them protection and still perform their assigned blocking mission. Under cover of machinegun fire, approximately 1 company of Viet Cong maneuvered into a position which pinned down the friendly platoons from 3 sides. A dwindling ammunition supply, coupled with a Viet Cong mortar barrage, which inflicted heavy losses on the exposed friendly troops, caused many of the irregulars to withdraw. Seriously wounded and ordered to withdraw himself, Sgt. Yntema refused to leave his fallen comrades. Under withering small arms and machinegun fire, he carried the wounded Vietnamese commander and a mortally wounded American Special Forces adviser to a small gully 50 meters away in order to shield them from the enemy fire. Sgt. Yntema then continued to repulse the attacking Viet Cong attempting to overrun his position until, out of ammunition and surrounded, he was offered the opportunity to surrender. Refusing, Sgt. Yntema stood his ground, using his rifle as a club to fight the approximately 15 Viet Cong attempting his capture. His resistance was so fierce that the Viet Cong were forced to shoot in order to overcome him. Sgt. Yntema's personal bravery in the face of insurmountable odds and supreme self-sacrifice were in keeping with the highest traditions of the military service and reflect the utmost credit upon himself, the 1st Special Forces, and the U.S. Army."

Source
Medal of Honor Citation.

York, Alvin Cullum (1887–1964) *Corporal, United States Army, assistant squad leader, Company G, 328th Infantry, 82nd Infantry Division, American Expeditionary Force, so distinguished in combat, during World War I, that he was awarded the Medal of Honor for his heroic actions.*

Born: December 13, 1887, Fentress County, Tenn., **Entered service at:** Pall Mall, Tenn.; **Place and date:** Chatel-Chehery, France, October 8, 1918. **G.O. No.:** 59, W.D., 1919.

"The American guards were astonished as the tall red-haired corporal marched his prisoners into camp. They had seen large groups of captured Germans before, but nothing like this. The date was October 8, 1918, in the first month of the Meuse-Argonne offensive. Alvin C. York, a sharp-shooting blacksmith from the Tennessee hamlet of Pall Mall, was about to become Sergeant York, the greatest hero of the Great War.

"York's colonel visited the site where York had fought, counted the German bodies and abandoned guns, and talked to other Americans who were on the scene. They explained that after capturing several Germans they had been pinned down by machinegun fire from the top of a ridge. York had pressed forward alone, shooting enemy soldiers whenever they appeared over the trenches. At last a German major promised to order his men to surrender if York would stop picking them off. In less than three hours Corporal York had single-handedly killed twenty-five Germans, silenced thirty-five machineguns and taken 132 prisoners.

"York was quickly promoted to sergeant and awarded the Medal of Honor. He became the toast of Europe, lauded by President Wilson in Paris and by people all across the continent. Marshal Ferdinand Foch told him, 'What you did was the greatest thing accomplished by any private soldier of all armies of Europe.'

"York was an unlikely war hero. He had registered for the draft as a conscientious objector, explaining that the Bible forbade killing. At boot camp, his captain quoted various Scripture passages concerning righteous war, which, he argued, were applicable to the conflict at hand. After much deliberation, York pronounced himself satisfied and went off to France.

"America was waiting for Alvin York when his troopship pulled up to a Hoboken dock on May 22, 1919. Rushed by photographers, dignitaries, and spectators, he was whisked to the Waldorf-Astoria Hotel and given a suite adjacent to the one reserved for the president. Then came a staggering line-up of public appearances. At the stock exchange, trading was suspended and members paraded York around the floor on their shoulders. Earlier he had expressed a desire to see the city's famous subway system; transit officials obliged with a tour in a private car. York admitted, 'New York is certainly a great city, but it do tire a fellow out some.' He and his congressman traveled to Washington, where he was applauded on the floor of the House of Representatives. After making the rounds of the capital, York said that he had, 'seen it all.'

"York was deluged with offers for lectures, tours, and books but wanted none of it. 'This uniform ain't for sale,' he said, and boarded a train back to Pall Mall. There he was paraded through town in a caravan of automobiles and mules. To his beloved mother and neighbors, the national hero was still 'the same old Al.'

"But the rest of the nation had followed York to Tennessee. The state presented him with a fully stocked 400-acre farm. When his long-time girlfriend agreed to marry him, the news made front pages across the country. Though they had planned to have the ceremony in the simple chapel where York had converted to the Church of Christ in Christian Union, Alvin and Gracie York were married on their new farm, in a rite performed by the governor of Tennessee before 3,000 people. The couple turned down a complimentary honeymoon to Salt Lake City, calling the journey 'merely a vainglorious call of the world and of the devil.'

"Instead, the Yorks stayed in Pall Mall, where Alvin continued farming and blacksmithing, the trades of his late father, and teaching Bible school. Dignitaries and curious visitors frequently sought him out in the fields; according to one later account, 'It became obligatory for Tennessee politicians running for office to pose for campaign pictures with him.' But York shunned politics, declining the vice-presidential nomination of the Prohibition Party in 1936.

Alvin Cullum York

"It took another world war to draw Sergeant York back onto public stage. At age fifty-four he registered for the draft at the same country store where twenty-five years earlier he had signed up as a conscientious objector. 'If they want me for active duty, I'm ready to go,' York declared. 'I'm in a mighty different mood now from that other time.' Though he was never called, York served as head of the local draft board and sent two of his sons off to war.

"A series of strokes in the 1950s confined him to a wheel chair, and on September 2, 1964, Alvin York died in a Nashville, Tennessee, veteran's hospital. To millions of Americans, he was Sergeant York, an American hero; to his neighbors in Pall Mall, Tennessee, he was just 'the same old Al.'"

Citation: "After his platoon had suffered heavy casualties and 3 other noncommissioned officers had become casualties, Cpl. York assumed command. Fearlessly leading 7 men, he charged with great daring a machinegun nest, which was pouring deadly and incessant fire upon his platoon. In this heroic feat the machinegun nest was taken, together with 4 officers and 128 men and several guns."

Source and Additional Reading
Medal of Honor Citation.
Editors. *Above and Beyond.* Boston: Boston Publishing, 1985.

Young, Gerald O. (b. 1930) *Captain, United States Air Force, 37th ARS, Da Nang Air Force Base, so distinguished himself in aerial combat, during the Vietnam War, that he was awarded the Medal of Honor for his heroic actions.*

Born: May 9, 1930, Chicago, Ill.; **Entered service at:** Colorado Springs, Colo.; **Place and date:** Khe Sanh, November 9, 1967.

Citation: "For conspicuous gallantry and intrepidity at the risk of his life above and beyond the call of duty. Capt. Young distinguished himself while serving as a helicopter rescue crew commander. Capt. Young was flying escort for another helicopter attempting the night rescue of an Army ground reconnaissance team in imminent danger of death or capture. Previous attempts had resulted in the loss of 2 helicopters to hostile ground fire. The endangered team was positioned on the side of a steep slope that required unusual airmanship on the part of Capt. Young to effect pickup. Heavy automatic weapons fire from the surrounding enemy severely damaged 1 rescue helicopter, but it was able to extract 3 of the team. The commander of this aircraft recommended to Capt. Young that further rescue attempts be abandoned because it was not possible to suppress the concentrated fire from enemy automatic weapons. With full knowledge of the danger involved, and the fact that supporting helicopter gunships were low on fuel and ordnance, Capt. Young hovered under intense fire until the remaining survivors were aboard. As he maneuvered the aircraft for takeoff, the enemy appeared at point-blank range and raked the aircraft with automatic weapons fire. The aircraft crashed, inverted, and burst into flames. Capt. Young escaped through a window of the burning aircraft. Disregarding serious burns, Capt. Young aided one of the wounded men and attempted to lead the hostile forces away from his position. Later, despite intense pain from his burns, he declined to accept rescue because he had observed hostile forces setting up automatic weapons positions to entrap any rescue aircraft. For more than 17 hours he evaded the enemy until rescue aircraft could be brought into the area. Through his extraordinary heroism, aggressiveness, and concern for his fellow man, Capt. Young reflected the highest credit upon himself, the U.S. Air Force, and the Armed Forces of his country."

Source
Medal of Honor Citation.

Young, Robert H. (1929–1950) *Private first class, United States Army, Company E, Eighth Cavalry Regiment, First Cavalry Division, so distinguished himself in combat, during the Korean War, that he was awarded (posthumously) the Medal of Honor for his heroic actions.*

Born: March 4, 1929, Oroville. Calif.; **Entered service at:** Vallejo, Calif.: **Place and date:** North of Kaesong, Korea, October 9, 1950. **G.O. No.:** 65 August 2, 1951.

Citation: "Pfc. Young distinguished himself by conspicuous gallantry and intrepidity above and beyond the call of duty in action. His company, spearheading a battalion drive deep in enemy territory, suddenly came under a devastating barrage of enemy mortar and automatic weapons crossfire which inflicted heavy casualties among his comrades and wounded him in the face and shoulder. Refusing to be evacuated, Pfc. Young remained in position and continued to fire at the enemy until wounded a second time. As he awaited first aid near the company command post the enemy attempted an enveloping movement. Disregarding medical tratment he took an exposed position and firing with deadly accuracy killed 5 of the enemy. During this action he was again hit by hostile fire which knocked him to the ground and destroyed his helmet. Later when supporting tanks moved forward, Pfc. Young, his wounds still unattended, directed tank fire which destroyed 3 enemy gun positions and enabled the company to advance. Wounded again by an enemy mortar burst, and while aiding several of his injured comrades, he demanded that all others be evacuated first. Throughout the course of this action the leadership and combative instinct displayed by Pfc. Young exerted a profound influence on the conduct of the company. His aggressive example affected the whole course of the action and was responsible for its success. Pfc. Young's dauntless courage and intrepidity reflect the highest credit upon himself and uphold the esteemed traditions of the U.S. Army."

Source
Medal of Honor Citation.

Z

★ ★ ★ ★

Zabitosky, Fred William (b. 1942) *Sergeant first class (then staff sergeant), United States Army, Fifth Special Forces Group (Airborne), so distinguished himself in combat, during the Vietnam War, that he was awarded the Medal of Honor for his heroic actions.*

Born: October 27, 1942, Trenton, N.J.; **Entered service at:** Trenton, N.J.; **Place and date:** Republic of Vietnam, February 19, 1968.

Citation: "For conspicuous gallantry and intrepidity in action at the risk of his life above and beyond the call of duty. Sfc. Zabitosky, U.S. Army, distinguished himself while serving as an assistant team leader of a 9-man Special Forces long-range reconnaissance patrol. Sfc. Zabitosky's patrol was operating deep within enemy-controlled territory when they were attacked by a numerically superior North Vietnamese Army unit. Sfc. Zabitosky rallied his team members, deployed them into defensive positions, and, exposing himself to concentrated enemy automatic weapons fire, directed their return fire. Realizing the gravity of the situation, Sfc. Zabitosky ordered his patrol to move to a landing zone for helicopter extraction while he covered their withdrawal with rifle fire and grenades. Rejoining the patrol under increasing enemy pressure, he positioned each man in a tight perimeter defense and continually moved from man to man, encouraging them and controlling their defensive fire. Mainly due to his example, the outnumbered patrol maintained its precarious position until the arrival of tactical air support and a helicopter extraction team. As the rescue helicopters arrived, the determined North Vietnamese pressed their attack. Sfc. Zabitosky repeatedly exposed himself to their fire to adjust suppressive helicopter gunship fire around the landing zone. After boarding 1 of the rescue helicopters, he positioned himself in the door delivering fire on the enemy as the ship took off. The helicopter was engulfed in a hail of bullets and Sfc. Zabitosky was thrown from the craft as it spun out of control and crashed. Recovering consciousness, he ignored his extremely painful injuries and moved to the flaming wreckage. Heedless of the danger of exploding ordance and fuel, he pulled the severely wounded pilot from the searing blaze and made repeated attempts to rescue his patrol members but was driven back by the intense heat. Despite his serious burns and crushed ribs, he carried and dragged the unconscious pilot through a curtain of enemy fire to

Fred William Zabitosky

within 10 feet of a hovering rescue helicopter before collapsing. Sfc. Zabitosky's extraordinary heroism and devotion to duty were in keeping with the highest traditions of the military service and reflect great credit upon himself, his unit, and the U.S. Army."

Source
Medal of Honor Citation.

Zussman, Raymond (d. 1944) *Second lieutenant, United States Army, 756th Tank Battalion, so distinguished himself in combat, during World War II, that he was awarded (posthumously) the Medal of Honor for his heroic actions.*

   Born: Hamtramck, Mich.; **Entered service at:** Detroit, Mich.; **Place and date:** Noroy le Bourg, France, September 12, 1944. **G.O. No.:** 42, May 24, 1945.

Citation: "On 12 September 1944, 2d Lt. Zussman was in command of 2 tanks operating with an infantry company in the attack on enemy forces occupying the town of Noroy le Bourg, France. At 7 p.m., his command tank bogged down. Throughout the ensuing action, armed only with a carbine, he reconnoitered alone on foot far in advance of his remaining tank and the infantry. Returning only from time to time to designate targets, he directed the action of the tank and turned over to the infantry the numerous German soldiers he had caused to surrender. He located a roadblock and directed his tanks to destroy it. Fully exposed to fire from enemy positions only 50 yards distant, he stood by his tank directing its fire. Three Germans were killed and 8 surrendered. Again he walked before his tank, leading it against an enemy-held group of houses, machinegun and small arms fire kicking up dust at his feet. The tank fire broke the resistance and 20 enemy surrendered. Going forward again alone he passed an enemy-occupied house from which Germans fired on him and threw grenades in his path. After a brief fire fight, he signaled his tank to come up and fire on the house.

Raymond Zussman

Eleven German soldiers were killed and 15 surrendered. Going on alone, he disappeared around a street corner. The fire of his carbine could be heard and in a few minutes he reappeared driving 30 prisoners before him. Under 2d Lt. Zussman's heroic and inspiring leadership, 18 enemy soldiers were killed and 92 captured."

Source
Medal of Honor Citation.

Appendix: American War Statistics

★ ★ ★ ★

American Revolution (1775–1784)

Participants	290,000
Deaths in Service	4,000

Last Veteran, Daniel F. Bakeman,
    died April 5, 1869, age 109
Last Widow, Catherine S. Damon,
    died November 11, 1906, age 92
Last Dependent, Phoebe M. Palmeter,
    died April 25, 1911, age 90

War of 1812 (1812–1815)

Participants	287,000
Deaths in Service	2,000

Last Veteran, Hiram Cronk,
    died May, 13, 1905, age 105
Last Widow, Carolina King,
    died June 28, 1936, age unknown
Last Dependent, Esther A. H. Morgan,
    died March 12, 1946, age 89

Indian Wars (Approx. 1817–1898)

Participants	106,000
Deaths in Service	1,000

Last Veteran, Fredrak Fraske,
    died June 18, 1973, age 101

Mexican War (1846–1848)

Participants	79,000
Deaths in Service	13,000

Last Veteran, Owen Thomas Edgar,
    died June 3, 1929, age 98

Last Widow, Lena James Theobald,
    died June 20, 1963, age 89
Last Dependent, Jesse G. Bivens,
    died November 1, 1962, age 94

Civil War (1861–1865)

Participants (Union)	2,213,000
Deaths in Service (Union)	364,000
Participants (Confederate)	1,000,000
Deaths in Service (Confederate)	133,821

Last Union Veteran, Albert Woolson
    died August 2, 1956, age 109
Last Confederate Veteran, John Salling
    died March 16, 1958, age 112

(Authoritative statistics for Confederate Forces not available. Estimated 28,000 Confederate personnel died in Union prisons.)

Spanish-American War (1898–1902)

Participants	392,000
Deaths in Service	11,000

Last Spanish-American War Era Veteran,
    Nathan E. Cook, died September 10, 1992,
    age 106

World War I (1917–1918)

Participants	4,744,000
Deaths in Service	116,000
Living Veterans	13,000

(Living Veterans do not include World War I veterans with military service in other eras.)

WORLD WAR II (SEPTEMBER 16, 1940, TO JULY 25, 1947)

Participants	16,535,000
Deaths in Service	406,000 (a)
Living Veterans	7,433,000 (b,c)

KOREAN CONFLICT (JUNE 27, 1950, TO JANUARY 31, 1955)

Participants	6,807,000 (a,d)
Deaths in Service	55,000
Living Veterans	4,499,000 (b, c, e, i)

VIETNAM ERA (AUGUST 5, 1964, TO MAY 7, 1975)

Participants	9,200,000 (d)
Deaths in Service	109,000
Living Veterans	8,273,000 (b, e, h, i)

PERSIAN GULF WAR ERA (STARTING DATE AUGUST 2, 1990, TO DATE TO BE DETERMINED)

Participants	3,700,000 (f)
Deaths in Service	6,526 (g)
Living Veterans	1,450,000 (h, i)

AMERICA'S WARS TOTAL (THROUGH JULY 1, 1994)

War Participants	41,746,000 (f)
Deaths in Service	1,087,526 (g)
Living War Veterans	20,169,000
Living Ex-Service members	26,198,000

Note: Figures on the number of living veterans reflect final 1990 Census data and include only veterans living in the United States. Detail may not add to total because of rounding.

Source: Veterans and Dependents on the Compensation and Pension Rolls as of October 1, 1995:
ERA Veterans
Children
Parents
Surviving Spouses

FOOTNOTES

Persons who served in more than one war period are counted only once.

A child connotes a minor or a helpless adult.

a Includes 1,476,000 who served in World War II and the Korean Conflict.

b Includes 217,000 who served in World War II, the Korean Conflict, and the Vietnam Era.

c Includes 518,000 who served in both World War II and the Korean Conflict.

d Includes 887,000 who served in the Korean Conflict and the Vietnam Era.

e Includes 303,000 who served in both the Korean Conflict and the Vietnam Era.

f Through end of December 1995.

g During Fiscal Years 1991 through for Persian Gulf War.

h Includes 244,000 who served in both the Persian Gulf War and the Vietnam Era.

i Includes small number who served in the Persian Gulf War, Vietnam Era, and the Korean Conflict.

Source: VA Information.

BIBLIOGRAPHY

Asprey, Robert. *At Belleau Wood*. New York: G. P. Putnam, 1965.

Astor, Gerald. *The Right to Fight*. Novator, Calif.: Presidio Press, 1998.

Ballendorf, Dirk A., and Bartlett, Merrill. *Pete Ellis, an Amphibious Warfare Prophet 1880–1923*. Annapolis, MD.: Naval Institute Press, 1997.

Bartlett, Merrill L. *Lejeune: A Marine's Life*. Annapolis, MD.: Naval Institute Press, 1996.

Belden, Bauman L. *United States War Medals*. New York: The American Numismatic Society, 1916.

Bennett, William J. *Our Sacred Honor*. New York: Simon & Schuster, 1997.

———. *The Children's Book of Virtues*. New York: Simon & Schuster. 1997.

———. *The Spirit of America*. New York: Simon & Schuster, 1997.

Beyer, Walter F., and Keydel, Oscar F. *Deeds of Valor*. 2 vols. Detroit, Mich.: Perrien-Keydel, 1906.

Blakeney, Jane. *Heroes: U.S. Marine Corps 1861–1955*. Washington, D.C., 1956.

Boatner, Mark M., III. *The Civil War Dictionary*. New York David McKay, 1959.

———. *The Biographical Dictionary of World War II*. New York: David McKay, 1970.

Borts, Lawrence H., and Foster, Col. Frank C. *U.S. Medals 1939 to Present*. Fountain Inn, SC.: Medals of America Press, 1998.

Editors of Boston Publishing Company. *Above and Beyond*. Boston: Boston Publishing, 1985.

Boswell, Rolfe. *Medals for Marines*. New York, Crowell, 1945.

Bourke, John G. *On the Border with Crook*. Lincoln: University of Nebraska Press, 1971.

Boyington, Gregory Pappy. *Baa Baa Black Sheep*. New York: Bantam Books, 1990.

Chambers, John Whiteclay III. *The Oxford Companion to American Military History*. New York, Oxford University Press, 1999.

Clark, George B. *Devil Dogs: Fighting Marines of World War I*. Novato, Calif.: Presidio Press, 1999.

Connelly, Thomas L. *The Marble Man, Robert E. Lee and His Image in American Society*. Baton Rouge: Louisiana State University Press, 1978.

Davis, Burke. *Marine! The Life of Chesty Puller*. New York: Bantam Books, 1991.

Donovan, Frank. *The Medal*. New York: Dodd Mead, 1962.

Dupuy, Trevor N., Johnson, Curt, and Bongard, David L, *The Harper Encyclopedia of Military Biography*. New York: HarperCollins, 1995.

Dvorchak, Robert J. *Battle for Korea*. Conshohocken, Pa.: Combined Books, 2000.

Foote, Shelby. *The Civil War*. 3 vols. New York: Vintage Books, 1986.

Freeman, Douglas Southall. *Lee's Lieutenants*. 3 vols. New York: Scribners, 1997.

Gamble, Bruce. *The Black Sheep*. Novato, Calif.: Presidio Press, 2000.

Grossman, LtCol. Dave. *On Killing*. Boston: Little, Brown, 1996.

Hackworth, Col. David H., and Sherman, Julie. *About Face*. New York: Touchstone, 1990.

Hackworth, Col. David H., and Matthews, Tom L. *Hazardous Duty*. New York: Avon Books, 1997.

Heinl, Col. Robert D. *Victory at High Tide*. Baltimore: Nautical and Aviation Publishing Company of America, 1979.

Henderson, G. F. R. *Stonewall Jackson and the American Civil War*. New York: Da Capo Press, 1988.

Hodgins, Michael C. *Reluctant Warrior*. New York: Fawcett, 1996.

Hoffman, Jon T., and Boomer, Walter E. *Once a Legend*. Novato, Calif.: Presidio Press, 2001.

Hoopes, Townsend, and Brinkley, Douglas. *Driven Patriot: The Life and Times of James Forrestal*. Annapolis, MD.: Naval Institute Press, 2000.

Heatley, C. J. *Forged in Steel: U.S. Marine Corps Aviation*. Charlottesville, Va.: Howell Press, 1998.

Hynes, Samuel. *The Soldiers' Tale.* New York: Penguin USA, 1998.

Isaacs, Edouard V. *Escape.* Boston: Houghton Mifflin, 1919.

Jordan, Kenneth N. Sr. *Forgotten Heroes: 131 Men Awarded the Medal of Honor.* West Chester, Pa.: Schiffer, 1995.

Jordan, Kenneth N. Sr. *Heroes of Our Time: 239 Men of the Vietnam War Awarded the Medal of Honor 1964–1972.* West Chester, Pa.: Schiffer, 1978.

Ketchum, Richard M. *Saratoga: Turning Point of America's Revolutionary War.* New York: Henry Holt, 1997.

Knox, Donald. *The Korean War: Pusan to Chosin.* Harvest Books, 1987.

Knox, Donald, and Coppel, Alfred. *The Korean War: Uncertain Victory.* New York: Harvest Books, 1991.

Krulak, Lt. Gen. Victor H. *First To Fight.* Annapolis, Md.: Naval Institute Press, 1984.

Leckie, Robert. *Conflict: The History of the Korean War.* New York: Da Capo Press, 1996.

Lee, Lt. Col. Alex. *Force Recon Command.* Annapolis, Md.: Naval Institute Press, 1995.

Lee, Irvin. *Negro Medal of Honor Men.* New York: Dodd, Mead, 1967.

Lehrack, Otto J. *No Shining Armor.* Lawrence: University of Kansas, 1992.

Lejeune, MajGen. John A. *The Reminiscences of a Marine.* Salen, N.H.: Ayer, 1979.

Lemon, Peter C. *Beyond the Medal.* Golden, Colorado: Fulcrum Publishing, 1997.

Lindbergh, Charles A. *The Spirit of Saint Louis.* New York: Charles Scribner's Sons, 1953.

Lowther, William A. "A Medal for Roy Benavidez." *Reader's Digest,* April 1983.

Manchester, William. *American Caesar: Douglas MacArthur, 1880–1964.* New York: Dell, 1983.

Marshall, S. L. A. *Crimson Prairie.* New York: Charles Scribner's Sons, 1972.

———. *The Soldier's Load and Mobility of a Nation.* Washington: Combat Forces Press, 1950.

Marszalek, John F. *Sherman: A Soldier's Passion for Order.* New York: Vintage Books, 1995.

McPherson, James M. *Battle Cry of Freedom.* New York: Ballantine Books, 1989.

Marine Corps Recruit Depot Museum Historical Society. *The History of Marine Corps Recruit Depot.* San Diego, Calif.: 1997.

Mersky, Peter B. *U.S. Marine Corps Aviation.* Baltimore: Nautical and Aviation Publishing Company of America, 1997.

Messimer, Dwight R. *Escape.* Annapolis, Md.: Naval Institute Press, 1994.

Middlekauff, Robert. *The Glorious Cause: The American Revolution 1763–1789.* New York: Oxford University Press, 1982.

Miller, John Grider. *The Bridge at Dong Ha.* Annapolis, Md.: Naval Institute Press, 1996.

Millett, Allan R. *Semper Fidelis.* New York: Macmillan, 1980.

Montross, Lynn, and Canzona, Nicholas A. *The Chosin Reservoir Campaign.* Nashville, Tenn.: Battery Press, 1987.

Moore, Lt. Gen. Harold G., and Galloway, Joe L. *We Were Soldiers Once . . . and Young.* New York: Harperpernnial, 1990.

Moran, Lord. *Anatomy of Courage.* London: Constable, 1945.

Moskin, J. Robert. *The U.S. Marine Corps Story.* New York: McGraw-Hill, 1977.

Norton, Maj. Bruce H. *Force Recon Diary, 1969.* New York: Ballantine, 1991.

———. *Force Recon Diary, 1970.* New York: Ballantine, 1992.

———. *Grown Gray in War.* Annapolis, Md.: Naval Institute Press, 1997.

———. *One Tough Marine.* New York: Ballantine Books, 1993.

———. *Sergeant Major U. S. Marines.* New York: Ivy Books, 1995.

———. *Stingray.* New York: Ballantine, 2000.

Nye, Roger H. *The Patton Mind.* New York: Putnam, Penguin, 1992.

Potter, E. B. *Nimitz.* Annapolis, Md.: Naval Institute Press, 1988.

Puller, Lewis B., Jr. *Fortunate Son: The Autobiography of Lewis B. Puller, Jr.* New York: Grove Weidenfeld, 1996.

Robertson, James I. *Stonewall Jackson; The Man, The Soldier, The Legend.* New York: Simon & Schuster, 1999.

Ross, Bill D. *Iwo Jima.* New York: Random House, 1986.

Saluzzi, Joseph. *Red Blood . . . Purple Hearts.* Chapel Hill, University of North Carolina Press, 1990.

Schmidt, Hans. *Maverick Marine; Gen. Smedley Butler and the Contradictions of American Military History.* Louisville: University Press of Kentucky, 1998.

Smith, Maj. Gen. Holland M., and Finch, Perry. *Coral and Brass.* New York: Scribers, 1948.

Stevens, Paul Drew, ed. *The Navy Cross: Vietnam Citations of Awards to Men of the United States Marine Corps, 1964–1973.* Forest Ranch, Calif: Sharp & Dunnigan, 1987.

Stockdale, Jim, and Stockdale, Sybil. *In Love and War.* New York: Harper & Row, 1984.

Stubbe, Ray William, and Lanning, M. Lee. *Inside Force Recon.* New York: Ballantine, 1989.

Thomas, Lowell. *Old Gimlet Eye.* New York: Farrar & Rinehart, 1933.

Thompson, James G. *Decorations, Medals, Ribbons, Badges, and Insignia of the United States Marine Corps.* Fountain Inn, S.C.: Medals of America Press, 1998.

Toland, John. *In Mortal Combat: Korea, 1950–1953.* New York: Doubleday, 1980.

Trulock, Alice Rains. *In the Hands of Providence: Joshua L. Chamberlain and the American Civil War.* Chapel Hill: University of North Carolina Press, 1992.

Twinning, Gen. Merrill B. *No Bended Knee: The Battle for Guadalcanal.* Novato, Calif: Presido Press, 1996.

Vandergrift, A. A. *Once a Marine. The Memoirs of General A.A. Vandergrift USMC.* New York: Norton, 1964.

U.S. Department of the Army, Public Info Division. *The Medal of Honor of the United States Army.* Washington, D.C.: Government Printing Office, Washington, D.C.: 1948.

U.S. Department of the Navy, Bureau of Naval Personnel. *Medal of Honor 1861–1949.* Washington, D. C.: Government Printing Office, 1949.

Ward, Geoffrey C. *The Civil War: An Illustrated History.* New York: Knopf, 1990.

Warner, Ezra J. *Generals in Blue.* Baton Rouge: Louisiana State University Press, 1964.

———. *Generals in Gray.* Baton Rouge: Louisiana State University Press, 1966.

www.inexpress.net
www.civilwarhome.com/athens/4795
www.biography.com
www.thehistorynet.com/wildwest
www.members.aol.com/teachernet
www.sunsite.utk.edu/civilwar
www.korea50.army.mil/personnel/def
www.hqmc.usmc.mil
www.ibiblio.org/hyperwar/usmc
www.harrisonheritage.com
www.citadel.edu/archivesandmuseum
www.tons.com/encyclopedia
www.deovindice.org/archives
www.webpages.homestead.com
www.hunley.org/html
www.pownetwork.org/bios

WEBSITES USED IN RESEARCH

www.history.navy.mil/index
www.army.mil/cmh-pg/moh

INDEX BY ERA

✩ ✩ ✩ ✩

COLONIAL WARS (1640–1763)
Church, Benjamin, Citizen-soldier, New England Army 49
Greene, Nathanael, Major General, Continental Army 102
Revere, Paul, Citizen-soldier 209

AMERICAN REVOLUTION (1764–1783)
Allen, Ethan, Citizen-soldier 3
Gates, Horatio, General, Continental Army 96
Hale, Nathan, Captain, Continental Army 105
Hopkins, Esek, Commodore, United States Navy 119
Jones, John Paul, Captain, United States Navy 133
Knox, Henry, General, Continental Army 142
Lee, Henry Lee, III, Colonel, Continental Army 145
Marion, Francis, Colonel, Continental Army 168
Moultrie, William, General, Colonial Regiment 179
Pitcher, Molly 201
Washington, George, General, Continental Army 253
Wayne, Anthony, Brigadier General, Continental Army 257

WAR OF 1812
Black Hawk 21
Brown, Jacob J., General, United States Army 29
Decatur, Stephen, Captain, United States Navy 70
Hull, Isaac, Captain, United States Navy 122
Osceola, Seminole Chief 194
Perry, Oliver Hazard, Admiral, United States Navy 199
Tecumseh, Shawnee Chief 237

CIVIL WAR (1861–1865)
Anderson, Richard Heron, General, Confederate States Army 5
Anderson, Robert, General, Union Army 6

Andrews's Raiders, Union Army 6
Archer, James Jay, General, Confederate States Army 9
Armistead, Lewis A., General, Confederate States Army 9
Barton, Clarissa Clara Harlow, nurse 13
Beauregard, Pierre G. T., General, Confederate States Army 17
Boyd, Belle, Confederate spy 24
Bragg, Braxton, General, Confederate States Army 26
Buckner, Simon Bolivar, General, Confederate States Army 31
Chamberlain, Joshua Lawrence, General, Union Army 41
Cleburne, Patrick R., General, Confederate States Army 49
Custer, George A. General, Union Army 57
Custer, Thomas W., Lieutenant Colonel, Union Army 58
Dixon, George, Lieutenant, Confederate States Army 73
Early, Jubal Anderson, General, Confederate States Army 81
Edmonds, Sarah Emma, spy, Union Army 82
Ewell, Richard Stoddert, General, Confederate States Army 87
Farragut, David Glasgow, Admiral, Union Navy 89
Forrest, Nathan Bedford, General, Confederate States Army 91
Frémont, John Charles, General, Union Army 93
Gordon, John Brown, General, Confederate States Army 98
Grant, Ulysses Simpson, General, Union Army 99
Greenhow, Rose O'Neal, Confederate spy 102
Hampton, Wade, General, Confederate States Army 110
Hancock, Winfield Scott, Major General, Union Army 111
Hardee, William Joseph, General, Confederate States Army 113

Hill, Daniel Harvey, General, Confederate States Army 117

Hooker, Joseph, General, Union Army 118

Jackson, Thomas Jonathan "Stonewall," General, Confederate States Army 127

Johnston, Joseph Eggleston, General, Confederate States Army 131

Lee, Robert E., General, Confederate States Army 147

Longstreet, James, General, Confederate States Army 150

MacArthur, Arthur, Jr., Lieutenant General, United States Army 153

McCausland, John, Brigadier General, Confederate States Army 159

McClellan, George Brinton, General, Union Army 160

Mosby, John Singleton, Colonel, Confederate States Army 178

Pelham, John, Major, Confederate States Army 199

Pettigrew, James Johnston, General, Confederate States Army 201

Pickett, George Edward, General, Confederate States Army 201

Pope, John, General, Union Army 203

Roosevelt, George W., First Sergeant, Union Army 212

Rosecrans, William Starke, General, Union Army 213

Safford, Mary Jane, nurse 215

Sedgwick, John, General, Union Army 216

Shaw, Robert Gould, Colonel, Union Army 217

Sheridan, Philip Henry, General, Union Army 220

Sherman, William Tecumseh, General, Union Army 221

Sickles, Daniel Edgar, General, Union Army 226

Smith, Edmund Kirby, General, Confederate States Army 229

Stuart, James Ewell Brown, General, Confederate States Army 235

Thomas, George Henry, Major General, Union Army 237

Tompkins, Sally Louisa, Captain, Confederate Army 239

Van Lew, Elizabeth, Union spy 246

Walker, Mary E., Surgeon, Union Army 251

Webster, Timothy, Union spy 259

Wheeler, Joseph, General, Confederate States Army 260

MEXICAN WAR (1846–1847)

Kearny, Phillip, General, United States Army 137

INDIAN WARS (1865–1890)

Cochise, Apache Chief 50

Crazy Horse, Chief, Oglala Sioux 54

Crook, George, General, United States Army 55

Gall, Chief, Lakota Sioux 95

Geronimo, Chief, Apache 97

Joseph, Chief, Nez Percé 48

Red Cloud, Chief, Oglala Sioux 208

Sitting Bull, Chief, Hunkpapa Lakota Sioux 228

SPANISH-AMERICAN WAR (1898–1902)

Bearss, Hiram Iddings, General, United States Marine Corps 15

Butler, Smedley Darlington, Major General, United States Marine Corps 34

Dewey, George, Admiral, United States Navy 71

Winans, Roswell, First Sergeant, United States Marine Corps 266

WORLD WAR I (U.S. INVOLVEMENT, 1917–1919)

Allex, Jake, Corporal, United States Army 4

Anderson, Johannes S., First Sergeant, United States Army 5

Bronson, Deming, First Lieutenant, United States Army 29

Burke, Frank, First Lieutenant, United States Army 32

Call, Donald M., Corporal, United States Army 38

Cukela, Louis, Major, United States Marine Corps 55

Daly, Daniel Joseph, Sergeant Major, United States Marine Corps 59

Edwards, Daniel R., Private First Class, United States Army 85

Gaffney, Frank, Private First Class, United States Army 95

Hulbert, Henry Louis, First Lieutenant, United States Marine Corps 121

Izac, Edouard Victor Michel, Lieutenant, United States Navy 126

Luke, Frank, Jr., Second Lieutenant, United States Army Air Corps 152

Maker, Raymond Whitney, Private First Class, United States Army 166

Manning, Sidney E., Corporal, United States Army 167

Miles, L. Wardlaw, Captain, United States Army 172

Pershing, John J., General, United States Army 200

Rickenbacker, Edward V., First Lieutenant, United States Army Air Corps 211

Woodfill, Samuel, First Lieutenant, United States Army 267

York, Alvin Cullum, Sergeant, United States Army 270

BETWEEN WORLD WARS (1919–1940)

Eadie, Thomas, Chief Gunner's Mate, United States Navy 81

Ellis, "Pete" Earl Hancock, Major, United States Marine Corps 85

Lindbergh, Charles, Captain, United States Army Air Corps   148

McGuire, Fred Henry, Hospital Apprentice, United States Navy   162

WORLD WAR II (1941–1946)

Abrams, Creighton W., Jr., General, U.S. Army   1

Anderson, Beaufort T., Technical Sergeant, United States Army   5

Antrim, Richard N., Commander, United States Navy   8

Baker, Thomas A., Sergeant, United States Army   11

Basilone, John, Gunnery Sergeant, United States Marine Corps   14

Beaudoin, Raymond O., First Lieutenant, United States Army   16

Bertoldo, Vito R., Master Sergeant, United States Army   19

Bigelow, Elmer C., Watertender First Class, United States Navy   20

Bolton, Cecil H., First Lieutenant, United States Army   21

Bonnyman, Alexander, Jr., First Lieutenant, United States Marine Corps   23

Boyington, Gregory, Major, United States Marine Corps   24

Bradley, Omar N., General, United States Army   25

Browner, Ralph L., Private First Class, United States Marine Corps   30

Burke, Arleigh, Admiral, United States Navy   32

Bush, George H. W., Lieutenant (Jg), United States Navy   33

Bush, Robert Eugene, Hospital Apprentice, United States Navy   34

Carlson, Evans Fordyce, Brigadier General, United States Marine Corps   39

Carswell, Horace S., Jr., Major, U.S. Army Air Corps   39

Chamberlain, Reid C., Corporal, United States Marine Corps   44

Christian, Herbert F., Private, United States Army   47

Choate, Clyde L., Staff Sergeant, United States Army   48

Clark, Mark W., General, United States Army   49

Connor, James P., Sergeant, United States Army   52

Cromwell, John Philip, Captain, United States Navy   54

Dalessondro, Peter J., Technical Sergeant, United States Army   59

David, Benjamin O., Jr., Lieutenant General, United States Air Force   61

Day, James L., Major General, United States Marine Corps   67

Dealey, Samuel D., Commander, United States Navy   68

Dervishian, Ernest H., Second Lieutenant, United States Army   70

Doolittle, James Harold, General, United States Army Air Corps   75

Doss, Desmond T., Private First Class, United States Army   76

Dunham, Russell E., Technical Sergeant, United States Army   77

Dusenbury, Julian D., Captain, United States Marine Corps   78

Edson, Merritt Austin, General, United States Marine Corps   84

Fisher, Almond E., Second Lieutenant, United States Army   90

Fluckey, Eugene Bennett, Commander, United States Navy   91

Fox, John R., First Lieutenant United States Army   92

Funk, Leonard A., Jr., First Sergeant United States Army   93

Garman, Harold A., Private, United States Army   95

Geiger, Roy S., General, United States Marine Corps   96

Gibson, Eric G., Technical Sergeant, United States Army   97

Gilmore, Howard W., Commander, U. S. Navy   97

Gordon, Nathan Green, Lieutenant, U. S. Navy,   99

Gray, Ross, Sergeant, United States Marine Corps   101

Gregg, Stephen, Second Lieutenant, United States Army   103

Hagerty, Robert Fleming, Lieutenant, U. S. Navy   105

Halsey, William F., Jr., Admiral, U. S. Navy   107

Halyburton, William D., Jr., Pharmacist's Mate Second Class, U. S. Navy   107

Hammerberg, Owen Francis P., Boatswain's Mate Second Class, U. S. Navy   110

Hansen, Dale M., Private, United States Marine Corps   112

Harrell, William G., Sergeant, United States Marine Corps   114

Hawkins, William Deane, First Lieutenant, United States Marine Corps   116

Herring, Rufus G., Lieutenant, United States Navy   117

Jackson, Arthur J., Private First Class, United States Marine Corps   127

Jacobson, Douglas T., Private First Class, United States Marine Corps   129

Kandle, Victor L., First Lieutenant United States Army   137

Kennedy, John F., Lieutenant, United States Navy   139

Lopez, Jose M., Sergeant, United States Army   151

MacArthur, Douglas, General, United States Army   153

McCarter, Lloyd G., Private United States Army   159

McGill, Troy A., Sergeant, United States Army   161

McKinney, John R., Sergeant, United States Army   163

Marquez, Eleuterio J., Pharmacist's Mate Third Class, United States Navy   169

Merrill, Frank Dow, General, United States Army   171

Michael, Edward S., First Lieutenant, United States Army Air Corps   171

Miller, Andrew, Staff Sergeant, United States Army   172

Miller, Doris, Petty Officer Third Class, United States Navy   173

Montgomery, Jack C., First Lieutenant, United States Army   176

Moon, Harold J., Private, United States Army   177

Morgan John C., Second Lieutenant, United States Army Air Corps   177

Moskala, Edward J., Private First Class, United States Army   179

Munro, Douglas Albert, Signalman First Class, United States Coast Guard   179

Murphy, Audie Leon, Second Lieutenant, United States Army   180

Nimitz, Chester William, Admiral, United States Navy   184

O'Callahan, Joseph Timothy, Commander, United States Navy   189

O'Hare, Edward Henry, Lieutenant, United States Navy   190

Ortiz, Peter Julien, Major, United States Marine Corps   191

Paige, Mitchell, Platoon Sergeant, United States Marine Corps   197

Patton, George S., Jr., General, United States Army   197

Peters, George J., Private, United States Army   200

Pollock, Edwin, General, United States Marine Corps   202

Puller, Lewis B., General, United States Marine Corps   203

Pyle, Ernie, journalist   206

Ramage, Lawson P., Commander, United States Navy   207

Reese, John N., Jr., Private First Class, United States Army   209

Ridgway, Mathew B., General, United States Army   211

Roosevelt, Theodore, Jr., Brigadier General, United States Army   212

Shofner, Austin C., Brigadier General, United States Marine Corps   223

Smith, Holland McTyeire, General, United States Marine Corps   230

Smith, Nathan R., Colonel, United States Marine Corps   231

Spruance, Raymond Ames, Admiral, United States Navy   231

Stilwell, Joseph, General, United States Army   232

Street, George Levick, III, Commander, United States Navy   234

Sullivan Brothers, United States Navy   236

Thomas, William H., Private First Class, United States Army   238

Treadwell, Jack L., Captain, United States Army   239

Turner, Day G., Sergeant United States Army   240

Twining, Merrill B., General, United States Marine Corps   240

Urban, Matt, Lieutenant Colonel, United States Army   243

Vandergrift, Alexander Archer, General, United States Marine Corps   245

Wahlen, George Edward, Pharmacist's Mate Second Class, United States Navy   249

Wainwright, Jonathan Mayhew, IV, General, United States Army   249

Watson, Wilson Douglas, Private, United States Marine Corps   256

Wilkin, Edward G., Corporal, United States Army   261

Wilson, Louis Hugh, Jr., General, United States Marine Corps   265

Yeager, Charles E., General, United States Air Force   269

Zussman, Raymond, Second Lieutenant, United States Army   274

KOREAN WAR (1950–1953)

Adams, Stanley T., Master Sergeant, United States Army   3

Barber, William E., Captain, United States Marine Corps   12

Benfold, Edward C., Hospitalman Third Class, United States Navy   19

Brittin, Nelson V., Sergeant First Class, United States Army   29

Burke, Lloyd L., First Lieutenant, United States Army   33

Cafferata, Hector A., Jr., Private, United States Marine Corps   37

Charette, William R., Hospitalman Third Class, United States Navy   45

Charlton, Cornelius H., Sergeant, United States Army   46

Collier, Gilbert G., Sergeant, United States Army   51

Commiskey, Henry Alfred, First Lieutenant, United States Marine Corps   51

Corey, Russell E., Captain, United States Marine Corps   52

Craft, Clarence B., Private First Class, United States Army   53

Davis, George Andrew, Jr., Major, United States Air Force   62

Davis, Raymond G., Major General, United States Marine Corps   62

Dean, William F., Major General, United States Army   69

Dewert, Richard D., Hospitalman Third Class, United States Navy   71

Evans, Andrew J., Major General, United States Air Force   86

Faith, Don C., Jr., Lieutenant Colonel, United States Army   89

Handrich, Melvin O., Master Sergeant, United States Army   112

Hanson, Jack G., Private First Class, United States Army 113

Hernandez, Rodolfo P., Corporal, U.S. Army 117

Houghton, Kenneth J., Major General, United States Marine Corps 120

Ingman, Einar H., Jr., Sergeant, United States Army 125

Jackson, Willis, First Lieutenant, United States Army 128

Johnson, Oscar G., Sergeant, United States Army 131

Keathley, George D., Staff Sergeant United States Army 138

Knight, Noah O., Private First Class, United States Army 142

Kouma, Ernest R., Master Sergeant, United States Army 143

Larsen, David R., Gunner,s Mate Third Class, United States Navy 145

Lee, Hubert L., Master Sergeant, United States Army 146

Lourim, William, Sergeant, United States Marine Corps 151

McLaughlin, Alford L., Private First Class, United States Marine Corps 164

Maffioli, Leonard J., Master Gunnery Sergeant, United States Marine Corps 165

Matthews, Daniel P., Sergeant, United States Marine Corps 170

Millett, Lewis L., Captain, United States Army 173

Miyamura, Hiroshi H., Corporal, United States Army 174

Mize, Ola L., Master Sergeant, United States Army 174

Murphy, Raymond G., Second Lieutenant, United States Marine Corps 180

Murray, Charles P., Jr., First Lieutenant, United States Army 181

Neppel, Ralph G. ,Sergeant, United States Army 183

O'Brien, George H., Jr., Second Lieutenant, United States Marine Corps 189

Thomas, William H., Private First Class, United States Army 238

Tominac, John J., First Lieutenant, United States Army 239

Van Winkle, Archie, Staff Sergeant, United States Marine Corps 247

Watkins, Travis E., Master Sergeant, United States Army 256

Williams, Hershel Woodrow, Corporal, United States Marine Corps 262

Wilson, Benjamin F., First Lieutenant, United States Army 264

Womack, Bryant E., Private First Class, United States Army 266

Young, Robert H., Private First Class, United States Army 272

VIETNAM WAR (1964–1975)

Adams, John T., Corporal, United States Marine Corps 2

Adams, Laurence R., III, Captain, United States Marine Corps 2

Alspaugh, Timothy D., Seaman, United States Navy 4

Ambrose, Gerald D., Lance Corporal, United States Marine Corps 4

Antonio, Joseph J., Sergeant, United States Army 7

Armstrong, Russell P., Staff Sergeant, United States Marine Corps 10

Ashby, James W., Hospitalman Third Class, United States Navy 10

Badnek, Samuel J., Private, United States Marine Corps 11

Barnum, Harvey C., Captain, United States Marine Corps 13

Benavidez, Roy P., Master Sergeant, United States Army 17

Bennett, Steven L., Captain, U.S. Air Force 19

Bird, William C., Private First Class, United States Marine Corps 20

Bolton, Gilbert, Chief Warrant Officer 4, United States Marine Corps 22

Bondsteel, James L., Staff Sergeant, United States Army 23

Brady, Patrick Henry, Major, United States Army 25

Brandtner, Martin L., Lieutenant General, United States Marine Corps 27

Buchanan, Richard W., Corporal, United States Marine Corps 30

Caine, Lawrence B., III, Corporal, United States Marine Corps 38

Capodanno, Vincent R., Lieutenant, United States Navy 38

Casebolt, Henry C., Corporal, United States Marine Corps 40

Castillo, William, Private First Class, United States Marine Corps 40

Cavaiani, Jon R., Staff Sergeant, United States Army 41

Cheatham, Ernest C., Jr., Colonel, United States Marine Corps 46

Christmas, George R., Lieutenant General, United States Marine Corps 47

Coffman, Clovis C., Jr., Lieutenant Colonel, United States Marine Corps 50

Conran, Philip J., Colonel, United States Air Force 52

Crockett, Joseph R., Jr., Sergeant, United States Marine Corps 54

Danner, David J., Sergeant, United States Marine Corps 61

Davis, Stephen Winfield, First Lieutenant, United States Army 63

Day, George Everett, Colonel, United States Air Force 65

De Bona, Andrew D., Captain, United States Marine Corps 69

Deibert, Charles L., Captain, United States Army 70

Dillard, Henry C., Corporal, United States Marine Corps 72

Dix, Drew Dennis, Staff Sergeant, United States Army 72

Donlon, Roger Hugh C., Captain, United States Army 74

Donovan, Joseph P., First Lieutenant, United States Marine Corps 74

Dunn, John, Captain, United States Marine Corps 77

Ebbert, Terry J., First Lieutenant, United States Marine Corps 82

Fox, Wesley L., Captain, United States Marine Corps 92

Hamblen, Donald J., First Sergeant, United States Marine Corps 108

Harrington, Myron Charles, Colonel, United States Marine Corps 114

Howard, Jimmie E., Gunnery Sergeant, United States Marine Corps 120

Ingram, Robert R., Hospitalman Third Class, United States Navy 125

Jacques, Maurice J., Sergeant Major, United States Marine Corps 130

Keaveney, Paul S., Lance Corporal, United States Marine Corps 137

Keys, William M., Lieutenant General, United States Marine Corps 141

Liteky, Charles, Captain, United States Army 149

Livingston, James E., Captain, United States Marine Corps 150

McCaffery, Barry H., Captain, United States Army 156

McCain, John Sidney, III, Lieutenant, United States Navy 156

McGinty, John J., III, Second Lieutenant, United States Marine Corps 162

McKibben, Ray, Sergeant, United States Army 163

McWethy, Edgar Lee, Jr., Specialist Fifth Class, United States Army 164

Marm, Walter J., Jr., First Lieutenant, United States Army 168

Martin, Cecil H., Machinist Mate First Class, United States Navy 169

Martini, Gary W., Private First Class, United States Marine Corps 169

Maxam, Larry Leonard, Corporal, United States Marine Corps 170

Modrzejewski, Robert J., Colonel, United States Marine Corps 175

Morris, Charles B., Staff Sergeant, United States Army 177

Newlin, Melvin Earl, Private First Class, United States Marine Corps 183

Norris, Gleason, Gunnery Sergeant, United States Marine Corps 185

Norton, John J., Captain, United States Marine Corps 186

Novosel, Michael J., CWO, United States Army 187

O'Malley, Robert E., Sergeant, United States Marine Corps 191

Ouellet, David George, Seaman, United States Navy 195

Rascon, Alfred V., Specialist Fourth Class, United States Army 207

Richards, Thomas A., Corporal, United States Marine Corps 210

Schwartzkopf, H. Norman, General, United States Army 215

Sexton, Charles T., Corporal, United States Marine Corps 217

Shields, Marvin G., Construction Mechanic 3rd Class, United States Navy 223

Sijan, Lance Peter, Lieutenant, United States Air Force 227

Smith, Chester B., Captain, United States Navy 229

Stockdale, James Bond, Vice Admiral, United States Navy 232

Thompson, Robert H., Colonel, United States Marine Corps 238

Vargas, Jay, Major, United States Marine Corps 247

Walt, Lewis W., Lieutenant General, United States Marine Corps 251

Watters, Charles Joseph, Major, United States Army 256

Webb, James H., Jr., Captain, United States Marine Corps 258

Wetzel, Gary George, Specialist Fourth Class, United States Army 260

Williams, Charles Q., First Lieutenant, United States Army 262

Williams, James E., Boatswain's Mate First Class, United States Navy 263

Wright, Raymond R., Specialist Fourth Class, United States Army 267

Yabes, Maximo, First Sergeant, United States Army 269

Yntema, Gordon Douglas, Sergeant, United States Army 270

Young, Gerald O., Captain, United States Air Force 272

Zabitosky, Fred William, Sergeant First Class, United States Army 273

Post-Vietnam 1975–2002

Gordon, Gary I., Master Sergeant, United States Army 98

Shughart, Randall D., Sergeant First Class, United States Army 226.

INDEX

★ ★ ★ ★

Note: Page numbers in *italics* refer to illustrations. **Boldface** page numbers indicate extensive treatment of a topic.

A

Abenaki people 49
Abrams, Creighton Williams, Jr. **1**, 157
Abshire, Bobby W. **2**
Acadia, invasion of 49
Adams, John T. **2**
Adams, Laurence R., III **2–3**
Adams, Samuel 209, 210
Adams, Stanley T. *3*, **3**
Admiralty Islands, battle for 154
Aisne-Marne, engagement of 60, 167, 230
Albert, Raymond 140
Alfred (U.S. frigate) 133
Algerian War (1815) 70
Allen, Ethan **3–4**, 142
ALLEN BROOK (Operation) 30
Allex, Jake **4**
Alligator (Seminole chief) 195
Alspaugh, Timothy D. **4**
Amagiri (Japanese destroyer) 140
Ambrose, Gerald D. **4–5**
America (U.S. ship) 134
American Expeditionary Forces (AEF) 200
American Red Cross, founding of 14
Anderson, Beaufort T. **5**
Anderson, Johannes S. **5**
Anderson, Richard Heron **5–6**, 213
Anderson, Robert **6**, 222
André, John 102
Andrew, John A. 219
Andrews, George 192
Andrews, James J. 7
Andrews's Raiders **6–7**
Angaur, attack on 107
"Angel of Cairo" 215
Antietam, battle of 6, 9, 14, 99, 111, 118, 128, 151, 161, 199, 217, 218, 219, 235
Antonio, Joseph J. **7–8**, *8*
Antrim, Richard Not **8–9**

Apache 50, 55, 97
Appomattox surrender 99, 101, 148, 151, 160, 201, 221, 222
Arcelin, Joseph 192
Archer, James Jay **9**
Ardennes counteroffensive 198
Ariel (U.S. ship) 134
Arizona (U.S. ship) 32
Arkansas Post, attack on 222
Armistead, Lewis Addison **9**, 201
Armstrong, John W. 227
Armstrong, Russell P. **10**
Army of Central Kentucky 50
Army of the Cumberland 55, 118, 119, 214, 221, 237, 238
Army of the Mississippi 26, 31, 50, 113, 114, 203, 214, 220, 222, 261
Army of Northeastern Virginia 222
Army of Northern Virginia 6, 9, 41, 81, 87, 99, 118, 127, 148, 150, 199, 203
Army of the Ohio 220, 237
Army of Pensacola 26
Army of the Potomac 17, 41, 81, 87, 101, 111, 118, 132, 150, 160, 203, 214, 216, 217, 221, 227, 229, 237
Army of the Shenandoah 17, 127, 131, 132, 229
Army of Southwest Missouri 203, 220
Army of Tennessee 7, 26, 27, 31, 50, 100, 113, 114, 118, 119, 121, 132, 150, 201, 222, 230, 237, 238, 261
Army of Virginia 118, 203
Army of West Virginia 55
Arnold, Benedict 4, 135, 254
Ashby, James W. **10**
Ashby, Turner 128
Atkinson, Henry 21
Atlanta Campaign 50, 58, 114, 119, 121, 222, 238, 261
Augusta (U.S. ship) 184, 204

B

Bad Axe River, battle of 21
Badnek, Samuel J. **11**
Baker, Thomas A. **11–12**
Baltimore (U.S. ship) 184
Bangs, George 260
Banks, Nathaniel P. 230
Barb (U.S. ship) 91
Barbary Wars 122
Barber, William E. *12*, **12–13**
Barlow, Francis C. 99
Barnum, Harvey C., Jr. *13*, **13**
Barron, James 70
Barton, Clarissa "Clara" Harlow **13–14**
Barton, Raymond O. 213
Basilone (U.S. destroyer) 15
Basilone, John *14*, **14–15**
Bataan, American stand on 250
BAXTER GARDEN (Operation) 186
Bearss, Hiram Iddings **15–16**
Beaudoin, Raymond O. **16–17**
Beaufort, battle of 179
Beauregard, Pierre Gustave Toutant **17**, 103, 118, 128, 132
Beaver Dam Creek, battle of 9, 148
Becker, Arnold 74
Bee, Barnard 128
Beito Island, attack on 116
Belkirk, earl of 133
Belleau Wood, Château-Thierry Sector 60, 122
Belmont, battle of 215
Benavidez, Roy P. **17–19**, *18*
Benfold, Edward C. **19**
Bennet, Queenie 73
Bennett, Steven L. **19**
Bensinger, William 6
Benton, Thomas Hart 93
Bentonville, battle of 114
Bertoldo, Vito R. **19–20**
Bickerdyke, Mary Ann 215
Big Bethel, battle of 118
Big Black River Bridge, battle of 101

Bigelow, Elmer Charles **20**
Bird, William C. **20–21**
Blackburn's Ford 151
Black Hawk (Sauk and Fox war chief) **21**
Black Hawk War (1832) 6
Black Hills Expedition 57
Black Kettle (Cheyenne chief) 57
Black Mingo, battle of 168
black regiments, in Civil War 219–220
Black Sheep Squadron 224
Blanc Mont, battle of 122
Bleeding Kansas 235
Blue Savannah, battle of 168
Bodnar, John 192, 193, 194
Bolívar, Simón 122
Bolton, Cecil H. **21–22**
Bolton, Gilbert **22–23**, 23
Bonaparte, Charles J. 133
Bondsteel, James Leroy **23**
Bonhomme Richard (ship) 133, 134
Bonnyman, Alexander, Jr. **23–24**
Bonus Army, rout of 154
Boston, siege of 102, 106
Boston Massacre 209
Boston Tea Party 210
Boxer Rebellion 34
Boyd, Belle 24
Boyington, Gregory **24–25**, 224
Bozeman Trail 54, 208
Braddock, Edward 253
Bradley, Omar Nelson **25**, 198, 212
Brady, Patrick Henry **25–26**
Bragg, Braxton **26–27**, 31, 91, 113, 114, 117, 132, 151, 230, 261
Bragg, Thomas 27
Brandtner, Martin L. **27–28**
Brandy Station, battle of 235
Brandywine, battle of 102, 142, 254, 257
Brice's Crossroads, battle of 91, 259
Bristoe Campaign 148

Brittin, Nelson V. 29
Bronson, Deming 29
Brook Farm 218
Brown, Jacob Jennings 29–30
Brown, John 235
Browner, Ralph L. 30
Brunner, Fred 192, 193
Buchanan, James 93
Buchanan, Richard W. 30
Buckner, Simon Bolivar 27, 31
Buell, Don Carlos 6, 17
Buffalo Bill (William F. Cody) 229
Buffum, Robert 6
Bull Run (Manassas)
    first battle of 81, 99, 103,
        118, 121, 128, 132, 151,
        160, 199, 201, 212, 230,
        235
    second battle of 6, 9, 81, 87,
        118, 119, 128, 138, 148,
        151, 161, 199, 203, 235
Bunker Hill, battle of 106
Burgoyne, George 96
Burke, Arleigh 32
Burke, Frank (Francis X.) 32–33
Burke, Lloyd L. 33
Burnside, Ambrose 83, 119, 161,
    222
Bush, George H. W. 33–34
Bush, Robert Eugene 34
Butler, Benjamin F. 17, 247
Butler, Smedley Darlington
    34–36, 35, 59
Butterfield, Daniel 227

C

C. Turner Joy (U.S. ship) 232–233
Cabanatuan (Camp of Death)
    225, 226
Cafferata, Hector Albert, Jr. 37,
    37
Caine, Lawrence B., III 38
Calhoun, James 57
Calhoun, John C. 103
Call, Donald M. 38
Camden, battle of 102
Camp of Death (Cabanatuan)
    225, 226
Camp Pendleton (California)
    108, 109, 110, 205, 231, 241,
    252
Cape Gloucester (New Britain
    Island) 204, 205, 252
Capodanno, Vincent R. 38–39
Carlson, C. F. 74
Carlson, Evans Fordyce 39
Carolinas Campaign 121
Carswell, Horace S., Jr. 39–40
Carter, Jimmy 251
Casebolt, Henry C. 40
Castillo, William 40
Cavaiani, Jon R. 41
Cedar Creek, battle of 55, 82, 99,
    221
Cedar Mountain, battle of 9, 81,
    87, 128, 203, 218
Central Army of Kentucky 31,
    113
Centron (France) 193, 194

Cerro Gordo, battle of 131
Chamberlain, Joshua Lawrence
    41, 41–44
Chamberlain, Reid C. 44–45
Chamberlain, Tom 42
Chambersburg (Pennsylvania),
    destruction of 160
Champion's Hill 101
Chancellorsville, battle of 6, 9,
    99, 111, 121, 128, 148, 217,
    227, 235
Chantilly, battle of 139
Chaplain's Medal for Heroism 45
Chapultepec, battle of 9, 17, 100,
    131, 147
Charette, William R. 45–46, 46
Charleston, defense of 17
Charlton, Cornelius H. 46
Château-Thierry, engagements of
    60, 122
Chattanooga, siege of 26, 58, 101,
    114, 132, 221, 222, 238, 261
Cheatham, Ernest C., Jr. 46–47
Cheat Mountain Campaign 147
Cherokee 179
Chesapeake affair (1807) 70
Chiang Kai-shek 232
Chicago (U.S. ship) 184
Chickamauga, battle of 26, 31,
    50, 55, 58, 91, 214, 221, 238
Chickasaw Bluffs, battle of 222
Chief Joseph (Nez Percé chief) 48
China, operations in 39, 232,
    240, 245
Choate, Clyde L. 48–49
Chosin Reservoir Campaign 165,
    204
Christian, Herbert F. 47
Christmas, George R. 47, 47–48
Church, Benjamin 49
Churchill, Sir Winston 49
Churubusco, battle of 17, 137
City of Memphis (transport ship)
    215
Clarence K. Bronson (U.S. ship)
    33
Cleburne, Patrick Ronayne
    49–50
Cleveland (U.S. ship) 60
Clinch, Duncan Lamon 195
Clinton, Sir Henry 254
Cochise (Chiracahua Apache
    chief) 50, 55
Code of Conduct, for prisoners of
    war 233
Cody, William F. (Buffalo Bill) 229
Coffman, Clovis C., Jr. 50–51
Cohen, William S. 61
Cold Harbor, battle of 6, 81, 99,
    101, 160
Collier, Gilbert G. 51
Collins, Frank 74
Columbia (South Carolina), burn-
    ing of 222
Commiskey, Henry Alfred 51–52
Concord, battle of 106
Condor (blockade runner) 103
Confederate Army of Tennessee.
    See Army of Tennessee

Confederate States Army (CSA)
    26, 31, 74, 81, 87, 99, 113,
    118, 127, 131, 147, 150, 235
Connecticut (U.S. ship) 36
Connor, James P. 52
Conran, Philip J. 52
Constellation (U.S. aircraft carrier)
    232, 233
Constitution (U.S. ship) 122, 210
Continental Congress 119, 146,
    254
Conway Cabal 96, 254
Cook, George 54
Cooke, John Rogers 235
Cooke, Philip St. George 235
Coolidge, John 192, 193
Cooper, Samuel 132
Coral Sea, battle of 184
Corey, Russell E. 52–53
Corinth, battle of 214, 222, 261
Cornwallis, Charles 102, 254
Corregidor (Philippine Islands)
    159, 225, 250–251
Cothran, John 73
Countess of Scarborough (British
    ship of war) 133, 134
Craft, Clarence B. 53
Crane, Stephen 180
Crazy Horse (Sioux war chief)
    54, 55, 95, 209, 228
Crescent City (U.S. ship) 116
Crimean War 134, 160
Crockett, Joseph R., Jr. 54
Cromwell, John Philip 54–55
Crook, George 55, 97, 178
Cross Keys, battle of 128
CSA. See Confederate States Army
Cukela, Louis 55–57, 56
Cumberland, Army of 55, 118,
    119, 214, 221, 237, 238
Cushing's battery 9
Custer, Boston 57, 58
Custer, George Armstrong 54, 57,
    95, 178, 229
Custer, Thomas Ward 57, 58

D

Dade, Francis 195
Dalessondro, Peter J. 59
Daly, Daniel "Dan" Joseph 59–60
Danner, David J. 61
Darien, battle of 219, 220
Davao Penal Colony 225
Davis, Benjamin, Sr. 61
Davis, Benjamin O., Jr. 61–62
Davis, Elnora, Sr. 61
Davis, Franklin M., Jr. 63, 65
Davis, George Andrew, Jr. 62, 62
Davis, Jefferson 31, 103, 117,
    132, 247
    and Beauregard 17
    and Bragg 27
    and Cleburne 50
    and Hill 118
    and Johnston 132
    and Lee 147, 148
    and Smith 230
    and Tompkins 239
Davis, Nathaniel A. 64

Davis, Raymond G. 62–63, 63
Davis, Stephen Winfield 63–65
Dawes, William 209, 210
Day, George "Bud" Everett 65–67,
    158
Day, George E., Jr. 66
Day, James L. 67–68, 68
Day, Sandra M. 66
Day, Sonja M. 66
Day, Steven 66
D-Day 24, 192, 212, 213, 252
Dealey, Samuel David 68–69
Dean, Wiliam F. 69
De Bona, Andrew D. 69, 186
Decatur (U.S. ship) 184
Decatur, Stephen 70
Deibert, Charles L. 70
Delaney, John 33
Delaware River, crossing of 142,
    254
Denver (U.S. ship) 84, 184
De Priest, Oscar 6
Dervishian, Ernest H. 70–71
Desert Shield 216
Desert Storm 1, 141, 216
Dewert, Richard David 71
Dewey, George 71–72
Diachenko (U.S. ship) 130
Dillard, Henry C. 72
Dinwiddie, Robert 253
Dinwiddie Courthouse, battle of
    55
Dix, Drew Dennis 72–73
Dixon, George E. 73–74
Dominican Republic, operations
    in 230, 266
Donlon, Roger Hugh C. 74
Donovan, Joseph P. 74–75
Doolittle, James Harold "Jimmy"
    75–76
Doss, Desmond T. 76–77
Doubleday, Abner 213
Douglass, Frederick 219
Drake (British warship) 133
Drysdale, Douglas B. 165
Dunham, Russell E. 77
Dunn, John F. 77–78
Durham Station, surrender at 222
Dusenbury, Julian D. 78–79

E

Eadie, Thomas 81
Early, Jubal Anderson 81–82, 221
Eastern New Guinea Campaign
    204
Eaton, William 122
Ebbert, Terry J. 82
Edmonds, Sarah Emma 82–84
Edson, Merritt Austin "Red Mike"
    84–85, 202
Edwards, Daniel R. 85
Eisenhower, Dwight D. 25, 32, 49,
    154, 155, 198, 212, 241–242
Ellis, "Pete" Earl Hancock 85–86
Eltham's Landing, battle of 9
Emancipation Proclamation 219
Emerson, Ralph Waldo 218
Empress Augusta Bay
    (Bougainville) 245–246

Enterprise (U.S. aircraft carrier) 107
Erie Maru (Japanese freighter) 225
Erskine, Graves B. 109
Essex (frigate) 90
Estaing, Jean-Baptiste-Charles-Henri-Hector, comte d' 254
Eutaw Springs, battle of 168
Evans, Andrew J. 86–87
Evans, Arthur Reginald 140
Ewell, Richard Stoddert 87, 128
Ewing, Thomas 221

F

Faith, Don D., Jr. 89
Fallen Timbers, battle of 257
Falling Rock, battle of 160
Farmington, battle of 55
Farragut, David Glasgow 89–90
Fertig, Wendell W. 44
Fetterman Fight 54
54th Massachusetts 219–220
Finback (U.S. lifeguard submarine) 33
First Bull Run (Manassas), battle of 81, 87, 99, 103, 118, 121, 128, 132, 151, 160, 199, 201, 212, 230, 235
First Winchester, battle of 128
Fisher, Almond E. 90–91
Fisher's Hill, battle of 55, 82, 99, 221
Fitzpatrick, John C. 255
Five Forks, battle of 55, 160, 221
Fletcher (U.S. ship) 20
Floyd, John B. 31, 147
Fluckey, Eugene Bennett 91
Flying Tigers (China) 224
Foch, Ferdinand 271
Foch, Marshal 122
Fonda, Henry 212, 213
Forbes, John 254
Forrest, Nathan Bedford 91, 223, 261
Fort Delaware 261
Fort Dipitie 35
Fort Donelson 31, 100, 215
Fort Erie 30
Fort Fisher 27
Fort Kearney 208
Fort Laramie Treaty 54
Fort Le Boeuf 253
Fort McKinley 199, 200
Fort Motte 168
Fort Necessity 253
Fort Pillow, battle of 91
Fort Rivière 35
Fort Sumter 5, 6, 201, 219, 222, 246
Fort Ticonderoga 142, 254
Fort Wagner, battle of 217, 220
Fort Watson 168
Foster, Wynn 233
Fox, George L. 45
Fox, John R. 92
Fox, Wesley L. 92, 92–93
Franco-Prussian War 221
Franklin (U.S. ship) 189, 190

Franklin, battle of 50
Franklin, William B. 138
Frayer's Farm, battle of 9
Fredericksburg, battle of 9, 119, 128, 151, 199, 217, 218, 227, 235
Frémont, John Charles 93, 128
French and Indian War 4, 253–254
Front Royal, battle of 128, 218
Fuller, Margaret 218
Fuller, William 7
Funk, Leonard A., Jr. 93–94, *94*

G

Gaffney, Frank 95
Gage, Thomas 210
Gaines' Mill, battle of 9, 148
Gall (Lakota Sioux warrior) 95, 228
Garman, Harold A. 95–96
Garnett, Richard B. 128, 201
Gates, Horatio 96, 102, 254
Gavutu, battle of 245
Geiger, Roy S. 96
The General (Confederate train) 7
Genêt, Edmond 255
George III (king of Britain) 106
Georgetown, battle of 168
Germantown, battle of 102, 142, 254, 257
Geronimo (Apache leader) 55, 97
Gettysburg, battle of 6, 9, 41–42, 43, 87, 99, 119, 148, 201, 212, 217, 227, 235
    significance of 43–44
Gibson, Eric G. 97
Gilbert Islands, assault on 231
Gillmore, Quincy A. 219
Gilmore, Howard Walter 97–98
Glasgow (British ship) 119
Glendale, battle of 148
Glowin, Joseph A. 266
Goode, Rabbi Alexander D. 45
Gordon, Gary I. 98
Gordon, John Brown 98–99
Graffenstein, Gene 109
Granger, Gordon 221
Grant, Ulysses Simpson 99–101, *100*, 160, 237, 238
    vs. Beauregard 17
    vs. Bragg 26
    and Buckner 31
    and Chamberlain 43
    vs. Hancock 111
    and Longstreet 151
    and Mosby 179
    and Rosecrans 214
    and Sheridan 221
    and Sherman 222
Grasse, François-Joseph-Paul de, 135
Grattan massacre 54
Gray, Ross Franklin 101–102
Great Savannah, battle of 168
Greene, Nathanael 102, 168, 254
Greenhow, Rose O'Neal 102–103
Green Mountain Boys 4
Greenville, Treaty of 258

Gregg, Stephen R. 103
Grenada Operation 216
Gridley, Charles V. 72
Gripsholm (U.S. ship) 44
Gritz, James "Bo" 228
Groveton, battle of 87
Growler (U.S. ship) 98
Guadalcanal 14–15, 39, 69, 96, 116, 179, 202, 204, 205, 241, 245, 252, 265
Guam, invasion of 67, 185, 231, 265, 266
Guantanamo Bay 231
Guerrière (British frigate) 70, 122, 123
Guilford Courthouse, battle of 102

H

Haferkamp, Johann 109
Hagerty, Robert Fleming *105,* 105
Haiti, operations in 35, 204, 245
Hale, Nathan 105–107
Hale, Samuel 106
Halfway Swamp, battle of 168
Hall, Mark Clark 49
Halleck, Henry W. 100, 203, 222, 238
Halsey, William F. "Bull," Jr. 107
Halyburton, William David, Jr. 107–108
Hamblen, Donald J. "Woody" 108–110
Hamilton, Alexander 255
Hammerberg, Owen Francis Patrick 110
Hampton, Wade 110–111, 222
Hancock, John 133, 209
Hancock, Winfield Scott 111
Handrich, Melvin O. *112,* 112
Hansen, Dale Merlin 112–113
Hanson, Jack G. 113
Hardee, William Joseph 27, 50, 113–114
Harder (U.S. ship) 68
Hardinge, Samuel 24
Harper's Ferry raid 9, 119, 127, 128, 132, 147, 148, 161, 235
Harrell, William George 114
Harrington, Myron Charles 114–116, *115*
Harris, Charles A. 140
Harrison, William Henry 199–200, 237
Hasley, William 154
HASTINGS (Operation) 175
Hawkins, William Deane 116–117
Hawthorne, Nathaniel 218
Hayes, Rutherford B. 213, 214
Hayes, Webb C. 213
Hazel Dell (U.S. ship) 215
Heitzelman, Samuel P. 138
Hernandez, Joseph 195
Hernandez. Rodolfo P. 117
Hill, A. P. 151
Hill, Daniel Harvey 117–118, 213
H. L. Hunley (Confederate ship) 73–74

Hokkaido, attack on 107
Honshu, attack on 107
Hood, John B. 132, 222
Hooker, Joseph 118–119, 148, 217, 227
Hoover, Herbert 154
Hopkins, Esek 119
Hornet (U.S. aircraft carrier) 76, 107
Houghton, Kenneth J. 120
Housatonic (Union ship) 73
Howard, Jimmie E. 120–121, *121*
Howard, O. O. 50, 111, 119, 121
Howard University 121
Howe, Sir William 254
HUE CITY (Operation) 46, 47, 238
Hue City, battle for 115
Huerta, Adolfo de la 35
Hulbert, Henry Louis 121–122
Hull, Isaac 122–123
Hull, William 106
Hunley (Confederate ship) 73–74
Hutchinson, Thomas 210

I

I-26 (Japanese submarine) 236
Ichiki, Kiyano 202
Illinois Volunteers 6
Inchon, assault landing at 204, 205
Indianapolis (U.S. ship) 173
Ingman, Einar H., Jr. 125
Ingram, Robert R. 125–126
International Committee of the Red Cross 14
Into the Mouth of the Cat (McConnell) 228
Iuka, battle of 214
Iwo Jima 14, 45, 101, 109, 114, 129, 185, 231, 249, 256, 263
Izac, Edouard Victor Michel 126

J

Jackson, Andrew 21, 30
Jackson, Arthur J. 127
Jackson, Donald 255
Jackson, Thomas Jonathan ("Stonewall") 24, 50, 87, 93, 119, 127–128, *128*, 132, 147, 203, 235
Jackson, Willis 128–129
Jacobson, Douglas T. *129,* 129–130
Jacques, Maurice J. *130,* 130–131
Japan, U.S. occupation of 155, 211
Jay's Treaty (1794) 255, 258
Jefferson, Thomas 134, 255
Jeffords, Thomas 50
Jenkins, A. G. 159
Jessup, Thomas S. 195
Johnson, Albert Sidney 132, 159
Johnson, Andrew 43, 101, 110, 121, 251
Johnson, Lyndon B. 155, 233, 252
Johnson, Oscar G. 131
Johnston, Albert Sidney 17
Johnston, Joseph Eggleston 17, 26, 27, 101, 114, 118, 127, 131–133, 147–148, 222, 230

Johnston, William 140
Jones, John Paul 133–135
Jumonville, Joseph Coulon de Villiers de 253
Jumper (Seminole chief) 195
Juneau (U.S. ship) 236

K

Kandle, Victor L. 137
KANSAS (Operation) 130
Kawajalein, assaults on 230
Kearny, Philip 137–138
Kearny, Stephen Watts 137
Keathley, George D. 138
Keaveney, Paul S. 138–139, 139
Kelly's Ford, battle of 199
Kemper, James L. 201
Kennedy, John F. 139–141
Kentucky, Central, Army of 31, 50, 113
Keokuk (Sauk chief) 21
Kettle Hill, battle of 200, 213
Key, Philip Barton 227
Keys, William M. 141–142
King, Ernest J. 185
King Philip's War 49
King William's War 49
Kirk, Alan 139
Kirksey, Andrew Jackson 140
Knight, Noah O. 142
Knight, William 6
Know, Henry 254
Knowlton, Thomas 106
Knox, Henry 142–143
Knoxville, siege of 31, 101, 151
Kouma, Ernest R. 143
Ku Klux Klan 91

L

Lafayette, marquis de 254
Laos, Americans lost in 228
Larsen, David R. 145
La Salle, Robert 192
Lawrence (U.S. ship) 199
Lebanon Operation (1958) 231
Lee, Charles 254
Lee, Henry Lee, III 145–146, 147, 168
Lee, Hubert L. 146, 146
Lee, Matilda 145, 146
Lee, Robert Edward 41, 87, 147, 147–148, 235, 237
    and Anderson 6
    and Early 82
    and Gordon 98, 99
    vs. Hooker 119
    and Jackson 127, 128
    and Longstreet 151
    vs. McClellan 161
    and Pelham 199
    and Pickett 201
    and Pope 203
    and Sedgwick 217
Lejeune, John A. 59, 86
Letcher, John 147
Lewis, C. 260
Lexington, battle of 106
Leyte Gulf, battle of 107, 154–155, 185, 191

Libby Prison 246
Lincoln, Abraham 14, 93, 178, 203, 219, 259
    and Hooker 118, 119
    and McClellan 160, 161, 203
Lindbergh, Charles 148, 215
Liscome Bay (U.S. ship) 173
Liteky, Charles 149
Little Big Horn, battle of 54, 58, 95, 229
Livingston, James E. 150, 150
Long Beach (U.S. ship) 141
The Longest Day (Ryan) 213
Longfellow, Henry Wadsworth 209
Long Island, battle of 102, 106
Long Room Club 210
Longstreet, James A. 6, 7, 9, 27, 41, 82, 128, 150–151, 151, 201, 213, 214, 227
Lookout Mountain, battle of 119
Lopez, Jose M. 151
Loring, William 128, 147
Louisiana Militia 25
Louisiana Purchase Exposition 97
Lourim, William 151–152
Luke, Frank, Jr. 152
Luzon (Philippine Islands) 199

M

MacArthur, Arthur, Jr. 153, 155
MacArthur, Douglas 44, 107, 153–155, 211, 224, 231
    and Wainwright 250, 251
McCaffrey, Barry H. 156
McCain, John Sidney, Jr. 157
McCain, John Sidney, III 156–158
McCain, William Alexander 157
McCarter, Lloyd G. 159
McCauly, Mary Hays. See Pitcher, Molly
McCausland, John 159–160
McCiernand, John A. 222
McClaws, Lafayette 213
McClellan, George Brinton 83, 100, 118, 128, 132, 148, 160–161, 203, 214, 259
McConnell, Malcolm 228
McCulloch, Ben 229
McDonald, Wesley L. 233
McDowell, Irvin 132
McGill, Troy A. 161–162
McGinty, John J., III 162
McGuire, Fred Henry 162–163
McKean, William B. 241
McKibben, Ray 163
McKinley, William 214
McKinney, John R. 163–164
McLaughlin, Alford L. 164
McMahon, Patrick Henry 140
McNamara, Robert 258
McWethy, Edgar Lee, Jr. 164–165
Macedonia (British ship of war) 70
Machias (U.S. ship) 60
Macomb, Alexander 137
Maddox (U.S. ship) 232, 233

Maffioli, Leonard J. 165–166
Magruder, John B. 132
Maguire, John E. 140
Maine Volunteer Infantry Regiment 41–42, 43
Maker, Raymond Whitney 166–167, 167
Malvern Hill, battle of 81, 119, 148, 161
Manassas, battles of. See Bull Run
Manila Bay, battle of 72
Manning, Sidney E. 167–168
Marietta (U.S. ship) 60
Marion, Francis 168–169
Marion Rifles 214
Marm, Walter Joseph, Jr. 168–169
Marney, Harold W. 140
Marquez, Eleuterio Joe 169
Marshall, George C. 49
Marshall Islands, assault on 231
Martin, Cecil H. 169
Martini, Gary W. 169–170
Marye's Heights, battle of 111
Matteson, Joel 215
Matthews, Daniel P. 170
Matthews, Stanley 214
Mauer, Edgar 140
Maumee (U.S. ship) 184
Maxam, Larry Leonard 170–171
Maximilian (emperor of Mexico) 221
Meade, George G. 41, 101, 151, 221, 227
Merrill, Frank Dow 171
Metacom (Wampanoag chief) 49
Meuse-Argonne Offensive 60, 122, 167, 198, 230, 243, 244, 249, 250, 270
Mexican civil war 35
Mexican War 5, 6, 9, 99, 113, 117, 131, 137, 160, 203, 221, 229, 237
Micanopy (Seminole chief) 195
Michael, Edward S. 171–172
Midway, battle of 231
Mikasa (Japanese ship of war) 185
Miles, L. Wardlaw 172
Miles, Nelson A. 54, 55, 95, 97
Miller (U.S. ship) 173
Miller, Andrew 172–173
Miller, Doris 173
Millett, Lewis L. 173, 173–174
Mill Run Campaign 148
Missionary Ridge, battle of 153, 221, 222, 238
MISSISSIPPI (Operation) 78
Mississippi (U.S. ship) 60, 72
Mississippi, Army of 26, 31, 50, 113, 114, 203, 214, 220, 222, 261
Missouri (U.S. ship) 107, 155, 157, 185, 251
Missouri, Southwest, Army of 203, 220
Mitchell, William ("Billy") 211
Mitsuru (Japanese commander)

78
Miyamura, Hiroshi H. 174, 174
Mize, Ola L. 174–175, 175
Modrzejewski, Robert J. 175–176, 176
Molino del Rey, battle of 6, 100
Monmouth Court House, battle of 102, 142, 201–202, 254, 257
Monocacy, battle of 99
Montgomery, Bernard Law 25
Montgomery, Jack C. 176
Montgomery, James 219
Moon, Harold, Jr. 177
Morgan, John C. 177
Morill, Walter G. 42
Mormon Expedition 216
Morris, Charles B. 177–178
Morristown, battle of 102
Mosby, John Singleton 178–179
Moskala, Edward J. 179
Moultrie, William 179
Moultrie Creek Treaty 194
Mount Vernon 253, 254, 255
Munro, Douglas Albert 179–180
Murfreesboro, battle of 221, 261
Murphy, Audie Leon 180
Murphy, Raymond G. 180–181
Murray, Charles P., Jr. 181, 181–182
Murray, John, fourth earl of Dunmore 119

N

Napoleon Bonaparte 137
Narragansett 49
Narragansett (Union sloop) 72
Narwhal (U.S. ship) 184
Neppel, Ralph G. 183
Nevada Cities, battle of 130
Newark (U.S. ship) 60
New Berne, battle of 201
New England Rangers 106
New Guinea Campaign 154
Newlin, Melvin Earl 183–184
Newton, John 213
New York City, defense of 102, 106
Neyland, Bob 223–224
Nez Percé 48
Niagara (U.S. ship) 199
Niagara, battle of 30
Nicaragua, operations in 35, 202, 204, 245
Nickerson, Herman, Jr. 108–110
Nimitz, Chester William 184–185, 231
Nixon, Richard M. 62, 253
Normandy Invasion 25, 212, 213, 243
Norris, Gleason 185–186
North Africa, Allied invasion of 49, 76, 198
North Atlantic Treaty Organization (NATO) 25, 258
North End Caucus 210
Northern Virginia Campaign 218
Norton, John J. 186–187
Novosel, Michael J. 187, 187

O

Oates, William C. 42
O'Brien, George H., Jr. **189**
O'Callahan, Joseph Timothy **189–190**
O'Connor, Pat 42
Oglala Sioux tribe 54
O'Hare, Edward Henry **190**
Ohio (U.S. ship) 60, 184
Ohio, Army of 220, 237
O'Kane, Richard Hetherington *190*, **190–191**
Okinawa, operations on 34, 53, 67, 68, 76, 78–79, 96, 105, 107, 108, 112, 179, 185, 226, 231, 232
Oklahoma (U.S. ship) 224
Olustee (Ocean Pond), battle of 220
O'Malley, Robert E. *191*, **191**
Operation ALLEN BROOK 30
Operation BAXTER GARDEN 186
Operation Desert Shield 216
Operation Desert Storm 1, 141, 216
Operation HASTINGS 175
Operation HUE CITY 46, 47, 238
Operation KANSAS 130
Operation Lumberjack 25
Operation MISSISSIPPI 78
Operation PRAIRE II 141
Operation PRAIRE IV 72
Operation STARLITE 11
Operation Torch 76
Operation UNION 38, 78, 170, 192
Operation UNION II 120, 192, 193
Operation WATCHTOWER 202
Oriskany (U.S. ship) 232, 233
Ortiz, Peter Julien **191–194**
Osceola (Seminole leader) **194–195**
Otis, James 210
Ouellet, David George Seman **195**
Overland Campaign 101, 111, 221
Overly, Norris 158

P

Pacific Fleet Amphibious Force 230
Paco Railroad Station, attack on 209
Paige, Mitchell **197**
Paimer, John M. 31
Pampang (U.S. ship) 163
Panay (U.S. ship) 184
Panther (U.S. ship) 60
Paoli Massacre 257
Parche (U.S. ship) 207
Paris, liberation of 25
Parrott, Jacob 6
Pathet Lao 228
Pathfinders Platoon 108
Patterson, Robert 132

Patton, George Smith, Jr. 1, **197–198**
Paull, Jerome 109
Paulus Hook, battle of 145
Payes Landing, Treaty of 194
PBR 105 263
PBR 775 145
Pearl Harbor 116, 130, 154, 171, 173, 184, 205, 224, 241
Pearson, Richard 134
Peebles' Farm, battle of 9
Peleliu Island, battle of 79, 96, 107, 204, 205, 225
Pelham, John **199**
Pendleton, Joseph E. 35
Peninsula Campaign 121, 138, 151, 178
Pensacola (Union sloop) 72
Pensacola, Army of 26
Pequot War 49
Perkins, Constantine 122
Perry, Charles 192
Perry, Oliver Hazard **199–200**
Perryville, battle of 114, 221, 238, 261
Pershing, John Joseph 16, 39, 122, 198, **200**, 211
Persian Gulf War 1, 141, 216
Peters, George J. **200**
Petersburg, battle of 111, 201
Pettigrew, James Johnston **201**
Philadelphia (U.S. ship) 70, 122
Philippines, operations in 34, 107, 153, 154, 159, 185, 199, 200, 230
Philippine Sea, battle of 185
Phillips, Nash W. 15
Pickett, George Edward **201**
Pickett's Charge 9
Pillow, Gideon J. 31
Pinkerton, Allan 259–260
Pinkney's Treaty (1795) 255
Pitcher, Molly **201–202**
Pittinger, William 6
Plunger (U.S. ship) 184
Polaris submarine-based ballistic missile 32
Poling, Clark V. 45
Polk, Leonides 27, 114
Pollock, Edwin **202**
Pope, John 93, 128, 148, 161, **203**, 213, 235
Porter, David 89, 90
Porter, Fitz-John 203
Port Republic, battle of 128, 160
Potomac, Army of 17, 41, 81, 87, 101, 111, 118, 132, 150, 160, 203, 214, 216, 217, 221, 227, 229, 237
POWs. *See* prisoners of war
PRAIRE II (Operation) 141
PRAIRE IV (Operation) 72
Prescott, Samuel 209, 210
President (U.S. ship) 70
President Adams (U.S. ship) 45
President Lincoln (U.S. ship) 126
President Madison (U.S. ship) 224
Price, Sterling 230
Princeton, battle of 142

prisoners of war (POWs)
    in North Korea 165–166
    in Vietnam 65–66, 157–158, 228, 233–234
    in World War II 192, 194, 224, 225
Proctor, Redfield 72
Providence (sloop of war) 133
Provisional Army of the Confederate States (PACS) 178, 230
PT 59 140
PT 109 140
Pulitzer Prize 200, 206
Puller, Lewis B. 130, **203–206**, *205*
Pyle, Ernie **206**

Q

Queen Anne's War 49
Queen's Rangers 106

R

Raccoon Roughs 98
Ramage, Lawson Paterson **207**
Ranger (U.S. ship) 133, 134, 184
Rappahannock Bridge, battle of 217
Rascon, Alfred V. *207*, **207–208**
Reconstruction 110, 221
The Red Badge of Courage (Crane) 180
Red Cloud (Sioux chief) 54, *208*, **208–209**
Red River Campaign 230
Reed, Autie 57
Reese, John N., Jr. **209**
Revenge (U.S. ship) 199
Revere, Paul **209–210**
Reynolds, John F. 111
Richards, Thomas A. **211**
Rich Mountain, battle of 214
Rickenbacker, Edward V. **211**
Ridgeway, Joseph 74
Ridgway, Matthew Bunker **211–212**
Rigel (U.S. ship) 184
Risler, Jack 192, 193, 194
Robertson Hospital 239
Robinson, Thomas G. 260
Rochambeau (U.S. ship) 140
Rochambeau, Jean-Baptiste-Donatien de Vimeur, comte de 254
Rochester (U.S. ship) 84
Rogers, Robert 106
Rommel, Erwin 198
Roosevelt, Franklin D. 15, 39, 61, 76, 154, 213, 236, 250
Roosevelt, George W. **212**
Roosevelt, Quentin 212
Roosevelt, Quentin, II 212
Roosevelt, Theodore 72, 97, 133, 200, 212
Roosevelt, Theodore, Jr. **212–213**
Rosebud Creek, battle of 54, 55
Rosecrans, William Starke 26, **213–214**, 238
Ross, George H. R. 140

Ross, Marion A. 6
Rosson, William R. 65
Russo-Japanese War 153
Ryan, Cornelius 213

S

S-4 (U.S. ship) 81
Safford, Mary Jane **215**
St. Clair, Arthur 257
Saint-Mihiel, engagement of 16, 56, 60, 167, 230, 249, 250
Saipan, battle of 30, 39, 120, 231
San Agustin Atlapulco, battle of 5
San Jacinto (U.S. ship) 33–34
San Juan Hill, battle of 200, 213
Santiago, battle of 249
Saratoga (U.S. aircraft carrier) 107
Saratoga, battle of 96, 254
Saulx de Vesoul, engagement of 239
Savage Station, battle of 148
Sayler's Creek, battle of 6, 58, 87, 201
Schwartzkopf, H. Norman **215–217**
Scone, Charles P. 217
Scott, Winfield 5–6, 17, 100, 118, 137, 138, 147, 160
Scully, C. 260
Sculpin (U.S. ship) 55
Second Bull Run (Manassas), battle of 6, 9, 81, 87, 118, 119, 128, 138, 148, 151, 161, 199, 203, 235
Second Massachusetts 218
Second Winchester, battle of 87
Sedgwick, John 119, **216–217**
Seeyle, Linus 83
Seminole Wars 113, 131, 195, 216, 237
Seoul, capture of 204
Seraph (British submarine) 49
Serapis (British frigate) 133, 134
Seven Days Campaign 6, 9, 87, 99, 118, 119, 128, 148, 151, 201, 227, 235
Seven Pines, battle of 6, 9, 99, 118, 119, 121, 132, 147, 151, 201, 217, 227
Seventh New York National Guard 218
Seventh New York National Guard 218
Sexton, Charles T. **217**
Shaw, Robert Gould **217–220**
Shawnee 237
Shenandoah, Army of 17, 127, 131, 132, 229
Shenandoah Valley Campaign 87, 93, 99, 128, 147, 218, 220, 221, 235
Shepherd, Lemuel C. 252
Shepherd, Lewis 223
Sheridan, Philip Henry 55, 57, 58, 82, 83, **220–221**, 235
Sherman, William Tecumseh 43, 100, 121, 132, 160, **221–223**, 251
    March to the Sea 114, 222, 261
Shields, Marvin G. **223**

Shiloh, battle of 26, 73, 91, 114, 215, 222, 237, 261
Shimomura, Sam 165
Shofner, Austin C. **223–226**
Shughart, Randall D. **226**
Sicily, invasion of 198
Sickles, Daniel Edgar 41, **226–227**
Sijan, Lance Peter **227–228**
Simpkins, C. 74
Sioux 54, 95, 208–209, 228–229
Sioux War of 1876 57
Sitting Bull (Sioux leader) 54, 57, 95, 208, **228–229**
Skipjack (U.S. ship) 184
Slim Buttes, battle of 54
Smith, Charles F. 100
Smith, Chester B. **229**
Smith, Edmund Kirby 31, **229–230**
Smith, Holland McTyeire **230–231**
Smith, Nathan R. **231**
Smith, Ralph C. 231
Soissons, engagement of 56
Solomon Islands, battle for 116, 154, 184, 197
Somervell, Brehon B. 45
Sons of Liberty 210
Sorenson, Doris Marlene 66
South Carolina (U.S. ship) 184
South Mountain, battle of 118, 151
Southwestern Army 230
The Spirit of St. Louis (airplane) 148, 149
Spotsylvania, battle of 6, 87, 101, 111, 217
Spurance, Raymond Ames **231–232**
St. Mihiel Offensive. *See* Saint-Mihiel
Stamp Act riots 210
Stanton, Edwin M. 101, 219, 227
Starkey, Ray L. 140
STARLITE (Operation) 11
Star of the West (federal supply ship) 6
Steuben, Friedrich Wilhelm, baron von 254
Stewart, Alexander P. 213
Stilwell, Joseph W. 96, 171, **232**
Stockdale, James Bond **232–234**
Stones River, battle of 58, 238
Stony Point, battle of 157, 257
Storz, Ron 234
Stoughton, Edwin H. 178
Street, George Levick, III **234–235**
Strong, George C. 220
Stuart, James Ewell Brown 110, 178, 199, 221, **235**
Sturgis, Samuel D. 91
Sugar Loaf Hill, battle of 68
Sullivan, Albert 236
Sullivan, Francis 236
Sullivan, George 236
Sullivan, Joseph 236

Sullivan, Madison 236
Sullivan Brothers **236**
Sykes, George 213
Tallmadge, Benjamin 106
Tang (U.S. ship) 190, 191
Tarawa, battle of 39, 120, 230
Taylor, Walter L. 194
Taylor, Zachary 99
Tearcoat Swamp 168
Tecumseh (Shawnee chief) 21, **237**
Tennessee, Army of 7, 26, 27, 31, 50, 100, 113, 114, 118, 119, 121, 132, 150, 201, 222, 230, 237, 238, 261
Tenskwatawa ("The Prophet") 237
Terrill, William R. 220
Terry, Alfred H. 55
Tet Offensive 1, 115
The Texas (Confederate train) 7
Thames, battle of the 237
Thanh Hoa (Dragon Jaw) Bridge 233
Third Winchester, battle of 9, 82, 221
Thom, Leonard Jay 140
Thomas, George Henry 222, **237–238**, 251
Thomas, William H. **238**
Thompson, Frank 82–84
Thompson, Robert H. **238**
Thompson, Wiley 194
Ticonderoga (U.S. aircraft carrier) 232–233
Tillman, "Pitchfork Ben" 110–111
Tinian, invasion of 231
Tippecanoe, battle of 237
Tirante (U.S. ship) 234–235
Todd, David H. 247
To Hell and Back (Murphy) 180
Tominac, John J. **239**
Tompkins, Sally Louisa 239
Trail of Tears 216
Treadwell, Jack L. **239–240**
Treaty of 1804 21
Truman, Harry 155, 185
Tulagi, battle of 245
Tullahoma Campaign 26, 50, 114, 214, 238, 261
Tunnel Hill, battle of 50, 222
Turnage, Allen H. 45
Turner, Ashby 24
Turner, Day G. **240**
Turner, Nat 237
Turner, Richmond K. 230
Tuskegee Airmen 61
Twining, Merrill B. **240–242**
Twining, Nathan F. 242
Twining, Robert 242
Twohig, Dorothy 255

U

U-90 (German submarine) 126
UNION (Operation) 38, 78, 170, 192

UNION II (Operation) 120, 192, 193
United Nations (UN) 185
United States (U.S. ship) 70
Urban, Matt **243–244**

V

Valley Forge, encampment at 254, 257
Vandergrift, Alexander Archer 44, 96, 202, 241, **245–246**, 246
Van Dorn, Earl 213
Van Lew, Elizabeth **246–247**, 260
Van Winkle, Archie 247
Vargas, Jay, Jr. **247–248**, 248
Vera Cruz, engagement of 35, 245
Verdun, battle of 167
Vermont, Ethan Allen and 4
Vesey, James 83
Vicksburg, battle of 83, 101, 132, 222
Villa, Pancho 200
Villers-Cotterets, engagement of 56–57
Virginia
  Army of 118, 203
  Northeastern, Army of 222
  Northern, Army of 6, 9, 41, 81, 87, 99, 118, 127, 148, 150, 199, 203
Virginia Light Dragoons 145
Virginia Volunteers 131

W

Wagon Box Fight 54
Wahlen, George Edward **249**
Wainwright, Jonathan Mayhew, IV 44, **249–251**, *250*
Wainwright, Robert 249
Walker, Dr. Mary E. **251**
Waller, L. W. T. 35
Walsh, W. J. 184
Walt, Lewis W. **251–253**
Warren, Joseph 210
Washington, Father John P. 45
Washington, George 4, 96, 102, 106, 134, 142, 145, 202, **253–255**
Washington and Lee University 148
Washita, battle of 57
WATCHTOWER (Operation) 202
Watkins, Travis E. **256**
Watson, Wilson Douglas **256**
Watters, Charles Joseph **256–257**
Wayne, Anthony **257–258**
Waynesboro, battle of 221
Webb, Charles 106
Webb, James H., Jr. **258–259**
Webster, Timothy **259–260**
Webster, Timothy, Sr. 259, 260
Weems, Mason L. 255
Westmoreland, William C. 1, 65
West Virginia (U.S. ship) 173
West Virginia, Army of 55
Wetzel, Gary George **260**
Wheeler, Joseph 55, **260–261**, 261

White, William 33
White Oak Swamp, battle of 148
Wicks, James A. 74
Wilderness, battle of the 81, 99, 101, 111, 151, 235
Wilkin, Edward G. **261–262**
Williams, Charles Q. **262**
Williams, Hershel Woodrow **262–263**
Williams, James E. *263*, **263–264**
Williams, Seth 213
Williamsburg, battle of 81, 99, 118, 132, 151
Wilson, Benjamin F. **264–265**
Wilson, James H. 91
Wilson, Louis Hugh, Jr. **265–266**
Wilson, Woodrow 271
Wilson's Creek, battle of 93
Winans, Roswell 266
Winchester, battles of 9, 55, 82, 87, 128, 221
Wolf Mountain, battle of 54
Womack, Bryant E. **266–267**
women
  in Civil War 14, 24, 82, 102, 215, 239, 246, 251
  in Revolutionary War 201–202
Wood, General 214
Woodfill, Samuel **267**
Wool, John 147
Wounded Knee massacre 209, 229
Wright, Raymond R. **267**

X

X-1 aircraft 269–270

Y

Yabes, Maximo **269**
Yeager, Charles E. **269–270**
Yellow Horse (Sioux warrior) 57
Yellowstone Expedition (1873) 57
Yellow Tavern, battle at 221, 235
Yntema, Gordon Douglas **270**
York, Alvin Cullum 180, 270–271, *271*
Yorktown
  battle of (Civil War) 118, 132, 151, 201, 217
  battle of (Revolutionary War) 135, 142, 257
Young, Gerald O. **272**
Young, Robert H. **272**

Z

Zabitosky, Fred William *273*, **273–274**
Zinser, Gerald E. 140
Zussman, Raymond *274*, **274**